Enigma Books

Also published by Enigma Books

Hitler's Table Talk: 1941–1944

In Stalin's Secret Service

Hitler and Mussolini: The Secret Meetings

The Jews in Fascist Italy: A History

The Man Behind the Rosenbergs

Roosevelt and Hopkins: An Intimate History

Diary 1937–1943 (Galeazzo Ciano)

Secret Affairs: FDR, Cordell Hull, and Sumner Welles

Hitler and His Generals: Military Conferences 1942–1945

Stalin and the Jews: The Red Book

The Secret Front: Nazi Political Espionage

Fighting the Nazis: French Intelligence and Counterintelligence

A Death in Washington: Walter G. Krivitsky and the Stalin Terror

The Battle of the Casbah: Terrorism and Counterterrorism in Algeria 1955–1957

Hitler's Second Book: The Unpublished Sequel to *Mein Kampf*

At Napoleon's Side in Russia: The Classic Eyewitness Account

The Atlantic Wall: Hitler's Defenses for D-Day

Double Lives: Stalin, Willi Münzenberg and the Seduction of the Intellectuals

France and the Nazi Threat: The Collapse of French Diplomacy 1932–1939

Mussolini: The Secrets of His Death

Top Nazi: Karl Wolff—The Man Between Hitler and Himmler

Empire on the Adriatic: Mussolini's Conquest of Yugoslavia

The Origins of the War of 1914 (3-volume set)

Hitler's Foreign Policy: 1933–1939—The Road to World War II

The Origins of Fascist Ideology 1918–1925

Max Corvo: OSS Italy 1942–1945

Hitler's Contract: The Secret History of the Italian Edition of *Mein Kampf*

Secret Intelligence and the Holocaust

Israel at High Noon

Wes Johnson

Balkan Inferno

Betrayal, War, and Intervention
1990–2005

Enigma Books

Printed in the United States of America

ISBN 1-929631-63-4
ISBN 978-1-929631-63-6

All photographs courtesy of the author.

Library of Congress Cataloging-in-Publication Data

Johnson, Wes.
  Balkan inferno : betrayal, war and intervention, 1990-2005 / Wes Johnson.

  p. : ill. ; cm.
  Includes bibliographical references and index.
  ISBN: 1-929631-63-4

1. Balkan Peninsula--History--1989- 2. Balkan Peninsula--Foreign relations--1989- 3. Balkan Peninsula--Politics and government--1989- 4. Yugoslav War, 1991-1995. I. Title.

DR48.6 .J64 2005
949.6/1039

To Sophia, who understood

Balkan Inferno

Betrayal, War, and Intervention
1990–2005

Table of Contents

Acknowledgments

A number of people have helped me in what has been a long journey, both in distance traveled physically, and in arriving at some understanding of a region filled with complexities and contradictions. I would like to thank Slobodan Markovic, formerly of Tanjug, for his encouragement when I first began to study and write about the Balkans. Wistfully, he still believes in a Yugoslavia and South Slav unity. Special thanks are due to Brana Markovic, whose *Yugoslav Crisis and the World* (Belgrade: Institute of International Politics and Economics) proved invaluable in threading my way through the thicket of events in ex-Yugoslavia. Basil Coranakis, the owner of *New Europe* newspaper provided me with technical support. There, Jennifer DeLay read my chapters. Theo Argytis, Nikos Katsifos, Tito Singh, Zoe Koulouris, and Despina Karra all had a hand, especially Costas Gkiokas, who made maps. I also must thank Lazar Antonic for his translation of Vuk Karadzic's *The Fall of the Serbian Empire*, which was first published in 1887. Lastly, thanks are owed to C. L. Sulzberger for my borrowings from his *A Long Row of Candles*. He remains without equal and is fondly remembered by those Greeks who knew him.

I wish to give heartfelt thanks to Robert Miller at Enigma, who saw merit in my book; and to chief editor Jay Wynshaw, who removed spelling errors and inconsistencies in the text.

Any errors of fact or interpretation were unintentional and are my own responsibility.

Excerpts from *Wartime* by Milovan Djilas (English translation by Michael B. Petrovich, Harcourt, Inc., 1977) reprinted by permission of the publisher.

Excerpts from *Njegos* by Milovan Djilas (Harcourt, Inc., 1966, renewed 1994.) reprinted by permission of the publisher.

Excerpt from *The Other Balkan Wars: A 1913 Carnegie Endowment Inquiry in Retrospect with a New Introduction and Reflections on the Present Conflict* (Washington, D.C.: Carnegie Endowment for International Peace, 1993) reprinted by permission of the publisher.

Preface

The twentieth century has ended as badly as it began, with a brutal war in the Balkans. The first two campaigns, in 1912–13, came about largely as a result of the accelerating collapse of the Ottoman Empire, a development that stirred the passions of the polyglot peoples living there and both fed hopes for liberation and nationalist ambitions aimed at the formation of larger states. A Greater Greece, a Greater Serbia, and a Greater Bulgaria were ideas that fired the imaginations of many, driving kings, statesmen, and land-hungry peasants along the path to war.

The recent slaughter we have witnessed in ex-Yugoslavia was the result of failing state structures in that country, compounded by severe economic dislocation and decline, played out against the backdrop of the collapse of communism throughout the Soviet Bloc. Yugoslavia's break up into its various components unleashed long-repressed sentiments for nationalist unity, ethnic fears of exclusion, and hatreds embodied in the memories and myths of the past. During the first Balkan wars, the major European powers were themselves engaged in empire building and expressed concern only as accounts of widespread massacre, pillage, ethnic cleansing, rape, and the mistreatment of civilians and prisoners made their way into the drawing rooms and parliaments of the West. This time, eighty years later, Europe once again demonstrated its inability to intervene impartially due to conflicting interests, which were driven as much by the past as by the future. Germany, Austria, the Vatican, Hungary, and Italy, individually or in concert, took actions in support of Slovene and Croatian separatism. And when, in 1994–95, Washington intervened, it allied itself with Croatia and the Bosnian Muslims against the Serbs. To do so, in what was essentially a civil war, served to re-establish the historic fault line dividing what was once the Austro-Hungarian Empire from that of the Ottomans and set Catholic Croats against Orthodox Serbs amidst a fragile construct called Bosnia. In the absence of a truly comprehensive and just settlement, it may well become a cause of renewed conflict in the future.

In a larger sense, the recent conflict served to disrupt a poor region of uneven economic development, interrupting traditional trade patterns at a time when its components were attempting to achieve a transition from communist, "command economies," to something approximating the market economies of the West. Almost all lost billions of dollars in missed business opportunities, even as they struggled to establish ties with the European Union. Inexperienced in the ways of Western-style democracy, the leaders floundered as they mimicked the forms of multiparty politics without understanding their substance. Some resorted to the crude, populist appeals of nationalism to gain and strengthen their grip on power. Out of the crisis, visions of a Greater Serbia, a Greater Croatia, and even a Greater Albania reappeared like ghosts from the past.

The shots fired at Sarajevo in June 1914 echoed across Europe, foreshadowing the end of crowned heads of state and the ultimate triumph of nationalism. An entire continent, a civilization, was plunged into a devastating war, and then was convulsed by another that brought even greater death and destruction within the short span of only twenty years. Throughout this century, tragedies large and small have been played out in the Balkans. For long decades, this drama took place behind an Iron Curtain out of sight of the West. Now, however, when integrative forces should hold sway, the area is again engulfed by nationalism. Unfortunately, its peoples are among the last in Europe to establish their boundaries and form their nation states, and it is fair to suggest that this process is yet to be completed.

However, it need not remain the source of bitter conflict and instability that we have known it to be. It requires economic development, time to learn the give-and-take of democracy, honest government, and a serious effort by the major powers to integrate it fully into European institutions. Historically, Western Europe has either ignored the Balkans, or has intervened in its affairs with disastrous results. It seems unfair that these strong-willed, vigorous men and women living on lands of such wild beauty, with their rich mosaic of culture and traditions, should all have such a dark destiny as if they were damned forever!

I apologize if this account seems to be a somewhat solitary tale. It is based on my impressions gained from eight years of travel and study in the area. Virtually all whom I talked to—on trains, buses, in dozens upon dozens of offices, on strange streets in little-known places—will never be encountered again. They have gone their separate ways, but remain indelibly etched in memory. I am grateful for their thoughts and opinions, their unfailing kindness, and their warm hospitality. May they one day live in the peace and security that they yearn for and deserve and which we, in the West, so take for granted. I hope that, by recording their comments, some have been given a voice concerning the events that have engulfed them, and that my experiences, however inadequately described, may give the reader a sense of the turmoil and tragedy of an area undergoing painful transition in the post-communist era. I have sought to underpin our "dialogue" with a brief account of what I consider to be the main chronological events, bolstered where I can by the observations of others concerning developments past and present. I will feel that I have succeeded if, in so doing, readers living outside the Balkans obtain a better understanding of the forces that are at work forging history, for better or for worse.

Athens, Greece
August 2005

The Balkans in 1989

Prologue

Astride the Powder Keg

Greek producer-director Theo Angelopoulos has an unforgettable scene in his greatly esteemed film, *Ulysses' Gaze*, which shows a giant, dismembered statue of Lenin being barged down the Danube to be junked. I described this to Theodoros Stassinopoulos, one of my Greek relatives, and said that, while I had liked it, I had thought it overlong. Lenin's head had dominated the screen, while the camera lingered over aspects of his physiognomy—his strong brow, commanding eyes, and cruel lips. It went on and on, while the barge seemed somehow suspended between blue water and blue sky.

Theodoros had also seen the film and exclaimed, "But, Wes, it's really just perfect! You must try to understand what it's like for us to see the collapse of Communism, to see the Soviet Union break up. Think of all of those who struggled within the system, who had hopes for some sort of a just, socialist society. Now it's over. It is just incredible!"

And so it must have seemed to millions. The social, economic, and political tectonic plates of much of the planet were shifting into unknown positions and relationships. Was it just the imaginings of US President Ronald Reagan—who had often liked to cast himself in the role of some film war hero, who had described the Soviet Union as that "Evil Empire," who had ordered the Pentagon to invent an invincible "Star Wars" anti-missile system—that had spent the Soviets into the ground? Or was Soviet Communist Party Secretary-General Mikhail Gorbachev, with his policies of *"glasnost"* and *"perestroika"* (openness and restructuring) responsible? It was he, after all, who had signed arms-reduction treaties with the West, and had admitted that even the Soviet leadership could be wrong. We have no real answer. Some day, we may conclude it was because of the daily struggle of thousands of dissidents throughout the Soviet Bloc, and of all the very extraordinary, ordinary people who simply said, "Enough!" At the American embassy in Athens, the rapid unfolding of events astonished most of us. Earlier, we had followed the dizzy rise of Lech Walesa's Solidarity movement in Poland and were not surprised by the imposition of martial law by General Wojciech Jaruzelski when the movement overreached itself. The subsequent repression was expected. What we were not prepared for, however, was that, after the amnesty and release of political prisoners in July 1986, within just three years Solidarity intellectual, Tadeusz Mazowiecki, would be asked to form a government, and that former Solidarity members, including Lech Walesa, would soon be voted into positions of power. A year earlier, in Hungary, an aged Janos Kadar, who had ruled since the failed uprising of October 1956, was removed by a group of young reformers. One of them, a then little-known foreign minister, Gyula Horn, from the spring until the autumn of 1989, opened the border with Austria to "visitors" from East Germany initiating what was at first a trickle, and then a flood, of refugees seeking life in the West. A Hungary bent on change had sealed the fate of its communist neighbor!

Looking back, the events of 1989 all seem telescoped in memory. When Gorbachev indicated he would not intervene in East Germany, the Bloc came apart like a house of cards. Once Erich Honecker fell, Czechoslovakia's communist leadership led by Gustav Husak followed quickly in a "Glorious Revolution" of only ten days. Bulgaria's Todor Zhivkov was forced out in November, and, before the year ended, the hated Ceaușescus were put up against a wall and shot. In Berlin, the Wall that had symbolized forty years of conflict and separation had been hammered down in a joyful night of bacchanalian defiance! It was as if the political laws of gravity no longer applied and an entire solar system had fallen out of orbit to its inevitable doom. The Cold War was in its last, terminal stage. After the cataclysm, I concluded that much of the daily blizzard of paper that was crossing my desk was no longer really very relevant. It was time for new experiences, time to explore my corner of Europe. After all, an entire region was now adrift. Who were these people who had been at the center of so much history in this century? What impulses would propel them, and in what direction?

The Balkans does not permit an easy conceptual understanding with its high headlands, which jut down from the Alps and rise sharply south of the plains of Hungary and Poland. There is little of the "soft underbelly of Europe" as famously stated by Winston Churchill. The countries are crisscrossed by mountains, rivers, and deep valleys. Only the Danube had provided an easy west-east avenue until the advent of the railway and motorcar. Even today, distance and time are not the same as elsewhere. Narrow, winding mountain roads add long hours to any journey. There is much rock and stone and endless forests and fields. The region is so divided. One can easily understand how tribes, clans, and families existed for generation after generation on their steep hillsides and pastoral highlands and were uprooted only by war or natural disaster. There is also the sprawl of cities old and new, like huge, extended villages, much of which, planned and unplanned, is given over to industrial and urban slum. The Adriatic and the Ionian Sea bound the peninsula on the west from Trieste down past Corfu and on to Crete. On the east are the Black Sea and the Aegean. Therein lies a whole world of dazzling diversity—and proud, passionate, people.

In the spring and early summer of 1991, press and television began to turn from the Middle East and the Gulf War to something much closer to the so-called civilized states structures of Western Europe. There, in Yugoslavia, people were taking up arms to fight their neighbors. The names of Milosevic and Tudjman were forcing themselves into our consciousness. People had already been killed for reasons beyond our understanding and comprehension. What did it all mean? Why were some saying that the Yugoslavia bequeathed by that "reluctant, old autocrat," Tito—the Yugoslavia of the 1984 Winter Olympics—was now an impossibility? Suddenly, here in Europe, where people talked endlessly of union and closer integration, were reappearing religious and ethnic extremism, fear and the specter of separatism. Why?

Austria-Hungary, Serbia 1914

PROVINCES OF THE SLOVENE
COUNTRIES
CARINTHIA
KRANJ
STYRIA AND
GORIZ WITH TRIESTE –
A PART OF THE "AUSTRIAN COAST"

DALMATIA AND ISTRIA
Dalmatia was a separate
province, while Istria was a
part of the "Austrian Coast"

DISTRICTS OF CROATIA AND
SLAVONIA
1. MODRUŠA - RIJEKA
2. LIKA - KRBAVSKA
3. ZAGREB
4. VARAŽDIN
5. KRIŽEVAC
6. POŽEGA
7. VIROVITICA
8. SREM

PROVINCES OF BOSNIA AND
HERZEGOVINA
1. BIHAĆ
2. BANJA LUKA
3. TRAVNIK
4. SARAJEVO
5. TUZLA
6. MOSTAR

HUNGARIAN DISTRICTS IN
VOJVODINA
I BAČKA – BODROŠ
II TORONTAL
III TAMIŠ
IV KRAŠOVO
V BARANJA

ADMINISTRATIVE
TERRITORIAL DIVISION

1. District of Ljubljana
2. District of Maribor
3. District of Primorsko-Krajiška
4. District of Zagreb
5. District of Osijek
6. District of Srem
7. District of Bačka
8. District of Beograd
9. District of Danube
10. District of Drina
11. District of Valjevo
12. District of Šumadija
13. District of Morava
14. District of Požarevac

15. District of Timok
16. District of Niš
17. District of Vranje
18. District of Kosovo
19. District of Skoplje
20. District of Bregalnica
21. District of Bitolj
22. District of Raška
23. District of Užice
24. District of Kruševac

25. District of Zeta
26. District of Split
27. District of Dubrovnik
28. District of Tuzla
29. District of Sarajevo
30. District of Mostar
31. District of Travnik
32. District of Vrbas
33. District of Bihać

Kingdom of Serbs, Croats & Slovenes, 1918

Ethnic distribution in B-H and Croatia, 1981

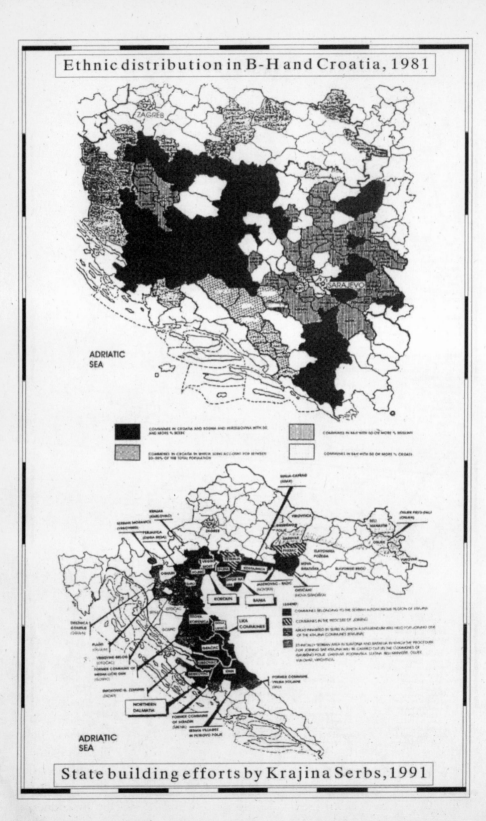

ADRIATIC
SEA

State building efforts by Krajina Serbs, 1991

ADRIATIC
SEA

Chapter 1

Back to the Future

Serbia, Slovenia, Croatia: July 1991

In the spring of 1941 the Ustashe—among them a good number of Muslim toughs—had killed many Serbs. Then the Chetniks occupied the little town and proceeded to slaughter the Muslims.

Wartime by Milovan Djilas,
speaking of Foca in Bosnia

"The Acropolis Express" from Athens to Belgrade is not much of an express and takes some twenty-four hours to cover the seven hundred miles northwards. Still, I thought it a better way to get into the crisis, which had recently erupted, than to be "dropped" from the sky after a flight of less than two hours.

It is worthwhile to be reminded of geography's hard reality: the Gorgopotamos Gorge in Thessaly, whose bridge was blown by the British and Greek guerrillas during World War Two to deny supplies to Rommel's Afrika Korps; Salonika, the port city on the Aegean prized by all during the Balkan Wars; Skopje and the Vardar River valley cited by Bismarck as the key to the Balkans; Nis, in southern Serbia, whose fortresses were built by Byzantines,

Serbs and Turks; and, finally, Beograde, the "white city," standing on its high hills overlooking the Danube. It is said to have been destroyed dozens of times in its two-thousand-year history, but has always been rebuilt again and again.

Dragomir Antonic is a bearded professor of religious archaeology and a huge bear of a man who has spent many years tracing the remnants of the Serbian Orthodox church in northern Greece. That warm summer morning, in his small apartment near Belgrade's old Skadarlija quarter of artists and writers, I found him in a very black mood. Over coffee and slivovitz or plum brandy, he tried to explain what had happened in recent days since, in the last week of June, the republics of Slovenia and Croatia had declared their independence from the socialist federation of Yugoslavia.

Even more ominous than the situation in Slovenia, which had seen the Yugoslav People's Army (JNA) given a humiliating kick in the shins by a smaller Slovenian territorial force, sharp fighting had broken out between Serbs and Croatian militia and police in Slavonia in eastern Croatia. He said that the country was on the verge of civil war. In the past ten days, thousands of Serb women and children had fled from their homes in Croatia to seek safety across the Danube in Serbia. With an anguished expression on his face, he said, "My friend, after fifty years, we have returned to 1941!"

Dragomir emotionally vented his anger against the leadership in Ljubljana and Zagreb who had broken with the federation, saying it is much like a man and a woman who have been married for years when one of them, suddenly, announces, "Okay, it's all over!" He thought that at least a year would be needed to disentangle the political, economic, and social claims of the two republics from those of the federation, if it was to be independence. It also angered him that politicians, the press and the radio-TV in Slovenia and Croatia were describing Serbs as "Bolsheviks." He said that most people had been born into the communist system, had wanted nothing to do with the party, or had joined organizations under pressure or to better their prospects. Croatia's President, Franjo Tudjman, had been a communist general close to Tito, and Slovenia's President, Milan Kucan, had also been a member of the League of Communists. "It's a lie and unfair," he said.

Explaining that his father had been a major in the Royal Yugoslav Army at the outbreak of World War Two, Dragomir said that he had spoken four languages and played the piano. In 1941, after Germany had overrun the country, and Italy and Bulgaria had joined in its occupation, the Croat Ustashe had arrested him and thrown him in a prison camp. After some months, he was released through the efforts of the Orthodox Church, rearrested by the Nazis, and sent to Dachau in Germany. He was fortunate to survive the ordeal, and was returned to Yugoslavia at the end of the war. Tito's communists, having come to power through their Partisan army's victory over the Germans and the Italians—and over their indigenous supporters—as well as over the Serb, royalist, Chetnik forces of Draza Mihailovic, had allowed him to work as a street sweeper, the job he had held until the day he died.

I asked where the New Democratic Movement for Serbia stood in all of this, the party in which he was active. He said they opposed war and did not want to participate in any "madness," adding that, if it came to it, he would go to fight rather than see his teenage son go off. I asked about Vuk Draskovic's Serbian Renewal Movement (SPO). Dragomir said that the SPO was calling for volunteers, claiming justification in that the Croats were arming themselves, and were sending gunmen into Serb villages to provoke incidents. Dragomir opened a map from the *Nin* weekly, which showed Yugoslavia's various national ethnic groups and how they intermingled in places and were spread across the boundaries of the republics. The blue, where the Serbs claimed to be a majority, extended into parts and pockets of northeastern and southwestern Croatia, and large areas in Bosnia. He circled a place on the map where the red of the Croats was broken by a finger of blue. "There's trouble here," he said. It was a town named Osijek.

Up a lane off Terazije, not far from the venerable Hotel Moskva, I located the moderate Democratic Party (DS). The young men and women working there were frantically answering phones and dashing from office to office. "We are in a race against time to prevent civil war," said one. "If war breaks out, it will be a disaster for everyone," said another. The staff of party leader, Dragoljub Micunovic, said they considered the ninety-day emergency moratorium that had been brokered between Slovenia, Croatia, and Yugoslavia by the European Community (EC) to be a lull before the storm, before the resumption of fighting and a full-scale war.

Citing the lack of reliable information, high tension, and the sheer political confusion as serious obstacles to finding out the actual situation, vivacious, dark-haired Vesna Marjanovic, DS's chief-of-staff, said that Micunovic had begun talks with Serbian President Slobodan Milosevic in the hope that the latter would agree to invite DS into his government. She said it was unclear what Milosevic would do, but that DS had decided it could not just watch the country slide into civil war without trying to prevent it. She said that Slovenia and Croatia were gaining support from the Western media, and that the DS was asking for the foreign and information ministries in an effort to project a better image of Belgrade's actual position. She hoped that Washington and Europe would immediately—and impartially—intervene in the crisis.

That evening, in my room in the Praq Hotel, I looked at a map of Yugoslavia and wondered if the train to Ljubljana would still be operating in the morning. The receptionist had heard rumors of shooting at Vinkovci. The next day, Belgrade's yellow, baroque-style station dating from the late nineteenth century was jammed with travelers, many with worried expressions on their faces. Gone were the carefree, holiday smiles and laughter of vacationers heading for Dubrovnik and the beaches of Yugoslavia's splendid string of islands in the Adriatic. There were JNA soldiers with field packs and slung AK-47 (M-70 variant) Kalashnikovs milling about. A middle-aged officer in a belted, double-breasted coat and high, parade hat was sweating profusely as he helped two young troopers push a cart loaded with ammunition cases.

The first hour was uneventful as the Ljubljana Express made slow, but steady progress across the rich farmland to the west. Cornfields, sunflowers, and small villages passed in procession. On this sunny Saturday, it was impossible to imagine that towns only a few miles to the north were already caught in the grip of rumor, fear and rising tensions. Approaching Vinkovci, however, there were indications of trouble in the area that put my travel companions on edge. The train slowed to a stop, waited, and then proceeded at an even slower pace. It stopped again. A militia man came through the car to check identities. I was told that, even under Tito, the practice had stopped years before. At Vinkovci, normally a bustling market town, the streets that could be seen from the train looked dead and deserted. We finally moved on.

A sour-looking, middle-aged Slovenian woman who sat opposite complained about the open window and our chain-smoking male companion who threw his butts to the wind, as if thinking that Yugoslavia was going up in flames and he might as well help it along. A woman from a mixed Serb-Croat marriage was going to Zagreb to collect two daughters who were visiting grandparents. A Greek young man was with us as well. He was startled when a wet, crimson blob appeared on his shoulder—then another. He inspected it with the tip of his finger, bringing it up to his nose. It was blood, real blood, coming from the luggage rack! After a stunned silence, the Slovenian woman took down an old, scuffed suitcase. It contained dead chickens, which still had their heads and feet, as well as their feathers! A putrid smell filled the warm compartment, suggestive of what was lying in wait for many in the months to come. It was so bizarre that I wondered what to expect from the Slovenes, a people who are said to act smug and consider themselves almost Austrian.

We reached Ljubljana in the late afternoon. It was lovely, with a fast flowing river running through the center of town and fine buildings from the Habsburg period. Some were being converted into trendy boutiques and restaurants. I enquired about a hotel, a cheap hotel, and set off with my bags in the direction of the nearby Park. Not far from the train station, I ran into my first "photo opportunity," a teenager in a gray shirt, dark gray pants, boots and belt, with a new-looking, folding-stock AK-47. I made sure that he knew I wanted to take his picture and made sure that he approved. As soon as I had cranked off two or three, his companion up the street started shouting, obviously asking what I was doing. My photo opportunity mustered some English and said that I must go with him to the police. I said that the only place I was going was my hotel. As I turned and walked away, the young guard shouted, "Remember, this is now Slovenia!"

From my hotel I made some futile phone calls to try to establish contact with people of interest. Government and party offices, of course, were closed for the weekend. A hotel employee suggested that I go to the Catholic cathedral in the morning and talk to the bishop, that he would know what was going on.

Sunday mass had already begun when I entered the church's white marble and ornate gold interior. Its beauty aside, I wished that I could fathom the minds of the worshippers. Were they praying to be delivered from the threat of war, or were they locked in personal thoughts? Did they realize that by seeking independence, Yugoslavia—the nation of the South Slavs—was being destroyed? Slovenia, on its own, has very limited prospects. Did it want to be an appendage of the Austria it so admires? The virulently anti-Slovene Austrians of Carinthia and Styria in the south would surely dominate them economically, and never treat them as equals. I had no answer.

I left and was surprised to see a cafe-bar opposite filled with men from the Territorial Defense Force (TDF). They were enjoying their drinks and willing to talk about their ten day "war" with the JNA. They said that the federal army came in like a poorly organized parade, with no idea of what they were supposed to do, except to take control of the border crossings and customhouses along the Italian and Austrian frontier. Many of the younger JNA soldiers hadn't wanted to fight and had surrendered. In short, the JNA had been chased back to their barracks where they were trying to decide what to do next. A TDF officer, dressed in camouflage and carrying a pistol on his belt, confirmed that they had captured several major JNA arms depots. He said confidently, "We've got plenty of weapons now. If the JNA wants to fight, we're ready. However, it won't come to that. I think it's all over."

I walked around and looked for signs that Slovenia might expect an attack. There were none. The huge, crossed-steel barricades that had blocked the roads had been pulled aside and people were out taking their Sunday morning strolls. Dogs chased pigeons in the park, and a large blue, white, and red Yugoslav tricolor still fluttered in the breeze near a monument to the Slovene communist leader Edvard Kardelj. There were no military vehicles. It all seemed surreal. I was told that Slovenia was on a long weekend holiday! I debated whether to remain in Ljubljana, or to go on to Zagreb. I decided for the latter when I learned that the train would leave that afternoon. Now heading eastward, I enjoyed the beautiful scenery along the Sava River with its high-forested hills and rushing water. Fishermen were trying their luck. Tents and campers were scattered along its banks. It was as idyllic a scene of peace as could be imagined anywhere.

Zagreb was full of flags, especially the red and white-checkered *sahovnica* of a brief medieval Croatian kingdom, which was also that of the Independent State of Croatia (NDH) of World War Two. Flags were flying from poles, from windows, and from Zagreb's fortress-like cathedral complex. Vendors were selling patriotic pins, pictures, emblems, and maps which showed how large Croatia once was, or ought to be, bordered with the faces of Croatia's historical great. A popular item was a black T-shirt with an Ustashe emblem. It was as if people felt compelled to show their ethnic identity. Bold newspaper headlines screamed of Serbian aggression. Cartoon strips depicted the JNA and the Serbs as war-crazed maniacs (all with a communist red star) bombing and shooting children. TV news program blared out the same. It was a city gripped by nationalist hysteria!

The Croatian Hina news agency had already cranked up a massive effort to influence the European press as to Croatia's "peace-loving, democratic, free enterprising, Roman Catholic, western" ways in contrast to those of Belgrade. The Croatians had immediately grasped the importance that the media had had in depicting Slovenia as "that brave little Catholic country of freedom fighters" and sought to duplicate their propaganda success. America also, since early 1991, had been learning about Croatia. It had been learning from Rudy Perpich, the former governor of Minnesota. Perpich had transmogrified himself into Rudi Perpich, emissary of Franjo Tudjman, the president of Croatia. A second generation, ethnic Croat, Perpich had turned down an offer to run the Foreign Ministry in order to sell Croatia to Western governments.

Working out of Croatia's Ministry of the Interior, Perpich already had assisted Britain's press baron, Robert Maxwell, to buy into Croatia's media. In Washington, he lobbied for US support for Zagreb's drive for independence. He also brought other Croatian-Americans and Croat government officials together. In May 1991, Perpich believed that the JNA would not fight to keep Yugoslavia together and was not worried about the possibility of war. He depicted "democratic" Zagreb as being "repressed" by Belgrade, making it a question of democracy against communism. This simple-minded explanation probably satisfied many, even US Congressmen, who considered Yugoslavia too unimportant or complicated to even bother thinking about. A photo, taken after the 19 May referendum had carried for independence, put the well-articulated good intentions of the Croats that I had met into better perspective. Two beefy, middle-aged men, each with a pistol in his hand, are shouting in mindless exultation and a Croatian flag flies from their car!

Osijek is seventy-five miles northwest of Belgrade in eastern Slavonia in Croatia. With its neat surrounding villages and peaceful cornfields, it would appear to be an unlikely place for a civil war. However, the presence of armed civilians at the railway station, the roving patrols of blue-shirted militiamen, and the Croatian National Guard (ZNG) in camouflage uniforms in front of city hall, said otherwise.

The daily press conference began shortly after 9 a.m. and Zlatko Kramaric, Osijek's mayor, police officials and civilians (ably assisted by translators) told a packed room of foreign and Yugoslav journalists the latest developments in what was the "opening round." The mayor stated that Croat villagers from "new" Tenja had attempted to return to their homes, but had been fired at by Serb "Chetniks" and forced to return to Osijek. He said a bomb had gone off outside a cafe the previous evening, but had caused no injuries. Serb "terrorists" had threatened a family to either leave their home, or have it burned down. He added that 125 homes had been torched so far. Police had been fired upon, and one attacker had been wounded. Machine-gun fire and RPGs had hit the city. He said that he was trying to talk to the "Chetniks" through intermediaries as well as learn their identities. He said people were frightened and afraid to talk. The Croats had formed armed, self-defense units. He said that many roads were blocked and the phones were out.

During the question period, the mayor accused the JNA of forming illegal "brigades" of Serb volunteers, arming them, and giving them military instruction. He said that these "terrorists" were provoking clashes by firing on Croat National Guard and police units, and that once the fighting had really got underway, the JNA had intervened on the side of the Serbs. He emphasized that if the JNA, which was then across the Danube along the border of eastern Croatia, stayed out of the situation, they would be able to take care of the "Chetniks" who were causing trouble. He claimed that Belgrade aimed to destroy Croatia in an effort to create a Greater Serbia. The mayor used the words "terrorists" and "Chetniks" interchangeably. The briefing was detailed and convincing. We were even told how many cows and pigs had been stolen, or had gone missing! An attractive, young, English-speaking guide from Zagreb TV volunteered to escort journalists around town.

Tenja is only a ten-minute drive from Osijek, and one end of the village was controlled by the Croats, the other by the Serbs. A few days earlier, fighting had broken out and the JNA had come in. At a Croat checkpoint in one of the houses, a dozen or so national guardsmen were lounging about. They were wearing new-looking camouflage uniforms, caps, boots, ammo belts, and had bayonets to go with their well-oiled, AK-47s. They showed me a number of cars and trucks that had been badly damaged, as well as the pockmarked walls of the houses and broken windows. The chewed-up asphalt from tracked vehicles and "splat" marks from where mortars had hit left little doubt that the JNA had made a persuasive show of force.

Some two hundred yards down the street, I got the attention of a Croat sniper behind a wall and told him that I was driving into the Serb positions. I had a white flag and a cardboard sign that said "Press." Farther down, at a cluster of houses and a barn, a bearded Serb in blue workman's overalls motioned me past his overturned farm wagon and an up-turned toothed rake. In contrast to the Croats, the men wore civilian clothing and had little in the way of weaponry. What they did carry, however, was amazing. A few did have AK-47s, but the others had shotguns, sporting rifles, an old British Sten gun, and what looked like Russian sub-machine guns from World War Two. They were dirty and tired and welcomed the little whisky and cigarettes that I had.

Their spokesman was a long-haired journalist who called himself Duga, a "writer-fighter." He wore green fatigues and carried an old US Thompson submachine gun. I found out years later that he was Neso Jeuric, who wrote for *Duga* magazine in Belgrade. He said the Croats had denied him entry into the area, so he had got off the main roads and come in through the woods to fight alongside his fellow Serbs and to get a story. While we were standing nearby, the Serb behind the wagon opened up on the Croats, so Duga offered me a guided tour. It was worse than "new" Tenja—smashed homes and shops, gutted by fire; holes from RPG or mortar rounds; broken furniture, strewn clothing, and personal effects. The bloodstains suggested that the fighting had been house-to-house. Duga said the Croats were trying to work in closer and that they were trying to keep them off balance through nightly probing action. He had no idea how it would end.

Over slivovitz, I asked Duga how it had started. He said it was his understanding that, a few weeks earlier, some Croats had driven into "old" Tenja in the late afternoon and shot at Serbs drinking coffee on their veranda, wounding several. Then, a few days later, talks were arranged by Osijek's police chief (a man liked by the Serbs) between himself, his Croat assistant and two Serbs. While driving into New Tenja, they were ambushed by a Croatian extremist who killed both policemen and one Serb, and wounded the other. After that, the village divided into two camps. Each side began to force their Croat or Serb neighbors to abandon their homes, with the result that ugly incidents had begun to erupt almost immediately.

Duga claimed that almost all of his irregulars were from Tenja. He did not say whether he was in contact with the JNA, but in my wandering around I did not see a radio. The Serb fighters and the non-combatants were equally nervous and did not want photos. He said that since serious differences had surfaced between Serbs and Croats over the past year, a psychological change had taken place between the two communities that would be difficult for an American to understand. He gave the example of one of the villagers who had gone on patrol with him a few nights earlier. The man had said that if he were wounded, Duga must shoot him. He didn't want to be captured by the Croats. Duga said that he had learned that the man's father had been wounded and taken by the Croats during World War Two. He was turned over to the Ustashe, spread-eagled across a table, and dismembered with a wood saw.

On my way out of Tenja, I stopped at the Croat checkpoint. The soldiers were young, certainly in their early twenties. I said that the Serbs were tired, and, understandably, very nervous. I urged these apple-cheeked, clean-cut young men to try to talk to them in order to arrange a ceasefire. One of them gave me a scornful look as though I didn't understand a thing and said, "We cannot talk to the Serbs—they are nothing but animals!"

Back in Osijek, I tried to grasp what I had seen and heard, but my mind didn't want to accept it. Here I was, sitting in the Turist Hotel and having an excellent meal and a bottle of wine, while, only a few minutes away, people were trying their very best to kill each other! The restaurant was deserted, except for myself and a police officer intent on entertaining two giggling prostitutes. A bottle was on the table and they were enjoying themselves. I thought to myself, *Welcome to the war!*

Back in Belgrade, I did as other journalists had done before me. I visited the apartment of Milovan Djilas, Eastern Europe's first prominent, anticommunist dissident. The stairs at 8 Palmoticeva were worn from use, and the walls suggested that the building had seen much of life. On the second floor, I found his name and rang the bell. After a moment, a slim, compactly built, man with the same brushed-back hair (now white), expressive face and intense, penetrating eyes that I had seen on the dust jackets of his books, opened the door. Djilas had been a young intellectual in the illegal Yugoslav

Communist Party before World War Two and had become one of Tito's top deputies during that terrible struggle. By 1948, he had helped engineer Tito's break with Stalin, fallen out with the party and then had written a devastating critique of Yugoslav communism in his *The New Class*. The book won him praise in the West and a seven-year jail sentence. Later, he was jailed for another three years. He wrote all of his life: politics and philosophy, poetry, short stories, novels, and autobiographical works. At eighty years old, he was still impressive.

Djilas said that federal Yugoslavia's dissolution had begun. But he was unsure if it meant the end of socialist state structures, Yugoslavia's social compact between its national communities, or both. He said that it was essential to find common ground during a transition to a new relationship. Djilas said that changes in the legal system and how the republics dealt with each other financially were required. He said Serbia did have serious reformers, citing the freer flow of public information and private ownership of small businesses. He said it was quite difficult to predict whether the fighting getting underway would be relatively short and sharp, or of a more prolonged nature. He said that the people didn't want war, but that the actions of the leaders at the republic level had brought them to this situation, especially in Croatia and Slovenia. He said, "The extremists are out of control and are encouraged by their every excess."

He didn't blame any one person for the crisis, saying that they all had made mistakes at different times. "I think they are all taking dangerous risks by encouraging nationalist extremism. They are leading our people to the abyss without listening to reason. They are determined to create second- and third-class states. However, concerning those states, where will the borders be? They will be difficult to determine, let alone establish. One thing is clear, however. Ideology is dead, and nationalism is driving our politics. But, as I said, the people don't want to fight, in spite of all of the propaganda. However, after what has happened in Slovenia and Croatia, the JNA could break up on ethnic lines, creating a very explosive situation. I can only hope that the republics realize that, if war really breaks out in earnest, it could prove to be long, destructive, and very brutal."

That evening I sat in a small garden restaurant to the rear of the Hotel Moskva and ate spicy *cevabcici*, or grilled meat kebabs; *shopska*, tomato, onion, and cucumber salad, a wonderful bread, and drank a cool white wine. A choral group was practicing in a building across the street and, with the windows open, their voices were filling the night air. It was so beautiful, and yet so sad, because events were now unfolding at such a pace one knew that catastrophe was just around the corner. Given Slovene and Croat independence, and the refusal of Serbs to accept second-class minority status, the three original, formative nations of Yugoslavia were moving inexorably towards tragedy!

Back in Athens, I reread my news clips. I needed to determine the events which, in only eighteen months, had acquired such a dynamic that it was likely that the Socialist Federal Republic of Yugoslavia (SFRY) as established by Josip Broz (Tito), with many historical antecedents dating back to the nineteenth century, was about to blow itself sky high! Why would a nation of twenty-five million people, with good prospects to achieve a respected and productive role in post-communist Europe, want to break up? Look at a map! There it is—a long, strategically placed country right on the Danube and the Adriatic, with seaports, river traffic, a main route by road to Europe, rail and air links, good industry, experience in heavy construction, international acceptance, beautiful women, great food and greater basketball players! A rugged country, yes, but one which, in many respects, is very well endowed by nature.

It didn't make any sense! Then, there was this other thing. As far back as I can remember, I had read of Yugoslavia and Yugoslavians. Now I had learned that there are Serbs, Croats, Slovenes, Montenegrins, Macedonians, Albanians, Hungarians, Romanians, Romanies, and, importantly, the Muslims of Bosnia-Herzegovina, whom some refer to as "Bosniaks" and others call "Turks." I am still stuck on the term "Yugoslavian"! I had also learned that there are literally hundreds of thousands of mixed marriages between all of the so-called national groups, including marriages between Muslims and non-Muslims. However, unfortunately, not many are calling themselves Yugoslavian today. I now knew that the Slovenes and the Croats are Roman Catholic and that the Serbs are Eastern Orthodox. But, they both speak the same language, Serbo-Croatian. Would religion alone be enough to set one against another? What was this nationality-religion fixation, this ethnic exclusiveness that had become so all-important in Ljubljana, Zagreb, and Belgrade? I was to eventually find out.

* * *

20–22 January 1990. The 14th Special Congress of the League of Communists of Yugoslavia (LCY) was held in Belgrade. Arguments erupted between various republic delegations over the question of a looser, confederal LCY organization in a multiparty system. Unable to gain acceptance, the Slovenes walked out and the Croats abstained. The congress ended in deadlock between Serbia, Montenegro and the two provinces of Vojvodina and Kosovo on one side, and Croatia, Bosnia-Herzegovina, Macedonia, and the JNA on the other.

In a country where the LCY had once exercised the main levers of power, the organizational distribution of that power was now at issue.

The congress was adjourned. It never met again in full session. It meant the end of the LCY, one of the main underpinnings of the state. Some republics began to organize variants of a socialist party, some more reformed than others. Others organized nationalist-oriented parties.[1]

24–25 February 1990. The newly organized Croatian Democratic Union (HDZ) convened in Zagreb and reconfirmed Franjo Tudjman as its president. A fervent nationalist, Tudjman made a speech that set alarm bells ringing within the Serb community when he claimed that the wartime NDH was not a fascist creation, but expressed the historical aspirations of the Croatian people. At the same time, the Croatian constitution was redrafted to state that sovereignty was to reside with the "Croatian people," replacing the previous language that had read "the Croatian people in brotherly unity with the Serbs of Croatia." Croatia's 600,000 Serbs were no longer to be a constituent people, but an ethnic minority.[2]

Concurrently, Serbian President Slobodan Milosevic was using the federal JNA (the other republics acquiesced in this) and control over Serbia's assembly and the republic's internal security apparatus to suppress a drive for republic status by the majority of Albanians of the province of Kosovo in southwest Serbia. Milosevic had come to power on a program of Serbian assertiveness and nationalism, promising to reintegrate Kosovo and Vojvodina (a province north of Belgrade with a Hungarian minority) into Serbia. Under a 1974 constitution, Kosovo enjoyed near-republic status. Serbia was reversing this, by rewriting its constitution and disbanding provincial political structures, often using a display of force. In Kosovo, over 20,000 Albanians demonstrated against Serbia's imposition of emergency rule, and the trial of their top leader Azem Vlasi. As a result of JNA intervention, 28 Albanians died and many were wounded. Besides the Slovenes and the Croats, the Serbs were also caught up in the throes of nationalism, and it had turned tragic.[3]

8 April–30 May 1990. Assembly and presidential elections were held in Slovenia. The Democratic Opposition Coalition of Slovenia (DEMOS) won handily and Milan Kucan was elected president. Kucan remained the main proponent for Slovenian independence. A few weeks later, similar elections took place in Croatia. The HDZ won only forty-two percent of the vote, but the electoral system gave it an unassailable majority in the assembly. The latter elected Franjo Tudjman president and Stipe Mesic prime minister. Slovenia and Croatia were now politically positioned to implement their drive towards independence.

29–30 June 1990. Croatian President Tudjman announced amendments to the constitution according to which Croatia would cease to be a "socialist republic." He also announced that the Partisan red star in the flag would be replaced by the Croatian *sahovnica*. The assembly president called for a Yugoslav confederation. A few days later, the Slovenian assembly adopted a declaration of state sovereignty, a verbal affirmation of the goal of independence.[4]

16–20 July 1990. The Serbian LCY and the Socialist Alliance of Working People merged into the Socialist Party of Serbia (SPS). Slobodan Milosevic was elected president. The Serbian assembly adopted a multiparty system. Like Slovenia and Croatia, the assembly declared the republic to be sovereign. These actions would normally have indicated to outside observers that Serbia had ended one party rule. However, this development was obscured by its denial, just days earlier, of republic status for the Albanians of Kosovo and the act of dissolving Kosovo's assembly.

25 July 1990. Indicative of rapidly increasing communal tension, the Serbian Democratic Party (SDS), under the growing influence of Milan Babic in the *krajina* (border) area of southwest Croatia, called for the independence of the Serbs of Croatia and the setting up of a Serbian National Council. As Babic was coordinating his efforts with Milosevic and others in Belgrade, this presented a challenge to the HDZ leadership in Zagreb, particularly to Tudjman. Babic moved quickly to turn an association of municipalities into an assembly, and deflected an undefined concept of nonterritorial autonomy by moderate Jovan Raskovic by pushing for separatism. In this, he had the support of a majority of Serbs, including many local policemen, who refused to wear the new black uniforms of the Croat police with its hated *sahovnica*.[5]

Tudjman, for his part, from March onwards had ignored Serb protests that objected to constitutional changes that would reduce their status to a national minority, and he and the HDZ refused consideration of Serbian autonomy. In fact, he sent Interior Ministry forces (MUP) into mixed Serb-Croat villages to disarm and replace Serb police and reservists with Croats. Some shots were fired. A delegation was sent to Krajina's main town of Knin to reassert Zagreb's authority. The meeting ended in heated anger, and, led by Babic and Knin police officer Milan Martic, the Krajina Serbs began to arm themselves, taking control of towns and villages.

Croats living there now found themselves to be in the minority. In August, the MUP tried to retake Benkovac, Obrovac, and Knin. Outnumbered and outgunned, with JNA jet fighters threatening to intervene, the Croats beat a humiliating, bloodless retreat. By the time the Serbs had barricaded roads leading into the area, Zagreb had lost a sizeable pocket of its republic's territory. On 1 October, a Serbian Autonomous Region of Krajina was declared.[6]

25 October 1990. While the Croatian Krajina became a backwoods battleground, the Croat Federal Prime Minister, Ante Markovic, had almost single-handedly brought Yugoslavia's runaway inflation under control. A political moderate, Markovic earned the admiration of Western governments and financial institutions for his new economic approach. However, his efforts to build a Yugoslav-wide reform party ran counter to the interests of republic leaders. Consequently, his efforts were undercut at every opportunity. He brought inflation down from 2,500 percent to near zero. Hard currency reserves rose and Yugoslavia's prodigious foreign debt fell to under US$16 billion for the first time in years. Indicative of economic and political strain, Serbia slapped a tariff on Croat and Slovenian goods, calling it compensation for selling raw materials and electric power at subsidized prices.

9–23 December 1990. Multiparty elections were held in Serbia and Montenegro, though the Albanian community boycotted them. On the second ballot, the SPS won forty-eight percent and a strong majority in the Serbian assembly. Milosevic was re-elected president with a majority of sixty-five percent. A former banker familiar with Western ways, Milosevic gained control of the communist party of Serbia much in the manner of a skilled *apparatchik*. He then turned the party upside down by tapping into a wellspring of repressed, Serbian nationalism. During the transition to modern, multiparty politics, Milosevic's effective use of the press, radio and TV, combined with his emotional, crowd-pleasing sloganeering, made him the most popular politician in Serbia. This, in addition to his skill in eliminating opponents and manipulating the machinery of the federal government, made him a regional power to be reckoned with. Milosevic developed his power-base among Serbia's poor, rural towns and villages, elements of the military, police and internal security and large, state-controlled companies. SPS became a large, well-organized machine. An American diplomat referred to him as "Serbia's Mayor Daley."[7]

Slovenia's "disassociation" referendum carried with 88 percent of those voting approving the question of independence.

17–28 January 1991. The Federal Defense Ministry issued orders, aimed mainly at Croatia, to disband "illegal paramilitary groups created along ethnic lines." The ministry threatened to use the JNA to enforce its directive, claiming that Croatia's actions to establish unauthorized self-defense units threatened to destroy the remaining fabric of the federation. Although the armed gangs of the Krajina Serbs were included, the JNA expressed specific alarm over the purchase of 36,000 Kalashnikov AK-47s by Croatia and Slovenia (some say the number was 80,000) from neighboring Hungary. Croatian President Tudjman promised that a 22,000-militia unit would be demobilized, although he placed Croatia's government installations under heavy guard in view of the JNA threat. The JNA also disclosed that Croatia's Defense Minister, General Martin Spegelj, had conspired with senior Croatian officials to murder certain Serb military officers and their families. The JNA accusation was backed by covertly televised conversations between Spegelj and others that have never been disproven.[8]

2 February–6 March 1991. Slovenia announced its intention to become independent, and Croatia stated it would then do the same. Serbia and Montenegro, in turn, agreed on a draft paper for Yugoslavia as a federation. Thus, a year later, the basic question remained as to the shape of this multinational state. Slovenia and Croatia demanded a loose confederation of states that would trade with each other, but each would have its own armed forces and be responsible for its own external affairs. Serbia wanted strong central controls. Croatia and Slovenia took turns to boycott meetings scheduled by the Federal President (Serb Borisav Jovic) that were intended to bridge the differences. Serbian President Milosevic began to talk of the need for all Serbs to live in one country and of the need to change internal borders if Croatia and Slovenia pulled out of the federation.[9]

Moreover, hotheads were taking matters into their own hands, with tensions escalating sharply in eastern Croatia, in Slavonia, and Baranja. The Krajina-based SDS began to organize rallies in Vukovar, Beli Manastir, and other towns. SDS-led Serbs took over the police force at Pakrac, disarming eighteen Croats. Croat specials took it back. The Croats deployed a police unit to the Plitvice national park in a predominantly Serb area over local protests. These developments led to violence. Within a few weeks, the Serbs ambushed a busload of police going into the park. In a brief firefight, a Serb and a Croat were killed, in effect the first fatalities of the civil war.

Ethnic incidents multiplied virtually unchecked. Serbs living in, or visiting Croatia, were at risk. Cars were vandalized and, more ominously, Croatian-Serbs by the hundreds began to be thrown out of their jobs and apartments. Under Yugoslavia's unique system of social property, a state-connected job normally included the use of an apartment. When loyalty oaths came into use, many Serbs refused them and were fired, even after many years of employment. The Latin Croatian script, which differs from the Serbian Cyrillic, became an issue. More racially pointed were the new Croatian school primers that read, "I am a little Croat... They are Serbs." Many thousands of mixed marriages were placed under great strain. When it became known that

Ljubljana had secretly printed its own money and passports, fear became even more palpable, as Croatia stated that it would break when Slovenia did. Barricades began going up across Slavonia as villagers prepared for the worst!

9–20 March 1991. Belgrade was rocked by a mass protest rally for greater access to the media and a more independent judiciary. Serbian President Milosevic deployed police and militia, staving off JNA moves not only to take action against dissidents, but to intervene against separatism in Slovenia and Croatia. Two persons died and a number were injured. Opposition leader, Vuk Draskovic, was arrested and released. Federal President Jovic resigned, and then was induced to return to his position. Amid great confusion, Milosevic promised to investigate police excesses. Little was done and Belgrade's anti-Milosevic activists were left frustrated and disappointed. The JNA knew that it and, more importantly, the Yugoslavia it had created, were in serious trouble. However, with power now in the hands of republic leaders, the existing federal machinery no longer had the clout to impose JNA views. Slovenia said it would no longer provide conscripts if they couldn't perform service at home. Croatia was inclined similarly. Zagreb still took no action against those accused of plotting against the JNA. Still bound by the constitutional order, the once powerful generals seethed with impotent anger as the JNA began to show the first signs of breaking up along ethnic lines.[10]

28 March–29 April 1991. Five so-called summit meetings of the republic presidents were held in various locations in Yugoslavia to try to resolve the issue as to Yugoslavia's future. Was it to remain within a federal framework, or become a loose confederation? The deadlock between Serbia on the one hand, and Slovenia and Croatia on the other, continued. The only thing they agreed upon was to hold referenda in the republics on the question by the end of May. The Krajina Serbs stirred the pot by announcing that they would stay in Yugoslavia and that the laws of Serbia and those of the SFRY would apply on its territory. The pro-SDS Serbs now had the upper hand in villages from southwestern Croatia over to Slavonia in the northeast. There were, however, areas where the Croats were stronger. Both sides were contesting for control.

2–19 May 1991. Incidents were unfolding at the Slavonian Serb village of Borovo Selo that would lead to war. In mid-April, a high-ranking HDZ official, Gojko Susak (one of Tudjman's closest advisors and fundraisers, who had made a fortune in a Canadian pizza chain), and his cohorts approached Borovo Selo at night and launched RPGs into the village. The Serbs then posted guards. On 1 May, a traditional holiday, flags were out in the village with the usual Yugoslav red star. That night, four Croat policemen from Osijek entered Borovo Selo to run up the Croat *sahovnica*. They met a hail of gunfire, and two were wounded and captured and two escaped. The next day, a busload of Croat policemen set out from Vinkovci to rescue their colleagues. The Serbs were waiting for them. A dozen Croats were killed and two dozen were wounded. The unfortunate incident that had begun with a Croatian pizza king wanting to play Rambo ended in an orgy of propaganda on both sides, with the Croats demonizing the "brutal, bandit, Chetnik, terrorists" and Serb nationalists congratulating themselves over their "victory." A psychological shift towards extremist solutions engulfed both Serbs and Croats.[11]

On 3 May, Serbian properties in Zadar and Sibenik were attacked by a Croat mob. On 6 May, violent demonstrations against the JNA broke out in Split. A young Macedonian conscript was pulled from his tank and murdered. The JNA said it would use force to protect its personnel. The federal presidency urged that only the JNA and federal police be used in contested areas in Croatia. As matters worsened, normal rotations into the federal presidency failed to take place. A Serb member for Kosovo was blocked by Albanians, Slovenia, and Croatia. In turn, on 15 May, the influential Croat Prime Minister Stipe Mesic (who threatened to crush the Serbs at Borovo Selo), failed to receive enough votes to assume the presidency. Not surprisingly, on 19 May, a stunning ninety-four percent of the Croat community voted for independence.

6–30 June 1991. Near Sarajevo, the sixth and last summit of republic presidents was held, and it failed to adopt proposals by Macedonian President Kiro Gligorov and Bosnian President Alija Izetbegovic for a "commonwealth of sovereign republics." On 12 June, Tudjman, Milosevic, and Izetbegovic held another unsuccessful meeting at Split. On 17 June, the extreme nationalist Croat Party of Rights (HSP) called for the "restoration and re-establishment of the Independent State of Croatia (NDH) on its entire historic and ethnic territory... with eastern borders stretching along the Subotica-Zemun-Drina-Sandzak-Boka Kotorska line." In the opening shot of the war of the maps, HSP advocated taking much of Bosnia and some of Serbia, as was the case during World War Two.

The next day, the Croat assembly hastily passed some sixty laws to facilitate separation. The federal presidency, still held by the Serb, Jovic, called for the adoption of the Gligorov-Izetbegovic plan and the election of Stipe Mesic as the federal President. However, the three main actors, Kucan, Tudjman and Milosevic, had been at loggerheads for too long. Positions had hardened on all sides. For far too many, past understanding gave way to fear and suspicion. And, most importantly, blood had been spilled.

On 25 June, Slovenia and Croatia declared independence. That night, Ljubljana saw a smart, military review of its small Territorial Defense Force (TDF)—70,000 men to protect a new nation of only two million. In Zagreb, a new *sahovnica* flag hung from government buildings, but an ominous silence also hung in the air. Croatia could muster some 80,000 national guardsmen and police out of a population of some five million, 600,000 of them Serbs. The JNA had 180,000 members from all of the six republics, 110,000 of them conscripts and many of them Serbs and Montenegrins from their larger population of over ten million. The JNA possessed an estimated 1,500 tanks, quantities of large artillery pieces, 300 fighter aircraft, 200 attack helicopters, and small naval vessels. It had stockpiles of arms throughout the country and its armaments factories were located in Serbia, Bosnia and breakaway Croatia. In Belgrade, the federal parliament called Slovenia's and Croatia's actions "constitutionally illegal," and Federal Prime Minister Ante Markovic authorized JNA intervention. With Slovenia and Croatia bracing themselves, sporadic shooting broke out between Croat militia and police and Serb irregulars.

Using a hastily assembled force of inexperienced conscripts, a relatively small JNA force moved out from several locations to regain control of Slovenia's border crossings, the main airport, and one small seaport. In a tragedy bordering on farce, dozens were killed and wounded. JNA vehicles were blocked and ambushed, and the Slovenes even downed a helicopter. During confused calls for a ceasefire, some JNA units didn't know whether to fight or not and many troopers were either captured, or simply gave up. Officers discussed operations with their Slovenian counterparts. Emboldened by its successes, the Slovene TDF talked its way into taking over three huge weapons depots without firing a shot.

However, after providing foreign journalists and photographers with the spectacle of armored vehicles smashing into Slovenian cars (and generally making a mess of things), the JNA slowly gained their objectives. Once in control of the borders, the JNA lacked the logistical support to stay there and made moves to return to their bases in Slovenia and Croatia. The Slovenes harassed them along the way, surrounded their compounds, and then cut off their electric power, water, and telephones. Tiny Slovenia had humbled the JNA, and had created the international impression that it really was an invasion and was really a war. JNA back-up plans to knock the stuffing out of Slovenia were never used. Serbian President Milosevic had already decided to let Ljubljana go.

The European Community (EC) "troika" of Luxembourg, the Netherlands, and Italy intervened on 27 June to preserve constitutional order and the integrity of Yugoslavia (precisely the reasons why the JNA had acted). EC consensus, however, began to crack over the need to use force. During a confused meeting in Zagreb, the EC got an almost meaningless assurance from Slovenia and Croatia to suspend independence for three months in return for a ceasefire. The only problem was that fighting continued.

On 30 June, Milosevic undercut the JNA generals and, with the troika EC foreign ministers present, gave the green light to the Croatian, Mesic, to take over the federal presidency. Within days, Mesic did become federal president; a ceasefire held in Slovenia; and a three-month "suspension" of what was already a fact was agreed upon.

On 7 July, this was solemnly formalized in writing on the island of Brioni. The declaration stated that the people of Yugoslavia had to decide their own future in peace. The EC agreed to monitor the situation and it sent a small group of unarmed observers dressed in white uniforms like ice cream vendors. With the JNA having agreed to pull out of Slovenia in ninety days, the EC congratulated itself. However, in reality, the "dogs of war" had been finally unleashed!

1–31 July 1991. It was to be a month of pious pronouncements, punctuated by instant death. The place was Slavonia in Croatia. Josip Reichl-Kir was an honest, hard-working policeman who, as police chief of Osijek, had the near impossible job of trying to keep the Serb and Croat communities from each other's throats. Nonetheless, he worked tirelessly, driving from one village to another trying to keep the peace. He was German-Slovene, but considered himself to be a good Croat. He was liked and respected by the Serbs for his fairness. Just before his murder, he had been trying to solve problems in Bijelo Brdo. The next day, he was working in Tenja. Returning to Tenja with his Croat assistant and two Serbs, his car was riddled with bullets by Antun Gudelj, the former head of the HDZ in Tenja and a close associate of Osijek HDZ fanatic, Branimir Glavas. With three dead and one Serb wounded, Gudelj simply walked away and vanished into thin air. It was to set "old" Serb Tenja and "new" Croat Tenja aflame.[12]

With the deal done between Kucan and Milosevic over Slovenia, the JNA began pulling out and relocating to Bosnia and Croatia. Zagreb screamed that it had been occupied by 70,000 Serb "bolsheviks." In truth, the JNA kept itself mostly to its established barrack cantonments, which the Croats almost immediately surrounded and began to harass. However, Croat accusations of aggression were picked up by the foreign media. Again, it was "little Croatia and big, bad Serbia." As the situation continued to deteriorate, JNA units on Croatia's border with Serbia began to get pulled into local firefights. The JNA intervened to separate the combatants, but ethnic Serb commanders were beginning to favor their Serbian brothers. Also, by this time, Milosevic and other Serb nationalist party leaders in Belgrade were actively organizing militias and channeling support to the Serbs in the Krajina and Slavonia. The hitherto unknown names of Lisanj, Kraljevcani, Petrinja, and Vidusevac began to be picked up by the world's wire services.

Slakovci is a Croat village of 1,700 people that sits side by side with the Serb village of Sremske Laze, population 900. For decades, they had lived in peace. They shared a school, a post office, an infirmary and a telephone exchange. In July 1991, however, friend was turning against friend and neighbor against neighbor. Mato Ivanic, a Croat teacher, told of the barricades being erected in each village and of his appeals to take them down. He said, "It doesn't matter who put them up first. What matters is to take them down. It takes years to build the harmony we had here. It can be destroyed in weeks. It will never, ever, be the same."[13]

I felt that I was getting closer to something basic, perhaps even universal. I had spent two weeks among Slovenes, Croats and Serbs, and the only thing I could really say was that they all seemed so outwardly normal. And yet, the very opposite of what we view as normal behavior had happened before my eyes. I decided that there must be some kind of unseen barrier between myself and those I had rubbed shoulders with that prevented me from grasping their thoughts and feelings. How could I acquire that empathy? How could I understand the collective mentality that could convince Slovenes they had no future in Yugoslavia? How could I comprehend Croatian passion for a red and white, checkered tribal symbol? What made Serbs flee their homes, erect barricades, and take up arms? What made a person willing to kill someone else? Was it conditioning? Was it the collective memory of a people? Was it myth? Was it all of these factors combined in extreme and unusual circumstances? I decided to dig into the past to try to find some answers.

* * *

Slavic tribes began to appear in the Balkans circa AD 500–600 fighting for farmland, cattle and horses, and secure settlement, sometimes migrating in their thousands, sometimes building fortified towns of strategic value. The area formed a divide between the western and eastern regions of the former Roman Empire. The remnants of the eastern region formed the Byzantine Empire at Constantinople and, after 1054, Roman Catholicism and Eastern Orthodoxy emphasized the old divisions. This religious demarcation, while never absolute, is generally considered to run from the Adriatic coast, along the Drina River, and then to the Sava and the Danube. While Byzantium waxed and waned, Bulgarian, Serb, and lesser kingdoms rose and fell accordingly. Strong Serbian kingdoms flourished for a time under the Nemanjic dynasty of Stefan I from 1170 until the death in battle of Prince Lazar in 1389. A Croat kingdom existed under Tomislav and Zvonimir until falling under Hungarian control in 1102. It would later remain under the Habsburgs. The Croatians and the Slovenes converted to Roman Catholicism and used the Latin script. The Serbs remained Orthodox and used Cyrillic. The two Slavonic languages (Serbo-Croatian) are mutually intelligible, but accented.[14]

In the fourteenth and fifteenth centuries, the Ottoman Turks pushed west and, by 1453, Constantinople had fallen and almost all of the Balkans had come under their control and administration. Holding the line against the farther advance of Islam were the Austrian Habsburgs and Hungary. The line of occupation followed, roughly, the imperial divide of old, but also included the westward bulge of Bosnia. For most Serbs, it meant almost five hundred years of rule by Muslim Turks. The Croatians and Slovenes were subordinated under a local nobility loyal to what would become the Austro-Hungarian Empire. The Croat, Slavonian and Banat lands (Vojvodina, north of Belgrade) became a strategic buffer and Serbian serfs could become free farmer-soldiers by serving along this long, defended frontier known as the Krajina. Serbs in great numbers lived on these lands for four hundred years. The Croats, therefore, took pride in their western, Roman Catholic orientation, the Serbs in their Orthodoxy, military prowess and freebooting ways. The Serbs and Croatians also lived in Bosnia-Herzegovina, but, there, Turkish *agas* and *begs* and Slav converts to Islam had the upper hand.

As the Ottoman Empire declined under its own weight and the constant warfare between itself and Christian kingdoms to the north, its restive subjects looked at last to throw off their yoke. Following Ottoman reverses at the hands of the Austrians and the Russians at the end of the eighteenth century, the Serbs around Belgrade wrung concessions from the Porte. Then, from 1804–6, a soldier swine-trader turned army chieftain from the clan of the Karadjordjevics raised a force of 30,000, first against abusive local janissaries, and finally against the Sultan's own troops. The small Serb peasant army proved successful and after Russia again declared against the Sultan, the Serbs were granted a wide-ranging autonomy. Later, an Obrenovic dynasty would alternate in leadership over what was to become an expanding Kingdom of Serbia.

21

Serbia registered small territorial gains to the south in 1833. It allied with the clans of Montenegro, who were fierce fighters and mostly Serbian. Both, however, began to encounter opposition to their aspirations from Austria, which saw the hand of Russian intrigue in developments in the Adriatic.

At that time, the Croats were still administered by the Hungarians and the Croatian nobility was a cosmopolitan assemblage of Croats, Italians, Germans, and Hungarians, essentially uninterested in Croatian national rights. However, as Vienna came under German influence (especially in language), Budapest pushed to replace the administrative use of Latin with Hungarian. In 1827–30, the Croat assembly made Hungarian compulsory in the schools. In opposition, the "Illyrian" movement grew amongst members of the lower nobility, the army, the professions and the clergy (Latin was the church language). Croats educated in Gratz and Vienna had come into contact with the romantic nationalist ideas of Germans such as Herder, and the Slovaks, Safarik, and Kollar. Its main theme was to recover Croatian "roots" before the arrival of Germanic and Hungarian influence. Its leader, Ljudevit Gaj, spoke grandly of a common Slavic culture from "Villach to Varna." They emphasized Serbo-Croatian in its three spoken dialects. Unable to acquire a wider following, the term "Illyrian" was dropped, and the movement became known as the National Party. It was to eventually advocate a more liberal regime within a Greater Croatia.[15]

The South Slavs were not untouched by the Revolution of 1848 that threw the Austro-Hungarian Empire into turmoil. A Slavic congress met in Prague and proposed the organization of the empire into a loose union of "nations." However, the court of Franz Joseph soon re-centralized control to the disadvantage of Hungary. A new Kingdom of Dalmatia, Croatia, and Slavonia was to be created with the Croats getting the port of Rijeka (Fiume) and prospects along the Adriatic. The Serbs had their eye on Vojvodina and the Banat (a fertile area populated by Serbs, Romanians, Germans and Hungarians). The Triune Kingdom was not established, however, and the Croat Sabor (assembly) ceased to meet as Croatia became merely six districts. Most vestiges of autonomy were abolished and its administration was taken over by Croats, Germans, Czechs and Slovenes. German became the official language and, apart from sweeping improvements for the peasantry and the granting of a bishopric at Zagreb, a real Croatian national program remained frustrated.

The Croat Bishop Josip Strossmayer led the National Party as a moderate proponent of equality and cooperation between the south Slavs, while Ante Starcevic broke off to establish the Party of Rights, which emphasized Croatian nationalism, historic claims, and the view that the South Slavs were really Croatian. Croatians continued to argue about these views, as well as about what should be their rightful relationship with Vienna and Budapest under the new Dual Monarchy. In this constitutional decision, Croatia was not consulted and it was handed back to Hungary. In 1868, Croatia's autonomy was widened internally somewhat, but Budapest continued to decide all matters of importance. In 1871, the Party of Rights led a local uprising that was suppressed, but it did induce Hungary to make additional concessions concerning the official use of Croatian and the power of the Sabor. Now deeply disillusioned, Bishop Strossmayer quit active politics to influence events from his pulpit. He remained an important voice until his death in 1905.

By 1877, the scene had shifted to Bosnia-Herzegovina and Serbian dissatisfaction under the Ottomans. During the first half of the nineteenth century, given Turkish defeats elsewhere in the empire, Bosnia-Herzegovina became a haven for displaced Turkish soldiers. Begs, janissaries, captaincies, and sipahis all vied for land and local power, even in opposition to the Porte. War and the exactions of overlords weighed heavily on the Serb peasants, who comprised a majority of the Christian population. Bosnia became part of Serbia's national project along with the Sanjak of Novi Pazar and "Old Serbia" to the south. If successful, Serbia would constitute a compact state in the center of the Balkans. In this, Belgrade had Montenegrin cooperation. In 1875, armed agrarian revolt broke out in Herzegovina and spread to Bosnia. Although its cause was economic in nature, tribal fighters arrived from mountainous border areas adjacent to Montenegro. It became a turning point in history for the whole region.

Within weeks, the major European powers of Germany, Austria, and Russia were embroiled in Bosnia, as the uprising continued on through summer until winter. Because of its location, Austria was given the lead in negotiations. Reform proposals made in December were rejected by the rebels, and those of May 1876 by the Porte. The revolt intensified and now Bulgaria was in upheaval as well. By July, Serbia and Montenegro could not resist what they saw as an opportunity and they attacked in concert. A Russian commander with 5,000 "volunteers" proved more hindrance than help, and Tsar Alexander II was forced to intervene to support Serbia. Although the Porte had not won decisively, the Three Emperors' Alliance, or *Dreikaiserbund*, forced the Turks into an armistice.

Next, when the extent of Turkish outrages in Bulgaria become known, events drove Russia to declare open war in April 1877. Russian troops crossed the Pruth River and gained early victories. By July, however, they were bogged down before Pleven, which held until December. However, under domestic pressure (and assuredly considering the carve-up to follow), Serbia broke its truce and Greece also came in. With the road open to Constantinople, the Sultan sued for peace.

What followed was the first comprehensive European effort to deal with the Eastern Question, that is, what should become of the vast territories of an Ottoman Empire now in decline and becoming increasingly unstable? Presumably because they had done most of the dying (37,000 lost in Bulgaria), the Russians were given the go-ahead to negotiate a settlement. What resulted at San Stefano in March 1878 was a Greater Bulgaria that included lands coveted by Serbia and Greece. Romania had to trade territory with St. Petersburg, to the advantage of Russia. Greece, Serbia, and Austria received little or nothing. After protests all round, and British saber-rattling, Russia backed down. The venue moved to Berlin.

By July, the deal was done. Greater Bulgaria was greatly reduced. Macedonia was given back to Turkey, under conditions. Montenegro, Serbia, and Romania became independent (but did trade territory). Russia's interests were recognized in the east and, to balance this off, Austria was invited to occupy Bosnia-Herzegovina and the Sanjak between Serbia and Montenegro. The Treaty of Berlin, executed under the eye of Germany's "honest broker" Chancellor Otto von Bismarck, was an earlier exercise in power politics.

After the Berlin Congress, Bosnia-Herzegovina became a subject of heated discussion, not only between Vienna and Budapest, but also among the ruling circles of Croatia and Serbia. Finally, Franz Joseph's views won out. Control of Bosnia-Herzegovina was viewed as just compensation given Russian gains and a way to stop Serbian expansionism. Its occupation proved as dramatic as the events leading up to it. The Croatian 13th Army Corps, stationed in Croatia and commanded by General Josip Filipovic, literally had to fight its way in against stiff Serb and Muslim opposition. With the enthusiastic approval of Croat public opinion, Filipovic set up a "provisional" government staffed by Croatians and quickly set about introducing Croatian law as well. Almost immediately, Zagreb pushed for full unification, with the support of the Slovenes. In Vienna and Budapest, debate raged on. In a compromise of sorts, Bosnia-Herzegovina's administration was given to the empire's joint-minister of finance. The titular head of Bosnia-Herzegovina was always the army commander, assisted by a ranking civil servant.[16]

From 1882–1903, Bosnia-Herzegovina was ruled by Benjamin Kallay, a Hungarian. Intent upon introducing the Austro-Hungarian way of doing things, the number of state employees rose from 120 to 9,533 by 1908. By far the majority at the administrative level were Croatian, but there were Czechs, Slovenes, and Poles as well. Kallay made very little effort to change the land tenure system (the cause of the revolt) and by 1914 there were still 93,368 peasant families. A great majority were Orthodox Serbs who worked one third of the cultivated land. In 1878, an estimated 85,000 families were broken down as 60,000 Serb and 23,000 Croat. The rest were Muslims. They all worked, mostly on large estates, for 6–7,000 *agas* and *begs*. Kallay built military roads and measured wood lots. He also built schools, and foreign loans made a railroad possible. Taxes increased five fold. As to the national question, Serbs and Croats found themselves increasingly at odds and both vied for support from the Muslims. Kallay tried to promote the idea of a Bosnian Muslim nationality, but it had little appeal at the time.[17]

In those years, the Habsburgs leaned towards their Croat and Slovene subjects and the position of the Catholic church. A number of Catholic churches and schools were built in Bosnia-Herzegovina, and militant clerics from Croatia began to replace the Franciscan order, which had been there since the 1300s. Nationalist-minded clerics and laymen promoted the idea of a union of Croatia, Bosnia, Slavonia, and Dalmatia.

In Croatia, Ante Starcevic and his Party of Rights took a strong anti-Serb stance. They viewed the Serbians as an obstacle to their own state-building. It must be remembered that Croats lived in Dalmatia on the Adriatic, in Croatia proper, and in Slavonia, in a semicircle around Bosnia. In the latter two areas, particularly in the Krajina, Serbs comprised a large segment of the population. Starcevic and others like him considered Serbs as second-class Croats, people who should convert to Catholicism and be Croaticized. Both Serbs and Croats had their eye on Bosnia. As an indication of how things were going, in 1894 (two years before Starcevic died), the Party of Rights split and Josip Frank established an even more anti-Serbian movement called the Pure Party of Rights![18]

The Austro-Hungarian annexation of Bosnia-Herzegovina in 1908 sent shockwaves through the Serbian communities and caused a crisis in Belgrade. Serb nationalists were inflamed as permanent annexation would foreclose any possibility that Serbia might one day inherit its lands in Bosnia. Serbs, after all, had done the fighting and now the Austrians were taking over. It appeared that, if anything, the area could eventually go to their Croat rivals. The latter, already entrenched in Bosnia-Herzegovina's administrative bureaucracy and now running much of their own internal affairs, had already succumbed to a steady diet of anti-Serb propaganda. Much of this was promoted by the Catholic church as directed by the Vatican. Starcevic, who had studied theology

25

in Budapest, had struck the name of the Serbian nation from his history of the South Slavs. The Party of Rights continued this tirade. This popular mindset was reinforced by pronouncements from the Papacy that questioned the legitimacy of the "schismatic Orthodox church" and lauded its Croat church as a bulwark of Christianity. A Croatian Catholic Congress in September 1900 in Zagreb announced its "agenda for the twentieth century" with anti-Orthodox appeals.[19]

Its ambitions frustrated in Bosnia, Serbia struck south. Under King Peter, the Serbs had fallen in with Montenegro, Greece, and Bulgaria in what was called the Balkan League. Their powerful northern neighbors (the Austro-Hungarian Empire and Russia) thought little would come of it. However, after signing secret protocols in the spring and summer of 1912, the three fell upon the Ottomans in October with a fervor fired by nationalism, religious righteousness, and the memory of centuries of cruelty and exploitation. The stated justification was to save the "oppressed Christians" of Macedonia and northern Greece.

The war was short, ferocious and successful. Its sanguinary nature and the resulting ravages among the civilian populations were soon lost in self-congratulations all round. Greece's land mass was doubled. Serbia gained "Old Serbia" and much of Macedonia. Bulgaria obtained the southern half of Macedonia. Then, in June 1913, feeling it had done most of the fighting, but was being denied its fair share of the spoils, Sofia took the disastrous step of attacking Serbia and Greece. Montenegro, Romania, and even the Ottomans piled in for a one-month massacre. Following big power intervention, minor adjustments were made to the possessions of victor and vanquished alike. The Balkan Wars served as a curtain-raiser for the crisis that was to come the following summer.[20]

Sarajevo seethed with discontent and had been under military rule since the Balkan Wars. In an atmosphere of clashing nationalism, young idealists joined secret societies bent on the removal of persons of authority through assassination. Croats and Serbs both had taken up the gun in an effort to change history. Some attempts had succeeded. Others had failed or had miscarried.

Austria was plotting as well. It had decided to hold summer military maneuvers in Bosnia-Herzegovina and the German and Austrian General Staffs were awaiting the opportunity to teach Serbia a lesson. Austrian Archduke Franz Ferdinand shared this view and no doubt thought he would enjoy his visit on 28 June, St. Vitus' Day (the anniversary of the battle of Kosovo and Serbia's national day). What is known now is that six Bosnian

Serbs had come into contact with a Colonel Dragutin Dimitrijevic (alias "Apis") who was the chief of intelligence on the Serbian General Staff and leader of the Black Hand. Dimitrijevic (later tried and executed), on his own, had armed them and sent them back to Sarajevo. They were young, happy-go-lucky amateurs actually, who, except for the vagaries of history, would have been discovered beforehand. A bomb thrown that morning bounced off the archducal car and wounded two staff officers. In the afternoon, Ferdinand decided to visit them at the hospital. His driver got lost, went up a narrow side street, and slowed to reverse in front of an amazed Gavrilo Princep. The Serb fired twice.[21]

In the aftermath of the murders, the full fury of the Austrians and their Croatian clients was vented on the Serbian communities and Belgrade. After discussions with Berlin, Austria decided for a short, localized war with Serbia that was to have the desired punitive effect. She attempted, unsuccessfully, to implicate the Serbian government in the plot and then put a number of stiff demands to Belgrade with the expectation they would be rejected. Although Serbia agreed to most of them, Austria declared war on 28 July. Pogroms broke out in Zagreb, Sarajevo and elsewhere, which raged on for days. Croat and Muslim mobs rampaged through the streets destroying Serbian homes, businesses and schools as well as assaulting individual Serb citizens. Unfortunately, these activities were supported by the Austrians and the civil authorities and, in many instances, by Catholic church leaders and their clerics.

In such an atmosphere, it was only a matter of time before Serbs were being hunted down and hanged from the trees and lampposts by the hundreds.[22]

But Austria and Germany were wrong in thinking it would be a walkover. As for Serbia, it was near exhaustion and in debt from the Balkan Wars and wanted peace. It now found itself, a nation of five million, against an empire of fifty. In 1914, it repelled two Austrian attacks and then pushed into Habsburg territory. It was thrown back, losing Belgrade and then it regained it again. In October 1915, the Austrian, German, and Bulgarian armies moved against the outnumbered Serbs. Overwhelmed, they fought their way for two months across Albania in winter with their king, their government and mules to where they could be evacuated by sea over to Corfu in Greece. Some 120,000 survived. However, many more were to die of wounds and disease.

Finally, in September 1918, twenty-eight Allied divisions took the offensive along the Salonika front. Nine divisions were Greek and six were Serbian. Under combined attack, the line of the Central Powers crumbled. Some say that the Serbs moved faster than the French motorized units. By November, their army was back in Belgrade, and it had occupied Bosnia-Herzegovina and Vojvodina as well.

Although Serbia had survived and even won, the war had taken a terrible toll. Its army had taken huge losses and many more wounded. In addition to the ravages of a typhus epidemic, which killed many thousands of civilians, the Austrian occupiers had been particularly brutal. In Serbia and Bosnia-Herzegovina, Europe saw its first concentration camps with Serbs even being sent to Hungary. Hundreds of villages were evacuated and the gruesome record suggests that even women, children, and the old were not spared, often being cut down on the road. Summary trials and executions continued for the entire duration of the war. Two thousand were killed near Nis alone for rebellion. The word had been given, "*Serbien muss sterben*" (Serbia must die) and die they did. The Croats and Slovenes, of course, had fought for the Central Powers, as had some Serbs from the Krajina who remained loyal to their units. The young state lost 1,264,000 people out of a pre-war population of 4,529,000. The country was devastated. However, out of the carnage came the idea of South Slav unity. During its exile on Corfu, the Serbian government had come into contact with Slovenes and Croats who had a different approach—who believed that their future should lie together. King Peter and his Regent, Prince Alexander, turned aside thoughts of a Serbia that reached to the sea and, on 1 December 1918, the Kingdom of the Serbs, Croats, and Slovenes was born.[23]

The new state was a constitutional monarchy under the Karadjordjevic dynasty. Its initial approach was democratic with universal male suffrage. However, real unity proved elusive. After much argument, district administrative units were established in 1919. Its many parties reflected not only internal division, but also the rough and tumble of the Balkan scene. Parliament was weakened by boycott and violence.

In 1929, King Alexander took over in the strongman style then sweeping Europe. The Kingdom of Yugoslavia was established (again with new internal borders), but in reality consensus was virtually nonexistent. This development was caused in no small measure by Croat opposition to a centralized state and the fact that Serbs were in a majority. Other national groups and the communists were also critical, but none was as intransigent as the Croats. The Slovenes, Bosnian Muslims and peasants had even gained under the system. In 1934, Alexander was assassinated in an Ustashe plot with links to Italy. In 1939, Peter II's regents tried to conciliate the Croats and redrew the borders. This late autonomy "understanding" ended with the outbreak of World War II.[24]

Yugoslavia found itself in a fascist vice. Mussolini's Italy was aiding the Croat Ustashe (Insurrection) movement in exile led by Ante Pavelic (the Frank wing of the Party of Rights), and German troops had stood on its border since the 1938 *Anschluss* with Austria. Neutrality bought eighteen months, but it was expected to capitulate in March 1941 when Hitler demanded that it throw its lot in with the Axis. He was going for Greece and wanted Belgrade in on it. A compromised coterie of ministers voted to agree, but Serb General Dusan Simovic staged an overnight coup that enabled Peter to form a new government. With anti-German demonstrators in the streets of Belgrade, and with Simovic swearing on everything Serbian, Berlin decided to invade. Belgrade was bombed on 6 April, Easter Sunday, and over 17,000 were killed. Within days, the country was overrun by the Germans, Italians, and Hungarians. Serb units were broken up, while the Croats and Slovenes offered little or no resistance. In Belgrade, the Germans met sullen-faced Serbs, while in Zagreb, they were cheered by large crowds of Croats.[25]

Following the surrender and the flight of the king, the country was partitioned. Italy took the Dalmatian coast and Montenegro. Albania took a large piece of southern Serbia. Bulgaria took much of Serbian Macedonia. Hungary part of Vojvodina. A large Independent State of Croatia (NDH) was established under Ustashe leader Pavelic; a collaborationist regime was set up in Serbia; and German military forces were assigned to strategic areas. As hopeless as the situation first appeared, the communist party under Tito began to organize itself for armed resistance and ex-members of the army began to rally to Colonel Mihailovic's Chetnik force.

In time, the Anti-Fascist Council for the National Liberation of Yugoslavia (AVNOJ) and its Partisan army, which had been forged in 1941–43, proved itself dominant politically and militarily and brought Tito to power in late 1944. Both the British and the Americans worked with and supplied the resistance, but Tito won against all comers even accepting the fact that the Soviet Red Army fought in the streets of Belgrade alongside the AVNOJ Partisans in October 1944. As for Mihailovic, he had cooperated with the Germans, lost Allied support and was executed after the end of the war. His Serbian supporters suffered accordingly.

This extraordinary account of unbelievable bravery, unsurpassed suffering and cruelty, endurance and betrayal has been told and retold elsewhere. To paraphrase Milovan Djilas, who fought it on behalf of AVNOJ, it was a war against the Axis, a civil war, and a revolution in an all-embracing inferno.

The single most searing aspect of that whole tragic episode was what happened to the Serb population at the hands of the Croat NDH and Ustashe.

This was no wartime expedient that was thrust upon the leaders of the Croat community and the Catholic church in extreme circumstances. This was planned mass murder and genocide. Pavelic had left Yugoslavia during the crisis of 1929 and placed himself at the disposal of Mussolini's Fascist Black Shirts. In Italy, Pavelic organized the Ustashe, the instrument that carried out Starcevic's policy of Croaticizing the Serbs. The Ustashe formula of his solution to the Serb problem was to eliminate one third, drive one third out of NDH, and baptize the remaining third Catholic.[26]

The NDH was established in April 1941 under Italian and German auspices, with the added trappings of an Italian kingdom (the Duke of Spoleto was renamed Tomislav II). It was enthusiastically welcomed by the Croats, and Pavelic was made *Poglavnik* or leader. He had only several hundred original cadres, so he was faced with the problem of setting up a government. However, Peasant Party leader, Vladko Macek, and the highest Catholic cleric, Archbishop Stepinac, urged the population to lend their support. The problem of control was difficult inasmuch as the NDH encompassed Croatia, a part of Serbia, and Bosnia-Herzegovina. Of 6.5 million people, 3.4 were Croats, 1.9 Serbs and 700,000 Muslims, and there were other minorities. Nevertheless, people flocked to join the movement. Mile Budak, Andrija Artukovic, Viktor Gutic, Dionisije Juricev, Krunoslav Draganovic, Stjepan Lackovic, Vjekoslav Luburic, Eugen Kvaternik, Slavko Kvaternik, Juraj Rukavina, Bozidar Cerovski, Ivan Herencic, Miroslav Filipovic-Majstorovic, Ivan Matkovic, Dinko Sakic, Ivica Brkljacic, Hinko Picili, and Jakov Dzal are but a few names of the more infamous members of the regime.[27]

In 1927, Pavelic had asked, "How can Croatia...full of Western culture, Latin and German culture, Italian humanist culture and German romanticism exist together with the Orthodox, ruthless and savage Serbs?" In 1941 he gave his answer. Within weeks, NDH-Ustashe fanatics moved against the Orthodox church shutting it down and either arresting or deporting its clergy. Orthodox churches were sacked and taken over. Over 200 priests and senior churchmen died. In the months and years that followed, the NDH-Ustashe regime would slaughter an estimated 500,000 Serbian men, women, and children, about 40,000 Jews, and some 100,000 gypsies. Camps were established at Gospić, Jadovo, Pag Island, Jasenovac, and in other locations. The Ustashe swept hundreds of villages and killed according to one's ethnic origins or religion. Lacking German efficiency, the executions were often done in the most brutal of fashions usually by club, knife, or strangulation following an orgy of torture and mutilation. Pavelic, who met with Hitler and collaborated with the Nazi executioner, Adolf Eichmann, once described a good Ustashe as one who can use his knife to cut a child out of the womb of his mother. To show their devotion, Pavelic's madmen once provided him with a basket full of eyes![28]

Like their Nazi mentors, the Ustashe kept records and photos of their handiwork. Catholic priests can be seen administering the sacrament of baptism in the mass conversion of Serbs (sometimes just before their execution)—"So that they can go to heaven." It is estimated that upwards of 200,000 were forcibly converted to Catholicism. The fortunate were those who were driven over into Milan Nedic's Serbia. Archbishop Stepinac is said to have come to question some of the methods of the regime, but he, his clerics and the Vatican had, by their actions, proven supportive of the NDH regime. Croats were recruited into the *Domobrani* (Home Guard) and many were trained in Germany. Having declared war against the Allies, Croats fought on the Russian front. However, the collapse of Italy in 1943 and the impending defeat of Hitler's Germany finally brought this monstrosity to an end and swift retribution to those unable to escape.[29]

Despite their wartime cooperation, relations between Tito and the West became tense. With 800,000 men under arms and a countrywide communist government, Yugoslavia had its eye on the prize port of Trieste, union with Bulgaria and support to the Greek communists. Another issue was that the Allies did not demonstrate interest in pursuing the many war crimes committed in Yugoslavia.

In 1945 a US army intelligence officer found Pavelic reading in the papal library, and stated in his report that, "Pavelic's contacts are so high… and so compromising to the Vatican that extradition would deal a staggering blow to the Roman Catholic Church." A US OSS officer was in active contact with Krunoslav Draganovic. The US also began to recruit Ustashe agents out of Italian refugee camps for anti-Tito activities. Ustashe-Vatican "rat-lines" were used to smuggle German Gestapo and SS officers out of Europe. By 1948, Andrija Artukovic would be in America. Pavelic would go to Argentina, where he helped to protect Adolf Eichmann.[30]

Once Tito turned against Stalin and the Soviet Union in 1947–49 and cut off support to the Greek guerrillas, Yugoslavia enjoyed a swing position between East and West, maneuvering this way and that amidst the tangle of Cold War politics. Tito put a lid on the nationalism of old, eliminated in one way or another any opposition, and set Yugoslavia on the path of building socialism. Yes, there were executions, but some, including even Stepinac, served jail sentences. Despite certain repressive aspects if one fell out of favor, or were found to be "out of step," there was considerable popular support for the regime, enthusiasm for unique, innovative approaches to federalism, and appreciation on the part of some that the establishment of six republics and two autonomous provinces was an attempt to balance, if not reconcile, national differences. However, limited democracy and "one-party" rule soon tended towards bureaucracy and, in time, the LCY lost the ability to renew itself and engendered regional dissent. Sensing this, Tito began to tinker with the system.

Yugoslavia's new 1974 constitution cut the Serbs down somewhat by boosting Kosovo (heavily Albanian-populated) and Vojvodina provinces to nearly that of republic status. Bosnia-Herzegovina's Muslims were given greater recognition as well. It is almost as if by decentralizing power somewhat, Tito was permitting the genie of nationalism to escape from the bottle. There had been earlier signs of trouble. In 1967, 130 Croat "intellectuals" asked that Serbo-Croatian be viewed as two languages and that Croatian be used in the schools. They wanted more political and economic power, demanding changes in banking, in taxation, the federal budget, and in currency regulations. The movement peaked in 1971 with the rebirth of Matica Hrvatska (founded in 1840), which turned into a nationalist party. By the end of the year, the republic planned changes to its constitution, which smacked too much of independence, including greater control over the Territorial Army (TDF). Tito cracked down hard, and then, he moved against Serbia for other reasons. A year after he died, in 1981, Kosovo's Albanians were to demand full republic status, which the Serbs read as separatism. Half-Croat, half-Slovene, Tito had held Yugoslavia together for forty-five years. In ten short years, his statue would be toppled from its pedestal.[31]

Federal Peoples Republic of Yugoslavia, 1946

Socialist Federal Republic of Yugoslavia, 1974

Early 1992, Serb-controlled territory

Late 1992, Serb-controlled territory in B-H

Chapter 2

Embattled Borderlands

Krajina, Slavonia, Kosovo: November 1992

"The Serbs die without complaint and kill without compunction."

Herbert Okun, a US diplomat

With Germany, Austria, and the Vatican all actively intriguing to advance the cause of Croatian and Slovenian independence, which meant, at the time, to openly foment the break up of Yugoslavia, only the American administration of President George Bush could have halted the country's precipitate slide into civil war. However, America's last ambassador, Warren Zimmerman, had arrived in Belgrade in 1989 with a new message for Yugoslavia's leaders that with the end of the Cold War and the transformation sweeping over Central and Eastern Europe, Yugoslavia no longer enjoyed the importance that the US had previously given it. Furthermore, the US placed human rights high on its agenda and strongly disapproved of what it considered to be Serbian repression of the Albanian majority community in Kosovo. Zimmerman did assert traditional US support for Yugoslavia's unity, independence and its territorial integrity, but added the new twist that the US would oppose unity imposed by force. His words were very much welcomed by the Kosovo Albanians, but so angered Serbian President Slobodan Milosevic that he refused to talk to the American for nearly a year.[1]

By that time, events had accelerated. With Ambassador Zimmerman admonishing Milosevic over Kosovo, and with Washington pressing its European friends to support Prime Minister Ante Markovic, the US lost leverage over the most important political figure in Yugoslavia. A year later, the league of communists had run itself onto the rocks of disagreement over Yugoslavia's future and nationalist passions were running rampant. The Slovenes and the Croats were rapidly cutting their ties to the federation and the Serbs had retaliated in turn. In early 1991, the US repeated its warning against the use of force to preserve unity, but began to look at Yugoslavia as a European problem.

Finally, on 21 June, four days before Slovenia and Croatia declared their independence, US Secretary of State James Baker diverted himself from a CSCE meeting in Berlin and a ceremonial visit to Albania to address the Yugoslav crisis, at his own staff's request. He held eleven meetings in a single day, which included all six leaders of the republics, the Kosovo Albanians, and two sets of meetings each with Prime Minister Markovic and Foreign Minister Budimir Loncar. Baker was at a loss when talking to Montenegrin Momir Bulatovic, having only two items in his briefing book—"The smallest republic in Yugoslavia. A possible vote for Mesic." It was a feeble, half-hearted, pro forma, last-minute exercise in futility.

In retrospect, Secretary Baker's time could have been much better spent with the Slovene leader, Milan Kucan, the Croat Franjo Tudjman and Milosevic in a closed room some months earlier where they should have been forcefully told that the US would not tolerate a civil war over Yugoslavia! They should have been told that a US-European summit would be held to work matters out in a peaceful way and that financial aid in the form of loans, direct investments, debt rescheduling and debt-forgiveness, and advice would become available to alleviate the serious financial strains between the republics. In other words, that the US stood ready to fix the problem. All of this, of course, did not happen and by November 1992, the war had spread from Croatia to Bosnia and the Serbs were pressing the attack.[2]

"We will never return our land to Croat control and we will never surrender our arms!" So said Zdravko Zecevic, Prime Minister of Republika Srbska Krajina (RSK) in his Terazije office in Belgrade. A short, compact, agricultural engineer in his mid-forties, Zecevic exuded exuberant confidence as he explained that the territory now held by the Krajina Serbs (including east and west Slavonia) extended from southwest Croatia where its capital of Knin was located, north to within forty kilometers of Zagreb, and then eastward over to the town of Vukovar on the Danube—across from Vojvodina in Serbia. "Here," he said, going on to explain the history of the military frontier, "Serbs have lived since the seventeenth century." Serb control was not complete, but it did comprise wide swathes of forested hills, rich farmland, a petroleum deposit, and a number of towns and villages with factories and infrastructure.

Zecevic's office walls were covered with peaceful rural scenes, reproductions of Orthodox icons, and war maps with plastic overlays of force dispositions which I tried to make some sense of. Zecevic admitted that the yet-to-be-recognized statelet suffered from severe economic dislocation, supply shortages, and loss of production as a result of seven months of fighting, and the fact that only 270,000 people were spread out over 5,000 square miles. He claimed that its population would more than double when its scattered refugee families returned. Left unsaid was the fact that the self declared "state" comprised almost one third of Croatia's territory which the JNA and Serbian militias had carved out from July 1991 until February 1992, linking the many areas where Serbs had lived as a majority within Croat populated territories.

He allowed that shortages of petroleum and electric power had made it difficult to get industrial enterprises back in operation, but nonetheless described the area's good potential in agriculture, meat and dairy produce, wood and forest products, and, when peace returned, tourism. Zecevic said that many homes and buildings remained damaged, and that schools lacked heating oil for the winter. He blamed UN sanctions for the slow return to normalcy and had little good to say about the effectiveness of the UN Protection Force (UNPROFOR) since the latter had interposed itself between the Serbs and the Croats in March 1992. Zecevic accused UNPROFOR of hypocrisy and claimed it was ignoring Croat incursions into the buffer zone. He said they had suffered 268 dead and 200 wounded as a result of some 800 incidents involving exchanges of fire. Zecevic claimed that the RSK had a common political and military agenda with the Bosnian Serbs, and stressed that it was essential that the latter clear a northern road corridor linking the Krajina, Serb-held territory in Bosnia, with Serbia itself. He pointed to the taking of Brcko, Biljeljina, Maglaj, Gradacac, and Bosanski Brod as operations designed to accomplish this objective before winter. Suggesting bold plans for the future, Zecevic said it was quite possible that the Krajina Serbs and the Bosnian Serbs would agree on a joint constitution—uniting Serbs on both sides of the Sava River. Before leaving with my "visa" to visit Slavonia (and a stack of RSK emblems of a crowned, double-headed eagle and shield), the ebullient "Prime Minister" urged me to visit Knin where, he said, they still enjoy good hunting in spite of the war![3]

The following day, I joined an UNPROFOR convoy out to Sector East headquarters at Erdut to hear its side of the story and see what the new republic looked like for myself. The stark contrast between the carefully ploughed fields of rich, upturned earth and a succession of shattered villages jarred one's sensibilities. It all didn't seem to fit, but the grim faces of Serb farmers in rough clothes and rubber boots driving their battered tractors indicated that a new war was in progress—one of grim survival. Checkpoints along the way were manned by armed men wearing a variety of mismatched uniforms, headgear, and military patches that I couldn't begin to describe. However poor their appearance, the UNPROFOR vehicles were checked carefully, including our "visas." There was no waving us through. Also, signs indicated that the formerly autonomous "Slavonia, Baranja, and Western Strem" had been placed under the command of Knin far to the southwest.

UNPROFOR had 15,000 men deployed in sectors south, north, west and east in the same southwest to northeast arc occupied by the Serbs, with the exception of a large chunk of Croat territory lying between sectors east and west. The situation was tenuous at best and UNPROFOR thought fighting could erupt at any time. Their mission, under the Vance Plan, was to separate the combatants; establish an "in-place" ceasefire; totally disarm the two sides; and see to the return of refugees. So far, it was not going very well. The UN had succeeded in getting the JNA to pull back and it had managed to collect the weapons of the TDFs at storage sites. However, the numbers of the Serbian paramilitary irregulars continued to grow and they were refusing to turn over their arms, just as Zecevic had said they would. Thus far, the UN had been unable to force their compliance.

Equally ominous were the number of incidents directed by Serbs against Croatians: the shooting and grenading of homes; dismissals from places of employment; the settling of Serbian families into homes vacated by Croatians; and the refusal to permit the return of Croatian refugees. The UNPROFOR officers openly admitted their sense of frustration and their pessimism for the future because of their inability to stem these practices. In Sector East, there were only two Russian and Belgian battalions of 1,500 soldiers, twenty civilians, 130 UN police and small communications, engineering, and medical support detachments. UNPROFOR was clearly no match for either the Croats or the Serbs. The biggest problem was said to be the increased number of Serb militia groups controlled by "warlord" commanders who ruled bits of turf and claimed autonomy from Belgrade. In effect, UNPROFOR was attempting to implement the Vance Plan with armed units operating outside a formal chain of command. It was difficult to judge whether Milosevic actually pulled all of the strings, or whether the militias were semi-independent. It was not a clear-cut case of black and white.

We returned to Belgrade via Vukovar, which had fallen to the Serbs a year earlier after three months of fighting that left the once-prosperous town on the Danube almost totally destroyed. We were told not to walk off the road because of the danger of mines. Even so, it was clear that the town was damaged beyond what I had imagined. Hardly a home was intact. There were bullet-pocked walls; gaping holes and broken window glass; charred rafters and missing roof tiles exposing the interiors to the rain and snow; blasted tree limbs, devoid of life. Very few people were moving about and, a year later I saw only one house undergoing what you could call real repair. To date, this had been Croatia's biggest defeat, and it had resulted in great physical destruction and high loss of life. Because the JNA siege of Vukovar had become symbolic in the Western press of what was described as the bludgeoning brutality of the Serbian military machine, I wanted to learn what had happened that had caused such devastation.

"Nidza," or Mikloj-Nikola Simijanovic, stands some six feet tall, has powerful shoulders, a deep chest, long black hair, and eyes that burn right through you. He is an artist, a sculptor from Vukovar who had lived there before the fighting started. I asked him to explain. He said that Vukovar had been one of the wealthiest towns in Yugoslavia and, as such, had developed a lively cultural community of artists and writers. He said that he had loved it, and the life there, up until 1990, when Zagreb attempted to rig the local elections in favor of the Croatian community. It became much worse, he claimed, when local Croat extremists began to acquire weapons. Non-Croats were intimidated and fired from their jobs. The JNA stood by, he said, and watched it all happen and eventually it holed up in its barracks complex once the fighting got underway.

My artist friend, who referred to himself as a "Hungarian," said that by September the military balance at Vukovar was roughly equal with the Croats dug in inside the city and elements of the JNA and the Serb militias strung out in Slavonia. However, in the following weeks, Zagreb was able to bring in upwards of 6,000 additional fighters from the Croatian National Guard and Party of Rights. Atrocities against Serb civilians, who were virtual hostages at that point, began to take place. Belgrade, however, was able to muster more manpower, artillery, and even aircraft and it became merely a question of time before the town would fall. It was clear that Tudjman had blundered in trying to hold it. That said, Nidza explained that the Croat defenders fought from underground bunkers that had been built after World War Two of extremely strong materials, and even from the sewers.

The town is right on the Danube across from Serbia and was boxed in on the other three sides by roads. Hence, according to Nidza, it was surrounded by the Serbs who continued to pour in ordnance. Nidza claimed that, at one point, the Croats were offered an exit out of town that they rejected. Finally, the Serbs proceeded to level the place street by street. By 20 November, it was all over.

He claimed that quantities of munitions were found stored in old buildings, a church, and the eighteenth-century museum residence of Count Heltz; that West German weapons were discovered; and that some NATO-issue food and medical supplies were found scattered about. Bodies of Serb civilians, who had been executed, were also found. We did not get into the question of what had happened to some two hundred Croat fighters who had surrendered and were herded into a warehouse. UNPROFOR had just discovered a patch of sunken earth outside Vukovar that it suspected to be a mass grave as well as the likely answer to the question of the missing men.[4]

His hands blackened and hardened from working with metal, Nidza showed me pieces of sculpture he had made in the images of war: twisted shards of shrapnel, shell casings, spent cartridges, and broken pieces of machinery, some welded into an anguished cry; the head of a soldier with what could be a raven perched on his helmet; an infernal machine, ready to explode, like Yugoslavia itself. As an artist, Nidza said he should belong to the world as a free and independent spirit. However, instead, he found himself fighting with the Serbs for what he claimed was his survival. His work was very strong and suggestive of the innate cruelty and destruction of war. I have wondered whether Nidza is still at his craft, welding torch in hand, or whether he also has died in the flames.

In Belgrade, the war dominated television, radio, the press, and what passed for national debate. Assuredly, what was referred to as "the situation" was on the minds and lips of everyone, but internal access to the media was limited and exploited shamelessly by Milosevic and his Serbian Socialist Party (SPS). Opposition newspapers and television tried their best, but Belgrade's city authorities breathed down their necks and were not always polite. Nevertheless, people were talking endlessly in the cafes, *boîtes de nuit*, and restaurants about the latest fight between David and Goliath! David, of course, was the Serb-American Federal Prime Minister Milan Panic and Goliath the

Serbian President Slobodan Milosevic. Their long-simmering disagreement over the direction of national policy had just re-erupted with renewed fury.

A few days after Milosevic's special police had cordoned off the Federal Ministry of the Interior building, the Serbian president's SPS and the rightwing extremist Serbian Radical Party (SRS) of Vojislav Seselj tried to oust Panic by a vote of no confidence in the lower house of parliament. This was overridden, however, on the following day by the Montenegrins of the upper house, not only saving Panic, but also increasing popular support for early elections. Panic, a self-made California millionaire, had been brought to Belgrade by Milosevic the previous June to help rump-Yugoslavia's (Serbia and Montenegro) international image, but not to take the bit in his teeth with regard to making real decisions. Nonetheless, Panic quickly proved to be his own man.

In July, he had showed up uninvited at a CSCE meeting in Helsinki, asked for their support and suggested that he could stop the war. He was rebuffed, but he astounded everyone by stating, "I'll do my job and Milosevic will do his—and God help him if he gets in my way." Since that time, he had taken several initiatives and had gained backing from the foreign media by making statements such as, "There is no idea worth killing for at the end of the twentieth century." Indicative of good intentions, but also naivety regarding the war, Panic once observed, "They're shooting! We just have to tell them to stop!" Since he was a real contrast to the usually stern-faced Milosevic, the opposition and students rallied to Panic's side and some polls even had him a two-to-one favorite. For a so-called dictator, Milosevic had his hands full.

Milosevic charged that Panic and Dobrica Cosic, a very popular Serbian writer whom Milosevic had promoted into becoming federal President, were conducting negotiations with the Croats and the Kosovo Albanians without consulting him. Foreign Minister Vladislav Jovanovic (yet another Milosevic protégé) had recently quit in angry protest, claiming that Panic was damaging Yugoslavia's interests at the Geneva peace talks. Whatever the actual case was, Milosevic was clearly trying to get rid of an unwanted competitor who was gaining in popularity. To this end, he was unwittingly assisted by the West Europeans and the US who were clamoring for early elections in the expectation that Panic might actually replace Milosevic. After getting over legal hurdles in typical Balkan fashion (laws and even constitutions are changed to the advantage of whoever is in power), Milosevic agreed. This should have bothered people, but it didn't. Somehow, many thought that Panic, a person who had lived in the US for thirty years; who spoke badly accented Serbian; who was unfamiliar with Yugoslavian affairs; who had no party organization;

who lacked a country-wide constituency; and who was being denied equal access to the media, especially TV, really had a chance to win.

Perhaps the views of the Democratic Party (DS) best typified the prevailing mood. They, and other oppositionists, regretted their boycott of elections the previous spring, and wanted to get back into the fight. Given the steadily rising level of anti-government demonstrations against Milosevic since the summer, it thought it could pull socialist deputies, even ministers, over to its side. It mistakenly thought that it was on a roll. Dusan Mihajlovic, the head of New Democracy (ND) was more realistic. He said that Milosevic held every advantage and thought that the election was not so much a fair contest as a popular referendum on Slobodan's policies since the beginning of the war as they affected peoples lives. Mihajlovic said that there was insufficient time to mount a real campaign and that with 141 parties of every description, it was asking too much of an inexperienced electorate to take it all in and make really informed choices.

Milosevic's message to his millions (mostly rural villagers) was short and simple, *"Sa nana nema neizvesnosti"* ("With us there is no uncertainty!"). Voters were faced with the formidable task of selecting the presidents of Serbia and Montenegro; hundreds of district councils; and all of the seats for both the federal and republican parliaments or assemblies. In Serbia alone, 250 deputies were to be chosen from 4,600 candidates, along with seven presidential contenders. Within days, this bewildering array had shaken down to forty-five political parties and alliances. At the federal level, the 138 members of the upper and lower houses had to be chosen from 12,786 candidates from twenty-eight parties. As for Panic (his student supporters had collected the required 10,000 signatures), he faced questions from Milosevic concerning his residency and the presence of an all-American campaign staff, which included a former US ambassador. Even so, he gave it his best shot. Panic spoke of free market economy and ethnic harmony, breaking into American English when his Serbian failed him. When it was over, Milosevic had blown him away with a fifty-five to thirty-five percent win. International observers said that only five percent of the vote was "flawed." It was a big win for Milosevic, a blow to the backers of Panic, and a big boost to the extreme-nationalist SRS, which won seventy-four seats in the federal assembly to Milosevic's one hundred. It forced the latter and his SPS to work with a party led by a madman, Vojislav Seselj.[5]

Nine days after the election, Milosevic's SPS and Seselj's SRS precipitated another vote of no confidence against Panic (the third such attempt) and removed him as prime minister. With the elections having had the result of shifting power further to the nationalist-right, many foreign observers braced themselves for the worst. However, in January, Milosevic confounded his critics by going to Geneva to throw his weight behind the Vance Plan. Speaking to reporters, Milosevic said, "I hope that all sides will use this opportunity to stop the war in Bosnia-Herzegovina." Sincere or insincere, good guy or bad guy, Milosevic has played it both ways and has tried to hold to the political center and on to power, amid an extremely complicated and volatile situation.

Buffered behind a complex constitutional structure, Milosevic was always quick to remind his critics of the "legal" limitations of his presidential powers, while accomplishing most of his plans for Croatia and Bosnia and fending off countermoves by the EC and the UN. There is no doubt that Serb militias were able to gain as much ground as they had only because of Belgrade's backing in men and war matériel, while conceding that much of it is where Serbs have been settled for centuries. Despite extensive external sanctions, Milosevic had thus far managed to keep the hardships of a sharply declining economy within tolerable limits. People explained that things never did work very well in Yugoslavia, and a great amount of getting around the system had existed. Consequently, there always was a black market and smuggling across its external borders. Serbia's self-sufficiency in food and the stockpiling of supplies had, thus far, taken the bite out of its isolation. The result of the election confirmed this as well as the existence of a bedrock of Serbian nationalist sentiment. Serbians were quite willing to sacrifice and, so far, a solid majority stood behind Slobodan.

I wanted to see where Milosevic had begun his rise to power; where he had tapped into a reservoir of Serbian resentment and passion that fused the past with the present; where he had called out to the Serbian nation not only to reclaim its history, but to claim its future. I wanted to see the object of his anger and wrath, the Albanians of Kosovo. I pushed my way onto the 11 p.m. bus for Pristina—four hours of standing room only as the bus rocked to the endless twists and turns in the road and endless tapes that blared out songs of Balkan sadness and joy. We were jam-packed. It must have been just before Podujevo when crossing into Kosovo that we pulled over to a checkpost. It was after 2 a.m. and cold. In the glare of lights, police militiamen in heavy, blue greatcoats looked at our driver's papers. Then, another, a pistol strapped to his side, climbed up to check our identity documents. He paid particular attention to the Albanians. Assisted by the driver, to the amusement of some, he called to a half dozen or so who had been huddled in the back, rousted them out, and told them to collect their luggage. This included one old man wearing a knitted skullcap. Only about half of them made it back aboard. Sometime after 3 a.m.,

I was dropped off at a deserted bus stop, and I headed, with my bags, in the supposed direction of a hotel.

Kosovo and Metohia (the Kosmet) comprises some 7,000 square miles of farmland and hills bounded by Montenegro, Macedonia, and Albania. Its two million inhabitants are ninety percent Albanian in the most densely populated rural area in the Balkans. It was always one of the poorer regions in Yugoslavia despite some industry and the famed Trepca mines with an estimated mineral wealth of US$5 billion. Besides being the severed "other half" of Albania (to include part of Montenegro and western Macedonia), it's also the heart of Old Serbia's medieval kingdoms and the site of some of Serbian Orthodoxy's most highly cherished churches and monasteries, Gracanica being one just a few miles outside of Pristina. It has been compared to the Israeli-occupied West Bank where two peoples, one indigenous, having lived there for hundreds of years, the other militant and determined to reclaim its roots, live on the same land and both call it their own. The Albanians, who converted to Islam under the Ottomans, have sustained a high population growth despite disaster. The Serbs, fewer in numbers, look at Kosovo as the endangered cradle of their civilization.

Pristina's Muslim mosques, Orthodox domes, ugly, communist-style apartment blocks, clutter of houses and shops of all descriptions, tacky, crumbling public buildings of gross proportions and heroic design, all juxtaposed with no apparent plan, suggest one is outside Europe's arc of affluence and approaching the marches of Asia Minor. The Grand Hotel Pristina (a "five-star" affair) is a typical example. Thirteen stories of decaying opulence, its huge, pretentious function rooms seemed grotesque considering its lack of guests. The barely heated rooms, broken telephones, and elevators that, when they work, often deliver you to a subterranean crypt before creeping up to the lobby, I have learned to regard as normal. I took to the sunshine and fresh air as soon as I could after breakfast even though I had no contacts and no idea where anything was located. If maps were once available, they no longer existed.

Pristina ("Prishtina" to the Kosova Albanians) is mostly a town of mean streets. Poorly clothed, unhappy-looking people jostled each other on the crowded, muddy pavements looking exhausted, old before their time and unhealthy, as if suffering from some baleful disorder. The reason for this malady made itself known, most unexpectedly, in minutes. Two burly militiamen, walking from the opposite direction grabbed an unsuspecting teenaged boy from behind by both of his arms and dragged him over to their vehicle. In he went, in a matter of seconds. I was so surprised that I managed to get my camera out only when it was almost over.

There was little or no commotion and no one tried to stop it, or protest, or even question the militiamen, as if it was normal and happened all the time. Two men, watching from across the street, crossed over and in broken English advised me to be careful. I explained that I was an American journalist and that I wanted to go to the office of Ibrahim Rugova, the leader of Kosovo's Albanians. They took me there in their car.

"Welcome to the only free fifty square meters in all of Kosova!" Dressed in a suit and shirt, with a carefully knotted tie, Dr. Shaqir Shaqiri extended a warm handshake as he greeted me in perfect English at the door of the headquarters of the Democratic League of Kosova (LDK)—a one-story building located next to a sports stadium. A professor of English and American Literature at Pristina University (before being jailed for the first time in 1982), he went on to depict how nearly two million Albanians had come to know a life of hell in a very small place. While waiting for coffee, I described what I had just witnessed. Shaqiri asked a middle-aged man to join us from another room. His face was cut and bruised. He explained that he had been hauled over on a dark country road the previous night by two Serbs who had pistol-whipped him and threatened his life. He was also honest enough to admit that his complaint had been listened to and that an arrest had already been made. He had come to the LDK to report the incident.

Under Serbia's "emergency" regulations, Kosovo's parliament was disbanded in 1989. Albanian declarations of full republic status in July 1990, and then complete independence in May 1992, were declared illegal by Belgrade. Additionally, Serbia passed a series of harsh laws that have made the "Kosovars" into non-persons who have been deprived of their legal and civil rights. Over 100,000 persons were removed from state employment. Machinery and equipment were removed from factories and sent elsewhere. Bank funds were transferred. Pristina's radio and TV stations, along with its newspapers and magazines, were shut down. The university and secondary schools were closed, libraries and archives looted and restrictions imposed regarding the use of the Albanian language. Cultural institutes were shut. Public attorneys, prosecutors and judges were dismissed. A ban was imposed regarding the disposal of real property. Meetings, rallies and demonstrations have been forbidden. Since the repression began in 1989, some 2,500 Albanians have been arrested, tried, and sentenced to jail, all according to the law.[6]

Shaqiri went on. As piecemeal and punitive Serbian efforts at recolonization made its impact, economic production and employment plummeted, as had standards of nutrition and public health care. With some 700,000 Albanians without adequate medical attention, infectious disease and infant mortality were on the rise. Fortunately, a small UN and CSCE presence had been established and some foreign voluntary agencies were beginning to provide assistance. UN mediators, Lord Owen and Cyrus Vance, were attempting to wrap a mantle of concern around Kosovo. As helpful as that might have been, it had not prevented the wounding and deaths of hundreds of Albanians who had protested about their plight. Nor was it to prevent SRS party boss Seselj from openly calling for the expulsion of 300,000 Albanians. Nor did it prevent "Arkan" (Zeljko Raznatovic), a "warlord" militia leader who was responsible for ethnic cleansing in Croatia and Bosnia, from becoming an elected member of parliament from Kosovo. Again, all according to the law.[7]

That night, I ate at the "Grand" Hotel. There were few guests in the dining room, so a powerfully built man of fifty or so, with close-cropped, steel-gray hair, dressed in a camouflage uniform and carrying a pistol stood out. If central casting in Hollywood had needed another "Kurtz," he would have fit the role. I tried to talk to him, but he wasn't having any of that. After he had finished his meal, he walked away without paying like so many of the security-men hanging around the hotel. Pristina had the atmosphere of a prison of inmates and armed guards. It was clear that, whatever the reasons, and I didn't have many answers yet, Milosevic's policies were not only destined for failure, but were overly harsh in their application. Milosevic could not ask for justice for the Serbs living in Croatia and Bosnia and deny the Kosovars their civil rights. Besides making a difficult internal problem even worse, it looked appallingly bad internationally.

It had been a brutal year and a half of slaughter and pillaging and the beginning of a callous trade in tormented human lives amid the lies of antagonists and certain members of the international community alike. I was certainly sobered by what I had seen and heard within the space of only a few weeks. How could I get a mental and emotional grip on events that had spun out of control, or had been orchestrated by Yugoslavia's more outrageous leaders and supposedly stalwart, respected and well-intentioned members of the West—including, surprisingly (or not so surprisingly), senior officials at the Vatican? A major country in the heart of Europe had been permitted to disintegrate, or perhaps had even been pushed along the path of destruction. What did it say about the future of others whose borders have changed in this century? Will they also become "balkanized"?

At the outset of the conflict, I was skeptical when Serbs pointed an accusing finger at Germany, Austria, and Rome. Now I was convinced that they, and others, had undertaken actions aimed at breaking up an established state, a state which, while certainly in need of considerable change, threatened no one. Indifference had led others to prefer simple expediency to international law, with the result that, as Yugoslavia broke up, ethnic communities in each republic began to struggle to salvage their own futures with little regard for previously applicable norms of behavior, relying predominantly on personal and local loyalties to legitimize their actions, however reprehensible.

The destruction of a state means the destruction of civil society and lives uprooted. It is a sudden twist of fate that means that your education and training, job and professional career, are wasted and count for nothing. A future that you thought you could reasonably plan for becomes a thing of the past. Your child's education and security for your ageing parents are impossibilities. Your home, savings and possessions vanish. Everything that you had ever built is gone. You may know every privation and never again have a feeling of peace and security. And, if you are a man, you will know the humiliation of being unable to protect your loved ones, let alone yourself. You will know fear, until that fear turns to hate. At that point, you will be guided by your own worst instincts and by others like you in the same situation.

* * *

3–29 August 1991. After assuming the Federal Presidency, Croat Stipe Mesic advised the Croatian assembly in Zagreb to refuse to accept Montenegrin Branko Kostic as chairman of the ceasefire committee. When Kostic was elected, Mesic walked out. Obviously not acting on behalf of all Yugoslavia's republics, he advised Zagreb to name Serbia as the prime aggressor. Mesic continued to use the Presidency to suit Zagreb's purposes. With more fighting in Slavonia, Zagreb began to discuss ways to grant the Serbs in Croatia some form of autonomy. However, as soon as Zagreb had announced it would cut off the JNA barracks in Croatia from their supply of food, water, and electricity, JNA-Serb militia forces in Slavonia began to move on Vukovar.

While the EC as a whole was trying to appear even-handed, the traditional central powers of "Mittel Europa," who had a history of involvement in the Balkans, were supporting Slovenia and Croatia. Slovenia's Foreign Minister, Dimitrij Rupel, was told in Vienna that Austria intended to take the initiative in lining up diplomatic recognition for Ljubljana and Zagreb. German Chancellor

Helmut Kohl and Foreign Minister Hans-Dietrich Genscher also began to urge early recognition. The Italian Foreign Minister, Gianni de Michelis, was doing the same.[8]

7 September–30 October 1991. The EC convened an international conference on Yugoslavia at The Hague under the chairmanship of Lord Peter Carrington that was attended by members of the SFRY Presidency, the federal government, the presidents of the six republics, members of the European Council, EC representatives, and those of the European Commission. The conference set itself the task of ending the conflict under the rubric: no unilateral changes in borders by the use of force; the protection of the rights of all Yugoslavians; and full respect for all legitimate interests and aspirations. Lofty as its intentions were, the EC was essentially attempting to square the circle. On 25 September, the United Nations Security Council declared events a threat to peace and called for an embargo on all military supplies. When the Brioni moratorium expired on 8 October, Croatia and Slovenia immediately re-declared their independence and followed this up with demands that the JNA leave their soil. Adding yet another factor that complicated matters even further, on 30 September, the Kosovo Albanians held a referendum for independence. In Bosnia-Herzegovina, on 14 October, with the Serb deputies refusing to participate, the Bosniak and Croat members of the assembly agreed to hold a referendum on the future of the republic. Then, the two sides adopted a "memorandum" that proposed independence. The Hague conference continued to reformulate statements describing how Yugoslavia should be reconstituted. Serbian President Milosevic opposed the idea of abolishing a state that had existed for seventy years. With Serbia dissenting, Lord Carrington urged a looser association of sovereign republics or states. By the end of October, the Serbs of Bosnia-Herzegovina had formed their own assembly.

5 November–24 December 1991. Plenary sessions at The Hague continued without reaching agreement. EC foreign ministers in Rome suspended trade, aid, and cooperation agreements with Yugoslavia and began to consider the application of economic sanctions and an oil embargo. On 9–10 November, Serbs in Bosnia-Herzegovina voted overwhelmingly to remain in Yugoslavia. The EC condemned continued Serbian military action against Dubrovnik, Vukovar, and other Croatian towns (Vukovar fell on 20 November). At Geneva on 23 November, Milosevic, Tudjman and JNA General Velijko Kadijevic signed an unconditional ceasefire in the presence of Lord Carrington and UN special envoy, Cyrus Vance. The latter proposed a UN force for Croatia. The EC Ministerial Council, on 2 December, singled out Serbia and Montenegro for economic sanctions. On 5 December, Stipe Mesic quit the presidency, with the comment that he had fulfilled his mission as, in his words, "...Yugoslavia no longer exists!"

On 11 December, the Vance Peace Plan was submitted to the UN Security Council. It proposed the deployment of peacekeeping forces into United Nations Protected Areas (UNPA)—that is, East and West Slavonia and the Krajina. All units of the JNA, Croatian National Guard and TDFs were to be withdrawn and all paramilitary units disbanded. Local police would maintain order assisted by the UN. Its intent was to foster conditions necessary for negotiations without prejudging their outcome. However, with Yugoslavia still in chaos and fighting continuing in Croatia, EC Foreign Ministers on 17 December, in Brussels, adopted sweeping guidelines for its early recognition of new states according to rules set out by the Hague conference arbitration commission (the Badinter commission). The Yugoslav republics were all invited to submit their applications by 23 December for review, pending decision by the EC Ministerial Council after 15 January. The SFRY Presidency protested that the EC decisions violated the UN Charter and international law, and that, by its meddling in Yugoslavia's internal affairs, the EC was supporting unilateral and unconstitutional secession and was attempting to abolish Yugoslavia's legal status.[9]

In a week of unilateral actions, the Serbian National Council on 19 December proclaimed itself as the Republic of Srpska Krajina with Milan Babic as its first president. The next day, Federal Prime Minister Ante Markovic resigned. On 21 December, the self-constituted Serbian assembly in Bosnia-Herzegovina adopted a resolution to form a republic within the framework of Federal Yugoslavia. To assert its leading position within the EC, and to accelerate secession, on 23 December Germany recognized the independence of Slovenia and Croatia with effect from 15 January. On 24 December, the EC announced it had received applications for recognition by Slovenia, Croatia, Bosnia-Herzegovina, and Macedonia. Serbia and Montenegro did not apply, pointing out they had been recognized at the Congress of Berlin in 1878 and claimed to have maintained full international continuity since that time.[10]

2 January–26 February 1992. This time in Sarajevo, and again in the presence of UN envoy Cyrus Vance, JNA General Andija Raseta and Croatian Defense Minister Gojko Susak signed a ceasefire with effect from 3 January. On 9 January, the UN Security Council, urged by its Secretary General agreed to send fifty officers to the contested areas of Croatia in preparation for the arrival of an anticipated 10,000 UN peacekeepers. That same day, the assembly of the Serb people of Bosnia-Herzegovina added substance to their previous resolution by declaring a "republic" within Federal Yugoslavia.

On 10 January, the Hague conference convened in Brussels. The so-called Badinter arbitration commission announced its opinions regarding Yugoslavia. In opinion 2, it stated that the Serbs of Bosnia-Herzegovina and Croatia had to enjoy all minority rights under the guidelines of the conference including, if need be, the right to "national determination." In opinion 3, it stated that the borders of Yugoslavia were to remain unchanged, or be changed only by mutual consent and that they were to assume the character of international boundaries. In other words, demarcations between republics that had the character of internal jurisdictional divisions became frontiers. In opinions 4–7, it stated that Slovenia and Macedonia met all conditions for recognition. Croatia would qualify with changes to its constitution in accordance with conference guidelines. Regarding Bosnia-Herzegovina, recognition had to await the outcome of a referendum.

The Vatican, on 13 January, was the first to recognize Slovenia and Croatia. Then, two days later, under "intense pressure" from Germany, the EC stated that it would "begin the process of recognition." However, before the day was out, the two breakaway republics were recognized by Austria, Belgium, the UK, and, subsequently, by all EC members and some fifty members of the world community. Not to be outdone, on 17 January, Italian President Francesco Cossiga crossed into Slovenia and Croatia in a high-speed, armed convoy for document-signing ceremonies with Slovenian President Milan Kucan and Croatian President Franjo Tudjman. He was the first European head of state to do so. It later was to become evident that Bonn had virtually stampeded the EC into following its lead.[11]

After three days of debate, rump-Yugoslav accepted the Vance Plan despite opposition from Krajina Serb President Milan Babic (head of the Krajina assembly, Mile Paspalj, voted for it). At Glina on 9 February, the Krajina assembly with eighty-seven members present, agreed to the Vance Plan. On 10 February, Babic's assembly supporters voted to hold a referendum on the question. On 11 February, Tudjman of Croatia confirmed in writing his acceptance. On 16 February, Paspalj's group voted Babic down, asking his "government" to resign. On 20 February, Babic's supporters at Knin voted against the Glina meeting. On 26 February, the anti-Babic faction met in assembly at Borovo Selo, amended the constitution, and made Goran Hadzic president. In effect, serious dissension was evident among the Krajina Serbs at a very critical point in the conflict.[12]

29 February–27 April 1992. From 29 February–1 March, a referendum on independence was held in Bosnia-Herzegovina, which most of the Serbs refused to participate in. Sixty-three percent of the population did vote, almost unanimously in favor. Tensions ran high during these three days, culminating in the death by shooting of Serb Nikola Gardovic by a Muslim gunman at his son's wedding outside a church at Bascarsija in Sarajevo. Within hours, barricades went up throughout the city guarded by armed civilians, Serbs on one side, Muslims on the other. Owing to the presence of joint police-JNA patrols, and the appeals of the Party for Democratic Action (SDA) leader, Alija Izetbegovic and Serbian Democratic Party (SDS) leader, Radovan Karadzic, further violence was narrowly averted.[13]

On 9 March at Brussels, the conference on Yugoslavia agreed on a framework to tackle institutional and economic issues and the rights of minorities. On 17 March, following five rounds of talks in Sarajevo, the leaders of the SDA, SDS and HDZ agreed to a declaration of principles for a new constitutional order (the Cutileiro Plan) whereby Bosnia-Herzegovina would be organized within its present borders into three national majority constituent units—Bosniak Muslim, Serbian, and Croatian—similar to Swiss-type cantons.

On 23 March in Helsinki, Slovenia and Croatia were admitted as full members of the CSCE. Rump-Yugoslavia remained shut out and was unable to defend itself from the CSCE's strident accusations. The CSCE during this period was much influenced by NATO military thinking and by new members from Central and Eastern Europe like the Czech Republic, Hungary, and Poland, who were eager to prove the "political correctness" of their pro-Western orientation.

On 27 March in Sarajevo, the Serbian assembly of Bosnia-Herzegovina adopted the constitution for its "republic." Some four hundred Muslim "intellectuals" gathered in protest. Local Serb intellectuals (and people who originated from the region) held a counter-meeting that proclaimed the common interests of Serbs wherever they lived. Again, this was a good example of the Balkan habit of mobilizing so-called intellectuals to argue a point.

On 30–31 March in Brussels, at session six on Bosnia-Herzegovina, the SDA, SDS and HDZ leaders proposed corrections to the Cutileiro Plan while confirming its general principles. It was agreed to establish a working group to define the three communities of Bosnia-Herzegovina according to national, economic and geographic principles, which were also to take into consideration historic, religious, cultural, educational, transportation and communications criteria. As difficult as this was in an ethnically mixed area like Bosnia, it was the only fair way. The war in Bosnia-Herzegovina essentially became a war of maps, the division of territory between three rival claimants and the respective rights of their national communities.

On 1 April, in Brussels, the eleventh session of the conference on Yugoslavia focused on the possibilities of renewed trade ties between the old republics and questions of succession. While UN-EC negotiating efforts slowly yielded results acceptable to all sides, the Ministerial Council of the EC on 6 April in Luxembourg pre-empted ongoing talks by recognizing Bosnia-Herzegovina within its existing borders, in effect granting full recognition to the existing alliance of Muslims and Croats to which a majority of Serbs were opposed. Armed clashes erupted in Sarajevo and elsewhere throughout Bosnia-Herzegovina, killing fourteen and wounding many more. A large group of Sarajevan citizens demonstrated for peace, occupied the assembly building and demanded a government of national salvation. Again, without Serbian participation, the Bosnia-Herzegovina "government" called for a ceasefire and introduced a state of emergency. In Belgrade, the remnants of the presidency met and concluded it was the intent of the EC to totally destroy Yugoslavia. The Presidency asserted that the problems in Bosnia-Herzegovina could be resolved only by peaceful means by all three constituent nations, Muslims, Serbs and Croats.[14]

On 7 April the Serbian assembly in Bosnia-Herzegovina met in Banya Luka and declared its independence and its right to enter into association with other entities in Yugoslavia. The assembly also announced that Biljana Plavsic and Nikola Koljevic had pulled out of the Bosnia-Herzegovina presidency in Sarajevo. That same day, US President George Bush granted full recognition to Slovenia, Croatia, and Bosnia-Herzegovina within the existing republican borders of the former Yugoslavia. With fighting in various areas, the Bosnia-Herzegovina presidency, on 8 April announced its emergency powers. EC representative Cutileiro met with all sides in Sarajevo on 11–12 April where agreement was reached regarding a ceasefire and on Bosnia-Herzegovina's future constituent, tripartite make-up. Unfortunately, as fighting increased, rational discussion proved to be more and more difficult.[15]

On 14 April, the US State Department cited Bosnia-Herzegovina's independence and internationally recognized borders, protesting the JNA's presence in that republic. After withdrawing from Slovenia and partially from Croatia, units had taken up positions at JNA bases in Bosnia-Herzegovina, including in Sarajevo. Bosnia was the main bastion of the JNA's large complex of military installations and armaments factories. If the Serbs could, they would try to prevent these assets from falling into the hands of the Croats or

Bosniaks. The US named Serbia as the main aggressor. A few days later, Serbia issued a retort and claimed that US policy was "one-sided, unobjective and biased." Serbia had entered an argument it couldn't win.

On 26 April, SFRY presidency representative Branko Kostic, JNA General Blagoj Adzic and Bosnia-Herzegovina President Alija Izetbegovic met in Skopje to work out plans for the disposition of the JNA in Bosnia-Herzegovina. Rump-Yugoslavia acknowledged that the JNA could not remain under the circumstances. Talk revolved around the division of military equipment and infrastructure heralding the JNA's final break up.

On 27 April, almost overlooked in the ongoing crisis, the new constitution for the Federal Republic of Yugoslavia (Serbia and Montenegro) was hastily adopted by the relevant assemblies.

2 May–29 June 1992. Izetbegovic requested to leave the Lisbon conference on Bosnia-Herzegovina for Sarajevo to deal with a Bosniak attack and the blockade of the JNA Second Army District in the city. Izetbegovic was abducted by the Serb JNA and detained in Lukavica barracks. With UNPROFOR and EC mediation, Izetbegovic and General Kukanjac agreed as to how the JNA would convoy its forces to Lukavica. As Izetbegovic was en route to his Presidency, Bosnia-Herzegovina TDF fighters fired on the JNA convoy and killed a number of officers, soldiers and civilians. Fighting spread in Sarajevo, Mostar, and elsewhere. The following day, Belgrade ordered its soldiers in the JNA to return to the federal republic within fifteen days and Bosnian Serbs to remain in Bosnia-Herzegovina. In effect, the bulk of the remaining JNA manpower and equipment was split between Serbia and the Bosnian Serbs.

On 5 May, Bosnia-Herzegovina presidency members, Fikret Abdic and Stjepan Klujle, JNA General Aksentijevic and an EC representative signed a ceasefire document for Bosnia-Herzegovina that would unblock barracks, Sarajevo airport and permit the exchange of the dead, wounded and captured. The next day, the Bosnian Serb Karadzic and Bosnian Croat leader Mate Boban met in Graz and agreed on a mutual truce under the EC, the ethnic division of Bosnia-Herzegovina, and territorial claims between Serbs and Croats agreeing to resolve matters peacefully. On 8 May, Milosevic purged the remnants of the JNA. Chief of Staff General Adzic, also acting defense minister, was retired and replaced by Lt. General Zivota Panic. Second Army District commander Kukanjac was sacked, and thirty-eight senior officers were summarily retired.

In separate actions on 11–12 May, the EC Ministerial Council from Brussels and the CSCE in Helsinki both slammed Serbia and the JNA for assisting irregular Serb forces in Bosnia-Herzegovina. Both accused Belgrade of aggression and threatened to undertake economic sanctions. The CSCE continued its harsh criticism of Serbia, while UN statements were more moderate, apportioning blame to all three sides. On 20 May, the US excluded Yugoslavia's JAT airline from US airspace.

On 27 May, in downtown Sarajevo's Vase Miskina Street, shellfire struck civilians waiting to buy bread. Sixteen were killed and 140 or more were wounded. It was not proven who was responsible, but the Western press accused the Serb military. The Lisbon conference on Bosnia-Herzegovina was again interrupted at the request of the Bosniak side. On 30 May, the UN Security Council imposed sanctions on the Federal Republic of Yugoslavia, completely severing it from world trade; freezing assets; cutting it off from all finance and banking; banning its aircraft and shipping; prohibiting its citizens from promoting business; as well as denying participation in scientific, cultural, and sporting activity. Belgrade denied the Security Council's charges and appealed to world opinion for the convening of an international conference. This was ignored and FR Yugoslavia became a pariah, an outcast. It was not even granted successor status to ex-Yugoslavia.[16]

On 2 June, Belgrade demanded that the Bosnian Serbs turn Sarajevo airport over to UNPROFOR, abstain from shelling Sarajevo and other towns, invite UNPROFOR observers to monitor the ceasefire they had proposed, and to insure the safe shipment of humanitarian supplies through their territory. On 5 June, all JNA units left the Marshal Tito barracks in Sarajevo for Serbia, supposedly the last to leave Bosnia-Herzegovina. It is worth noting that the report of UN Secretary General Boutros-Ghali cites the fact that armed units of the Croatian republic were fighting in Bosnia-Herzegovina. They failed to leave that territory, but no sanctions were imposed on Zagreb. Under pressure, the Bosnian Serbs implemented the forgoing roughly by the end of June after a month of almost continuous fighting.[17]

On 15 June, Croat President Tudjman and Bosnia-Herzegovina President Izetbegovic agreed to diplomatic relations and discussed the desirability of a military alliance against the Serbs. On 20 June, Izetbegovic proclaimed a state of war and ordered full mobilization and imposed emergency measures. On 21 June, Croat army units overran part of Krajina controlled by UNPROFOR. On 25 June, Lord Carrington met separately in Strasbourg with Tudjman, Milosevic, and Bosnia-Herzegovina Foreign Minister Haris Silajdzic, in place of Izetbegovic.

Milosevic denied FR Yugoslavia's involvement in Bosnia-Herzegovina and insisted that recognition of the latter must emerge from agreement between all three parties. On 27 June the Lisbon conference ended, not with agreement between the parties to the conflict, but with urgent appeals for humanitarian aid for Sarajevo. Blame was apportioned to all, but Serbia and the JNA came in for most of the criticism. The French president, François Mitterrand, made a dramatic visit to Sarajevo to highlight the seriousness of the situation.

On 28 June (Vidovdon's Day), the opposition political coalition DEPOS (Democratic Movement of Serbia) began eight days of demonstrations calling for Milosevic's resignation, the disbandment of the National Assembly and the formation of a government of "National Salvation."

On 29 June, elements of the US Mediterranean Sixth Fleet steamed into the Adriatic—a cruiser, a destroyer, and four amphibious troop carriers with 2,200 marines. The US began to flex its muscles to give the impression it was prepared to undertake military action. The Bush administration, however, did not view Yugoslavia as a problem warranting US military intervention.

3 July–27 August 1992. At a session in Grude, Bosnia-Herzegovina, the leaders of Croat Herzeg-Bosna adopted decisions establishing a Croatian "state." That same day, the Bosnia-Herzegovina presidency announced the creation of a single national army and called for the integration of the Croat Council of Defense (HVO) with its military.

On 11 July, immediately after NATO-West European Union talks on the margins of a CSCE summit at Helsinki, it was agreed to block off Yugoslavia's Adriatic coast. Italy was the first to place its ships on-station off Bar, Montenegro. A number of NATO vessels joined in. This effort was greatly expanded in November.

In Zagreb on 21 July, Presidents Tudjman and Izetbegovic signed a friendship agreement and further concluded that the Herzeg-Bosna HVO would integrate into a Bosnia-Herzegovina national army under joint command. On 3 August, Izetbegovic called for the lifting of the arms embargo for Bosnia-Herzegovina and again ordered full mobilization.

US President Bush on 6 August announced the establishment of diplomatic relations with Slovenia, Croatia and Bosnia-Herzegovina; and additionally called upon the CSCE to send observer missions to Vojvodina, Sandzak, and Macedonia. In Congress, the US Senate Foreign Relations Committee adopted a resolution calling upon Bush to convene the Security Council with the intention of taking all necessary measures, including the use of armed force, to ensure delivery of humanitarian aid to Bosnia-Herzegovina and an end to attacks on civilians. The Senate on 11 August approved Bush's UN initiative to use "all necessary means" to resolve the crisis.

At Prague on 13 August, the CSCE, after hearing reports on Kosovo, Vojvodina and Sandzak, agreed to a permanent Kosovo mission. In Novi Sad, the Reform Democratic Party of Vojvodina set out what constitutional changes were required to re-establish autonomy. A few days later, the Muslim National Council in Novi Pazar in the Sandzak, led by SDA head Suleyman Uglianin, asserted the Sandzak's desire for special status. Obviously, the recognition of minority rights had become contagious and, in this case, linked to Bosnia-Herzegovina.[18]

Throughout the rest of the month, Lord Carrington tried to revive his conference on Yugoslavia at Brussels and London by talking to all of the leaders involved in the conflict and by enlarging the scope of the meeting by inviting some thirty countries and organizations. Principles were adopted; committees and working groups were established; and Cyrus Vance (UN) and Lord David Owen (EC) became co-chairman permanently set up in Geneva. Carrington bowed out, presumably a very frustrated man. While this was going on, Srpska Republic leader Karadzic met with Herzeg-Bosna leader Mate Boban and agreed on a ceasefire and mutual collaboration to establish a Bosnia-Herzegovina compatible with previously agreed upon aims. Prisoners were exchanged between Belgrade and Zagreb. "Ethnic cleansing" and "death camps" were phrases working their way into the many news reports coming out of Bosnia-Herzegovina. Grave questions and accusations were being asked about the conduct of the war, mostly directed at Belgrade and the Bosnian Serbs.

1 September–24 October 1992. Bosnian Serb leader Karadzic met a UNPROFOR deputy commander on 1 September at Pale to discuss placing Serb artillery and 82 mm mortar batteries under UNPROFOR control in and around Sarajevo. This was accomplished at eleven depots by 12 September. The Serbs alleged that some 1,300 mujahideen, recruited abroad, were now fighting in Bosnia. It subsequently came to light that a large shipment of arms from Iran bound for Bosnia had been seized by the Croatian authorities at Zagreb airport.

On 16 September, the US State Department stated it would use its influence to eject FR Yugoslavia from the UN. Three days later, the UN Security Council took the position that as Yugoslavia no longer existed, FR Yugoslavia could not participate in UN affairs and must reapply for membership. On 22 September, the US asked the Secretary General to set-up a war crimes commission. The letter left little doubt that the US was now accusing the leaders of Serbia, the JNA, and the Serb leaders of the Krajina and Bosnia-Herzegovina with having committed war crimes. On 23 September, the UN General Assembly suspended FR Yugoslavia from further participation.

On 2 October, US President Bush proposed to the UNSC to ban all flights from Bosnia-Herzegovina airspace, except those approved by the UN and to enforce the ban with combat aircraft. Srpska Republic President Karadzic proposed to stand down its aircraft if the Bosniaks did also. He overruled air commander General Zivomir Ninkovic.

On 3 October, at International Red Cross headquarters in Geneva, the warring sides of Bosnia-Herzegovina agreed to free all civilian and military prisoners who hadn't committed offences. It was acknowledged that there were fifty-two POW camps in the territory—twenty-four Serb, nineteen Muslim and nine Croat.

The EC Council of Ministers on 5 October urged follow-up to what had been agreed to in London, and additionally requested a way to collect and analyze information on war crimes. The next day, the UNSC agreed to establish an international body to investigate war crimes in Yugoslavia (particularly in Bosnia-Herzegovina). On 9 October, a UN supervised "no-fly" zone was established over Bosnia-Herzegovina. On 12 October, talks began in Zagreb aimed at resolving issues between Croatia and FR Yugoslavia over traffic, finances, succession, ownership and property, and refugees. Serbia did not attend and criticized FR Yugoslavia participation on the grounds that Croatia had not withdrawn its forces from Bosnia-Herzegovina and that it continued to persecute Serbs in Croatia. In this, and in similar FR Yugoslavia dealings with the UN-EC at Geneva, and with CSCE officials concerned with Kosovo, it is clear that Milosevic was angry over the conduct of President Cosic and Prime Minister Panic. The latter were more moderate and accommodating, while Milosevic continued to take a harder line on most issues.

On 22 October, the US submitted war crimes evidence to the UN, all but one of the grave offences being attributed to Serbians. UN special envoy Tadeusz Mazowiecki requested experts to examine allegations of mass graves at Vukovar. On 24 October, a symbolic reopening of the Belgrade-Zagreb highway failed when buses ran into Krajina Serb roadblocks. Nor were telephone connections re-established, though attempted under the auspices of UNPROFOR, FR Yugoslavia and Croatia.

28 October 1992. Geneva conference co-chairmen Vance and Owen met in Belgrade with Cosic, Panic, Karadzic and JNA General Zivota Panic to discuss the status of Serb aircraft in Bosnia-Herzegovina. Vance met separately with Milosevic and gave him the just released plan for Bosnia-Herzegovina authored by the Finnish diplomat, Martti Ahtisaari. According to this paper, Bosnia-Herzegovina would be a decentralized state of seven to ten units, based on national considerations. The central authorities would be responsible for foreign affairs, defense, foreign trade and citizenship. It is likely that the need to control the reaction of FR Yugoslavia to this new plan added to the urgency, in Milosevic's mind, to get rid of Cosic and Panic. Two days later, the assemblies of Republika Srpska and Republic of Srpska Krajina met in joint session at Prijedor and adopted a declaration on unification. They announced that there would be plebiscites in both republics followed by elections for a constituent assembly.

2 November–29 December 1992. The combined political parties of Milosevic and Seselj attempted to dump Prime Minister Panic in a federal assembly vote of no confidence on 2–3 November. Ninety-three were for this motion, twenty-four voted against. In the Chamber of Republics, eighteen voted for and seventeen against (one ballot was invalid). Without the required votes, Panic and his "federal" cabinet survived.

On 16 November, the UNSC expressed concern over the enforcement of the economic embargo against FR Yugoslavia. The Security Council listed strategic items to be embargoed and set up additional ways to tighten control, including on the Danube River. By 22 November additional NATO ships were positioned in the Adriatic to seal off the coast.

On 26 November, the US State Department in commenting on Kosovo made its policy clear that it favored a return to full autonomy within FR Yugoslavia's present borders (Serbia), but not independence.

On 3 December, a ministerial conference of some fifty Islamic states concluded in Jiddah with an appeal to the UN to end the "genocide" against Muslims in Bosnia-Herzegovina and threatened to provide financial and military assistance on their own initiative.

On 11 December, the UNSC decided to deploy seven hundred UNPROFOR soldiers and other monitoring personnel to Macedonia. This was to be the UN's first effort at preventative peacekeeping. On the following day, the EC summit in Edinburgh called for military measures to protect the UN's mission and the establishment of safe-havens for refugees. Serbia and the Bosnian Serbs came in for renewed criticism. On 17 December, the NATO Ministerial Council stated it was ready to take military action in Bosnia-Herzegovina at the UN's request.

On 18 December, the UNGA resolved to request military support if Serbia and the Bosnian Serbs failed to comply with all UN orders in Bosnia-Herzegovina. One hundred and two General Assembly members voted for, and fifty-seven abstained. The latter included all EC members, Russia, China, Bulgaria, Romania, Sweden, Poland, the Czech Republic, and Canada. Of the permanent members of the Security Council, only the US voted for. This signaled to the Serb side that Europe, and Russia with its SC veto was not ready for military intervention. In UNSC Resolution 798, concern was expressed over reports of "massive, organized, and systematic detention and rape" of Muslim women in Bosnia-Herzegovina.

On 20 December, nationwide elections were held in FR Yugoslavia. At the federal level in the Chamber of Citizens, Milosevic's SPS won forty-seven seats and Seselj's SRS thirty-four, DEPOS twenty, the Democratic Party of Socialists (Montenegro) seventeen, Democratic Party of Serbia five, the Socialist Party of Montenegro five, the People's Party of Montenegro four, the Democratic Alliance of Hungarians of Volvodina three, the Democratic and Reformist Party two, and the Civil Alliance one. In the National Assembly, SPS won a hundred and one and SRS seventy-three. DEPOS won forty-nine, but the others won less than ten each. Milosevic was re-elected president with fifty-six percent of the vote (2.5 million votes). Panic took thirty-four percent (1.5 million votes). With a pronounced shift in power to the nationalist right, the well-intentioned, but inexperienced, Panic was ousted on 29 December.

* * *

In the early months of 1993, Slobodan Milosevic must have been pleased with how things looked from his presidential office in Belgrade. Serb forces held roughly thirty percent of Croatia and sixty-five percent of Bosnia. Western governments were in disarray over what to do (beyond providing humanitarian aid) and the "talk-fight" tactics of the Serbs had the UN tied in knots. Economic sanctions (always slow to yield results) were still bearable. With the war aims of the Serbs virtually accomplished, Milosevic was master of the game. He likely told his intimates that, while he did not start the war, he would finish it. He could argue that, while the Serbs had legitimate grievances under the constitutional order in the post-1974 SFRY, his initial instincts had been to preserve the federation. Then, when this had proved impossible, as a nationalist, he had done what he could to protect the Serbs. It was an argument that was lost amidst accusations of aggression, human-rights abuses and atrocities leveled at the Serbs. This is far from being the whole story, however.

As the Serbs consolidated their control over the Krajina in 1991, Croats did the same in territory that they held in Slavonia and elsewhere in Croatia, accompanied by atrocities and the expulsion of the Serb population. At the outset, there was the murder and mutilation of wounded and captured members of the JNA. Then, we learned of executions of Serb villagers at Vukovar, Borovo Naselje, Gospic, and elsewhere. It was the instruments of murder that shocked the most: hatchets, knives, strangulation devices, and tools to gouge out eyes and others to mutilate male genital organs. The ethnic cleansing began almost at once with expulsion orders from Croat crisis committees amid threats and intimidation. By August 1992, Serbs had been evicted from some two hundred villages in western Slavonia alone, a process accompanied by looting and the destruction of property, as well as acts of violence against individuals. By the end of 1994, 300,000 Serbs had been driven out of Croatia with upwards of 200,000 more to follow in 1995.

Vukovar itself encapsulates developments that provide useful context for the period 1990–91: the establishment of armed teams of Croat extremists whose purpose was to create an atmosphere of fear among the Serbs—to the point that they voluntarily departed; the initial breakdown of the JNA as an effective fighting force; the subsequent proliferation of militias and special action units on the Serb side; and an effective media campaign that served to isolate and satanize the Serb people. Serbs, of course, pointed to a long and distinguished presence in Vukovar county and town and argued that they even comprised a plurality. They claimed that, in March 1990, cadres of what would become the 204th Croatian National Guard (ZNG) (the paramilitary wing of the HDZ party) were formed under Tomislav Mercep for the purpose of intimidating the Serbian community. The need to create fear was borne out by local election results as the HDZ had come in only third with twenty-five percent and trailed behind the Communist League-Democratic Change Party and the Serbian Democratic Party (SDS).

It appears that the Mercep group's first major operation was the murder of Zeljko Ostojic in his Borovo Naselje flat shortly after the Spegelj arms assassination plot was exposed on TV on 25 January 1991 (Ostojic was involved in the JNA investigative effort). In February, Mercep (then HDZ head and defense secretary for Vukovar) met with Croat parliamentarians Vladimir Seks, Ivan Vekic, and Branimir Glavas and agreed that, where possible, Serbs would be fired from their jobs, harassment of Serbs would be combined with threats and other actions intended to induce them to leave the area; and that liquidation would be used as a last resort. On 10 March, some two thousand armed volunteers rallied at Bogdanovacka. Borovo Naselje was to set the pattern for other communities to be divided up by HDZ loyalists under the command of the ZNG and MUP. The Serb executives at the Borovo Combine were the first to go and company funds were then removed to buy arms. The dismissals spread to the public prosecutors, courts, police, the municipal secretariat for defense and other offices controlled by Zagreb including hospitals and those providing social services.[19]

To intensify the atmosphere, Serb-owned buildings (particularly bars and restaurants) were bombed. Newspapers and magazines from Belgrade were confiscated by armed gangs and the kiosks selling them were destroyed. HDZ activists took over Radio Vukovar on 2 May (in response to the armed clashes at Borovo Selo). On 25 July 1991, Zagreb dismissed Vukovar's city council and its Serb mayor, Slavko Dokmanovic, replacing him with Marin Vidic, who was a cohort of Mercep. On 15 August, men led by Zrnic Ivica waylaid two JNA soldiers who were ambling down the railroad track in Vukovar, apparently out shopping. At gunpoint, they were knocked unconscious and their throats were slit. Dismembered, the bodies were thrown in Petrovacka Dal. On 18 August, the men assaulted a young Serb woman, Sladjana Petrovic, raped her repeatedly for several days and then murdered and mutilated her. On 20 August, they murdered two teenaged boys in the custody of the ZNG in a shelter in Olajnica. After that, they shot a dozen or more Serbs who had witnessed the incident. The killings continued for the duration of the siege with gangs of murderers roving through the streets in search of victims. According to Belgrade military authorities, there may have been as many as forty such groups, which included members of the ZNG and MUP. They estimated that hundreds of Serbs died in this manner.[20]

The attack on Vukovar, because of its duration, destruction and civilian casualties, was criticized as being clumsy in execution and unnecessarily brutal. Because of the involvement of the JNA, it was viewed by the West as a major act of aggression by Serbia. However, the initial weakness of the opposing sides would seem to be borne out by the fact that the Serbs couldn't rescue their besieged barracks force of two battalions plus one company of JNA MPs, nor could the Croats overrun either them, or the Petrova Gora suburb. Ultimately, well over eight thousand Croats were committed to the defense of the area, including: the ZNG 204th Vukovar Brigade, the Vinkovci Brigade, the Zagreb Brigade, some 150 MUP, some 400 new recruits from Vukovar (partially trained), an unknown number of HOS, and, allegedly, some foreign neofascist mercenaries.

Before serious fighting got under way, some six thousand Croat children, women and elderly people were evacuated to the Adriatic coast. Serbian civilians were not permitted to leave, but some must have made it out. An estimated 12–14,000 civilians remained, many from mixed marriages. The JNA General Staff decided to deploy substantial forces to Vukovar on 14 September, immediately after the Croats cut off the barracks there from food, water and electricity. (The last delivery of fresh food was on 25 August.) Although Serb forces had reportedly begun to converge on the area earlier, another account states it was early October before the 12th Vojvodina Corps, the Elite Guard Brigade and supporting elements of the 1st Military Region were actually in place. Croat reinforcements entered the town and the Croat commander, Lt. Col. Mile Dedakovic, went to Zagreb as late as early November for talks with Tudjman. There was at least one humanitarian relief convoy in and out, so one wonders how tight the Serbian "siege" actually was.

The Croats used Vukovar's strongest buildings for fixed defense and underground corridors and sewers to maneuver their forces. Fire-zones overlapped and communications to underground command posts proved adequate. Thousands of civilians lived underground in the cellars of homes and buildings, and many survived in large bombproof shelters. Self-contained hospital units continued to function up until the end. The crisis committee operated from a bunker in the basement of the town-center hospital. Limited food stocks and water were available, but some tried to forage above ground, exposing themselves to gunfire.

On the Serb side, the JNA gave heavy fire-support to local Serb TDFs and militia volunteers. In the JNA, the desertion rate was high, morale and discipline were poor and the chain-of-command of what was once a good army was shambolic. General Zivota Panic, commander of the 1st Military Region, took over and organized an integrated assault force that by 17 November (after several weeks of block-to-block street fighting) had taken all but small pockets of resistance. Amid the thirteenth internationally brokered ceasefire, Vukovar surrendered on 20 November. On the previous night, several hundred Croatian fighters made it through the Serb lines to Vincovci.[21]

With non-Serb commanders and junior officers disobeying orders or otherwise failing to cooperate and conscripts refusing to report for duty or deserting from the front, a weakened and disorganized JNA became dependent largely on Serbs, Montenegrins and Bosnian Serbs who felt a loyalty to their own national community for its continued existence. Others, JNA officers wedded to the idea of Yugoslavia in the Titoist Partisan tradition, found themselves in limbo, being disinclined to lead, follow, or get out of the way, when they saw the JNA involved in what became an internecine nationalist struggle. It's no wonder that the JNA tended, more and more, to side with Serbs fighting in Krajina, Slavonia, and eventually in Bosnia as the war continued. The strain of the situation took its toll in suicides, self-inflicted wounds, escape abroad and betrayal. An instance of farce concerned one JNA soldier who commandeered a tank at the front and drove it to the federal parliament. An instance of tragedy concerned another, who informed to the Croats and brought death to his former friends.

The rise of nationalism, the subsequent break up of Yugoslavia and the disintegration of the JNA led to the formation of armed groups of volunteers, paramilitary organizations or militias on the part of the Serbs. Some were an expression of the legitimate need for self-defense. Others were the personal projections of political leaders who wanted to extend their power and influence across republican borders so as to pursue so-called patriotic agendas. And, a few were organized, trained, equipped and supported by the security apparatus of Serbian President Slobodan Milosevic. Serbs have a tradition of owning weapons as one of the rites of manhood. Tito's doctrine of local defense ensured that there were thousands and thousands of weapons stashed away in the armories of the TDFs and police. With compulsory military service and reserve obligations extending to middle-age, most Yugoslavs are familiar with weaponry, not just the Serbs.

The first such armed group was the Marticevci (the territorial defense force of the Krajina Republic), which got under way in the summer of 1990 under the police chief of Knin, Milan Martic. For a time, it was trained by a Yugoslavian who had been an infantry officer in the Australian army—Captain Dragan. By the summer of 1991, SRS head, Vojislav Seselj, was organizing his so-called Chetniks. Seselj was used by Milosevic for a time, and then jailed. Vuk Draskovic had his Serbian Guard, and then later thought better of paramilitary politics. There were White Eagles, the Dusan Silni, and others. The most notorious was the Serbian Volunteer Guard, or Arkanovci Tigers, under Zeljko Raznatovic, or "Arkan." A wanted international criminal, with close ties to the Milosevic regime, Raznatovic outdid others in organized looting, ethnic cleansing and special actions intended to terrorize civilians. Arkan's Tigers have also been used out in front to stiffen a defense, or sharpen an offence, but he became most infamous for operating against lightly defended civilians. After a battle, Arkan's forces moved in to persuade the local population to do the bidding of the Serbs by whatever means it took—the destruction of a house, physical abuse, or worse.[22]

While the bulk of the militias constituted an army of sorts in the making and had as their leaders politicians, former police and military officers, and volunteers from towns and villages, very few units, by the end of 1992, had a level of professional training, integrated organization, tactics, staff support and communications that qualified them as a modern fighting force.

More often than not, they conducted operations as marauders with heavy fire-support whose purpose was not just to gain territory, but also to empty it of its non-Serb population. It degenerated not only into a dirty war, but into one whose aims eventually were undermined by political struggles between its

Serb principals. First came Milosevic's power play to oust the Krajina Serbian, Milan Babic. Then there was his falling out with Seselj and with the Bosnian Serb, Radovan Karadzic. Adding to the confusion was the fact that militia warlords had to deal with their patrons in Belgrade—political bosses, JNA and police commanders, or senior members in the government for the bulk of their support.

By the time that the battle for Vukovar was over, the Serbs were isolated internationally and were already being vilified by the world press, having lost any real voice in what constitutes the centers of influence and decision-making in the West. This campaign had actually begun years ago, but the Serbs, it seems, remained unaware of it. From the mid-to-late 1980s, the Germans, the Austrians, and the Vatican discovered a coincidence of interests in expanding their influence in Central and Eastern Europe, including north Yugoslavia (Slovenia and Croatia). The Germans had the financial and economic power to set up many joint ventures with the Soviet Union and other countries in the Bloc and became a source of credits and economic persuasion long before the fall of the Berlin Wall. Its intelligence service, the BND, was active in Yugoslavia and brought selected Croatian officers into a special relationship with Bonn. This was to serve both services well during secession when Zagreb's need for arms became acute.[23]

Austria's ideas were rooted in the romanticism of *Mittel Europa*, Roman Catholicism, and the harder school of Habsburg tradition. Having existed precariously as a small, landlocked country for almost a century, it had long looked with favor on any prospect for the creation of even smaller buffer states on its southern flank between itself and the Serbs, especially given its sanguinary experiences in Yugoslavia in World Wars One and Two.

For the Vatican, it must have been viewed as a God-given opportunity and a spiritual affirmation of the church militant under Pope John Paul II when it saw its own son, Lech Walesa, come to power in Poland after his years of struggle as leader of the Solidarity movement. By 1989, the Hungarians and the Czechs were also again being considered as Catholic, not communist. The Vatican's attention naturally turned to the Slovenes and Croats, to the church of Cardinal Stepinac, which had been periodically repressed under Marshal Tito.

Austrian Foreign Minister Alois Mock had always been quick to say that, in his opinion, Yugoslavia had always been an "artificial" state. He repeated this often in 1990 and became the most outspoken advocate of Slovenian independence in Europe. He also was of the *Mittel Europa* school, believing that the Habsburg states of old would one day find themselves in a regional alignment. The two ideas came together easily and, as the People's Party leader, he, and Vice-chancellor Erhard Bussek, took the cause of Slovene and Croat independence to Bonn and Washington. The subject resonated well in Bavaria and Baden-Württemberg after German reunification as south Germans (staunch Roman Catholics) saw possibilities for increased influence in formulating Germany's foreign policy. In March 1991, Slovene President Kucan was given a big reception in Stuttgart. He then proceeded to Bonn where he was given promises of political and financial support. Jorg Reismuller, publisher of the *Frankfurter Allgemeine Zeitung* (Germany's most powerful newspaper), became a strong backer of Croat independence and mounted an aggressive campaign against the Serbs, which others imitated. Over 500,000 Croatian and Slovene guest workers lobbied as well. Of the former, many were organized into HDZ branches that worked to influence German politicians and their parties. All in all, it effectively shaped how the Germans looked at Yugoslavia.[24]

The Vatican had not been idle either. It had engaged in a long vigil in Yugoslavia under Tito, denouncing Stepinac's confinement to Krasic (his birthplace) in 1946, and elevating him to cardinal in January 1953. Upon his death in 1960, Stepinac was buried under the altar of Zagreb's cathedral. Rome issued statements supporting Stepinac and the Croatian church, and it never once apologized for its actions during World War Two. Through the 1980s, John Paul II refused to set foot in Yugoslavia unless he could pray at Stepinac's tomb. He found an energetic leader in Cardinal Franjo Kuharic, a man who politicized his flock with anti-Serb sentiments, told them to vote HDZ, and sent circular letters to Catholic bishops around the world requesting support. The Croat St. Jerome Institute in Rome hosted Franjo Tudjman's Vatican visit in May 1991 when he met John Paul II and held talks with the Acting Papal Secretary of State—a duplicate of Pavelic's visit in 1941 whose symbolism was not lost on the Serbs and the Orthodox church. By both statements and actions, John Paul II stood behind Croat separatism, personally giving his approval by recognizing the breakaway state on 13 January 1992 and by visiting Tudjman's Zagreb in September 1994.[25]

Germany's reunification in late 1989 greatly accelerated Bonn's (soon to be Berlin's) *drang nach osten*—drive towards the east. Even the US recognized that Bonn's economic and financial weight would pull former communist countries into its, and the West's, orbit and, from 1990 onwards, Washington encouraged it to be more assertive in the CSCE. Because central, eastern, and southeastern Europe were undergoing rapid transition, the situation in Yugoslavia became a topic of intense debate, first in the media and then in the German parliament (Bundestag) in the winter of 1990–91. Put briefly, Milosevic was portrayed as the communist bully on the block and the Croats and Slovenes as defenseless victims (albeit democratic and civilized) who were in need of help. The question asked by Green/Alternative and Social Democrats on the left, and the Bavarian Christian Social Union (CSU) and the Christian Democratic Union (CDU) on the right, was not only why Germany was remaining aloof from the plight of people struggling to assert their right to self-determination, but also why Bonn was not recognizing its historic, geographic and economic interests. The latter attitudes in the Catholic, conservative, nationalist CSU were cultivated through Episcopal conferences, which carried over into Chancellor Helmut Kohl's CDU with decisive results.[26]

During the Slovene-JNA confrontation, the Bundestag voted for Slovenian and Croatian recognition. Kohl, citing the experience of East Germany's decision for self-determination (in this case a referendum for reunification), pre-empted the issue from the political center. His foreign minister, Free Democratic Party (FDP) leader Hans-Dietrich Genscher, also asserted himself and pushed aggressively as much to demonstrate German leadership in Europe as out of conviction. The idea of *Mittel Europa* fitted here also, with its assumption that only Germany could provide the economic, financial and cultural umbrella needed by the smaller countries to the south. Small may be beautiful, but for Yugoslavia's fate to be debated by the "Alpe-Adria" was clearly absurd.[27]

In mid-November, Kohl let it be known that Bonn would recognize Slovenia and Croatia by Christmas. Genscher argued that granting recognition would internationalize the issue, force Milosevic to accept a fait accompli, and permit the EC and others to intervene without the agreement of Belgrade—leading to a ceasefire more quickly than through Lord Carrington's negotiations. Italy was the first to cave in and Prime Minister Giulio Andreotti convened a meeting in Rome to coordinate the positions of Italy, Austria and Germany, despite EC desire for a single policy. The US, UK, and the UN protested and appealed to the EC troika not to do anything to disrupt the efforts of Carrington and Vance. In early December, Bosnian President Izetbegovic expressed his concerns that early recognition would cause Bosnia to explode.

In the face of these warnings, Kohl and Genscher pressed on. They chose an EC foreign ministers summit in Brussels on 15–16 December to issue their ultimatum—either agree, or Germany would act on its own. Coming three days after marathon talks on the EC's future at Maastricht, no one stood up to Genscher. The UK undercut Carrington by being content to get concessions on monetary union and an opt-out on the EC's social charter. The others meekly asked Bonn to wait until 15 January, but blindly opened Pandora's box by inviting all six republics in Yugoslavia to apply for recognition according to criteria established by the Badinter commission. Bonn poked all of its EC colleagues in the eye by recognizing Slovenia and Croatia on 23 December. Genscher was quoted as gloating, gleefully, "We've done it!" The tune, "Danke Deutschland—Jetzt sind wir nicht mehr allein" (We're not alone anymore), blared from Zagreb TV and went to the top of the charts. Special envoy Klaus-Peter Klaiber came for the signing ceremony, which consigned seventy-three years of Yugoslavian history into the dustbin.[28]

The Germans, the Austrians and the Vatican had looked long and hard at the creaking edifice of Yugoslavia and then gave it one hefty shove over the edge into the abyss. Their actions were not limited to the diplomatic arena. Germany made available large amounts of East German arms to the Croats, including artillery, tanks and even MIG-21 aircraft. Arms purchasing offices were set-up in Prague, Budapest, and elsewhere. Despite the embargo, arms flowed in from Austria, countries formerly in the Soviet Bloc and such far-off places as Singapore, Argentina, and Nigeria. Slovenia purchased US$50 million worth of arms from Germany, Austria and other sources. Huge sums were involved for two small countries suffering from economic dislocation and severe losses in trade, and yet, the cash and credits were somehow available.[29]

On New Year's Eve, a concert for peace was held in Dubrovnik. An orchestra was brought in from Toulouse and Barbara Hendricks sang Mozart and Bach. The affair, held in the Franciscan church, was attended by a host of European dignitaries. A Serbian soprano was turned away by the Croat authorities. Sadly, there was no concert for the Serbs of Croatia. It would continue this way as Serbs, Croats, and the Bosniak Muslims began a descent into hell. A year later, US Secretary of State Lawrence Eagleburger labeled the Serbs "war criminals." Lady Margaret Thatcher called for NATO air strikes.[30]

Geographic Macedonia

Macedonia (FYROM)

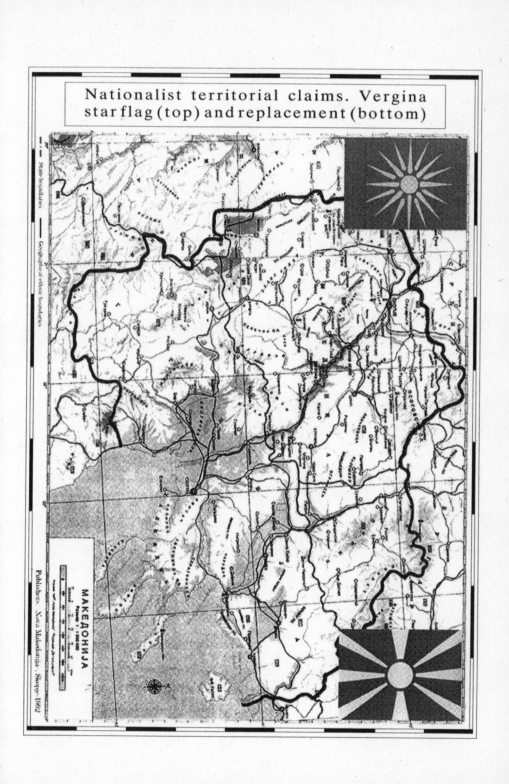

Nationalist territorial claims. Vergina
star flag (top) and replacement (bottom)

Chapter 3

Crossroads of Conflict

Macedonia: November 1992–May 1997

> The most natural solution of the Balkan imbroglio appeared to be the creation in Macedonia of a new autonomy or independent unity, side by side with the other unities realized in Bulgaria, Greece, Serbia, and Montenegro, all of which countries had previously been liberated, thanks to Russian or European intervention. But this solution had become impossible, owing first to the incapacity of the Turkish government, and then to the rival pretensions of the three neighboring States to this or that part of the Macedonian inheritance.
>
> Carnegie Commission Report on the Balkan Wars, 1914

A historic and strategic crossroads contested by Greeks, Romans, and Slavic tribes in ancient times and by the Byzantines, Bulgarians, Serbs, and Ottomans during the late Middle Ages, and having endured five hundred years of Turkish occupation, only to be divided between Greece, Serbia, and Bulgaria during the two Balkan Wars of 1912–13, newly independent Macedonia, which remains burdened with the awkward acronym FYROM (the Former Yugoslav Republic of Macedonia), again found itself to be an apple of discord in the southern Balkans as a result of Yugoslavia's break up, struggling against all odds amid political and economic pressure from every side.

Following multiparty elections in November 1990, and a successful referendum for independence in September 1991, Macedonia's cagey, longtime communist president, Kiro Gligorov, talked Milosevic into pulling the JNA out of this southernmost republic without so much as a broken window. However, the peaceful redeployment to Kosovo province, an hour to the north, belied Milosevic's true state of mind for the elections had brought forth a proliferation of political parties of every persuasion and ethnic coloration. A youthful, ultra-nationalist Internal Macedonian Revolutionary Organization-Democratic Program warned of Serbian, Bulgarian, and Greek plots and busied itself by resurrecting historical claims. The ethnic-Albanian community had boycotted the referendum, and threatened to secede if its constitutional demands were not met. Reform communists calling themselves "social democrats" tried to hold to a shaky center. And ominously, onlooking political leaders in neighboring Albania, Greece, and Bulgaria all sensed that Macedonia was vulnerable—unloved, unarmed and undefended, like a lone sheep surrounded by wolves.[1]

By road up from Lake Ohrid, winding through western Macedonia past tall stands of hardwoods, ploughed fields and picturesque farmlets hugging steep hillsides, until finally arriving at the wide avenues and broad, shady squares of Skopje, one didn't get the impression that this was a country struggling for survival. However, in July 1993, Macedonia was isolated and caught in the middle of a clash of regional interests. Blagoj Handziski, the amiable secretary-general of the Social Democratic Alliance of Macedonia (SDSM), set out the main problems facing this small, ethnically mixed, and largely unrecognized republic. At the top of the list, he cited the threat posed by the JNA and heavily armed Serb militias at that time, who, after overrunning much of Bosnia, might turn their attention to Kosovo and drive out its Albanian population. Because the Sar Mountains straddle the border between Kosovo and Albania, Handziski said that the bulk of any exodus would pour into Macedonia with a devastating effect.[2]

Darkly handsome, with a short, salt-and-pepper beard, Handziski said that Milosevic had threatened to do just that at a little publicized meeting at Lake Ohrid held on 31 May. Requesting a get-together at short notice, Milosevic insisted that the TV cameras keep their distance and that commentary be restricted to a voiceover, not the text of their conversation, which was to remain secret. Milosevic allegedly urged Gligorov to block US President Bill Clinton's plans to assign Americans to the newly established United Nations Preventative Deployment (UNPREDEP) force in Macedonia. Should Gligorov decide otherwise, Milosevic suggested that a large influx of Albanians from

Kosovo could irreversibly change Macedonia's demographic make-up in favor of its sizeable Albanian minority. The implication was that Macedonia would disintegrate in ethnic strife. However, despite Milosevic's hardball tactics, Gligorov welcomed the Americans in.

Regarding Macedonia's Albanian minority, some twenty percent out of a population of just over two million, Handziski said that a majority supported the ruling coalition, but the National Democratic Party (NDP) under Ilijaz Halimi had called for armed resistance in Kosovo and hinted at the same internally. Handziski said this would be dangerous should Albanian President Sali Berisha ever play his nationalist "card" in an attempt to unite Albania, Kosovo, and the Albanian-populated areas of Montenegro and Macedonia. As it was, he added, Berisha applied his influence and pressure on the Party of Democratic Prosperity (PDP) of Dzeladin Murati, which was part of the government. Alluding to the fact that the Albanians came boiling out of the bazaar in the old town across the river from time to time (there have been injuries and deaths by shooting during riots), Handziski voiced his concern should the situation really become radicalized. He said that it could become "explosive."[3]

He said Macedonian foreign policy was one of keeping "equidistant" from its immediate neighbors, explaining that they even refrained from leaning on Bulgaria for support—even though Sofia was one of the first to recognize them as a state. He said that Bulgaria refuses to recognize Macedonian as a nationality and their tongue as a distinct language, in effect questioning their legitimacy. The same was true for Greece, which was incensed that Skopje was using the sixteen-point Star of Vergina (the royal symbol of Alexander the Great) for their flag and called their republic "Macedonia," the name of Greece's northernmost province. He said he regretted their quarrel with Athens and that they might be willing to climb down on symbols, but never on *Makedonija*. He said it was unlikely that any government would control eighty-one votes in parliament (out of a total 120) so as to be able to amend the constitution.

Handziski said that the economic situation remained precarious, although it had improved somewhat since the winter when petrol and fuel oil were in very short supply. When I mentioned that I had seen dozens of Greek petrol trucks on the road, and backed-up at the Serbian border, Handziski admitted that Macedonia was not then enforcing UNSC Resolution 820, which had put in place broad economic sanctions against rump-Yugoslavia. He said that before the war, sixty-eight percent of Macedonia's trade had been with Yugoslavia. From 1990–93, he claimed it had grown to eighty-three percent—most of it with their putative enemy, Serbia. If sanctions were enforced, he claimed that unemployment would double from thirty to sixty percent, causing economic collapse and riots to erupt between Macedonians and the Albanian, Serb, Greek, Turk, Gypsy, and Vlach minorities.

I thought back to the previous November when I had visited Skopje on my return to Athens. I had hired a Pristina taxi for US$30 that had run out of fuel north of Skopje. The driver had just managed to make it to a small airfield where lines of cars were waiting. An hour later we were lucky to obtain a liter. Outside the Grand Hotel (grander than Pristina's!), a line of empty cars had been waiting for days. Taxi fares had shot up, and it made sense to walk this pleasant, small city. In fact, its cleanliness and the absence of heavy traffic had real appeal after Athens. Skopje is dominated by the Vardar River and a beautiful old, stone bridge dating from the Ottomans. Like the one described in Ivo Andric's *Bridge Over the Drina*, one can easily imagine that it has had a similar history and was once the center of events. Knowing that a rebel named Karpos had been impaled there on a sharpened, wooden pole in October 1689 authenticated its credentials.[4]

I wandered around the old town with its busy markets and mosques, not sensing any hostility from the swarms of swarthy merchants, shoppers and tough-looking, streetwise young men wearing gold chains around their necks and wrists, more often than not carrying wads of money—anything from denars to deutsche marks. If hungry, big steaming bowls of spicy goulash soup and huge hunks of crusty, white bread could be had for little or nothing. That evening, I had the good fortune to find one of the best restaurants in the Balkans, T'Ga Za Jug, run by Ljubomir Blazevski. Located in a rehabilitated Turkish caravanserai, the stone building was now given over to artists and artisans. When he learned I was a journalist, he rang Vladimir Petreski of the Macedonian Information Center who became my guru whenever I was in Skopje. Ljubomir's mixed-grill of lamb chops, liver, veal roll stuffed with cheese, salad, fluffy round loaves of bread, and Alexandria red wine was a great accompaniment to history and politics.

The opening up of the political system in Yugoslavia and the republic elections in 1990 had resulted in an upsurge in nationalist feeling in Macedonia as elsewhere. Students revived the Internal Macedonian Revolutionary Organization (VMRO), which had expired by World War Two. Under the slogan, "Macedonia for the Macedonians," they dredged up VMRO's historical aspirations and symbols—maps that included Pirin Macedonia in Bulgaria and Aegean Macedonia in Greece—with the "White Tower" of Thessaloniki (Greece's second city) as its centerpiece. Its rallies around its bold, red banner and rampant gold lion espoused nationalism and anti-communist reform.

VMRO's youthful exuberance expropriated the night with noisy crowds waving wine bottles and singing how they would regain old "Solun" (Salonika, Thessaloniki's old name). It was exciting, heady stuff, especially for twenty-five-year-old lecturer, Ljupco Georgievski, VMRO's president, who vowed to unite Macedonia "democratically, peacefully... without guns and violence."

VMRO, which soon changed its name to the impossible appellation of VMRO-DPMNE (Democratic Party for Macedonian National Unity), won a plurality of assembly seats in November 1990, gaining thirty-eight. The League of Communists of Macedonia (LCM) came second with thirty-one. PDP came third with seventeen, the balance being divided between six others. VMRO-DPMNE, however, was denied its opportunity to form a government largely through Gligorov and the existing establishment, who were not only unwilling to give up power, but who also maintained that VMRO's leadership lacked experience. A "technical" government was set up under Nikola Kljusev. It fell in July 1992, when the EC, at Lisbon, failed to recognize the new state's chosen name, "Macedonia." Since that time, Macedonia had been led by Prime Minister Branko Crvenkovski of the SDSM, who formed a coalition with the PDP/NDP, the Liberal Party (LP), and the Socialist Party of Macedonia (SPM).[5]

That brisk autumn day, drinking beer (*pivo*) behind the Grand, it was great fun to watch the never-ending procession of diplomats and foreign officials who were just discovering Macedonia. The top US official was CSCE ambassador Norman Anderson whose trim, blonde wife walked a large Alsatian with a grim, "don't get in my way" look. Newly arrived CSCE sanctions-monitoring staff played with their walkie-talkie radios, at first refusing to discuss their "secret" assignment and then, like a new customs man from London, admitted their glee over being given a three month, well-paid, "holiday" in far-off Macedonia. Without knowing the language, MACSAM's thirty-five inspectors had the task of sifting through mountains of documents (many of them bogus), and supposedly monitoring five road, and two rail routes, along 500 kilometers of border—without having any authority to do physical searches. They could only advise and assist if asked! Theoretically empowered to make spot-checks on a twenty-four-hour basis, MACSAM's "toothless" staff headed for the hotel around 9 p.m. for a shower, drinks, and dinner. According to a Norwegian UNPREDEP officer near the Serb border, from midnight until dawn the trucks roared north, loaded with oil, petrol, tires, steel, computers—you name it—an estimated hundred violations of strategic shipments a day. Smuggling had become a booming business!

By early 1993, the EC and NATO countries feared a wider war and were afraid that other countries might somehow get involved. At the center of their concern was Kosovo, and what Milosevic might, or might not do. US President Clinton laid down several markers beyond which the Serbs were not to go, and to prove he was serious, he began to deploy some 500 troops out of Europe to join the 700-man Nordic battalion of Swedes, Norwegians, Danes, and Finns, who were monitoring the Serbian-Macedonian border.

I taxied out to Skopje's small, but busy airport south of town to talk to the Americans who had arrived in June. Within minutes, I was drinking coffee with US Army Major Len Jeffery from Houston. With their gleaming, white "humvee" armored personnel carriers and camouflage uniforms, the guys and gals of "Able Sentry" gave the impression that they were ready to get up and go. About 200 had come out of the Berlin garrison and were crack troops![6]

However, halfway through my first cup, it began to sink in that "Able Sentry's" real purpose was to demonstrate to the Europeans that the US was willing to place some troops on the ground (well out of harm's way) in a symbolic gesture of resolve that did not exist. Jeffery explained that they would be in the country six months and then be replaced. They were then undergoing "familiarization" by the Scandinavians, although some had received peacekeeping training in Germany. He hoped they could take responsibility for a section of the border by September. UNPREDEP operated under the guidelines of total visibility in coordination with the Macedonian Defense Ministry. It had no responsibility for what went on in Kosovo, could not cross the border, and its sole mission was to observe and report. In fact, they did not expect to have any contact with the Serbs as such. It was essentially a UN "show the flag" operation. It did not train or assist Macedonia's police or militia, and had no internal responsibility other than to defend itself in an emergency.

For Macedonia, UNPREDEP forces (especially the Americans) were a needed "hands off" symbol of international and US concern that was thought would provide a "trip wire" in case Serbian forces crossed the border. Macedonia itself possessed only a lightly armed militia of 15,000 and lacked the financial resources to do much more. Indicative of their isolation, however, the Americans were blissfully unaware that the Serbian Democratic Party (SDP) and the Movement for Pan-Macedonian Action (MAAK) were opposed to their presence. They did not know that Albanian protests were put down with deadly force, and they knew nothing of arms-narcotics trafficking. Small in numbers and without heavy weapons, UNPREDEP seemed an unlikely deterrent to the Serbs. Nor would its presence bolster Skopje in the event of a breakdown in internal security. At best, it could help coordinate humanitarian aid in a crisis. It had a little bit of farce to it, just as a Washington wag had earlier referred to portly Acting Secretary of State Larry Eagleburger as "Lawrence of Macedonia." In actuality, Milosevic had been bluffing for he had no need to move against Macedonia. Clinton was also bluffing, for the last thing the new president wanted to do was to get US ground forces seriously involved in ex-Yugoslavia. "Able Sentry" was the thinnest of blue lines!

But Greece at that point was only half-bluffing for the quarrel over a name had gone on for a year and a half. In Skopje, school children were waving their gold sunburst on red flags, full of Alexander the Great. In Greece, hoary old men in military dress (full-skirted *foustanela*, blue, double-buttoned over blouse, leather belt, forage cap, and hobnailed, upturned, pom-pommed, *tsarouchia* shoes) came forth carrying the blue and white Greek Cross banner, led by bearded, robed, Orthodox clerics followed by thousands shouting, "Macedonia is Greek!"

As the fervor mounted (demonstrations were massive, with rallies of up to a million people held in Athens and Thessaloniki), virtually all were caught up in the hysteria. Claiming that Skopje's constitutional amendments, which explicitly disclaim territorial aspirations outside its borders, were still insufficient, Greece, in August 1992, began to block the shipment of petroleum to Macedonia through its port of Thessaloniki, impounding shipments already paid for. Macedonia is hot and dusty in summer and cold and windy in winter. Factories were forced to close, homes and schools lacked heating oil, and cars and tractors went without petrol. The economy plummeted![7]

Then, apparently, well-connected Greeks close to Prime Minister Constantine Mitsotakis realized how much money could be made by sanctions-busting and getting supplies to Greece's traditional ally Serbia. Under the cover of UN mediation between Athens and Skopje, Greece's oil embargo against Macedonia was dropped and all the stops were pulled out as Athens entered into a cozy arrangement with Gligorov that became profitable for all—Serbs, Greeks, and Macedonians. It quickly became so good that Mitsotakis began inching towards the acceptance of a compromise name for "FYROM," or the "Skopjians" as Greeks call them in a churlish way. It most likely would have been "New Macedonia," a name that would haunt Mitsotakis within months. His young, Harvard-educated, hardline nationalist and very ambitious ex-foreign minister, Antonis Samaras, angry at having his policy undone by the prime minister, resigned from the New Democracy party and ultimately brought the government down.[8]

Despite dire predictions from pundits and experts on the Balkans, Milosevic had no need to invite US intervention by expelling Albanians from Kosovo, or violating Macedonia's borders. He would have stirred up a hornet's nest, as Albania's Berisha had vowed to come to Kosovo's aid if need be. Albania could not mount military operations, but it could supply light arms and ammunition to all-comers. In practical terms, Milosevic lacked the money and people to fill Kosovo, even if they could be induced to go there. Additionally, he was already doing as he wanted with its largely passive population. As for Macedonia, he was getting quantities of whatever he needed through his southern neighbor. His threat to Gligorov was worth a try to keep the US out of UNPREDEP. However, it is unlikely that he seriously contemplated following through on it. It had cost him nothing and had put Gligorov under pressure to ignore the UN sanctions against rump-Yugoslavia. In July 1993, Macedonia was being singled out by CSCE MACSAM as the worst offender at sanctions-busting in the Balkans. How it came to that conclusion, given MACSAM's limited mode of operation, is a mystery, but that is the line that they were putting out.

A year later, Skopje found itself staggered by a total trade embargo imposed by Athens after Greece's aged and ailing socialist Pasok party leader, Andreas Papandreou, unexpectedly found himself once again prime minister. After a few months of heated rhetoric, Papandreou maliciously demonstrated his nationalist credentials by closing Greece's border with Macedonia, forcing this tiny country to put thousands of trucks on the road from the ports of Durres, Albania, to Burgas, Bulgaria, to stay alive. Greece was attempting to break the back of a tiny (2.2 million people), landlocked country, the poorest in ex-Yugoslavia, by economic warfare! By some miracle, the Macedonians (all of them) carried on somehow, creating a new class of enterprising, cross-border entrepreneurs (and money) out of dire necessity. Seemingly, in the Balkans, some always find opportunity in disaster. A Macedonian mafia became established with links to business and government. Staid, quiet Skopje saw its first "biznessmen" with BMWs and cordless phones. It was great! They could operate from their cars![9]

Amid near economic chaos, the Council of Europe decided to follow through with plans for a national census preparatory to general elections scheduled for autumn. The council thought that a census (an easy matter in Denmark) would be a useful tool for planning purposes. The dominant SDSM wanted it to lay to rest exaggerated population claims by the Albanians and the Serbs. In late June 1994, the census went forward as dozens upon dozens of European observers fanned out across the country to validate results. It took only hours to determine that the Albanians had decided to boycott the affair and no amount of cajoling on the part of the government and visiting dignitaries could persuade the PDP/NDP leaders otherwise. A chagrined and frustrated Gerd Ahrens, the UN Special Envoy for Minorities, said that the Albanians had linked the census to the question of citizenship, and were refusing to come forward to be counted. I mentioned that when I had crossed the Albanian border by bus, many ethnic Albanians from Macedonia used old Yugoslav passports, identity cards and even driving permits. National identity remains a major issue for Albanians![10]

The Albanians had boycotted a census in 1991—and the referendum on independence as well. They also objected to the new constitution on the grounds that it relegated them to minority status, failing to mention them as a constituent nation. They disapproved of the name "Macedonia," for they claimed it preempted their rights. Claiming to number 800,000 or forty percent of the total population, they would have the right to secede and join Albania if it were true. In actuality, they number around 450,000 or twenty-three percent. It has been crucially important for SDSM to keep them in the ruling coalition, for the PDP/NDP controlled twenty-three seats in the parliament and could make and unmake any government. In fact, the Albanian community was influenced by and manipulated, to some degree, by Berisha in Tirana, who had been working with the more nationalist wing of the PDP, led by Mendu Thaci. Within days after the attempt to conduct the census, the PDP/NDP walked out of the assembly in protest over sentences meted out to ten Albanians (including ex-Deputy Defense Minister Hysen Haskaj and an ex-PDP secretary-general) on charges of illegal arms possession and subversion![11]

Because VMRO-DPMNE, was, in actuality, the largest in parliament, I wanted to hear why they were always a "bridesmaid," but never a "bride." Party Vice-President Dosta Dimovska proved to be a fiery "bridesmaid" who lashed out at what she called a cabal of former communists who monopolized all of the levers of government to stay in power and were bent on destroying them as a political movement. Her dark eyes flashing, she went on non-stop, detailing what she claimed was a plot orchestrated by President Gligorov and Prime Minister Crvenkovski through Internal Affairs Minister Ljubomir Frchkovski and Deputy Minister for State Security Slobodan Bogoevski to discredit and split the party. She said that they had been subjected to a smear campaign—allegations that VMRO-DPMNE was in contact with Croatian and Austrian security and had set up a paramilitary organization. Dimovska said it was all a ludicrous lie, claiming the police had bought a few unemployed youths and had induced them to make false statements. She said that their phones were all tapped and claimed they had proof of the existence of the operation, which was provided by a security official, Bogdenko Gogov, who came forward on behalf of himself and others who didn't like being victimized themselves by being forced to participate in such a "dirty game."[12]

Dimovska claimed that after the 1990 elections, the agreement was for the SDSM to hold the presidency, for VMRO-DPMNE to have the prime ministership, and for the Liberal Party to name the president of the parliament. She said Gligorov went back on his word, naming Kljusev and then Crvenkovski. She said that VMRO-DPMNE had been ahead of everyone on the independence issue and they wanted rapid privatization of state-owned enterprises and compensation for those who had lost property under communism. She said that they wanted real democracy and an end to inter-ference by state security. They lacked a free press, had media controls and she claimed VMRO-DPMNE had beaten back a government attempt to impose an unconstitutional law for "verbal crime." Had this passed, sentences of three to five years would have been meted out to critics of the regime. In foreign affairs, Dimovska freely admitted VMRO-DPMNE's desire to have closer ties with Bulgaria, to have "really normal state-to-state relations," as she put it.[13]

When asked about her party's prospects in elections scheduled for autumn, Dimovska said she was not confident they could overcome the advantages held by the coalition. She said that the SDSM controlled the security and police and had most of the money; that the Liberals under Stojan Andov dominated the media, including radio and TV; and the PDP/NDP tended to focus only on Albanian interests. She explained that the coalition had failed to move towards a market economy; yet it put out a steady stream of propaganda trumpeting its supposed successes. "It's just like in the old days," Dimovska insisted. She said that despite their many problems, they, VMRO-DPMNE, remained the most popular party in the country and that because they respected their party's history and traditions, they would continue to be interested in the status of Macedonian minorities in neighboring countries. However, she said that they now accepted the fact that Macedonia had to exist within its present territory and abide by CSCE conventions on borders and human rights.

At a small, wayside restaurant on the road to Lake Ohrid, an old photo of VMRO's founder and martyred hero, Gotse Delchev, with his grave eyes and moustache, looked down from the wall. There were others as well—those who followed and fell in the short-lived Ilinden (Saint Elijah's Day) rising against the Turks, which began on 2 August 1903. Who were these men, still remembered some ninety years later? The Turks at that time called them "terrorist bandits." In Sofia, those for Greater Bulgaria ("Vrhovists") initially looked to them as "brothers." The Serbs, if they thought of them at all, considered them rival claimants to "Old Serbia." The Greeks were much the same, insisting on the supremacy of the Patriarchate in Constantinople and their claims to an ancient patrimony. Europe, to the north and west, had heard much of Macedonia in the closing decades of the nineteenth century, of Turkish "outrages" against its Christian subjects in a land hard to define, a land in-between, a crossroads of conflict. The French referred to "Macedoine" as an area of mixed races—and named a salad after it. One doubts that Gotse Delchev approved of this descriptive, but trivial approach.

* * *

Although rebels under Pop Georgiev Berovski had enjoyed success in the region around Razlovci at the time of the "April Uprising" in Bulgaria in May 1876, and at Kresna in October 1878, neither campaign had received Bulgarian or Russian support sufficient to sustain resistance for more than months. In fact, both attempted to use the Macedonians for their own ends. It was the young Delchev (one of six conspirators and a schoolmaster like Berovski) who at Shtip, southeast of Skopje, founded VMRO in 1893 and organized the first Macedonian liberation movement. Previously, anti-Turk rebels (Bulgarian as well as those living in Macedonia), thought little beyond the *cheti*, a band of armed men. Weapons were distributed to villagers who, on given command, attacked local targets in a limited way, pinpricks to avenge a rape by a Turkish irregular *bashibazouk*, or the depredations of a hated *chiftlik* overlord. Delchev and his co-conspirators had a larger purpose; a general, mass-uprising that would force the Porte to grant autonomy to all of Macedonia, a development intended to be a historic first step towards full independence.[14]

Born in Kukush (today, Kilkis in Greece) in 1872, Delchev operated from the large, polyglot port city of Salonika just to the south. Its site recognized the strategic importance of an outlet on the Aegean, the Vardar river valley running north (the route of a rail line connecting Salonika and Belgrade), and the Struma river valley to the east, which binds western Pirin to Macedonia's main heartland. It was a well-positioned land that, despite its undeveloped state, had the potential to rival Greece, Serbia, or Bulgaria. Obviously, these three were alive to the situation, and were determined not to be denied what they considered to be their "rightful claims." Even Austria, by then ensconced in Bosnia, was looking to the Aegean.

Although Delchev and his followers established bomb-making facilities, cached arms behind the Bulgarian frontier and attended congresses in an effort to reach a modus vivendi with the Bulgarians, VMRO's real strength was its ability to build an extensive network of members and supporters in Macedonia and to maintain an independent capability for action.

With Turkey beginning to totter, armed gangs of Greek "adartists" headed north under the banner of "Ethniki Etairia"—the National Society. Serbian chetniks went south, blessed by the Society of St. Sava. The Bulgarians, with German Prince Alexander of Battenberg on the throne (having united with Eastern Rumelia in 1885), sent *comitadjis* across the border to convince by arms those unswayed by the Cyril and Methodius Society. Scores of guerrilla bands fell upon isolated Turkish outposts, ambushed each other, and fought for the hearts and minds of Macedonia. Sofia's rival to VMRO, the External Macedonian Revolutionary Organization (MRO-External) (Vrhovists), also tried to gain the support of émigrés and considered Delchev to be a dangerous upstart who stood in the way of its plans for annexation. Political competition between the two turned into a violent struggle that lasted for several decades, existing even today in the realm of polemics.[15]

VMRO specialized in bombings, bank robberies and abductions. It won international notoriety when it kidnapped the American Protestant missionary, Ellen Stone, and her companion, Katerina Tsilka and kept the two hostages on the move for five months until ransom money of 14,000 Turkish liras in gold was forthcoming. It executed those collaborating with the Turks and clashed with MRO-External Vrhovists who attempted to enter VMRO territory. On the other side of the coin, it appealed for unity of action between Patriarchates and Exarchates alike and recruited members from both. It worked for social and economic reform, established schools, and agitated to raise the political consciousness of a very poor, underdeveloped part of the Ottoman Empire. VMRO committees provided material support for villages, even as they built up their coffers for the purchase of weapons. They established courts and even adjudicated interest on loans. In many respects, VMRO was becoming a state within a state.[16]

By the turn of the century, Turkey's ability to control Macedonia was increasingly being called into question by Europeans who were appalled at conditions there and were demanding reform. However, the Porte proved unable to stem the violence, lacked authority in many areas, and could dispatch its military detachments only from here to there in response to a given incident. By 1903, VMRO felt it time to assert its authority: oppression was rife; its rival, MRO-External, had attempted a rising the previous year, and all of the Balkan powers were becoming involved—including the Albanians and the Romanians. Delchev convinced his central committee to ready itself for an uprising. As fate would have it, he died in a border clash in May; killed in a hail of Turkish bullets says one account; captured and executed says another. In any case, preparations went forward and dozens of villages took up arms on Saint Elijah's day. It proved to be an impulsive, premature and tragic act. Although initially successful—much of the Bitola vilayet fell to rebel control—its leaders and many fighters were encircled at Krushevo where they had declared a republic. High in this mountain village in western Macedonia, they fought off the troops of Bahtijar Pasha until they were overrun. By December, it was all over. Although Europe failed to intervene, many protests were made over the orgy of Turkish reprisals that followed.[17]

In the aftermath of the slaughter, pillage and rape of suspect villages at the hands of the Turkish soldiery (thousands had been sent from Constantinople), concerned European powers, mainly the British, insisted that reforms be instituted. However, Sultan Abdul Hamid was in no mood to accept real change and, while going through the motions of accepting the "Murzsteg program," did what he could to delay and obstruct its implementation. The Europeans were far from united on the question as well. Austria and Germany did their best to undo the effort in light of Austria's desire to expand its influence to the Aegean and even eastward. Vienna was against the establishment of even limited autonomy in Macedonia. Under no compelling demands, the Sultan deployed the bulk of his troops to the province to sit on the problem. As for VMRO, it was to a large extent broken up, leaving individual members to go over to MRO-External, attempt an accommodation with the revolutionary Young Turk movement, or trade assassination for assassination with the MRO-External's supreme committee in Sofia.[18]

Amid the turmoil that existed in the run-up to the Balkan Wars, the interests of the major European powers, Russia and the Ottomans were sometimes mutually exclusive, sometimes intertwined. A few years earlier, Moscow had accommodated Vienna. Austria's 1908 annexation of Bosnia-Herzegovina reversed matters and the Tsar gave the go ahead to the Italians to take on the Turks in Tripoli in 1911 and encouraged its Balkan clients, Bulgaria, Serbia, and Greece, to form a front against the Habsburgs. In what was intended to be a defensive alliance against Austria, the three members of the "Balkan League" set about to prepare for war against the Turks and the division of Macedonia. Sofia favored autonomy, with the idea that a weak Macedonia would join Bulgaria. Belgrade was for partition, with secret clauses giving the land north of the Sar Mountains to Serbia, and that east of the Struma river to Bulgaria. In the event of a dispute, Russia was to mediate. In any war, Bulgaria would provide 200,000 troops and Serbia 150,000.[19]

In May 1912, Greece signed an agreement with Bulgaria, leaving territorial issues open. In October, Montenegro agreed and within days moved against the Turks. With 700,000 men under arms, the league allies were opposed by weakened Ottoman forces of half that number. Lord Kinross describes how the Greeks decimated the Turks and entered Salonika on the feast day of its patron Saint Demetrios, "to be pelted with roses by delirious Greek crowds in the streets." The Serbs came down the Vardar and were victorious at Kumanovo and Monastir, leaving Turkish survivors to flee into Albania. The Bulgarians took on major Turkish forces in Thrace and drove them back to a defensive line between the Black Sea and Mamara. While peace talks were going on in London in January 1913, the Young Turks, led by Enver Pasha, fell on the Sultan's war cabinet in a fit of rage, shot the war minister and forced Kamil Pasha to resign at gunpoint. They rejected the peace terms and fought until virtually all of European Turkey was lost. Bulgaria, dissatisfied with the carve-up, attacked Greece and Serbia on 30 June in an obstinate display of stupidity and arrogance that put them on the wrong side of victory for the next thirty years—from 1914 to 1944. Their Macedonian dream turned into a nightmare![20]

By September 1918, miles and miles of trenched fortifications had been dug across the brown, barren hills of southern Macedonia. At its widest point, the Salonika front had shifted only twenty-five miles in two years of static fighting. On the fourteenth, however, a six-hour artillery barrage rained down on the Bulgarian positions, signaling the start of an offensive that would do much to end the war. Serb, French, and Senegalese troops went forward at Vetrinek with fixed bayonets. On the sixteenth, two Bulgarian regiments mutinied and the German commander ordered a retreat. Appeals to the Austrians and the German General Staff for reinforcements were to no avail. The Bulgarians and Germans fought stubbornly, awaiting aid that failed to arrive in time to turn the tide of battle. By 28 September, the French and their Moroccan spahis had taken Skopje. Bulgaria was quitting. With Austria already angling for peace, the German generals Ludendorff and Hindenberg, aware that their Salonika front was broken and knowing that a massive Allied offensive in the west was underway, went to the Kaiser and told him they could not continue. In early October, the Allies were deep in Serbia as the Austrians and Germans steadily gave ground. On 31 October, the Serbs stood on the heights of Belgrade watching Austrian soldiers retreat north across the Danube.[21]

Conditions in Macedonia in 1919 were appalling beyond belief for poverty and years of war had reduced thousands to the state of animals. Most lived at the barest level of existence in makeshift tents, exposed to the weather without adequate food, medical care and sanitation. American army attaché Major Blinder had seen it when attached to the French-American Military Commissariat. Likewise Senator Louis Crenton of Michigan. Talk ensued that Macedonia would become an American mandate under the postwar League of Nations.

In early 1919, the well-known British journalist James Bourchier was prevailed upon to set out his views on autonomy. He saw a Macedonia from the Sar Mountains to the Struma, with Salonika as its capital, all under American protection. His paper was sent to President Wilson and the British. American professors submitted similar ideas. Colonel House, Wilson's advisor, became interested and sounded sympathetic. The chief US delegate to the Paris Peace talks, Frank Paulk, pushed the project, but ran into Allied opposition. Essentially, the Greeks and Yugoslavs blocked consideration of what would undo their territorial gains. The US soon lost interest in what would have been a very divisive issue.[22]

Incredibly, Macedonian independence stayed alive in dingy, smoke-filled, meeting halls abroad, in Europe, America and Canada where émigrés endlessly debated the reasons why disaster had befallen them. In America, a Macedonian Political Organization (MPO) arose from the remnants of VMRO formed by earlier immigrants who were working the mines, steel mills and railroads of their adopted country. It split into Vrhovist (fascist in orientation) and VMRO factions—with the latter becoming VMRO-United. The Vrhovists took similar names, penetrated its rival and collected money from a Macedonian community that was not only confused, but riven with disputes.

By the early 1930s, VMRO-United increasingly cooperated with the US Communist Party, as the latter followed the line laid down by the Communist International, which advocated an independent Macedonia within a Balkan federation. Equally incredible was the fact that VMRO-United kept in contact with cohorts in such places as Petric (Pirin Macedonia), arranged visits to political prisoners in Yugoslavia and Bulgaria via the League of Nations, and actively publicized the fact that a "white terror" was being conducted in Bulgaria with hired Vrhovist gunmen that was taking the lives of many of its supporters.[23]

World War Two opened a new chapter in the struggle of the Macedonian people. In April 1941, following German air raids and a rapid Wehrmacht advance that saw the Royal Yugoslav Army disintegrate, Skopje was occupied by the Bulgarian Fifth Army. Tito's communist party began to organize the resistance and sent Lazar Kolisevski into the city. By September, a Partisan group was set up. The war took its toll: Jordan Nikolov-Orce, Cvetan Dimov,

Straso Pindur, Mirce Acev, Rade Jovcevski-Korcagin, Kuzman Josifovski-Pitu, and countless others. Thousands of Jews were sent to Treblinka, never to return. However, by late 1944, the Germans were pulling out in an attempt to regroup northward. Bulgaria was overrun by the Red Army of the Soviet Union. A Partisan newspaper, *Nova Makedonija* (New Macedonia), appeared in the village of Vranovci. Skopje fell on 13 November, and within days, a symphony orchestra was organized!

In the beginning, the Anti-Fascist Council for the People's Liberation of Macedonia (ASNOM) was the main communist party vehicle for building socialism within a federal Yugoslavia. Interestingly, whereas the Bulgarian communists had attempted to interfere in a negative way at the outset of the war to reduce the status of the Macedonian communists, by late 1944, ASNOM had obtained the agreement of the Bulgarian Fatherland Front and the Bulgarian Workers' Party for the ultimate integration of Pirin Macedonia into Yugoslavia's Macedonian republic. The Macedonians now had a sense of their own success and identity. ASNOM set out in its formative statements that the Yugoslav Federal Republic of Macedonia was founded upon its own struggle (past and present) as part of the larger experience of the communist movement in Yugoslavia, and that of VMRO's fight for independence that had culminated at Krushevo. The two streams of Macedonian socialism and nationalism were merged.[24]

Full of revolutionary fervor, Tito and the Macedonian communists gave active support and sanctuary to their Greek comrades engaged in a ferocious civil war across the border. Aid was based on the idea of Macedonia within a communist Balkan federation that would include Yugoslavia, Bulgaria, and Greece, historic aspirations in Aegean Macedonia, and kinship with many who were fighting for the Macedonian Popular Liberation Front (SNOF) in Greece. This lasted until Tito broke with Stalin in 1949.

As for Gotse Delchev, his bones had an interesting itinerary. Given to Bulgaria by Greece in 1923, the communist Bulgarian leader Georgi Dimitrov returned them to Skopje where, on 10 August 1946, they were interred under a white block of carved stone in the sunken courtyard of the church of Saint Spas. Over a hundred years after the beginning of his struggle, it is hard to judge whether Delchev's ghost rests easy. Given his rebellious life, he probably still longs for the south.[25]

* * *

November 1990. The first multiparty elections were held on 11 November. In the second round on 25 November, VMRO-DPMNE came in first with thirty-seven seats, the League of Communists of Macedonia second with thirty-one. Macedonian republican representatives, elected or otherwise, participated in various federal bodies and in Yugoslav communist party structures. They served in the diplomatic corps and armed forces. Macedonia had its own small TDF. SFRM President Gligorov asked Nikola Kljusev to head a non-party government of experts.

8 January 1991. The first multiparty assembly of the Republic of Macedonia was constituted.

25 January 1991. Following the lead of Slovenia and Croatia, the Assembly of Macedonia adopted a declaration of independence and deliberated over the state of negotiations on the future of Yugoslavia

27 January 1991. The assembly elected Kiro Gligorov President of the Republic of Macedonia. Gligorov, it should be noted, sat on the SFRY presidency. Macedonia was still a constituent member of SFRY, which was then unraveling.

30 January 1991. Gligorov met Izetbegovic in Sarajevo where the two discussed prospects for preserving a "Yugoslavia." It appears that the two favored this approach if it was possible to achieve it.

3 June 1991. Gligorov and Izetbegovic jointly proposed a "Platform on the Future Yugoslav Community," whereby SFRY would become a commonwealth of sovereign republics. This idea was not adopted at the last meeting of the SFRY presidents held on 6 June.[26]

8 September 1991. A referendum on independence for the republic of Macedonia carried with seventy-four percent of those voting in favor. The Albanian community boycotted the affair, being reluctant to identify with a Macedonian state in which they were not named as a constituent nationality.

17 September 1991. The assembly of Macedonia declared its intention to accept existing borders, rejecting territorial claims on any neighboring states.

21 November 1991. The assembly of Macedonia announced its new constitution, which described the republic as a sovereign, democratic and social state. The Greek government found Article 49 objectionable: "The Republic cares for the status and rights of those persons belonging to the Macedonian people in neighboring countries, as well as Macedonian expatriates, assists their cultural development and promotes links with them." It also opposed Articles 3, 68, and 74, which provide for border changes. Greece insists it has no Macedonian minority, but has jailed persons who have attempted to promote Macedonian political activity.[27]

24 December 1991. Under the advice of the EC's Badinter commission, Macedonia and other ex-federal Yugoslavia entities applied for recognition by the EC.

6 January 1992. The Macedonian assembly added amendments to its constitution to the effect that they didn't have any territorial aspirations. Greece remained unsatisfied with the changes.

11 January 1992. The Badinter commission concluded that Macedonia met all EC requirements for recognition. However, because of Greek objections to its name, national symbols, and constitution, Macedonia's recognition was set aside as a matter to be negotiated between Skopje and Athens under UN auspices.

3–17 March 1992. Representatives of Serbia and Slovenia met separately with Macedonian officials to discuss outstanding issues. Serbia withheld recognition, but agreed to remove the JNA from Macedonian territory. Slovenia agreed to exchange diplomatic representatives at the full ambassadorial level.

26 March 1992. JNA forces left Macedonia, leaving a bare minimum of facilities and equipment behind for Macedonia's small TDF.

25 April 1992. The assembly of Macedonia passed legislation to create their own currency, replacing the Yugoslav dinar with the Macedonian denar. Over the next few years, Macedonia went through several issues of new currency to cope with inflation and fiscal instability. The controversial "White Tower" denar disappeared.

27 June 1992. The EC summit at Lisbon concluded without giving formal recognition to FYROM under its chosen name "Macedonia." This decision caused a furor in Skopje, with opposition parties, particularly VMRODPMNE, blaming Prime Minister Nikola Kljusev.

7 July 1992. A no-confidence motion was brought against Kljusev by twenty-five members of the assembly, which snowballed into a vote of ninety-nine votes for and only two votes against. Kljusev resigned, leaving Gligorov ten days to designate a new prime minister. Gligorov gave VMRO-DPMNE leader, Ljupco Georgievski, a mandate, but the latter failed to find sufficient numbers of people from other parties to work with. Next, Gligorov asked Democratic Party (DP) head Petar Gosev to try. He, also, failed.

6 August 1992. US President George Bush asked the CSCE to send an observer mission to Macedonia. His concern was the need to monitor economic sanctions against the Serbs.

21 August 1992. Greece "froze" petroleum shipments to Macedonia.

4 September 1992. SDSM party leader, Branko Crevnkovski, became prime minister following a two-month crisis. His new cabinet was approved by the assembly seventy-two for, five against, after VMRO-DPMNE, with thirty-seven votes, walked out in protest. Crvenkovski had been designated prime minister by Gligorov after earlier efforts to form a government had failed.

12 December 1992. The UN Security Council approved the UNPREDEP mission to Macedonia of 700 soldiers, thirty-five monitors and twenty-six civilian police. The EC at Edinburgh urged economic aid and UN mediation.

8–12 April 1993. The UN admitted Macedonia under the provisional acronym FYROM. In days, Greece and Macedonia began negotiations that turned into a marathon exercise in frustration that only a hardened optimist like Cyrus Vance could endure. We will not try to detail their many twists and turns. It is enough to know that they still continue, and that the name issue remains unresolved.

15 June 1993. 318 US troops arrived to join UNPREDEP. Two hundred were to follow. They joined 700 others who began to arrive in late 1992.

12 October 1993. Newly elected Greek Prime Minister Andreas Papandreou threatened to close the border with Macedonia if it refused to change its name. Anti-Macedonian demonstrations were organized. Opposition parties escalated the situation.

16 December 1993. Macedonia was recognized as FYROM by the UK, Germany, France, Italy, the Netherlands, and Denmark. Greece was incensed. Macedonia went on to be recognized by most of the UN community, many by its chosen name.

24 January 1994. Greek Prime Minister Papandreou stated that the problem with Macedonia was at an impasse. He demanded that Skopje stop using Greek symbols, revised what he claimed was "irredentist" language in its constitution, and guaranteed that there would never be an attempt to change the border between the two countries.

8–22 February 1994. The US recognized Macedonia as FYROM. Greece angrily broke off negotiations and, within a few days, sealed its border with Macedonia. The EU protested Greece's action saying Athens's action was illegal and demanded that the embargo be lifted.

18 March 1994. US President Bill Clinton appointed Matthew Nimitz as his special envoy for the Macedonian controversy.

23 April 1994. The legality of Greece's action was put before the European Court.

25–26 April 1994. A two-day official visit by President Gligorov to Bulgaria was marred when the two governments failed to agree on language to be used in the final communiqué. Gligorov insisted on Macedonian and Bulgarian texts. Sofia demanded a single Bulgarian text, insisting that there was no separate Macedonian language.

25 May 1994. Gligorov met Albanian President Sali Berisha at Lake Ohrid. The status of Albanians in Macedonia and in Kosovo was discussed. Both sides expressed satisfaction at the talks.

21 June 1994. The Council of Europe attempted to conduct a census in Macedonia. With the Albanians boycotting, it was "postponed."

29 June 1994. The European Court at Luxembourg ruled against the European Commission's request to issue a restraining order that would end Greece's embargo against Macedonia. The court accepted Greece's argument that the matter was political and concerned national security issues. Macedonia thought the decision "unfair."[28]

5 July 1994. Following their announced boycott of parliament in protest against sentences given ten Albanians accused of forming a paramilitary group, SDSM's Albanian coalition partner, PDP/NDP, pondered its next step. Their ministers did not resign, however, permitting the government to continue in power.

16–30 October 1994. Parliamentary and presidential elections were held in two rounds: SDSM fifty-eight seats, LP twenty-nine seats, SPM eight seats, PDP ten seats, NDP four seats, Independents seven seats, others four. VMRO/DPMNE, DP and MAAK boycotted the second round, allowing others to gain higher than normal parliamentary representation. Gligorov was re-elected president. The opposition charged gross "irregularities."[29]

13 November 1994. The results of the second attempt to conduct a census were announced: Macedonians 66.5 percent, Albanians 22.9 percent, Turks 4.0 percent, Gypsies 2.3 percent, Serbs 2.0 percent, 0.5 percent Vlachs, 1.8 percent others. It appears we are to believe there were no Bulgarians. On the official census forms, which cited six languages, Bulgarian was not listed as an option.[30]

18 November 1994. Greece, in Budapest, used its veto to prevent Macedonia from becoming a full member of CSCE. It remained with observer status.

14 December 1994. Albanian activists in the western Macedonian town of Tetovo attempted to begin construction of a "university." This was declared illegal by government authorities and a small, makeshift wooden structure was bulldozed to the ground over the protests of the organizers, some of whom were from Kosovo.

17 February 1995. Albanian demonstrators clashed with police at Tetovo over attempts to establish an ethnic-Albanian university. Approximately 1,500 protesters tried to prevent the police from closing private classrooms that had opened during the week. One Albanian youth was fatally shot and twenty-eight suffered injuries.

27 April 1995. Some 10,000 Albanians demonstrated outside a Tetovo court that tried Kosovo activist Fadil Suliemani on charges of incitement. He was subsequently sentenced to a year in jail.[31]

13 September 1995. At UN headquarters in New York, Macedonian and Greek foreign ministers agreed to normalize relations. In a signed agreement, mutual respect for all borders was emphasized. Skopje agreed to discard the star of Vergina as its state symbol and Greece agreed to end its economic blockade within one month. This was described as an interim accord. UN-sponsored talks over the name issue were to continue.

27 September 1995. Macedonia was admitted to the Council of Europe under the acronym FYROM.

2 October 1995. Presidents Gligorov and Milosevic met in Belgrade to discuss regional and bilateral affairs. They agreed to normalize relations. Because of Greek/UN factors it would take time.

3 October 1995. An attempt was made to assassinate President Gligorov. A powerful car bomb was detonated as Gligorov's car passed, killing his driver and seriously wounding the president. The president of the assembly, Stojan Andov, became the acting-President. Andov headed the coalition Liberal Party (LP).[32]

5–9 October 1995. In emergency sessions, the Macedonian assembly approved a new flag and ratified the agreement with Athens. There was protest activity by Macedonian nationalist elements following the announcement of the terms of the agreement.[33]

9–14 October 1995. After last-minute delays, Greece and Macedonia sign a "memorandum on implementation." A Macedonian delegation traveled to Athens to work out technical details. The border was to reopen at midnight on 14 October permitting normal travel, the shipment of goods and the establishment of diplomatic ties.

8–9 December 1995. Following the signing of the Dayton Accords, the Third International Conference on the Former Yugoslavia (its focus was peace implementation) was held in London. Macedonian Foreign Minister Stevo Crvenkovski was present.

14 February 1996. In a coalition rift that had been brewing for some time, Prime Minister Crvenkovski added SDSM members to the government, excluding LP leader Stojan Andov and others.[34]

8 April 1996. Yugoslavia extends recognition to the Republic of Macedonia using the latter's preferred name.

15 April 1997. Macedonia tightens its border owing to upheaval in Albania. There were a few shooting incidents and illegal crossings.

10 May 1997. A thousand soldiers from four NATO countries (US, Italy, Greece and Turkey) participated in a Partnership for Peace training exercise with Macedonia, Albania, Slovenia, Romania, and Bulgaria.

15 May 1997. Several thousand angry demonstrators protested in Skopje over money lost in a Bitola pyramid investment scheme. 23,000 people allegedly lost an estimated US$66 million.

26 May 1997. Ethnic Albanians and Turks clashed with Macedonian "nationalists" in the town of Gostivar west of Skopje. The latter removed Albanian and Turkish flags from the town hall, causing a fight to erupt. Macedonia's constitutional court ruled against displaying the flags, sparking anti-government demonstrations.[35]

27 May 1997. Amid accusations of corruption, Prime Minister Crvenkovski reshuffled his cabinet, replacing his foreign, economic, agriculture and health ministers among others. This was done in the wake of the pyramid scandal and demands for an investigation. Blagoj Handziski was moved from defense to foreign affairs.

29 June 1997. President Gligorov said that Greece could call his country whatever it liked and stated that the world community would use its chosen name, the Republic of Macedonia.[36]

* * *

An elderly, threadbare Macedonian attached himself to me as a guide, a gentleman named Jovan Popostefanovic. He told me that when he was born the Turks still ruled and his name was written in Macedonian style as Vane Popostefanija. After the First Balkan War, the Bulgars came and decreed that he must spell his name Ivan Popstefanov. Following the Second Balkan War, he was told by the Serbs to assume his present style of nomenclature. Alas, said Jovan, such is the fate of our dear Macedonia. No wonder the rest of the world calls stew a "Macedoine." We do not even any longer know our names, we the nation whose Alexander conquered the world entirely. When will we smash our fetters and gather around our capital in Solun?

C. L. Sulzberger, *A Long Row of Candles*, at Lake Ohrid in 1939

Macedonia might be called a house of mirrors where history and culture are reflected in different ways, depending on where one stands and in what direction one is looking. Actually, it seems that the remnants of Greek, Bulgarian, Serbian, Turkish and even Albanian influence have been refracted somehow, because when you shift again, you will see something strong, something very uniquely Macedonian—a composite. It is this "uniqueness" that finds its defenders in Skopje and its antagonists and questioners elsewhere. Although Webster's dates the word "Macedonian" from 1582, the argument has really raged for only the past one hundred years. The question arose as a nation was struggling to be born.

Arguably, the characteristics that define the Macedonian today are the tangible aspects of existence that affect people in their everyday lives: Orthodox churches and Muslim mosques; a school system; two major universities; an academy of science; research institutes; a state health system; over 200 radio and television stations, 310 newspapers, magazines, and periodicals, and the publication of some 600 new books a year; a film industry; a philharmonic orchestra; state opera and ballet groups; drama and dance companies; cultural clubs; museums and art galleries; libraries; old churches, monasteries, and antiquities in a country of more than two million who enjoy eight spoken languages. It seems both foolish and mean-spirited to question whether this is a nation. Many nations began as a state of mind!

President Kiro Gligorov is in many ways the father of this new country, for he charted a course, which, if it had been done differently, would have resulted in disaster. Macedonia avoided conflict such as engulfed others to the north. It has been difficult enough, however. Because of the war, efforts to move to a market economy and two blockades, its economy was badly hit, effectively cut in half. Some estimate its loss in legitimate business because of the UN sanctions against Serbia as high as US$4 billion. Greece's nineteen-month embargo cost some US$60 million a month, or over US$1 billion altogether. What it gained with sanctions-busting is hard to judge, as it was "black" money and unaccountable. It made some rich and permitted others to survive. Industrial production bottomed out at forty percent of pre-war levels.[37]

On 15 October 1995, the day the Greek border was opened, not one freight train moved north. There were few trucks as well. Mircela Casuleva tried to go to Greece. At the Greek border, at Idomeni, police turned her back, claiming they had not received instructions from Athens. However, they invited her to use the duty-free shop. When the sales clerk found out Mircela was from Skopje, she shouted, "Macedonia is Greek and will remain Greek!"

"It is so very demeaning," said Mircela, "to have people question the name of your country!"

A few days later, the situation was the same. Both sides were working out the details. I talked to Macedonia's heroes, its truck drivers, who were of the opinion it would be years before they would do any real business with the

Greeks. It could have been so different they said. Uneducated, but instinctively in tune, they have been proven absolutely correct.

The 3 October assassination attempt on Gligorov shattered hopes that the country could make a violence-free transition from being a Balkan question mark to a fully accepted member of the world community. Deputy Minister of the Interior, Stojan Trenevski, said that fulsome forensic assistance was being provided by the US, the UK, and Germany, but no suspects had been arrested, and no one had claimed responsibility. The attack had plunged the country into deep gloom and a sense of foreboding for its future. While it was possible that terrorists from a neighboring state had rigged the remote control ammonium nitrate car bomb that had wounded Gligorov, many thought that ultra-nationalists from Canada or Australia had done it. There had been angry accusations that Gligorov had betrayed his country by giving up the Star of Vergina.

VMRO-DPMNE leader Dimovska said that they had every reason to be against the government, but insisted that they had had nothing to do with it. "They would like to pin it on us," she said. Then she went on to detail the shabby conditions under which elections had been run the previous year. There were frauds and irregularities aplenty according to her. Petar Gosev, the leader of the DP, said the same, and so did journalists. My old friend, SDSM Minister of Defense Handziski, smiled and said it had not been all that bad, stating that in his view VMRO-DPMNE was its own worst enemy. He explained their splits and infighting and said that the SDSM/LP/PDP coalition had proved best for Macedonia's stability and for moving it towards the West. He reminded me of the harrowing times they had gone through. However, the big difference, he said, was that the US had become their "big brother"; that Washington's "hands-off" warning was the most welcome development since their independence. His desk laden with mementoes from the Pentagon, Handziski said that US military advisors were working in his ministry and that they had started many joint programs, including NATO's Partnership for Peace. He said he attended NATO sessions where he tried to emphasize the importance of the "Southern Tier" of Albania, Macedonia, and Bulgaria. He said even the US Chairman of the Joint Chiefs of Staff, General John Shalikashvili, visited Skopje. I asked what happened when the JNA had intruded at Cupino Brdo. Handziski smiled and said, "We told them to get out; and one day they packed up and left." On my way out, a young guard gave me his ripped-off Vergina star shoulder patch as a souvenir.[38]

A senior American diplomat sized up the situation in the following fashion. "Things are okay for now... as all are agreed on the need for stability.

However, events have underscored the fact that Mr. Gligorov won't be here forever. We naturally have some ambitious personalities, and it could become bruising. Handziski is attractive and able. Acting-President Stojan Andov is smart and well connected. Vasil Tupurkovski is very popular, but has no party organization and is not in parliament. We really wish that the Democratic Party (DP) and VMRO-DPMNE hadn't pulled out of the last election. We think it has hurt them. We did send DP chief, Petar Gosev, to the US to see how our party system works." When asked about US interests in this small country, he said, "We are not filling a power vacuum so much as simply making our presence felt. We do this so that others don't get aggressive ideas. Regarding Skopje and Athens, they both really wanted mediation. Unfortunately, it will take time for things to normalize. Greece could have been in the driver's seat here. Maybe they will catch up some day. Right now, however, we have the Gligorov problem. We are helping with medical support as well as investigative assistance. Gligorov is of crucial importance. He is the glue that has held things together!"

If Gligorov is the glue, then someone had thrown a well-aimed stone that could have shattered Macedonia's fragile stability. Was it outraged revenge, or part of a deeper plot? It was hard to say. So far, Macedonia had survived in the face of adversity. It was outwardly stable, although everyone was aware of the tensions that existed. The coalition, an assortment of ex-communists, business, banking, trade and the media had, until then, enjoyed a lock on power that was not seriously challenged. VMRO-DPMNE had been stymied because no one would work with them. This then was the arrangement that the US, the UK, and Germany has been propping up since independence. I wondered what people thought of it and how they viewed foreign political involvement.

I went out to Cyril and Methodius University, which I found to be of modern design, in gray stone and cement, set amid easy grassy slopes. It looked like a college somewhere in America and, as students do elsewhere, they wondered whether the big powers were being fair to them, and whether anyone understood Macedonia. Darko, for one, was dead against the deal with Athens. A MAAK supporter, he said Macedonia, a struggling, poor country had been subjected to great economic pressure and finally gave in. He questioned why the EU had not taken action against Greece to end the embargo and why the UN had not done something. He angrily added, "First they took our flag. Next it will be our name!"

Every country should have a Diogenes and in Macedonia it is Dr. Gjorgji Marjanovic, Professor of Criminal Law, who, without fear or favor tells things as they are. He is a big man, with bushy gray hair, bristling eyebrows, and a way of looking at you with an imperious glare, his glasses out on the end of his nose. His students adore him.

"The opposition was right to boycott the second round of the elections last year," he said. "Who you stand with, so are you," he intoned. "Real democracy, to begin with, is lawful procedure. The election process is prescribed by law—how the election must be conducted. This was power politics. It was an attack on the law."

Warming to the subject, he described how voting districts were redrawn a few days before the election to the advantage of the coalition. There was little or no prior notification of this, he said. Consequently, on election day, many were confused as to where they should vote. The voters lists were a shambles with names left out, duplicated, and written in by hand. Even dead people were listed. Some voted in several districts.

Marjanovic said that, by law, the results should have been out within eighteen hours after the polls closed. They took eighteen days and the results were so flawed, he said, that two election commissioners quit. This was an election that the CSCE supervised and attested was acceptable (UN Secretary General Boutros-Ghali expressed strong reservations over the results), he noted. Marjanovic said it was a shame that the regime had resorted to such tactics, especially Gligorov, who was generally well liked. Trying to put the best construction on it, he surmised that the coalition tried to win big so they would have enough assembly strength to get an agreement with Athens. Marjanovic did not believe such illegalities were justified, however, as he insisted it was this aspect of the past they had to break with. "We ate soap," he said.

As I sat with a puzzled look, he explained. "We all know what happened, but we have to swallow it!" He told a story of how a peasant traveled a long distance to a village to buy cheese. Riding along on his donkey and halfway home, he got hungry and bit into a piece. His mouth full of froth, he knew he had been cheated and given soap. But because he was hungry and had paid good money for it, he ate it anyhow. "In the Balkans, we are a little like that," he said.

A year later, by November 1996, some changes were discernible. Expensive new cars were on the road. A few foreign agencies had appeared. People dressed better and thronged Skopje's shopping center. The Grand Hotel had become too grand for my shoestring travel budget and I shifted over to the smaller Bristol Hotel, opposite the no-longer-used old train station. Built in 1923 as Skopje's first modern hotel, the Bristol had seen it all—the 1928 premier of Vasil Iljovski's play *Begalka* in Macedonian; the 1939 publication in *Nas Glas* (Our Voice) of the 1903 Krushevo Manifesto (Macedonia was then

Serbia's Vardar Banovina); the Second World War; and forty-five years of Tito's communism. It was sorely tested at 5:17 a.m. on 28 July 1963 when a nine-point Mercali scale earthquake hit the city; 1,070 people died—some 3,500 were injured. The train station came down (its clock hands tell the time of the disaster), except for part of its front façade. The Bristol had some cracks, but survived. More recently, the Gligorov car bomb went off, breaking glass. I enjoyed its garden and the shade of its chestnut tree in summer. When it was cold, I dug into its *soorba* soup for breakfast—barley, beef, and tripe—and bread. It filled your backbone. Don't forget the vinegar and hot peppers! Its staff still worked for the government tourist agency, and try as I might, no one knew the family name of the hotel's original owner. If, when, privatization comes, someone will ask.

By the end of April 1997, I had logged some six trips to Skopje in four and a half years. At the outset, the odds were that the country would not be permitted to survive; that landlocked and with a weak economy it would collapse, or be pulled apart. It did not happen. Today, there is light at the end of the tunnel. The new Yugoslavia has recognized it, and has dropped talk about its small Serb minority. Albania has imploded into economic collapse and anarchy. Bulgaria came close to doing the same, but may now right itself with a serious, reform-minded government in power. Greece has yet to come to grips with reality, but at least it lets trade cross its northern border. There is still the name, and Macedonia must thread its way through a diplomatic thicket every time it attends an international conference, a trade fair, even a sporting event. Its UN-approved acronym, The FYROM, places it between Thailand and Togo. When it becomes known as the Republic of Macedonia, it will still be a long way from the salt, but its name will be true to history, and to itself.

At Orthodox Easter, it was "big Friday" at Skopje's church of St. Dimitrija at the entrance to the old bazaar. The faithful were lighting candles, as women stooped low to pass under Christ's raised bier. Others bought red-colored eggs, or religious trinkets from a priest, depositing coins and tattered denar notes in a basket. It was a lively scene, while the panoply of all of the saints and the heavenly host looked on from their painted positions on the smoke-stained walls. It bespoke life and hope, not death. On Saturday night at Lake Ohrid, the thirteenth-century stone church of St. Clement was packed with people. Priests and singers told the gospel story in spite of an ancient graybeard who got off the track and had to be led back by his nearby brother in embroidered satin vestments. At midnight, holy fire appeared, and by the time everyone's candle was lit, it was a miracle that the place hadn't been burned down. People praised Christ, kissed, cracked their eggs, and then went home to eat. It was the same throughout the Orthodox world.

Lake Ohrid, 289 meters deep, a UNESCO treasure, lies serenely under the backdrop of the snow-capped mountains of Albania. Its Orthodox churches and monasteries were founded by the disciples of Cyril and Methodius, the creators of the Cyrillic alphabet, and date from the late ninth century onward. St. Naum, St. Clement, St. Sophia, and others together comprise an unrivalled collection of icons, frescos, and mosaics. A Slavic university was founded in AD 893. Bulgarian, Byzantine and Serbian kingdoms existed before the Ottomans, creating a rich tapestry of cultures and customs. Here Ohrid thrived and remains today. At the north end of the lake is Struga, site of an annual international poetry festival. At the south end of the surrounding steep slopes is St. Naum on the Albanian border. Around its shores are traditional inns and restaurants with heavy wooden beams, stone walls and overhanging upper floors. Charcoaled lake trout or spitted lamb is great in the open air. For evening, go up the cobbled street close to St. Sophia to the Anteka. Its old-style ambience is as excellent as its food and its musicians work their magic well into the night. Macedonia no longer exists "behind God's back."

Contrary to alarmist predictions, destitute and desperate Albanians did not pour over the border in April. And, significantly, most of Macedonia's hitherto outspoken Albanian oppositionists suddenly lost their voice when they realized that Berisha was in deep trouble. This will not continue for long, however, and the government would be wise to moderate its stance on an Albanian university. It should do so while pressure from Tirana on the PDP/NDP has slacked off. Similarly, while Bulgaria is finding its political and economic feet, it should examine ways to better its relations with Sofia. It is just not the language issue. It is the view (mainly SDSM) that the VMRO-DPMNE gravitates towards Sofia as a party that puts many off. Skopje's allegations that Bulgaria may have had a hand in the Gligorov attempt did not serve them well. Sofia, for its part, has stuck to its "Macedonian state, but not a nation" line, but has not tried to throw its weight around. It has played a waiting game, moving with the momentum of a nascent Turkish, Bulgarian, Albanian axis that sits astride Serbian-Greek interests. The nexus is Macedonia; and, in part, this is why the US has entered the game.

As of late 1995, the US Defense Department already had some thirty programs going—Macedonians attend staff courses, service schools, senior seminars and even West Point military academy. This, and NATO's Partnership for Peace will orient Macedonia's small armed forces along US lines. Handziski said they wanted to join NATO and that all of their security considerations aim in that direction. He said that they would accept a NATO base on their territory and he hedged his answer when asked about the then rumored US interest in a former JNA facility at Krivolac. (It will be used by NATO in the Kosovo crisis.) In addition to US assistance, Handziski said that they have obtained training and equipment from Ankara. They would like a similar arrangement with Greece.

In only seven years Macedonia has ceased being part of an able, well-equipped JNA and is now a country with no arms industry and little money to spend, but it must somehow defend itself. With the dissolution of Yugoslavia, Macedonia found itself adrift in a sea of uncertainty. It no doubt needs and welcomes the security of its friendship with Washington, symbolic as it is. It is sort of a symbiotic relationship, like a tickbird and an elephant. Yugoslavia needs stability on its southern flank. It would be unhappy if Macedonia's Albanians became separatist so as to impact on Kosovo, or on Montenegro for that matter. Since the war, it is even more dependent on uninterrupted access to Thessaloniki than it was before. Thus, good relations with Macedonia and Greece are important, even given its plans to expand its use of the Danube. Greece, as a full member of NATO and the EU, is in a position to help or hurt. Athens greatly angered the European Commission when it ran its embargoes against Skopje, the European Court's overly tolerant decision notwithstanding. There has even been talk of an east-west highway project across Albania, Macedonia and Bulgaria that would reduce the importance of Thessaloniki. Because Greece has its own east-west "Egnatia" highway partially completed, it would probably oppose substantial funding or financing by the EU.

Greece will eventually have to accept its northern neighbor, despite the fact that its major political parties remain a hostage to the nationalist hysteria they themselves fostered. In much of the Balkans, ethnic and historical stereotype thinking lurks just below the surface, needing little encouragement to bring it out. After five years of acidic Greek commentary concerning FYROM and the "Skopjians," we were recently reminded yet again of the mischievous capriciousness of Balkan reality when it was rediscovered that Nikos Kazantzakis's fictional *Zorba the Greek* was modeled on the real life George Zorbas, a Greek mining engineer, who lived much of his life in Macedonia. He was buried in Skopje after a long life amid many women. Observers in Skopje were quick to note that Kazantzakis's Macedonia included Mount Olympus, Mount Athos, and Thessaloniki. Greeks were equally quick to comment that Kazantzakis and Zorbas are Greek, and that Macedonia is Greek!

Then, to his great credit, Greek composer Mikis Theodorakis went to Skopje and directed his "Alexis Zorbas" symphony, which featured in Michalis Cacoyannis's Oscar-winning film from 1963. A national orchestra performed with a twelve-minute standing ovation at the end. Finally, as if life were imitating art, Anthony Quinn arrived on the island of Crete and danced a slow Khasapiko. Greece took the aged American actor into their hearts and made him a Greek and Zorba a Cretan. Macedonia was momentarily forgotten.

Demonstrating amazing toughness and tenacity, Gligorov not only recuperated, but recovered sufficiently to resume office within a few months. To the surprise of those who expected him to bow out, his return prompted his young prime minister, Crvenkovski, to oust coalition kingpin Andov in February 1996 and to pack his cabinet with more SDSM members. Andov, a much older, experienced ex-communist had apparently acquired too much influence for the liking of the SDSM while acting president, adding to a long-simmering situation wherein the Liberals had begun flirting with the DP/VMRO-DPMNE opposition and had accused an SDSM minister of finance of appropriating public monies intended for LP activity for his own party's benefit. A year later, the SDSM-dominated coalition was fighting off charges of collusion concerning the collapse of several dodgy pyramid investment schemes. It seems a Bitola banker invited an undetermined number of officials to join his scheme at the outset—including the vice governor of the Central Bank, helping them rake in huge profits before the collapse. In May 1997, Crvenkovski predictably reshuffled his cabinet and promised an investigation.[39]

As Macedonia's foreign fronts improve, its domestic shortcomings become of increasingly greater significance. The SDSM rules the roost in a manner that is perhaps the most moderate and least chauvinistic in ex-Yugoslavia, but which has its obvious faults. When meeting and demonstration permits are arbitrarily cancelled; when efforts are undertaken to undermine the opposition; when an election process is unfairly manipulated; when minority rights are slighted; democracy suffers. Presently, it may be the best that can be expected for a country that is inexperienced in democracy, one that struggled for over one hundred years to assert its identity in the face of repeated efforts to deny its existence.[40]

Because of the might of the word, though in an unrecognized tongue,
I still select sound on the Macedonian lyre.
It is my shield, the equal of your might,
Mighty tyrants! For the grave will gather you in with all the rest.

I act out tranquility for you, even seek harmonies,
For the mysterious name hidden somewhere in this place.
This is my wager in the gruesome game.
This the thought that I've constantly pursued.

"Resistance" by Blaze Koneski from Crn Oven (Black Ram), 1993

Albania

Regional Ethnic Overlap

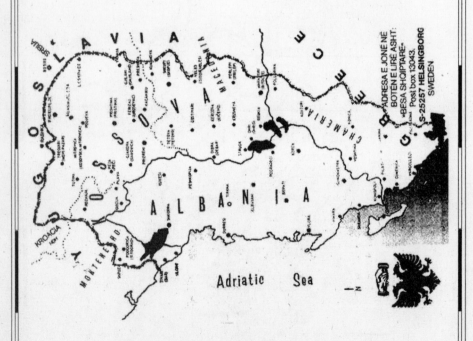

Nationalist Claims

Chapter 4

Europe's Orphan

Albania: July 1993–November 1997

Morn dawns; and with it stern Albania's hills,
Dark Suli's rocks, and Pindus' inland peak,
Rob'd half in mist, bedew'd with snowy rills,
Array'd in many a dun and purple streak,
Arise; and, as the clouds along them break,
Disclose the dwelling of the mountaineer:
Here roams the wolf, the eagle whets his beak,
Birds, beasts of prey, and wilder men appear,
And gathering storms around convulse the
Closeing year.

George Gordon, Lord Byron (1788–1824)

Lord Byron became enthralled with things Albanian and, as many English gentleman orientalists were once wont to do, he loved to wear a rich, red jacket of velvet and heavy gold brocade; a long, flowing, fustenella skirt; boots and leg wrappings of a fetching design; a broad sash to cradle an inlaid, short sword and pistol; and a silken, multicolored, head wrap which hung down to one side of his dark, handsome head. He had been traveling rough since he had entered his maturity and would lay down his life upon the altar of Greek independence amid a malarial swamp at Mesolonghi. In that short span, however, his poetry inspired a generation of romantic artists who painted landscapes, ancient ruins and the people of the Balkans. Clan chieftains and mountain fighters fired their imaginations from his evocative "Childe Harold's Pilgrimage": "Land of Albania! let me bend mine eyes on thee thou rugged nurse of savage men! ...Where is the foe who ever saw their back? ...Unshaken, rushing on where'er their chief may lead."[1]

Indeed, a barely known exotic race was found to exist on Europe's very doorstep, hidden away in their walled redoubts, Muslim, Catholic, and Orthodox, whose origins are shrouded in the mists of time and who are said to be descended from the ancient Illyrians. Most had converted to Islam and a succession of Albanians served as grand viziers to the Ottoman Empire. They also produced a host of fine soldiers who were famous for their ferocity and loyalty. Select troops guarded the Sultans and garrisoned Constantinople. Theirs was the dynasty of Mehmet Ali of Egypt. Skanderbeg, their national hero, covered them in glory and entrusted them with his black, double-headed eagle on scarlet flag from the fifteenth century. It was a proud heritage that spanned many centuries!

However, of the peoples of the Balkans, the Albanians are among the last to reach self-awareness as a nation. Isolated in their mountain fastness, a tribal society that was essentially feudal existed into the early twentieth century. Theirs was a life more in harmony with medieval ways than the modernity that was suddenly thrust upon them. The personal honor that a man was expected to uphold to avenge a wrong often led to a *hakmarrje* (blood feud), and when they were not fighting the Serbs, or Montenegrins, they fought each other in a felicitous anarchy. It is said that during World War One, when the retreating Serbs captured Albanians who had fired on their column, that the latter would neither grimace nor turn their heads as throats were slit. Djilas recalls how, in World War Two, in Montenegro, Partisans were pursued by Albanians who came cursing and shouting, "Moracani, Moracani!" in remembrance of a long bygone clan battle!

The northern Ghegs, many of them Catholic, tended to be the most xenophobic and fiercely independent of all. The Tosks, who were almost all Muslim, except for an Orthodox minority, held fiefs along the coastal plain and in the south. While many Albanians were willing to serve the Porte, local rulers maintained a good measure of autonomy and resisted Ottoman efforts to subdue them. This or that pasha would come and go, making depredations in this or that district, but without bending the populace to his will. The tradition of constant warfare, natural when enemies existed on every side, served to inhibit the wider growth of husbandry, civil government and modern education. Even so, Albanian men in the latter part of the nineteenth century were often photographed with a rifle in one hand and a book in the other, as if aspiring to a knowledge of the written word. A contemporary referred to them as "savage children," for they were of an earlier age.

Their luck, soon to be mixed with misfortune, turned in 1878 when their leaders gathered to form the League of Prizren. Although it expressed their early nationalism, it came about as a reaction to the treaties of San Stefano and Berlin, which presaged the coming break up of Ottoman rule and the inevitable partition of lands where Albanians had long been living. However, the Albanians had arrived late to the business of state building and faced Balkan and European rivals who were stronger and better organized. Also, unlike others, the Albanians never rallied around a single religious institution that bore their culture and served to unify its people, so that, while the league asserted its claim to autonomy by force of arms, it failed to gain complete clan support and was put down. Unfortunately, just then, it was also at cross purposes with the Great Powers. And lastly, Albania's association with the Ottomans, and the fact that most were Muslim, made them the odd man out in the Balkans, adding to their alienation.

By the turn of the century, however, the Albanian question became an adjunct to the larger Eastern Question for Austria and Italy, for their own strategic purposes, became interested in who would control the eastern littoral of the Adriatic. Austria wanted to shut out the Serbs and Italy wanted to exclude the Austrians. As for the Albanians, they were alive to Serbo-Montenegrin designs in the north and Greek interest in Epirus, its Orthodox south. It needed outside protection. The Balkan Wars confirmed this, as Montenegro took Shkoder; the Serbs a part of the northern border; the Greeks the south as far as Korce; while Albanians in Kosovo and Macedonia were absorbed into a new "Old Serbia." Austria led a Great Power dictat, which restored the status quo in Albania, as well as a move, in 1912, to assert its independence. A German army major, Prince Wilhelm of Wied, was chosen to be its ruler. He lasted only six months amid growing internal strife. Then, an Albanian, Eshad Pasha Toptani (with Serbian backing), took power in a situation approaching anarchy.

World War One saw Albania first occupied by the Allies; enduring a push by the Central Powers; and then being reoccupied by the victors. Rival Albanian delegates argued their cause at Versailles and it was only due to the insistence of US President Woodrow Wilson that Albanian independence was reaffirmed and the country not partitioned. Instability and limited intervention by Yugoslavia and Greece continued even as the Tosk Orthodox Bishop, Fan Noli (a Harvard graduate), formed the first post-war government in 1921.

However, Noli's short-lived coalitions were increasingly undermined by antireform landowners. At the end of 1924, a gigantic Gheg tribal chieftain, Ahmed Zogu, gained power and, with the backing of the Italians, he ultimately became king.[2]

It was unfortunate that Albania had been supported by a defeated Austria-Germany, by an American president who soon died and then by an Italy that within a decade became a fascist dictatorship. Italy made a poor dependency out of the country and had as its only interest its economic exploitation as a producer of agricultural products, primary minerals and certain features for military use. Consequently, the once-proud "Arnaut" chieftains within only one generation became exploitative begs who, under a corrupt king who lived off foreign subventions, saw the people sink ever lower into poverty, illiteracy and poor health. On Good Friday in April 1939, Italy began its military occupation of the country. Thereupon, King Zogu packed as much gold and clothing as his caravan of cars could carry and fled to Greece.

World War Two saw fascist-collaborationist regimes set up with a Greater Albania taking in portions of Yugoslavia under the protection of first an Italian, and then a German occupation force. Tirana even contributed the Skanderbeg SS division to the German Wehrmacht, which committed atrocities against Serbs living in Kosovo. Ultimately, however, Albanian communist Partisans won against collaborators and nationalists alike, taking over an impoverished, factionalized country at the end of the war. Led by leaders whose worldview had been formed by Marxist-Leninism and Stalin, Albanians were force-fed an alien ideology as they were harnessed to the task of socialist transformation. They were the captives of a regime that became the most rigidly authoritarian in the communist world, its so-called dictatorship of the proletariat creating a population that was socially pulverized in Europe's worst jail. The sentence, from 1949 to 1989, amounted to forty years of hard labor, with no amnesty, and no time off for good behavior.[3]

By December 1989, the Albanian Party of Labor's (APL) Tosk taskmaster, Enver Hoxha, had been dead for four years. Nevertheless, his "clan" of communist minions were trying to prevent their pyramid of power from collapsing as it was doing everywhere to the east. Albanian President and APL First Secretary, Ramiz Alia, suggested that Albania's level of development was so advanced that it was immune to the crisis occurring elsewhere. His ignorance combined with arrogance was astonishing. However, changes Alia himself had permitted allowed the people to walk around, so to speak, without their leg irons and, when they became aware of what had happened throughout Europe, they were soon climbing over the walls of the foreign embassies in

Tirana with only one thought, to escape! Multiparty elections eventually ousted the reorganized Socialist Party and brought a northern Gheg physician-turned-politician to power, President Sali Berisha of the Democratic Party (DP).[4]

Politics, however, proved to be no palliative for empty stomachs and, as Albania's chimerical workers' paradise collapsed in chaos, hungry mobs looted food stores, broke into warehouses and then turned their fury on the factories where they had long toiled to fill quotas, but never their family's needs. Law and order disintegrated and even the shooting of dozens failed to quell roving gangs of rioters who carried away anything of value. What couldn't be moved was often disabled or broken. Public buildings, utilities and even schools were damaged. Desperate crowds, often verging on hysteria, commandeered ships and forced the crews to take them to Italy. Others braved the Grammos mountains between Albania and Greece in the dead of winter, fording icy streams and threading their way by night past border guards to finally arrive exhausted on the outskirts of Igoumenitsa, Ioannina, and Florina. In their thin jackets, bellbottoms and muddy, sodden, shoes, they asked for any kind of work at any kind of wage. And, unfortunately, some had become a brutalized rabble.

Through 1991–3 the disorder spread, not only in urban areas, but into the countryside as well. And while Sali Berisha's DP had gained in urban popularity, respect for official authority was almost non-existent. Foreigners were not excluded. A number were robbed and a few, unfortunately, were murdered for their meager personal possessions. With the collapse of institutional order, skyrocketing unemployment and rampant crime, desperate breadwinners looked for any conceivable escape hatch. What at first was a trickle of refugees coming across the border into Greece soon became a flood. It went on for a year. We saw them in the streets and on the construction sites doing dirty, backbreaking jobs for half that being asked by Greeks. Of medium build, slim and wiry, some even ran to blond hair and blue eyes. They walked well, even with their ragged clothing, but they also had a look about them that told you they were out on the edge and capable of almost anything. They were Europe's orphans![5]

By July 1993, I had decided I needed to know what circumstances had driven the Albanians to the lower depths. I decided not just to fly to Tirana, but to go first to Ioannina in northwest Greece, and from there to retrace the refugee route in reverse.

The Olympic flight took less than an hour and, that day, it was hot, almost 100°F. Ioannina was building a new terminal and, we waited for our bags in a windswept, dirty parking lot. The sweat running down my chest and the dust caking my face helped to make the needed transition from the comfort of my home in Athens. An airport taxi driver disingenuously attempted to tell me that it was three hours by bus to the border. In fact, it is one hour to Kakavia and it cost very little. The drive was undramatic, a winding road through low, wooded, mountains, the Grammos. I wondered how things would be at the border, as Greece had just rounded up and thrown out some 20,000 Albanians after Tirana had expelled a Greek Orthodox priest for subversion. As many of the Albanians had been in Greece quite legally, it was much more than a tit-for-tat reaction on the part of Athens.

At Kakavia, the vehicles were backed up in both directions. One had to get chopped out of a Greek police post and get chopped in on the Albanian side. A Greek officer shook his head as he fixed his stamp and told me I was crazy. The Albanian police were even more incredulous. After repeated, but polite questioning, I got them to understand that I was a journalist. As I sat on a dust-covered, dilapidated plastic sofa, two policemen carefully examined my passport and made entries in a tattered notebook. After five minutes, they smilingly issued a *permis de circulation pour les etrangers a sejour provisoire* by the Republika E Shqiperise Ministeria E. R. Publik, and another obscure piece of paper that I never understood. For Americans, a visa was free. Others paid as much as US$40. Lugging my bags, I climbed over a few strands of barbed wire and then past a young army conscript with a Kalashnikov who looked at me as if I were some man from Mars.

Then, without warning, three hire-car drivers appeared from nowhere and began to argue over whose fare I was. In Greek, I asked about a bus for Gjirokaster, the scene of protests over the expelled priest. They shook their heads and broke up in laughter. Seeing only an ancient bus that obviously had not moved in years and no identifiable taxis, my resolve melted in the hot sun and I chose a driver that I knew I could punch out if I had to, finally agreeing on US$20 for the twenty-mile ride. He made room for me in his back seat amidst a barrel of olive oil, some boxes and a spare tire, and assigned an Albanian passenger to the front. I wanted to be in the back, believing it would be safer in the event of a head-on collision. I had read that Albanian roads were littered with the wreckage of cars as a result of drivers having tested their skills without the benefit of any lessons.

Upon entering Albania, one goes through something of a time warp. Three hours earlier, I had been in Ioannina. Now, along the road, I was seeing utter ruin, desolation and decay on every side. I mean, this was Europe after all, some four hundred kilometers from Athens and only seventy-five from Italy. What had gone wrong here in these mountains and coastal plains? The old

Opel Rekord groaned up the steep hillside to Gjirokaster, Enver Hoxha's birthplace. To a sizeable Orthodox, ethnic-Greek minority, it is Agyrocastro. It is situated high on rocky outcrops, typically Epirotic. To my shouts for a hotel, a *xenodoxeion*, my driver stopped at the Hotel Alupi, a large, old, Albturist affair. I entered a painfully bare lobby whose few sofas and chairs were all occupied by policemen and security types who were sprawled out, relaxing. I gave my passport to a female receptionist and asked for a room. After a pause, she said to wait and walked out with my documents. While waiting, I noticed that there were no keys in the customary cubbyholes. Also, the only *kart regjistrimi* that I saw had been used as scrap paper. For the next half hour, the same woman would come and go. To my questions, she would smile and say, "Yes, it is a hotel. Please wait!" It seemed an odd hotel, as the police had accosted a man who attempted to go upstairs and insisted on examining his identity papers. An argument had erupted.

Finally, smiling Hadji rescued me. He explained in broken English that he ran a "hotel," a better hotel that would cost only US$15 a day, including meals. It was a deal; and off we went up a narrow, cobblestone lane that looped above the town to what must be one of the better houses in Gjirokaster with massive stone and white plaster walls, timber-framed windows and eaves, and a heavy slate roof. It was set in a walled garden with shade and fruit trees. It was clean and quiet and had hot water. It was great! After a shower, I stretched out on my bed, looked out over the town and imagined that this was how an Illyrian eagle, a real *buljukbasa* clan leader must live. However, curiosity soon triumphed and I left to see the sights. The shops were nearly bare, but the place had a charm with its overhanging upper stories, its several mosques and a large castle crowning an overlooking hilltop.

I went back to the Alupi, to learn where the Greek consulate was located, so that I might find out about the expulsion of the priest. To my surprise, I was directed upstairs past the police. Thereupon, I found two harassed and obviously overworked Greeks who were examining Albanian visa applications. On the floor was a huge cardboard box containing hundreds of passports and paper files. That explained the police presence. As the phone jangled, I was told that they could not discuss the case of Archimandrite Chrysostomos ("the golden tongued") Maidonis, but, if I returned at 7 p.m., the consul might be available. When I returned, I found a young man dressed in a white T-shirt, white slacks, white shoes and carrying a white, cordless phone, an item that must have been quite a status symbol in Gjirokaster. He was very abrupt, stating in less than ten seconds, "No, I don't have time to talk. It's all over, really over. I'm off for vacation!" I thanked him and wondered how to make a story out of that.

Back at Hadji's, I talked to his Orthodox wife and his eleven-year-old daughter, Julia. The latter, who spoke good English, would make any parent proud. Hadji arrived and we took to the garden where I shared my Scotch and cigarettes. Being a Muslim was no impediment. We were soon joined by a neighboring woman who taught at a school. Hadji's toddler son, Taran, provided music from a much-abused 78 rpm, wind up victrola. I explained that I had met the head of the Democratic Party of Gjirokaster, Sotiris Hronis, in Athens two years earlier. I also asked about Andreas Zarbalas, the Greek Omonia Party leader. It seemed that the much-publicized plight of Albania's Greek minority was yet another aspect of the overwhelming problems affecting the entire populace as they faced the need to both reinvent society and rebuild their country. Even young Julia was aware that local government officials had claimed that her school's window glass had been replaced, when it hadn't.

Hadji described his plans to convert his home into a first-class hostel. I like to think he will succeed one day. He had worked at the Alupi, but had got into trouble because he had once carried on a mail correspondence with a foreigner. Now, he was just a helper and there was no business. The staff showed up just to collect their meager salaries. However, Hadji's house had possibilities. For dinner, his wife served excellently seasoned fried eggplant, zucchini and green peppers, a cool yogurt soup, sliced tomatoes, cucumbers and onions, fresh bread, red wine and watermelon. In Albania, there is food if you have money. For money, you need to work. No job, no food. At the time, there was massive unemployment, widespread hunger and some starvation. Had Hoxha's prison provided a better daily diet? I wondered if it had been better under Zogu. Did Albanians look back to some imaginary pastoral past as they were once told to look forward to an industrialized future? Progress is never linear. Society can easily regress under certain circumstances.

At 4 a.m. the next morning, there were dozens of people huddled near the Alupi waiting for the bus, or waiting to line up for a visa. At 4:30, the bus lumbered into the square, already half full. Hadji had prepared me for the shoving match that followed. With him pushing from behind and shouting to the driver, I made it in. The ticket for the hundred miles to Tirana was US$2.50. It was worth a hundred times that in education. The scenery was an array of broken down, deserted factories; rusting machinery; lifeless villages; untilled fields; and, most memorably, the lost and listless, sitting by the road, ragged, some without shoes, sitting with a dazed expression on their faces. They weren't begging. In fact, they weren't doing anything, just sitting, like shell-shocked survivors of an artillery attack. It was a bleak testimony to the failure of an institutionalized ideology. I was witnessing a man-made disaster.

The road was narrow, winding, potholed and broken at the edges. We traveled at a slow speed and stopped frequently to pour water in the radiator, allow people to relieve themselves and to pick up or drop off passengers. In addition to that, the bus collapsed four times en route. At one point, some beered-up young men in the back pushed forward to assault the driver, but others blocked the aisle and shouted them down with a variety of well-chosen oaths. Some of us managed to flag down another bus at around 4 p.m., and we were in Tirana in another hour. We were dropped off at a vacant lot in a squalid section of the city comprising ugly apartment blocks. As my fellow passengers started walking off in different directions, I soon found myself virtually alone. As luck had it, however, a block away I was able to hail a cruising taxi. I was only minutes away from Tirana's center, Skanderbeg Square.

I inquired at one or two cheap hotels that were back off the square, but they were beyond the pale for even someone like myself who had traveled in the Middle East and India. The Hotel Tirana, a very large pseudo-modern affair was full. Tirana, it seems, was awash with foreign advisors and aid givers. After a few hours, however, the desk did some juggling and I had a room. It was large, comfortable and replete with Chinese-made bathroom fixtures. It overlooked the square, which was filling up for that early evening time when Albanians like to take their *korzo*, their stroll. Trucks and buses, cars, horse carts, wagons (both pushed or pulled by their owners), but mostly just people walking were crisscrossing from all angles. It wasn't noisy. It was as if, after the heat of the day had subsided, everyone was willing to give way and wait a little. Later, I had a good schnitzel and a bottle of wine for US$5.

The dining room had only foreigners for guests and most of them seemed intent upon reading thick file folders, presumably new proposals and reports about how Albania was to be rescued by the West. I thought about the appalling sights I had seen in the past two days. I remembered reading that someone in the 1930s had said that Albania is a place where people with no shoes walk on gold! It has oil, maybe more offshore. I had seen a few pumps working and sending their spillage down the hillside into a riverbed, an environmental eyesore. Albania has a lot of chrome and other minerals. Would Berisha, who had thrown the door open to western capitalism, be able to turn things around? I thought of Hadji, of how nice his family and neighbors were. I thought about two young men I had met on the bus. One was a classical violinist who had been playing in a restaurant in Greece. He said that he had once given a concert in France. The other had been working as a waiter in

Athens. He said that he was a five-year university graduate in physics. He planned to approach the American embassy about scholarship possibilities. I wondered what was the survival rate for people being carried along like so much human flotsam?

As if economic collapse weren't trouble enough, relations with the Greeks were constantly in turmoil because of illegal immigration and the aggressive activities of certain senior Greek clerics and right-wing nationalists who were attempting to undermine Albanian authority in the southern part of the country. This was not only detrimental to Albanian relations with the West (Greece belongs to the EU and NATO and can either help or hurt), but also put the larger ethnic-Greek community at risk, opening them to charges of disloyalty. One of the main instigators was the old Metropolitan Sevastianos in Konitsa who ran a political center and a powerful radio station that never lacked for funds. He and his supporters simply wanted to take over north Epirus, which they claim is Greek. More than that, they distributed pamphlets and maps that showed Greek territory running up to the Skhumbini River, thirty kilometers from Tirana! They printed books, distributed video cassettes and beamed their tirade from Ioannina and Corfu as well. Greeks and selected ethnic-Greek Albanians were run through what amounted to indoctrination courses. Sevastianos also offered visa assistance and helped to obtain residence and work permits as inducements.

Sevastianos's crusade was backed by Greece's most senior cleric, Metropolitan Seraphim in Athens. I had listened to the latter deliver a fiery sermon and watched his supporters from the Pan-Hellenic Association of Northern Epirus walk from the cathedral to Syntagma Square. There, at the tomb of the unknown soldier, with flags flying, they swore to regain north Epirus. Then, all repaired to the nearby Grande Bretagne Hotel for more speeches and refreshments. Boy scouts; Red Cross nurses; old men dressed in military uniforms; robed priests in their stovepipe hats—it made for a merry occasion, this talk about marching north. Apparently, Chrysostomos "the golden tongued" was very much involved in all of this. He had arrived in Durres as Costas Stamos in the summer of 1991 as a teacher at the Albanian Orthodox seminary. He zealously promoted the Greek church over the Albanian and proselytized shamelessly among his students. Moving to Gjirokaster, he was promoted to Archimandrite. There, he asserted responsibility for all southern Albania. He actively distributed Sevastianos's propaganda material and allegedly met often with ethnic-Greek Albanian separatists. He also worked closely with the Greek consulate in Gjirokaster in ways said to be inconsistent with his religious status.[6]

Sevastianos and others had struggled against Albania during the Cold War and they decided it was opportune to spread Hellenism and Orthodoxy after communism's collapse. This coincided in part with the plight of some ethnic-Greeks who felt threatened by the resurgence of Islamic and Catholic-centered social activism. By April 1992, Sotir Qiriazati (the chairman of the ethnic-Greek Omonia organization) had urged Greek Prime Minister Constantine Mitsotakis to intervene officially so as to establish a program of economic development and autonomy for north Epirus. The Greek government blew hot and cold on any kind of aid to Albania and any tentative moves towards Tirana came to a halt whenever the Greek press cranked up on alleged harassment of the ethnic-Greek minority. Much ink was expended assessing the true size of this community. Greek figures ran from 300–500,000, while Tirana put it at no more than 65,000, almost all in the south near the Greek border.[7]

While I met Albanian officialdom during my visit, I wanted to wander around to get some feeling for this city of 300,000. The broad plaza adjacent to the hotel, Skanderbeg Square, is surrounded by modern-looking buildings that give a deceptive air of progress to the city's center. This veneer, however, does not extend more than a kilometer or so in any direction and then the reality of Tirana takes over. Opposite the Hotel Tirana was the Ethem Bey mosque. What struck one as unusual was its large signboard outside showing eleven positions for prayer. Its instructions were in Albanian and Arabic. Some young men entered to pray, but not very many. Farther down, old office buildings given over to government (in a yellow ochre, Italianate style) lined both sides of the street. They looked charming until you got up close to their peeling plaster. Off to one side was the foreign ministry. A little farther down was the ministry of defense and then the presidency. At the far end of this long boulevard was the university. It could all be seen in an easy morning's stroll. It was that small.

The thing to do is to take a side street and keep going. Tirana apartment buildings are not a very pretty sight. They all have a sordid, deserted look to them: stained walls; tiny balconies for air and to hang the washing; tiny windows; a forest of TV antennas on top of the roof. Many flats have small TV satellite dishes to widen their window on the world. Boys were playing dirt court basketball at the Ismail Qemali School with a battered ball and a broken backboard. Their playground was refuse strewn and many of the windows in the building were out, either completely missing, or broken. The Librari bookstore had little that looked interesting. I examined graffiti on the sides of the buildings wondering if they might help decipher the detritus of disaster: Florenci; Blendi; Partizani; Demokraci. Could it explain what Albania's young were thinking? Pink Floyd. Wall. David Gilmore. Breakdown. Tonight You Will See Your Birth, Life, Death. Life = WC. Doors. We Don't Care (upturned index finger). The Party's Over So Get The Fuck Out! Much of it was in English. It was scrawled everywhere, especially on monuments once intended to impress. Is English a form of elite escapism? Is graffiti the weapon of the weak?

The next morning I took a shared taxi, an old van, and headed for Skopje by way of Lake Ohrid. The sights were more of the same. To cite the most striking, one would have to mention the large iron and steel works at Elbasan. This Chinese-built aid project looked like a dinosaur dying in the desert. Its smokestacks were idle and, even from afar, you could see and feel that it was wasting away in the elements, its furnaces, huge halls, railroad lines and overhead cranes giving way to inactivity and neglect. It was a weekday and no workers could be seen. It was as if thousands had suddenly downed their tools and walked away. Out of Elbasan, the road narrowed and twisted up into scrub-covered hills. As we approached the Macedonian border, more of the people's pillboxes were in evidence up on the hillside, located at what some local APL official must have thought was a good defensive position. The country is dotted with thousands of these igloos with a gun slot, which were obsolete in terms of modern warfare on the day their concrete was poured. What a mad waste of labor and material! They dotted the beaches south of Durres. In most cases, their location made little military sense, even if they could have withstood a TOW rocket hit. Were they built on weekends on a quota system? Like China's backyard furnaces of the Cultural Revolution which were intended to make the country self-sufficient in iron, was this the influence of the idea of the People's War, the naive belief that armed workers in their pillboxes could defend an Albania ringed by its supposed enemies?[8]

Land of Albania! let me bend mine eyes: a crowd pressed against the security grill of a bakery to be first in line to buy bread. A teenaged girl, both legs cut off at the thighs, begs beneath the statue of Skanderbeg. Sometimes she leans against the stone, asleep, exhausted by her efforts to keep upright and move about. A street was lined with trees reduced to rows of stumps due to the scarcity of fuel in winter. Ragged children were standing by the roadside to watch the bus go by. Their pale skin and thin faces tell you they are hungry. They don't wave. They just stand and stare.

* * *

114

The Albanians, an admixture of people descended from the Illyrians, are among the oldest races of Europe. The Macedons ran up against them around 400 BC, as did the Romans a little later. They were regarded as savage fighters and piratical. Rome mounted several punitive expeditions against them and finally enlisted their sullen accession during the Third Macedonian War in about 167 BC. Illyria became part of Caesar's proconsulship while it was being organized into the empire. However, in AD 6, they rose up in revolt under the leadership of their chief, Bato and forced the Emperor Augustus to recall his stepson Tiberius from the German frontier. It was three years before the Illyrian generals once again accepted Roman rule. Peace must have prevailed, for in AD 270 an Illyrian cavalry commander was made emperor. For five years Aurelian ruled ably and well. He was simple and frugal in his personal habits. Some regarded him as the best ruler since Septimius Severus despite his ill-fated decision to declare himself a "sun god," an act that led to his untimely murder. Ten years later, another Illyrian, Diocletian, the son of an ex-slave, was elevated and ruled for twenty years. He is less well regarded for he set up a system of rotating dictators, which were linked by marriage, and which also favored his fellow Illyrians. However, even detractors credit him with bringing order out of anarchy.

Illyria, or Illyricum under Rome, was deepened and extended south to Crete long before Justinian ruled from the east. Its administration sometimes changed, but, under Roman rule, it enjoyed peace and prosperity. The Via Egnatia, the roadway linking Dyrrhachium (Durres), Thessalonica, and Byzantium made Illyria a crossroads for commerce for many hundreds of years. However, Germanic tribes from the north were to eventually make their inroads. The empire was divided in AD 395, and Rome was sacked by the Visigoths in AD 410. An Illyrian, Orestes, named his son emperor. Romulus, or Little Augustus, ruled only months until Odovacar, a German chief, was named king on 22 October, 476. An age had ended. The Illyrian lands had traditionally extended from the Danube-Morava rivers to the Adriatic. This hinterland, presumably less Romanized than the coastal areas, was now subjected to successive waves of invading Goths, Huns, Avars, Slavs, and Bulgars. As an old empire broke up, the remnants of Illyricum found themselves straddling the fault-line dividing the emerging Catholic kingdoms of the West from the Eastern Orthodoxy of Constantinople.[9]

With the weight of invasion, the collapse of far-flung commerce and trade and the break up of the large, slave-owning estates, feudalism emerged as the dominant political and economic system throughout the Balkans, including the lands of the "Albanoi." The tenth and eleventh centuries witnessed wars between the Bulgars and Byzantium. Crusader armies arrived from the north, establishing fortified way stations along the route to the Holy Land. The Albanoi (later known as Arber, Arberi, Arberish) tried to assert themselves during these tumultuous times. Albanian principalities rose briefly, but were overrun by others, including the Serb King Stefan Dusan. However, after his death in 1355, Albanian chiefs again established themselves: the Balshajs from Shkodra, Topiajs from Durres, Muzakajs from Berat and the Shpatajs from Arta.

Albanians had long lived in Kosovo (the Dardania of Roman times) in unbroken settlement from the time of its Illyrian antecedents. However, its fertile farmland was contested by many and, by the late fourteenth century, the Ottoman Turks had arrived. In an effort to turn the tide, a combined army of Serbs, Bosnians, and Albanians, under Serbian Prince Lazar met and were defeated by the Ottomans at Kosovo Polje (The Field of Blackbirds) in June 1389. The Ottoman advance, with intervals, was to continue in successive waves. The Albanians (Catholic and Orthodox), resisted with the others, the Austrians, Hungarians, Serbians, and Romanians until their defeat at Varna in 1444 broke up this Christian coalition. It was in this period that Skanderbeg became famous for his steadfast leadership and outstanding military exploits.[10]

Gjerge (George) Kastrioti was the son of an Albanian vassal to the Turks who, as a child, had been taken to Constantinople as a hostage. He served in their army, won plaudits and was made a beg. At some point, probably in his youth, he converted to Islam and was given the name Skander. Hence, the name Skanderbeg. It is said that after fighting against the Hungarians at Nis in 1443, he led 300 Albanians home and began to raise a rebellion against the Ottomans. Another account has him sent back as an official, whereupon he began to conspire and sought the support of Venice and Hungary. By 1444, he had organized other notables into an Albanian League and into open revolt. At Torvioll plain, an Ottoman army of 25,000 was routed by 10,000 Albanians led by Skanderbeg. He remained the leader of the Albanian clan chiefs for the next twenty-five years until his death in 1468. The Ottomans led successive campaigns into the Albanian highlands, but failed in their objectives, often beaten back by less numerous forces. George Kastrioti became the toast of Rome and Venice (his likeness has been found in paintings, etchings, and other works of art) and his league was supported by the Italian states and the papacy.[11]

In an imponderable "if" of history, one wonders what might have been Albania's fate if its people had not converted to Islam. Would Rome's powerful Popes, princes of the realm, worked a greater influence on the course of events? Although Ottoman rule was extended into Albania by the middle of the sixteenth century, the latter's leaders remained unruly and often rebelled against an imposed foreign authority. Would they have been regarded as the "Bravehearts" of the Balkans when they took up arms against the hated timar system, which required regular contributions of taxes and manpower? With outside support, would they have been able to keep the Turks at bay? Would the Porte have decided that the Sar Planina was a mountain range too far? Might the Albanians have worked out an alliance with the wealthy Venetians up the coast at Dubrovnik? Later, trading on a tradition of Catholicism and their early Latin heritage, could they have made common cause with the Croats and Slovenians, securing Habsburg and Hungarian assistance? Might not they have advanced more as a people and have been better prepared for the end of the empire? The Maronites of Lebanon, an equally fierce tribe of mountain fighters, survived somehow for over 1,500 years and, as Christians, came to enjoy the patronage of Popes and eventually, even faraway France.

Skanderbeg's son, Gjon Kastrioti, carried on the struggle, as did a grandson, Gjerge. However, the main centers of resistance eventually succumbed and grudgingly accepted Ottoman suzerainty. After one hundred years of fighting, from Kosovo to the Adriatic coast, the country was in ruins, causing many to leave for Italy and the Greek islands. Amid economic and cultural decline, many were converted to Islam and much of Albania's Catholic and Orthodox past was trodden into the ground, though some areas retained self rule because they had continued to resist, paying only token tribute. Gradually local chiefs began to assert themselves. This became especially so as the Ottoman empire began its slow decline. The creation of large pashaliks towards the end of the eighteenth century accelerated this tendency. Examples of semi-autonomous rule are Ali Pasha Tepelena at Yannina (Ioannina) and the Bushatllis from Skhodra, who both enjoyed considerable independence for several decades until they, too, were put down. In 1832, the Porte ended the timar system, which sustained the feudal nobility and attempted to centralize control under the so-called "Tanzimat" reforms. After four hundred years of timar exactions, Tanzimat created a new army of tax farmers open to the corruption of Constantinople. Peasant risings took place but they were spontaneous and uncoordinated.[12]

According to the Treaty of San Stefano in 1878, Montenegro was to be greatly enlarged (taking Albanian villages), Serbia was given part of the Sandjak of Prishtina (Kosovo), and Bulgaria got most of Macedonia, including areas populated by Albanians. The Treaty of Berlin would undo much of this, but San Stefano's effect was to compel Albanians to organize themselves to gain control over their areas before someone else took them first. To this end, the Albanian League convened at Prizren on 10 June 1878, preceded by secret meetings of Albanians living in Constantinople led by Abdul Frasheri. The Great Powers gathered in Berlin on 13 June to meet for one month. The Albanians, still subjects of the Sublime Porte, were ignored. However, some eighty notables set up an organizational structure with the authority to levy taxes so as to raise an army. Given its wide representation, some sought to emphasize their loyalty to the empire and a willingness to defend Ottoman interests. Frasheri, on the other hand, asserted Albanian nationalism and articulated Albanian national goals. When the results of Berlin became known, Albanian fighters assembled in the north and south, provisionally joining together in common cause.[13]

With typical Great Power aplomb, the Europeans expected the Turks to enforce the Berlin Treaty and, in August, wanted the latter to facilitate drawing a new Montenegrin-Turkish border. Instead, the Turks (spread thin militarily in any case) gave the Albanians arms, approved their efforts to collect taxes and turned control of their soon-to-be-lost territory over to the rebels. The latter defended it stoutly against Cetinje causing Europe to juggle the territories involved. When the Albanians refused this they awoke one morning to see a European flotilla blockading their harbors. Problems arose in the south as well, when they were forced to face up to Greek claims. Once again, the Albanians were given arms. They were willing to see Thessaly go to the Greeks, but not Epirus. Greece did get Thessaly and Arta in south Epirus in 1888.

The Turks, for their part, were under stiff European pressure to get the Albanians in line and became alarmed at talk of uniting all the Albanian lands under a capital at Bitola. Opinion within the league divided between the followers of Frasheri, who wanted full autonomy, and the conservatives, who emerged as a majority by October 1880. Acting out of expediency, a large Ottoman army led by Devish Pasha was sent in which was joined by the loyalists. It took Prishtina in April 1881 and drove on to the coast. Those who had been loyal to Frasheri were jailed, or sent into exile. Even in defeat, however, the League of Prizren had made its mark. Many of Albania's leaders had awakened to the call for independence!

If awakened, Albanians were for the most part unlettered. After the repression of the league, efforts were made not only to set up schools and an educational system, but to establish Albanian in an accepted linguistic form. Progress was painfully slow in Albania itself. A few schools taught in Albanian by the turn of the century, but even these were closed by the authorities who preferred a scattering of religious schools that taught Turkish, Greek and

Italian. Albanian expatriates helped their language to flower abroad, but in their homeland the soil was stony indeed. Seeing its neighbors on the move, a new generation of Albanians secretly set up the Committee for the Liberation of Albania in Bitola in 1905 and established armed bands under Bajo Topulli. Initially, Topulli was encouraged to cooperate with the Young Turks. This lasted for only a few years until the latter reasserted control by Constantinople and engaged in the same excesses as had always existed. However, with the Ottoman hold on Albania growing increasingly uncertain, Sultan Hamid II himself visited Kosovo in 1911 and made concessions over education and taxes. It was a belated effort that was soon overtaken by events.

The two Balkan Wars and World War One brought independence to the Albanians under less than auspicious circumstances. Their lands remained as divided as they were themselves. Comments made by the British Foreign Secretary, Sir Edward Grey, in August 1913—"The difficulty of coming to an agreement about particular frontiers has been very great... It will be open on many points to a great deal of criticism from anyone with local knowledge... It is to be borne in mind that in making that agreement, the primary essential was to preserve agreement between the Great Powers..."—could have been made again in 1920. A decade later, the Allies had finished with its infant and had entrusted its care to the Italians. In succeeding years, Italy and King Zogu looted their charge as best they could. According to the then young American cub reporter, C. L. Sulzberger, who knew Albania's royal family, Zogu solved his political problems by assassinating exiles, and then by assassinating his assassins, a process which could go on for some time! In retrospect, however, this system was not so different from what followed under the communists.[14]

In 1924, when Bishop Noli fled west, a few of his followers went to Moscow, the beacon of revolution. There they became associated with the Balkan Federation of communist parties and the Comintern. Included were Sejfullah Maleshova (Noli's poet-secretary), Lazar Fundo, and the self educated Ali Kelmendi. Kelmendi, a Gheg, returned home to organize a communist party, but escaped Zogu's anger by fleeing in 1936. He joined the International Brigade in Spain and then went to France. There, he led a small group of Albanian communists, including Enver Hoxha who was a student. In 1938, Kelmendi and Maleshova tried to have Fundo killed by the Soviet NKVD in Moscow, but Georgi Dimitrov intervened. Hoxha, a negligent student it seems, knocked about, and then returned home to teach French. Mehmet Shehu, who was to become prime minister, was in and out of military schools and also fought in Spain. Both Hoxha and Shehu were middle class Tosks. On the eve of World War Two, the Yugoslav communists made contact with their movement. By 1941, Tito found the Albanians quarrelling and in need of advice. He finally forged unity between factionalized groups and got an Albanian party started in November. Its program drove the richer Gheg chieftains and land-owning Tosk begs over to the side of the Italians and Germans. Nevertheless, with British and Yugoslavian help, the communists emerged on top at the end of the war, with Hoxha as party secretary.[15]

Till 1949, Albania was a Yugoslav satellite, receiving aid and assistance. Axis war needs had improved the extractive industry and the country's roads and bridges (a copper plant was started, as was one for cement, adding to a capacity in chrome, oil, and bitumen). It was all nationalized overnight. Efforts were made to extend agriculture by draining marshlands. Thus, although there was devastation, a small industrial base did exist. At first, Tirana received UNRRA and Allied aid as well. Tito, it seems, wanted to bring it into a Balkan Federation as a republic, which would have included the controversial Kosovo region. Hoxha, however (never a favorite of Tito), amid much factional infighting, opted for Stalin's patronage, protection and ideological purity, and followed the latter's denunciation of Belgrade. The political casualties of the time included Naku Spiru (by suicide), Koce Xoxe (a Tosk tinsmith), who was executed after a secret trial, and many others who were purged from the leadership. Thus, Albania became part of the Soviet system, benefiting and suffering by turns. It's true to admit, however, that because of, or despite, draconian internal conditions, a people once largely illiterate became educated within the confines of the communist system, and vastly improved health care extended life expectancy. It was a jail system, which wanted its inmates to be capable of long, arduous labor.

The following decade, of course, saw Stalin's death, the demise of Beria and Malenkov, and Khrushchev's speech to the twentieth CPSU Congress. It also saw problems in Poland, East Germany, and Hungary. Hoxha had to tread carefully through a political minefield as well as to keep a flagging Soviet interest in Albania alive. Again, events outside Albania led to serious ideological turmoil. Tuk Jakova (a Gheg carpenter), Bedri Spahiu, and Panajot Plaku were purged, while Liri Gega (a woman) and Dali Ndreu were shot. The Soviet Union's subsequent denunciation of Stalinism and its reconciliation with Belgrade posed new problems and dangers. In the late 1950s, however, Mao Tse-tung swerved to the left with his Great Leap Forward and Hoxha hitched himself to a new star.

As Hoxha got out from under Tito, he broke from Moscow. It soon turned into a three-way slanging match between Moscow, Tirana, and Peking. By 1961, Soviet advisors and experts were sent packing. It was only months before China stepped into the breach with grains, soft-loans, and technicians willing to live as modestly as Albanians themselves. During the Chinese Cultural Revolution, Hoxha urged Albanians to exert themselves anew. It went well for a while between this Mutt and Jeff of the communist world. However, China eventually became as pragmatic as Albania was doctrinaire. Its ardor cooled. This time, Tirana was the jilted party. In July 1978, Peking called it quits, rolled up project plans and sent its technicians home. Albania was on its own.

Hoxha's response was to lash out with revolutionary exhortations which he enforced with his Sigurimi secret police. Little Albania would stand alone. With a population of only three and a half million, a society already under serious stress and strain was sent into overdrive: quotas, banners, work brigades; a forty-eight hour working week, plus unpaid overtime; student volunteers; men and women brought out of their retirement; factories running three shifts around the clock; men, trucks and tractors shifted from site to site to maintain rigid schedules and a lot of strenuous manual labor with pick and shovel. As for Hoxha, he published several more volumes of his speeches and polemics. Undoubtedly, he actually thought that he had raised Marxism-Leninism to new heights. It was no secret that his pyramid of power (excepting the execution of Defense Minister General Beqir Ballaku in 1974 and the "suicide" of Prime Minister Mehmet Shehu in 1981) had become one of the most stable ruling cliques in the world. And, he had only some 1,000 political prisoners!

During the 1960s, when Tirana and Moscow were throwing brickbats at each other, *Pravda* publicized the nepotism and interlocking nature of the regime:

> Half or more of the fifty-three members of the APL central committee are related. First we have four couples. Enver Hoxha and his wife Nexhmije; Mehmet Shehu and his wife Fiqrete; Hysni Kapo and his wife Vito; and Josif Pashko and his wife Eleni Terezi. The wives of Manush Myftiu, politbureau member, and Pilo Peristeri, candidate member, are sisters. Kadri Hasbiu, candidate member and minister of internal affairs, is the husband of Mehmet Shehu's sister. The brother of Hysni Kapos's wife is Piro Kondi, also a member of the central committee.

The article goes on to cite Nexhmije Hoxha's additional positions and other officials related to her. The same was true for the Shehu and Kapo couples. The system extended to the Sigurimi and police, the military, the youth movement and to every organization of any importance in the country. The system became known as the Albanian pyramid.[16]

By the late 1980s, a few of the younger leaders had begun to face the facts: declining agricultural production on the large state-owned latifundia; industry beset with low output and often crippled by a lack of spare parts and technical problems; the country's physical plants obsolete and in need of modernization; roads and other infrastructure needing repair. And, most importantly, people were simply tired and exhausted, and heading for a breakdown. The entire edifice of state and society was ready to collapse!

A year later, in July, I returned to Tirana by way of a bus from Skopje that passed Lake Ohrid's eastern shore. At the Albanian border, there was the usual confusion regarding documents and the inspection of baggage. A businessman held us up while officials argued over a small machine he wanted to bring into the country. Once underway, everyone's mood improved as we wound our way down through the hills. Things looked better outside the bus as well. Occasionally, a roadside stand would appear, with someone selling something—cigarettes, soft drinks and various small food items. People were back working the fields, mostly with hand implements that have been replaced long ago in luckier lands to the north. Men in shirtsleeves swung long-bladed scythes. Women in trousers and headscarves gathered grain into small bundles. It was a scene, one would think, from the past, but it meant bread. In Tirana, it was evident that the improvements were more than marginal. People were dressed better. They appeared less stressed-out, no longer having that look of acute anxiety around the eyes. There were a few new cars in the street, cafes with umbrellas and new plastic chairs and real open markets with things to sell—a lot of fruit and vegetables and sweets and biscuits from Greece and Italy. There were imported electrical appliances that people had never seen before. Even children, with stalls made from cardboard boxes, were busy becoming "biznessmen."

I stayed at the Dajti Hotel, which used to house state guests. It had been built before World War Two and needed repair. My small room had hot and cold running cockroaches, depending on which faucet you opened. The Tirana Hotel was under renovation and there was a hole in the ground for a five-star affair. Barring minor inconveniences, Tirana was beginning to function for foreigners. For example, a taxi driver insisted on giving me a receipt, something I never got in Athens. Things were happening under Berisha. In the big scheme of things, Albania looked to the United States as its superpower patron in the Balkans and Europe. The US had accepted this role on condition that Berisha cooperated closely on the worsening situation in Kosovo and that Albania allowed it to set up support facilities connected with the conflict in Bosnia. With the backing of an able, strongly anti-communist ambassador in

William Ryerson, Berisha believed that America (and its Albanian-American community) would work the transformation that would make Albania a part of Western Europe. As a harbinger of Western investment to come, Coca-Cola agreed to build a plant outside of Durres to replace the Joy-Cola that people called "Joke."

Moreover, Albania had applied to join NATO and had begun to reorganize its military under Washington's guidance. While waiting to visit Colonel Sali Dika at the Ministry of Defense, several American military officers swept by to their waiting staff car. The Albanian guards gave them a snappy salute as they drove off. Dika explained that Americans were rotating in and out of the ministry on a "Memorandum of Understanding." He said that US equipment was on the way and that Albania was getting ready for NATO's Partnership for Peace program. Defense Minister Safet Zhulali had been to the US, and US Defense Secretary William Perry was expected. Dika crowed, "We are already working as a NATO member!"

Eqerem Mete at the foreign ministry had briefed me on the problem of Albanian-Greek relations. He said things had plummeted since the previous April when a team of armed men from the previously unknown Front for the Liberation of Epirus (MAVI) infiltrated an army camp at Episkopi near the Greek border at night and killed two Albanian trainees in their barracks and wounded others. What he failed to explain was in what connection, and upon what grounds, the authorities had arrested five ethnic-Greek Albanian members of Omonia and had charged them with conspiracy, illegal possession of arms and espionage. The charges were unprecedented since the days of the Cold War. One of the accused was a US-Albanian citizen. Another had been jailed for eight years under Hoxha. All were from the southwest pocket of north Epirus. In the presidential palace, the mood was no better. Berisha's advisor-spokesman, Gence Pollo, fulminated over obstructionist tactics by the Greek government within the EU whereby loan and grant funds voted for Albania had been blocked by Athens time and time again with the allegation that ethnic-Greeks were being repressed by Tirana. It appeared that an unfortunate backlash was taking place.

In Gjirokaster, Professor Selfo Cocoli said that most people were getting along reasonably well with each other as individuals, regardless of religion or ethnic background. However, since the fall of communism, ethnic-Greek leaders had pushed for autonomy. But nowhere, he pointed out, has autonomy been granted when that same group comprised a minority of the population. He said that the majority of Orthodox Albanians think themselves Albanian. He estimated the number of ethnic-Greeks at 60,000. He thought that Sotiris

Qiriazati was taking Omonia in a direction that would lead to conflict, not only with the government, but with the overwhelming majority of Albanians. Cocoli explained how, at the end of World War Two, the Albanian Chams had been driven out of south Epirus and that a succession of Greek governments had refused to even discuss the issue. A port official in nearby Saranda echoed Cocoli's comments, explaining that everyone had been going through difficult times. He said that the Greeks have their share of officials, doctors, teachers, and police and are now getting their churches and schools repaired. An exception was in the military where, over the past several years, Greek officers had been transferred, or retired, but not replaced by Greeks.

Panaiotis Barkas, a member of Omonia, was far less reassured. He claimed the five had been arrested with unlawful procedures and that Berisha intended to make scapegoats of the minorities. He cited the difficulty they have had acquiring the official documents needed to go to Greece. Educational levels had fallen. He said they felt threatened and squeezed by the Muslims. He said they will have to leave one day to the only refuge they know, Greece. His sense of despair was such that he even suggested that the American CIA was involved. How different, I thought, from an ethnic-Greek whose older brother had earned enough money in Italy to buy two used buses that they were now operating up and down the length of the country. At Kakavia, I came upon young gypsies who had acquired stoves, refrigerators and washing machines and were headed back to Albania. They flashed a smile and gave me a thumbs-up!

As I turned them over one by one, my clippings on Albania resembled some scrapbook from a family of relatives who are always down on their luck somehow, where nothing seems to go right. For them, it has been one disaster after another.

* * *

19 December 1990. After only four days of student protests over university and social conditions, a panicky regime began to grant emergency concessions including the right to organize political parties in opposition to an APL, which had governed for forty-six years. Some 50,000 Albanians rallied in the street around Sali Berisha, a cardiologist and a founder of the Democratic Party (DP). A week later, Gramoz Pashko met with authorities to secure registration. Other demands made were the disbanding of local APL committees, the removal of a statue of Stalin from central Tirana, release of political prisoners, and talks between officials and opposition leaders. Amid destructive rioting, followed by many arrests, new elections were set for 10 February, a matter of only weeks![17]

9 January 1991. Greek Bishop Anastasios Yannoulatos was summoned to the Patriarchate in Istanbul where he was made Archbishop of Albania and given a charter to revive the Greek Orthodox Church. His martyred predecessor, Archbishop Christoforos, died alone in an Albanian prison in 1954. Officially, Albania had been atheist.

15 January 1991. Greek Prime Minister Constantine Mitsotakis, in an effort to stem the tide of refugees, pledges help to Albania's plummeting economy. Mitsotakis ended a visit to Tirana by telling ethnic-Greeks in the south to hold on in Epirus. Earlier, a Greek government spokesman accused Tirana of pressuring ethnic-Greeks to leave Albania so as to influence the outcome of the election.

10 February 1991. Sliding its date back until the end of March, President Ramiz Alia announced that Albania would invite outside observers to monitor the first, free, post-communist multiparty election. In a move to relieve acute shortages, Alia stated that returnees from abroad would no longer pay customs duty on their personal effects. Amid organizational confusion, the APL was opposed by the Democrats, the Republicans, Omonia, and even an Ecology Party. In the face of growing opposition, the APL proposed a new constitution that will now emphasize legality and human rights.[18]

31 March 1991. Amid accusations of vote rigging, the APL won 169 of 250 seats to the People's Assembly. Widespread protest erupted in the northern city of Shkoder where four demonstrators were shot by the police. Opposition Democrats called for a general strike. In Shkoder, the local APL office was ransacked and torched. A young, reform-minded APL economist, Fatos Nano, was again named premier.[19]

18 April 1991. After weeks of unrest and uncertainty, DP agrees to enter into a coalition. Ending a boycott, DP sent seventy-five deputies to the assembly. Ramiz Alia, who began the reform process, failed to be elected. The APL refused to name those responsible for the shooting deaths at Shkoder. The DP blamed the Sigurimi. The DP's role remained unclear. It took weeks to form a government. Amid mutual distrust, the APL attempted to limit the DP's influence.

5 December 1991. The DP pulled seven ministers out of the coalition, leaving the APL (now renamed the Socialist Party) to govern amid a collapsed economy, soaring crime and spreading civil unrest. An Italian army unit began distributing food to slow up the flood of refugees to Italy. Some 200 deaths resulted from revenge killings, many from land disputes. Others occurred during food riots. Hardline communists, including Nexhmije Hoxha, were arrested on charges of corruption. In later trials she was sentenced to eleven years. Given near anarchy, the Socialists agreed to new elections.[20]

22 March 1992. The DP, which earlier saw Gramoz Pashko exit in anger over Berisha's decision to quit the coalition, won decisively in national elections with ninety-two seats. Aleksander Meksi, an engineer, was appointed Prime Minister. Berisha is easily elected president. The Republicans and Social Democrats receive one portfolio each. Omonia (renamed the Union of Human Rights) is snarled in red tape and is reduced from three to two representatives. Socialists get thirty-eight seats under both a direct and proportional system. Five other small parties (Agrarian, Communist, Christian Democrat, Ecology, National Unity) fail to obtain the required percentage of votes.[21]

1 August 1992. Reflecting its lack of local organization and its ill-timed decision to double the price of bread as part of price deregulation, the DP was beaten in local elections by the Socialists. Albanians per capita consume the most bread in Europe (1lb. 6oz. per day). The word for bread in Albanian, *buke*, means food.

4 September 1992. Dissidents within the DP openly split from the Berisha-led party and form the Democratic Alliance. At a DP party conference in August, eight members (including four MPs) were expelled in anger and accused of being neo-communists. Seven joined the new Alliance led by DP co-founder, Gramoz Pashko.

17 December 1992. Albania became the first ex-communist country to apply for NATO membership. While visiting NATO headquarters, President Berisha urged peacekeeping troops for Kosovo. He said Albania would not tolerate the ethnic cleansing of the majority Albanian population and, should this happen, a wider war would result. Albania had earlier recognized Kosovo's "independence."

4 February 1993. Albania renewed its call for UN intervention in Kosovo. Foreign Minister Alfred Serreqi urged demilitarization of the province. Minister of Defense, Safet Zhulali, attempted to downplay Albania's Warsaw Pact membership and appealed for admission to NATO. The US and Turkey offered to upgrade its army.[22]

20 March 1993. Visiting Tirana, NATO Secretary-General, Manfred Woerner, promised assistance to Albania's small military forces. He urged continued restraint by Tirana concerning Kosovo.

8 May 1993. In Rome, President Berisha thanked Pope John Paul for the support of the Papacy. As part of a European tour, he asked the Council of Europe for continued assistance. Repeating an oft-stated position on ex-

Yugoslavia, Berisha called for the recognition of an independent Kosovo. He again named Serbia an aggressor.

28 June 1993. Following the expulsion of Archimandrite Chrysostomos, Greek police began "Operation Broom," a general round-up of Albanians working in Greece. Within days, some 20,000 were sent across the border with little regard for their legal status. Albania appealed for UN intervention. In northern Epirus, ethnic-Greeks and police clashed. Concurrently, representatives of the son of King Zogu, Leka I, began a tour of Albania. They implausibly claimed that a restoration of the monarchy was not on their agenda.[23]

30 July 1993. Ex-premier Fatos Nano was jailed and charged with "abuse of power and falsification of documents" concerning the distribution of Italian food aid involving around US$9 million. Three others were arrested with him. Within weeks, seven former APL members, including four politbureau members, were jailed. Former president, Ramiz Alia, and two others were moved from house arrest to prison. Ultimately, the entire former politbureau was locked up. Vague charges of corruption were made. It was apparent that Berisha planned to jail not only old communists from the APL, but reformist Socialists as well. Opposition journalists were harassed, even the foreign media if it had provided critical coverage of events.[24]

19 October 1993. Increasingly, the new Albanian security service (SHIK) functioned as an adjunct of the DP of President Berisha. It was accused of surveilling opposition politicians and journalists, tapping phones, opening mail and causing people to be dismissed from their jobs. It made efforts to have the license of lawyer Spartak Ngjela revoked. Once imprisoned under Hoxha, Ngjela had taken the cases of persons who ran foul of the government, e.g., dismissed state prosecutor, Maks Haxhia, and *Koha Jone* editor, Aleksander Frangaj. Journalists complained that their telephones had been disconnected for no valid reason.

12 November 1993. Albania became involved in a row with neighboring Macedonia when ethnic-Albanians in that country were found with quantities of weapons. Former deputy defense minister, Hysen Haskaj, was arrested with eight others. They were charged with forming an illegal paramilitary organization. Three hundred AK-47s, said to have been received from Albania, were seized. Tirana denied complicity.

10 April 1994. The previously unknown North Epirus Liberation Front (MAVI) claimed responsibility for an attack on an Albanian army camp at Peshkepia (Episkopi) just inside the border. During the night raid in which two conscripts were killed and three were wounded, the attackers shouted, "This is for Epirus. We have not forgotten!" MAVI accused Athens of abandoning northern Epirus. An angry Albanian government accused Athens of being responsible, expelling a Greek diplomat working in Gjirokaster. In return, an Albanian diplomat was expelled from his embassy in Athens.

21 April 1994. Albanian security authorities questioned some fifty members of the ethnic-Greek Omonia organization. After a month, during which those detained were denied counsel or contact with their families, six were formally charged with treason, espionage and fomenting separatism. The US rebuffed Greek charges of persecution of ethnic-Greeks but insisted on a fair trial for the six.

15 June 1994. Amnesty International questioned Albania's public prosecutor concerning the six's arrest; interrogation; specific charges under the law; and the absence of legal counsel for the accused. Tirana proved slow to respond to AI's request.

3 July 1994. Former president, Ramiz Alia, was given nine years for "abuse of power." Nine other ex-communists receive three to nine years.

7 October 1994. In the aftermath of a two-week trial that began in mid-August, a Tirana appeals court upheld convictions of five ethnic-Greek Albanians who had been charged with espionage and illegal arms possession. This major trial was criticized as to its procedure and the presentation of evidence. It also became known that the accused had been beaten, threatened and deprived of sleep—factors that may have led to their initial confessions. They were: Theodoros Besianis, aged sixty-two and an American citizen, father of two and an ex-chairman of Omonia in Gjirokaster; Vangelis Papachristos, aged fifty-one, a school teacher, father of four and general secretary of Omonia in Saranda; Panayiotis Martos, aged fifty-five, father of four from Delvina; Iraklis Syrmos, aged fifty-five, farmer and father of three from Dervitsani, been jailed for seventeen years under Hoxha; Costa Kyriakou, aged thirty-nine, also a farmer from Dervitsani and a Gjirokaster activist. The sentences ranged from six to eight years, which were reduced in all cases to five to seven years on appeal. A sixth person, Costas Tsavos, was tried separately and sentenced for one year for lacking proper papers for a new hunting rifle purchased in Greece. The evidence produced in court was either vague, or in dispute (Confessions were disowned by the accused in court, and SHIK TV tapes of Omonia meetings were denied by the defense). The trial atmosphere was bad: Attacks in the press, deportations of hundreds of Albanians from Greece, and very harsh words from both governments. Greek-Albanian relations hit an all-time low. AI and Helsinki Watch look at the case. Washington expresses concern.[25]

5 November 1994. Lacking a required two-thirds majority in the parliament, President Berisha opted to hold a referendum on a new constitution that broadened presidential powers. It was rejected by some sixty percent of those voting. This setback for Berisha was hailed by the opposition as a mandate for new elections. In yet another case that showed shortcomings in the legal system, three members of the constitutional court resigned in protest, claiming the court had sat on legal challenges made by the Socialists and Social Democrats. The chief justice refused to examine the legality of their appeals to the court, which denied them a hearing.

6 December 1994. The Social Democrats with seven seats, and the Republicans with one, gave up their two ministerial portfolios and quit the ruling coalition. The DP, with an absolute majority in the 140-member assembly, was not affected. Social Democrat dissident Teodor Laco subsequently formed the Social Democratic Union.

30 January 1995. US military personnel participated in a search-and-rescue exercise with Albanian units and other NATO elements. This was the first Albanian-NATO exercise under the Partnership for Peace program. It provided Berisha with a publicity boost.

9 February 1995. Because of international criticism, Albania's Supreme Court suspended the sentences of the Omonia Five. It had earlier reduced their sentences by one third and had released one prisoner who had been jailed under Hoxha. Berisha publicly admitted that Albanian judicial procedures needed to be reformed. He was probably responding to a letter from US President Clinton, which urged that the five be released.

21 March 1995. Three Greeks and four ethnic-Greek Albanians were arrested in possession of weapons near the Albanian border by a Greek border patrol in the early hours of the morning. The men, several of whom had military and police backgrounds, had nine assault rifles, pistols, and a quantity of ammunition. A follow-up raid in Athens uncovered more weapons and linked them to MAVI. Greek Prime Minister Andreas Papandreou ordered an investigation of the ultra-nationalist suspects, whom some think are involved with the Greek National Intelligence Agency (EYP). Subsequently, a Greek diplomat assigned to Tirana was recalled when he was found with a quantity of MAVI propaganda materials in his embassy office.[26]

22 March 1995. President Berisha reduced the sentences of Nexhmije Hoxha and Fatos Nano by two years each. Two ex-politbureau members charged with embezzlement were released. In April, Hoxha's son, Ilir, was placed under house arrest for having given a press interview, which the government claimed was unlawful.

2 June 1995. A new penal code was put in place that reduced the jail terms meted out to former communists. In July, Ramiz Alia was freed from prison, only to die soon thereafter of a heart ailment.

14 June 1995. Albania was admitted to the Council of Europe. Albania was in the process of economic recovery, and even some growth in capital accumulation. Starting from an abysmally low base, Albania had come to chart an improvement of about twelve percent a year. The World Bank estimated per capita income at US$300 annually. Inflation had dropped from 400 to twenty-five percent. Optimists praised the "mom and pop" street stands and kiosks as the baby steps of capitalism. Others said that the remittances from workers abroad and money made from UN sanctions-busting is what keeps Albania afloat, specifically petrol, diesel fuel, and kerosene, which are smuggled across Lake Shkodra into Montenegro. They point out that foreign debt had risen by ten times that of all exports annually. Few foreign investors expressed any interest in the country's factories and mines, which require modernization. Berisha noted that Albania's lack of infrastructure discouraged investment and it was impossible to build infrastructure without foreign investment. The problem was indeed circular.[27]

13 September 1995. In an official visit to Washington, Berisha offered NATO whatever facilities it required in his little country. Besides meeting President Clinton, Berisha met Defense Secretary William Perry. It became known that unmanned CIA spy planes operated out of Albania over Bosnia. Albania rushed into a US embrace, anticipating US equipment, more base facilities and an American presence that would provide continuing support.[28]

20 September 1995. A government-controlled parliamentary panel ruled that Albania's Supreme Court had no jurisdiction to hear a judicial appeal by jailed Socialist leader Fatos Nano. In effect, parliament began to act on constitutional matters, arguing that a new penal code eliminated the supreme court's appellate powers. It was clear that judicial decisions were politically inspired. The DP-controlled parliament had begun to usurp authority that had been exercised by the court system. Parliament passed a law on communist "genocide," which barred any official serving in the government in March 1991 from running for political office until 2002. It was similar to laws passed in other ex-communist countries.

13 October 1995. President Berisha called for the Kosovo question to be included in an overall Yugoslav peace settlement.

1 April 1996. US Secretary of Defense William Perry attended a regional meeting of defense ministers in Tirana. Italy, Turkey, Bulgaria, Macedonia, Albania, and the US attended. Greece was absent.

3 May 1996. Pre-election polls showed the DP leading with thirty-eight percent to twenty percent for the Socialists. Berisha was given thirty-one percent to fifteen percent for jailed socialist leader Fatos Nano. The election atmosphere was marred by accusations of police harassment of the opposition in the run-up to the 26 May polling date.

2 June 1996. With opposition candidates on a hunger strike and calling for a boycott of the second round, OSCE monitors stated that the 26 May election was flawed with irregularities and had to be rerun in three districts. The DP took sixty-eight percent in the first round, amid accusations of fraud. Opposition rallies were broken up and candidates were beaten by the police. Only the DP, the Union of Human Rights and a rightist alliance went into the second round sharing out of seats. The US criticized the conduct of the election.

5 June 1996. The DP took six of nine seats in the final round. Socialist oppositionists held a well-publicized hunger strike amid calls by the US and the EU for new elections in three constituencies. Berisha denied poll-rigging, as DP prepared to own the 140-seat assembly with its 122 seats. Berisha agreed to a partial rerun on 16 June in seventeen districts owing to "irregularities" specified by the central election commission. However, the opposition boycotted and demanded a completely new election. It started a protest campaign.

23 June 1996. At a prestigious meeting of European government and business leaders at Crans-Montana, Switzerland, Berisha vowed he would not hold a new election. He was backed by the German and Austrian delegates. He was dismissive of international criticism.

20 October 1996. OSCE observers pulled out of local elections amid dismay on behalf of the Council of Europe monitors. OSCE protested the limitations placed on their activities by the Albanian authorities. With foreign officials at odds as to the propriety of the political process, Berisha's DP again won heavily. Ethnic-Greeks lost in north Epirus as the Union for Human Rights and Omonia's candidates were swept from office. President Berisha called it a vindication of the election of the previous May–June. Since then, the Socialists have boycotted parliament, refusing to take the ten seats they had won. In the general election, OSCE concluded that half of the election law's seventy-nine articles had been violated, some grossly. Gradually, Berisha found himself on the defensive with the Socialists having gained the benefit of sympathetic foreign media coverage.

30 October 1996. The International Monetary Fund (IMF) sounded an alarm regarding various so-called pyramid investment schemes in operation since 1993. Because of competition and the need to gain new customers, the schemes increasingly offered prodigiously high interest rates. Many thousands of Albanians had used savings and had even sold apartments and land in order to get into what they thought was a way to get rich quick.

15 November 1996. Hers was the first to go. Maksude Kadena, aged thirty-six, had once been a worker in a shoe factory. Somewhere, somehow, she got the idea to start a pyramid investment scheme similar to that of Bernie Cornfeld's Investors Overseas Trust in the 1960s. The idea was deceptively simple and alluring. For a membership fee of say US$500 and up, one needed simply to rope in six more people who would do the same. Soon the money was rolling in and lucky were those few who got in first and then got out. Presumably believing that they had found the path to capitalist enrichment, relatives and neighbors by the hundreds signed on and sank in their all. As long as people kept coming and money was being pumped through the system, some made high profits in the beginning. An Albanian BBC reporter claimed that even foreign diplomats invested money. With such an appeal, other schemes sprouted up. Some, more sophisticated, started imaginative scams. They had foreign names, large offices and drove big cars. Policemen guarded their buildings; and many thought that they were endorsed by the government because of ads run on state television. Some funds were connected to DP members of parliament, even ministers. Massive sums of money from DP rip offs, UN sanctions-busting, illicit drugs trafficking and the Italian mafia were involved. In Mrs. Kadena's case, some 18,904 investors had won or lost. Within weeks, by Christmas, others had collapsed as well. At the end, an estimated US$1.5 billion went down the drain... or was diverted into investments elsewhere.[29]

28 January 1997. Like wildfire, protest riots erupted over the collapsing schemes. Thousands demanded that Berisha resign. Government officials were assaulted, but, more frequently, defrauded depositors took out their anger on public buildings and government property. Pyramids were declared illegal and President Berisha pushed a law through parliament that promised to pay the public for its losses. The DP mounted counter-demonstrations. Police and security personnel arrested hundreds.

8 February 1997. Protest spread south. In Vlore, the Gjallica fund failed with a reported loss of US$175 million. A local DP member of parliament stated, "It's like wheat. You plant it in October and reap it in June. You can't reap it in February just because people demand it!" A few companies began to distribute partial repayments. However, thousands received nothing.

27 February 1997. The US stepped up its pressure on the Berisha government to hold new elections. Over the preceding months, Washington had increasingly distanced itself from its former protégé. The State Department's annual human rights report stated, "The flawed May elections coming at a time of further government pressure on the judiciary and the press were major steps backward for democracy." The EU countries tended to be less critical, mentioning police repression of protestors, but not demanding new polls. Many called for the release from jail of Socialist leader, Fatos Nano.[30]

2 March 1997. Hundreds of armed Albanians, after looting an army depot, took on the police in pitched battles and effectively gained control of Vlore. A SHIK office was attacked and six security men were killed: three by gunfire; two from fire inside their building; and one who was beaten to death by a mob. Some claimed the incident was caused by a SHIK officer who stabbed a man near the university. Berisha dismissed the government of Alexander Mexhi. A state of emergency was imposed and a news clampdown began.

4 March 1997. Amid mounting chaos, President Berisha was re-elected by a DP-controlled parliament to another five-year term. While Berisha talked of emergency measures by the army and the police to reassert his control, these elements of support melted away before thousands of armed civilians who began to loot arms depots. Italian helicopters evacuated thirty-six, including fifteen journalists out of the southern city of Vlore. It is controlled by a mafia mob.

7 March 1997. Berisha called a halt to ineffective army and police operations as much of the country went over to anti-government elements who had seized thousands of weapons, tanks, artillery, planes and even coastal vessels. A truce of sorts was declared and Berisha agreed to talk to an opposition grouping called the Democratic Alliance. Berisha's seaside home (formerly used by Hoxha) was sacked by an angry mob that carries off anything of value before setting it on fire.

12 March 1997. Berisha appointed Bashkim Fino, a socialist from Gjirokaster, as caretaker prime minister until new elections were held. DP member Belul Cela was interior minister and Sheqir Vukaj (also a socialist) was defense minister. In fact, there was little for government to run as authority and administration disintegrated. A watching world was treated to photos and television coverage of a bedlam of flying bullets where even small boys carried AK-47s. The rebel National Salvation Committee called on Berisha to quit.

15 March 1997. Former Austrian chancellor Franz Vranitzky, now an OSCE envoy, was named to visit Tirana to explore ways to restore order. Foreign diplomats and families were evacuated by US, UK, French, Italian, German and Greek military units. Albania was virtually cut off from the world. Refugees again tried to make it over to Italy by boat. Fatos Nano was released from jail.

19 March 1997. With an EU delegation in Tirana, government grain stocks were looted from warehouses. Gangs stole aid supplies being delivered to Durres. Armed rebels appeared aimless and leaderless.[31]

2 April 1997. Prime Minister Bashkim Fino went south to talk to the rebels. SHIK was disbanded upon the resignations of Bashkim Gazidede and his deputy Bujar Rama. Fino thought that June polls, as had been agreed, might prove impossible given the situation.

5 April 1997. A UN-approved multinational force led by Italy was expected to deploy in Albania by mid-April. It would secure the ports and roads for delivery of humanitarian aid and consist of Italy, France, Greece, Spain, Turkey, Romania, Austria, Denmark, and Bulgaria.

13 April 1997. As foreign forces began to arrive, King Leka I returned from exile. Met at the airport by some 1,000 supporters, the tall, bespectacled, fifty eight- year-old vows he will save Albania. He had left as a tiny infant when his father fled in 1939.[32]

18 April 1997. OSCE envoy Franz Vranitzky announced an agreement that emergency elections would be held on 29 June. The Austrian met Berisha, Nano and Fino in an effort to bridge over differences. A referendum would also be held on the restoration of a monarchy.

22 May 1997. Prime Minister Fino met with opposition leaders who were unhappy with the Berisha government's election law. They threatened to not participate unless changes were made. Vranitzky shuttled in and out to break the political deadlock.

27 May 1997. Italy recalled its ambassador as phone taps surfaced in the Italian press of his conversations with DP leader Tritan Sehu (an aide to Berisha) in which he urged Sehu not to sign an all-party accord on elections. The taps also linked the envoy to illicit financial dealings with Italian businessmen in Tirana.[33]

24 June 1997. Socialist leader Nano, DP head Sehu and Skender Gjinushi of the Social Democrats met in Rome and agreed to hold elections five days later. OSCE and others were to send observers. An ethnic-Greek was kidnapped to keep his daughter off the ballot. More violence erupted in southern Albanian towns. OSCE admitted that the elections were being held in very unfavorable circumstances.

1 July 1997. Socialists swept the elections, gaining a two-thirds majority. The referendum rejected the restoration of a monarchy. A second round was held for some seats. In the final tally, the Socialists won 117 in a parliament that now had 155 seats. The DP, which won twenty-seven, claimed the polls were conducted amid Socialist violence directed at their party. Now it was their turn to threaten to boycott.

25 July 1997. With Fatos Nano prime minister, parliament elected an unknown academic, Rexhep Mejdami, as president. A Nano cabinet was sworn in as Western governments voiced support. Berisha resigned as expected and took his place as a MP with the DP opposition.

1 August 1997. With foreign military forces out, random violence and lawlessness continued. Perhaps some 2,000 have died since 1 January. Reports claimed that upwards of one million guns have been stolen. Some entered the illicit arms market. Albania was in ruins.[34]

* * *

The *Mimosa* rocked to and fro as it ploughed the choppy waters of the Corfu channel on its northeasterly course for Agia Saranda on the Albanian coast opposite Kerkyra. A leaden sky threatened rain and the late November wind had driven its passengers inside. Only a dozen or so were crossing, unlike an earlier Easter when my boat was loaded with returning Albanians and an amazing collection of deck cargo—luggage, huge bundles, boxes, a wooden bed, a big overstuffed chair and even glassed-in window frames. Then, the young were wearing new clothing and many were in a holiday mood sharing out their food. This time, we had only a few small bags, some pipes, some paint, and a mattress. A business accounting and computer student said she was visiting her uncle, but was unsure whether she would ever want to return home again. Following those optimistic days of 1995 to the present, two things had happened: The DP government under President Berisha had regressed to semi-dictatorial, one-party rule (the traditional clan-power pyramid), and then, disastrously (amid widespread official corruption), a number of dodgy investment schemes had collapsed one after another. Thousands lost virtually everything that they had put into Sude, Populi, Gjallica, Xhaferi, Kamberi, and the biggest of all, Vefa.

As I crossed the harbor mole I searched for something familiar. Saranda had actually never looked inviting, but some two years later it looked positively awful. Overlooking the port customs enclosure was an iron railing ringed by several dozen young men who appeared desperate beyond belief. They stood there, silent in their soiled clothing, eyes intent, watching and measuring. Expecting to be accosted (I wasn't, by them, or by anyone else), I gripped my pack strap and quickened my pace. The streets were inches deep in mud in many places and strewn with rocks. Garbage and debris were heaped in mounds—uncollected. Buildings and cars, were holed by bullets, window glass broken. What I took for government offices had been trashed and were empty, floors littered with torn documents of one kind or another. A few kiosks, small shops and cafe-bars were open. Some men wore souvenirs of the recent disorder—camouflage pants, shirts and army boots. For now, however, the weapons were off the street and out of sight. A man shrugged in skepticism, saying anything could still happen. No one expressed regret that Berisha had gone. Some said that Fatos Nano was a good man. However, all expressed doubt about the future.

I was told that weapons had been turned in. I suspected, however, that many were stashed away for future use. The few police that I saw were armed. However, their demeanor suggested that they would disappear if any trouble erupted. They stood chatting with their friends, who were just hanging around amongst dozens of other men who were just hanging around. They gave the impression that there was nothing to do and no money to do it with. Buses and taxis were working, but telephones were still out in many areas. One could not phone Tirana, or even to Gjirokaster only thirty kilometers away. A great many things were broken and there were few indications they would get fixed any time soon. A truck driver perhaps said it all with the American flag that he had pinned up inside his cab. The flag was upside down, an unintentional, or intentional, signal of distress. He could just as well have been speaking for the entire country!

Unsure where I would spend the night, I asked about the place I stayed at in 1994—the Hotel Butrint. It had been burned down in June. It stood across the bay, with black smudges around its windows. I thought back to that pleasant summer evening when I had eaten dinner on its terrace that looked out over the Adriatic Sea. The wine had been good and I had been content to sit watching the guests.

A man at the far end had caught my eye as he sat with his friends. He was flamboyantly spectacular in his striped, bright-colored sports coat; a sky blue silk vest; a fuchsia shirt with matching tie; and a gold-knobbed walking stick. About forty-five, his obviously dyed blond hair completed the effect. Unable to contain myself, I walked over and made an introduction. He proved unwilling to talk at length to a complete stranger, let alone an American journalist, but he did tell me that he was Dr. Amsterdam Armstrong (PhD) of New York City, an "international citizen" who published a US-Albanian business magazine. He claimed to be the personal guest of the president. I made a mental note at the time that if Berisha was surrounding himself with such people, Albania was going to be in real trouble.

Early on, there had been large advertisements in the international press that described Albania as an investors' paradise, a land where even pristine, undeveloped coastal property was dirt cheap. Big business and high profits awaited. In a country starting from zero, fortunes were to be made, or so it was suggested. It is not surprising that the Italian Mafia moved in and people such as the Kosovar Hajdin Sejdija, in his Rolls-Royce, drove around Tirana's rutted streets to have a look. Besides ordinary crime (theft of government property, food commodities, imported goods and stolen cars from abroad), large profits were being made drug trafficking (controlled by the Kosovar Albanian Swiss-based Mafia) and semi-officially condoned UN sanctions-busting of commodities bound for Yugoslavia. With the addition of remittances from some 400,000 Albanians working abroad, considerable amounts of hard currency were in circulation as early as 1994. In a country without any experience of a stock market, or personal investments of any kind, and totally lacking a regulatory system, the pyramids were just waiting to happen. As Albania received considerable foreign financial aid from 1992 onward, questions should be asked of the World Bank, the International Monetary Fund and the major powers as to why this was permitted to happen.[35]

For the most part, average Albanians are charmingly naive and refreshingly unsophisticated, isolated from the world. They are curious, awed and too trusting of foreigners. When they saw how the Berisha regime won the West's support (especially from the US) and how this regime gave its explicit approval to the schemes while Tirana was crawling with foreign financial experts, many equated capitalism with quick and easy profits. At the same time, they are by temperament hot-tempered and violent when they feel they have been wronged. As a result, they vented their fury on a regime that they felt was responsible for their losses. However, now that their orgy of destruction has seemingly spent itself, their situation is even more desperate than before. The country is at absolute rock bottom and has nowhere to go but up.

All Albanians have the normal desire to gain the material means to improve their lives. Their concern is their immediate family and friends. They are totally disillusioned with government and politics. And, because the struggle for survival has taken many abroad, while others search for jobs that do not exist, few are seized with the desire to become actively involved building civil society. This is a luxurious concept applicable elsewhere. At most, they take to the street to demonstrate, or vote. The educated professionals, of course, have their organizations and comprise an elite. It is they, those who grew up under communism, who involve themselves with party politics. They are, themselves, the sons and daughters of an older elite. It is they who vie for position, power and international attention. But this is a very small pool of talent. Fatos Nano, an acclaimed economist, bought Italian foodstuffs at three times the world market price.

Because this orphan sits on Europe's doorstep, the spotlight of attention has focused on its recent misfortunes. But because it is of Europe, but not yet in Europe, those who are in a position to provide a helping hand have the obligation to do so. In the context of eventual EU accession, Brussels should provide a pool of expert advisors that can set Albania on the path of social reconstructtion. A new constitution, an independent judiciary, a professional police force, a supervised securities and banking system, harmonization of Albania's laws with those of the EU, are only a few of the urgent tasks that need to be undertaken. Additionally, the authority of the EU must stand firmly behind any body charged with the responsibility of ensuring that the Albanians adhere closely to applicable norms. And lastly, however long it may take, Albania must be assured that it will not be excluded from admission to the EU.[36]

One day, Albanians will take their rightful place in Europe and they will surprise many. They came of age amid wars, revolution, and repression, and in spite of everything, they have made rapid strides in the arts and sciences. I have met any number that do impress. A studious-looking young lady tossed off that she had read Thomas Hardy's *Tess of the D'Urbervilles* in high school and proceeded to recite a synopsis. A boat captain, in response to my question about some sacks of white, granular material, said that it was a base for PVC and proceeded to write *polyvinyl chloride* out in English. I have also been asked what one should think of Jesus and whether I am afraid when I fly by air. And, they can be polite. I once offered cigarettes to two soiled sweaty workers who were digging on a plot of land. They smiled broadly in appreciation, but insisted that I take two of theirs first. I have been with taxi drivers who have stopped to talk to an elderly acquaintance, obvious in their friendship and concern. I have also seen the dire results of their anger and frustration. Albania is today the youngest, fastest-growing country in Europe. Almost two-thirds of its population is less than twenty-five years of age. It has both the strengths and weaknesses of youth.

> Fierce are Albania's children, yet they lack
> Not virtues, were those virtues more mature.[37]

Tenja village, Croatia, July 1991.

Vukovar, Croatia, November 1992.

Slovene militiaman, Lubljana, July 1991.

Vukovar, Croatia, November 1992.

Armed civilians and police, Osijek, Croatia, July 1991.

Line outside a Belgrade bank, November 1992.

Croat soldier standing guard.

Croat soldier inspecting a car.

Croat policeman checking train passengers.

Old Vukovar train station, November 1992.

Milovan Djilas in his Belgrade apartment, July 1991.

Tenja village, Croatia, July 1991.

Mosque in Skopje, Macedonia.

Truck drivers in Skopje during the Greek embargo.

Country tavern in Macedonia. On the wall are old pictures of
Gotse Delchev and his fellow rebels.

Old town bazaar in Skopje, Macedonia.

Albanian men line up for Greek visas in Girokaster.

Apartment block in Tirana, Albania.

Albanian boys in Gjirokaster.

Roma gypsies at the Greek-Albanian border.

Gutted building in Grbavica, Sarajevo.

UN position near the Miljacka River, Sarajevo.

Boy scouts in Belgrade.

SARAJEVO

Bosna R.

BOSNIA-HERZEGOVINA

0 — Miles — 2

MUSLIM HELD

Miljacka R.

Sarajevo

Airport

Mt. Igman

Lukavica
Serb barracks

SERBIAN HELD

Rapid Reaction Force artillery

CROATIA

Demilitarized Zone — **Bihac**

Bihac town

1 mile — Safe Haven

Coralica

Bihac

Bosanska Krupa

Concentration of Krajina Serb forces

Grahovo

KRAJINA

Zadar

Knin

Glamoc

Serb-held Bosnia

Muslim/Croat Federation-held

Serb-held Croatia (Krajina)

Croatian Army attacks

Split

Operation "Storm", August 1995

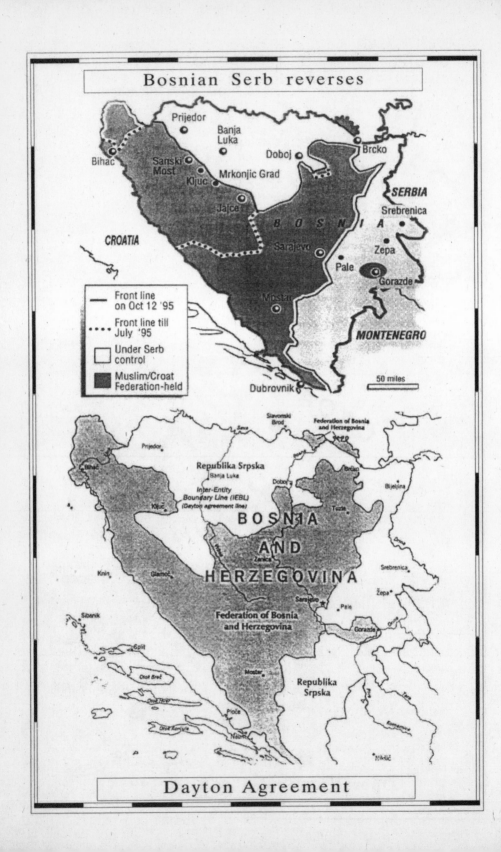

Bosnian Serb reverses

Prijedor

Banja
Luka

Doboj

Brcko

Bihac

Sanski
Most

Mrkonjic Grad

Kljuc

Jajce

B O S N I A

SERBIA

Srebrenica

Sarajevo

Zepa

Pale

Gorazde

Mostar

CROATIA

MONTENEGRO

Dubrovnik

Front line
on Oct 12 '95

Front line till
July '95

Under Serb
control

Muslim/Croat
Federation-held

50 miles

Dayton Agreement

Slavonski
Brod

Sava

Federation of Bosnia
and Herzegovina

Prijedor

Republika Srpska

Bihac

Banja Luka

Doboj

Brcko

Bijeljina

Inter-Entity
Boundary Line (IEBL)
(Dayton agreement line)

Tuzla

Kljuc

B O S N I A

Knin

Glamoc

A N D

Zenica

Srebrenica

H E R Z E G O V I N A

Zepa

Sibenik

Sarajevo

Pale

Split

Federation of Bosnia
and Herzegovina

Gorazde

Drina

Otok Brac

Otok Hvar

Mostar

Republika
Srpska

Otok Korcula

Ploce

Neum

Tara

Niksic

Chapter 5

The Heart of Darkness

Bosnia: January 1992–December 1995

These people are just like us.

Luc Delahaye, photographer

It was the casually callous aspect of the murders that riveted my eyes to the photo, a photo that depicted the war in Bosnia in all of its wanton brutality and horror. It was early April 1992. Ron Haviv of Saba Press had traveled to Bijeljina in northeast Bosnia across the Drina from Serbia. Arkan's Tigers had entered the small town and had begun their campaign of ethnic cleansing that, in coming weeks, would sweep south, leaving a trail of death and destruction as eastern Bosnia's Muslim population was driven out. Most were told to leave immediately or die. Some were dragged from their homes one by one and shot. Others were subjected to the murderous brutality of detention camps. Haviv was ordered to clear out. He did, but amid shouts and screams, he was able to record some of the slaughter.

A man and two women have been shot and are lying face down on the sidewalk. Blood has begun to pool under their bodies. A tall young Serb in camouflage clothing is kicking one woman to see if she is still alive. He has his rifle barrel close to her head, ready to squeeze off another round. He has a lit cigarette in his left hand. A pair of wrap-around white-rimmed sunglasses are positioned jauntily up on his forehead. He has his black knit cap tucked neatly under the shoulder strap of his jacket. There are bullet impact marks and smears of blood on the wall above where the bodies have fallen. Two other soldiers stand nearby, looking in another direction. They are not ragtag irregulars. They are well-equipped, wear uniform patches, and look very professional, like the hired killers they are.[1]

Another photo, this one taken by Luc Delahaye in Sarajevo, shows two middle-aged people, a man and a woman, lying bleeding after a mortar round has hit. Both victims are very still. The woman's mouth is open, but her eyes appear to be closed. Her head rests on a bloody left arm. Her right arm is twisted under her body. It would appear that she has fallen heavily on the pavement. The man is bald with a fringe of white hair. His face is flat down in his own blood. The photo is a low angle close-up shot, which helped to win Delahaye that year's Robert Capa Gold Medal. It has an added interest, since a fashionably dressed woman clutching her handbag is running for safety between the victims.

"It's strange to have this kind of war in Europe," said Delahaye. "These people are just like us." He added, "Now the Muslims and the Croats are much less recaptive to the press... They know the world won't like what they're doing."

Haviv had commented, "At first, the fighting was the local butcher against the local barber... But then this unit of highly trained commandos, the Tigers, arrived and in eight hours finished the first battle of the Bosnian War."[2]

Haviv may be forgiven for thinking that Bijeljina was the first. On 26 March, Croatia's 108th Brigade entered Bosnia and took Bosanski Broad. It then surrounded Sijekovac and the local Muslims and Croats killed fifteen of their Serb neighbors. On 3 April fifty-five Serb civilians were murdered near Kupres and over one hundred went missing, again at the hands of their neighbors. By the end of April, events had escalated sharply, culminating in the entry of Serb formations into Sarajevo and attacks by Bosniak units on the JNA as it was attempting to withdraw from the city. In fact, all sides began to grab territory by ridding those areas of unwanted civilian inhabitants. The time-honored Balkan custom of ethnic cleansing was well underway. The Serbs were soon to have the best of it. Given their clear superiority in artillery, tanks, fighting vehicles, helicopters, and transport, their rapid advance was not seriously impeded as the Bosnian Serb Army (BSA) and the militias drove 700,000 displaced civilians before them. Again, they spared their own troops by first softening up their targets with heavy weapons and then sent "specials" in to apply their terror tactics. In a dirty war, all sides have dirty hands![3]

Looking at an ethnic map of pre-war Bosnia-Herzegovina, one can understand the logic of BSA commander General Ratko Mladic's deployment of his forces, which came to number 120,000 men, for his overriding need was to create an economically viable and defensible state that would be contiguous to Serbia and the Serb-held Krajina. For if the project succeeded, a Greater Serbia would be possible. Serbs did live in strength in eastern Bosnia-Herzegovina, but so did Muslims in the Drina river valley. And as stated above, they were "cleansed" in the opening weeks of the war. Then, in early May, the BSA forces attempted to divide Sarajevo into a larger Serbian area with some industrial depth (including the airport) and an older Muslim area north of the Miljacka River and east of Marijidvor. This met with only partial success because of stubborn resistance by the Bosniak fighters and interference by UN/UNPROFOR, which was trying to call a halt to the Serbian offensive. To the south, a Serb move on Mostar (the gateway to the sea) was blocked by the Croats and ultimately failed to carry. Most importantly however, in the north, a corridor was forced through linking the separate "lungs" of Serb-held territory in the east with that in northwestern Bosnia-Herzegovina. Over the weeks, the Serbs consolidated their hold on Brcko, even though their lifeline was a precarious fifteen kilometers wide at the narrowest point.

In the north, ethnic cleansing took place on even a larger scale, sometimes with brutality and acts of violence, sometimes not. In some towns and cities, the process took weeks and months because of sheer numbers. Offices were set up where those cleansed were made to sign away their homes, apartments and land, in addition to being robbed of personal possessions and having the privilege of purchasing their ticket to safety for large amounts of money. In more chaotic circumstances, hundreds might be pointed down a road with little or no food, water, or adequate clothing to face the elements across little known and often dangerous terrain in close proximity to the fighting. It was done on such a scale in full view of the TV camera that the Serbs were rightly condemned.

With the ongoing assimilation of JNA Serb officers and conscripts into the BSA (with JNA weapons and supplies), plus the threat posed by Serbian paramilitary forces, Bosnian President Izetbegovic was faced with the stark possibility that the predominantly Muslim-populated centers such as Sarajevo,

Tuzla, Zenica, Gorazde, Zepa, and Srebrenica might soon become isolated and forced to an early surrender. Unless they could secure defense in depth and hang on in Sarajevo, all of the international recognition would count for nothing in terms of the survival of the new state. Izetbegovic and his SDA had accepted the probability of war since mid-1991. Hence, the Bosnian leader and his party cadres were not totally unprepared for the events of April and May. Izetbegovic had set up an SDA National Defense Council in June of the preceding year and had begun to illegally buy arms from Slovenia in the autumn. An SDA militia named the Patriotic League came into being and later the Green Berets. However, the bulk of the Bosniak army was built from local TDFs using existing weapon stocks. In addition, Izetbegovic's SDA put weapons into the hands of Sarajevo's street gangs who were praised as heroes as they committed wholesale theft and atrocities against the city's noncombatant Serbs, took over the black market, and expanded their criminal activities.[4]

Forced on the defensive in the first months of the fighting, and having to cope with the emergency needs of thousands of refugees, Izetbegovic sought help from wherever he could find it. First of all, the US, the EC and the UN saw Bosnia-Herzegovina almost solely as a victim under attack by the stronger Bosnian Serbs and Belgrade. Besides rushing in food, medicine and emergency supplies through UNHCR and a host of volunteer agencies, the UN and the Western powers (even though there was a lack of a consensus over how to stop the war and inconsistency in carrying out decisions) gave critically needed moral and political support to Sarajevo. UNPROFOR deployed by increments to facilitate the distribution of humanitarian aid and soon Serb commanders had to deal with British and French army officers who disputed their control over the battlefield. The Bosnia-Herzegovina side used this advantage with great skill, sheltering behind and, indeed, manipulating the situation to gain sympathy and support. Although the Bosnia-Herzegovina side should share in the blame for precipitating the bloodshed, this fact was lost on most of the onlooking world.[5]

Secondly, the Muslim-Croat political front of 1991 continued as a marriage of convenience into 1992. Izetbegovic's SDA-dominated regime harbored few illusions about Croat ambitions in Bosnia-Herzegovina (and past understandings between Tudjman and Milosevic), but it knew it was dependent on Zagreb for the delivery of critically needed war materiel. Ultimately, Izetbegovic had to give the Croats fifty to seventy percent of all military supplies coming in through Croatian channels, channels that somehow circumvented a UN arms embargo. At that time, both were attempting to contain the Serb advance, local agreements between Serb and Croat leaders notwithstanding.

Thirdly, Izetbegovic reached out to the Islamic world where he was already well known, and appealed for aid. It took months for the Organization of the Islamic Conference (OIC) to pass resolutions and governments to provide funds and set up covert channels, but Turkey, Iran, Saudi Arabia, and others responded generously.[6]

Croat President Tudjman looked with scorn at the idea of a Muslim-dominated Bosnia-Herzegovina, and considered the concept to lack historical legitimacy. Furthermore, the thought that the Croat seventeen percent of Bosnia-Herzegovina would have minority status was unacceptable both to him and to the Croats of western Herzegovina and north-central Bosnia. But first Serb positions along the Neretva River had to be rolled back. The HVO forced the Serbs out of a divided Mostar in mid-June and the HDZ led by Mate Boban expanded its area of control. A statelet of Herzeg-Bosna was set up and armed by Zagreb. Muslims were driven from their jobs and apartments. The same occurred on a wide scale in central Bosnia, even in areas where the Muslims were a majority. With two armies eyeing each other amid an influx of refugees, it was inevitable that clashes would occur. On 25 October, fighting erupted at Prozor over rival gang control of petrol. Disagreement led to the loss of Jajce to the Serbs. Mutual recriminations were heated and, as winter set in, the Croat and Serb sides seemed to accept any and all gains made at the expense of the Muslims. And, to underline the cynicism of wartime loyalties, at Kiseljak near Sarajevo, all three sides made black market deals that penetrated roadblocks, sustained civilian populations and fuelled the war.

In April 1993, the Croat HVO asserted its claim to Kiseljak and Vitez by going on a rampage of murder and looting against Muslims. The latter fled to Travnik and Zenica after their villages were torched. Enraged, Muslims who had been cleansed elsewhere in 1992, along with the Bosniak army, drove the HVO out. As Bosnia was about to be ground down into isolated enclaves, men who had been hounded from their villages and who had survived the worst that Serb detention camps had to offer, formed themselves into an army and began to fight. At Travnik, the 17th Krajiska Brigade was organized. At Zenica, a 7th Muslim Brigade was formed, which assumed an extreme nationalist-Islamic orientation. This Third Corps began to carve out a triangle of territory from Tuzla in the northeast, to Mostar in the south, to Travnik in the center. Bypassing the Croatian Vitez pocket, they swept around it using the same scorched earth tactics that they had been subjected to. The Croats took murderous revenge at Vares and Stupni Do. Vital road supply communications from Travnik to Tuzla were won at a very heavy cost. Some civilians had been displaced two or three times and large numbers of semi-trained Bosniak fighters were captured and were now seeing the inside of Croat camps.[7]

With the Serbs holding seventy percent of Bosnia by the end of 1993, and the Croats and Muslims fighting over the rest of it, the US administration of President Clinton pressured Tudjman and Izetbegovic to stop fighting each other and face off against a BSA that had remained in static positions for almost a year. Promising substantial support if they did, or a disaster if they didn't (a hint of sanctions was made against Zagreb, since it had 30,000 of its troops in Bosnia-Herzegovina), Clinton brought the two leaders together at the White House in February 1994 to sign solemn agreements that set out a political and governmental framework for a federation. While much of it would be honored in the breach, it stopped the fighting and provided a fig leaf for Washington to provide overt and covert support to both. It was the turning point of the war.

President Clinton, who did not want his domestic agenda affected by a war in the Balkans, which his advisors felt did not then concern US strategic interests, was pressured into action by Congress and opinion makers who were being bombarded by a slick anti-Serb publicity campaign run by Ruder-Finn Global Public Affairs and Hill and Knowlton, two Washington public relations firms. In a made-for-television war of very simplistic explanations, the media meant everything. Ruder-Finn had been retained by Zagreb in 1991 and the government of Bosnia-Herzegovina hired both firms in the spring of 1992. In terms of impact, they were of crucial importance to Sarajevo. After adopting the EC-UN policy of containment after inauguration, Clinton inched towards intervention with every incident perceived as a new Bosnian Serb "outrage" in a war depicted as being caused by Belgrade. In US eyes, it was white hats against black hats. The year would see the continued "strangulation" of Sarajevo and, in April, a Serb move against the "unprotected" enclave of Gorazde. There, 10,000 Bosniak fighters sheltered behind 80,000 civilians and attacked Serb villages in the hope of provoking Serb retaliation and in return, NATO air attacks on Serb targets across the board.[8]

Therefore, instead of intervening as an impartial neutral in 1991, the US now opted to intervene directly against the Bosnian Serbs. The reasons for doing so are by themselves complex, but revolved around the following considerations. The US wished to assert its leadership in Europe through its dominant role in NATO. An aspect of this was to award its German ally a secondary role as Zagreb's advisor-patron in Europe. This fitted in with Bonn's position in Central Europe and, by extension, to Slovenia and Croatia that it supported in 1990–91. US aid to Sarajevo gained influence in the Middle East where Saudi Arabia and others viewed Bosnia-Herzegovina not only as endangered, but as their opportunity to establish Islam in Europe (a payback for support given to the US in Afghanistan). Lastly, Clinton had to be responsive to key Catholic and Jewish constituents and fund raisers during increasingly difficult days in Congress. Clinton could not appear soft on "Serb aggression." Washington gradually became more determined and duplicitous.[9]

The second major development in 1994 was the superseding of the Vance-Owen plan of January 1993 and the Vance-Stoltenberg plan of July 1993 by the Contact Group (US, UK, France, Germany, Russia) plan of July 1994. Not only did Belgrade agree to the fifty-one percent (Croat-Muslim federation) to forty-nine percent (Srpska Republika) split for Bosnia-Herzegovina, but it cut off the Bosnian Serbs from their supplies of weaponry and strategic materials such as petrol so as to force Bosnian Serb leader, Radovan Karadzic, to the negotiating table. It caused an open breach and ended four years of close cooperation, precipitating a crisis in morale among the Bosnian Serbs and an unraveling of its until then superior military position based on control of seventy percent of Bosnia-Herzegovina. Milosevic gambled that he could end the war as a winner vis-à-vis Croatia and Sarajevo and end the imposition of crippling UN-EU sanctions—after having supported both the Krajina and Bosnian Serbs. However, ever suspicious of Milosevic's motives, the US's main concern after the Bosniaks were pushed back to Bihac in late November was to change the situation on the ground so that the Serbs would have to accept "the plan."

By early 1995, rumors abounded of American advisor-technicians at Bosniak military bases. American civilians were also sighted riding the back roads of Bosnia in UN vehicles, an obvious way to obtain ground knowledge needed to augment overhead satellite data and intelligence reports. Journalists claimed they were CIA. More telling, a senior CIA official in Vienna (who had once help arm Jonas Savimbi's UNITA in Angola) made frequent visits to Zagreb and Sarajevo. Functioning as the main arms conduit, Croatia dealt with the German arms supplier, Ernst Glatt, whom the CIA had used in the 1980s to supply the Afghan mujahideen and Nicaraguan contras. Also, UNPROFOR military officers cited repeated flights of giant C-130 cargo planes into Tuzla, which today we know were part of a massive military supply program for Sarajevo. Just how these aircraft circumvented the NATO-enforced UN no-fly zone over Bosnia has never been explained by UN-NATO officials. With military equipment paid for by Saudi Arabia and other Muslim countries now pouring in, the BSA and the Krajina Serbs were soon hard pressed to hold off the more numerous Croatian and Bosniak forces.[10]

By early 1995, the US had already announced its withdrawal from the UNNATO naval blockade in the Adriatic, signaling that the US would no longer prevent weapons from reaching Croatian ports. Next, a group of middle-aged Americans with a military bearing arrived in Zagreb. Led by Lt. General Richard Griffitts (retired), they were an advance party from Military Professional Resources Inc. (MPRI), which had ostensibly been hired by the Croatian government to revamp the Croat armed forces around its rapidly growing arms inventory. MPRI put out the amusing cover story that it was there to reorganize the Croat defense ministry and assist them in making a transition to democracy. Additionally, the US Department of State contracted MPRI to monitor the cut-off of supplies from Belgrade to the Bosnian Serbs. Chosen because of their combat experience, MPRI's military commanders possessed the knowledge of how to coordinate armor, artillery and infantry, along with the ability to plan offensive operations. The first demonstration of Croat resolve (with obvious backing by Washington) came on 1 May when, without warning, the HVO broke through the UNPA buffer forces in Sector West and overran the Pacrak pocket in western Slavonia. Taken by surprise, Srpska Krajina units scattered and left some 6,000 civilians to fend for themselves as best they could. Four hundred were killed.[11]

At the end of the month, the focus of attention moved to Sarajevo where BSA and Bosniak forces exchanged heavy artillery fire along the line of separation inside the exclusion zone. Both were told to desist by UN official Yasushi Akashi, but the order to the BSA was reinforced by NATO missile attacks and air strikes near Pale. This led to the humiliating spectacle of several hundred UNPROFOR soldiers being taken hostage by the Serbs where they took turns being tied to military targets. It caused a backlash against the Bosnian Serbs whereby the previously cautious French and British moved to bring to bear a heavily armed UN Rapid Reaction Force as well as to agree to the increased use of NATO air power. With the UN mission in a state of crisis over the possibility of withdrawal, the US administration asserted its authority (and NATO's) over the UN in a most effective and forceful power play.

Events were now aligning themselves for a showdown. The Bosnian Serbs were isolated from Belgrade and marginalized politically. Sarajevo knew it had the support of the US and could risk taking provocative action calculated to bring NATO fully in on its side. The US and its NATO commanders were poised to pound the Bosnian Serbs in preparation for an assault by Croat and Bosniak forces. The offensive, if successful, would change the situation on the ground so that Pale would either have to accept the Contact Group plan, or risk losing an unacceptable amount of territory. General Mladic played into the hands of the US by responding to each and every Bosniak probing attack, as Pale felt it had to do from the time Sarajevo broke the ceasefire earlier in the spring. In fact, Pale believed it had been deceived into accepting a ceasefire in the mistaken belief that former US President Jimmy Carter could sell its modifications to the Contact Group plan to Washington. For its part, Sarajevo used the time to regroup its forces after the failure of its Bihac offensive. Disappointed, frustrated and enraged (and becoming desperate and reckless), the Bosnian Serbs went on the offensive determined to take an eye for a tooth!

At Srebrenica, the BSA had put on the pressure because of Bosniak raids on surrounding Serb villages. This included intentional harassment of a Dutch UNPROFOR battalion, which (as at the other enclaves) proved unable, or unwilling, to prevent attacks from being made from inside the so-called "safe haven." In early June, the Serbs pushed the Dutch up to the perimeter. In fact, all of the enclaves had angered the Serbs for three years, particularly so after the Croatians had been permitted to keep UNPA Sector West. BSA General Mladic was now determined to overrun them and finish them off once and for all, regardless of the UN and NATO. This would consolidate Serb territory and eliminate the sure prospect they would become a bigger problem in a longer war of attrition. Srebrenica fell in ten days in July and Zepa a week later. Some 40,000 Muslims were cleansed and thousands (soldiers and civilians) were captured and massacred. The Serb atrocity was so enormous and blatant that even the Russians no longer strenuously objected to NATO's involvement. The US moved to retaliate.[12]

It was not long in coming. Following a lengthy military build-up, Zagreb's Operation "Storm" struck at the Serbs' weakest point—along the Krajina front with Knin at its center. On 4 August, a combined air, artillery and infantry attack went in from several directions. Amidst political-military disarray on the part of the Krajina Serb leadership, the front collapsed after only sporadic resistance as soldiers and civilians fled in confusion. The push took only four days as 180,000 Serbs in cars, trucks and tractors made their way into Bosnia, or on to safety in Serbia. Amid widespread looting by the HVO, those Serbs who had stayed (mostly the elderly) were killed and their homes were burned. The final weeks of the war first saw the BSA yield ground to the Bosniaks north of Bihac. Then, after a mortar struck Sarajevo's Markale market, NATO aircraft attacked BSA targets on an around-the-clock basis. Under intense political and military pressure, the Bosnian Serbs finally agreed to "the plan" and fell back to positions close to the fifty-one to forty-nine percent split. An unnecessary war had finally ended.[13]

The bridge over the Drina at Zvornik is a narrow link between the Serbs. The checkpoints at each end between Serbia and the Srpska Republika are within shouting distance. However, in late October 1994, the Bosnian Serbs were feeling the first bite of a blockade imposed by Slobodan Milosevic because of their refusal to accept the Contact Group plan. A river that had just separated friends and relatives had become a formidable frontier when differences with Belgrade had widened it into a chasm. Serb militiamen carefully checked documents while customs men inspected the buses to insure they contained only personal belongings. Anything intended for resale was removed—sacks of coffee and the like. This was punitive, and tighter than the stated policy to permit food, clothing and medicine. "We are being very strict," said one Serb. "Only a blackbird can cross freely." Phone connections had also been cut, impacting on all kinds of business, official and private. The one remaining Srpska Republika office in Belgrade had to use a military radio and indirect lines to obtain my travel permit.

The Bosnian Serbs at the Karakaj checkpoint referred to those on the other side as brothers, but ruefully admitted that they had received a hard blow. The trucks of all description that had been plying the road were now gone. However, I saw two incidents laden with poignancy. A VJ vehicle delivered a soldier's body to a BSA van. After carefully transferring the polished wood casket with its white coverlet, wreath and wooden cross, the two uniformed details saluted, embraced and departed in opposite directions. At Mali Zvornik, on the Serbian side, a well-built, gray-haired, black-mustached fighter from Bosnia got down from a bus in his camouflage clothing and pistol belt, carrying his kit-bag. He was met by a young girl who covered him with hugs and kisses. They walked hand in hand to a small farmhouse not far from the road. With 200,000 Bosnian Serb refugees in Serbia, it seemed that the sanctions set by Belgrade would be impossible to maintain. Yet it had happened. However, it still seemed likely that Serbian blood would prove thicker than politics, or the Drina, for that matter.

South of Zvornik, the scenery is spectacular with a narrow river gorge and abrupt upward-thrusting cliffs on the Bosnian side. It is breathtakingly beautiful as the bus grinds up the steep incline of pine, rock and mountain streams. Some six miles on is Drinjaca. There you see clusters of devastated homes, bullet-pocked and holed by shellfire. The roofs have collapsed onto burned interiors and the empty window openings stare like accusing eyes. Drinjaca and Zvornik and Vlasenica, like dozens of other villages, had been ethnically cleansed in the opening weeks of the war. It had all been aimed at Muslims and it was selective, brutal and complete. I searched to detect emotion on the faces of the travelers, but I concluded they had seen it many times before. A work detail of uniformed men walked through a field harvesting potatoes. A crew loaded roof tiles from a ruined house into a truck. BSA troopers drilled in a bare compound. Farther on, and still climbing, small homes hugged the hillsides, or were spread out on high mountain meadows. Crops were planted on slopes of forty-five degrees. This is the Bosnia of the mountain Serb who claims legal title to some sixty percent of the total land area of Bosnia-Herzegovina.[14]

Three hours later and seven hours out of Belgrade, we arrived in Pale as the sun was going down. It was once a nice resort town where people from Sarajevo would drive up to picnic, kick a soccer ball, or spend their holiday. In 1994, its small houses, shops, public buildings and few hotels were crowded to overflowing with Serbian refugees, mostly from Sarajevo, who were living in cramped, makeshift accommodations. For they had been cleansed as well, leaving out of fear and intimidation. Gordana Draskovic, a petite blonde who worked for Srpska TV, told me her personal story. She has been sharing one small room and a tiny bathroom (with no hot water) with another woman for over two and a half years.

She said that immediately after Bosnia's Muslims and Croats had declared independence in March 1992, the city was in a state of sheer confusion and fear. There were many rumors and reports of clashes between armed groups and of casualties. She was living with her relatively well-off parents in their home on the Muslim side of Sarajevo and was employed in the assembly, or parliament, as an SDS party worker. A few weeks later, a Muslim friend warned her that she was going to be arrested because she was considered to be "political." Within the space of an hour or so, she crammed her car with clothing and personal belongings and said goodbye to life as she had known it.

Armed men from the SDA came searching over the next several days and vented their anger on her parents when they found out she had gone. Others returned a few days later. They assaulted her ailing father, knocking him down, and ordered her parents to move to the basement. Two Muslim families moved into the other two floors. A few months later, her parents fled across the Miljacka to Serbian-controlled Grbavica where they lived in a two-room apartment. There they survived on little food, money, or medicine. She saw them when she could. She misses the family photos, which somehow got left behind. They were burned by their new "house guests." Now, with winter coming on, she wishes she had a warmer pair of boots. She works every day, is rarely paid, and eats in a communal mess. Gordana and her parents are luckier than some. They are alive.

The next morning the sun shone brightly, but everyone's breath was steaming as they walked along in the chill air. Pale's press center was housed in a tiny building and one needed only a quick look around to know that they had few resources to work with, despite the fact that President Karadzic's daughter, Sonya, was said to be in charge. An interview was arranged for myself and a Chinese journalist with cabinet advisor, Slavisa Rakovic, and then Zoran Tesanovic, a center guide, was going to show us Sarajevo.

Rakovic was informal and friendly, a Sarajevo businessman who had got into politics after the outbreak of war. Putting on a brave face, he admitted that Milosevic's action had been a psychological shock to the Serb community, but he said that the great majority of those across the Drina still stood with them. "We feel betrayed, sold out for just what we don't know." He argued that the reopening of Yugoslavia's airline and participation in sporting and cultural events was nothing in exchange for accepting the Contact Group plan.

Should the situation become critical, Rakovic predicted it would strengthen their radical elements who wanted an all-out military victory rather than a negotiated political solution. He said that the worst outcome of a civil war is for one side to emerge the winner and the other to be beaten. He said they were willing to give up territory they had won by blood to achieve an acceptable settlement. He cited the following modifications to the plan as minimum demands: guaranteed Serb control of the corridor linking east and west Srpska Republika, the division of Sarajevo between the Muslims and the Serbs, an outlet to the Adriatic sea, and the Muslim enclaves in eastern Bosnia-Herzegovina were to become Serb territory.

Rakovic said that Belgrade was engaging in wishful thinking if it believed that pressure would make them accept the plan. "We were never a creation of Milosevic," he insisted, adding that they had an elected leadership that had the overwhelming support of its people. He said that the international community now knew they existed and knew they couldn't be defeated militarily. "The US knows this too, but they are trying to stack the cards against us," he added. "This won't work. We will look to our own future."

When asked how the BSA would manage to supply itself, he claimed this had been anticipated after problems with Milosevic during the Vance-Owen period, stating they had stockpiled plenty of everything. "We can fight a long time if we have to," he insisted. However, he said they believed that the war was essentially over because both sides had now achieved a semblance of a strategic balance. Therefore, they expected NATO to be neutral and not back up the Muslim-Croat alliance. He urged the major powers to look at the reality of the situation, to not read "Greater Serbia" into everything they did. He added, "Whatever happens, we will survive it all." With Rakovic's words of defiance still ringing in my ears, we headed for Sarajevo.[15]

The road into Sarajevo comes twisting down from a high elevation. After the last checkpoint, vehicles speed up to avoid snipers, or that odd mortar round. Earth and wood barriers have been erected for protection. The Serb lines are just off the road. The Bosniak side is some 200–300 yards farther down the slope. It had been two weeks since a Bosniak unit had infiltrated at dawn and had got into the BSA positions on Mount Igman. Of the few survivors, two were nurses who had been wounded and left for dead. One cannot speak. The other only remembers the name of her village.

From above, looking down on the living and those doomed to die, the city was obviously very vulnerable to artillery attack from its surrounding hills, which were held by the Serbs. Farther down, in the built-up areas of the broken city, the odds evened out where the two sides were engaged in street fighting. There, like in Beirut, heavy barricades blocked off streets, and buildings had their windows sandbagged, bricked, or boarded up along the lines of confrontation for protection and to prevent observation. There they sniped at each other and at civilians who entered their gun sights. Mortar rounds were lobbed back and forth and when really heavy statements were to be made, there was always the artillery.[16]

We drove past Grbavica's apartment blocks with their blackened, gaping holes and shattered windows. It was a quiet day and yet not many people were out in the rubble-strewn streets. We threaded our way over to the UNPROFOR checkpoint. There, at the river, French and BSA soldiers supervised a crossing point. Older men and women waited patiently as their names were checked against a list. Would they soon sprint down the infamous "Sniper's Alley"? Hardly. But it did seem risky. Everyone was very calm, as though they were waiting to buy a ticket to the cinema. Nearby, there was a small covered market that had very little to offer—a few pieces of fruit, vegetables, eggs, bread, and household soap. Still, people talked among themselves and even laughed. Over to one side was a small low building, which was the only remaining Orthodox church in Grbavica. It had been relocated in order to get closer to the protective presence of UNPROFOR. Nonetheless (with a brave little bell donated from Greece), its bullet-pocked walls suggested that its guardian angel was off duty. Inside was a simple altar, a few wooden icons on the walls and a few chairs. A young Serb soldier held his son in his arms as he lit his candles. When he saw I was taking his photo, he looked at me and as he remembered his loved ones, both the living and the dead, he held his fingers in the flames not only once, but three times. Given their fight against ever-increasing odds, this seemed to symbolize the way of the Bosnian Serbs—to live by a fierce faith and a terrible fire!

That November saw the Bosniak Fifth Corps break out of Bihac and drive south. This largest Muslim offensive to date was cheered on by a Western media that thought it saw the war turning around. A patient General Mladic allowed his opponents to overreach themselves, and then rounded on them unmercifully. The Krajina Serbs jumped on, as well as 5,000 Muslims loyal to Fikret Abdic. Over Christmas, Carter's mission came out. He gave Pale the impression that Washington might listen to them. A four-month ceasefire was put in place, and then all disappeared like the snow in early spring.

In mid-March, Bosniak forces attacked northeast of Tuzla and near Travnik and Konjic. With small-scale actions also occurring along the Sava River valley corridor, the ceasefire slowly eroded until BSA and Bosniak forces began exchanging artillery fire in Sarajevo. At the end of May, NATO aircraft were attacking Pale.[17]

Again I took the 11:30. In Belgrade, he was the first to get on, assisted up by his friends. He was young, athletic-looking and handsome with his dark hair and black T-shirt. His jeans were cut off below the knee where his right leg used to be. The plaster around his stump was antiseptic white. The usual scrawled names and cartoons, as after a skiing accident, were absent. I offered him a cigarette and asked how it had happened. He stared at his leg in an odd way and said it had been a landmine. He had had his pre-prosthesis treatment at a Belgrade hospital.

It's hard to see an old woman cry, but cry she did. She was around seventy years old and all in black. She wore a headscarf that set off her white hair and made her square, lined face even more impressive. She hugged her granddaughter and her daughter and her tears flowed freely down her cheeks.

When it was time to go, she climbed up and gave a long, sad wave. Even her handkerchief was black.

Over in Bosnia, I noticed the new graves as we went along—an old person who had lived out his life in a close-knit community, or someone home from the front, I couldn't tell. You knew only that any death was a recognized loss to this small, scattered people. The bus stopped often to pick up soldiers heading back to their units. In camouflage and carrying kit-bags, they handled their AK-47s with ease. One gave me a shoulder patch—a double-headed eagle, crown, crossed swords and a shield with four Cyrillic Cs—"Samo Sloga Srbina Spasava" (only unity can save the Serb). They were quiet and clean-cut, mostly in their late teens and early twenties. I asked a woman who was forty, or so, where she was going. She said she was from Sarajevo, but the recent fighting had forced her to find temporary refuge in Pale. When I asked why she would again risk Grbavica, she unhesitatingly replied, "We want to stay—it is our place." With growing emotion, she said, "We don't hate the Muslims—we only refuse to leave what is ours." She said, "We are not monsters as people outside are saying. We want to live in peace." As tears flooded her eyes, she said, "My brother has lost a leg." Then, she could no longer speak.

In Pale, dozens of journalists were trying to find out the whereabouts and welfare of nearly 400 UNPROFOR soldiers who had been taken captive to prevent more NATO air strikes. The Bosnian Serb leadership was issuing tersely worded warning statements and few details. Then, amid all the secrecy, we heard that a Greek TV crew had filmed some of the hostages. The press center was in an uproar. The Greeks, now smugly satisfied, were sent home and the major networks were left to stare at one another. Finally, I got to Slavisa. He scoffed at the possibility that any UNPROFOR personnel would be harmed. He said they had been tied up only in the beginning to get the message across. As for themselves, at Pale they had four dead and over a dozen wounded, or so he claimed. Then Slavisa delivered his message: they were ready to use the Contact Group plan as a point of departure for negotiations. Pale had fully expected that after the Carter visit they would gain equal status with Sarajevo and, importantly, the linking of Srpska Republika with Belgrade as an accepted option for the future. He heatedly pointed out, however, that when all sides regrouped in the spring that the plan and the map were back on the table on a take-it-or-leave-it basis—returning, in effect, to June 1994.

Rakovic said it was their assessment that this reversal came as a result of US pressure, combined with Croat-Muslim maneuvering, which served to undo what had been accomplished by Carter. After all, he pointed out, the Croat-Muslim federation had clear links to Zagreb. Where was the fairness in this, he wanted to know? He stressed that no one could force the Contact Group plan on them. Concerning the air strikes of 25–26 May, Rakovic said that the US and NATO were wrong to view their seizure of their heavy weapons from the UNPROFOR storage sites in isolation. He pointed out that Sarajevo had broken the ceasefire and had begun attacking. He cited Debelo Brdo, Mount Treskovica, the Jewish cemetery, and the Pale link road as places where Sarajevo had initiated action. He said Bosniak forces had seized control of the road on occasions in recent weeks. Turning to broader issues, he said that Zagreb's take-over of Western Slavonia and increasing pressure by Sarajevo now made it more urgent for them to unite with the Krajina Serbs. Up until now, he explained, they had each dealt with their problems on a piecemeal basis, cooperating militarily only when necessary. This must change, he added for emphasis. He frankly admitted that Zagreb's offensive in Slavonia placed the Brcko corridor at risk. He said that they would take steps to correct this problem.[18]

At Pale, I stayed with the Skipina family. They had lived on the Muslim side of Sarajevo. At the outbreak of the fighting, the mother and her son were arrested and interned behind barbed wire because her husband was a JNA officer. After one month, they were exchanged for a Muslim couple. They had been living in Pale just over three years, occupying the upper floor of a house owned by a Muslim family that they had never seen. The sparsely furnished rooms were spotlessly clean, the wooden floors scrubbed white. Starched white curtains hung in the windows, an Orthodox icon and a religious calendar on the wall of their main room. The husband was at the front, but their son Slobodan was on leave. An AK-47 stood in the corner. That night for dinner, we ate garden greens, a type of pasta and freshly baked bread. There was no meat, but it didn't seem to matter somehow. The wine was good, and there was fruit for dessert. The water was so cold and clear that I suggested they export it to Evian. Later, there was TV—Charlie Chaplin in *The Great Dictator*. Somehow, the grainy black-and-white film, which pokes fun at fascism, seemed unfunny knowing there were people in the world who wanted to drop high explosives on the heads of these people.

The events of summer and autumn fell swiftly on top of each other— Sarajevo, Srebrenica, Zepa, Tuzla, Knin. After the Markale market incident on 28 August, NATO's Southern Command in Italy had gone into high gear as its aircraft (mostly American) struck at BSA targets throughout Bosnia-Herzegovina to soften up the Serbs for a final Croat-Bosniak assault. The US State Department spokesman stated, "...there is no military victory in sight for them; the tide of war has turned against them; their dream of a Greater Serbia is no more..." Indeed, even after their heavy weapons were withdrawn from Sarajevo and they had given Milosevic authority to deal with the Contact Group on their behalf, the bombing continued. A confident Izetbegovic, now openly demonstrating the increasingly Islamic orientation of his regime, tacked on additional demands. Heavy weapons, ammunition dumps, radar and air defense sites were hit. Tudjman, flushed from the success of his Krajina campaign, ordered additional HVO units into northwest Bosnia for an attack on Banya Luka. The Split-based 4th Brigade teamed up with the Bosniak 5th Corps from the Bihac area. The 7th Corps was expected from central Bosnia-Herzegovina.

Sarajevo's tall buildings and apartment blocks were shrouded in mist when Zoran and I drove down and looked like a city set amidst clouds. It was the haze that made it look so decidedly seductive. We stopped for coffee. The cafe boasted a mural of a topless woman by a swimming pool in cool blues and greens. It was a cruel reminder of how Sarajevans had vacationed on the Adriatic just a few hours away. Neno Zdrale, a dentist, was asked what he thought of the peace talks scheduled for Dayton. "Maybe sheer necessity will lead us to cooperate with the Muslims, but we must keep our areas of the city under our own control," was his only comment. Zdrale said his family had lost many in the fighting. One was an uncle who had given food and old clothing to a poor Muslim family who had lived near him. "He was killed defending his house," he said. "We didn't mind them being here, but now it is obvious that they mind us."

Farther down in Grbavica, there were gaping holes in the sides of the buildings, broken windows covered over with plastic, pockmarked walls and shot-up cars down on their axles. It was eerily quiet. Two elderly men were filling water bottles from a hose. On most days there was intermittent gas and electric power. We met a bearded fighter with an AK-47 who, at seventy-one, claimed to be the oldest soldier on the Serb side. He had fought with Tito. There were splat marks from mortars in almost every street. It was clear that residential areas hadn't been spared. Blankets and large carpets hung across the streets, building to building, to prevent observation. People had learned to take the safest routes, cutting through buildings to avoid exposed areas. Sometimes knowing wasn't enough. Two old women were killed by a mortar round while cooking in a garage. A young Srdjan Tovljevic, aged eight, was killed by a sniper while playing at his house. The Bosniaks controlled areas close to Grbavica.

We visited Zoran's parents. Their house was back from the river, but out in the open. Sheet metal barriers had been erected nearby for protection. Still, they had had some hits. We sat around the table for coffee and cigarettes. Zoran's sister and her children lived there also. A bottle of brandy was produced as everyone caught up on the news. A girl of eleven was excited at the prospect of a holiday in Greece where she would live with a Greek family. Everyone was ready for the war to end but were concerned as to what the terms might be. Zoran thought they would probably be sold out. On the way back to Pale, we stopped and talked to a few fighters up on the link road. Their bunkers were built of logs, cement blocks and earth. Inside was a rough bed, a cook stove and a chair. Through a slot, they pointed out the positions of the Bosniaks. They said the Muslims had become better fighters and that their equipment and tactics had improved. On leaving, they gave me a Bosnian Serb thumbs-up, three-finger salute.

Back in Pale, I talked to Vera Ninkovic who teaches English at the elementary school. We discussed the effects of the war on her students, many of whom were originally from Sarajevo. She said that some had difficulty concentrating; had trouble breathing; and were now afraid of loud noises. A few had reverted to bed-wetting. I remarked on the American logos I had seen on clothing worn by the younger set and the teenagers—and the Donald Duck and the Davy Crockett comic books (in Serbo-Croatian) at the news kiosk. Ninkovic said that Americans had always been held in awe by the Serbs but that even the attitudes of younger people had changed since talk began of President Clinton's support for Sarajevo and Zagreb. Ninkovic said that with NATO jets overhead and now Pale having been bombed, the war had thrust itself on the kids.

Ognjen Tesanovic, 12, said that what he missed most from Sarajevo was his father, who had been killed in the fighting. His voice catching a little, he said that he had no idea how the war began. He wanted to be a doctor when he grew up.

Danka Blagojevic, 12, only wanted the war to stop. She didn't know how it had started, or what she could do to stop it. She remembered her house in Sarajevo and wished that she could return. She said that she had made new friends, but felt as though her childhood had been destroyed.

Jelena Micic, 12, also wanted the war to stop. She wanted people to know that the Serbs want to live in peace. She realized that the Croat and Muslim children were not guilty of wrongdoing.

While walking through town, I asked a pretty, dark-haired girl to pose for my camera. In her jacket, jeans and sneakers, she threw her hip out ever so slightly, perhaps suggestive of her fast-approaching womanhood. As she smiled, I wondered what her future would be. Something approaching normalcy, or more war?

The accords signed on 21 November on a US air force base at Dayton brought a halt to the fighting and imposed the obligations of an uneasy peace and an uncertain future. As imperfect a document as it was, an end to killing, maiming, and the destruction of a poor country carried argumentative weight in its favor. There was scope for rebuilding shattered societies if Messrs Milosevic, Tudjman and Izetbegovic had the will to do so. The accords set out the following provisions:

A. Bosnia-Herzegovina is to remain a single state within its present borders. It is governed by a federal constitution, which provides for a two-chamber parliament, a constitutional court, a rotating tripartite presidency, a single currency and a central bank.

B. It consists of two entities, a Croat-Muslim federation, which controls fifty-one percent of the land area and Srpska Republika, which controls forty-nine percent. Sarajevo is under the Croat-Muslim federation, while Gorazde is linked to the Croat-Muslim federation by a land corridor. The Serbs retain Srebrenica, Zepa, and Pale outside Sarajevo.

C. Democratic elections are to govern the political allocation of elective positions of responsibility. Persons indicted as possible war criminals are excluded from holding public office.

D. The question of control of Brcko is to be decided by international arbitration. All refugees have the right to return home. A NATO Multinational Military Implementation Force (IFOR) is to function as a peacekeeping force until June 1998. Most sanctions against Yugoslavia are lifted, others remain.

The Serbs gave up Grbavica, Nedarici, Ilidza, and Vogoscra in Sarajevo. At the end, they dug up the bones of their dead and left.

* * *

Slav settlement began in Bosnia-Herzegovina in the seventh century. In AD 960, it was detached from Serbia and became a separate entity, uniting for a time with the Serb principalities of Rashka and Zeta. Hungarian inroads into Bosnia began from the mid-twelfth century, bringing Laszlo and Kulin as "bans," or representatives, of Hungary's king. A trade agreement was concluded with Serbian Dubrovnik (Ragusa). With the rise of Hungarian influence, the Papacy wanted to extend the Latin rite, placing Bosnia under a Hungarian archbishop instead of the Slavonic archbishop at Dubrovnik. In reaction to this, Kulin embraced the Bogomil heresy, placing Bosnia between two religious authorities. Pope Innocent III preached a crusade and Kulin caved in. However, heresy spread and Pope Honorius III again called for a crusade. War was avoided by accepting the Hungarian archbishop of Kalocsa, although Bogomilism in Bosnia continued, making many apostate in the eyes of Rome, which considered Bosnia "overgrown with thorns and nettles and a breed of vipers." Ban Ninoslav was to recant, but refused under popular pressure, a situation that led to a none-too-successful military expedition by Hungary. A compromise of sorts saw a Catholic bishopric set up at Djakovo.[19]

A succession of Hungarian bans established the Kotromanic dynasty in Bosnia and extended Bosnia south by conquering the Serbian principality of Hum (the future Herzegovina) by 1326. Hungary's hold on Bosnia-Herzegovina was greatly aided by Byzantine attacks on Serb prince Stefan Dusan to the east. The Kotromanics coined money and ruled from the Sava to the sea and from Cetina to the Drina. Soon after Tvrtko took over, he fell out with Hungary's Louis I, who had given Hum as a dowry for his wife (Stephan Kotromanic's daughter). At first, Tvrtko held off Hungarian attacks, but a revolt of nobles amid family intrigue forced him to leave the country. Eventually, he was restored by Louis. Thereupon, in 1377, at the tomb of Saint Sava, he declared himself "King of the Serbs and Bosnia, and of the Coastlands." In 1382, to promote trade, he built the town of Novi (today's Hercegnovi) at the entrance to Kotor bay in Montenegro.

In 1386, the Ottoman Turks invaded Bosnia. In two years, they were at the Neretva River, but Tvrtko held them off at Belica. Tvrtko, like others, sent forces to help Prince Lazar, but the Serbs were disastrously beaten at Kosovo's Field of Blackbirds in June 1389. Undeterred, Tvrtko turned north and took Split, Trogir, Sibenik and the coastal islands. He claimed the title of King of Rashka, Bosnia, Dalmatia, Croatia and the Coast before dying in 1391. At this point, Bosnia was at its zenith. It didn't last long. Sigismund of Hungary (the future Holy Roman Emperor) was beaten by the Turks at Nikopol and Bosnia fell prey to internal dissension. A succession of pretenders and magnates vied for power, some siding with Sigismund, some with the Turks. In time, the Turks took Constantinople and Serbia. A claimant, Stephan Tomasevic, appealed to Pope Pius II for help. Pius sent a crown, which Stephan assumed in 1461. Ending his tribute to the Sultan, he appealed to Venice. He also appealed to the Turks for a fifteen-year armistice. After his envoys had left the Porte with a promise of peace, Sultan Mohammed II invaded Bosnia. Tomasevic surrendered with the promise of his life and was promptly beheaded. The Turks had conquered the south by 1482 and took the two remaining banats from Hungary in 1512 and 1528.

The Turkish governor, or pasha, first ruled from Banya Luka and then from Sarajevo. The latter is located on the shortest route from the Pannonian plain to the north to the Adriatic. Circa 1460, the Turks built a settlement, which consisted of a castle, mosque, public bath, a bridge, a hostelry for traders and a water supply. The name Sarajevo means "the field around the castle." The Bosnian pashalik was divided into eight sanjaks and much power was in the hands of forty-eight hereditary kapetans, or captaincies—held feudally. The Bosnian nobility (mostly Bogomils on the wrong side of Rome) apostatized as a class to preserve their landed power, adopting Islam. As many serfs followed their masters, they became Muslim also. Under Ottoman rule, Bosnia slowly slipped into decline. Its mining disappeared and trade dried up. Its only importance was as a Turkish outpost during unending wars against the Habsburgs and Venice. When Hungary was won back from the Turks, the Austrians under Prince Eugene of Savoy sacked and burned Sarajevo in 1697. At the 1699 Treaty of Karlowitz, the Sava became the northernmost limit of the Ottoman Empire. At the Treaty of Passarowitz, lands east of the Una and Hercegnovi were ceded to Austria. These were restored to Turkey in 1739 and remained as such until 1878.

In the early nineteenth century, Bosnian nobles periodically rebelled against the Porte. Husein Gradascevic (the Dragon of Bosnia) led the landowners in a protest against the proposed reforms of Mahmud II in 1831. He and Mustafa Pasha Bushati of Shkoder joined their forces in north Albania and Macedonia. In 1837, when Abdul Mejid abolished captaincies, even more trouble erupted. In Herzegovina, Ali Pasha Risvanbegovic became virtually independent. However, Mehmed Reshid restored the Sultan's rule in Albania and turned Risvanbegovic and Smail Aga Cengic against Husein, who fled into Croatia (he was banished to Trabzon). Omar Pasha had restored control by 1850–51 (he finished off Risvanbegovic and began to invade a rebellious Montenegro) but replaced the feudal regime with a centralized administration that subjected the peasantry to even greater exactions and more arbitrary demands. In 1862, the Serb, Luka Vukalovic, led a peasant revolt that was harshly repressed and caused even greater resentment. Even some Muslims sided with the Serbs despite their religious and social differences.

The advent of Habsburg rule in Bosnia-Herzegovina has been dealt with earlier. However, it must be stressed that efforts by the Porte to impose administrative reform (the Tanzimat system), to organize a modern army, and its failure to introduce land reform are fundamental to understanding the discontent and upheaval in the Ottoman Empire's European lands. The feudal system of power and obligation were to be ended (which directly affected the land-owning nobility), while the rural peasantry was being exploited more than ever. Bosnia's land tenure had changed little since the eighteenth century. There were two types of estates, agaliks and begliks. On the first, the serfs had certain land rights. On begliks, the serf worked on terms set by the owner, giving much of his produce to the beg and owing him labor as well. The tax burden was heavy, compounded as it was by tax farming abuses. Looking out for their own interests, nobles often converted their agaliks to begliks.

Although schools, roads and a railway were built, for most, life was abysmally backward.[20]

Arguably the best book dealing with the imposition of Ottoman and Austro-Hungarian rule in Bosnia and the social interaction of all affected thereby is Ivo Andric's *Bridge Over the Drina*. Andric was awarded a Nobel prize in 1961, largely on the strength of this work. As William H. McNeill has said, "Every episode rings true, from the role of terror in fastening Turkish power on the land to the role of an Austrian whorehouse in corrupting the old ways." The book begins with the building of the bridge and the impalement of the rebel Radisav, and ends with the opening of World War One and the hunting down of Serbs. Andric himself was interned for three years in an Austrian camp.

In 1945, when his book was first published, he had been through a second catastrophe. As McNeill states, "Andric (a Bosnian Serb) grew up in a world where rival and mutually incompatible world views found themselves in acute conflict." In his "Letter From 1920," Andric writes about a Jewish friend who left Sarajevo forever, an aspiring medical student who called Bosnia a land of hatred and fear. As for his Sarajevo, his friend recalled how Catholic, Orthodox, and Muslim clocks all tolled the time differently, as different as their calendars and prayers. He likened it to a deadly endemic disease. I cite this cautionary tale in the context of much recently written material describing pre-1992 Sarajevo as a city of ethnic harmony.[21]

During World War One, the Muslim community had generally sided with Austria and the Croats. So, within the Austro-Hungarian army were Croats, Slovenes and even Muslims. The end of that conflict saw Muslims and Catholics turn this way and that to preserve their interests vis-à-vis Serbia. Consequently they grasped the Trialist kingdom of Serbs, Croats and Slovenes, while Muslims debated whether to call themselves Serb or Croat. The Muslims were led by Mehmet Spaho, who founded the Yugoslav Muslim Organization (YMO) in 1919. Serb occupation was not without incident. Retribution took place against Muslims who, along with the Croats, had belonged to the Schutzkorps (local militia), which had achieved murderous results against Serbs in eastern Bosnia. However, the violence ended with land reform (4,000 Muslim owners were paid compensation) and the absorption of energy into inter-war politics. The Serbs followed their Radical Party, which pushed social reform based on the old Mlada Bosna movement. The Croats argued fiercely for a confederal arrangement and, with the adoption of the 1921 constitution, they began to boycott parliament. The kingdom was divided into thirty-three districts whereby only Bosnia retained its original outline.[22]

The subsequent two decades saw the sad failure of democracy and a semidictatorship under King Alexander. However, Bosnian Muslims acquired better education (including studies abroad) and many were affected by the modernizing influence of Ataturk in Turkey. A Muslim prima donna, Bahrija Nuri Hadzic, even sang at the opera house in Belgrade. Spaho and the YMO were in a pivotal position, helping to make and unmake governments. Alexander ended the chaos in 1929 by assuming wide powers. He announced a new "Yugoslavia" and made the kingdom over into nine banovines, or banates. The Italian-backed Ustashe succeeded in killing him in 1934. Five years later, moves towards a fundamental compromise proposed a redrawing of boundaries that would have included parts of Bosnia in Croatia.

Spaho died in June of that year when negotiations had reached a critical stage. His successor, Dzafer Kulenovic, attempted to get a special banovina for Bosnia, but this failed because the Serb majority in the affected areas did not want to be separated from adjoining Serb banovinas (This might sound familiar to us today). However, the "Sporazum" (Agreement) of 1939 was adopted. In 1940, Kulenovic stopped attending cabinet meetings. He claimed that the YMO was not getting its fair share of patronage and again demanded a Muslim banovina, which would include the Sandzak of Novi Pazar. When he was turned down, Kulenovic became embittered and held a deep grudge against Serbia. The situation continued into 1941 amid inconclusive debate and non-implementation of the Sporazum. War came in the spring and Sarajevo was bombed with a heavy loss of life. Nevertheless when Bosnia-Herzegovina was incorporated into the Croatian fascist NDH, Muslim opposition to this and to the regime's cruel excesses was muted. Moreover, many lent their active support.[23]

Serbs, Jews, and Gypsies by the hundreds of thousands soon went to their deaths. In the mountains, guerrilla warfare went on against the occupiers and between the Partisan bands of Tito and Chetnik leader Draza Mihailovic. Because of Muslim acquiescence to NDH, Serbs in Herzegovina turned on them during a brief armed revolt in the summer of 1941, killing 600 at Bileca and 500 at Visegrad. In general, the Chetniks continued this practice throughout the war when and where they could. The Partisans were against this and later many Muslims joined the communists. However, many more threw their lot in with the NDH and the Axis powers. Dzafer Kulenovic became a NDH vice-president. He was backed by a YMO businessman, Uzeiraga Hadzihazanovic. Hakija Hadzic became the Ustashe commander for Bosnia. Muslims joined its ranks.

In October 1942, a Muslim Volunteer League was set-up by the Germans, which fought more against the Partisans than the Chetniks (some 4,000 Muslims eventually went over to Draza). A similar, but more independent, unit existed north of Bihac. The Muslims appealed directly to Hitler for aid. In 1943, Hitler moved the Prinz Eugen SS division of Germans from Romania to Bosnia for the purpose (at Himmler's suggestion) of training two Muslim divisions. The 13th SS "Handzar" Division was organized with the blessing of the virulently anti-Jewish Grand Mufti of Jerusalem, El-Huseini. By April, it came to number 21,000 Muslims. After training, it was assigned to northern and eastern Bosnia, where it engaged in atrocities against thousands of Serbs. However, as the tide of war turned in late 1944, all of the Muslim units disintegrated. Remnants were forcibly returned from Allied-occupied Austria in April–May 1945; and many were then killed by the communists along with Croat Ustashe members.[24]

Tito viewed Islam as retrograde during a period of repression of the Catholic church and the crude manipulation of the Orthodox. As Islam is not only a private faith, but a public way of life, its religious law courts were shut down and women were forbidden to wear the veil. Koranic elementary schools were closed as well. The dervish tekke orders were banned, as were Muslim cultural and educational societies. The state controlled the training of its clergy and allowed only one organization. Printing houses were closed and there were no Islamic textbooks until 1964. However, despite YCL efforts at suppression, texts circulated, teaching went on in mosques, and the dervish tekkes went into private homes. That said, a great many Muslim private properties were lost through state nationalization (this affected all ethnic communities). A factor that alleviated much of this over time was Yugoslavia's role in the Non-Aligned Movement. As Belgrade developed relations with Egypt, India, and Indonesia, religious conditions improved. By the 1960s, Muslims were needed as diplomats and envoys. And, with their higher birth rate, they became a majority in Bosnia.

As official permissiveness increased, Muslim thinkers like Alija Izetbegovic began to put down their thoughts on Islam and Bosnia. The 1971 census saw Muslims identifying themselves as such. The Muslim Bosnian identity was given a further boost with the 1974 constitution, which gave impetus to regional power and expression. Muslims were now better represented in the Bosnian YLC. They were permitted to study at Arab universities abroad and, in 1977, an Islamic theological school was built in Sarajevo by the Saudis. All of this coalesced around the idea that Bosnia-Herzegovina should carry more weight politically within the SFRY and gain more economically. A surge of investment and construction did occur on funds borrowed on unrealistic expectations. As Muslims asserted themselves, the Croats complained that they were not getting a fair shake. There was significant Serb migration out as Muslims from the Sandzak flocked in. Additionally, the Iranian revolution of 1979 made its impact on what was an increasingly tense political situation.[25]

In 1983, the YLC cracked down on what it saw as excessive Muslim nationalism. A trial took place in Sarajevo whereby thirteen leading Muslim activists were convicted of counter-revolution. The most well-known was Izetbegovic, who had belonged to an anti-communist Young Muslims' organization after World War Two and who had privately circulated his *Islamic Declaration* for thirteen years among Muslim intellectuals. The show trial resulted in Izetbegovic being sentenced to fourteen years (reduced to eleven on appeal). The careers of senior Muslim communists were given an official boost, but several became mired in financial scandals similar to the Albanians in Kosovo. Fikret Abdic's Agrokomerc, with 13,000 employees and a number of Bosnia-Herzegovina officials on the take, finally went broke owing US$300 million. Izetbegovic's release in 1988 came at a time of growing economic stagnation (US$33 billion in foreign debt), a credit crunch and increasing economic dislocation. As people questioned their mutual relationships, ethnic nationalism began to assert itself in a more exclusive and extremist manner.

In Bosnia in 1990, the three ethnic communities established their own parties: the Croats an offshoot of the HDZ, the Serbs an SDS—as was set up in Krajina, the Muslims the SDA. Izetbegovic became its almost unopposed leader. Early on, the SDA adopted Islamic symbols of identity—giant green banners and the crescent. It boasted an overnight membership of 700,000. An émigré millionaire, Adil Zulfikarpasic, broke from the SDA and attempted to form a secularly oriented party called the Bosnian Muslim Organization (BMO). However, the publication of Izetbegovic's *Islamic Declaration* was viewed as an SDA political manifesto and overwhelmed the BMO with its impact.[26]

* * *

3 January 1993. At Geneva, co-chairmen of the Conference on the Former Yugoslavia, Cyrus Vance and David Owen presented a proposed division of Bosnia-Herzegovina into ten provinces. Bosnia-Herzegovina's government would be decentralized with Sarajevo only having responsibility for its own taxes, foreign affairs and foreign trade. Sarajevo province would be ethnically mixed around an open city. Bosniak Muslim provinces were separated—one in the northwest surrounding Bihac and a large central-east province (irregular in shape), which included lands lost to the Serbs along the Drina valley. The Croat provinces were separated within Bosnia-Herzegovina, but contiguous to Croatia in the southwest (Mostar and Travnik were its two main cities) and in the north. A Serb share-out would consist of a large province in the northwest around Banya Luka, one in the east contiguous with Serbia, a dot inside a Muslim province, and two provinces adjacent to Sarajevo, but both separated.[27]

Vance-Owen tried to give everyone something. The Muslims got the industrial towns of Tuzla and Zenica. They also got coal mines. Most of the hydroelectric plants went to the Croats. The Serbs got a mixture of industrial facilities around Banya Luka. Bosnia-Herzegovina's arms plants were at Travnik, Vitez, Konjic, Bugojno, and Goradze. Under pressure from Belgrade to accept, the Bosnian Serbs dragged their feet and insisted on consultations. Their main problem with the proposal was that their provinces would be separated. On 20 January, at Pale, the assembly of Srpska Republika voted fifty-five to fifteen for nine of Vance-Owen's constitutional proposals. The Croat-Muslim side had accepted the constitutional arrangements on 10–12 January. On 30 January, talks broke off. The Croats had agreed to both the principles and the map. The Serbs agreed only to the principles. The Muslims soon rejected both the principles and the map. Vance and Owen continued to meet through subsequent weeks and the two chairmen exerted much effort in separate sessions with all of the principals involved. From time to time, a plenum was cancelled due to the failure of a participant to attend.

22 January 1993. Croat forces came through UNPROFOR lines in the Krajina intending to seize the Maslenica Bridge, an airport at Zadar and Peruca dam. The action continued over UN resolutions. Fighting also erupted between Croats and Muslims at Gornji Vakuf in central Bosnia-Herzegovina amid rising tension and mutual hostage taking.

10 February 1993. US Secretary of State, Warren Christopher, said that the US intended to become more involved in seeking a solution to the Bosnian war and that, towards that end, President Clinton had appointed Richard Bartholomew as a special envoy. As the US began to airdrop supplies to Muslim refugees in eastern Bosnia, Washington talked about putting more pressure on Milosevic.

25 March 1993. Vance-Owen presented minor changes to the map and an annex on interim arrangements. The Croats and the Muslim sides accepted the entire plan. Bosnian Serb leader, Radovan Karadzic, still objected to the map and viewed the interim arrangements as another collective presidency that they had objected to earlier. The Bosnian Serb concern was that they would always be outvoted. An angered UN Security Council urged the Bosnian Serbs to agree.

26 March 1993. Following talks in Belgrade, a ceasefire for Bosnia-Herzegovina was to take effect on 28 March. With minor exceptions, the ceasefire was observed. Unfortunately, it would become one of many.

6 April 1993. Verbal agreement was reached between Croatia and Srpska Republika Krajina concerning an end to the fighting; the withdrawal of Croat HVO forces; the use of Maslenica Bridge and Zemunik airport; and the use of Peruca dam's roads by civilians.

12 April 1993. US, French and Dutch aircraft flew out of NATO bases in Italy to enforce the ban on flights over Bosnia-Herzegovina air space.

16 April 1993. A serious clash broke out between Serb and Muslim forces at Srebrenica. With over fifty dead, UNPROFOR stated that the Bosniak side had provoked artillery fire from the Serb side. The UN Security Council expressed alarm and declared that Srebrenica was to be considered a safe area. The following day, Bosnian Serb General Ratko Mladic and General Sefer Halilovic signed a ceasefire agreement concerning Srebrenica in the presence of General Lars Valgren that specified that the town would be demilitarized and all weapons surrendered to UNPROFOR within seventy-two hours.

18 April 1993. The UN Security Council stated that if Radovan Karadzic failed to sign Vance-Owen within nine days, additional sanctions would be imposed on Yugoslavia. Adding to protests by Belgrade, Karadzic said that should this happen, he would abandon the peace talks. Additional sanctions went into effect on 26 April.

20 April 1993. Hard fighting took place between Bosniak and HVO Croat forces at Vitez, Kiseljak, Jablanica, Mostar, and Konjic. As this was going on, Milosevic made repeated appeals to the Bosnian Serbs to reconsider. Yugoslavia was ejected from more UN forums.

30 April 1993. US President Clinton said that his advisors were considering a range of military options to end the war in Bosnia-Herzegovina. A list of Bosnian Serb military targets was under review.

1–2 May 1993. A conference opened in Athens to attempt to obtain Bosnian Serb agreement to Vance-Owen. After talks which included Mate Boban, Izetbegovic, Karadzic, US-Russian envoys Bartholomew and Vitaly Churkin, the co-chairmen (Owen's EC successor Thorvald Stoltenberg was also present), Milosevic and Tudjman, the Bosnian Serb president signed the agreement on condition that it would be approved by the Srpska Republika assembly on 5 May.

5–6 May 1993. The Bosnian Serb assembly (Milosevic, Montenegrin President Momir Bulatovic, Yugoslav federal President Dobrica Cosic, and Greek Prime Minister Mitsotakis were present) debated Vance-Owen for seventeen hours. Amid appeals by the aforementioned for acceptance, the assembly voted fifty-one to two (twelve abstentions) to stick with its Bijelina decision to hold a national referendum. Back from Pale that same day (6 May), Milosevic warned that he would cut off all aid except food, medicine and assistance to refugees. He later claimed that the border was being closed, but this was for international consumption. His support continued.

6 May 1993. The UN Security Council announced that Sarajevo and the towns of Tuzla, Zepa, Goradze, Bihac, and Srebrenica were safe areas and ordered the withdrawal of Bosnian Serb forces. Generals Ratko Mladic and Sefer Halilovic signed a ceasefire and accords dealing with the so-called safe havens, or safe areas. A second agreement on a ceasefire and prisoner exchanges was signed within days, attesting to both a shaky situation and practical progress. Finally, President Izetbegovic refused to disarm the safe havens.

10 May 1993. The UN Security Council ordered a halt to a Croat HVO offensive against the Bosniak Muslims in the Mostar area. A ceasefire signed by Bosniak General Halilovic and Croat General Milivoj Petkovic was ignored by the HVO. BSA units observed the fighting from hills overlooking Mostar, but stayed out of it.

16–17 May 1993. With Yugoslavia's assemblies urging adoption (extremists walked out of a joint session attended by MPs from Bosnia and Krajina), the Bosnian Serbs overwhelmingly rejected Vance-Owen. The latter believed they could hold out for more and that Milosevic could not risk cutting off their support.

22 May 1993. After indications that the US was unwilling to put its own troops into Bosnia-Herzegovina, a five-nation (US, UK, France, Russia, and Spain) action plan was adopted in Washington. Agreement was reached to provide heavily armed UNPROFOR troops for safe areas.

8 June 1993. Hundreds of Croat civilians and HVO crossed into Serb territory after losing Travnik. British UNPROFOR troops saw Bosniak fighters shooting Croat civilians and intervened to save some 170 at Guce Gora. Major fighting between the two sides soon erupted at Zavidovici, Zepce, and Maglaj in north-central Bosnia.

11 June 1993. Meeting at Athens, NATO's foreign ministers agreed to provide air support for UNPROFOR if authorized by the UN. The US pushed the plan, but the UK and France remained very skeptical, thinking it would provoke retaliation against their own troops by the BSA. Under US pressure, NATO continued to discuss the option.

16 June 1993. Owen and Stoltenberg opened talks at Geneva with Milosevic, Tudjman and Izetbegovic regarding how to remake Vance-Owen into an agreement for a confederation of three ethnic republics. It included the Bosnia-Herzegovina presidency members, Mate Boban and Karadzic. After ten days, agreement was won from the Serbs and Croats, but Izetbegovic stuck with hard-liners Ejup Ganic and military chief Rasim Delic and refused to return to Geneva. The new Bosnia-Herzegovina would have a council of ministers, a prime minister, a foreign minister and a court to adjudicate constitutional matters. The top positions would rotate between the three entities. Karadzic claimed he was ready to give land and that the Muslims would have forty towns. With the Serbs and the Croats drawing the map, Tudjman said that the Muslim side would have an area surrounding Sarajevo, land to the northwest and the Bihac pocket. For his part, Izetbegovic wanted to hold out for a loose federal state and used fighting with the Serbs as an excuse to stay away. As his army overran Croat-held areas, Izetbegovic also pushed for a lifting of the arms embargo.

10 July 1993. After days of delay, Izetbegovic convinced his Bosnia-Herzegovina rump presidency (the ten-member body did include Croat member, Miro Lasic, and Serb, Miro Lazovic) to agree seven to three to not accept Owen-Stoltenberg. In a speech to his supporters, he said he would ask for a federation, but not three units and not on an ethnic basis. He called it "unacceptable and an ugly option." He praised the US for having a better appreciation of the situation than the EC. The Bosniak leader no doubt believed that the Croats and Serbs would link up with Zagreb and Belgrade, leaving the Muslims with a small state surrounded by stronger antagonists. He also wanted an outlet to the sea; access to the Sava; an undivided Sarajevo; and return of lost territory—a total of over forty percent of Bosnia-Herzegovina.[28]

During this diplomatic impasse (and fighting between Muslims and Croats), US President Clinton and German Chancellor Kohl bluntly told Zagreb that it would be punished economically if they and the Serbs carved up Bosnia-Herzegovina. Later in the month, Izetbegovic stated that he was willing to return to the negotiating table. Finally, at the end of July, the parties returned to Geneva. Compromise language offered by Owen-Stoltenberg that proposed Bosnia-Herzegovina become a "union of three republics" was accepted by all. The problem now was to agree on the map, the actual division of territory.

4–5 August 1993. Izetbegovic pulled out of Geneva after the BSA took the heights of Mounts Igman and Bjelasnica above Sarajevo. Karadzic agreed to turn the areas over to UNPROFOR to prevent the Bosniaks from taking them. This was done and tripartite (Serb, Croat, Muslim) military agreements were signed in anticipation of a political breakthrough at Geneva.

20 August 1993. After intense talks, Owen-Stoltenberg presented a comprehensive peace package (including maps) and requested that all sides consult with their assemblies and meet in ten days for a final conference. The Croats quickly officially proclaimed their Croat Republic of Herzeg-Bosna. Meeting now at Pale, the Bosnian Serbs voted 55–14 for the agreement (three abstained). The Muslim-dominated assembly in Sarajevo voted for more talks, but against the agreement in its present form. In effect, they rejected it.

8 September 1993. At the White House in Washington, US President Clinton advised visiting Alija Izetbegovic to return to Geneva in the expectation that US pressure on the Serbs and Croats would win more territorial concessions favorable to Sarajevo.

9–10 September 1993. Croat HVO overran the Serb-held villages of Divoselo, Citluk and Pocitelj near Gospic. The BSA responded with artillery in the Karlovac sector. In Banya Luka, BSA troops and officers demanded improved conditions and an end to profiteering. By mid-month, Izetbegovic had met separately with Tudjman and the Serb Momcilo Krajisnik and expressed his desire to make a deal.

20–29 September 1993. After all parties had convened aboard HMS *Invincible* in the Adriatic (including US envoy Charles Redman and Russian diplomat Vitaly Churkin), Izetbegovic stated he had to put the plan to his assembly. As it stood, it was rejected sixty-nine to eleven.

1–2 October 1993. Mate Granic of Croatia, meeting at Neum, and the Serbs at Banya Luka, withdrew all concessions that had been on offer to Sarajevo.

21–22 October 1993. Following the convening of 400 delegates at Velika Kladusa (Bihac pocket) under Fikret Abdic to proclaim an "Autonomus Province of West Bosnia," Abdic met in Zagreb with the Bosnia-Herzegovina Croat leader Mate Boban and Croat president Tudjman. The next day, Abdic went to Belgrade and signed a pact with Karadzic and Milosevic. Clearly a move was afoot to undercut Izetbegovic. Many Muslims with Abdic took up arms against the Bosniak 5th Corps.

2 November 1993. After fitful UN-sponsored talks between Croatia and Srpska Krajina, the two sides met alone in Oslo. Tudjman said the Serbs could have full autonomy where they were in a majority.

17 November 1993. An international court for war crimes in ex-Yugoslavia opened at The Hague with 30 judges and some 300 staff.

25 November 1993. Expressing bitterness and frustration, Lord Owen accused the US of fostering a dominant Muslim state in Bosnia-Herzegovina.

29–30 November 1993. Owen-Stoltenberg reconvened at Geneva with an even larger cast of invitees (UNPROFOR, UNHCR, the Red Cross).

21–22 December 1993. At Geneva, the Croat and Serb sides agreed on a 17 percent Croat, 33.3 percent Muslim, 49.7 percent Serb division of Bosnia-Herzegovina.

20–26 December 1993. At the initiative of the Islamic countries, the UN general assembly passed a resolution condemning primarily the Serbs and secondly the Croats for war in Bosnia-Herzegovina, and called for the lifting of the arms embargo—109 voted for, fifty-seven abstained (including all permanent members of the Security Council, except the US, and all EU members). In Dubai, the Organization of the Islamic Conference urged the UN Security Council to end the arms embargo.

5–10 January 1994. Bosnia-Herzegovina Prime Minister Haris Silajdzic and Foreign Minister Mate Granic of Croatia met in Vienna and agreed on an end to hostilities between their two sides. Tudjman and Izetbegovic then met in Bonn. The latter refused to agree to the plan, but did agree to a general ceasefire.

11 January 1994. After two days at Brussels, NATO again placed air units at the disposal of the UN to protect safe areas in Bosnia-Herzegovina. The UN Secretary General Boutros Boutros-Ghali alerted NATO that he might call on them to open Tuzla airport and protect convoys into Srebrenica and Zepa. British General Michael Rose became the new commander of UNPROFOR.

18–19 January 1994. At Geneva, side agreements were made between the parties that would become undone with changed circumstances.

31 January 1994. Having said earlier that it was withdrawing its offer of 33.3 percent of Bosnia-Herzegovina to the Bosniak Muslims, the Bosnian Serbs called for a general mobilization of its population.

5 February 1994. A large explosion took place at Markale market in Sarajevo, killing 68 and wounding almost 200. It was reported by the press as a 120mm mortar fired from Serbian lines. UNPROFOR could not fix responsibility. The world community blamed the BSA despite the unusual aspects to the tragedy. The UN threatened air strikes as the Serbs pulled back their heavy weapons twenty kilometers.[29]

26 February 1994. At US urging, Prime Minister Haris Silajdzic of Bosnia-Herzegovina, Croat Foreign Minister Mate Granic and Kresimir Zubak of Herzeg-Bosna met in New York to discuss proposals for federation.

2 March 1994. After four days of talks in Washington, the same representatives signed a preliminary agreement establishing a Muslim-Croat federation of cantons under a central government.

18 March 1994. US President Bill Clinton, his senior officials, along with Croat President Franjo Tudjman and Bosnia-Herzegovina President Alija Izetbegovic signed agreements at the White House on federation. It would give the Muslims four cantons, the Croats two, and two were to be mixed. Its proposed boundaries included fifty-eight percent of prewar Bosnia-Herzegovina.[30]

19 March 1994. The UN Secretary General reported that operations in Bosnia-Herzegovina had cost US$1.6 billion, 79 UNPROFOR dead and 924 wounded.

7–11 April 1994. The UN Security Council condemned continued ethnic cleansing by Serbs at Banya Luka and Prijedor and warned the BSA to call off its attack on Gorazde. Over two days, NATO aircraft made limited attacks on BSA forces at Gorazde. The BSA did pull back, although General Ratko Mladic was furious.

12 May 1994. The US Senate voted fifty-one to forty-nine to lift the embargo on arms for Bosnia-Herzegovina. It also voted to press for UN and Allied approval.

23 May 1994. With Owen-Stoltenberg stalled, the US, UK, France, Germany, and Russia asserted their leadership much in the manner of the European powers of the nineteenth century in an attempt to find a solution to the conflict. This Contact Group came up with a new plan that gave the Croat-Muslim federation fifty-one percent, the Serbs forty-nine. Initially, Izetbegovic rejected this proposed division. Owen-Stoltenberg continued to convene under its own momentum.[31]

9 June 1994. The US House of Representatives voted 244 for and 178 against lifting the arms embargo for Bosnia-Herzegovina.

29 June 1994. The Contact Group announced that it would present its plan to all of the parties concerned. The plan was ratified by their respective foreign ministers at Geneva on 5 July. It was further agreed that Bosnia-Herzegovina remain a single state within its borders.

10 July 1994. The Contact Group plan was adopted by the G-7 plus Russia meeting at Naples. Thus, the major powers backed it.

30 July 1994. At Geneva, the Contact Group welcomed acceptance by the Croat-Muslim federation and urged the Serb side to agree. With Belgrade urging acceptance, Pale insisted it needed changes.

4 August 1994. After debate over the plan, Belgrade said it was cutting the Bosnian Serbs off from all material aid except food, clothing and medicine. This time they meant it.[32]

5 August 1994. NATO aircraft hit BSA positions around Sarajevo after heavy weapons were removed from an UNPROFOR storage site. The UN Secretary General tersely suggested that NATO take over in Bosnia-Herzegovina (using its own troops) since the Contact Group plan replaced Owen-Stoltenberg. More than just a little pique was apparent.

10–11 August 1994. The US announced a possible lifting of a few sanctions against Yugoslavia, if it sealed its border with the Bosnian Serbs. President Clinton stated that he would request the UN Security Council to lift the arms embargo in Bosnia-Herzegovina if the Serbs didn't agree to the Contact Group plan by 15 October.

21 August 1994. Bosniak forces took Velika Kladusa, driving out Fikret Abdic's men. Some 60,000 Muslim refugees poured into the adjoining territory under control of Srpska Krajina.

27–28 August 1994. A referendum on the Contact Group plan by the Bosnian Serbs rejected it by ninety-six percent. They wanted a new map.

3 September 1994. The Russian Foreign Minister Andre Kozyrev said they would pull out their peacekeeping forces in Bosnia-Herzegovina if the arms embargo was lifted. In NATO, only the US and Germany were for it. The US was also in a minority in the UN Security Council.

26 September 1994. Presidents Clinton and Izetbegovic met in New York and agreed to retain the arms embargo for another six months. Izetbegovic said additional arms were needed, but admitted that a strategic balance now existed between his Bosniaks and the BSA.[33]

5 October 1994. While placing added sanctions on the Bosnian Serbs, the UN Security Council restored Yugoslav air traffic (no cargo), participation in sport and cultural events, and limited Adriatic ferry traffic—to be extended at intervals.

15 November 1994. The US announced its intention to pull out of the monitoring of ship traffic bound for ports in ex-Yugoslavia.

16 November 1994. Abdic forces retook Velika Kadusa and 30,000 Muslim refugees returned to this pocket within a pocket. In days, NATO aircraft hit an airport in Krajina to pressure the Serbs to ease off their counter-offensive against Bihac. The Bosnian Serbs were also bombed after they tracked two UK planes. The Serbs were condemned by the UN for attacking the Bihac safe area.

2 December 1994. After months of talks, agreement was reached between Croatia and the Krajina Serbs regarding restoring water, power, an oil pipeline, and rail and road traffic facilities. It was co-signed by the US and Russian ambassadors to Croatia.

18–31 December 1994. Former US President Jimmy Carter discussed "the plan" with all concerned. A four-month ceasefire was set.

11 January 1995. Bosnian Serb leader Radovan Karadzic said that he accepted the Contact Group plan as a basis for negotiations. The next day, Croat President Tudjman announced that UNPROFOR's mandate in Croatia would not be renewed after 31 March.

30 January 1995. The draft plan of the so-called "Z-4" to end hostilities was put to Zagreb and the Krajina Serbs. The latter said they would not consider it unless UNPROFOR stayed in the UNPA. Srpska Krajina subsequently decided to break off economic talks. Neither were the Croats happy. They claimed that Z-4 broke up Croatia. Inconclusive talks dragged on through winter and on into the spring.

13 February 1995. The Hague tribunal cited charges against twenty-one Serbs accused of crimes that had occurred in Bosnia-Herzegovina detention camps.

12 March 1995. After meeting with US Vice-President Al Gore in Copenhagen, Tudjman agreed to extend UNPROFOR's Croatia mandate.

16 March 1995. The first anniversary of the Croat-Muslim pact was celebrated in New York. Alija Izetbegovic visited Germany. He met with Chancellor Kohl and spoke before the German Bundestag.

20 March 1995. UN spokesman Fred Ekhard said that the ceasefire in Bosnia-Herzegovina had been violated by Bosniak attacks near Tuzla. The Serbs responded by sending mortar rounds into the town.

30 March 1995. Upon expiry of UNPROFOR in Croatia amid administrative reorganization, the UN Security Council adopted language that changed the UN's role to support Croatia's territorial integrity no matter whether Croats were a majority, or a minority. Croatian Foreign Minister Mate Granic expressed Zagreb's satisfaction.

25 April 1995. The Hague Tribunal stated it would examine the roles of Radovan Karadzic and Ratko Mladic regarding war crimes.

28 April 1995. The UN Security Council announced that UNCRO (UN Confidence Restoration Operation) in Croatia (ex-UNPROFOR) would reduce its personnel from 12,000 to 8,750.

1 May 1995. Croat HVO attacked Sector West (western Slavonia), coming in through a UN-controlled buffer zone. Tactical surprise carried the day. The Krajina Serbs hit Zagreb with rockets, killing four persons. Several hundred

Serb civilians died during and after this operation. The UN voiced criticism, but did little.[34]

9 May 1995. The Hague Tribunal opened investigations into Croatian ethnic cleansing of Muslims in the Lasva Valley of Bosnia-Herzegovina in 1992–3.

24 May 1995. BSA and Bosniak artillery were engaged at Sarajevo. After the expiry of the deadline, NATO aircraft hit Serb targets.

26–27 May 1995. UN special envoy Yasushi Akashi ordered Bosniaks and Serbs to return their heavy weapons to storage. Two hours before the deadline, NATO aircraft hit targets at Pale. BSA General Mladic took UNPROFOR soldiers hostage, claiming NATO was biased.

2 June 1995. The BSA began to release UNPROFOR personnel. Near Mrkonjic-Grad, Serb air defense downed a NATO F-16. USAF Captain Scott Grady was extracted by a special air unit after six days.

5 June 1995. The Croat HVO began a probing attack in Sector South.

16 June 1995. The UN authorized (with US-French-UK urging) the establishment of a well-armed Rapid Reaction Force (RRF). Many in UN-NATO believed that UN and aid personnel might have to withdraw from Bosnia-Herzegovina if the cooperation of the warring sides soon collapsed.

30 June 1995. The German Bundestag agreed with the government's decision to deploy German air and medical units to ex-Yugoslavia.

11 July 1995. The BSA took the Srebrenica safe area, rounding up thousands of Muslim civilians, and a Dutch UNPROFOR battalion.[35]

21 July 1995. Stoltenberg-Bildt met in London. It urged a return to negotiations and warned Pale not to attack the Goradze safe area.

22 July 1995. Tudjman and Izetbegovic with senior officials from the Bosnia-Herzegovina federation met at Split and agreed to coordinate military operations, particularly around Bihac.

24 July 1995. Forces of the UN-RRF deployed on Mount Igman to protect UNPROFOR personnel still assigned to the Sarajevo area.

25 July 1995. The BSA took the Zepa safe area, driving out some 15,000 Muslim civilians. Atrocities took place as at Srebrenica.[36]

28 July 1995. The Croat HVO overran Grahovo and Glamoc in Krajina. The Serbs began to prepare for a possible attack. To the north, they agreed, under UN pressure, to disengage from Bihac.

3 August 1995. Srpska Krajina Prime Minister Milan Babic said from Belgrade that the RSK was ready to negotiate with Croatia on a modified Z-4 plan, which had been tabled by mediators. He said the RSK agreed to include the economic measures that had been discussed in the winter. At the venue of the talks in Geneva, Croat Ivica Pasalic concluded the day's discussions by rejecting Thorvald Stoltenberg's seven-point proposals with the argument that an additional paragraph should be added citing the proposed peaceful integration of the occupied territories into Croatia.[37]

4 August 1995. At 0500 hours, Croatian forces opened a ground and air attack against RSK units on a wide front in western Krajina. Every fifteen minutes, Zagreb radio repeated President Tudjman's speech wherein he accused RSK of refusing to accept reintegration with Croatia. Tudjman told the Serbs to surrender and to be prepared to face trial (to be pardoned, or jailed). At the outset of the attack, NATO aircraft hit two Serb radars that had locked on to the orbiting aircraft. Actually, the only UN-NATO casualties were UNPROFOR (a dead Dane and two Poles) soldiers shot by the Croats. Carl Bilt condemned the attack and accused the Croats of negotiating in bad faith. The US "regretted" Zagreb's resort to force.[38]

5 August 1995. In the face of light resistance, as Serb civilians and soldiers took to the roads in retreat, the Croatian HVO were in Knin by 1230 hours. As a diversionary tactic, the HVO opened a second front by mounting probing attacks in Sector East (Baranja, Slavonia, Western Strem). In Bosnia-Herzegovina, the Bosnian Serbs were divided as to what to do. Karadzic tried to take direct command of the BSA and wanted to move forces to the Krajina. General Mladic and eighteen of his generals refused to accept Karadzic's action and rejected getting involved in the Krajina campaign. After a week, Karadzic climbed down from his position and restored Mladic's command. As a further indication of dissension amongst the Serbs, RSK Prime Minister Milan Babic accused President Milan Martic of ordering the evacuation of Srpska Krajina without putting up a real fight.[39]

7 August 1995. Croat Defense Minister Gojko Susak announced that Operation Storm was over, stating they had sustained 118 dead and 620 wounded (no apology for the UN deaths). That day the Bosniak 5th Corps forces retook Velika Kladusa from Abdic's fighters. It was reported by UNPROFOR that the Croat HVO and elements of the 5th Corps fired on a column of 12,000 retreating Krajina Serbs near Bojna.

12–13 August 1995. US National Security Advisor Anthony Lake (in Europe to advise allies of US aims in ex-Yugoslavia) met Andrei Kozyrev at Sochi. The two sides were reportedly close together in their views, except that Moscow wanted more sanctions on Belgrade lifted. The US continued to use sanctions as leverage.

16–19 August 1995. A team headed by Assistant Secretary of State Richard Holbrooke began intense peace talks in Belgrade, Sarajevo and Zagreb with

Milosevic, Izetbegovic, and Tudjman. In Sarajevo, US special envoy Robert Frazure slid off the road in an UNPROFOR vehicle and was killed.

28 August 1995. A mortar hit Marcale market killing thirty-seven and wounding eighty-six. The Muslim side blamed the BSA. General Mladic denied it and asked for a joint investigation. (UNPROFOR initially stated it was unable to assign responsibility.) Amid argument over the evidence, the BSA was blamed for the tragedy. Mladic's request was rejected.[40]

29 August 1995. As NATO air strikes against the Serbs were about to get underway, Karadzic led a delegation to Belgrade (including General Mladic) that in the presence of Orthodox Patriarch Pavle, agreed to give authority to Milosevic to end the conflict.[41]

30 August 1995. NATO aircraft hit a wide range of Serb targets. General Mladic responded by shelling three UNPROFOR positions in Sarajevo in retaliation for the air attacks and shelling by RFF artillery. Two NATO aircraft were downed by ground fire. The BSA pulled their heavy weapons back twenty kilometers from Sarajevo by 20 September, but only on condition that the Bosniaks also stopped fighting.[42]

8 September 1995. At Geneva, the foreign ministers of Croatia, Bosnia-Herzegovina and Yugoslavia (representing also the Bosnian Serbs) met with representatives of the Contact Group, plus Carl Bildt, and gave verbal assent to the basic principles for the arrangement of Bosnia-Herzegovina.

26 September 1995. In New York, foreign ministers from Croatia, Bosnia-Herzegovina, and Yugoslavia met with the Contact Group led by Holbrooke and Bildt adopting an agreement for constitutional arrangements in Bosnia-Herzegovina. The agreement provided for holding free elections in both entities when conditions permitted. The Croat-Muslim federation would elect two thirds of the members of the Bosnia-Herzegovina assembly and the Serbs one third. The assembly would be guided by majority rule, provided that one third of the members of each entity had voted. The Bosnia-Herzegovina presidency would operate in the same manner. However, any decision could be blocked by a one-third minority if the assembly of that entity voted against it by a two-thirds majority.

29 September 1995. The UN Security Council criticized Croatia's decision to abolish refugee status for about 100,000 Muslims in its country. The UN also criticized its new laws concerning Serb properties in Krajina that amounted to confiscation.

3 October 1995. Stoltenberg and the US ambassador to Croatia met representatives of Strem-Baranja and Croatia at Erdut to discuss transitional arrangements aimed at reintegrating it with Croatia. Several meetings were required before an agreement was reached.

5 October 1995. After several days of talks led by Holbrooke, a Bosnia-Herzegovina ceasefire agreement was reached with all parties. Included were provisions for restoration of gas-power to Sarajevo, free road passage between Sarajevo and Goradze, and the exchange of prisoners. The ceasefire aspect was finally signed 11 October. All sides attempted to position their forces to their own advantage. Violations occurred and it did not take hold until 20 October.

13 November 1995. The Hague Tribunal brought charges against six Croats accused of committing war crimes against Muslims in the Lasva valley (Vitez, Busovaca, and Zenica) from May 1992 to May 1993.

20 November 1995. After twenty days of seclusion at a US air base at Dayton, Ohio, all parties to the conflict initialed a general framework agreement for Bosnia-Herzegovina. Underpinning the document were the UN Charter, the Helsinki final act, as well as OSCE guidelines.

8–9 December 1995. An international peace conference concerning ex-Yugoslavia was held in London with forty-three nations and twelve international organizations participating. It dealt with implementation of the Dayton agreement and requirements for postwar reconstruction. Also present was the Organization of the Islamic Conference, which also attended the subsequent signing of the Dayton agreement at Paris.

14 December 1995. The Dayton Accord with twelve annexes was signed in Paris, ending four and a half years of war in Bosnia-Herzegovina and Croatia. The next day, the UN Security Council authorized the establishment of NATO's Implementation Force (IFOR) and the appointment of Carl Bildt as High Representative for Bosnia. NATO began to deploy IFOR for an initial twelve-month period, taking over from UNPROFOR.[43]

21 December 1995. The UN Security Council condemned the Bosnian Serbs for killings at Srebrenica, Zepa, Banya Luka, and elsewhere.

Ethnic groups in Yugoslavia, pre-1991

0   100
kms

SLOVENIA
Ljubljana   Zagreb

CROATIA

VOJVODINA

Novi Sad

Belgrade

BOSNIA

Sarajevo

SERBIA

Sanzak

MONTE-
NEGRO

Pristina

Podgorica

KOSOVO

Skopje

MACEDONIA

	Macedonians		Serbs
	Albanians		Croats
	Hungarians		Muslims
	Bulgarians		Slovenes
	Romanians, Slovaks		Montenegrins

Roma gypsies not shown
Based on SFRY 1981 census data

BOSNIA-HERZEGOVINA

SERBIA

Pljevlja

Berane

Niksic

Kotor

Cetinje

Prevlaka

Boka Kotorska

Podgorica

Adriatic Sea

Bar

Ulcinj

ALBANIA

Albanian

Serbian

Mitrovica
Mitrovicë

Peć
Pejë

Priština
Prishtinë

KOSOVO
KOSOVË

Djakovica
Gjakovë

Uroševac
Ferizaj

Gnjilane
Gilan

Prizren
Prizren

Contested Kosovo

Chapter 6

Serbia's "Addams Family"

Belgrade and Beyond: January 1993–June 1998

In response to Slovenia's and Croatia's separatist moves towards independence, Serbian president Slobodan Milosevic asserted that he would act to protect Serbs living in the other republics. In practical terms this meant providing arms and logistical support to the Serbs in the Krajina and Slavonia who were fast becoming disadvantaged minorities at risk. Subsequently, it held true for Bosnia as well. The underlying idea, given the disintegration of the SFRY—and without calling it Greater Serbia—posited that the ethnic-Serbs, the leading formative people of the original Yugoslavia of 1918, should all live securely under one roof.[1]

Milosevic had recognized and seized on Serb resentment and discontent as early as the late 1980s, for events had conspired to put him at the very center of resurgent Serb nationalism. He had been quick to exploit this new assertiveness first voiced by Serbian intellectuals and then by the larger population, using it as a lever to power.

By mid-1989, his "anti-bureaucratic" coup against the ossified leadership of the communist party of Serbia neared completion. Building on unquestioned popular support, he created the mass-based SPS and moved to reintegrate Kosovo and Vojvodina firmly under the control of Belgrade.

By so doing, under the federal constitution, Serbia would retain the votes of Kosovo and Vojvodina in the presidency and, with like-minded supporters soon to take over in Montenegro, he could command four of eight votes in what was supposedly the country's most powerful institution. This step would give the more than ten million citizens of Serbia and Montenegro a predominant political voice vis-à-vis the other republics. And, if the large Serbian communities in Bosnia and Croatia were taken into consideration, Milosevic was destined to emerge as the strongest leader whether the republics remained together as a federation, or ultimately went their separate ways. This was both a careful calculation and an extremely risky gamble.[2]

It all came back to Kosovo, for as communism was collapsing, the Serbs looked to their past, back to their history for renewal and reassurance that the threads of their old traditions still remained intact in songs, epic poetry, myths and the deeds of kings and warriors. The sacred ark of its people had been borne by the Serbian Orthodox church down through the ages. Its prayers, bread and salt had consecrated Serbia's leaders. Milosevic, a skilful, tough apparatchik, assumed the mantle of the dead King Miliutin.

For a time it went well. In the early winter of 1993 in Belgrade, the streets hummed with the flow of traffic. Taxis, streetcars, and buses made their rounds. The hotels and public buildings were heated. Passers-by wore warm jackets, woolens and furs to ward off the cold. Food shops were full, as were cafes and restaurants. Along the Kneza Mihaila, the smart boutiques still displayed items from Paris, London, and Rome. However, unemployment and inflation had shot up, along with a roaring black market. People queued up outside banks trying to determine the best way to protect their savings. In time, many would be wiped out, while newly wealthy profiteers involved in smuggling, sanctions-busting, and the war effort would pile up fortunes. Some were clearly Milosevic's men.[3]

A year later, the Serbs were hurting. Respectable-looking elderly men and women picked through the trash looking for food, or something of value. Men in old suits, frayed collars and carefully knotted ties—most often wearing worn athletic shoes—took care to replace bin lids. Out of embarrassment, the women avoided eye contact as they examined an item and carefully placed it in a shopping bag.

Streten Marinkovic was not one of the aged who were to die because they could no longer obtain dialysis. In his early sixties, he was still healthy. However, the American company that had sold heavy equipment had closed three years earlier and he had been jobless ever since. He was clearly worried. He and his wife had used up their savings and had sold whatever they could. He asked, "Why did Washington insist on blaming them for the outbreak of war?" His voice ached with sadness, adding, "The one country we truly admire is America!" It was beyond his comprehension! There, in Belgrade, two million ethnic Serbs, Croats, Albanians, Hungarians, Romanians, Bulgarians, Muslims, and Roma gypsies struggled to survive.

Elsewhere in Serbia and Montenegro the situation was not as bad, but still the cumulative effect of sanctions was to reduce living standards by half, to about US$1,250 per capita annually. Productivity had plunged, so that even if sanctions were removed, it would take Yugoslavia until the year 2010 to attain the same level as 1990. While the nation had been collectively denied its future, individuals were being denied life itself. At University Children's Hospital on Tirsova, Dr. Slavko Simeunovic remembered Milica who was born with transposition of the heart arteries. If she had undergone an operation at three or four months, she would have been fine. However, he explained, they could no longer do extra-corporal circulation, operate the hospital's respirator, or obtain special medicines. She died. Dr. Zoran Milosavljevic said that each order for medicine, supplies, or a piece of equipment had to be approved by the UN sanctions committee. It was supposed to take ten to fifteen days, but, in practice, it takes months, if it is ever approved at all. Besides lacking money, orders got hung up on foreign exchange problems. This had affected the availability of cytotoxins for cancer. Diagnostic antibodies were often unavailable. They could no longer store bone marrow. For some, who were all looked upon equally by a national health service, it meant dying unnecessarily.

Statistics tell the story. After years of decline, infant mortality was up sharply. So was tetanus and polio. Infectious disease rose 142 percent between 1989 and 1993. The number of operations dropped seventy-five percent. For the population at large, psychiatric illness had risen. Dr. Svetomir Bojanin said that due to stress, loss of self-esteem and social dislocation, a sharp rise in adverse behavior had been noted. The overall death rate had gone up by 5,500 persons per year. Some of the aged simply wanted to die and committed suicide. Because of their deplorable condition, many hospitals and clinics would be closed down if they were located in the US. In addition, the medical profession, like all others, had been cut off from the international community and effectively denied scientific and technical data. Prevented from working, some of Yugoslavia's best and brightest talent packed up and left. For those remaining, it will take years to renew contacts abroad given the prejudice that has been built up in the West. Sanctions are a blunt instrument. They affect all, including the forty percent non-Serbian population in what is left of Yugoslavia. It is UN-approved murder!

I also learned that the Yugoslavia no one talked about except in the worst way possible was coping with an influx of over 500,000 refugees, no matter where they had come from, or what their ethnic origin. The United Nations High Commissioner for Refugees (UNHCR) admitted that Yugoslavia's response to the situation was superb and unprecedented. They said that ninety-five percent were living in homes, or apartments, with other families, and that only five percent were in temporary accommodations such as hotels, resorts and camps. This suggested a residual tolerance among most at a time when Serbs in Croatia were still being driven from their jobs and apartments. The refugee numbers were: Serbs–368,000; Muslims–36,000; Croats–10,000; others–46,000. Montenegro had another 44,000. The majority were located in and around Belgrade. UNHCR estimated that another 200,000 remained unregistered and were living with families or friends.[4]

Seventy-four percent of the refugees were from Bosnia and twenty-five percent out of Croatia. Numbers were almost evenly split between eighteen and under, and eighteen and above. Of the latter, the majority were women. At one end, there had been 10,000 new births. At the other, 50,000 were old and infirm and considered at high risk. Sixty percent had been refugees for two and a half years. A majority were professionally qualified, but only fifteen percent had found full-time employment. Nearly half had no source of income (having used up any cash and possessions) and were dependent on their host families, municipalities and religious organizations. Seventy percent of the hosts were related in some way, however distant; ten percent were friends; twenty percent were total strangers. Some of the hosts had themselves been refugees during World War Two. They were old and expected their guests to help them eke out a living. UNHCR, the Red Cross and the Muslim Merhamet organization have been able to provide only limited assistance.

As for living under one roof, almost all were crammed into tight quarters averaging six persons. Sixty-five percent lived as one big family, while thirty-five percent chose to have separate households. The economic situation for all was proving precarious as half of the host families were earning around US$75 a month. Out of that had to come food, medicine, housewares, a little clothing and school supplies. In an amazing forty-four percent of UNHCR cases, the hosts provided all household expenses. Municipalities helped by providing utility subsidies (gas, electric power and water). Of special concern to all were the young to ensure they emerge from the situation as normal children. Host comments quoted by UNHCR were: "I consider it only being human... Everyone has to help out in this mess... One cannot overlook human disaster... When asked, we could not refuse." And these are the same people being systematically vilified by the international community!

I was asked to go to the Zvezdara neighborhood to see how Serbs were donating food and clothing to Muslim refugees from Bosnia. I didn't. But I did visit the large mosque in old Starigrad and I saw Muslims on the street elsewhere. Croatian refugees were less numerous, but have entered Serbia both as families and as members of mixed marriages. I spoke to a Croat woman who had been living in Belgrade since before the war. She said that she could sense that things were not quite the same with her neighbors and work colleagues, but that no one had ill-treated her. In my visits to Belgrade the worst slur I heard about ethnic-Croats was a joke: "If a Serbian invites you to his house for soup, you get soup, meat, potatoes, wine, brandy, and coffee. If a Croat invites you for soup, you're sure to end up just eating soup!"

A Serb taxi driver in his early forties once related how the war had affected him. He was tall and dressed in the athletic warm-ups and sneakers that many in Yugoslavia like to wear. He had been in middle management at a factory that was forced to close down because of the lack of imported spare parts and supplies. Besides driving a cab, he played evenings in a band. While regretting he had to work out of his profession, he said that he was spending more time with his children and had even picked up basketball again. When he learned that I was an American journalist, he told me how he had once driven a woman from CNN television around for two days. He said they had talked to refugees, hospitals, schools, business offices and to many people right off of the street. She came away with an understanding of life under sanctions and was convinced of the essential decency of most. She said that she wanted to get a camera crew in and do a story. However, when she discussed it with her boss back in Atlanta, she was told, "That may well be all very interesting, but we can't run that kind of stuff!"

I wondered how this robust, emotional and very proud people would hold up? There were the women, sensibly dressed in coveralls and headscarves, planting flowers at the public buildings and gardens. Municipal workers, some of darker complexions, were out cleaning the streets, but with bright orange jackets and work gloves. Even the walkways under the broad avenues were free of litter and given over to shops and vendors. The people did not appear to be outwardly aggressive. They waited in lines, waited for the lights to change and did not shoulder you aside as people do in Athens. There were sex and "Rambo"-type magazines at the kiosks, but also good book stores that always seemed to have customers. I learned that this is a people not easily pushed around, a people who will stubbornly defend their rights and stand their ground. And surprisingly, I saw very few people actually begging in the streets.

Still, the "situation" and the strain were always there. It was not evident coming north by train, for from the window, a beautiful, lush countryside passed by—the Shumadiya of central Serbia so often depicted in quaint, idyllic paintings where the haystacks are perfectly shaped and the cows fat and contented. The fields were almost always being tended, in either rain or shine. It was very much a family affair, whether with machinery or hand implements.

They worked their smallholdings from sunrise until sunset and over weekends—small houses, small numbers of livestock and small Yugo cars parked in the drive. It was a hardy, Spartan life for young and old alike, but the physical exertion made for strong bodies in a people who are close to nature. Most of the men liked to hunt and fish. Young boys, devoid of "designer" labels, swam in rivers or ponds, or played soccer. The girls were usually slim and often beautiful. The womenfolk were the real keepers of hearth and home. Almost all go to church—and special were the baptisms, weddings, and name and feast days. There was much wine, meat and merriment. Village men didn't pale at the sight of blood and slit the throats of their farm animals with one swift, easy stroke. They remained the backbone of the Serb people, and Milosevic's main support.

Belgrade had advantages and problems like cities everywhere. However, the war had accentuated the problems (big city SPS machine politics; people with hallucinatory ideas or solutions; and crime and corruption). On the day that you run into well-scrubbed boy and girl scouts out orienteering historical sites, a gang member might be found riddled by a Kalashnikov. Its ambience is Balkan. The brilliant, surrealistic film *Underground* by Bosnian Muslim director, Emir Kusturica, went out on the artistic edge to depict a Yugoslavian society descending into the insanity of civil war—a demimonde where Marko and Blacky operate amidst a variety of characters, good and bad. Most journalists have likewise fixated on the tragic, the sensational and the bizarre that the war has thrown up. The once peaceful neighbors do appear homicidal, and, with a little imagination, one can envisage the "Addams family" living in that big gloomy house on the corner who are locked in a bitter quarrel with those Croats and Muslims who live just across the back alley. There are any number of stories of how it all began![5]

Slobodan Milosevic and his wife and lifelong companion, Dr. Mira Markovic, unquestionably ruled over the rambunctious "family" that lived under their roof, some of whom are scary, weird, or really comical characters. The place is a ramshackle affair with rooms filled with friends, relations and unexpected guests—a creaky staircase leads up to the attic, and another goes down to a deep, dark cellar. Some see ghosts, have opened old trunks and are all dressed up as hajduk bandit heroes, or Chetnik guerrilla fighters like their great grandfathers. Few venture to the cellar that no one talks about! But an analogy can be carried too far. Slobodan, "Slobo" to his friends and supporters, was a formidable leader who somehow managed to survive the problems of permanent crisis, meting out rewards and punishment as need be, often skillfully controlling or channeling the sound and fury of challengers and dissenters in ways that even served to increase his grip on power. At least it certainly seemed so at the time. Milosevic was almost always obdurate and implacable, a very serious politician.

Mira Markovic keeps her hair jet black and wears the same color. She has a doctorate in sociology from the University of Belgrade. Dr. Mira, as many call her, heads the United Yugoslav Left (JUL) party. Its numbers are small, but its influence is considerable because of her very intense, intertwined relationship with Milosevic and frequent participation in talks with his political intimates. Mira expressed her ideas, observations and concerns in a column in the mass circulation *Duga* magazine and, periodically, has had them published in book form. She advocates a vague, ill-defined communism and thinks that the reconfiguration of Yugoslavia (all of the former republics) need be only a few years away. Because JUL has failed to articulate a program to address the worldwide impact of a liberal market economy and globalization, many think that Dr. Mira's musings are nostalgic at best. Her critics add that for anyone to say that South Slav unity is just around the corner is to betray an inexcusable lack of awareness of the depth of mistrust and hatred that now exists and to be oblivious of the years of slaughter. Still, Dr. Mira is also very, very serious.

President Milosevic and Dr. Mira were then in their mid-fifties. Both have rounded faces and that solid Slavic look. Much has been made of Milosevic's even features, his shock of gray hair, and brown eyes that leap out of the TV set, or off political posters to convince millions. Mira, with straight bangs, out of feminist convictions eschews the make-up, furs, and jewelry so beloved by Balkan women. Usually in black, she looks as if she is in mourning.

Rumors and stories abound, for it seems that the two are something of a mystery. Both came from Pozarevac south of Belgrade and both have tragic childhood backgrounds. Mira's parents were Partisans during World War Two.

One account has her mother executed by the Nazis, another by the Partisans themselves as a traitor. Mira's father abandoned her in infancy and did not acknowledge the relationship until many years later. Slobodan's father is said to have been a failed priest who also committed suicide. Years afterward, his mother did the same. Mira denies this is what happened. Whatever the actual truth, the two were childhood sweethearts and became inseparable.

Neither of the Milosevics mix much with the people. Their public appearances are well staged. While they do have children, neither the daughter nor the son has added luster to the family's image as leaders. Marija tried journalism, but seldom wrote. Then she was a disk jockey with her own radio station. Later, she had a disco. A rumor has her flying to Tokyo with a suitcase full of deutsche marks during the war. Her conduct was scandalous. Marko, the son, is said to be addicted to fast cars and loves guns. He supposedly owns a nightclub. For reasons unexplained, Marko escaped doing his military service. To people living a life of privation, they appear as willful, spoiled brats. Consequently, many ridiculed Dr. Mira when she wrote of being so terribly worried when Marko left to holiday in Salonika wearing a T-shirt, without a jacket to keep him warm. This was when thousands were dying in Bosnia or fleeing their homes with only what they could carry. People were asking, is she really a sociologist? Did she really do all of the scholarship to earn her PhD? One thing is certain. She often nailed people in her column just before they fell from power!

Multiparty politics in Yugoslavia is a rough and tumble affair. There are dozens of parties of all political stripes, but, since 1990, the scene has been dominated by Milosevic's SPS, which is a mixed crowd representing essentially "establishment" interests. While nationalists within the party have a viewpoint, the party was backed at the outset by the state corporations, business and banking, the rural population and the pensioners, undergirded, of course, by a purged JNA, a massive paramilitary police and a not overly obtrusive internal security service. SPS members view it as their "apparat" or "their thing." People have entered the front door and left by the back, or by a window. Milan Panic, Dobrica Cosic and a number of generals come to mind. The regime worked, but increasingly in a shambolic fashion. For, as it still faced a stiff outer wall of sanctions that effectively denies it access to international finance and investment, life has been a make-do, roll with the punches affair. As such, politicians have reinvented their personae according to changing circumstances.

The *enfants terribles* of Serbian politics are Vojislav Seselj and Vuk Draskovic, two brash demagogues who, as intellectuals, are more akin to the

Katzenjammer Kids. Of the two, Seselj is clearly dangerous. They were both raised in the cradle of communism, but turned to fervid (Draskovic) and rabid (Seselj) Serb nationalism. Together, they founded the Chetnik movement and traveled to the US and Canada in 1990 in an effort to drum up support from exile elements. Seselj was anointed "Vojvoda," or "Duke" (the equal of field marshal in military terminology!) by Momcilo Dujic, one of the few living Chetnik leaders to have survived World War Two. However, he and Vuk (which means "Wolf") immediately quarreled over money collected, or pledged, which the new Vojvoda says ended up in the hands of Draskovic's wife, Danica. The two broke up, with Seselj forming the Serbian Radical Party (SRS) and the volunteer Chetnik paramilitary organization. Draskovic set up the Serbian Renewal Movement (SPO) and the Serbian Guards. Both wrapped themselves in the trappings of bygone military regalia, which attracted a claque of bearded "kapetanos" who did the same. The effect was bizarre!

Seselj, a gangling, paunchy giant of six feet four inches, with short sandy hair, spectacles and a hair-trigger temper escaped obscurity because the communist system assisted him in obtaining a PhD. His thesis is verbosely entitled the "Political Essence of Militarism and Fascism, A Contribution to the Analysis of Marxian Criticism of the Political Forms of Civic Democracy." At Sarajevo University, his constant clamoring that the constitutional order was unfair to the Serbs resulted in 1984 in a show trial and an eight-year jail term, of which he served twenty months. Seselj moved to Belgrade and joined its small, not remarkably repressed, dissident community. By age thirty-two, he had already ditched communism and was searching for a satisfactory replacement. This led him to rediscover the Chetniks. For a time, he even espoused the return of the monarchy. An ultra-nationalist extremist and an aggressive opportunist, Seselj took the name of Serbia's respected pre-World War Two Radical Party for his own. And, when the Chetnik militia was setup, Seselj had an instrument out on the cutting edge of Greater Serbia, as well as the armed muscle to back up his arguments!

Besides his linkage to Chetnik atrocities in Croatia and Bosnia, Seselj has advocated taking over all of Bosnia-Herzegovina and much of Croatia (up to the Karlobag-Ogulin-Virovitica line), a mirror image of the Croatian Party of Rights. At one point, he talked of the need to eject some 300,000 Albanians from Kosovo and 100,000 Croats. Today he accepts minorities, but only if they agree to a strongly centralized government. He also disputes a Macedonia and a Montenegro separate from Serbia. His party newspaper, *Greater Serbia*, blamed Milosevic for the loss of Krajina, the isolation of the Bosnian Serbs, and for accepting a Dayton agreement that he claims is a sell-out. Seselj's tactics are insults, unfounded accusations, backstabbing and outrageous heckling in parliament. Seselj has spat at fellow deputies, dribbled water on them and has snapped microphone wires after being cut off for violating the time limit, or topic. He packs a pistol and has engaged in any number of public scuffles. If he ever came to power, Seselj would try to march the Serbs off to feed his crazed fantasies!

Outrageous though his behavior is, no one has accused Seselj of trying to enrich himself. As a former mayor of the Zemun municipality, he had the reputation of running a clean local administration. And, if he wears a shiny suit in parliament, he often mingles in shirtsleeves with his estimated one million supporters. Unlike most men, he doesn't drink or smoke, and there are no stories of other women in his life. He is huge, but ungainly. A photo of the Vojvoda in helmet and combat fatigues would be comic, except for what he represents. Other photos of him in Chetnik outfits are ludicrous to the point of being embarrassing. Yet, many have voted for this monster. At the outset of the war, Milosevic used the Chetniks in Croatia. As a reward, Milosevic permitted Seselj to enter parliament in 1992 by running a weaker candidate for the Belgrade-Rakovica by-election. Milosevic's idea was that Seselj would disrupt the opposition, which is exactly what he proceeded to do. Moreover, when the SRS won big in December, Milosevic used Seselj to help dump Panic and Cosic. Then, when Seselj got too big for his boots, Milosevic removed his parliamentary immunity and jailed him for a number of months. A hero to his loyal supporters, who held nightly vigils outside his SRS office until his release, he was permitted to return to his role as parliamentary spoiler. He has since come on to challenge Milosevic's own SPS's popularity as a deputy premier. He is a Frankenstein of Milosevic's own making!

Likewise, Draskovic came up through the communist system. A very intense individual with long, flowing black hair and beard in a Rasputin style, Vuk started out as a journalist for *Tanjug* in the 1960s. Rumor has it that he didn't last long because on a trip to Africa he invented a coup that didn't happen. Nevertheless, he continued to write for other publications (even against the World War Two Chetniks), became ensconced as PR advisor to the president of the YLC trade union confederation, and then turned to fiction to give vent to his considerable powers of imagination. His first novel was called *Noz* (The Knife) and depicts the slaughter of Serbs in Herzegovina (like Seselj, also Draskovic's home) during World War Two. He continued to write of Serbia's tribulations. Then, as the YLC began to collapse under the pressures of separatism, Draskovic threw himself into politics. His resurrection of the Chetniks and the subsequent establishment of the Serbian Guards militia we have already mentioned. Of official support and encouragement during the crucial transitional time when Milosevic was consolidating his SPS, we can only guess. It takes a lot of money to arm and equip thousands of fighters. It didn't all come from abroad![6]

Draskovic, with an admitted flair for the dramatic, brought the claimant to the Yugoslav throne, Prince Alexander Karadjordjevic, to Belgrade expecting to be swept away in adulation. People came out of curiosity, but they seemed to have had enough of kings. Vuk's SPO trailed way back in the polls in December 1990, despite his having depicted his party as being tied to the chariot of the Serbian Orthodox church. With emotionally loaded rhetoric, Vuk reminded listeners that Serbia must extend west to the farthest Serbian grave. Recalling Ustashe and Muslim crimes during World War Two, Draskovic proclaimed the soil containing Serb bones (in Bosnia and Croatia) as "Heavenly Serbia," the spiritual home of the Serbs, which must be physically reunited with Serbia. He used the same powerful simile as the 600-year-old epic poem in which the prophet Elijah asks Prince Lazar to choose between an earthly or heavenly kingdom. Lazar embraced the latter and he and his men fell to the Ottoman Turks at the Field of Blackbirds at Kosovo. Draskovic rallied his Serbian Guards to cross the Drina in order to protect the Serbs from Croatia's new "Ustashe" and the Muslim "Turks" of Bosnia-Herzegovina: "Only the Serbian banner is to be seen on these roads! Should any hand lift any other banner, that hand shall be cut off!" Both Draskovic and Seselj outdid Milosevic with their emotional symbolism, nationalist excess and sheer demagoguery.

There is Vuk, dressed in black, carrying the flag-draped casket of Serbian Guard leader Branislav Matic, who was not killed over in Bosnia, but in front of his Belgrade home in August 1991. By that time, Draskovic had already been jailed for three days for leading the mass anti-Milosevic demonstrations in March. Shouting himself hoarse against Milosevic's "red bandits"—Croats, Muslims and the Kosovo Albanians—Vuk had helped to get the genie out of the bottle. Perhaps it frightened him a little, for in the months to come he began to distance himself from his Serbian Guards and from paramilitary activity in general. This wasn't the stuff of a novel. This was real blood and gore! Yugoslav expert Dusko Doder once called Draskovic the Jekyll and Hyde of Serbian politics. He asserts that Vuk is very changeable—reasonable and extreme by turns. However, Draskovic eventually moderated his talk about a Greater Serbia and conceded the impossibility of separating out the Croats, Muslims and Serbs without violence. He went over to the other extreme by suggesting ethnic cantons for the whole of Yugoslavia in some sort of federation. He would break it all up into tiny bits, with a constitutional monarch for the Serbs!

As the war burned on, Vuk and Danica's SPO formed coalitions with other opposition groups, but were muffled by Milosevic's monopoly of the media. In June 1993, the SPO and others were again back in the streets. A demonstration turned into a riot. A policeman died and thirty people were injured. Both were jailed and roughed up while in prison. Facing a stiff sentence if tried, Vuk went on a hunger strike and gained attention abroad. France's president, François Mitterrand, sent his redoubtable Danielle to Belgrade and protests came in from other quarters. Already being castigated daily by a hostile international community over the war, Milosevic pardoned the couple to defuse the issue. A very pale Vuk, with a dramatically placed bandage on his head, waved from his hospital bed. The month in jail ended in a victory of sorts, for now the couple had celebrity status and traveled to meet Western political leaders. Vuk even attended a prayer breakfast with US President Clinton in Washington. The Draskovics had survived the cellar!

In late October of 1994, the weather in Belgrade was still balmy and beautiful. Dragomir and his bosom buddy, Dusan Davidovic, were waiting at the Washington, a definitely downscale eatery just off from Skadarlija. It was Serbian rules. He who invites pays. The table was already covered with dishes when I sat down and the white wine was both cold and good. The kebabs, fried peppers and *mutchkalitsa* liver stew were fine, and followed by more wine. Dusan, or "David," as he is called, is also an academic. Bearded, big armed, broad-chested and well over six feet tall, he would have made a great football linebacker in his younger days.

As I had arrived from Pristina, he told how in 1981 he was doing his JNA service and had been sent to Kosovo to maintain order after several days of demonstrations by the Albanians. Everyone was on edge, but David said they had strict orders not to use force. He said it was a new experience to be jeered, cursed and spat at. However, it was decided to hold a soccer match to show the JNA's goodwill. After about five minutes into the game, the Albanians started screaming bloody murder and showered the army players with stones and beer bottles. "They really hated us... They waved Albanian flags and shouted Ko-so-va! Re-pub-lik-a!"

David wore a look of exasperation and launched into a Serb history lesson. We marched through victory, retreat and final victory in World War One. We viewed the end of that conflict, with Serbia holding old Serbia and Macedonia, Bosnia, and Herzegovina, and even some parts of Croatia and Slovenia. Then we invited the Slovenes and Croats in as equal partners, because we trusted them and believed in Yugoslavia and South Slav unity. We saw how they got out from under the Austrians and Hungarians and escaped from paying any war reparations, even though they had fought against the Allies. We took satisfaction in their new-found respectability, for they could now hold their heads high. "Then, they turned on us," said David. He drained his glass and slammed it down in disgust. "And they betrayed us in World War Two!" He drained his glass again. This time the table shook. "You know the rest!" He poured himself another.

Dragomir pulled a gypsy threesome in off of the street. The songs came one after another, songs from Macedonia, from Kosovo. David, Dragomir and others joined in. We poured out wine and shared our food. The trumpet was from Skopje. He had married many times and had twelve children. The trombone was from Nis. The accordion was a youngster from Belgrade. They were all Muslims. As David sang, tears ran down his cheeks. He cried, "They do... they do have souls!"

Pristina was like a town that had lost its soul. It was neither this, nor that, a place of torment, a battlefield. It was as ugly as ever, a civic shambles. The pavements had crumbled. The plaza lights at the Grand Hotel were shattered, bulbs removed. There was another water shortage. Serbs and Albanians alike gathered around the few workable spigots with plastic pails and bottles. From the time under Tito when the Albanians, according to the new constitution of 1974, had been permitted to run Kosovo virtually with the same powers as a republic, the Yugoslav federal government pumped US$1.5 million a day into the province to bring it up to the level of the others. This went on for fifteen years. Most of the money, however, went into the pockets of Albanian provincial officials to build their personal villas and dozens of projects that fed Albanian nationalism, not basic infrastructure that would serve everyone. Instead of good roads and a water system, Kosovo got plenty of tinsel on a grandiose scale. And when given authority, Albanians flocked in and 45,000 Serbs moved elsewhere. Serbs claim that their churches, even graveyards were vandalized; that crops were burned, and livestock killed, or stolen; that individual Serbs were singled out and assaulted; that they had become a disadvantaged minority in what was actually Serbia![7] Pristina's potholed and unpaved streets, its erratic electricity and mounds of garbage, its entire dilapidated condition, suggested that things went wrong here that couldn't be blamed on the war. I asked a Serb hotel employee why he continued to live in such a place. Surprised, he explained that he had been born in Pristina, had his job and a small apartment. "I have nowhere to go," he said. Another young Serb, very poorly dressed, worked the reception window of a large office building. He wore a gold ring with the four Cyrillic "Cs." I wondered if they had gathered at the town of Kosovo Polje in 1987 and heard an up-and-coming Serb communist named Milosevic vow that "…Nobody, either now, or in the future, has the right to beat you!" By 1990, he had forced the Albanian authorities in Kosovo to capitulate. Thousands quit, or were thrown out of work. It had since been run by emergency rule ratified by Serbia's assemblies, which were being boycotted by the Albanians. It amounted to de facto re-annexation backed up by police specials and the army (VJ). However onerous the Serbian grievances, and they were probably quite real, Milosevic's approach had caused society to separate even further into two antagonistic camps. It had turned into an ugly standoff interspersed by acts of violence. Kosovo's tottering economy had virtually collapsed.

Llilyana Staletovic and Branko Vujovic of *Jedinstvo* newspaper said that the situation was better now because the Albanians had stopped their protest demonstrations. They felt that the LDK leader, Ibrahim Rugova, had lost ground. "The Albanians are back," Branko insisted. "They have their own newspapers in this building." He also pointed out that Basri Plana had joined the SPS and was a deputy for Kosovo. "You should talk to him," he said. Llilyana said that Belgrade was ready to negotiate with the Albanians, but would not agree to secession. She explained that even educational matters were at an impasse, as the Albanians wanted the same system as in Tirana. She said they had opened their own private schools. Branko asserted that, despite Pristina's shoddy appearance, the Albanians had money and held most of all private business. He said that a few Serbs had joined in as partners. He claimed that Serbs were returning, but that jobs were still very scarce. "The basic problem here," he said, "is political… for control." He called Rugova a "fanatic," and claimed that the LDK had sent men to fight in Bosnia. He said that the Albanians trained fighters at Elbasan and at Korca, and that the Turkish government did the same. He also claimed that Suleyman Uglianin, the Muslim SDA leader in the Sandzak, had also sent people to Bosnia. Very strong words!

LDK presidential advisor Alush Gashi told a different story. The US-educated physician said, "Serbia is the one-man show of Slobodan Milosevic, his mafia, and his police… a system based on fear!" He said that LDK's claim to independence is not aimed at the Serbs, but will actually stave off popular demands for formal union with Albania. The well-dressed, smooth-talking Gashi said he had tried to convince Washington of this, from taxi drivers up to the White House. He said that they are proud of what they have accomplished and believe that non-violence will work. "We are a strong, dedicated people," he said. While denying LDK had sent people to Bosnia, he couldn't speak for the Sandzak. He thought that Albanians living up in Bosnia must have sided with Sarajevo. As I was leaving, two late-model automobiles wheeled up in front of the LDK building. Young men with suits and ties jumped out to escort "President" Rugova inside. The slender, dark-haired man with glasses and a signature scarf wrapped around his neck strode inside. At the entrance, his security men stood with bowed heads, their arms pressed tightly to their sides out of respect. He did have an intensity about him!

Almost a year later I met him under tragic circumstances. The Croatian army's Operation Storm of early August had driven some 170,000 Serbs out of the Krajina. Some had been relocated to a sports complex in Pristina. An old man's hand shook as he tried to get a spoonful of soup up to his mouth. His listless eyes were sunk in his head, his cheeks hollow and his whole demeanor one of utter exhaustion. Upon entering the Krajina's capital of Knin, an exultant Croat president Franjo Tudjman had kissed his *sahovnica* and crowed, "The Serbs ran so fast they left their money and dirty underwear!" So much for the Serbs whose forebears had lived in the Krajina for 400 years. I asked Dusko Milailov who had worked with the UN what had happened. He said he had been in the northern sector at the time trying to arrange an exchange of prisoners. On 4 August, about mid-morning, he saw RSK troops starting to pull out from their positions. He said that there was not even any fighting. He was told that everyone had to get out. It turned to chaos! Dusko made it to Petrova Gora and luckily found his wife and four children after four days. Then they joined thousands of others running a gauntlet of spit, stones and Croat curses. They got to Novi Sad in Vojvodina in a truck that belonged to a friend.

Marko Bicko is a railway worker with a wife and two children from Knin. Early on 4 August, artillery rounds started to come in from several directions. In an hour or so, the word was to run for it! Serb soldiers said they didn't know what was going on, only that they had orders to withdraw. Almost immediately, roads were jammed with army vehicles, cars, vans, trucks, tractors—some pulling wagons or carts—anything that could move. Marko called it a panic situation, adding bitterly that their leaders were the first to go. It took six days to get to Novi Sad. He said he would not return to the Krajina under any circumstances. He said that his children still suffer from the shock of their exodus. I left what food and cigarettes I had with the two families and visited those who were camping on the floor of a gymnasium. Their small bundles of personal belongings sat beside gray sleeping bags. An elderly woman was busy with her knitting. Some looked at me as if I could help them. I left feeling I had intruded on their misery.

Rugova complained that the refugees were sheltered in "Albanian" public buildings. "Next, they will be given a job, some land, or an apartment." He thought that this was just the beginning and that more would come. However, this wasn't his main message. Kosovo, he said, was not an isolated problem. It had to be solved within the context of an overall settlement for all of ex-Yugoslavia. He cited the damage to Kosovo's economy over the past several years and the lack of a legitimate, functioning, civil administration. "We are looking for solutions," he said, "for a regime (FRY) that is falling apart. We have our educational system, which works," he insisted, "and our independent state is the people, not buildings." He said they were conducting a non-violent revolution against the Serbs, who themselves needed emancipation from their past. "But, we cannot go back to the autonomy of previous years because federal Yugoslavia no longer exists," he explained. He said they could accept an interim international administration under the UN, EU, or the Contact Group and that Serbia had to accept their demands.

"We expect respect for what has been created democratically, all of it under international observation. An independent Kosovo will have a calming effect on the Albanians in Macedonia and in Montenegro." He went on soothingly without explaining what would prevent all of the Albanians from wanting to unite together. "We want a peaceful transfer of power from the Serbs to ourselves," he said. He thoughtfully explained that they had reserved fourteen out of 144 seats in their non-recognized assembly if the Serbs agreed. Rugova left little doubt that he was counting on the continued disintegration of rump-Yugoslavia to achieve his ends. Thus, he wanted the Contact Group (especially the US) to pressure the FRY into making concessions. He believed that time was on their side. "Having been victims," he said, "we have set up our system under Serbian occupation in conformity with Western guidelines. We will be small, but wealthy enough, neutral and equidistant from the other states in the region. And," he mused, "if unification with Albania does happen, the capital might be right here in Kosovo." Such is the man, and such are his dreams!

I had told Gashi that I had spoken to Rugova's rival, Basri Plana. Gashi spoke icily, almost hissing! "He represents no one, only himself. He can do what he is doing," Alush said, "but he must know he is working against the interests of his own people!"

Plana was a heavy-set physician of forty-five with a PhD in psychiatry. He had been elected unopposed to the republic and federal assemblies for the SPS and sat under a photograph of Slobodan Milosevic. I was prepared to dislike him, but went away thinking differently.

He claimed he had reluctantly entered politics five years earlier when, after the YLC's collapse, separatist-minded activists took Kosovo on the path of the "politics of self-destruction." Europe, he said, should be trying to integrate, not create smaller and smaller entities. Many had asked him, he said, why they should go to bleed for new borders when Yugoslavia was then a multiethnic society in one nation of six republics? Consequently, Plana said he and friends—Albanians, Serbs, Roma (gypsies), and Turks—set up a broad coalition that served as a launching pad to run on the SPS ticket. He admitted that their turnout was small compared to the LDK which boycotted all elections conducted by Belgrade. He and Rugova were poles apart in their respective political beliefs.

"The problem with separatism," he asserted, "is that it is driven by the idea of Greater Albania, uniting Kosovo, parts of Macedonia and Montenegro with Albania proper (as happened in World War Two with Italian and German backing). You would re-draw the borders of four states," he noted. "Rugova holds his Albanians hostage to all of this. He has placed them on a direct collision course with the Serbian authorities, oftentimes with tragic consequences." He claimed that there were no legal, or constitutional obstacles preventing Albanians from fully participating in society. "We can have a normal life for the asking," he insisted. He claimed that people were becoming disillusioned with Rugova, that a shift in opinion was underway. Albanians, he maintained, now held about half of the total number of state jobs in Kosovo and that even their professors were returning to their positions at Pristina University. He said that Trepca mines were hiring some 3,000 new workers. "We can get things done," he said. "We are the future!"

Plana claimed he had challenged Rugova to a televised debate, but the LDK had not responded. "We hold out an officially recognized school curriculum, a job, law and order, a positive orientation towards life, not conflict and deprivation. Can any country," he asked, "survive with half-educated children with certificates which no one accepts; with its youth held captive to the illusion of a self-declared independence; with heavy emigration because there is no future for them here? How can Rugova preserve society by preaching exclusion for the Serbs when we should be striving for social and, more importantly, mental integration?" he asked. "I am trying to be a bridge between Belgrade and the Albanians. I am not in it for money. My house has been stoned and shot at, and some of my supporters have been killed. We offer a real life, not an early grave. I can take you to villages and show you where the boys who died in Bosnia are buried. They're there. And as for the refugees from the Krajina, this is a humanitarian problem. I believe there is room for them here. When Hoxha was in power, a lot of Albanians came to Kosovo." That was Basri Plana. I had now heard a different side and it had come from an Albanian! Rugova, the "velvet revolutionary," just might be leading his people up a dead-end street that would eventually explode in a blood bath!

I stood inside the 700-year-old Serbian chapel of Grachanitsa and looked up at a dome that gave an amazing impression of height in a church that is actually small in size. Its ancient wall frescos and icons wedded the story of Christ and his sacrifice to that of King Miliutin and the Serbian nation. From there, it was minutes to Kosovo Polje, the "Field of Blackbirds" at Gazimestan. There, on 28 June 1989, the six-hundredth anniversary of that epic battle, a million people gathered to hear Slobodan Milosevic summon them to struggle: "…We are again engaged in battles and quarrels. They are not armed battles, but this cannot be excluded yet." The gray square castle tower monument stands on a courtyard of more rough-hewn stone. It overlooks a broad expanse of undulating grassland and stunted trees where, on that fateful day, 35,000 soldiers loyal to Prince Lazar fell. On the monument is written Knez Lazar's own summons:

> "Whoever is Serb and of Serbian birth,
> And who does not come to Kosovo Polje to do battle against the Turk,
> Let him have neither a male nor a female offspring,
> Let him have no crop…"

The tower is surrounded by hollow cement cylinders emblazoned with swords and the four Cyrillic Cs and the dates 1389–1989. On some days, when the wind is strong, you hear a muffled, wailing sound, as if the Serbs are still mourning for their dead.

In Belgrade, I spoke to Captain Dragan Vasiljkovic about the RSK debacle. Vasiljkovic, or "Captain Dragan" as he is known was one of the early military organizers in the Krajina in 1990–91. He is a former career officer in the Australian army, an infantryman expert in unconventional warfare. He had served with South Africa as a mercenary and has flown solo across the Atlantic. After the early Serbian successes, he was told that his help was no longer needed. A World War Two orphan, he returned to Belgrade and established a foundation for disabled fighters and the families of the dead. His administrator is a woman who once cared for him in his youth. When I saw him, he was at a foundation workshop wearing a US army West Point sweatshirt. "I used to like it," he said, "but now I don't care if it gets dirty. In fact, I am totally turned off by Washington." I could tell that he really didn't want to talk to me, an American. Finally, after some waiting, his better side got the best of him. He wiped his hands on West Point and talked.

"Look," he said. "This was no conventional force. This was an army of farmers and villagers. They were ill trained and ill equipped. Some didn't have proper boots. After the first year, they somehow thought they had won. Officers were no longer working with their troops and those that did only knew outdated Partisan-Soviet tactics. War is a tremendously expensive business… We simply didn't have enough money to go around. Soldiers went unpaid and morale was low. After four years of sanctions, and pressure from NATO, how long could people like this hold out? Then, last year, Belgrade cut us off. Everyone was tired. What would you expect to happen?"

It was hard to fault his logic and easy to credit rumors of how some fighters had sold equipment, petrol, and even weapons to survive. He said there had been recent changes in the chain of command that had not been smoothly accepted. Others said that, when the word went out that the Croats were attacking in force, there was utter confusion and communications broke down. It turned into a rout! "It's not that we didn't know of the Croat buildup," he said. "We heard that they had American advisors and were getting US equipment. The question was what do to about it? We tried last-minute negotiations to hold them off. It didn't work. The Krajina is gone." Dragan said he didn't blame the Bosnian Serbs for not helping them. "They had problems of their own." He had been in Knin for several weeks before the collapse and said that he had seen it coming. He had gone to Belgrade and was on his way back when the roof fell in. There, on the road, he met Serbs making their way out. He realized then that it was all over.

At face value, Vasiljkovic's comments concerning General Mladic seemed charitable. At the time, Krajina Serbs were fighting in support of their Bosnian brothers at Bihac. When the Croats came in, Radovan Karadzic had favored sending in some of his forces to assist the RSK. Probably on Milosevic's orders, Mladic refused. Karadzic tried to take over the BSA. Mladic remained opposed, but did allow Radovan to salvage some pride by portraying himself as some sort of "coordinator" between the BSA and RSK armies. After two days, it was too late. The front had collapsed and the roads were clogged with civilians, as well as troops who had lost contact with their units. The Bosnian and Krajina Serbs had had three years to craft a common military strategy. The same was true of an alliance that would have driven the Greater Serbia project forward. They had failed in both, mainly because of their own fractious leadership and quarrels with Belgrade. President Milosevic's decision to cut off his support put paid to the whole idea. It was finished! Peter Njegos, a nineteenth-century Bishop of Montenegro, is the most admired poet of the Serbian people, and his "Mountain Wreath" is arguably his most famous:

> Our God has poured his wrath upon the Serbs,
> For deadly sins withdrawn His favor from us,
> Our Rulers trampled underfoot all law,
> With bloody hatred fought each other down,
> Tore from fraternal brows the living eyes,
> Authority and Law they caste aside,
> Instead chose folly as their rule and guide!
> And those who served our kings became untrue,
> Crimson they bathed themselves in kingly blood!
> Our noblemen—God's curse be on their souls—
> Did tear and rend the kingdom to pieces,
> And wasted wantonly our peoples' power.
> The Serbian magnates—may their names rot out!
> They scattered broadcast Discord's evil seed,
> And poisoned thus the life-springs of our race.

British scholar R. G. D. Laffan, at the Salonika front in 1917, called the Serbs heroes whom they had learned to love and respect. Likewise, at the start of World War Two, the English writer Rebecca West's *Black Lamb and Grey Falcon* sing their praises. More to the point today, their past is fused to their future by a fiery present, by a messianic effort to attain their perceived national destiny.

I returned to Bosnia a year after Dayton. The Skipina family was still there. It was November and a pile of wood was stacked up in a large circular mound of perfect splits just outside their door. A jumble of footwear stood inside, some of them flattened out into Turkish-style slippers. A hog had been killed. Men tended a fire rendering its fat into lard. A brandy bottle was out.

We stood around and drank toasts. "*Zhivelli!*" (To your health!) The next morning was overcast, drizzling, with gusting wind. Winter was just around the corner. I used a new UNHCR bus service to get into Sarajevo. It crossed the Inter Entity Boundary Line (IEBL) and was set up to encourage refugees to return to their homes. The bus was almost full and all passengers were checked against a list. The driver was a cheery Dane who had previously driven aid trucks for a volag. He said that, when they first got started, Serbs were being harassed as they got off in the city. Bosnia-Herzegovina security had tried to take their names. The Office of the High Representative (OHR) remonstrated strongly and it had stopped.

From Grbavica, I walked across the Miljacka and headed for the Holiday Inn where in America it promises "no surprises." It had taken some hits on the side facing the river, but had survived intact and had provided rooms to visiting journalists. Just for laughs, I priced a single. It was still impossibly high. There, in the parking lot, a mortar splat had been painted red for all to see. It was a reminder of the recent past. I walked beyond Marshal Tito and was guided by giggling schoolgirls to the US embassy. From there, I went to the OHR and waited for Jock Covey to return. Jock and I had served together in Jerusalem. He had been pulled as principal officer in Berlin to assist Carl Bildt. When he arrived, his year in Sarajevo showed in his red-rimmed eyes that bespoke exhaustion. He expressed his frustration at trying to get an international effort to pull in one direction, as many assigned to OHR retained their own national outlooks.

Criticism aside, Jock said progress had to be measured by each and every small success that helped to get a devastated society functioning again, anything that helped to overcome the hatred, fear and lack of trust on all sides. A year into Dayton, he said it was the assessment of the US and the OHR that should the Republika Srpska (RS) attempt to pull out of Bosnia-Herzegovina down the road, the Bosniak Muslims would attack. Jock said its army would be fully capable of overrunning the Serbs by then. "Consequently," said Covey, "it is absolutely essential for IFOR to stay on." He likened the RS to the Israeli hardline, nationalist Likud party. Like Likud, RS was both determined and very adept at pushing its own agenda, in this case towards a link-up with FRY. RS, Jock said, had recently taken the position that Bosnia-Herzegovina consists of three separate entities. It acted accordingly and, as a result, it was being penalized in the distribution of aid. He said that Momcilo Krajisnik had come within only 40,000 votes of being elected president of Bosnia-Herzegovina. That would have undercut Izetbegovic and shredded the Contact Group's policy. Another US diplomat said that RS must be "kept in a box" like Saddam Hussein. He repeated the formula used in getting Radovan Karadzic to step down. "We discredit them, isolate them and then put the pressure on. It always works!"[8]

As I walked about, the question of what kind of regime Washington was building with its input of financial aid and weaponry kept turning over in my mind. For openers, Sarajevo was certainly not the devastated city I had thought from watching television. It was along the Miljacka that the tall office towers were gutted by fire. Other buildings had been hit. Still, it was not Beirut and much of it (except for specific targets) was intact, or relatively undamaged. A year after the war, its streets were full of people. Its shops had things to sell, even expensive bathroom fixtures. Public transportation was up and running. There was a real bustle to the place. Despite over three years of war—shellfire, the irreplaceable loss of human lives and cultural treasures—Sarajevo had survived and was still very much a city.[9]

But it had changed. Its new orientation was obvious. Its streets, with their green and white signs, had been renamed to suit its Islamic present and Ottoman past. Turkey's crescent flew from several sandbagged military positions and the interior of IFOR's press center had become Ankara's showpiece. The Saudi Arabian aid office displayed King Saud's green banner, its Koranic verse and sword. The Iranians were there. SDA slogans stabbed the air. SDA Forever! An all-green outline of Bosnia with a curved crescent set off an SDA office in the center of town. Another SDA complex was low, modern and spanking new. Its building on Titova had a professional staff that knew how to make a visiting journalist happy. I was provided with glossy SDA publications (in English) and an excellent cup of Turkish coffee. Even the sugar was in an SDA wrapper–*SDA za BiH!* Jasmina Ahmetbasic, smartly dressed and wearing a headscarf, knew her job. It all said money. I went back to the Holiday Inn with the sun already low on the horizon. Its lobby lounge was filled with a dozen, or more, young men having coffee, beer, or soft drinks. As several were amputees in wheelchairs, it was obvious they were Bosniak war veterans. I asked how they felt. They made exactly the same comments as the men in Pale: they were glad that the war was over. Very few had jobs to go to. And, they didn't want to fight again, but if they had to, they would. I recalled to mind what Jock had said![10]

RS president Krajisnik is a sturdy-looking, no-nonsense Serb who had come into his own since Karadzic had been forced out. I had asked him about Dayton. He thought that it is unfair, that the cards were stacked against them. He commented, "We lost Serbian land and our part of Sarajevo. We failed to gain access to the sea. Brcko must be negotiated. Our borders are illogical. Nevertheless, we signed it and we wish to implement it. Dayton brought peace. We are grateful for that. It is even working out better than we had expected. We can find ourselves in this agreement." But, he also cited serious problems. "Prisoners are being held. The Bosniaks want to absorb us into Bosnia-Herzegovina. We are totally against a tight union with Sarajevo. We will not accept it. It is hard to deal with a framework agreement. A lot is not spelled out. But, so far, we have done what was expected of us. The military balance bothers us. The US will train and equip the Muslims, but we must reduce our forces. We do want to cooperate, but we will reject any aspect that fails to meet our minimum security requirements."

I had also asked him about the rumored, so-called understanding between Milosevic and Tudjman to divide Bosnia-Herzegovina suggesting that possibly this would be more important in the long run than what was signed at Dayton. "We would be against this," he said, "for it would give us a large Muslim minority, a source of tension and instability. We don't want this and, personally, I don't think that the conduct of the war can be explained on this basis. By the same token, however, we think a federation between Croats and Muslims is very artificial and will fail. If the Muslims want to be on their own, we have no objection. Our goal, that of RS, is to be as independent as possible. Should we ever decide that we cannot continue in association with Bosnia-Herzegovina, neither IFOR or anyone else can prevent us from leaving. We know our friends, and our enemies. Ultimately, the Muslims want our downfall, our defeat. Their problem is that they have lived only as masters, or slaves. We Serbs demand equality and want to live as free men. We may only be a small nation, but we are a great people!"[11]

I asked Betsy Grew, a Dutch member of UNHCR in Pale, if RS was out of step with OHR-IFOR efforts on minority returns. She said that, except in a small way, none of the parties to the conflict wanted it. She explained that some mixed-marriage families had been allowed to come back, and a few others, but nothing really significant by any side. This was separately confirmed by Even Laurtzsen of the Norwegian Red Cross. Elections that past autumn had definitely reflected hardened nationalist attitudes on all sides. In Mostar, the Croats refused even minimal cooperation with the Muslims. A number of violent incidents had taken place. In Pale, there was disinterest in most OHR-IFOR projects, while down in Sarajevo, at least from the press handouts, Bosnia-Herzegovina was the object of hundreds of caseworkers with ideas and money. IFOR engineers were fixing roads and schools. There were escorted outings for kids. Special psychologists worked with women to overcome trauma. A center had been set up to determine the status of lost properties. People were being given do-it-yourself packages for patching up homes. Volags talked of confidence-building measures. The UNHCR bus was a good example. It provided secure mobility for seeing the old neighborhood, for shopping and for getting a look at what is still enemy-occupied territory for most people.

Mrs. Skipina had somehow found a trout. She had grilled it; had put together a salad from her garden, and had baked bread. It was really good— *dobra*. Afterwards, I coaxed her into having a glass of scotch. I had brought a stack of newspapers with me back from Sarajevo, the first she had seen from there in a long, long, time. Later, when I said good night, she tried to hide her tears. She was undoubtedly thinking of the past, of a life, of work, of a home, and of a lost familiarity. Her husband had said that they would never go back.

In the morning after breakfast, I walked to the press center. I was talking to Branko Mandic when he was notified that Prime Minister Biljana Plavsic had just dismissed BSA commander Mladic. We stared at each other, not knowing what it meant. Up until then, he was thought to be irreplaceable. A change was obviously underway that might not be accepted by the BSA. An internal army revolt was not unthinkable.[12]

As the bus was making its way back to Belgrade, I concluded that the RS was engaged in an uphill struggle that ran counter to the will of Washington. This would cost them needed aid, assistance and access to international finance, not to mention opposition from the Contact Group and many others at every turn. They ran the risk of remaining locked in isolation, economically stagnant, while the Sarajevo side gathered its strength. It was not at all clear if this would change any time soon. Approaching Zvornik, I saw something that suggested that Kusturica's "Underground" was very close to the mark. It was the shell of a completely gutted house. Its roof, and those of others nearby, had collapsed into its interior. All of its window frames were gone. Its walls were pocked with bullet holes and charred by fire. On the side facing the road, an appeal had been written to vote for the Serb Unity Party of Arkan Raznatovic. I subsequently learned that he had received an OHR handout to help conduct his election campaign![13]

Moreover, that November in Serbia, the previously unthinkable was happening! For while Milosevic's SPS, with Dr. Mira's JUL and a small New Democracy party had romped home free in elections to the FRY federal assembly, the voting in two rounds of local elections had swung solidly against Milosevic in the larger urban centers, including Belgrade, Nis and half a dozen others. For the first time, Milosevic's SPS had failed to do its homework, and it was Vuk's SPO and Zoran Djindjic's splinter Democratic Party (DS) in yet another coalition, this time called "Zajedno" (Together), which had finally turned the trick! On the evening of the seventeenth, thousands of exuberant voters took to the streets in Belgrade to celebrate! If the SPS had miscalculated, Milosevic miscalculated again, badly. For, instead of trying to demonstrate he was a democrat by handing local administrations over to Zajedno and permitting it to make a mess of things, like the quarrelsome kids they proved to be, he did Mayor Daley even better by brazenly moving to annul what had freely taken place at the polls! As an unrepentant strongman, he could not resist the temptation to try to hang onto all of the power, and the many jobs held by his SPS minions!

The official results were delayed amid SPS accusations of massive irregularities. Then, on cue, local election commissions and the judges nodded their agreement, which the courts were obligingly quick to confirm. It was robbery and everyone knew it! Milosevic had been given the benefit of the doubt on many occasions, but on this he had gone too far! Serbia's urban middle class was stung into action, led by tens of thousands of young people who had awaited an opportunity to protest against a regime that, in the main, remained unresponsive to their needs. Milosevic ordered a rerun, which was mostly boycotted. He offered a parliamentary commission, which the SPS could control. Western leaders cried "foul" in protest.

Then Milosevic invited the OSCE in to investigate, led by a not-to-be bamboozled Filipe Gonzales of Spain. The OSCE's findings backed Zajedno. Milosevic fulminated unconvincingly about foreign plots. He glowered glumly, showing his worst side, while the days of protest became weeks, and weeks became months. It appeared that the master of the game was finally losing his grip! Lashing out, he ousted any who had the temerity to disagree with him.

Who can ever forget the thousands who braved the cold day after day to send Milosevic a message by jumping in unison, chanting, booing and pitching raw eggs at the purveyors of official lies. Many dressed in zany costumes, creating a carnival atmosphere. It was theatre! However, Milosevic remained Milosevic. He ordered the police to get them out of the streets. It had already started to get rough. Ivica Lazovic, a Zajedno activist, was shot in the head by an SPS supporter from Kosovo, but survived. Another was not so lucky and was beaten to death. The police shoved forwards, batons swinging. Many must have remembered Milosevic at Kosovo Polje ten years earlier telling the people that the police had no right to beat them. It tore at their conscience. VJ head Lt. General Perisic told the students that they would stay out of it. The Serbian Orthodox church came out for Zajedno. Finally, Milosevic did what he would have done at first if he had thought it through, if he had not followed his gut reaction to refuse to accept SPS defeat. After some official mumbo-jumbo, he gave up Belgrade, Nis, Novi Sad, Kragujevac, and ten other towns.

Milosevic's stocktaking entailed the dismissal of no less than seven ministers. However, he kept a justice minister who had annulled the election results and a police minister whose men had beaten up peaceful demonstrators. But instead of easing in real reforms on media control and use, party financing and voting laws, and OSCE approved monitoring of the tally (including an electoral court), Milosevic became caught up with the need to shift the seat of his power to the federal structure as his term as president of Serbia was due to end on 31 December 1997. Even the coalition parties of Zajedno began to jostle for position for the soon-to-be-vacant job of Serbian president. In fact, after they had taken down the red star atop Belgrade's city assembly building, many began to lose interest in running mundane affairs such as the municipal trash service. By autumn the coalition had split up and SPO's Draskovic and DS's Djindjic were not even talking to each other. Worse, they accused each other of wanting to get into bed with Milosevic!

In August, Milosevic was sworn-in as FRY president by both houses of the federal assembly, having been elected in mid-July. He made piecemeal adjustments to reflect his actual authority relative to a position that had been very limited in power. He was an expert at this. Then, he had to tidy up this transition by finessing the elections to the Serbian assembly, as well as the high profile Serbian presidency. Seventeen candidates were scrambling for his old job, but only three were serious contenders: Zoran Lilic, who had been FRY president, was the SPS man; Seselj of SRS; and Draskovic of SPO. On 21 September, the lackluster Lilic polled less than a million and a half votes. Seselj, the scariest guy around, got over a million. Vuk, to his chagrin, was third with 853,000. Then Vuk did a real number! To improve relations with Milosevic, he stage-managed the ouster of Djindjic as the mayor of Belgrade and then took over the independent Studio B TV station and packed it with his own people. It was a shameless display of spite and opportunism. Then, in the next presidential round, Seselj (whose SRS had increased its standing in the assembly) nosed out Lilic in an election that failed to produce a turn out of fifty percent.[14]

It no doubt caused Milosevic considerable consternation to see Seselj edge ahead of SPS. As crafty as ever, he stood on the constitution (having bent it in the past) and ordered a third round. He shoved Lilic aside and ran a member of his Montenegrin mafia, Foreign Minister Milan Milutinovic. Even so, it took two cliffhanging rounds in December to get his own man in. Finally, on the second ballot, SPS's machine got another half million voters out and Milan won big! Milosevic, as well as his critics abroad, all breathed a collective sigh of relief when Seselj was shut out!

A disaster had been narrowly averted. But now, trouble was looming in mountainous Montenegro! The ruling pro-Milosevic Democratic Socialist Party (DPS) had been split since spring owing to a power struggle between Milosevic's young protégés—Momir Bulatovic, who, as Montenegrin president, had stood by Milosevic since 1989, and Prime Minister Milo Djukanovic, who had run much of the very lucrative UN sanctions-busting operations there during the war. The latter now controlled most of the DPS party organization and was aiming for the Montenegrin presidency. Handsome, smooth, and well-financed, Milo boosted his popularity by playing to younger voters over on the nationalist right, promising reform and to fight for tiny Montenegro's equality at the federal level, right where Milosevic had installed himself with enhanced authority! It promised to become a problem because besides sitting on the FRY presidency and the supreme council of defense, the Montenegrin president is in a position to both influence and obstruct legislation in the upper federal assembly, the Chamber of Republics. Milosevic needed to control this body, particularly regarding constitutional change.

In the first round, on 5 October, Bulatovic won by a razor-thin margin of 2,000 votes. But a rerun was required because the result had fallen below the fifty percent threshold. In the next, Djukanovic nosed out Momir by some 5,000 votes, produced at the last moment by the addition of 8,000 Albanians and Croats to the rolls. Over noisy protests, the OSCE observers and the US warned that the results must stand. In fact, Milo had already visited Washington. He had vowed to abide by Dayton and had revealed his plans to move Montenegro (Crna Gora) into the US-EU's orbit. This stance was rewarded by the US as soon as Milo assumed office in January 1998. UN sanctions were eased. And soon, USAID was dangling project proposals before his eyes. It was obvious that Washington planned to treat thirty-five-year-old Milo almost like the president of that separate state that some Montenegrins wanted it to be. It was an approach that threatened to further reduce Milosevic's strength and Yugoslavia's power as a state.

Montenegro has a short, but strategically important, border with neighboring Croatia abutting the Prevlaka peninsula. It has naval facilities at Kotor and Bar and VJ bases elsewhere. It comprises a bulwark of defensive depth for RS in Bosnia. And, except for the Danube, it is FRY's only outlet to the sea. Montenegro under unfriendly influence is a dagger aimed at Belgrade. Serbia would never willingly allow it to go independent. It is unthinkable! Therefore, the FRY maintained substantial military capabilities there and took care to insure that its officers from Crna Gora remained relatively content. Montenegro went to the very heart of things!

In September 1997, I traveled there from Pristina. By bus it was over seven hours through the high wooded hills of western Kosovo and then the spectacular gorges of Montenegro itself. Vertigo and verticality merged as our bus twisted around endless turns amidst the spectacle of geologic upheaval—sheer cliffs and ravines, and rock that jutted up beyond where the eye could see. The roadway hugged the mountainside, or bored through some two dozen tunnels that had been blasted out from solid rock. Its grey-black slabs denoted its name: Montenegro, Crna Gora, "Black Mountain." I made Podgorica by midnight. 650,000 people. 13,500 square kilometers. Tiny villages amid pine and towns that date from the Middle Ages. Here was Zeta, the coastal region of a Serbian kingdom. Budva and Hercegnovi are archaeological jewels set on a superb, small coastline on the Adriatic. Its alpine upland is an environmental treasure. Its people, mostly of Serbian stock, fought for their freedom for over 400 years, never submitting to the Ottomans. I was told that Montenegro has produced splendid generals, poets, artists—and smugglers. The latter remain a proud tradition.

In recent years, Montenegro has been discovered by Sophia Loren, Claudia Schiffer, and Sylvester Stallone. This attention has convinced the disco set that Montenegro should cut itself loose from Serbia and go it alone. They talk of a tourist trade that would surely fall into the hands of wealthy Italians overnight. They talk of shipping. But most of the Montenegrin-owned boats at Bar are of the small, fast kind used for smuggling cigarettes. They talk of an old king and claim that Serbia still owes them gold from World War One! It is the same nationalist nonsense that splintered the South Slavs into what some today regard as Balkan banana republics! Djukanovic, they said, will make Montenegro into a businessman's paradise. I wondered listening to this if he might emulate Milo Minderbinder of Joseph Heller's *Catch-22*—the slick young genius who arranged for the US Air Corps to bomb itself for the Germans while he cornered Egypt's cotton market and bought eggs on Malta. After all, Djukanovic's economic expertise had revolved around smuggling petrol and many other commodities throughout the war. He has called his old boss Slobodan Milosevic "yesterday's politician"!

Montenegro was asserting a new mood. It was saying it should be the equal of Serbia. This is like saying little Rhode Island should be equal to New York State, for the population ratio is the same, eighteen to one. Nevertheless, in the FRY parliamentary assembly's upper Chamber of Republics, each has twenty members. In the lower Chamber of Citizens, Montenegro is constitutionally required to have thirty members, one deputy for every 65,000 voters. A quick and dirty calculation suggests that Montenegro has 1,950,000 voters. But it doesn't. It has 470,000, suggesting that it is grossly over-represented at the federal level. In fact, it has a lock on any planned legislation. Until recently, except for minor bumps in the road, Milosevic and Bulatovic worked in relative harmony. It appeared that Djukanovic might be a different matter. He related to those who had no memory of World War Two, who barely remembered Tito, those only dimly aware that Belgrade built their roads, their ports and a money-spinning aluminum plant. For them, to become "Western" far outweighed events in Bosnia, Croatia, or Kosovo.[15]

Milosevic suffers from a generation gap. The same man who in the mid-1980s was considered by official Washington, the World Bank, the International Monetary Fund, and other foreign creditors, to be the best hope for a modernized, liberal economy in Yugoslavia (especially given their advice that SFRY recentralize its financial controls in order to get a handle on its foreign debt problem and to exert strict financial discipline over the republics, i.e., for Belgrade to again have a strong say in things), now found himself depicted in the world press as a dictator and criticized for not opening FRY up to global financial and market forces that would be independent of its control. Like others in Central and Eastern Europe, he was expected to offer carte blanche entry to virtually nameless and faceless investors whose intentions must be accepted on faith as benign. This he was reluctant to do, for it would impact on his power base and also erode what Yugoslavia's socialists consider as sacrosanct. His problem with Djukanovic was related to this. Milo Minderbinder was the West's opening wedge![16]

Slobodan Milosevic isn't all gruffness and growls. Those who have dealt with him say that this pugnacious populist has a charming side as well. Besides exuding warmth over lavish tables loaded with wine and slivovitz, he is credited with being an excellent negotiator, puffing his favorite cigarillo while blowing smoke, and calling on choice expletives and table pounding to make his point. During the war, he usually delivered on what was promised. US special Balkan envoy, Richard C. Holbrooke, thinks that if Milosevic had been born in the US, he would have been a political success—more than a mayor Daley! But Milosevic is Serb and entangled in centuries of Balkan drama. At times, when he is candid, he has admitted that he has made mistakes. Certainly, the same could be said for Tudjman and Izetbegovic, but if they have expressed regrets, they have not yet found their way into print. Only Milosevic is reviled by the West's press and by its politicians as the result of an eight-year propaganda campaign. He is certainly no angel, but neither is he always the devil he has been depicted to be.

Milosevic stands accused of having started the war. He and others did wave the spectre of Serb nationalism. But when he was intent on reintegrating Serbia (Kosovo and Vojvodya provinces), Croatian and Slovenian separatism was already well advanced. Although he had made bellicose statements, fighting broke out because of acts against ethnic-Serbs in Croatia, and Slovenia's determination to breakaway. Once war had begun, and Yugoslavia's internal borders came into question, Bosnia was dragged into the conflict as well. Now, after Dayton, Serb nationalists, and not only Seselj, accuse Milosevic of permitting the Greater Serbia project to fail and that, as a calculating banker, he decided to cut his losses when sanctions threatened to bring absolute ruin and his own political downfall. However, for Greater Serbia to succeed, he would have had to go in with the VJ and invite a direct confrontation with NATO. It would not have been an easy choice, especially for a leader whose own commitment to nationalism was related to an internal political struggle. Again, he wanted SFRY to stay together for reasons of personal power, and because he also believed that the future of the South Slavs would be better served by a strong federal state.

He has been unswerving in this. And he remains confrontational with any competition, meeting Djukanovic's challenge head on. First, he denigrated him to undercut his federal authority. Next, in early May 1998, he and Bulatovic brought a no-confidence vote against Federal Prime Minister Radoje Kontic, who leaned towards Djukanovic. This passed and led to his ouster. Then, Milosevic named Momir for the job and it was approved by both assemblies. Milo claimed this was illegal and below the belt, announcing that Montenegro would boycott the federal government. In return, Milosevic began to reduce the flow of federal funds, including pension payments on the eve of a republic parliamentary election that the Djukanovic-led DPS-Liberal Alliance won by forty-nine percent to Bulatovic's thirty-six! It all threatened to end in a constitutional crisis, a serious situation indeed![17]

If Montenegro became Milosevic and Dr. Mira's rumpus room, Kosovo was the grease fire in the kitchen that threatened to burn down the whole house! Milosevic's crackdown on separatist aspirations, a decade of repression, the realization that a parallel society is going nowhere, and Bosnia, all have had time to do their work. For some five years, the Kosovo Liberation Army (KLA) was rumor and shadow. The LDK said it didn't exist. They said it was a plot by Serb security, a "plot" that attacked its own police and killed pro-Serb Albanians! However, in recent months, the KLA had come out of the closet.

Previously, they had attacked lone police cars on country roads, or isolated police stations. Occasionally, they killed Albanians who were accused of collaboration. This had now changed because of the virtual collapse of authority in Albania. A difficult-to-control border straddles a tangle of mountain trails and small villages where sworn secrecy is traditional. Secure sanctuary was there for the asking. And now Albania was awash with weapons in the hands of criminal gangs, or last year's looters who sell AK-47s like packs of cigarettes. Hundreds went over to the KLA. Albanian villages became quasi-KLA base camps, a ready refuge.

After being on the receiving end of isolated pinprick attacks from February 1998 on, special police and VJ units moved against villages in western Kosovo which were harboring what Belgrade was calling terrorists. Its indiscriminate use of heavy weapons to flush out KLA fighters from fortress-like farmhouses caused high civilian casualties. Mass demonstrations erupted in Pristina in protest. Next, KLA gunmen tried to contest the road between Pec and Pristina, gaining control of perhaps a third of the province. Belgrade stepped up its operations in an effort to seal off the border. In turn, Rugova broke off his talks with Milosevic, which had been brokered by the Contact Group. Many differences separated the two. Moreover, the loss of KLA fighters, some 500 civilian deaths and 50,000 refugees made it difficult for Rugova to accept autonomy. He began to be undercut by the KLA, which called for immediate independence within a Greater Albania and was waging an open-ended war of attrition![18]

* * *

The Serbian knights sweltered in their helmets and heavy mail as they gathered at Kosovo Polje in late June 1389, for the sun was well into its arc and the air, dust-filled from thousands of hooves, was stifling. 35,000 cavalry and foot soldiers milled about amidst the flags and pennants of princely houses. Some Bosnians were there, and some Albanians. But others, who had promised to come, had failed to appear. To the south, and eastward, in the haze, were the Turks. They wore a lighter armor and rode smaller Mongolian ponies that could wheel with lightning speed, like the slash of a curved scimitar. After an interminable wait, the ranks were assembled and the order to advance was given amid oaths, curses and prayers, like armies everywhere. It began. The tide swung to and fro, until finally the Serbian center surged forward. However, the right flank faltered and by afternoon, Ottoman cavalry were cutting at the flanks of Prince Lazar's army. In an act of desperation, Lazar's aide, Milos Obilic, rode into Murad's camp. When brought before the Sultan, he plunged his dagger deep into Murad's side. The Turks cut off his head on the spot. Then Murad's own heir, Bayezit the "Thunderer," took command. The Turks, with superior numbers, broke into the Serbian ranks and rode them down. Lazar was captured and also beheaded. Sultan Murad died of his wound. Thus, 28 June has come to be known as St. Vitus' (Vidovdan) Day and is immortalized by the most famous epic poem of the Serbian people:[19]

> There flies a black bird, a falcon, from Holy Jerusalem,
> And it bears a swallow.
> But that is no falcon, no black bird,
> It is the Saint Elijah.

And he carries not a swallow,
But a book from the Mother of God.
He took it to the Tsar at Kosovo and laid it on his knees.
The book asked unto the Tsar:
Tsar Lazar of honorable stock,
Of what kind will you have your kingdom?
Do you want a heavenly kingdom?
Or an earthly kingdom?
(Then Tsar Lazar pondered long about heaven and earth.)
The Tsar chose a heavenly kingdom,
Not an earthly kingdom.
He built a church at Kosovo…
(One that would have a floor of silk and scarlet)
Then Lazar was overwhelmed by the Turks,
And Tsar Lazar himself was destroyed,
He and His seventy and seven thousand soldiers.
All was honorable and holy and God's goodness was
fulfilled.

Sultan Murad's entrails buried nearby became a Muslim shrine. The rest of him was taken off to Bursa in Turkey. Lazar's head and body came to rest in a monastery in the Frushka Gora foothills northwest of Belgrade. On 28 June 1988, black and hard as old leather, it began a year's pilgrimage through towns and villages before returning to its original resting place at Ravanica. Milosevic knew what moves the Serbs and even gave his backing for the renewed construction of a huge Orthodox cathedral in Belgrade.

In the late seventeenth century, the Austrians challenged Ottoman rule south of the Danube and penetrated as far as Kosovo and Skopje in 1689. However, they and Serb rebels failed to prevail, leaving a Serb peasant population vulnerable to the vengeance of the Turks and their Albanian vassals. In 1690, under Patriarch Arsenije III, 200,000 Serbs began what is known as the Great Serbian Exodus, moving north to today's Vojvodina and Slavonia. As a consequence, Albanians from the highlands and Turks resettled the farmlands of the south, in Old Serbia. As mostly Muslims, the Albanians had the upper hand over any Serbs remaining there, or arriving later.

With the creation of the Serbian state in the early nineteenth century, and its subsequent expansion south, it became a question of time before Serb nationalism would reassert itself in its historical heartland. In fact, it would clash in the exact place and at the exact time that Albanian national feeling was first stirring.

The first incidence was in 1878 when Serbs settled lands southwest of Nis, evicting Albanian villagers in the process. Serb success in the Balkan Wars, and the collapse of the Ottoman Empire, only accelerated the process. After World War One, Serbia attempted to redress its severe population losses by negotiating the transfer of some 300,000 Albanians and Turks to the Turkish mainland. Also, 50,000 Albanians left for their new state under Tirana. Land grants, and tax relief, attracted an estimated 65,000 Serbs (11,000 families) to settle in Kosovo. (Albanians claim 200,000 hectares, or 500,000 acres were seized.) The 1908 Ottoman, and 1916 Austrian, censuses of Kosovo's population were 505,000 and 460,000 respectively, of which eighty percent were Albanian. Serbian censuses in the 1920s and 1930s showed populations of 435,000 and 550,000, of which at least sixty percent were Albanian, despite Serb colonization efforts. World War Two brought demographic change and tragedy to both communities.[20]

Kosovo's annexation to Italian-controlled Albania and atrocities against Serbs by the Albanian fascists have already been touched on. Suffice it to say that communist AVNOJ forces in 1945 hunted down Ballists and other nationalists, taking revenge against an Albanian population that was in active revolt. In effect, Kosovo was re-annexed by force. Underground resistance by the Albanian National Democratic Committee continued until the 1950s when it was uncovered and its leaders were executed, or imprisoned. Even earlier, some Albanian communists were singled out and jailed as Stalinists in an effort to mould a malleable local leadership. Serbs vigorously argued that they were discouraged in various ways from returning to Kosovo in the decades following World War Two because Tito wanted the Socialist Autonomous Province to settle down. The Albanians argued, just as strenuously, that they were subjected to show trials, police brutality and other forms of coercion and that thousands became "Turks" and were resettled in Anatolia. Although Tito later recruited many Albanians into his security apparatus, the seeds of ethnic discord had been sown very deep![21]

Nevertheless, Albanian aspirations received official encouragement with the new constitution of 1974. They had recently won a university and their new powers stood just short of republic status. However, instead of fostering good feelings, it ultimately fed separatism! Almost overnight, Albanian officials, managers, police, university professors, TV and radio personalities, and those involved in the arts assumed unimagined prominence and powers of authority. Newspapers and magazines appeared, all in the Albanian language. Federal money poured in and loans on easy terms were granted. The border with Albania opened and cultural exchanges of artists and intellectuals became almost routine. In 1978, the centenary of the League of Prizren was celebrated. Still, then, as now, the Albanians had one of the highest birth rates in Europe and Kosovo continued to slide behind the curve in economic development. In fact, according to the plan, Kosovo's GDP was supposed to grow by ten percent a year when, in actuality, it continued to decline in per capita terms as compared with the other republics. Despite investment in new industrial plants, and the famed Trepca mining complex, unemployment remained high. Only one Albanian in ten held what amounted to a full-time job! Many women remained uneducated.[22]

The incidents of April 1981 began almost accidentally. University students, unhappy with their dormitory conditions, began to air a list of grievances over life in Kosovo—poverty, lack of work, low development—that soon became a demand for republic status. A march on KLC headquarters was broken up by Albanian police. Then, because party leaders feared trouble on the anniversary of Tito's death, they ordered the police to arrest suspected troublemakers. On the 23 March commemoration, hundreds of student demonstrators demanded the release of their friends and shouted for a republic. The police, unprepared and panicky, fired tear gas and live rounds. More arrests were made, and by 2 April the province had erupted in rioting. Pristina urgently requested reinforcements from the SFRY federal government, calling it a general revolt. On 3 April, the province was placed under martial law. Units were sent in from all of the republics and so was the federal paramilitary All Yugoslav Security Force. When it was over, several hundred lay dead or wounded. Arrests were made, including some university professors who were given harsh sentences. Kosovo entered a cycle of protests, arrests, and jailings under its own Albanian KLC, which was backed by the six republics and the federal government. This, in effect, raised serious questions over its status and its future.

In October 1985, some 2,000 Serbs from the Kosmet petitioned the assemblies of Serbia and SFRY to examine and put an end to what they described as unbearable conditions of unrest and uncertainty in the province. Their appeal was met with indifference on the part of Yugoslavia's ruling communists, including Serbia's, and with threats by Albanian leaders in Kosovo. In January 1986, over 200 prominent Belgrade academics and intellectuals signed another petition that deplored official inaction on Kosovo's appeal and elaborated on conditions which threatened the Serbian community, namely: an absence of law and order, inequality before the law, in employment, and education, incidents of vandalism, theft and assault which were passed off as misdemeanors; and the creation of ethnically pure Albanian villages. The signatories used strong language, evoking "genocide," and claimed that the

Serbs had been persecuted by a "rigged political trial" for decades. They called for thoroughgoing changes in the province's administration.[23]

Even more basic issues were raised by a seventy-four-page missive that came to be known as the "Memorandum of the Serbian Academy of Science and Arts." Circulated secretly as an unfinished draft setting out Serbian complaints, it was somehow published in September 1986 in the mass circulation daily *Vecernje Novosti*. It stirred up such a controversy that YLC leaders were forced to take a stand on its assertions. It claimed that since 1945 Croats and Slovenes had taken unfair political and economic advantage of the Serbs, that the Serbs had, over the past century, fought and died in far greater numbers than others for South Slav independence and, instead of being rewarded, had been dealt with unfairly, that in Kosovo the Serbs faced gradual genocide; and in Croatia "...The resolution of their [Serb] national status must be a priority political question. If a solution is not found, the consequences will be damaging on many levels... not only for relations within Croatia, but also for all Yugoslavia."[24]

The president of Serbia, Ivan Stambolic, had been criticized in the memo as being ineffective. Stung, as by an insult, Stambolic and Belgrade's party boss (who also supervised the media), Dragisa Pavlovic, commenced an attack on both the memo and the academy. They were immediately joined by the Croats and Slovenes and other YLC leaders throughout Yugoslavia. Milosevic, head of the Serbian party, maintained a studied silence, allowing others to express the required politically correct "consensus" view. He was waiting.

The opportunity presented itself in April 1987 when Stambolic casually asked his former protégé to go down to Kosovo to calm unrest and dissatisfaction among the Serbian community there. A large crowd gathered at Kosovo Polje while Milosevic talked inside the House of Culture with local leaders. Albanian police were positioned uneasily outside and used their batons as Serbs pushed forward. They began to shout and then started throwing stones. Amid the din, those inside argued in nervous confusion over what to do. Finally Milosevic went outside to see for himself and then launched into his famous speech. He told them that he understood them. He told them to remain on their land, in their homes, despite injustice and degradation, for the sake of their ancestors and children despite all the obstacles and problems and, most significantly, they should work with him to change the situation. He galvanized popular support almost overnight!

Few realized that Milosevic had arranged this confrontation through a cadre of local Serb supporters. He raised the stakes again in June at a Belgrade YLC meeting being held to discuss the Kosovo problem. This time, 3,000

Kosovo Serbs were on hand to noisily make their protests known while the YLC was deliberating nearby. Stambolic became clearly rattled, not understanding that Milosevic had staged the entire scenario. In September, an Albanian army recruit went berserk and killed four of his barracks mates with his service rifle, including one young Serb. Belgrade's press and TV played the incident up, giving it an anti-Albanian twist. Ten thousand people attended the funeral. Pavlovic called the media in, on public television, and told them to put a stop to it and that the situation in Kosovo could explode.

Slobodan and Mira worked out their plan of attack over a weekend, and on the Monday *Politika Ekspres* published a stinging article aimed at Pavlovic, accusing him of extinguishing the "frail hopes of these poor, oppressed people," the Serbs of Kosovo. An editor had signed it, but it was Mira's. Defiantly, the daily *Politika* reran it. With Stambolic's approval, Pavlovic called a meeting of the Belgrade party leadership, armed with a letter of support from the president. The majority did line up with Pavlovic. However, a close friend of Milosevic arranged for the presidency of the Serbian central committee to meet the following day. A very nervous Stambolic phoned Milosevic and was given assurances. In fact, Milosevic and his allies were already soliciting support from each and every member of the collegium. With Slobodan presiding, it went on for two days, with forty-nine persons speaking and twenty armed with voting authority. A showdown was shaping up.

President Stambolic spoke early, making pathetic, silly remarks about the need for Milosevic and Dragisa to meet every day for coffee or lemonade to resolve their differences. Milosevic cut him short, stating, "This question cannot be minimized by describing it as a personal conflict, as two kids having a squabble... This is not personal animosity or sympathy and these are not things that can be simplified in that manner." Milosevic got on the phone and briefed Mira. She told him that he must press on, that there was no going back. Overnight, Milosevic and his friends discussed a situation that was still not clearly in their favor. However, the next morning, they got to four members of the Belgrade committee who agreed to sign a letter stating Stambolic had forced them to back Pavlovic.

When the meeting resumed, Milosevic cut the debate short and went for the jugular. Careful and circumspect, he revealed the letter with all of its implications for Stambolic and Pavlovic, and called for the latter's expulsion from the party. The vote went eleven for, five against, with four abstentions. The Albanian, Azem Vlasi, voted against. The matter was deferred to a central committee plenum.

Milosevic and his men worked day and night throughout Serbia in personal contact with district and regional committee members to ensure that things went their way at the eighth session of the SLC central committee. Stambolic, seemingly in a trance, expressed the view that people should just say what they wanted to. It was not enough. Dramatically, Milosevic had arranged for the proceedings to be televised and so be open to public view for the first time ever in Yugoslavia. People sat transfixed before their sets as if it were the World Cup! Belgrade TV edited in support of Milosevic. Stambolic sat like a zombie, unable to grasp what was happening. In fact, Tito's legacy was used as a political football with, by implication, Stambolic and Pavlovic standing accused of violating party unity. Milosevic's people displayed relentless determination by lobbying at every break with whoever they could talk to. Milosevic tried Vlasi, but it ended in insults.

With expressions of support pouring in from all over Serbia, SLC members jumped on the bandwagon. Pavlovic was ousted. Stambolic was to follow. Milosevic well understood the magic of mass appeal and the power of the press and TV. Serbia was soon to become his!

* * *

17 November 1988. Earlier, Kosovo's provincial KLC leaders had announced that the SAP was economically bankrupt. With approval from the YLC and federal government, Milosevic's Serbia was about to re-centralize the republic. A meeting of the provincial KLC was held in Pristina to discuss the resignations of Kosovo president Kaqusha Jashari, and her named successor, Azem Vlasi. Hundreds of miners from Trepca came out of their pits in protest and walked thirty miles to Pristina to express their opposition. Crowds of young university students and school children joined them. However, the resignations went forward because of heavy pressure from the YLC.

23 February 1989. The Trepca miners had struck two days earlier. Thirteen hundred remained below ground to protest reintegration with Serbia. They initially insisted that KLC leader, Rahman Morina, resign and that SFRY president, Raif Dizdarevic, talk to them. It turned into a general strike, which shut down the province.

They demanded: no retreat from the 1974 constitution; that Morina, Husamedin Azemi (boss of Pristina), and Ali Shukria (YLC central committee) should resign; that Stipe Suvar (YLC leader), Milosevic (SLC leader), and republican central committee representatives (including SAP Vojvodina) talk to them; explanations for the resignations of Jashari and Vlasi; that Kosovo's leadership be selected locally, not by the other republics, and most importantly that Milosevic's policy towards Kosovo be reversed.

President Dizdarevic, Suvar and Milosevic did go to Kosovo, but failed to dissuade them. Milosevic told the Albanians that they would not lose any of their rights, but the Serbs would regain theirs. The strike went on until 28 February when Morina, Azemi, and Shukria resigned. However, Serbia suspended this. Amid renewed protests, federal paramilitary units arrived in early March. Twenty-four (official figures) demonstrators were killed in clashes. Dozens were arrested, including Azem Vlasi. Finally, a state of emergency was declared. Any possibility of a peaceful reintegration of the Kosovo SAP was over.[25]

23 March 1989. With federal troops and armor in the streets, the Kosovo assembly met and approved amendments to its constitution that permitted Serbia to take over, so voting itself into oblivion. As it was done under duress, Albanians call it the "Constitution of the Tanks." The next day, Serbia adopted its new constitution. Kosovo's constitutional court tried to question the legality of the vote (some unauthorized persons participated and no official tally was compiled), but it was abolished. Demonstrations erupted and twenty-eight people were killed, including three small children, with reportedly 300 injured. A curfew was put in place. Within weeks, the KLC party organization collapsed amidst continuing protests.

21–23 June 1989. The disbanded Kosovo assembly attempted to meet to overturn the events of March. They were obstructed by some of their own members and harassed by an electricity cut-off.

23 December 1989. A gathering of Albanian intellectuals met to establish the first non-communist party in Kosovo. The LDK came into being with Dr. Rugova (PhD), the head of the Albanian Writers' Association, as its chairman. With the KLC completely discredited, the LDK rapidly gained in popularity throughout the province.[26]

2 July 1990. In the face of a continuing state of emergency and curfew, and enabling acts by Serbia, members of Kosovo's disbanded assembly met and declared Kosovo a republic within the SFRY. Locked out of the building, the delegates stood outside to make their proclamation. Thus, the Albanian leadership asserted their equality with the other six republics in an act that went unrecognized within the SFRY, but which was reported by the media.

3 September 1990. Following daily demonstrations, candlelight vigils and the like, a general strike was organized for all but essential workers. Independent Trade Unions of Kosovo President Dr. Hajrullah Gorani was arrested.

7 September 1990. Kosovo's assembly members met at Kacanik and adopted a constitution for their unrecognized SFRY republic. Four died in police actions.

100,000 attended the funerals, in spite of an effort by the Serbian authorities to block them off.

26–30 September 1991. Kosovo's assembly resolved to conduct a referendum on independence as a sovereign republic. This was done over several days with 914,802 (eighty-seven percent of those claimed to be eligible) voting. According to LDK, it was carried by 99.87 percent.

24 May 1992. Elections for the assembly and president of the now self-declared Republic of Kosovo were held. 762,257 (eighty-nine percent) in Kosovo and 105,300 living abroad voted. Dr. Ibrahim Rugova was declared president. LDK took ninety-six of one hundred seats directly and twenty-five more by plurality. Fourteen seats were reserved for other nationalities, mainly the Serbs. The elections were observed by eight foreign teams. Several other political parties participated. By this time, many direct action organizations had been formed: the Kosovo Helsinki Committee, the Forum of Albanian Intellectuals, the Movement of Greens, the Association of Independent Lawyers, and the Council for the Defense of Human Rights and Freedoms. Adem Demaci headed the latter organization, after being jailed for twenty-eight years. He had been released in 1990 and has since played a prominent role.

24 June 1992. A month after the elections, the elected members of the Kosovo assembly attempted to meet in Pristina. Paramilitary police armed with clubs prevented this, beating several MPs and their staff assistants.

Kosovo had now been under Serbian occupation for three years. Its Albanian population refused to recognize the legality of the FRY administration, grudgingly dealing with it only when forced to. They boycotted every single election, whereas their participation could have reduced Milosevic's power. Emergency rule was harsh and demeaning. Opposition demonstrations were repressed by lethal force, arrests and official harassment. The Albanians responded by organizing a parallel society centered around a makeshift private school system. Although their Republic of Kosovo was recognized only by Albania, the LDK and Dr. Rugova gained foreign support and recognition as leaders of the Albanian community. LDK's nonviolent approach was commended by many. Dr. Rugova met several western leaders, including Pope John Paul II.

Because injuries and deaths often occurred during demonstrations, by 1995 Rugova had taken his people off the streets. A sullen attitude of live and let live had set in. Albanian students were returning to university and others were going back to work. The level of violence was down. However, talks between the Albanians and Belgrade were stalled, the former insisting on international mediation. Still, arrests continued. In July–September 1993, some ninety had been arrested on charges of arms smuggling, possession of arms, and intent to organize an armed revolt. By February 1994, six groups and two individuals (twenty-seven people) had been sentenced for up to five years. Pre-trial and trial proceedings were criticized as being flawed because psychological and physical coercion were often used. Membership in a National Movement for the Liberation of Kosovo (NMKR) was outlawed by the Serbian authorities. A number of the arrestees were members of the LDK. The leaders of the LDK claimed that they were being unjustly accused and imprisoned.[27]

23 January 1998. The Serb district council member from Zvecan, Desko Vasic, was assassinated in his car on the Klina-Srbica road. This followed a police action in which an Albanian died. Tit-for-tat incidents continued into early February, with six dead on both sides. The KLA took credit for several Serbian deaths.

28 February 1998. KLA gunmen attacked Serb police at Likoshane. The latter raided a village. By 2 March, twenty Albanians and four Serbs had died. A few days later, helicopters and armored vehicles were being used and the toll went to fifty. The Serbs claimed twenty KLA members had been killed. Pristina erupted in protest. However, this time the police acted with restraint. VJ units deployed west of Pristina.

9 March 1998. With eighty Albanians dead, the EU and the Contact Group acted to reimpose sanctions on Yugoslavia, banning credits, investments and any arms trade. They also froze assets abroad. Russia took exception. Belgrade sent a delegation to Pristina, but it was rebuffed. At Prekas, fifty-three bodies (including women and children) were reinterred by Albanian family members. They had been buried in coffins by the Serbs after the Albanians had refused to touch them, demanding that autopsies be performed by foreigners.

23 March 1998. The Contact Group gave Milosevic one month to end the fighting in Kosovo, threatening additional sanctions and intervention. Albania again called for a NATO peacekeeping force. FRY invited foreign forensic experts and offered talks to the LDK. Shoring up his position, Rugova was again re-elected "president." A deal was struck, returning Albanians to the public school system. Concurrently, the KLA warned Rugova he could not accept anything less than independence and killed six Albanian so-called collaborators.

15 April 1998. Ethnic-Serbs abandoned homes in the Decani area as armed KLA members took control of western Kosovo. KLA men, many of them masked, try to take over the Pristina-Pec highway.

23 April 1998. In a show of strength for Milosevic, a Serbian referendum polled ninety-five percent against international mediation for the crisis in Kosovo. Over sixty percent of the voters participated.

23 April 1998. Serb forces broke up a band of an estimated 200 KLA fighters crossing the border from Albania. Sporadic fighting caused casualties on both sides. Refugees crossed into Albania.

29 April 1998. Contact Group imposed new sanctions on Belgrade.

3 May 1998. There was heavy fighting as Serb forces moved on Drenica area. Albanian villagers took up arms alongside KLA fighters. Both Serb forces and KLA fighters contested for control of the border.

15 May 1998. Milosevic and Rugova met directly in Pristina. The talks were brokered by US Bosnia negotiator, Richard C. Holbrooke. The US softened sanctions on FRY, angering some Europeans. Rugova broke off talks because of stepped-up Serb military operations.

28 May 1998. NATO deliberated over Kosovo and decided to send additional personnel to Macedonia. NATO opened a base at Krivolac.

21 May 1998. KLA spokesman Jakup Nura, speaking to the Albanian newspaper *Kombi*, stated that Rugova should press for independence. Reports cited KLA attacks against neutral Albanian villages.[28]

29 May 1998. Dr. Rugova met in Washington with US President Clinton who urged him to return to talks with Milosevic.

10 June 1998. Serb security forces ended a five-day sweep of border area, which caused some 10,000 villagers to cross over to Albania. This brought charges of use of disproportionate force and intent to conduct ethnic cleansing from NATO and Western observers. By mid-month, the count was up to 20,000 or more. The Serbs laid landmines in an attempt to create a security zone aimed at preventing attacks from across the border by KLA infiltrators.[29]

15 June 1998. Eighty-three aircraft from thirteen NATO countries conducted mock air attacks over Albania and Macedonia in a display of strength designed to pressure Milosevic into halting military actions in western Kosovo. President Milosevic assured Russian President Boris Yeltsin he would protect Albanian civilians and work for a political solution acceptable to both communities, insisting, however, that FRY territorial integrity be preserved intact. He stated that his forces would continue their military activity. This fell short of what NATO wanted. Planning for NATO air strikes continued. Members expressed the need to obtain an UN mandate, which would permit intervention in the internal affairs of Yugoslavia. It was likely that Russia would veto this in the UN Security Council.

23 June 1998. KLA rebel fighters continued to hold villages west and southwest of Pristina as up to 50,000 Serbian police and army personnel deployed armor and heavy artillery in preparation for an assault against ethnic-Albanians armed with lighter weapons.

30 June 1998. Holbrooke talked briefly to KLA fighters at Junik and then to LDK and Serbian representatives in Switzerland in an effort to get negotiations started. The Contact Group stated it was opposed to independence, but admitted the importance of the KLA.

"Vote for Arkan," Eastern Bosnia near Zvornik.

Serb refugee from Krajina in Pristina, Kosovo.

Market stalls in Grbavica, Sarajevo.

Signboards of the Democratic Action Party in Sarajevo.

British IFOR unit near Sarajevo.

Pro-coalition marchers in Sofia,
Bulgaria, February 1997.

Demonstration in Sofia, Bulgaria, February 1997.

VMRO-CDM party office in Bansko, Bulgaria.

Victory celebration in front of the Nevski cathedral in Sofia, February 1997.

Miron Cosma, head of the coal miners union at Petrosani, Romania.

Ceauşescu's mammoth "House of the People" in Bucharest, Romania.

Romanian miner outside the Dalja mine in
Petrosani.

Young boy in front of workers' homes in
Petrosani, Romania.

Demonstration in Athens, Greece, 17 November 1990.

Athens riot police ready to
move against anarchists,
17 November 1990.

Anti-government trade union demonstration in Athens, April 1991.

Trial of George Koskotas. The accused is seated under the arm of the prosecutor. Athens, Greece, January 1992.

Yugoslav police position at Komorane, Kosovo, August 1998.

Yugoslav police armored vehicle at
Kormorane, Kosovo, August 1998.

Yugoslav police guarding farmers during harvest in Belacevic, Kosovo, August 1998.

Albanian family at Kormorane, Kosovo, August 1998.

Serbian Ministry of Information building in Belgrade after
NATO bombing, August 1998.

Yugoslav government building in Pristina
after NATO bombing, August 1999.

Graffiti in Pristina, Kosovo, August 1999.

Ransacked USIS center in Belgrade, August 1999.

Kingdom of Yugoslavia, 1929, 1939

Banovina of Drava

LJUBLJANA

ZAGREB

Rijeka

Banovina of Croatia

Banovina of Danube

NOVI SAD

City of Beograd Authority

Zemun · Pančevo

BELGRADE

BANJA LUKA

Banovina of Vrbas

Banovina of Drina

SARAJEVO

Banovina of Morava

Zadar (Italy)

Coastal banovina

SPLIT

NIŠ

Banovina of Zeta

Lastovo (Italy)

CETINJE

SKOPLJE

Banovina of Vardar

LEGEND:

Bounderies of banovinas* established in 1929

Bunderies of the banovina of Croatia since 1939

* Large administrative unit headed by ban

Occupied Yugoslavia, 1941

MARIBOR

LJUBLJANA

ZAGREB

N.Gradiška

Jasenovac

NOVI SAD

Sr. Mitrovica

BEOGRAD

Jajinci

Rab

SARAJEVO

NIŠ

SPLIT

Mostar

CETINJE

PRIŠTINA

SKOPJE

Banat under German Administration

Territory annexed to Hungary

Serbia under German occupation with the quisling government

Territory annexed to Germany

Territory annexed to Italy

Montenegro with the Italian governor

Territory annexed to the Italian 'Great Albania'

So-called 'Independent State of Croatia'

Territory annexed to Bulgaria

Demarcation line between German and Italian spheres of influence

Main concentration camps

Jasenovac Concentration Camp

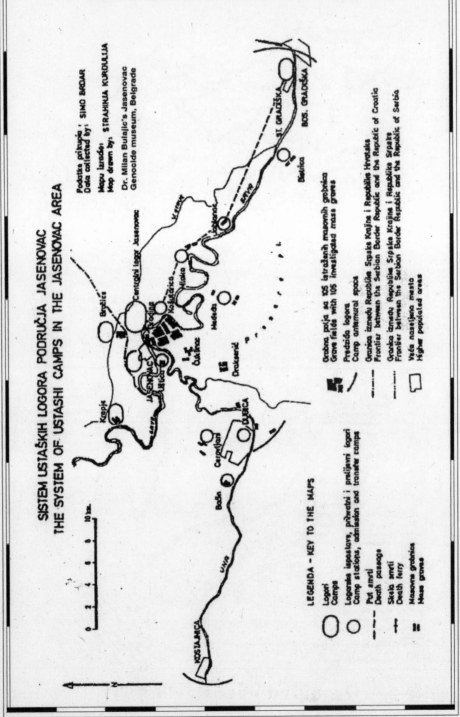

Chapter 7

The Fascist Phoenix

Croatia: January 1993–October 1998

I was sitting outside at the Esplanade Hotel's Bistro cafe on a warm summer evening in Zagreb. It was early August 1998. A cold carafe of dry white wine had been served by a waiter with very pale skin, pale blue eyes and bleached blond hair. He was slim, polite, and feminine in manner. He wore a waiter's uniform whose origin was probably Austrian. As I admired the provincial rococo and fin de siècle buildings across the street, the sounds of a piano intruded on my attention. No, it couldn't be! But yes, it was! The lilting strains of "Lili Marlene" floated in the air as if to provide a fitting accompaniment for the shiny Mercedes Benzes and BMWs that were gliding up to the entrance. Also suggesting Zagreb's ostensible orientation were conspicuously displayed advertisements for MasterCard, DHL, and Delta airlines. Delta doesn't go there. But never mind. It is nice for some to think that it will one day and that Americans and other wealthy Westerners will rediscover the splendors of the Esplanade as some did during Tito's time.

After a good grilled trout, I lingered on to avoid returning to my hotel room by the tram tracks and examined the usual handout describing Zagreb's events and performances for July and August.

On the cover was the statue of one of Croatia's national heroes, Ban (governor) Baron Josip Jelacic who, during the revolutions of 1848, took command of the Krajina military frontier and led mostly Serbian soldier-peasants into Hungary at Vienna's behest to share with the Russians the bloody task of repressing Hungarian freedom fighters led by Lajos Kossuth. The Croat patriot served reaction. Just recently, Croat author, Predrag Raos, described how a youthful Austrian Emperor Franz Joseph, having found out that the fifty-something general's mistress was only sixteen, played a prank and announced their nuptials. Never one to disobey Vienna, Jelacic married the girl and tragically gave her and their only child syphilis to which they both succumbed. Vienna further rewarded Croatian loyalty by narrowing their already limited liberty and placing them even more securely under the heel of the Dual Monarchy, in fact the Hungarians! There, at Jelacic Square (until a few years ago, Republic Square), the Ban, his sword and horse are facing south—never north.[1]

Its first pages were devoted to one Adolf Mosinsky who had built Zagreb's sewer system at the end of the nineteenth century. An ad for Dr. Zeljko Takac's (MSc.) treatment of nervous disease ("nerves and brain") hinted at *Mittel Europa*'s traditional anxieties. Next were schedules for summer and folklore festivals—the theatre, museums and galleries. But apart from foreign performances, Croat was the only ethnicity cited. The same went for libraries and Zagreb's other public places. And, instead of listing the availability of religious services for different faiths, it noted only Holy Mass and the twenty-four Catholic churches one might visit. It suggested that Serbs, Jews, and others no longer existed in the mind of Zagreb's official tourist office.

Over more wine, I turned to the *Croatia Weekly*, published by the Institute for Culture and Information. Just as when Rebecca West was visiting in 1938, it headlined that the Austrians and Germans were thronging the Adriatic beaches. Eerily, like the Nazi Germany of that day, it editorialized its concern about Croatia's birth rate and urged every married couple to have more than three children. Readers were assured that recently rocky relations with the US had improved after Croatian Foreign Minister Mate Granic had met with Secretary of State Madeleine Albright, and that President Tudjman would probably make an official visit to Washington the following January. Croatia, it said, was being congratulated after having submitted its first draft of its Return of Refugees and Reconstruction Plan to the international community.

226

There was, however, great concern in Zagreb over the future of the Croatian community in Bosnia-Herzegovina, and it alleged how the previous March the Croat member of the Bosnia-Herzegovina presidency, Kresimir Zubak, had been badly bullied and insulted by the US special envoy for the Balkans, Robert Gelbard.

Another article lashed out at the departing IHR's man in Mostar, Martin Gorrod, calling him unjustifiably biased against Croats. It reported that Tommy Baer, head of B'nai B'rith's international department, had visited Zagreb in connection with the pending trial of World War Two Ustashe war criminal, Dinko Sakic, who had been handed over to Croatia by Argentina. And there were pieces about the coming beatification of Cardinal Stepinac. Given its overall content and tone, the newspaper strongly suggested that, while Croatia might claim that it is part of the West it is still firmly rooted in the Balkans with all that this means. In the past, it had always belonged to something larger. Today, however, it is just another small country obsessed with its own sense of nationalism.

However, if one man can be credited with willing its independence into being, it is Croat President Franjo Tudjman. He fought as a Partisan officer in World War Two and became the JNA's youngest general, having passed through the "inferno" described by Milovan Djilas: a war against the fascist occupiers, a civil war, and a national revolution. To understand the predicament of Croat communists at the time, one should recall the genocide conducted by the NDH (by one's own people); the retribution meted out to upwards of 30,000 Croat Ustashe, Domobrani, and family members (on one's own people) who were prevented from escaping to Austria by the British army at Bleiburg; and the fate of the Croat communist leader, Andrija Hebrang, who, in 1946, was found guilty of wartime cowardice and collaboration with the Ustashe. Tudjman, however, was a zealous communist and moved up rapidly in the ranks. He became the JNA's chief political commissar, a convinced ideologue. He was a vain, pompous, narrow-minded man, and given to emotional ranting.

Tudjman acquired a PhD in history in the 1950s. While in the JNA he insistently began to immerse himself in aspects of wartime Yugoslavia that Tito and others thought best kept buried. He went into the archives at Zagreb military academy and became convinced that the official version of the misdeeds of the NDH, and what happened at Jasenovac concentration camp, was a plot to blacken and repress the Croats. He claimed that only 30–40,000 had died there, many at the hands of Jewish "kapos," or trustees. Tudjman's scholarship has been discredited by many, but writings that he began publishing as early as 1963 provide needed insight into his conversion into a Croat ultra-nationalist with a fascist philosophy. He participated in the resurgence of Croat political consciousness referred to previously that finally led to Tito's crackdown on Matica Hrvatska and the Maspok movement. As one of its leaders, he was jailed and thrown out of the LCY. He went to jail again in the 1980s (but with very lenient treatment) and was released at the time Milosevic was rising to power in Serbia.

A man with a mission, he used his passport to travel abroad for the purpose of gaining the support of Croat-exile organizations located around the world. The stiff, gray-haired, bespectacled, former general with a crooked smile and strained demeanor must have seemed like an ageing schoolmaster to Croats in Canada, the US, Australia, Western Europe, and Latin America for they were the remnants and second-generation sons of uncompromising anticommunists, including extremists who had engaged in terrorist activity against Tito's Yugoslavia. In all likelihood, Tudjman's military bearing, solid dissident credentials and his absolute belief that he had unlocked the truth of Croatia's past—that he alone understood how Croatian history was being played out—convinced them to get behind him. As the League of Communists of Croatia (LCC) collapsed, he formed his Croatian Democratic Union (HDZ). For the presidential election of April 1990, he had US$4 million available, most of it from Croats abroad and in Germany.

Tudjman risked everything by inviting dozens of exiles to Zagreb to attend the first HDZ congress on 24 February 1990. He warmly embraced their presence. He told a packed hall of 2,500 delegates in emotionally loaded language that they would seek independence. He went on to wed the NDH's darkest World War Two past with the present by saying, "Our opponents see nothing in our program but the claim for the restoration of the independent Croatian Ustashe state... These people fail to see that the state was not the creation of fascist criminals; it also stood for the historic aspirations of the Croatian people for an independent state... They knew that Hitler planned to build a new European order..."[2]

His words, and the return of the exiles, not only rallied the Croatian population. It caused widespread fear in a Serbian community that felt that it was being threatened. In retrospect, their concerns were justified. They were written out of the new constitution and made to accept second-class citizenship. Those refusing to take loyalty oaths were hounded from their jobs and apartments. They were subjected to attacks on their properties, homes and persons. A campaign of persecution was instituted.

It is interesting to compare Tudjman's philosophical outlook with the romantic nationalists of nineteenth-century Prussia and some of the national socialists of the Nazi movement, for there is a startling similarity of thought at some points. The Croat president's most famous, or infamous, book—depending on one's point of view—is his *Wastelands of Historical Realities*, published in 1989. It is a distillation of his earlier writings and represents the core of his worldview on the eve of Yugoslavia's destruction. Tudjman returns to the Old Testament of the Bible to trace the efforts of the Jewish nation to eradicate its enemies. He describes this as a genocide ordained by God who used the instrument of his chosen people. Indeed, this is applicable for all peoples, from those of ancient times up to our modern age. He sees it as a natural phenomenon, like famine or flood. He concludes, "Firstly, in history there have always existed attempts to devise a final solution for foreign or undesirable racial, ethnic or religious groups through expulsion, extermination and conversion to the true faith."[3]

Tudjman draws on a hodgepodge of sources to bolster his argument, even Marx, and turns to Frederich Nietzsche to say, "he [Nietzsche] thought that any struggle and war and any violence in the form of the imposition of one's will on others, was an objective law of life and history." Tudjman quotes Nietzsche's dictum, "Life is a consequence of war, and society is a means of war." Consequently, he is not overly critical of the Nazi era and does not look upon it as an aberration. He is at pains to explain how Germany tried to solve the Jewish "question" territorially through their forced immigration, and then by their transfer to concentration camps or ghetto areas. He argues that Germany came to its "final solution" because of the non-cooperation of others and the hostility of the Allies. If only the Jews had been deported to British Palestine, Ethiopia, or Madagascar (four million were to be sent there), that tragedy could have been avoided. Even as late as April 1944, he argues, Hitler offered a million Jews for only 10,000 trucks. And finally, in yet another travesty of historiography, Tudjman states that the six million dead of the Holocaust is a gross exaggeration and links up his historical revisionism with moral relativism by calling the Holocaust the *shoah*, a "burnt offering" like the sacrificial offerings of ancient times.

Tudjman's rewriting of history was not limited to books alone. In 1991, the Jasenovac war memorial ceased to exist, becoming part of Lonjsko national park. Funding for the memorial ceased. Then, in September, after the war was under way, Croatian forces took the area and destroyed its museum, library, and other buildings containing evidence of the genocide that had taken place there. Documents and exhibits were obliterated or stolen. Back in Serb control by December (but before UNPROFOR inspected the site), it was blasted by HVO tank, artillery and rocket fire. However, the Croat president-historian's effort to erase the past failed, for the shelling unearthed a previously unknown mass grave containing the remains of hundreds of victims. Undeterred, Tudjman took the opportunity during the opening session of the UN peace conference on Yugoslavia at The Hague in November 1991 to insist that Croat deaths during World War Two equaled those of the Serbs.

The Croat president's perverted philosophy permeated his regime and its attitude towards the possibility of peace with Belgrade. At the bottom of it is an implacable hatred towards everything that is Serbian: its Orthodoxy; its more firmly rooted past; the fact that Serbian centralism dominated the first Yugoslavia and Belgrade the second. This hatred stems also from his belief in Croatian superiority because of its Roman Catholicism and its linkage to the Habsburgs and Germanic peoples to the north. Then there's the simple fact that Croatia continues to be at odds with Belgrade over the future of Bosnia. Tudjman wrote, "...It was no accident that the great Roman Empire split into its eastern and western parts on this soil [or] that Christianity split into its eastern and western wings along this same watershed." Tudjman brings his depiction of religious and ethnic oil and water up to date with references to Serbian expansionism since the early nineteenth century, requoting a Croat who said that mutual struggle between the two peoples was inevitable "until extermination, ours or yours"[4]

Apart from Serbs, international Jewish organizations and Israel were outraged when Tudjman's thinking finally circulated to the outside world. France and the UK were irritated and the US was embarrassed. Germany was less so, but it was not very happy with the image that its protégé had acquired. Subsequently, an effort was made to recast the Croat leader as a democrat by a PR campaign designed to convince people that Tudjman had really jettisoned his anti-Semitism and racist views. In 1993, as the US attempted to organize international support for Zagreb, Tudjman was induced to make an apology of sorts to Tel Aviv. To the disgust of many, he was then invited to the opening of the US Holocaust museum in Washington. Next, in May 1995, he attended the fiftieth anniversary celebrations of the Allied victory over Nazi Germany, leaving behind a memento of his thinking—a hastily drawn diagram of how a supposedly independent state of Bosnia-Herzegovina would be carved up one day. And, in 1996, an extensively revised version of his *Wastelands* was published in the US with a lengthy introduction by former US ambassador to the Vatican (1989–93), Thomas Melady, who described Tudjman in glowing terms as a courageous anti-communist and true European statesman. It was another effort to placate the Jewish community and its influential Congressional lobby. The Croat head of state had yet to be accepted by world Zionism, however, despite diplomatic relations having been established between Zagreb and Tel Aviv in 1997. Croatia is still very much on probation.[5]

In this context, a problem was laid on Zagreb's doorstep in June 1998 when Argentina extradited known World War Two Ustashe war criminal, Dinko Sakic, back to his homeland for trial. The circumstances of his return remain unclear in a situation where Sakic had openly bragged of his past, Nazi hunter Simon Wiesenthal and others held derogatory information on him, and Argentinean President Carlos Menem's government remained under a cloud due to unsolved bombing outrages against the Jewish-Israeli presence in that country. If Sakic's (and his wife's) return was meant to test Tudjman's stance on this issue, there were already indications that the charges would probably be framed in such a way so as to minimize the Ustashe commander's guilt. Having written his book, Tudjman could not do otherwise.

In a real sense, Tudjman himself had accepted much of the NDH's past as part of Croatia's struggle for independence. But just who are Dinko and Nada Sakic? Evading justice through ratlines run by Monsignor Krunoslav Draganovic, Sakic arrived in Argentina on the ship *Takuman* out of Genoa in 1947. For a time, he lived under the name Ljubomir Bilanovic, but later he took his own back and became acquainted with Argentine President Juan Peron and ex-Paraguayan dictator Alfred Stroessner. Dinko and Nada had three children and lived comfortably for decades. Franjo Tudjman met Sakic in 1994 while visiting Buenos Aires. Sakic, in turn, visited Croatia in 1995 and stated that he was not only proud of his deeds in World War Two but would repeat them today. He extolled president Tudjman and said that the NDH regime of his time had laid the foundation for today's Croatia. Tudjman said much the same, calling it an "integral part of Croatian history." He went on to state, "…in the Ustashe movement were noble people, pursuing noble goals who coveted a free Croatia." Tudjman explained the origin of the NDH's extermination of the Serbs as due to the war and the "collision of two historically interdependent, exclusive, and intransigent state programs." He suggested it was natural for the NDH to fall in with Hitler because Germany fulfilled the historic territorial aspirations of the Croats, giving it Bosnia and the Sandzak.[6]

Sakic was then seventy-seven years old. In the early days of World War Two, he was the brother-in-law and aide-de-camp of Major Vjekoslav Maks Luburic, NDH commander of the concentration camp system (Ustashe Defense) and perhaps the most notorious of the NDH's mass murderers. Sakic arrived at Jasenovac in February 1942 and was made deputy of the Stara Gradiska section. In November, he went to Jasenovac's Camp III as deputy. By mid-1944 he was commander of the entire complex of killing grounds spread over 110 square kilometers where daily hundreds of its unfortunate inmates went to their destruction. In April of 1945, Sakic was instructed to destroy the camp as Partisan forces closed in. He completed his work amid the execution of prisoners who had failed to escape when camp security began breaking down. Elements of the 4th Serbian Brigade entered the camp on 2 May and found a scene of destruction, its buildings burned and the Sava clogged with dead bodies. A terrible stench filled the air. Years later, an examination of the files of the International Red Cross in Geneva yielded only propaganda photos of a "work camp" where healthy looking men and women were busy at their tasks. A snapshot from that time shows a handsome Lieutenant Sakic in his black uniform, Gestapo-like dress hat, leather-belted blouse, breeches, and jackboots. He carries what appears to be a leather switch or swagger stick. Standing next to him is his pretty wife, Nada, who, with her sister, Maya, were guards at Jasenovac. There exists extensive information about him in Yugoslavia's archives and a half dozen or so people are still alive who remember him as a murderer. The litany is long: the time he shot down Leon Perer and Avram Montiljo, Jews aged seventeen and sixteen; the many times that he ordered the hanging of prisoners; the time he shot and killed the Croat poet, Mihovil Miskin; and the time he quartered a child of one of the Serbs captured on Kozara mountain. In March 1947, the Croatian state war crimes commission declared him a war criminal and ordered proceedings against him in the People's Court.

Following Sakic's extradition, several demonstrations took place on his behalf. Miroslav Rozhic of the extremist Party of Rights wanted Sakic amnestied. However, he stood indicted for ordering executions, attending them, and not preventing them. Sakic's wife, Nada (now "Esperanza"), who worked at Stara Gradiska reportedly committed repeated acts of extreme brutality to female prisoners and engaged in personal executions, often robbing the victims as they entered the camp. It is hard to imagine Nada with a Schmeiser automatic and a killing knife, but much of the horror of Jasenovac was revealed at her sister, Maya's, trial after the war. Efraim Zurof, director of the Simon Wiesenthal Center in Jerusalem (who located where Sakic lived in Argentina), viewed the pre-trial situation with considerable foreboding. He found it very unnerving that no one had spoken up against the demonstrations for Sakic. He was also amazed to learn that a woman who had assisted Tudjman on his *Wastelands* book, and was officially responsible for Croat-

Jewish affairs, served thirteen years for airplane hijacking and murder after 1976 as a member of an extremist organization. It was another aspect of Croatian experience that Tudjman accepted.

Croat clerics and the Vatican facilitated the exfiltration of many Ustashe members out of the country in 1945 as Tito's AVNOJ regime was taking power and oppositionists were being hunted down. False documents, money and safe conduct were provided. Ustashe were also recruited out of internment camps by Western intelligence services for anti-Yugoslav activity. By 1950, Ante Pavelic (the *Poglavnik*, or leader, of the wartime NDH) had set up the Croatian Liberation Movement (HOP) with General Drinjanin (Maks Luburic) as its military commander. HOP was reorganized in 1967 by Dr. Stjepan Hefer, Pavelic's successor. A long series of assassinations, bombings, airplane hijackings, and armed attacks on Yugoslav embassies, missions and clubs ensued, too numerous to mention here. There were terrorist operations inside the country from 1974 onward as well. Stjepan Bilandzic of the Croat National Resistance in Germany spoke for all: "Yugoslavia must be destroyed either with the help of the Russians, or the Americans, with the help of communists, non-communists, or anti-communists, with the help of anyone willing to destroy it, to destroy it by dialectics, or by dynamite… but destroy it at all costs!"[7]

By the 1980s, there were many Croat exile centers in action. It was this receptive environment that Tudjman found waiting as he traveled abroad for support, spreading the word that the time was fast approaching when Croatia would become independent. In Zagreb, Croat separatists hired the ex-Austrian Consul-General Johann Josef Dengler to facilitate contacts with Vienna and Bonn. Tudjman and Archbishop Franjo Kuharic acted for state and church. Dengler played a key role with Helmut Kohl's ruling CDU. He also advised Tudjman to launch his HDZ on his own, not in a coalition and prepared an agenda, which with hindsight proved very prophetic:

1. Declare Croatia's independence and sovereignty;
2. Tactically, propose a confederation;
3. Draft a new constitution and hold a referendum before requesting international recognition;
4. Zagreb should secede while Serbia is occupied with its Kosovo problem;
5. Lastly, quickly privatize property to attract foreign capital.[8]

A few years ago, an American diplomat returning to Athens after visiting Zagreb had commented, "Fascism is so thick up there, you can actually smell it!" I felt for the young officer whose duty it was to defend US policy. Was

Washington blind to what others were seeing, namely, that during the war, hundreds of neo-Nazis fought alongside the Croats; that often, Croat fighters were wearing Ustashe-type uniforms, even with swastikas on their helmets; that a Mile Budak Foundation had been established "to promote the real values of Croatian culture and literature"; that a school and a street had been named after the former NDH Minister of Education and Religion who urged that "A third of the Serb population be killed, a third converted to Catholicism and the remaining third expelled"; that Budak's books have been republished; that a dean of Zagreb's medical school cited racial differences between Croat and Serb skulls; that a team of Croat scholars claimed to have discovered racial links between the Croats and the Persians in an attempt to claim Aryan, non-Slav origins for the Croatians; that hundreds upon hundreds of anti-fascist names of streets had been changed and similarly named memorials torn down; that a new morbidly pagan "Altar of the Fatherland" has been erected at the old fortress of Medvedgrad; that Tudjman's "Great Guard of Honor" has been uniformed in a splendor matched only by the megalomania of the president's own "whites," which even outdid Marshal Tito; that state television's film library had been recently purged of materials relating to Croatia's World War Two NDH and Ustashe past? There was even worse in a nation of five million that had come more and more to emulate the dictatorships of Europe's dark past.

Although Croatia was a client of Bonn and Washington, the latter had increasingly criticized Zagreb's record on human rights, particularly concerning its dwindling Serb minority. In August of 1998, an American diplomat in Zagreb gave me a copy of the State Department's annual report for 1997 with the comment that it would read virtually the same for that year. It was a strong indictment that unfortunately will not significantly influence US policy as long as Croatia is viewed as a useful ally against Belgrade.

Its twenty-three pages can be summarized as follows: Croatia is democratic only in appearance. Its powerful presidency and the domination of the HDZ preclude a real opposition. Its last presidential election was fundamentally flawed. The regime's powers, its control of TV and its increased control of radio and press, make the system, in reality, authoritarian. The Serb minority in Slavonia and Krajina is being subjected to threats, looting, beatings and even murder. Few arrests have been made by a politically controlled police and judiciary. Judges and state attorneys have been purged. Although Serbs in east Slavonia have now been provided with documents, only a small percentage of those who fled in 1995 have been permitted to return. Forced evictions and dispossession of property continue.[9]

The dream, indeed the belief, that all of the South Slavs would live in peace and prosper together is effectively over for now. The memory of that great, urbane Bishop Strossmayer who stood up to Franz Josef and warned that his misrule in Bosnia would cause Austro-Hungary's collapse, the man who fought anti-Serb racism and anti-Semitism, has been lost amid extremism and clericalism.[10]

That August, in the hot sun, I ignored the beckoning cafes with their walnut crepes and strukli pastries and trudged up to The Kaptol to visit Zagreb's twin-steepled cathedral, for soon there would be an event that, in addition to bestowing the Vatican's implicit blessing on the Tudjman regime, would divide the Croat Catholics from the Orthodox Serbs like nothing else. That was the pending elevation of Cardinal Alojzije Stepinac by Pope John Paul II to one step below sainthood. In no other place in Croatia do history, tradition, piety, a momentous evil, and the yearnings of a people coexist more vividly. The light inside was dim and I moved in the gothic gloom as if in a room filled with ghosts of the past. Against one wall was a bas stone relief of Stepinac being blessed by Jesus, which had been done in a naive style by Ivan Mestrovic. It had been donated by Croatian-Americans from Detroit. It was here that Stepinac had been buried in 1960. Now, however, in preparation for his beatification, he had been moved behind the main altar and rested on a catafalque in an ornate silver casket. At the end facing the altar, Stepinac, wearing his cardinal's hat, gazed down serenely in a golden death mask. The sides of the casket were embossed with the faces of his flock. I thought of the untold dead at Jasenovac and wondered what had gone on in the mind of this man who had stood by while hundreds of thousands were being murdered? It is a question asked by many.

Stepinac was born in 1898 into a wealthy peasant family. He was called up during World War One and served with other Croats in the Austrian army. However, he deserted, and ended up alongside the Serbs on the Salonika front. He later studied agriculture and joined a Catholic student association. He acquired a reputation for having an excessively pious, priggish personality. In 1924, he broke his engagement with his intended and entered the priesthood, spending seven years at the Jesuit Gregorian University in Rome. After his graduation, at age thirty-two, Zagreb Archbishop Antun Bauer brought him to the Cathedral. He became the Archbishop's assistant two years later. There, Stepinac organized a campaign against offences like swearing, sunbathing and mixed swimming. He also believed, like almost all Croat clergymen, that the Serbians were apostate and should be converted to Catholicism. He viewed Orthodoxy as having a pernicious influence in the region. It is indeed possible that his dogmatism even increased after the Vatican signed a sweeping Concordat with the Yugoslav government only to see it withdrawn because of Orthodox opposition. Likewise, the concessions to the Croats contained in the Sporazum of 1939 were undone by the entry of Yugoslavia into World War Two in April 1941.[11]

Thus, as the country was overrun by German, Italian, Bulgarian, and Hungarian forces, Zagreb's Archbishop was a relatively young, inexperienced man whose only moral and political terms of reference were the Vatican in Rome and the church's militant experience in his own homeland, Yugoslavia. He records in his diary on 9 April 1941: "...the Yugoslav army is very weak. Croatian soldiers do not want to fight. The Croats are surrendering to the Germans, or are even going over to their side to fight against the Serbs. The state is disintegrating, which is exclusively the responsibility of the Serbs and their barbarian conduct towards the Croats."[12]

Stepinac had, years earlier, sworn an oath to uphold Yugoslavia and the Royal Yugoslav Army. But, in April 1941, he writes nothing of how his own priests were rallying to the Ustashe who had set up a recruiting office a stone's throw from the cathedral at Kaptol 4. The Franciscan monastery at Cuntic also went over to the Ustashe. Reverends Herman and Benko are singled out for praise. Earlier, the high schools had been prepared by the Franciscan Dr. Radoslav Glavas. Dr. Viktor Gutic had recruited the villages and sworn to secrecy monastery friars and parish priests. In the euphoria of a new dawn, others like Friar Berkovic of Drnis and Reverend Vilim Cecelja of Hrastovica proclaimed they had been Ustashe for years. Dr. Dragutin Kamber wrote, "A large majority of Catholic priests were among those who prepared the creation of the NDH." Even the Archbishop himself had interceded on behalf of the jailed Budak. On 10 April, Ustashe leader Slavko Kvaternik proclaimed the NDH: "Due to God's providence and the will of our allies!" Stepinac wrote, "...This day represents a turning point in the life of the Croatian nation... The people welcomed the proclamation... and also welcomed the German army. The Ustashe are taking over in all fields." The next day, the new authorities told the populace over the radio to turn to their parish priests for instructions.

Immediately, Archbishop Stepinac extended his support to the NDH. He visited the head of the police, Milovan Zanik, and personally congratulated Kvaternik. Stepinac described that Easter Sunday as being very festive. The Cathedral was packed with high officials. General Kvaternik (who acted for Pavelic until the *Poglavnik* had arrived from Italy) sat in the cathedral's shrine and was blessed by Stepinac. Numerous photos show Stepinac standing or sitting at the right hand of ranking Ustashe, German and Italian officers.

Likewise Stepinac's subordinates are shown blessing Ustashe-NDH functions and being sworn in as curates to military units. Even as Stepinac wined and dined NDH functionaries at his palace, a number of his underlings enthusiastically became Ustashe killers in priest's clothing. Friar Miroslav ("Satan") Filipovic commanded Jasenovac for four months and, according to his own confession, 20–30,000 people were killed during that time. It is simply not credible to believe that Stepinac remained unaware of the horror that began within only days of the NDH's coming to power.

Indeed, Stepinac took the initiative to introduce himself to the *Poglavnik* upon his arrival on 16 April, a day before the final surrender of the Yugoslav army of which Stepinac was chief vicar. He wished God's blessing on Pavelic's endeavors and said that the church would refrain from interfering in politics, even while his minions were involving themselves at all levels. Pavelic said that he would support the church fully and vowed to get rid of an "Old Catholic" sect that allowed divorce and to crackdown on an Orthodox Church, which he viewed as a political organization. That same day, Stepinac wrote in his diary, "If that man rules Croatia for ten years, as he said he would, Croatia will be a paradise on earth." Pavelic's NDH established a hell on earth for the next four years whose excesses shocked some of the most hardened Italians and Germans. On 28 April, Stepinac told his clergy, "God has done this and our eyes are full of admiration."

By that date, 260 Serbs had been executed at Glina and a genocide was being organized. Stepinac made a mild protest about this on 14 May and then visited Pavelic on 26 July and heaped praise on him. This is the pattern that would continue throughout the war. A slaughter would be described as a "mistake." The church's paper *Katolicki List* threw its weight behind the regime. It detailed events and published the speeches, announcements and edicts of a NDH government that claimed its racial policies (pogroms) were more advanced than in Germany. On 5 May, the Bishop of Banya Luka, Platon Jovanovic (68), was dragged to the Vrbanja River and killed. The Metropolitan of Sarajevo, Petar Zimonjic (75), was killed. The Bishop of Gornji Karlovac, Svetozar-Sava Trlajic, was tortured at Gospic and herded off with 2,000 others to Velebit Mountain and killed. Again, the Catholic episcopate in November 1941 chided a regime already soaked in blood over the "mistakes" and the "lack of success" of the mass conversions because of some "irresponsible" acts, but then praised Pavelic, absolved the regime of blame, and said what had happened was a reaction to twenty years of Serbian repression. On 28 November, Stepinac again countered criticism: "It is not drunkards, nor murderers, nor thieves, usurpers, fornicators, nor card players who form the firm foundation of our fatherland… but hard-working, sober, honest, and conscientious men." *Bog I Hrvati* (God and the Croats) became the watchword!

The oath upon joining the Ustashe was taken with a crucifix, knife and pistol. Before going off to slaughter or force a conversion, Ustashe members were blessed by a priest. After the deed, they were given the communion sacrament and absolved of guilt. This, at least, was the theory. Many murderous orgies dispensed with the fine words and were sustained solely by the beast that dwells in man. Consequently, thousands of conversions where priests were present were followed by a quick execution. Others were permitted to live. In May 1944, Stepinac reportedly notified the Holy See that 244,000 conversions had taken place. In fact, this had been a program that Pope Pius XII had taken great interest in. There was considerable correspondence between the Vatican and Stepinac and Italian prelates in Zagreb. It also became a matter of some controversy between Stepinac and the regime where it pertained to Jews who had converted to Catholicism and those of mixed Jewish-Catholic marriages. These people were at risk of being taken off to concentration camps and Stepinac availed himself of legalisms to save some 300 persons. In a similar vein, he made an official appeal that "non-Aryans" (Serbs) who were married to Catholics be dealt with "administratively" differently from those who had no such relationship. Stepinac even offered to bring the church's investigative powers to bear to separate the so-called "worthy" from the "unworthy." Another appeal regarding 200 Jewish orphan children went awry when the Catholic church helped collect them, and they were then sent to Jasenovac where they all perished.[13]

Stepinac wrote some letters of veiled criticism and he talked around these issues in several sermons. However, he never took a resolute stand and said, "This I cannot permit!" He continued to officiate as the regime's highest ranking cleric, expressing great concern for the future of the NDH right up until the end.

In October 1946, Stepinac was sentenced to sixteen years' hard labor for his "offence against the people and the state." During his trial, Stepinac and his defense lawyer described his many contacts with NDH's leadership as merely perfunctory to keep communications open so that Stepinac could help people. Ignoring the fact that NDH's conversion program was carried out in close cooperation with the church (in fact planned by Stepinac as head of the episcopal conferences), and orchestrated by Pope Pius XII at the Vatican, Stepinac again defended it as a way to save lives. And, when accused of treason because, as the vicar of the royal army, he was sworn to defend Yugoslavia, Stepinac took refuge in his religious duties of rendering "spiritual aid" to the

Catholic soldiers of the NDH. Stepinac stated that his conscience was clear on all counts. It has been reported, and it is no doubt true, that Stepinac would not have been tried if he had agreed to Tito's offer to head a Catholic church under state control, as was the case with the Orthodox church under communism. This he refused.

Rome responded immediately by excommunicating those responsible, ignoring Tito's offer to release Stepinac to a Vatican exile. In the event, Stepinac was placed in solitary confinement for five years and then he was released to live out his days in his home village of Krasic. In December 1952, Pope Pius XII made Stepinac a cardinal. Marshal Tito, in turn, broke off relations a month later. Then, having made Stepinac into a martyr against communism, Pius XII, as did John XXIII who followed, continued to remember their son Alojzije in their public prayers and pronouncements. On 10 February 1960, Stepinac died and was to be buried at Krasic. However, an autopsy was performed first in Zagreb on the morning of 11 February, during which his heart was removed and given to Archbishop Seper. The corpse was sent back to Krasic for burial. Somehow, the police were informed of what happened and they made Seper hand over what was obviously intended to bolster the myth of Stepinac's martyrdom. Alive to the political implications, the regime relented and permitted Stepinac to be buried in the Kaptol Cathedral on Friday, 12 March. His heart vanished!

Milan's Archbishop, Giovanni Montini (later Pope Paul VI), compared Stepinac's trial to that of Socrates and Christ. John XXIII made a statement of how he had personally prayed for the blessed soul of Stepinac at St. Peter's Basilica. So it continued. Stepinac's almost pathological fear of communism was remembered by Pope John Paul II, who was himself deeply involved in opposing the communist regimes of Central and Eastern Europe. Regarding Yugoslavia, he continued the policy of his predecessors by not apologizing for the role of the church during World War Two. He took the position that he would visit Yugoslavia only if he would be permitted to pray at Stepinac's tomb. In other words, a stubborn confrontation between the Vatican and a changed and changing Yugoslavia continued into the late 1980s. When the Berlin Wall fell in 1989, and there was upheaval in the communist world, Yugoslavia was poised to be the first to join the European Community and all of its institutions. However, amid internal economic and political strains that were little noted or ignored by the international community, Croatian and Slovenian separatists were plotting secession.

In February 1991, the Croat bishops, led by Archbishop Kuharic, sent a letter to their colleagues abroad that posed the dangers of the "forcible imposition of a communist dictatorship"; told of the church's "difficult historical experience" in the first and second Yugoslavia; and raised the prospect of independence. It also singled out the threat posed by "Serbian interests," "its politicians, army officers and... certain leading figures in the Serbian Orthodox church." It emphasized the threat of "communist ideology, greater Serbian aspirations, and military force," saying "...they are firmly opposing Western cultural tradition and those with a pronounced West European tradition." It also claimed that the "Serbo-communists" were engaged in a relentless, vulgar propaganda campaign against the church, the Holy Father and the Vatican. The letter made mention of mass hatred directed against Catholics because of "the desire of Slovenia and Croatia to become independent." And so it began all over again.

At the time of the May referendum for independence, the church's newspaper in Zagreb, *Glas Koncila*, disabused its readers of the possibility of Catholics living happily in Yugoslavia. It called the vision of "...Strossmayer, naive Catholics and non-Catholic Croats" an unachievable dream, and claimed that the church and Catholics would always be disadvantaged. It stated that it would be a "sin to repeat unsuccessful experiments" and instructed its congregation exactly how to mark the ballot papers, and provided an example in blue ink marked "for" (independence). Naturally, the ballot paper to be marked "against" (Yugoslavia) had been printed in red. It cited guidance from the Second Vatican Council and, as a final argument, it incredibly reached back to the tragic June 1928 death by shooting of Stjepan Radic at the hands of a Serb MP during a session of parliament to suggest that all Serbs are crazed murderers.

Within a few days of the successful referendum, President Tudjman was at the Vatican and met with John Paul II. He held discussions with Monsignor Angel Sodan, acting papal Secretary of State, and then he visited the famous, or infamous, St. Jerome Institute, which has figured in so much Croat Catholic church history. There he met Monsignor Ratko Peric and talk of mutual cooperation took place. A month later, Tudjman's announcement of secession was immediately supported by Archbishop Kuharic, who summoned a bishops' conference that declared that federal Yugoslavia was "dead," and that any attempt at armed opposition by Belgrade was immoral, against human rights and against a right to self-determination.

It also called on the international community for support. On 26 July, John Paul II spoke out in support of Croatian "freedom and democracy." And as the fighting began, Kuharic and his bishops spoke out in ever-shriller tones to catch the ears of Catholics around the world. In the months to come, support for Zagreb was mobilized not only by the Vatican, but by other Catholics abroad.

On 3 October 1998, Pope John Paul II beatified Cardinal Stepinac at a ceremony held at the shrine of Marija Bistrica near Zagreb before an estimated crowd of 350,000. The Pope praised Stepinac as a martyr to communism over an appeal by the Simon Wiesenthal Center that Stepinac's war record be exhaustively examined first.[14]

* * *

If Serbs trace their lineage back to Stefan Dusan and earlier to assert a historic legitimacy to their lands, the Croats point to their Pacta Conventa, which, from 1102 when the Croat nobles made agreements with Koloman the king of Hungary, set out their feudal rights and duties under Hungarian suzerainty. Under the pact, the nobles paid no taxes and had other benefits in return for serving in the king's army. They were considered equal to the Hungarian nobility. In the eighteenth and nineteenth centuries, a larger and stronger Hungary attempted to absorb Croatia. However, the pact was valid on paper until the end of the Austro-Hungarian empire in 1918. A legal document, therefore, underpinned Croat claims to statehood. In fact, it was the fear of being completely absorbed by Vienna and Budapest, or being overshadowed by an expanding Serb state that gave rise to the nationalist movements of the late 1800s. A Party of Croatian Rights was set up by Ante Starcevic, whom we have mentioned earlier. This father of the modern Croat state was also the intellectual fount of the anti-Serb fanaticism that has flourished in this century.

Thus, in 1918, when the Kingdom of the Serbs, Croats, and Slovenes was proclaimed, there were two strong strains of nationalism that contended under an overarching Yugoslavism—Serb and Croatian. The Serbs, no doubt, viewed their military success and territorial expansion with satisfaction (despite catastrophic war losses) and went about with the weight of their greater population to create a centralized state and a strong standing army, concepts they had adopted decades earlier under the influence of Ilija Garasanin.

For most Croatian politicians, trying to salvage their pride in the ruins of military defeat and a dead Pacta Conventa, an early enthusiasm for Yugoslavism soon evaporated and they viewed it as the hegemony and chauvinism of the Serbian bourgeoisie and their king. They failed to appreciate the prospect of building a state in cooperation with others and continued to view things through the narrow prism of an endangered nationalism, which came to be expressed by a virulent strain of ethnic and religious prejudice.

Their largest political party, the Croatian Peasant Party (CPP), which had been set up by the brothers Ante and Stjepan Radic in 1904, immediately opposed a unitary government and insisted that Croatia be given autonomy within a federal state. In this, he was backed by the more extreme Party of Croatian Rights and the Pure Party of Rights. Several arrests set an unfortunate precedent.[15]

In Serbia, a popular broad-based Radical Party under Nicola Pasic had dominated politics since the turn of the century. It and the other main parties all believed in Serbian and, by extension, Yugoslav unity under the Karadjordjevic dynasty of King Alexander. The tasks at hand were enormous: post-war reconstruction, repayment of debts, development and modernization of a largely peasant economy, and the need to protect themselves from Italian inroads in the Adriatic. A strong state was necessary. In the first free election under universal suffrage (ethnic Hungarians and Germans were denied the vote) in 1920, Serbian Democrats won ninety-four seats, Serbian Radicals eighty-nine, the Communist Party fifty-eight, the Croat Peasant Party fifty, Slovenian and Croatian clerics twenty-seven, Bosnian Muslims twenty-four, and Social Democrats ten. A government was formed under the Serbian Democrats and Radicals led by Pasic. Parliamentary democracy again got off to a bad start when Radic's peasant party boycotted the assembly and the communists were declared illegal. The CPP-led Croats were almost all rejectionists. The communists soon went underground.

Given a free hand, the Serbian parties drew up a constitution to their liking. It passed 223 to thirty-five, with only 258 present out of 419 originally elected. It set forth a constitutional monarchy (a king with strong authority) and a unicameral assembly of 315 delegates elected every four years by direct, secret ballot. King Alexander took his oath on 28 June 1921 (Vidovdan Day) and power was concentrated in Belgrade, mainly under the control of Serbian politicians and appointed officials. Belgrade imposed its will on an unreconciled populace. Civil liberties were whittled away as the country became more and more authoritarian because of Serb-Croat confrontation. Radic returned to the assembly only to walk out again. He went to jail, this strange, uncompromising, charismatic man whose forte was merciless verbal abuse. "Swine," "gamblers," "gangsters," "tyrants," and "foreign agents" were among his favorite epithets. On 20 June 1928 a Montenegrin MP accused of corruption took his revolver into the assembly and shot Radic, killed two members outright, and wounded another. Radic lingered on for weeks and uttered words and wishes, which were seized upon by the Serbians and Croatians alike. His death was traumatic.

In January 1929, most probably in sorrow, the king shut down parliament, suspended the constitution and placed even greater limitations on political activity. Democracy was put on the shelf for another time, perhaps. His declaration of a Kingdom of Yugoslavia meant little to people who continued to think mostly in ethnic terms. New internal boundaries (banovinas) were devised and gerrymandered to give Serbs control of six regions, the Croats two, the Slovenes one, and Muslims none. The arrangement continued to favor the Serbs, as did changes in 1931 that saw the establishment of a bicameral assembly that did nothing to change the status quo. The death of Radic and the advent of what was virtually a dictatorship caused the Croats to become even more disdainful of Yugoslavism. None of them thought of restoring parliamentary democracy. They all wanted the downfall of the king, the destruction of Yugoslavia and a Croat state of their own. Dr. Ante Pavelic, who headed the Frank wing of the Croatian Party of Rights, went abroad and established in Italy under Mussolini's control what came to be known as the Ustashe ("Insurrection") Croatian Revolutionary Movement (UHRO).[16]

Pavelic had first contacted the Fascist Party in 1927. He worked through Senator Forges Davanzatti and by 1932 had set up a camp at Borgotaro in Parma province. In December 1933, he sent Petar Oreb to make an attempt on the life of Aleksandar, who was visiting Zagreb. It failed amid fatalities and Oreb told all. Pavelic moved camp, but established a propaganda center in Milan. Earlier, there had been a raid near Gospic that ended with arrests and much publicity for those captured, who were depicted as heroes by both the Croats and the Communist Party. Now also active in Hungary, UHRO and the Macedonian VMRO assassinated King Alexander and French Foreign Minister Louis Barthou in Marseilles on 9 October 1934.

The assassination of Alexander was condemned in the West and by the League of Nations. Mussolini was forced to intern the UHRO in Italy on the island of Lipari and place Pavelic under arrest. He was not sent to France, however, where he was wanted for murder, and he and his family were relocated to Cava dei Tirreni and kept under control. The camp at Janka Puszta in Hungary was closed. It forced Pavelic and his intimate associates to explain themselves and their political philosophy. A constitution had been written in 1932. A year later, Pavelic announced the "Principles of the Croatian Ustashe Movement." The documents expressed two salient aims: the racial purity of a Croat nation and the absolute power of the state. Ethnically, the Croats were declared a nation unto themselves unlike any other. Only ethnic Croats were to vote and have "sovereign rights." Given their unique Aryan nature, they were not bound by international law. Their goal was to liberate Croatia by any means and exclude other ethnic groups. Pavelic, the Leader, took his oath of office on the "principles" in April 1941. Absolute obedience was required of UHRO members, who swore to execute Pavelic's orders with the help of "Almighty God and all of the saints." If one broke the oath, the punishment was death.

There were economic and social welfare aspects also. All material and intellectual property was to belong to the state for its use. Natural resources were not subject to private exploitation. Also, the land was to belong only to those working it and their family. The Ustashe thereupon made inroads into Catholic organizations as well as the CPP. The latter, if it articulated a philosophy, held to a Croat folk nation, a state of peasants on the land. Croatian soil and a close association with nature made the peasant and his family a purer, superior being. Like many of the Ustashe beliefs, it also had a mystical appeal. Therefore, at the popular level, particularly among people with limited education, religion, race and special bonds to the Croat soil became fused. Many who joined the Ustashe were from farms and villages. It later became known that Radic's successor, Vladko Macek, had met Pavelic in Vienna in 1930 and proposed cooperation. This was preceded by a proposal by the CPP's Stjepan Kosutic in 1927 that Pavelic form a fighting wing for the party. Other CPP exiles like Juraj Krnjevic had contacted Pavelic as well. The two movements shared the same goal, a Croat state, even though the autocratic Macek's attitude toward Pavelic went up and down. By 1936, the CPP had set up armed formations of its own, the Peasant's Defense and the Citizen's Defense, both of which were modeled on the Austrian Heimwehr and Hungarian Honwed and which would later throw their lot in with the Ustashe, or the army of the NDH. By ideology and organization, the Croatians were preparing an armed revolt.[17]

The European context in which this was happening was the spread of fascism and a growing threat to democracy and world peace. Hitler had reoccupied the Rhineland in 1936 and was rapidly rearming. He would unite Germany and Austria in the Anschluss of 1938 and take Sudeten Czechoslovakia after the Munich agreement. Italy had sent troops into Ethiopia in 1935 and was building an African empire. Italy had also occupied nearby Albania. Both supported the rebel forces of Franco in Spain. World war was only months away.

Given the gathering storm clouds abroad, and the realization on the part of Prince Pavle and Serbia's ruling elite that Croatians could not be induced to accept a Yugoslav national identity, the need for political compromise assumed utmost urgency. Macek, the leading Croat politician, also headed the United Opposition, which amounted to a coalition of Croat and Serb parties against

Pavle's government. Without even a common program, they won 1,364,524 votes to the regime's 1,643,783 in 1938. Macek was given a splendid welcome by Serbs in Belgrade. In February 1939, Pavle dismissed Prime Minister Milan Stojadinovic and replaced him with Dragisa Cvetkovic, who had been the prince's protégé. Macek would hardly think of embracing his Serb brothers, but he did sense it was time to accept the 1931 constitution and gain Serb concessions.[18]

He and Cvetkovic entered into talks lasting from April to August of 1939. Out of those negotiations came the Sporazum, or the "agreement," an understanding that amended the constitution and created the Banovina of Croatia, the only such in Yugoslavia to have an ethnic name. It combined the banovinas of Savska and Primorska with parts of Bosnia-Herzegovina. The boundary was not finally fixed, however, as plebiscites were to take place in a few districts in Bosnia. It was to be self-governing, with Croats filling its administrative posts. A ban, nominally under the king, headed an executive council responsible to an autonomous assembly, or Sabor. Only defense and foreign affairs remained in the hands of Belgrade. Leaving the opposition, Deputy Prime Minister Macek brought five CPP members into a Cvetkovic cabinet to join the Radical Union, Agrarians, the Slovenian Peoples Party, the Yugoslav Muslim Organization, and one independent. Unfortunately, Macek viewed the situation from Croatia's own interests and only secondarily for the advancement of Yugoslavia. Macek clearly dominated Croatian politics and maintained his complete control of the CPP.

Interestingly, the Banovina of Croatia was set up as a unitary, centralist state, as Serbia had been, with no provisions for local rule for its large Serbian minority. In fact, under Macek, no effort was made to promote civil liberty and the formation of democratic institutions. Ranking members of the CPP and Croatian officials sympathized with the Ustashe and Frankovci (the Frank wing of the Croatian Party of Rights). The agreement was immediately criticized by Serb politicians, the army and the Orthodox church who felt it weakened both Yugoslavia's national and Serbian interests. Others disliked it on democratic grounds as a deal done between Macek and the crown, pointing out that Macek had not been elected to rule Croatia, but appointed by Pavle. Macek, adapting to the temper of the times, repressed the left and tolerated right-wing separatists. Pro-Italian and pro-German sympathizers openly made propaganda. Although World War Two began a month after the Sporazum was signed, Macek blindly continued to look at everything exclusively from the viewpoint of Croat nationalism. By the spring of 1941, Yugoslavia was under great pressure to join the Axis. Pavle and the government gave in and

Cvetkovic signed the Tripartite pact in secret. A Serbian military coup swept them from power. Macek fought on to protect Croatia and his Sporazum.[19]

Fifty years later, the second independent state of Croatia became established on the ruins of the second Yugoslavia. At the outset, it lost a short war with Belgrade for control of the Krajina and Slavonia. By 1992, its armed forces had intervened in Bosnia in an effort to expand an existing Croat Herzegovinan enclave. Again, Zagreb thought in terms of Croat territories under the Sporazum and the Greater Croatia that had come to exist in World War Two under the NDH. In 1993 and after, the echoes of ideas that had been discussed at Karadjordjevo hunting lodge by Tudjman and Milosevic in March of 1991 continued to ricochet off the hard realities of more recent events. Although Tudjman lost more territory in Bosnia-Herzegovina, he was not overly pessimistic about the future, for he had strong friends in Washington and Bonn that could hardly ignore him after the Serbs had won a dominant position by force of arms. Besides the Krajina and Slavonia, they controlled close to seventy percent of Bosnia. Surely, the West would not allow that situation to stand!

Despite its setbacks on the battlefield, Croatia was establishing itself on the diplomatic front. In 1992, the Republic of Croatia had won worldwide recognition by successfully playing the role of the aggrieved victim. In February 1993, Zagreb had taken another important step forward by accepting the instruments of accession to the Council of Europe, which it had been invited to join. Many observers believed that because of Croatia's known human rights violations and its involvement in the then ongoing conflict that this was premature, but the EC committee of ministers apparently somehow thought otherwise. As mentioned earlier, steps were taken to improve Croatia's and Tudjman's image. Concurrently, Croatian HVO pushed past UNPROFOR in sector south (Krajina) near Zadar. It continued to argue it was justified in doing so, despite any ceasefire as it was recapturing Croatian territory. It was seldom really challenged, in spite of UN resolutions and reprimands. HVO and Croat paramilitary forces were increasingly coming up against Bosniak forces contesting territory in central Bosnia-Herzegovina. With very few military gains to show against increasing domestic hardships, in March Tudjman was faced with the resignation of his government.[20]

At bottom, it seems, was the discontent felt by many who thought that they had been promised a European life-style when, instead, they found themselves still mired in Balkan blood. Inflation had climbed to over 2,000 percent and had impoverished all but those making money on the black market. A third of the school children were malnourished. Power failures were frequent and the Dalmatian coast, where people once frolicked, was not only dead, but within artillery range of the Serbs. Domestic prices had doubled, while production had halved. The country was trying to cope with an influx of thousands of refugees from Bosnia and the third of Croatia occupied by the Serbs. The average wage had fallen to US$60 a week, a quarter of what was needed for a family of four. And only HDZ insiders were becoming wealthy. Even the Krajina attack was criticized because the Serbs blew the Peruca dam in return, causing even more power cuts. In May, the Croats attacked their Muslim allies at Mostar. But the Bosniaks countered fiercely in central Bosnia-Herzegovina, and Tudjman had to suffer the ignominy of seeing his soldiers and civilians flee to the Serbians to save themselves.

Maja Freundlich, a senior Croat foreign ministry official, in a mid-year article in the *European* newspaper of London, repeated at great length the Croats as democracy-loving victims of aggression, argument. This time, however, he added that the duplicitous Serbs had even managed to turn the Muslims against the Croats. Croatia used the same explanation regarding Mostar, where they had clearly initiated hostilities. The EC's presidency (led by Denmark at the time) never went beyond a letter to Tudjman that held out vague possibilities of sanctions. German Foreign Minister Klaus Kinkel was quick to take the sting out of the EC's "threat" by observing that the Croats were only partially responsible for the problem. This situation seemed to have stuck in the craw of US Secretary of State Warren Christopher, who stated that it was Germany that had helped bring on the Yugoslav catastrophe by their insistent push to recognize Croatia and Slovenia, and then Bosnia-Herzegovina. Christopher was hinting in his lawyerly language that Bonn should do more to control the Croats. This raised the ire of Chancellor Kohl, who immediately rejected the allegation, but in July joined US President Clinton in warning Zagreb not to try to divide Bosnia. Croatia attempted to play Bonn and Washington off against each other like a favored nephew does with his indulgent rich uncles. There on the ground, a French UN helicopter was downed by Croat fire while taking wounded Muslim civilians out of Zepa. Likewise, UN Spanish army Lieutenant Arturo Muñoz Castellanos, 28, died of wounds suffered as he attempted to deliver medical supplies to a Muslim hospital in Mostar. Again, everything was overlooked.

Croatia's intent became clearer at the end of August when HDZ chief in Herzegovina, Mate Boban, convened a meeting of Croatian delegates at Grude who announced they would form the "Croatian Republic of Herzeg-Bosna." They rejected what was being offered at Geneva and stated that their borders would be defined later. It meant that the Croats, with Zagreb's help, would continue to fight. It didn't go well for them, even with Serb help. By early winter, the Bosniaks were winning and holding what they had won. At the year's end, Tudjman and Milosevic offered Izetbegovic thirty-three percent of Bosnia-Herzegovina, and the EU tacked on the prospect of access to the Sava, the sea at Ploce, and more land around the enclaves. The Bosniaks, now being built into a real army, pressed on.

In January 1994, the situation at Vitez became critical and Zagreb broke UN-NATO's air exclusion ruling to fly close air support. Tudjman announced that his forces would enter the fray, only confirming what he had been doing since 1992. In fact, the HVO in Herzeg-Bosna had grown to four brigades under the command of General Ante Rosso, a veteran of the French Foreign Legion. But so had the Bosniaks, who now had almost 100,000 troops fighting against the Croats alone. It was time for Tudjman to cut a deal.

Within weeks, Tudjman and Izetbegovic were in Washington and the Croat-Muslim war was over. US persuasion over the winter months, and both the appeal and logic of a traditional Catholic-Islamic alliance against the Orthodox Serbs won the day. Explaining this amazing turnabout to the nation, Tudjman stated, "We have clearly been promised a range of firm assistance for the early recovery of zones under UN protection." He meant American assistance!

Tudjman immediately took another step, which even a critic would have to admit was skilful. At a UN-brokered meeting in Zagreb, he signed a ceasefire agreement with the Krajina Serbs that in the months to come would lull the latter's fractious leadership into believing that they had won their war and that a political agreement would be forthcoming that would give them independence. He did so having been promised US-supplied arms and the prospect of associate status with the EU. By May, military cooperation between the two members of the Bosnian federation was more and more a reality. At Brcko, Bosniak infantry went in against the Serbs after a Croat artillery barrage. A wounded Croat veteran, Kresimir Zubak, was made the first president of the federation. And, as if to underline the new reality, the Contact Group laid out its final offer of fifty-one percent of Bosnia for the Muslim-Croat entity and forty-nine percent for the Serbs. It would remain the Contact Group's fundamental position until the end of the conflict.

The new Croat-Muslim cooperation was demonstrated dramatically in November as a vital adjunct to a Bosniak offence launched out of the Bihac pocket. Combined Croat-Muslim forces took Kupres in central Bosnia-Herzegovina after HVO artillery pounded the Serbs. For the latter, it was the single most serious setback in thirty-one months of fighting. In fact, the Croats supplied quantities of T-55 tanks, artillery and rocket launchers, which gave the Bosniak infantry assaults an added punch. To the northwest, the BSA was backed up at Bosanska Krupa and had called on the Krajina Serbs for help. Seven thousand Serbs came over from Yugoslavia as well. Then, three weeks after being thrown back along the Bihac-Bosanska Petrovac road, the combined Serb force had Bihac, the Bosniak Fifth Corps, and about 180,000 civilians surrounded. UN-NATO officers requested Croat permission to use its airspace to protect Bihac, which again resorted to its "safe area" status. To stem the counter-attack, the Contact Group offered the Bosnian Serbs the right to link up with Belgrade in the same way that the Bosnia-Herzegovina federation had with Croatia. The EU's input to the pot was to suggest reduced sanctions on Yugoslavia. As winter came on (making further large-scale fighting unlikely), Serbian fortunes had hit a high point amid Western disunity. The Bosnian Serb leadership should have accepted the Contact Group's plan then and there and bargained from a position of strength.[21]

But it didn't. And by the time the Bosniaks broke the Carter ceasefire and began their spring offensive, the Contact Group was denying it had ever offered additional concessions. Karadzic and company had fallen for the oldest game in the Balkans, the same lies and deception that they had often used themselves. The Croat HVO's Operation Flash, which overran western Slavonia in early May, should have been sufficient warning. But General Mladic's BSA was busy blunting Bosniak attacks and his blood lust had blinded him from seeing the reality of what was happening.

Finally, Washington pushed the UN aside. NATO, with Washington's lead, took over and unmistakably sided with Sarajevo and Zagreb against the Serbians. Mladic gave it every excuse. The Croatian build-up around sectors north and south in the Krajina had gone on for weeks. And, after the HVO took Grahovo, Storm came like an August thunderclap. The Krajina fell. And in a few weeks, the Serbs agreed to go to Dayton.

After the peace had been signed, and after the last of the Serbs had left Sarajevo, the most obvious point of tension was between the Bosniak and Croat allies in the divided city of Mostar in south Bosnia, Herzegovina to be more precise. There the EU had taken up the task of rebuilding the city and its lovely, centuries-old bridge, which the Croats had destroyed much, much, earlier. In fact, the bridge, to German administrator Hans Koshnik (a former mayor of Bremen), seemed to symbolize the bonds of cooperation he hoped would come to exist between the Croatian and Muslim communities. On New Year's Day, 1996, a Muslim youth was shot dead by a Croat gunman. Days later, a car was shot up in which two Muslim policemen were wounded. A

Croatian policeman was killed in return. After RPGs were fired into the eastern Muslim side of the city, local Croat leaders demanded complete separation. Koshnik's car was mobbed by angry Croats after he insisted that a dual administration must be installed. Again, Klaus Kinkel weakened the EU's own stance by claiming that Zagreb had only limited influence in Mostar.

Given the fact that the Croats and Muslims fought for ten months over Mostar in 1993, its reunification and integration was viewed as a litmus test for the survival of the federation and of Dayton itself. There, in February, a Croatian hardliner in a Hitler mask stood at Mostar's main checkpost shouting, "Muslims back!" March came with the checkposts still in place and the police extorting money and setting conditions for travel. If the Croats refused to disband Herzeg-Bosna, so, too, had Sarajevo refused to disband its secret police. Tit-for-tat house burning and ethnic cleansing became commonplace, as did kidnapping. The worst offenders were the police. In July, elections for a joint city council served only to confirm entrenched ethnic loyalty. West Mostar became a Croat crime center whose activities went unchecked by the EU's 180 unarmed policemen. Mostar became Europe's stolen car capital, only outdone in turnover by an illegal Croat tax on goods entering the area. Werner Stock, a German police captain, admitted that Herzeg-Bosna under its local HDZ organization was a mafia state. Koshnik, a good man who was undercut by his own government, left, his life threatened. The Croat mayor of west Mostar, Mijo Brajkovic, vowed that they would never give their part of Mostar to the Muslims.

With Bosnia-Herzegovina's first countrywide elections scheduled for September, Tudjman, Izetbegovic, and Milosevic were called to Geneva. There, under strong US pressure, Tudjman was forced to disband Herzeg-Bosna, an illegal entity under the Dayton agreement. However, this had no effect on the outcome of the polls in the federation where support for the HDZ and SDA was reinforced. Non-national parties were marginalized. In fact, Tudjman continued to run the Croatian zone and the HDZ as his "fiefdom" (adjacent as it is to Croatia proper and sharing a common border) as if Herzeg-Bosna still existed. His local supporters couldn't agree more, the idea being to extend the de facto Herzeg-Bosna's power and influence further into federation affairs, hence assuring the future of the Croat community. The stuff of assurance was a February 1997 attack on Muslim visitors to a cemetery organized by HDZ mafia leader Marko Radic. One Muslim died and thirty were injured. A month later Tudjman began his presidential election campaign at Mostar.

That spring, Croats exulted in their new-found power and ethnic authority. Leading the way were HDZ stalwarts and the neo-Nazis of the extreme right.

Back again were the ceremonials, salutes and slogans of the Ustashe era. There, dressed in black uniforms, were men ready to fight and die for the fatherland. Stiff-armed, Hitlerian salutes shot out—"For Home!"—"Ready!" Photos of former Ustashe hung in military barracks. Those still alive held public office. Others received a special pension. Tudjman wanted Pavelic's remains returned from Spain. In his campaign speeches, he repeated his historical explanations supportive of a Greater Croatia. He brushed off US criticism of the ethnic cleansing of surviving Serbs in Krajina and Herzegovina by again claiming it was themselves who were the victims. By both word and deed, Tudjman made it clear that his regime was the successor to the NDH.[22]

The seventy-six-year-old leader would have liked to leave his mark in history as the man who led Croatia into the West. On the contrary, however, his actions betrayed any real vision in that direction. The press was muzzled, except for a few courageous newspapers like the *Feral Tribune* in Split. Those who attempted to speak out were fined, jailed and assaulted. Television and three major dailies were in Tudjman's hands. If Tudjman was not embarrassed over not permitting the opposition to take over Zagreb after a city election they had won, why would he have been embarrassed when his HZD supporters beat political competitors? Minor political setbacks meant nothing to a man whom even ex-supporter, Stipe Mesic, said ruled as a dictator by decree. Judges were dismissed; radio stations closed down.

It was hardly a surprise when, on the first round on 15 July, with a low turnout, that Tudjman won sixty-one percent of the vote. The opposition took a distant second and third—Social Democrats twenty-one and Liberals seventeen. At the time of writing, there was no political center. The HDZ was dominant, with a predicted trend towards the extreme right—the Croatian Party of Rights, the Croatian Pure Party of Rights, Croat Christians, and Tomislav Mercep's new Croatian Popular Party. It was not what one would have liked to see relative to prospects for democracy.[23]

One reason why Tudjman kept as tight a control over the media as Belgrade was to prevent the truth about war crimes and corruption from leaking out to the public and to Croatia's foreign allies. The regime was not always successful. In September 1997, the *Feral Tribune* published another bombshell. A Miro Bajramovic, a former member of the 1st Zagreb Special Unit of the Ministry of the Interior under Mercep, described in detail how they had slaughtered some 400 Serb civilians at Pakracka Poljana detention camp in central Croatia in late 1991. Bajramovic, who claimed eighty-six victims, stated that his unit killed another ninety at Gospic and thirteen at Slano near Dubrovnik. The *Feral Tribune* reported that Mercep was prominent in the

HDZ, was then close to Interior Minister Ivan Vekic, and had been decorated by Tudjman. The paper explained that Mercep, in August 1991, was defense secretary for Vukovar municipality. He had been involved in the robbing and execution of Serbs and his extra-judicial excesses led to his brief detention. He was released by security boss Josip Manolic (Tudjman's closest aide) and flown to Zagreb, where he received new orders. Mercep's men were deployed to the Pakrac area of west Slavonia in October, where ethnic cleansing of Serbs, robbery, detention, torture and eventual execution became routine. Mercep amassed a small fortune from murder. He was subsequently appointed to parliament by Tudjman.[24]

Presumably to deflect international criticism and US pressure, Tudjman began to surrender selected Croat war crime suspects to the International Tribunal at The Hague in the autumn of 1997. No one went willingly, but Dario Kordic, and nine other indictees, surrendered in October. Kordic, a protégé of Minister of Defense Gojko Susak, was accused of involvement in the ethnic cleansing and murder of over a hundred Muslims in Bosnia's Lasva valley in April 1993. In December, IFOR soldiers seized Vladko Kupreskic and Anto Furundzija in central Bosnia. There were others as well. Similarly, by spring 1998, Croatia had issued new directives for providing citizenship documents to Serbs who had fled during the war and who now wanted to return. However, in the former UNTAES of East Slavonia, which was returned to Croat control on 1 January 1998 under the Erdut agreement, nearly half of the 120,000 Serbs who had lived there two years earlier had packed up and left. UNTAES had been billed as a showcase of ethnic reintegration, but even US$450 million in reconstruction aid did not restore trust and confidence. The daily departure of families continued and Croat persecution hurried them on their way.[25]

From time to time, Tudjman had said he was an admirer of Franco of Spain. Both were the youngest generals of their day. Both opposed communism—Tito's Yugoslavia and a left-leaning Republic. Both were fervent Catholic nationalists. Both rose through discipline and will power and were puritanical and bookish. Both had seen war at its worst—Tudjman as a Partisan, Franco as a Legionnaire in Spanish Morocco. Both read history. Both combined a fox-like caution with daring. Just as Franco had done after the civil war, Tudjman wanted to mix the bones of Jasenovac's victims with those of their Ustashe murderers in a vain attempt to twist history to fit his own philosophy. He would then claim this as the reconciliation of Croatia's past with the present. This why World War Two, the NDH, Stepinac, the Vatican, and what is happening today, are all of a piece; why a conference in Split in

June 1998 sponsored by the German Frederich Naumann Foundation entitled "Catholicism and Liberalism in Croatia" proved so controversial; why an agreement between Croatia and the Vatican for the restitution, or return, of all church property plus state subsidies, was retrograde and looked back to the past.[26]

The man then at the helm of the new Croatia didn't live to see Bosnia redivided as he desired. For Tudjman had a form of cancer that was not under control. Nonetheless he must have believed he had accomplished much for his people even though it did require a tremendous toll in death and destruction and a hate that is still burning hard and bright. And there were other rewards: his white and gold uniform; Tito's villa on the island of Brioni; his two sons and a daughter who live well as part of his extended family of sycophants; his wife, Ankica, whom he permitted to keep US$300,000 in eleven bank accounts as "pin money"; a Sabor, which raised his salary to US$198,000 a year (just below the US presidency). He must have felt that his God was smiling down on him, very well pleased.[27]

* * *

5 January 1996. A hail of bullets from the Croat side of Mostar struck a Bosniak police vehicle in the night, seriously wounding two Muslim officers who were patrolling the confrontation line. In the city, Spanish NATO-IFOR and West European Union police try to prevent the situation from getting out of control.
30 January 1996. Serb General Djordje Djukic and Colonel Aleksa Krsmanovic were arrested in Muslim-held Sarajevo, turned over to IFOR, and subsequently flown to The Hague as possible war crimes suspects. Srpska Republika and Belgrade protested.
1 February 1996. The Bosnia-Herzegovina Muslim-Croat federation chose a ruling body almost equally divided between the two communities. Prime Minister Izudin Kapetanovic's fourteen-member body had seven Muslims and six Croats—and one Serb. In Sarajevo, the Serbian population pulled out before the handover of its area to federation authorities.
28 March 1996. German Foreign Minister Klaus Kinkel cancelled a meeting designed to reduce tensions in divided Mostar because the Muslim and Croat sides were too far apart. The Vice President of Herzeg-Bosna, Pero Markovic, stated his intent to use a property commission established under Dayton to move Croats from areas of mixed populations to areas purely Croatian. Markovic, the former mayor of Capljina, had run a concentration camp outside

of Mostar where thousands of Muslim military-age men had been held. Many of them had died from beatings, torture and starvation.

3 April 1996. US Secretary of Commerce Ronald H. Brown died when his US military transport crashed near Dubrovnik. Thirty-five passengers and crew were killed while on an investment-reconstruction tour of Bosnia-Herzegovina and Croatia. On board were a number of senior executives. The following July, US Commerce Secretary Mickey Kantor completed the mission, again with the participation of US businessmen.

30 June 1996. An election for a joint city council in Mostar saw the Bosniak SDA win forty-eight percent of the vote to the Croat HDZ's forty-five. The OSCE ensured that Muslim and Croats will each hold sixteen seats, and each control three city municipalities. Turnout was sixty percent.

27 July 1996. Croatia inaugurated a new investment agency, which attracted little interest from its business community. The sale of state property was mostly benefiting senior HDZ party leaders. Since the war began in 1991, Croatia had received US$1.4 billion in direct investment. Growth had been sluggish, mired in red tape.

31 July 1996. The International Police Task Force (IPTF) asked for the dismissal of the Croat police chief of west Mostar for kidnapping, as well as that of the Muslim deputy at Bogojno for illegal eviction of a Croat family and for threatening IPTF personnel.

1 August 1996. US envoy John Kornblum obtained the agreement of Croat leaders in Bosnia-Herzegovina to disband Herzeg-Bosna before elections set for September 14. In Washington, President Clinton at a meeting scheduled at the White House was expected to urge Croat President Tudjman to halt his unilateral expansion of Zagreb's power in Bosnia-Herzegovina.

6 August 1996. US envoy John Kornblum and EU officials obtained the agreement of Muslim and Croat leaders to form an administrative council at Mostar.

7 August 1996. In Athens, Croatian President Tudjman and Serbian President Milosevic agreed on a framework expected to lead to the restoration of diplomatic and trade relations. The final document, which ended five years of hostilities, was signed on 23 August.

14 September 1996. Croat Kresimir Zubak was elected to the three-man Bosnia-Herzegovina presidency.

22 October 1996. US envoy Robert Frowick, who heads OSCE Bosnia, announced that local elections scheduled for late November would be postponed because of lack of cooperation between the parties. Lack of freedom of movement, voting irregularities, and disagreement over procedures were given as the main reasons.

23 November 1996. Thousands of Croat demonstrators gathered in Zagreb's central square to protest against government efforts to close independent Radio 101. The station had criticized Tudjman's use of technicalities to maintain control of Zagreb's municipal council after a coalition pulled a surprise upset in 1995. It had been vocal on other subjects as well. New press laws additionally restricted the ability of newspapers to operate freely.[28]

9 January 1997. Former warring parties from Yugoslavia, Croatia and Bosnia signed a far-reaching agreement on arms reduction and limitation in Florence. The agreement followed six months of talks in Vienna under OSCE auspices. Sarajevo had been difficult as it wanted three signatures only—Yugoslavia, Croatia, and Bosnia. Finally, owing to US pressure, five entities were noted—Croatia, Yugoslavia, Srpska Republika, Muslim-Croat federation, and Bosnia-Herzegovina.

10 February 1997. Violence erupted in Mostar when 500 Muslim pilgrims en route to Liska cemetery were blocked by 700 Croats who had been participating in a Roman Catholic carnival parade. Shots fired at the Muslims killed one. Thirty others suffered gunshot, club and knife wounds when they were attacked by a special army unit. The Muslim holiday of Bairam (when Islam mourns its dead) was the reason for the visit to west Mostar. The Croats called it an open provocation.

15 April 1997. After local elections two days earlier, the State electoral commission announced that an opposition coalition had nudged out Tudjman's HDZ for control of the Zagreb city assembly. Social Democrats took 24.1 percent and the Social Liberals 12.58 for a combined 36.7 percent compared with the HDZ's 35.67 percent. Polls in east Slavonia where Serbs were to vote for the first since the war, were delayed by a shortage of ballot papers and incorrect voting lists. The UN claimed it was an intentional attempt by the government to manipulate the outcome. Zagreb denied the charge.[29]

15 June 1997. Tudjman was re-elected president on the first round with sixty-one percent. Turnout was fifty-five percent of 3.8 million voters.

1 July 1997. The UNTAES mandate for east Slavonia was extended another six months because the Croatian government had failed to take steps to permit the return of an estimated 350,000 Serbs to the country. During his presidential campaign, Tudjman promised the Croats that they would be able to move to the east by 15 July. Earlier, when being read a demarche by Western ambassadors, Tudjman twiddled his thumbs and then told the envoys that he thought it unlikely that the Croats would permit Serbs to return.[30]

10 October 1997. A new press law was announced which contained provisions to force newspapers to make corrections and clarifications. It also set out the qualifications for chief editors.

1 January 1998. UNTAES turned east Slavonia over to Croatian control, although OSCE would monitor the situation, and IPTF (UN civilian police) were to remain there for nine more months.

29 March 1998. Following a meeting with President Tudjman, US envoy Robert Gelbard stated that he had been promised that Serb refugees would be permitted to return to Croatia. Croatia had increasingly come under pressure from the Western community, particularly the US government, and had been threatened with unspecified sanctions. Croatia wanted to join the EU, NATO Partnership for Peace, and the World Trade Organization and had to appear to comply. However, Carlos Westendorp, the IHR for Bosnia, noted that Serbs living in Srpska Republika were turned back by Croat policemen when they attempted to visit their homes in Krajina.

24 April 1998. Rioting Croats overturned UN vehicles and burned buildings in Drvar in protest after a Catholic procession to the town of Derventa some eighty miles away were stoned by Serbians. Seventeen busloads of Croats, accompanied by Cardinal Vinko Puljic, had taken refuge in the war damaged church that they were visiting. Against UN advice the Croats had gone into a Serb majority area. Drvar is now a Croat majority town where the UN was trying to settle Serbians. Before the war it was almost completely a Serb town. The incident pointed up the difficulties involved in refugee return.

3 May 1998. Gojko Susak, 53, Croatian defense minister, died of cancer. Susak, from Herzegovina, had lived in Canada where he was a very successful businessman. He returned to Croatia and helped to finance the HDZ. He was close to president Tudjman and, as a leader in the HDZ's right wing, he was influential in Bosnia.

20 May 1998. The Croatian government issued new instructions concerning the return of Serb refugees: how they could obtain Croat citizenship papers, time limits for "administrative" actions; and clarifications regarding suspect war criminals. In April, the government adopted orders that departed from a draft that had been worked out with the international community. Envoys on the scene believed that Tudjman himself had tried to deviate from the earlier plan. Tudjman was personally strongly opposed to the return of Serbs and probably relented in the belief that he could defeat the program's implementation by allowing the terrorizing of Serbs remaining in Croatia. The Serbs were afraid to return.[31]

1 August 1998. The owner of one of Croatia's largest newspapers, *Slobodna Dalmacija*, had to sign over his thirty-five percent holdings to the government in payment for US$130 million owed to the state-owned Dubrovacka Banka. The bank, the country's fifth largest, was US$250 million in debt due to bad management and corruption. The newspaper's owner, Miroslav Kutle, was once a friend of Tudjman. He had owned a small restaurant. This development had served to increase government control of the press. Ivana Trump, a wealthy American, owns thirty-three percent of the paper. Remaining shares are held by the paper's employees.

20 August 1998. Slovenia and Croatia, the two countries who felt it was impossible to live in Yugoslavia, have fallen out over a number of issues. Each now had a list of grievances: a border either by sea or land has not been fixed; approximately US$2 billion in property disputes were outstanding; some US$200 million in Croat deposits were stuck in Slovenian banks; the Slovenians claimed the Croats were not paying their fair share of operating costs for a mutually owned nuclear power plant; and competition between Ljubljana and Zagreb as to which country is the true bulwark of the West. Slovenia, of course, thinks of itself as almost a part of Austria. Croatia, situated as it is on the fault-line between East and West, only sees itself in epic terms.

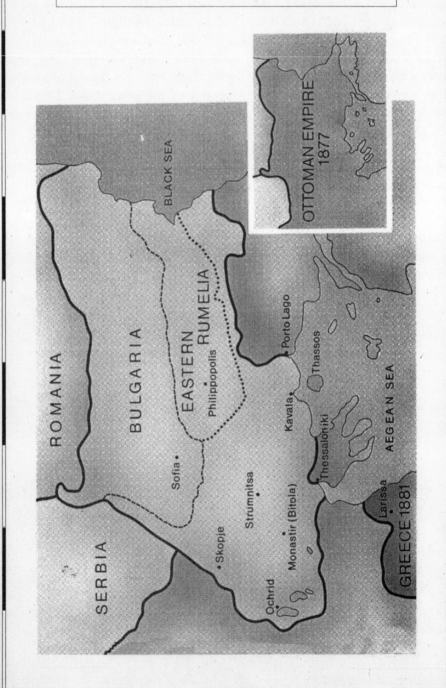

Bulgaria. San Stefano and Berlin (1878) and After

OTTOMAN EMPIRE 1877

BLACK SEA

ROMANIA

SERBIA

BULGARIA

EASTERN RUMELIA

Philippopolis

Sofia

Skopje

Strumnitsa

Monastir (Bitola)

Ochrid

Porto Lago

Thassos

Kavala

Thessaloniki

AEGEAN SEA

Larissa

GREECE 1881

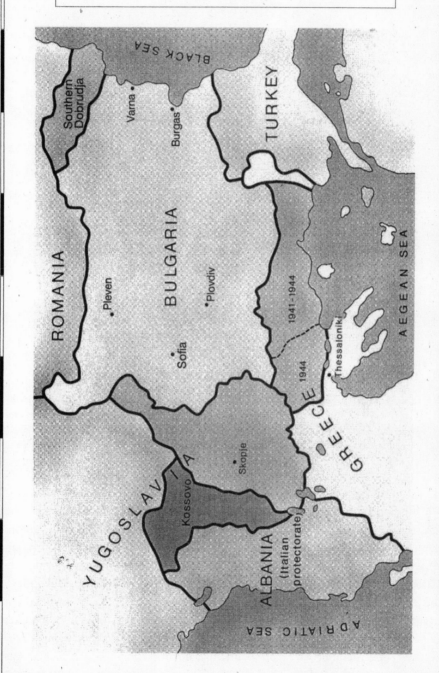

Bulgaria. 1941-1944
and Today

Chapter 8

The Good, the Bad, and the Ugly

Bulgaria: October 1993–June 1997

A Serbian peasant had been honest and hard working all of his life. One day God spoke to him and said, "Jovan, you are a very good man and I will grant you one wish… anything that you desire. But you must know that in doing this, I will do twice as much for your Bulgarian neighbor living across the road." After considering the matter, Jovan said, "God, please remove one of my eyes!"

The Bulgarians have long been loathed by their neighbors, the Greeks, the Serbs, the Romanians and, of course, the "Terrible Turks." Was it more than just a bad press in the past, when the Bulgar was accused of hiring assassins for this job or that: members of the MRO-External during the 1930s—the Vrahovists; the poison pellet on the tip of an umbrella jabbed into the leg of anti-communist dissident and BBC correspondent Georgi Markov in London in 1978 by an agent of Bulgarian security; and the strange plot to kill Pope John Paul II in 1981 using a member of the Turkish ultra-right "Grey Wolves" one Mehmet Ali Agca?[1] Certainly, not too long ago, the feeling was reciprocated by the Bulgarians themselves. Somehow, only the Russians were liked and spoken of with affection, as reflected by the old saying: "Cico Ivan ot Mockva sliza ot Dunava"—Uncle Ivan in Moscow is coming up the Danube (to help us). And Bulgaria has needed help… most often after having chosen the wrong side and finding itself left in the lurch. It came to lack self-confidence.[2]

As the American correspondent C. L. Sulzberger once observed, the Bulgarians are a tough, dour and glum people who have been very unlucky since becoming a modern state, even though they were hard workers, good soldiers and took pride in calling themselves the Prussians of the Balkans. On occasions, they seemed destined for greatness, only to have it all fall apart. By the mid-1990s, their Russian big brother, who had looked on them as the sixteenth republic of the Soviet Union, was no longer able to help. Bulgaria found itself adrift between East and West. I, for one, wanted to see it for myself to determine the good, bad or ugly aspects of its situation. Certainly, a country that invented aerial bombing during the Balkan Wars and then went on to produce the great opera singer Boris Christoff had to be unique.

In mid-February of 1994, I found myself amid shimmering snow on the Markoudjik ski run at Borovets in the Rila Mountains just a stone's throw from the former hunting lodge of Prince Kiro. The nearby peaks floated above the clouds in their unearthly beauty, blotting out, for a time, Bulgaria's past and its present problems. The lift had climbed some three miles over very dense stands of towering pine, lending additional majesty to the scene.

The snow was well maintained, the attendants unfailingly helpful and observant, and the accommodations and food both comfortable and excellent in that order. An evening bottle of red wine along with *papazyaniya* meat and vegetable stew, or some other tasty dish, accompanied by an ensemble playing mostly Bulgarian music did wonders to rest tired muscles as well as ease memories of the madness going on elsewhere in the Balkans. It was inexpensive by Western standards—perhaps a third of what it would cost in The Arlberg, or at Garmish. The five days went by too quickly and I returned to another reality wishing I could have bought a sweatshirt that proclaimed that I had been "Bruised At Borovets."

"Bulgaria is the only country not infected with the Balkan virus. For us, at the end of the twentieth century, this is something that we absolutely refuse to succumb to." So stated Georgi Yuroukov, head of the southeastern Europe section at the Bulgarian Ministry of Foreign Affairs. "For ourselves," he said, "our borders are fixed and final," adding that the Macedonian issue, which had bedeviled Bulgarian politics for decades, is now a "closed book." "Today," he said, "we want only to expand relations with the West so we truly become part of Europe." He allowed how Sofia had been one of the first to recognize the ex-Yugoslav republic of Macedonia as "Macedonia" out of respect for an old idea—"paying their dues so to speak"—but added that while it recognizes the state of Macedonia, they do not view it as a "nation," or "people," as such. To an American, it was truly a Balkan nuance.

Yuroukov said that their recognition of Skopje was intended to remove question marks about the region, to dissuade others from moving against what some might view as a "gray area" (he clearly had Yugoslavia and Greece in mind). He stressed that Sofia wasn't interested in old, historical arguments any longer, but was very concerned with questions of regional stability. He said that if one were to make a survey, every third or fourth Bulgarian would admit to Macedonian roots. He explained that, in 1946, Stalin was seized with the idea of a Balkan federation led by Bulgaria and Yugoslavia that would then redraw their borders. The 250,000 or so living in the Pirin mountains of southwest Bulgaria were told to call themselves "Macedonian" whether they wanted to, or not. Some refused and were punished. Yuroukov said others retained a Macedonian identity after it became politically incorrect to do so, and that pockets of Macedonian nationalists existed who agitated under the banner of what they called the "UMO-Illinden"—United Macedonian Organization-Illinden. He said the same had happened in Yugoslavia when Tito decided to create a Macedonian republic—a million Bulgarians in Vardar Macedonia had to become "Macedonian." He said that Bulgarians were now free to call themselves what they wanted and that this was better all around.[3]

Compared to the orderly, cloistered hush of the foreign ministry, the sound and fury of the Sabranie, Bulgaria's national assembly, or parliament, made quite a contrast. Under Todor Zhivkov it had been nothing but a rubber stamp for the Bulgarian Communist Party (BCP). Now, however, its members freely and fiercely debated the issues almost without restraint, causing US Deputy Secretary of State Lawrence Eagleburger to note two years earlier that, "The Bulgarian revolution has traveled the furthest distance of any country in eastern Europe," calling it a well-kept secret. I didn't agree with the US secretary's hyperbole, but multiparty democracy had taken hold in an essentially violence-free fashion. The only problem was that the political right and left had been butting heads for four years and little in the way of structural reform of a stagnating economy had been accomplished. Just then, the Sabranie was an anvil of clashing views that threatened to collapse the nonparty government of Prime Minister Lyuben Berov, a respected, elderly professor of economics. I sat high in the gallery as speaker after speaker had his, or her, say.

Berov was doing his best to pass a mass privatization bill and the Union of Democratic Forces (UDF), a coalition of pro-market, pro-capitalist parties, were trying to defeat it and bring him down. While this was surprising enough, Bulgarian Socialist Party (BSP)—reform wing—MP Elena Poptodorova told me that they are for membership in NATO and the EU and that the recent visit of the Russian ultra-nationalist Vladimir Zhirinovsky, had "sent chills down their spines." The West had really won the Cold War, she pointed out, and claimed that Bulgarians now expected it to consolidate its gains instead of acting with cautious hesitation, or showing little interest. She thought that NATO's Partnership for Peace might prove too "platonic," whereas they wanted to move things to the "bedroom." Her party colleague, Filip Bokov, said it was the BSP that had drafted parliament's recent pro-NATO statements. This, from former communists, left me amazed!

UDF parliamentary boss and Democratic Party (DP) head, Stefan Savov, said they were fighting to regain power and had (unsuccessfully) brought five votes of no confidence against the Berov government, a government, he explained, that depended on the socialists for its survival. He said UDF was beating Berov over the head on the issue of the rise of organized crime and would soon try again. I asked why the UDF wouldn't work with him, to which Savov stated that they disagreed over the budget and Berov's slower approach to privatization. Moreover, Savov (who had served fifteen years' hard labor under the communists) said that the UDF's liberal, free market orientation was the only political force that could attract the western investment and technology needed to move Bulgaria into the twenty-first century. He was very adamant in his views.

It was an education to move around this small, Renaissance-style, Sabranie and listen to people who, four years earlier, were talking openly only to their close friends in hushed tones behind closed doors or during a walk in the park. It was clear that this simple, unostentatious white building on Tsar Osvoboditel Boulevard had a new central importance, perhaps, for the first time ever.

Representing the linchpin of the Berov government, Movement for Rights and Freedoms (MRF) MP, and deputy chairman of the foreign relations commission, Yunal Lyufti roundly criticized the lack of a bipartisan approach to issues. The MRF, said Lyufti, wasn't just a party for ethnic-Turks, but addressed all national problems—he called it a party for change. He said that moving the country to a market economy and a full democracy really meant restructuring, not only the economy and political practices, but society itself. People were basically conservative and loath to change their ways, he asserted. Currently cooperating with the BSP to keep Berov in power, Lyufti did not rule out working with the UDF again if it refrained from adopting the patronizing attitude towards the MRF it had held during their 1991–92 coalition government. Lyufti said they had repeatedly protested to UDF head and Prime Minister Filip Dimitrov about the lack of consultation and coordination. As for new elections, Lyufti said that they expected to win some twenty-four seats in the next election. The MRF, he said, as a modern party, was a strong advocate of democratic pluralism and minority rights.

With about twenty-eight liberals and independents that voted on either side of the aisle, and a sharp dichotomy between the UDF and the BSP, the MRF had come to enjoy a swing position that made and unmade governments. Consequently, there were constant rumors of shifts in position in a situation that was both static, and subject to change, like a river under the ice. In any case, over the past four years, strongman rule had been stood on its head and while the government could propose, parliament now disposed of any and all matters of any importance. The other big change, of course, was the freedom to take to the streets to demonstrate and strike. In February, 18,000 students from St. Kliment Ohridski (Sofia University) began striking over Berov's austerity measures and shut the school down. They were joined by 4,000 professors and lecturers who also opposed budgetary cuts to higher education. It continued into a third week, closing Bulgaria's first and most prestigious academic institute. It was the second time ever that its staff had struck, having once walked out for four months in 1922! The students were just beginning to feel their strength.

According to Katerina Katceva, a third-year law student and a member of the strike committee, their strike was brought on by drastic cuts in scholarship funds and student subsidies, a situation they had discussed with the government months before their action. She explained that normally tuition was free and that dormitory and dining hall costs were state subsidized. She also cited additional scholarship aid and tax exemptions for poor students. Anton Ivanov, a fourth-year chemistry student, said that many would now attempt to go abroad, exporting Bulgaria's intellectual potential overseas to the detriment of the nation's future. Both said that their strike was apolitical and was not backed by any of the parties. Regarding the much-debated budget of Berov—it had yet to pass its first reading in parliament despite appeals from the International Monetary Fund (IMF) and other financial organizations that it be finalized by the end of February so that other supportive measures could go forward. This had become the pattern that obstructed needed structural reform.

Eagleburger had been half right. Bulgaria had traveled a long way, but it was more like being on a political treadmill. Much energy and many words had been expended, but comparatively little had yet been accomplished.

Nonetheless, they were trying. In June 1990, Bulgaria held its first, free elections. In a real sense, it was a contest between entrenched apparatchiks in the BSP, former communists who were only grudgingly giving way to reformers within the party, and their own sons and daughters who supported a plethora of small new parties grouped together under the UDF. In part, it was generational. The BSP had experience. It controlled state organizations in the old way, even as it tried to appear as new look "socialists." It offered safety and security to rural villages, farmers and elderly pensioners. The UDF was poorly organized and then led by the ex-dissident philosopher, Zhelyu Zhelev, who later became president. It stressed anti-communism and swore that it would make Bulgaria capitalist by the shortest possible route: privatizing the economy, returning expropriated property to its rightful owners, and by opening the country up to foreign investment. It wanted to do it all overnight.

The 1990 election was fiercely, but fairly fought, considering that Bulgaria had very little experience with democracy. It was made even more interesting when the US government under President George Bush sent a group of advisors that some have likened to a SWAT team to Sofia to assist the UDF. This effort to ensure a UDF win came under the Congressional National Endowment for Democracy, which expended an estimated US$1 million during the campaign. It is likely that US intervention was prompted by the BSP's announcement months earlier that its government planned to impose a moratorium on its US$11 billion foreign debt.

When the votes were counted, the BSP had clearly won. Many young people, however, thought it should have been otherwise. A tent city of protesters, the "City of Truth," installed itself in the center of Sofia. The BSP made Zhelev president to take some heat out of the opposition and the UDF's leadership split. This, amid a plummeting economy and living standards, forced the BSP to form its first-ever coalition as it tried to hold on until new elections were called.[4]

In October 1991, the UDF under Dimitrov nudged out the BSP. Amid jubilation on the political right, the UDF formed a government with Ahmed Dogan's MRF. Impatient and inexperienced, it lasted only ten months when the MRF pulled out. With both major parties at an impasse, a government of so-called "experts" was put together under Berov in December 1992. The Berov team began to assess what was needed to save a sinking ship (Bulgaria was virtually broke), while a deadlocked Sabranie leisurely locked horns three days a week. In this effort, Berov was joined by the World Bank, the IMF, the EC, and other agencies. Bulgaria gained some breathing space as bridge loans and expertise became available. In March 1993 it became an associate member of the EC and talked confidently of privatization and the need to orient its trade towards the West. By early 1994, reform had just started to take hold. Restitution for confiscated property was underway, some state firms had been sold, and a Czech-style privatization scheme was finally agreed upon. Some modest foreign investment had begun to trickle in.

But out in the street it was difficult to find much to be really hopeful about. Money exchanges were everywhere, but the value of the lev was being driven lower and lower. People scoffed at the privatization scheme. Not only did they not understand it, they were convinced that the share coupons were virtually worthless. They looked upon it as a way for the government to fob indebted companies off on the public while insiders grabbed what was good. Everyone feared for his job, that his workplace might be closed, or sold to foreigners who would hire and fire them at will. Unemployment was climbing steadily. The shops were stocked with basics, but people enjoyed less and less purchasing power. In a country that a few years earlier was forging ahead in high-technology computers, plastic bags became unobtainable. A people who had struggled with the system under communism to secure for themselves a modicum of comfort were seeing the underpinnings of society being removed one by one. This country of 9 million, 7,650,000 Bulgarians and 900,000 Turks had never known a decent life under the Ottomans, its foreign royalty, or communism. And now, capitalism was a question mark. No one knew how it worked.

Adding to the uncertainty, a new American ambassador had arrived who, during his US Senate confirmation hearing, had stated that he would work to change Bulgaria's constitution to improve the lot of ethnic political groups, meaning the rights of Turks, Macedonians and Roma to form ethnic parties. In the previous October, Ambassador William Montgomery had been hooted and jeered by BSP protestors with placards as he went into the presidential palace to present his credentials to the professor of philosophy, Zhelev.[5] Berov's spokesman, Raicho Raikov, a big man with an easy avuncular manner, appealed for understanding and assistance from the US. He cited the fact that Bulgaria had lost an estimated US$4 billion in trade because of the fighting in the former Yugoslavia, adding that they had complied with the UN sanctions and were not out to make money out of the war. Bulgaria, he said, needed access to Western markets, specifically the EU and US, to survive. He noted that they were still waiting for their EU association agreement to go into effect. He hoped that Montgomery would prove to be a friend.[6]

Raikov adroitly demolished suggestions emanating from the newly elected Greek prime minister, Andreas Papandreou, that a special political axis should exist between the two countries. Raikov said they opposed forming a regional axis, stating that Zhelev's vision of Greece, Turkey, and Bulgaria as a "triangle of security" simply meant good, friendly relations which should include Skopje as well. He hoped that axes were a thing of the past, pointing to the wars, which had erupted in the Balkans because of such alliances. "We need financial assistance," he noted, "but more than that we want trade and investment." He cited plans to build a new Warsaw-to-Athens north-south highway and east west Bulgaria-to-Albania road and rail links. He called Bulgaria a blank spot on the map for investors and said it had endless possibilities to be a real "gold mine." As to their foreign debt, which now stood at US$13 billion, Raikov gave me a wry smile and repeated an old peasant saying: "It is better to divide a debt into small pieces, rather than risking losing the whole!"

So far, Bulgaria hadn't quite matched its bogeyman reputation. Its people were friendly enough without being effusive and much of Sofia—before it spread out in a jumble of ramshackle stucco and wood houses, dreary apartment blocks and industrial sprawl that had the look and smell of a slum—was positively charming. Sure, there were dilapidated rubber-tired horse carts; old Ladas and Moskva cars wheezing their last, broken down trucks and buses, and muddy rivulets running in cobblestone streets. There were poor people dressed in worn, nondescript clothing wondering how they were going to make it through the week and collectors of scrap metal, cardboard and newspaper—anything of value, no matter how small. Some lived right on the refuse dumps. I thought of my boyhood in St. Paul where Irish, Germans, Swedes, Slovaks, Poles, and Russians rubbed elbows in our working-class neighborhood. In those days, men who sold ice, sharpened knives and gathered rags and paper were a familiar sight. Sofia was far from frightening.[7]

And Sofia (from the Greek *sophia*, meaning wisdom), has a better side to show. The center is a compact rectangle of ancient archaeology, history and the imprint of Bulgaria as a modern state. Sofia University and its immediate environs north to the Vasil Levsky monument, west to St. Petka Samardjiiska church on Vitosha, south to the national museum of history, and east, again to the university, contain the president's and prime minister's offices, the parliament, the Alexsandar Nevski cathedral, the ministries, the central bank, the opera, the Ivan Vazov theatre, and a dozen additional points of interest—all within walking distance. It was great to work from the luxurious lobby of the Sheraton with its reliable telephones to make appointments, and to walk my rounds up yellow, glazed brick streets, through shaded parks of chestnuts, and past buildings whose glories had certainly faded, but still looked impressive. Sofia offered an easy familiarity.

The communist era had seen Sofia grow from some 300,000 to over a million. They had built broad avenues, but kept the old parks and green areas, and added new ones to offset huge, high-rise hotels that are outdone only by a monstrous National Palace of Culture, which is now owned by South Koreans. Although the city is huge, inexpensive taxis, buses and electric streetcars reduce the distance. The latter with their hard, wooden seats and dirty windows are recommended because everyone rides and no one pays. A scant half hour brought me above Boyana to the lower slopes of Vitosha Mountain where people can ski in winter. A stony walking path upwards uncovered old villas hidden in the trees, springs of water coursing down their leaf-clogged channels, and an inn which had great beef and mushroom *djuvetch*, with melted cheese (baked in a clay pot) and a good red wine. I had quite by accident stumbled on another of Sofia's hidden delights.

Furthermore, this closed off, very secretive society was proving reasonably accessible to this foreign journalist whose only words in the Bulgarian tongue were *da* and *nyet*. Nowhere else in the Balkans had I found as many officials who were actually at their offices and were willing to give me their time. It might require phone calls from their reception rooms, but the doors opened.

It was February 1996. Because of fog, our Balkan airlines flight had been diverted to Plovdiv to the south. Two Greek hunters got off for what they said would be splendid duck shooting. On the way in, we had an excellent view of the Balkan Mountains, which give their name to the entire region. Three hours later, we were airborne and I was fretting over whether I would make the last public bus for Samokov and Borovets.

After landing, I pushed my way through immigration whose staff take their time to scrutinize arrivals. It's necessary because Bulgaria is a destination for narcotics, which usually enter from Turkey. Once through, I took the usual meterless taxi and negotiated a hotel drop off for my suit bag—then a mad dash to a bus station in south Sofia. I was lucky. In less than an hour, the bus turned onto a road that became more and more narrow as it wound its way through steep, wooded hills close to the Iskar River. Drab, but once-frequented cafes looked empty and abandoned. A spillway, dam and power station spanned the Iskar. Scaled logs were piled, ready for the sawmill. Off to the side, monuments topped by a red star paid tribute to workers whose names were now known only to their families and a few friends. I arrived at Borovets long after dark, but, from the headlights, one could see that the snow was deep and still falling.

Back again in Sofia, I watched the snowfall from the window of my room at the Grand Hotel Bulgaria as a dozen dogs frolicked in a small park just opposite. In the street, it turned to slush. The hotel was far from grand, but was conveniently located and fitted my budget. As usual, tea (*chai*) was better than the coffee and one should arrive early for the breakfast buffet. Outside, a long line had formed at a shop that sold cheaper cigarettes. The customers stood hunched against the cold, hoping to work their way inside before the supply ran out. I walked past the forlorn-looking military club and the tomb of Georgi Dimitrov, once covered with graffiti and littered with trash, but now cleaned up, painted white, and guarded by a single police car. It told anyone who cared to know that the socialists were back in power.[8] An ailing, exhausted Berov had quit in November 1994 after being pushed from pillar to post and finally confessing his inability to continue. In early elections in December, the BSP trounced the UDF, with the socialists taking 125 of 240 seats and the UDF having its parliamentary strength reduced from 110 to only sixty-nine.

To get an objective appraisal of what had happened, I taxied out past the railway station to a sprawling, slab-concrete apartment complex in Hadzi Dimitar to talk to Renata Indzhova, who to me was Sofia's "first lady." Forty-two years old, and combative, Indzhova was named to run Berov's privatization agency over men controlled by various political and business interests. She did an able job, first as deputy, in a situation where a legal framework (detailed laws) had to be passed by parliament line by line. Then, when Berov quit, she became interim premier (the first woman to hold that position) with the mandate to oversee elections and run the government until the winner took over. During her short time in office, Indzhova fired several senior officials who were trying to block privatization. And, she shook up the establishment when she embarked on a personal crusade against organized crime.

Hadzi Dimitar is not the address of the rich. It is ugly and depressing, further evidence that Indzhova had remained clean of corruption. A year after stepping down, she still seethed in anger over the direction she saw her country going. The UDF, she said, was too diffuse; it lacked unity and failed to pull together, even for a national election. It was full of would-be leaders, she added. I gathered from what she had said that the BSP had won because of the UDF's mistakes and the former's appeal for older people. Moreover, in the past year BSP reformers had been sidelined, or shoved aside and the old communist nomenklatura had taken over after they put up thirty-five-year-old Zhan Videnov as their prime minister. The BSP, she said, was not interested in honest privatization. "We are now controlled by Bulgarian, Russian, and Ukrainian mafia," she claimed, "that go right up to the prime minister's office. They are not only buying the best state properties, but are doing it with big loans from state banks, which they are not repaying." In short, she said that the country was being "ripped-off" by a pack of crooked politicians, businessmen and government bureaucrats.

Corruption had existed under communism, but it was kept within bounds by a strict party hierarchy and the knowledge that almost anyone might unexpectedly be called to account for his actions. Today, however, there were no rules and people were grabbing what they could. Because of a massive hemorrhage of non-performing loans, the state banking system was mired in non-recoverable debt. At the same time, people who knew next to nothing about banking were now in business and had attracted depositors because of their flashy offices and come-on. Several had already collapsed and people stood outside trying to get their money back. At the same time, foreign exchange offices were ubiquitous. They all had customers (almost all Bulgarian) who were changing leva into hard currency, or vice versa. This said that somehow money was being generated (legally, or illegally) in a country that was officially close to bankruptcy. A few were making it big. The rest remained poor.

Government spokesman Nikola Baltov tried to put the best spin on things. Handsome, with a good haircut, loosely knotted tie and his shirt sleeves rolled up, Baltov said that one year was not enough to make massive changes. He said that inflation had been over a hundred percent, but was now at thirty-two. The lending rate had been seventy-two percent, but was now thirty-four. He cited a US$500 million trade surplus at the end of 1995. He claimed they had done well consolidating several state banks, but that the private sector lacked discipline and liquidity. He referred to the large number of bad loans that he claimed were made in late 1993. He explained the need for laws to govern banking, business and a securities market, and went on to express confidence in Bulgaria's voucher privatization scheme, which had yet to get off the ground. He described various options that voucher holders could exercise when the government put over a thousand firms on the auction block—a third of the total economy. Crime, he said, was related to social conditions, particularly the collapse of a state system, which had yet to be replaced. He defended BSP's backtracking on NATO membership. He said people were divided on this, claiming the BSP did not want to be diverted from economic issues. He argued that it had taken Spain decades to join.

UDF Vice-Chairman and MP Alexander Boshkov admitted that their election defeat had been disastrous. Not only had they been beaten, but Savov had quit, taking his DP out of the UDF to work with the Agrarian Peoples Union (APU) (forming a People's Union, which had won eighteen seats). "We are still like young children, politically," said Boshkov, a dark, heavy-set man with boundless energy. "We still lack organization, discipline, good archives, and finances and logistics that we can rely upon." He said UDF leader Filip Dimitrov's replacement by Ivan Kostov was the result not so much of a power struggle as the realization that Dimitrov had had his day and had lost. The UDF youth league was weak, he admitted, when, in his opinion, it should provide enthusiastic young cadres, the future leaders. "How can we ask them to sacrifice themselves, or even study, when a young man can join a gang, carry a baseball bat, have a good car, and all of the money and girls he wants? It is the reality that we are up against. Many people are now out to make a killing, run, and just disappear!"

In front of the Sheraton, beggars stood around in the snow while well dressed men and woman exited cars and hurried on past to the entrance. There in the underpass, gypsy children were huddled in a corner sniffing glue. A few discarded syringes were scattered about. Peddlers hawked their wares amid pickpockets and under-age prostitutes. Up again, at street level, musicians scratched out their tunes on crude wooden stringed instruments, or creaky old accordions. I saw my first dancing bear—a pathetic animal with a chain attached to a ring in his nose. He shuffled in a circle on his hind legs, pawing the air, his eyes rheumy and his coat falling out in patches. A man sat by his bathroom scale. People pushed past each other on Vitosha. Stalls crowded the sidewalks, symbolic of a new economic system that was still trying to raise its head. Some months before, there had been a serious shortage of bread that went on for weeks. Videnov's government had sold off Bulgaria's grain reserve to earn hard currency. It miscalculated the harvest and then was forced to import wheat at an even higher price. Bread now cost more and people were still angry. I asked myself how one should assess Baltov's trade surplus.[9]

Velko Ivanov was a fifth-year law student at Sofia University. He was general-secretary of the students' federation and had a paper clipping of George Washington addressing the Continental Congress hanging on the inside of his battered office door. He was well built, very good-looking, spoke excellent English with confidence and maturity and had fallen in love with America during a student exchange spent in Ohio. Over the next hour or so, he hammered home the following points: both the BSP and the UDF were failing in their duty to provide responsible leadership, the BSP had changed, but it still had authoritarian tendencies, many BSP members were unreformed communists who occupied critical positions in the state bureaucracy, they opposed change. The UDF, he said, was unfortunate to have started with Dimitrov. He was abrasive, even antagonistic, when he should have been trying to make friends. The UDF had little in the way of a plan or program, he insisted, other than to be pro-capitalist and anti-communist. "The two, each in different ways, are both inadequate," he said.

That night, I got myself to Fridtjof Nansen to the "Fram" which is claimed to date from 1888. Some young Bulgarians had bought its name, and while it lacked the ambience of age, it made it up in friendliness. I drank the red wine, didn't fuss about the food, and enjoyed the conversation. They, like others, were trying to launch a business of their own as the state sector collapsed. They had put all of their savings into the place. I refrained from asking if they paid protection to any one of the so-called security companies now in operation, most of which were being run by former members of state security (Darzhavna Sigurnost) who kept martial arts and wrestler strong-arm enforcers on their payrolls. Their fears, if they had any, were hidden behind warm smiles. Ominously, earlier that day, Todor Zhivkov had been acquitted of all charges of corruption and released from house arrest!

The former dictator had been sentenced to seven years in 1992 and had been permitted to appeal charges of spending US$24 million in public funds on luxury apartments, cars and entertainment for his family and friends. Supposedly because of his fragile health and age (he was then eighty years old), he was confined to the comfort of his granddaughter's house where he occasionally was interviewed by the media. Upon his release, Zhivkov stated that his trial had been directed against the Bulgarian people, not himself. The charges had been very narrowly framed, without any reference to the thousands that Zhivkov had sent to jail, labor camps, or internal exile, many of whom did not survive. In rendering its verdict, the Supreme Court ruled that its decision was final and could not be appealed. The court also ruled in favor of Zhivkov's aide, ex-Politbureau member Milko Balev, who had been given only a slap on the wrist—an eighteen-month suspended sentence followed by four years' probation. With communist security files still sealed, former BCP Central Committee member Aleksandar Lilov (a powerful BSP member of parliament who operated behind the scenes) bragged openly on TV that Videnov and the cabinet belonged to him![10]

Bulgaria was proving to be a mixture of the good, the bad, and the ugly, with generous amounts in each category. Much of it is beautiful including the mountains and the Black Sea's golden coast. It has ample mineral, water and agricultural resources and produces metals, grains, fruits, tobacco, textiles, chemicals and machinery. It had a large food processing and armaments industry, much of it going to Soviet Bloc and Arab markets. It sought sophistication. Its DS agents had aggressively stolen computer technology. On the cultural side, Sofia still offered concerts, opera, ballet, drama and art. Villages preserved their folkways, handicrafts, song, and dance. A choral liturgy at Aleksandar Nevski is awesome. But now there was spreading poverty and crime. People felt they were in the grip of what they called a mafia—the collusion of big business, politics and crime, which had become the new "system." Bulgaria's only entry at the 1996 Berlin film festival was Ivan Tscherkelow's *Rolling Thunder*, which speaks to the problems of social change and old age. A man, in his seventies, leaves his wife of many years and goes off to a solitary suicide. His alienated sons try to talk him out of it, but are confronted with his unshakeable belief that life no longer has a meaning. This also is Bulgaria.

By early 1996, cynicism had again replaced the optimism that had existed after communism had collapsed in Eastern Europe. It had been a naive belief held by many that the West was eager and waiting to become their new steadfast partner. Boshkov put it best. I had asked him if, in retrospect, the UDF had been hurt by Washington's involvement in the controversial 1990 election campaign. "Yes," he said, "the US jumped in, made a big splash and then forgot us when we lost." He said that both had had high expectations. He said they had thought that heavy investment would come in, that EC and NATO membership would follow. And when it didn't, he said, they felt disappointed and let down. Later, he explained, a well-meaning US ambassador was simply not enough. "We needed top level support... US banks, investors, the Overseas Private Insurance Corporation (OPIC)... But," he said, "they are all looking at the cost, and profits. The European Bank for Reconstruction and Development (EBRD) is no different. They talk big until it's time for action and then they begin to look at you like you are a highly developed country like Denmark. Out come the surveys... a million questions. And then, we have to pay for their consultants and their studies... There is no end to it. Again, we were disappointed!" And now, he noted, the US had not even bothered to replace its ambassador.

In the intervening years, the old "top-down" leaders in the BSP had regrouped. They were backing off from NATO. They claimed good relations with the North Atlantic Cooperation Council, but opposed President Zhelev's every effort to move closer. It now cited Russian sensitivity and the need to protect trade that Bulgaria had with that country. It said it was for privatization, but its projections still left much in the public sector. It went about the task at a snail's pace, suggesting it was a time-consuming job to put good "insider" deals together. One such was Orion group's sale of a piece of Bulgarian telephone to the Intracom Company in Greece in a way that was far from transparent. The commissions, and kickbacks, were said to be substantial. The BSP had even come up with a US$10 million state loan to lubricate the deal. It was trying to keep control of state farms and the agro-businesses—vital to its grip on power in the rural areas—by making them into cooperatives. Since regaining power, it had taken over the national radio and television stations; the national news agency; the privatization agency; the state savings bank; the accounting board; the agency for foreign aid; and were making a move on the central bank. The so-called "socialists" seemed unassailable.[11]

But then a typically Balkan phenomenon began to happen, aided by the accumulated rot of an economy that was approaching free fall. A June presidential primary election, almost a non-event, became pivotal to a turnabout in Bulgarian politics. President Zhelev, having distanced himself from the UDF over leadership issues, put his reputation on the line with UDF deputy Petar Stoyanov and lost. This meant that in an election for a president with very limited constitutional power, Bulgarians would again have the opportunity to express their preference—right, or left. With a confidence born of arrogance, the BSP paid little attention to the event in an election atmosphere supercharged by the gangland-style death by shooting of Bulgaria's first post-communist premier, Andrei Lukanov.

The murder of the wealthy BSP MP at his home (in an area swarming with police) raised questions about crime and corruption that the BSP candidate— lackluster Minister of Culture Ivan Marazov—was ill-prepared to answer. In the first round, Stoyanov took forty-four percent and Marazov twenty-seven percent with millionaire wheeler-dealer Georgi Ganev of the Bulgarian Business Bloc splitting voters and taking twenty-three percent. Ten other candidates dropped by the wayside. Because nobody had gained a majority, a second round was held. Close to the run-off date, a bomb destroyed the car of the chief liquidator of the Bulgarian Agricultural and Industrial Bank, an official who also sat on the electoral board. Voters were again reminded of crime and corruption. In early November, Stoyanov won a resounding sixty percent to Marazov's forty. A lawyer from Plovdiv, Stoyanov saw the situation as a "new beginning" and appealed for popular support from all of the parties of the right to force an early election. During the year, the lev had gone from seventy to the dollar to 240. Even Marazov admitted the vote was a protest against BSP policy.[12]

In the wake of defeat, Videnov vowed to seek a vote of confidence before the BSP leadership and hold a party congress in January to assess its program. His comments were made amid criticism over a failure to institute reform (this coming from party dissidents) and expressed doubts over the leadership abilities of the thirty-eight-year-old prime minister (this coming from the conservative old guard).

A marathon BSP plenum in November narrowly backed Videnov, but the former communist youth leader immediately found himself being questioned about his connections to the Orion group. At a two-day BSP congress in late December, Videnov submitted his resignation both as party leader and prime minister. This development stunned the BSP, and threw its government into confusion as Videnov's action would require the selection of a new premier and cabinet. Sensing that the BSP was now on the run, the UDF began to mount mass demonstrations, which demanded early elections. Stoyanov started to lead his supporters into the street at Plovdiv. In two months time, the lev had gone to 485 to the dollar.

The UDF was armed with the argument that, by failing to meet its reform targets, the BSP had made it impossible for the World Bank and IMF to grant desperately needed funding to finance Bulgaria's foreign debt. In fact, the IMF had been in Sofia since the autumn waiting for the government to get its act together. The country was again close to default. Confidence collapsed as banks closed their doors[13] and although it was clear that the BSP was discredited domestically and internationally, its leaders took the position that it was determined to serve out its remaining twenty-one months.

At that point patience ran out and the people realized that they had to take matters into their own hands. Normally passive, those who had spent hours each day standing in lines (even old BSP voters) now joined the crowds who were swelling Bulgaria's squares. On 8 January the BSP named Nikolai Dobrev as the new prime minister. His cabinet refused a joint "salvation declaration" that the UDF urged it to accept. The BSP intended to brazen the situation out. On 10 January the UDF walked out of the Sabranie apparently timing its action with the arrival of hired thugs who provoked those who were demonstrating outside to break into the building.

In the mêlée that took place between protestors, militiamen and police, dozens were injured. Filip Dimitrov was felled by a blow on the head. Several windows were broken, the entrance forced and furniture was smashed. The authorities were restrained and no one was shot. But Ivan Kostov's UDF had crossed the line into extra-parliamentary action, setting a troubling precedent in a new democracy. Many thousands continued to surround parliament. Aleksandar Nevski and Narodna Sabranie filled to overflowing, always with university students out in front taking the brunt of blows from the police and counter-demonstrators. Outgoing President Zhelev talked to the party leaders, the police and the military in an effort to restore order. But as Stoyanov's swearing-in on 19 January approached, the UDF's ranks were swelled by miners, port employees, factory workers and many others. Stoyanov's inauguration was akin to the crowning of a king, with a blessing both from Patriarch Pimen, who had broken from the communists in 1989, and Patriarch Maxim who had served like a puppet under Zhivkov. With the political crisis still unresolved, the lev fell from 800 per dollar, to 1,500, to 3,000, before stabilizing at around 2,500.

I had arrived at the end of January 1997 and was met at the airport by a driver who took me to Bansko in the Pirin Mountains. The BSP government had become shakier and shakier, but snow is for skiing. I had left Athens knowing that strikes and massive anti-government demonstrations were in progress, not only in Sofia, but all over the country. The truckers, who had swung to the UDF, had begun to block the major highways, bringing the country to its knees. With the main roads and rail lines blocked, Bulgaria was cut off from its neighbors. With Niko at the wheel of his old Opel, we got on Sofia's ring road intending to take the highway south to Blagoevgrad. About a half hour out of the city, we joined a line of hundreds of cars whose progress was blocked by strikers who had put trailer trucks across the road. The stranded drivers were calm, as were the police. Others, in battered old Ladas and Zastavas, escaped the jam by leaving the road and bumping their way over trackless, barren, brown hills to their villages on the southwest side of Vitosha Mountain. It was an amazing display of don't-give-a-damn determination!

I was inclined to try to get through on the strength of my press card, but Niko doubted we could squeeze by to talk to someone. He found two other cars going in our direction—young men with their girlfriends. Over a cigarette, it was decided to try from the opposite side of Sofia on the highway to Plovdiv. So back we went, in a convoy, this time headed southeast. Just short of an hour later, a smaller road began angling southwest again. We were now in steep, forested, hills, which the sun didn't penetrate. Piled snow narrowed the way to a single lane of rutted ice. We skidded our way through, tires spinning, engine accelerating to a roar as Niko sought traction. A rally driver couldn't have done better. Arriving in Bansko after dark, I offered him drinks and dinner. He was determined to head back, however, hoping to make Sofia by midnight. He said he would be back on Saturday. He was as good as his word under bad conditions that gave him every excuse to quit. Perhaps there is some "Prussian" in the Bulgarians after all!

Bansko was great. Superb skiing under the expert eye of Mihail Trenchev who took me to places I thought were beyond my capability. His co-op of men and women also taught trekking, rock climbing, mountaineering and ran an "outward bound" school. They were all local sport enthusiasts who, in the off season, made money working on construction, logging, the saw mill, making wood furniture—whatever was available. They believed in the center's potential and were fighting for developmental investment; the need to keep development in harmony with environmental concerns and privatization that would not exclude them from the picture. They had all helped to build Bansko and felt that they had a stake in it. And as villagers, they were surviving the economic crisis better than those in the city. Trenchev's father was an ex-army full colonel whose pension was equivalent to US$20 a month. But they had a garden, fruit trees, livestock and a few chickens. One woman told me about her father who had worked in a uranium mine and had silicosis. His pension was US$6 a month, half of which went for medicine. Many city people were at absolute rock bottom.

Bansko also was great because the village is quite beautiful—a type of rustic timbered and stone construction I had not seen before. Much of it dated from the nineteenth century. And, maybe not so surprisingly, I found the Macedonian question still flourishing at the local headquarters of VMRO-CMD (Internal Macedonian Revolutionary Organization). To counter the UMO-Illinden and its sympathizers in Skopje (VMRO-DPNE and alleged official support), a pro-Bulgarian VMRO was back in operation churning out political tracts written by a band of believers who lived in villages like Bansko in the southwest. Stefan Zahov welcomed me to his rough-hewn, log office, which was above a small restaurant. On the wall were old photos, a VMRO calendar and a shelf of dusty books. Zahov, a journalist, gave me a short rundown on VMRO's history, including the fact it had been legalized again only in 1988. Now, he explained, it stood with the anti-BSP coalition. Young, with long brown hair and moustache, Zahov looked like a Vrahovist of old there beside his maroon and black VMRO flag. He was warm and friendly and gave me an enormous book on the subject by the Bulgarian Academy of Science, a copy of the "Macedonian Review," booklets, and some VMRO "baseball" cards—a Gotse Delchev, a Todor Aleksandrov and a Dame Gruev—their old heroes who will never die!

In Sofia, the BSP finally caved in and agreed to April elections. Then, President Stoyanov took the constitutionally correct, but risky, course of offering Dobrev the mandate to form an interim caretaker government. As a result of behind-the-scenes talks with Stoyanov, Dobrev allowed his mandate to expire and then told the BSP, "I know that you will think me a traitor, but I will not have my hands dipped in blood." Previously an interior minister, most considered him to be an honest policeman. In fact, within the BSP, he had access to the party's secret files. Many think he was chosen as Premier in December because he was about to bring corruption charges against the BSP's top leaders and that as prime minister he wouldn't turn on the party. He did even better; he turned the game over to the UDF. With the 7 February announcement that the UDF would form an interim government; Sofia went absolutely wild!

That evening, UDF supporters carried Stoyanov on their shoulders and danced in the streets. UDF head, Kostov—a vegetarian and a jogger—said, "I do not promise that you will be richer, or live better. I do promise that under the next government, I will be honest and that you will be master of your lives." The following afternoon, a victory celebration was held in front of Nevski Cathedral. In a square thronged by thousands, pop music competed with Nevski's booming bells. Demonstrators dressed their zaniest—red, white, and green face paint, crazy hats and clothing—and carried banners and flags from all of the parties, and placards that read, "No Left Turn!" and "Communism, Never Again!" A huge national flag floated from Nevski's gold dome. Bulgarians of all ages, usually a somewhat stolid people, literally jumped for joy. They interrupted speaker after speaker with their chants—all jumping in unison—forcing politicians and their wives dressed in suits and furs to do the same. For once, the people were in control. The leaders knew it. Towards the end, Kostov struggled with the cork of a champagne bottle and then sprayed the crowd.

Not everyone had been there, however. Automobiles, trolley cars, and pedestrians moved through the streets. Verdi's *Rigoletto* was playing that night at the Ivan Vasov. The Los Vegas Casino offered roulette, blackjack, and poker. Over at the Rodina Hotel, a young man built like a refrigerator—bald head, earring, in black leather—clinked glasses with a stunning blonde. Outside, sitting in the backseat of a chauffeured car, a beauty with long black hair ran her slender white fingers through her address book while cradling her mobile phone. At the Preslav restaurant at the Sheraton there was fillet of guinea fowl and prawns with fettuccine and Madagascar sauce. Dessert was bourbon over chocolate mousse, or raspberry and peach coulis. For others, mostly the elderly, there were rubbish bins to pick through. On Monday morning, the big automobiles were again sliding up in front of parliament. It was still a cliffhanger, for at that moment, power was suspended somewhere between the street, the president's office, UDF headquarters, and the men and women who were crowding the corridors of the assembly. Such is the raw chemistry of Balkan politics.

Boshkov admitted the urgency of finding common ground among their loose coalition of parties. The UDF would hold a party congress aimed at organizational changes to achieve greater unity and cooperation. It sounded all too familiar. Filip Dimitrov (with a nasty scar on his head) said that because of how things had turned out, he felt completely vindicated that his own reform policies were correct. He said Bulgaria would need help from the IMF, the World Bank and the G-7. He hoped they were more familiar with the country now than they were in 1991. He said conditions would continue to be very difficult, but that, ultimately, Bulgaria would have to learn to stand on its own feet. I asked Lilov if he thought that his BSP had been dealt with unfairly. He glared at me and refused to comment. The BSP had started a boycott even though they still had 122 to 125 votes in the 240-seat assembly. They said that this was much like 1990–91, when President Petar Mladenov and Prime Minister Lukanov were forced out at the time of the "City of Truth" protests. Then, in August 1990, an angry mob had sacked the BSP's party headquarters.

Velko's eyes were red from loss of sleep, but he was happy. "This is a national cause," he said, "and we have tried our best to act in the national interest for everyone." The UDF's Kostov, he admitted, had tried very hard to get them under the coalition umbrella, but so far they had succeeded in staying neutral without any splits. "We are working to create a civil society, a real democracy." He said he and others had been threatened, but he had laughed it off explaining that his days and nights had been so chaotic that any surveillance would have been impossible. Still, he had often been out in front when clubs were being swung. It had been dangerous and dozens of students had been injured. He admitted that the "demo" of 10 January had been joined by about 150 paid thugs who had forced their way into the assembly and caused damage. His partner, Boris Petrakiev, who handled contacts with student organizations abroad said that they had come to realize for the first time that they could change the course of events and that they could exert real power. He said they were determined to defend their rights even if they have to turn on the UDF if they failed to fulfill their promises.

In the weeks that followed, another interim government awaited new parliamentary elections. The difference, however, this time was that the IMF immediately flew in to offer standby credits to temporary ministers who had just taken up their portfolios. In only three weeks, Bulgaria had been assured US$650 million in support. By April, Prime Minister Stefan Sofianski, who also doubled as Sofia's mayor, had won pledges amounting to US$1.2 billion. The UDF had also agreed to institute a strict exchange rate to help stabilize inflation. At the end of April, it won by a landslide—137 seats to fifty-seven for the BSP. Laudatory comments were made by foreign investors who were already looking to make money on Bulgarian debt. A currency board, which would allow appointed international experts to regulate monetary matters, was also in the works. Prime Minister Kostov (who some claimed could control as many as 179 votes in parliament) promised to privatize, close loss-making industries and sell off the state banks to foreign, "strategic" investors by the end of 1998.[14]

I returned in June, sitting in on a business conference that was trying to boost Bulgaria's economic prospects. A number of government officials had been invited. Most failed to show up, without any explanation. Boshkov, now a deputy prime minister, came and urged the attendees to drop their cash at the casino. His remark jarred on my ears. An Israeli (who knew some of my friends in Jerusalem), with Bulgarian forebears, stood up and broke down in tears telling of the difficulties he had experienced trying to do business in Bulgaria. He shouted at the officials on the podium, calling them "liars." Then the American manager for Amoco petroleum told how he had succeeded in opening a gas station (combined with a McDonald's) in record time. He said it was identical to those in America, down to the last detail. I wished those of the new regime well, but I didn't go to the closing dinner. I walked to Graf Ignatiev and sat alone again at an old journalist's club. I was pleased to add my signature to the many comments, cartoons and sketches that hang on its walls. It seemed my face had become familiar.

* * *

Like the Slavs, the Bulgarians entered Europe in AD 500–600, drifting westward in small groups from their homeland above the Amu Darya in Central Asia. They were Turanian, a Turkic people, who were displaced by the Khazars who had settled between the Sea of Azov and the Kuban. Near the mouth of the Danube, they collided with border forces of the Byzantine empire and defeated them. A small Bulgarian state was established at Pliska. Under Khan Krum, from 803–814 it expanded into lands inhabited by Slavic people.

Both peoples were pagan under a Bulgarian prince and a nobility. Within a short time, they were assimilated and all became Christian and spoke Slavic. Boris briefly flirted with Rome, but soon adhered to the Patriarchate in Constantinople and Eastern Orthodoxy. He welcomed scholarship and Slavic culture flourished. Disciples of Cyril and Methodius relocated from Moravia to Preslav, which by 893 had become the new capital. The Glagolitic tongue of the two brothers was modified and "Greekified" to the Cyrillic alphabet used by the Bulgarians, Serbs, and Russians of today.

Under Simeon, 893–927, their first empire held all of the lands south of the Danube from the Black Sea to beyond Belgrade, down below Albania (excepting a slice of the coast), northern Greece—angling from below Janina to above Thessaloniki and Adrianople—and to the Black Sea again. Simeon tried to take Constantinople and failed. He proclaimed himself emperor, however, and raised the archbishopric to that of a patriarchate. In time, resources were stretched thin and some nobles came to resist centralized authority. Also, Bogomilism broke out as a direct challenge to established religion and the powers supporting it.

This upstart empire was attacked by the Hungarians, Pechenegs, and Russians from the north and the Byzantines from the south. The Russ took Preslav (and Boris II prisoner) and then were driven out by the Byzantines who gained control of the area. Samuel at Ohrid (991–1014) raised rebel forces against Basil II (963–1025) and after some success was beaten in a major battle in 1014. Fourteen thousand men were captured and Basil (the "Bulgar Killer") blinded them all save one man in a hundred left with one eye so as to be able to guide the shattered army home. Samuel died of shock and horror when he learned what had happened.[15]

After 150 years of Byzantine rule, Petar and Ivan Asen mounted a revolt of the nobles, which established a second empire at Turnovo at the time when Constantinople was beginning to crumble. It was at its zenith under John Asen II (1218–1241) and was once again the strongest Balkan power. It didn't last long, however, and it broke up amongst rivals with much of it passing to the Serbs. Just decades later, mounted Turks and sea raiders began arriving at the edge of Europe, out for hire or booty. The Ottoman was different, however. They did not immediately foray westward. They stood at the Bosphorus for seven years until they were invited across by the usurper John Cantacuzene, who gave his own daughter to Sultan Orkhan. He then used Orkhan's help to win a share of the imperial power at Constantinople with John Palaeologue. The Turk was soon tied to three royal houses by marriage. Then, when the Serbian Stefan Dusan intrigued with him against Byzantium, he concluded that the duplicitous Christians would be a pushover.[16]

Orkhan continued to play the game with Cantacuzene, the Genoese, and later with Palaeologue, and all the while Constantinople was becoming weaker. In 1353, Orkhan's son came across and soon Turkish settlers in waves that later became a flood. The Ottoman armies threaded their way into Thrace and up the valleys leading to the Danube and introduced a new social order in the wake of their depredations. Orkhan's second son, Murad, turned north toward Bulgaria, a country then divided between three rival brothers and beset with a Hungarian invasion in the west that had been blessed by the Pope. There, Franciscans forcibly converted 200,000 Orthodox Christians to the Latin rite. By 1369, Murad had taken the Maritza Valley and south Bulgaria. One brother, Sisman, became a vassal, his daughter entering the Sultan's harem on the one condition that she be allowed to remain a Christian. He and Murad drove the Hungarians out, but Sisman failed to gain land from his younger sibling. He and the Serbs then attacked Murad at Samokov, but were beaten. The passes leading up to Sofia were now open.

But Murad, like his father, was a masterful strategist. He first wanted to ensure that he would not be outflanked by the Serbians and invaded Macedonia up to the Vardar River. The Serbians, themselves in turmoil after the death of Dusan, marched against him at the Maritza in 1371 and lost. In 1372, Murad moved northwest across the Vardar, pressing up against Prince Lazar who had succeeded Dusan but had not secured the loyalty of all of the nobility. Murad waited while internal problems in Anatolia were resolved, while colonists were brought out to occupy the new territories, and while his new empire was consolidated. A revolt in Thrace by his own son, Cuntaz, and a rival son of the Byzantine co-emperor, one Andronicus, was nipped in the bud. Murad blinded his son and then beheaded him. The fathers of other Turkish rebels were dealt with likewise. The Greeks were bound together and thrown into the Maritza. Murad played with Andronicus and his father; and both came to serve a larger purpose for the Ottomans as vassals.

After a decade, Murad moved on Sofia, having first taken Prilep and Monastir. Sofia is near a knot of mountain ranges, strategic valleys, and rivers running to the Danube and the Mediterranean. It should have been defended mightily, but, in 1385, it fell to Murad without a struggle after its commander was murdered outside its walls by a young Turkish falconer who had won his trust. Nis was next and the heads of its Serb defenders were embedded in its fortifications. Again, Murad pressed Lazar for more lands and more tribute. Following the execution of Serbian mercenaries in a dispute over booty (Christians fought for the Turks as Turks had fought for Christians), Murad's commander took his troops into Bosnia, but was outnumbered and decimated at Plochnik by a Christian coalition led by Prince Lazar. Murad waited, turned on the Bulgarian Sisman and pushed up north to the Danube. With the Bulgarians neutralized, Murad bided his time until, in June 1389, at age 70, he moved up to the Field of Blackbirds. He had both Bulgarians and rebel Serbs in his ranks. Lazar's were mixed, but all Christian. Although Sultan Murad died in this battle, his son Bayezid proved an able and ruthless leader. He simply executed Sisman and then took the rest of Bulgaria before Hungary did.[17]

As a conquered people, Bulgarians bore the full brunt of Ottoman rule given their close proximity to Constantinople and the fact Bulgaria was the main route both west and north for the Sultan's armies. It was also the military object of periodic forays from Western powers, which failed to rescue its Christian population, caused great death and destruction, and resulted in an even worse situation than they had before. Crops were destroyed, or confiscated, trade was disrupted, and the women were ravaged with equal rapaciousness by Christian crusaders and Muslims alike.

Sigismund of Hungary's 100,000-strong international crusade of 1396 set the pattern. When Bayezid failed to appear, they set off to find him, sacking Nis and slaughtering its population. Then, north at the Danube, the fortresses of Vidin and Rahova fell, again amidst much butchering of Muslims and Christians. They continued to Nicopolis, reveling in drink and debauchery and thinking that Bayezid was far away, only to have him and his horde of 200,000 appear from nowhere. Knights from France and Scotland charged off straight into the fray, mindless of tactics. Bayezid caught them just over the crest of a hill where the Christians, unhorsed and in heavy armor, were either cut down where they stood or beheaded at leisure on the following day after having been taken prisoner.[18]

Janos Hunyadi's column came down in 1443 and occupied Sofia before marching into the Balkan Mountains and winter. There, they often won against the odds, and the elements, but it could not be long sustained and they returned to Buda only with Turkish banners to show for their bravery. In 1444, Hunyadi's Hungarians marched again with the Wallachians under Ladislas III, then king of both Poland and Hungary. This campaign was instigated by a Papal Legate, Cardinal Julian, who was much involved in Balkan affairs and determined to break a treaty between Ladislas and Murad II. A fleet was even sent into the Black Sea to block the Bosphorus to prevent the Turks from crossing the Hellespont to Europe. To their surprise, Murad's men appeared before them at Varna after having bought off the Genoese, who brought them across. Ladislas was outnumbered three to one and his main charge broke against a wall of Janissaries. Ladislav, unhorsed, was slain, his severed head put atop a lance and a copy of the treaty atop another. Vlad Dracul, the Wallachian leader, escaped with Hunyadi. Julian was never seen again, perhaps unaware that his crusading champion's head was sent as a trophy to Bursa, the first Ottoman capital.[19]

Following the fall of Constantinople in 1453, Bulgaria lay buried for 400 years. Under the lash, its people labored to provide endless levies; supplied endless requisitions of grain and foodstuffs; and paid endless taxes. The system was serfdom for the *raya* (flocks) and service under the Sultan for the few— semi-autonomous rulers, converts to Islam, or male children taken from their parents for Janissary service under a conscription system that was cruel and capricious. Other unfortunates fed the insatiable demands of the slave markets to the east—men, women, and children. Even their independent church was returned to the Greek Patriarchate, itself compelled to obey if it wished to continue to reign from the Phanar. That which remained "Bulgarian" was circumscribed by laws and, because it was "Christian," was forever inferior.[20]

Still, like others in the Balkans, Bulgarians kept their folkways and legends alive in song, poetry and dance, and adhered to the Christian faith when it would have been easier to apostatize. The church remained the source of education in written Old Slavonic, and the vernacular. Christians and Muslims necessarily dealt with each other daily, but most lived separate lives. The seasons came and went in an ordered routine, except when war or disease, or an unforeseen incident brought disaster. A word in anger between a Christian farmer and his Muslim sipahi overlord could result in death. A broken cart blocking a road, or a spilled load of grain, or a look fixed upon a woman that ended with her being forced to her master's will could explode in violence. The added injustices and instability caused by the introduction of the Tanzimat system had by the mid-nineteenth century, caused others to rise in revolt. Finally, in the 1870s, the Bulgarians arose from the dead.

Vasil Levsky is not mentioned in Western literature. Even Lord Kinross's masterful *Ottoman Centuries* gives him a miss. However, the Bulgarians regard him as a national hero, and every 19 February they heap flowers on his monument in Sofia in memory of the day in 1873 when the Turks took him and hanged him by his neck. For Levsky, only in his thirties, had rebelled and taken his Bulgarian Revolutionary Central Committee into the Stara Planina mountains. Levsky's revolt was suppressed, but he inspired others who felt that freedom was worth fighting and dying for, like life itself. By 1876, revolt had spread, the sparks turning into flames. The Turks responded both with regulars, and irregular *bashibazouks*, who raped, burned, slaughtered and looted to make the Bulgarians pay the full price for daring to take up arms. In a month alone some 12,000 civilians died. At Batak, hundreds were incinerated after they had taken refuge in a church. There, 5,000 of 7,000 inhabitants perished, their tangled bodies were described by a correspondent from the English *Daily News*. British public opinion was outraged and many MPs, goaded on by the Liberal leader William Gladstone, demanded that someone—even the Russians—do something![21]

It was a time of confusion in Constantinople. Sultan Murad, who had replaced the profligate fool, Sultan Abdul Aziz, in a palace coup, had a nervous breakdown abetted by drink and was deposed by his reactionary younger brother, Abdul Hamid. There had been a succession of Grand Viziers, revolt in Bosnia, protests by the theological students, talk of a constitution, default on an enormous foreign debt, and the ouster and assassination of top officials, along with drought, famine, and a winter so severe that wolves roamed in packs through the suburbs of the city. The new Sultan did promulgate a constitution to throw a European six-power conference of his critics off balance, for they had come to Istanbul to press Abdul Hamid to treat his Christians better. The British and the French, however, refused to accept an action plan drafted by Austria, Germany and Russia, and London sent ships from its Mediterranean fleet up the Dardanelles to forestall outright intervention. As today in the Balkans, each had interests apart from concern about human rights. Britain convened a counter conference, which collapsed, and Russia, just waiting and eager to extend its influence, prepared to liberate Bulgaria.

In April 1877, Russian armies invaded from the north across the River Pruth and in the Caucasus, aiming at easternmost Armenia. Romania, then only Wallachia and Moldavia, joined in and declared independence. We cite this campaign again only to stress that it was extremely brutal and hard fought. After a circular movement through the mountains to Thrace, the Shipka pass, and the Maritza, which was joined by the Bulgarians, General Mehmet Ali rolled the Russians back to the Balkan Mountains. Likewise after good gains, the Russians to the north found Osman Pasha dug in at Pleven and impossible to dislodge. There the Turks had breech-loading rifles from America that were superior to the Russian muzzle-loaders. A joint Russian-Romanian attack commanded by Romanian Prince Carol came close to success, but was beaten back by a ferocious counter-attack. Out of admiration for their dogged defense, public opinion in Britain, influenced by the press as during the Crimean War, began to swing back in support of the Ottoman Empire. Encircled in winter, desperately low on food and ammunition, with no hope of relief, Osman attempted a breakout at night in early December. It, too, almost succeeded, but Osman was wounded, his men panicked, and thousands died in the snow, or were killed by Bulgarians.[22]

After Pleven, the Russians went over the mountains to take Sofia, while another army won at Shipka again and then at Adrianople to threaten Istanbul itself. At the start, the Russians set up local governing authorities of Bulgarians, who were enraptured of their Russian liberators. Thousands rallied to hastily organized *chetis*, which served to augment the Russian regulars, but which were also influenced by nationalist committees that sprung into existence. With Grand Duke Nicholas closing on Istanbul, Abdul Hamid called for intervention under the Paris treaty of 1871. But with Prussia opposed and the British cabinet divided from the outset, Nicholas marched on. The Sultan appealed to the British, even Queen Victoria herself. Finally, when the Russians were at San Stefano, just outside the city, Prime Minister Benjamin Disraeli won approval to send five warships into the Sea of Marmara where they positioned themselves within range of the Russian guns. Although an armistice of sorts had been struck, another Russian advance caused the London stock market to panic. England voted war credits, its army and navy were put on alert, and there was talk of an expeditionary force to Gallipoli. Patriotic feeling and anti-Russian fervor swept England.[23]

This British show of force averted war and forestalled the entry of the Tsar's army into Istanbul. As it was, however, Russia dictated terms at San Stefano in March 1878 that gave it Kars, Batum, and Ardahan in the Caucasus; independence for Serbia and Romania; promises of reform in Bosnia; and a Greater Bulgaria that would be a powerful surrogate state. In theory, Bulgaria was to be autonomous. But with a prince selected by the Tsar; Russian occupation for two years; and a Russified administration reaching from the Black Sea to the Aegean, including Macedonia over to Albania, it would have dominated the Balkans. Naturally, the Bulgarians were enthusiastic over the recreation of their first empire. It was what all Balkan countries aspired to; to again become as large as what had existed sometime in the past—and even more so!

When the impact of San Stefano had sunk in, the major powers agreed that it could not stand. Consequently, Prussia's Bismarck called the interested parties to Berlin within only months amid serious tension. The most dramatic result of the conference was to break Bulgaria's "empire" into three zones, which varied in the extent of control by the Sultan. Bulgaria north of the Stara Planina, to include Sofia, was to be autonomous under a minor prince selected with the participation of the Porte and pay a "tribute" in taxes. Southern Bulgaria was to be called Eastern Rumelia, with a semi-autonomous regime under an Ottoman-appointed Christian governor, and also pay taxes. Thrace and Macedonia were returned to direct rule. It is easy to understand why the Bulgarians were angered when they saw how the English, Austrians, and Russians had taken care of themselves, while they (supposedly the main reason for the conflict) were given short shrift. Consequently, the national committees began to cast about for ways to resume their struggle when and where they could in a country that seethed with hatred for the Turks and suspicion of their neighbors to the west—the Greeks and the Serbians.[24]

Initially, they had the good sense to begin building up a state apparatus and an army on that territory most firmly under their control—the north, cooperating with Russian officials sent for that purpose. Prince Alexander of Battenberg came out from Germany after being selected as Bulgaria's sovereign, none too pleased with the extent of Russian influence. A constitution was drawn up. In Eastern Rumelia, a commission from the great powers was to somehow supervise the situation. In sum, Europe was very much involved with Bulgarian affairs. In Sofia, Alexander became assertive vis-à-vis the Russians and the national assembly while at the same time talking in nationalist terms. A movement began to unify north and south, which soon assumed the aspect of a Balkan comic opera. In Philippopolis, the Christian Gavril Pasha was installed by the Sultan, only to fall into disfavor with his subjects. In Turkish style, he felt free to veto those laws that displeased him. In turn, the Bulgarians insisted on flying their flag. At a moment of confrontation, Alexander came down with his troops and declared for union, which was immediately approved by the assembly. Gavril was unceremoniously carted through the streets with an unsheathed sword at his side and then sent across the border. Amazingly, instead of invading, Abdul Hamid appointed Alexander governor for five years. The assembly moved to Sofia.

Serbia took offence at Bulgaria's success and sent a detachment across the frontier. Prince Battenberg, to everyone's surprise, took Bulgaria's raw troops in hand (the Russian officers had been withdrawn in pique) and pushed the Serbs back towards Belgrade. To prevent real damage being done, Austria immediately intervened and restored the status quo. This didn't end the matter, however. The Russians kidnapped Alexander, took him over the border, and made him abdicate. This affront so aroused the Bulgarians (led by the rebel, Stefan Stambolov) that Alexander was quickly returned and his captors, including the Russian military attaché, were jailed. It would appear however, that Alexander, now exhausted, decided that what had happened was not in his job description. He quit.

Amid the confusion, a three-member regency was set up headed by Stambolov and the national assembly decided that it would choose its prince. The Russians responded by sending its fleet to Varna and continued to try to intimidate the fledgling government. It failed, however, and the Russian liberators broke off relations and withdrew their officials and advisors.

Unswayed, the assembly chose Prince Ferdinand of Coburg. This, in 1887, went unrecognized by Russia and Turkey, but the other European powers did so, as Ferdinand was related to Queen Victoria. Stambolov, as prime minister, ruled for seven more years. Although the British called him the Bismarck of Bulgaria, his end was no better than that of a bandit.[25]

Having achieved union between north and south Bulgaria, many now looked to Macedonia. Henceforth, the revolutionary committees devoted their energy to the formation of a liberation movement that would fend off Greek and Serb inroads while extending its reach to Ohrid to reclaim "Greater Bulgaria." Unfortunately, the MRO-External (Vrahovists) who were "statist" and run out of Sofia (and again involved with Russian advisors) were unable to control their VMRO brothers west of the Pirin Mountains, and the movement split into factions (despite unity congresses) and descended into an internal struggle that resulted in much violence. Back home, Bulgarian peasants bore the financial burden of paying off former Turkish landowners, railroad construction, foreign loans and state administration (including the army) that, while onerous, served to raise their political consciousness. Aided by teachers and other intellectuals, the Bulgarian Agrarian National Union (BANU) under Alexander Stamboliski set down its populist roots in the run up to the Balkan Wars. The older Conservatives and Liberals broke up into weaker competing groups to the satisfaction of a Ferdinand who, in 1908, declared Bulgaria fully independent of the Ottomans.

Now a Tsar, Ferdinand gave his ear to Russian diplomatic envoys who encouraged anti-Ottoman understandings with the Serbians and the Greeks that in 1912 were turned into treaties for making war. The results of this were related earlier, but great stress should be placed on the blunder by Bulgaria to attack Greece and Serbia on the night of 30 June 1913 because of disappointment over its share of Ottoman territory. Misjudging its military capabilities and the amount of support from Russia, it initiated hostilities that resulted in its defeat in only one month. At the Treaty of Bucharest in August, Bulgaria's war gains in the west were reduced to some land in the Struma Valley and eighty miles of coastline on the Aegean, which included Dedeagatch (Alexandropolis). If that were not bad enough, during the brief but bloody campaign Romania had crossed the Danube and had taken Pleven and had driven to the outskirts of Sofia itself. As a result, Romania got southern Dobrudja. The Porte, having lost enormous territories, had to be content with regaining Adrianople. But Bulgaria's losses were not only measured in land and its strategic war aims. It was a great blow as well to its national pride. Greater Bulgaria, the dream of centuries, lay in ashes. And part of Bulgaria below the

Danube was now in the hands of the Romanians. Altogether, it would lead to Bulgaria lining up with the Central Powers during World War One. That would be another mistake of incalculable consequences.

After the guns of August 1914 sounded, the first to side with the Central Powers were the Turks under Enver Pasha. By November, the Straits were closed to Allied ships, cutting a vital link with Russia. In February 1915, a British naval effort to get through aborted with four vessels sunk. Britain then dusted off its old Gallipoli plan, which in execution proved a disaster that resulted in enormous casualties before a humiliating withdrawal. Given the stalemate in France, the Balkans became of great importance. Italy was induced to join the Allies. Bulgaria's value lay in its proximity to the Straits and in its flanking position vis-à-vis Serbia, then locked in a death struggle with the Austro-Hungarians. Any Bulgarian decision would also affect Greece and Romania. The war, in effect, offered Sofia a chance to acquire Macedonia and regain Dobrudja, if the Central Powers were victorious. The issue was keenly debated by the king and the national leaders amid very divided opinions.

The Agrarian leader, Stamboliski, and the socialists were opposed. Ferdinand, a German, and his premier were for, and they were able to bring others around. In September 1915, Bulgaria signed on in return for a promise of Macedonia, and even more if it turned out that Greece and Romania went with the Allies. October saw a massive offensive against the Serbs that drove them across Albania. The British and French, in turn, landed troops at Salonika against the wishes of the pro-German Greek King Constantine, but were unable to push north on this front until autumn 1918. It is indeed ironic that the Bulgarians held much of Macedonia during the war, only to lose it again when the tide of battle turned against them. Having barely recovered from the debacle it had suffered during the Balkan Wars, 1918 brought complete disaster. Outmanned and outgunned, Bulgaria was knocked out of the war by September. In October, Ferdinand abdicated in favor of his son, Boris. As a result of the Treaty of Neuilly of 1919, Bulgaria had to pay over US$450 million in reparations. It lost its access to the sea, it ceded strategic points to Yugoslavia—and its army was restricted in size. It was both beaten and humiliated.[26]

Stamboliski (jailed for his opposition to joining the war) was sent to Paris to sign the peace treaty. In fact, his Agrarians, the communists and the socialists emerged as the most popular parties. The communists immediately clashed with the government coalition and stirred up the trade unions. During the general strike of December 1919, Stamboliski countered with his Orange Guards—peasants with heavy clubs. In the elections of 1920, Stamboliski invalidated the results of nine communist deputies and ended up with a majority, forming his own government. His ideal was a peasant state where everything revolved around rural life. His radical populist vision fell short of accomplishment, but he did do much to improve life in the villages, particularly in education. He brought Bulgarians back to some respectability by being the first of the defeated to join the League of Nations. He also tried to patch up relations with Yugoslavia and prevent MRO-External raids into Macedonian territory now controlled by Belgrade. For this, the Vrahovists despised him. By 1923, amid charges of abuse of power and corruption, a military coup took power and Stamboliski was brutally murdered.[27]

The 1920s were increasingly turbulent. Boris III had been behind the coup, but could not control it. A coalition called Democratic Concord took power and was anything but. Agrarians were arrested and suppressed. The communists, who had stood by, were criticized by the Soviet Union and the Comintern and were told to organize a rebellion. Their amateurish plotting was uncovered and the party was banned. A bomb explosion at Aleksander Nevski killed 128 and two communists were charged for the crime. Repression against the party was swift and widespread. However, the main destabilizing factor was fighting between Vrahovist centralists, who wanted to annex Macedonia to Bulgaria, and the VMRO, which wanted autonomy or some form of separate identity. They were numerous and spread from southwest Bulgaria to the slums of Sofia. They murdered each other and intimidated every regime that came along. By the early 1930s, the communists had reemerged as the Bulgarian Workers' Party. It had strength in the trade unions and began to attract the peasant vote. When it gained a plurality in Sofia in 1931, the government refused to accept the results. In May 1934, another military coup took place and, in 1935, Boris installed an authoritarian regime.

Boris III was able to take over because of the existing divisions amongst the coup-makers. He returned the country to civilian rule and abolished the Military League. He ran a dictatorship, but he permitted elections to an assembly (party identities were known, but unstated) that convened in a consultative capacity only. However, in 1938, when leftists and Agrarians, were again elected, he drove some of the delegates into foreign exile. Thus, on the eve of World War Two, Bulgaria was being governed by Boris and people whose mindset reached back to San Stefano, people seemingly isolated from what had happened during the past sixty years. It should be noted in this context that, while Germany was extending its power in the Balkans, the Soviet Union was doing the same because their pact of August 1939 divided Poland and assigned the Baltic countries and Bessarabia to Russia, but failed to address the future of the wider region following France's defeat and the British evacuation at Dunkirk in May 1940. The Balkans, bereft of any allies, was vulnerable to political and military penetration.

As part of the carve up of what would result in a rump Romania, in September 1940 southern Dobrudja was given back to Bulgaria. This helped to boost already considerable German influence. But Boris was afraid of the Soviets and Turkey and played for time. The winter saw Italy invade Greece and then get pushed back into Albania, greatly complicating German plans for North Africa and the invasion of Russia. Russia again pressured Bulgaria to agree to a mutual assistance pact and talked about Turkish and Greek territory in Thrace that might become Bulgarian. Germany, having decided to invade Greece through Bulgaria, sent soldiers in civvies into the country to make preparations. When Moscow learned of this, it protested to Berlin. In January, it stated that Bulgaria was in its zone of interest and that stationing troops there, or in the Straits, would threaten its security. Nonetheless, Boris agreed to permit German troops transit and on 1 March 1941, signed on with the Axis powers in return for access to the Aegean. The assembly approved of this, 140 to twenty.

The invasion was swift and sealed the fate of Yugoslavia and Greece. Bulgarian forces occupied Skopje on 19 April and then took up occupation duties in Macedonia and Thrace. In Yugoslavia, Bulgaria simply annexed a large part of southern Serbia. In Greece, Bulgaria took back the territory it had lost in the Balkan Wars from the Pirin mountains south to the sea. German troops, as a precaution, occupied a narrow buffer in eastern Thrace to separate the Bulgarians from the Turks. In the areas under its control, the Bulgarian army was often brutal and harsh towards civilians. Settlers were brought out and attempts were made to impose the Bulgarian language on the existing population. Thus, Bulgaria's aims were concentrated on consolidating lands that it considered to be part of its old empire. It also started schools and churches in an effort to Bulgarize the population. To the east, because of the pro-Russian sympathy among many, Bulgaria was not required to fight on that front. Thus, for two years Sofia was able to view its new borders with satisfaction, only to see them jeopardized when an Axis defeat loomed large.

After Stalingrad and Russian advances, and the Allied invasions of North Africa and Italy, some began to think that the Germans might lose after all. Boris and his cabinet ministers considered how to do an Italian exit without, however, losing their war gains. Bulgaria was, in fact, an unusual place—a dictatorship with pro-German sympathies, but nothing like a fascist movement. In fact, various political tendencies were tolerated. It continued to have diplomatic relations with the Soviets even after a group of communists were infiltrated into the country and caught by the police. Bulgarians tried to avoid taking measures against Jews, who were exiled internally, but avoided the gas chamber. Boris's unexpected death in August 1943 and the appointment of a regency made it even more difficult to deal with the situation. In late 1943, heavy Allied bombing told the Bulgarians exactly where they stood. Many reacted in panic. The communists raised their heads again, trying assassination and then trying to establish Partisan groups in the mountains. They were not very successful in their accomplishments, but they provided the myth upon which the post-war BCP was founded.

In August 1944 a coup took Romania out of the war and Bucharest was occupied by the Red Army. Following months of dithering, this caused Sofia to announce that it was no longer at war with the US and Britain and it tardily tried to form an all-party regime. A communist-creation of small parties called the Fatherland Front stayed out. On 2 September the Soviets declared war and began to occupy the country against an unresisting Bulgarian army. Only a few days later after a few strikes, the Fatherland Front (led by communists, socialists, agrarians, and other factions) simply took over with the cooperation of the police and discredited old regime politicians. The Soviets forced an unprepared army to turn on the Germans then retreating from Yugoslavia. Some 30,000 died. In the months following, the BCP consolidated its power in the shadow of the Red Army, conducting mass purges and executions. The reputation of the great Georgi Dimitrov was stained forever. In 1954, Todor Zhivkov took over and ruled for another thirty-five years.[28]

* * *

10 November 1989. The day after the Berlin Wall came down, Petar Mladenov (foreign minister) and others ganged up on an aged and astounded BCP Secretary-General Todor Zhivkov at a meeting of the Politbureau and voted him out. Serious strain had emerged among the ruling elite: the party, state security and interior, and the military. Mladenov, with Moscow's approval, seized the proximate cause of the crisis—Zhivkov's renewed attack on the Turkish community, which saw riots against forced assimilation; the deaths of dozens of demonstrators; and demands by thousands that they be allowed to emigrate to Turkey. This racist policy, which began in the mid-eighties (and backfired), was put in motion in its latest stage by Zhivkov and his aide Milko Balef without any party discussion. Many had tired of Zhivkov's lavish spending on his family and his coterie of sycophants at a time when Bulgaria owed US$10 billion abroad. Finally, it was all enough to get rid of him.[29]

10–17 June 1990. Delegates to the national assembly were elected in two rounds. Two hundred seats by proportional representation and 200 by simple majority. The BSP took 52.75 percent (211 seats); the UDF 36 percent (144 seats); the MRF 5.75 percent (twenty-three seats); Agrarians 4 percent (sixteen seats); and four parties 1.5 percent (six seats). Some 91 percent of the electorate voted. The communists had legalized the establishment of other parties after Zhivkov's removal. The UDF grouped together some sixteen parties.

20 December 1990. After a summer of protest, the appointment of Zhelev as president, and the resignation of BSP Prime Minister Andrei Lukanov (who had led the post-10 November government) in the face of strikes and demonstrations, a coalition government headed by independent Prime Minister Dimitar Popov was sworn in, with eight ministers from BSP, three UDF, and two from the Agrarians. Bulgaria had been essentially rudderless for a year. Food and power shortages, and other disruptions, contributed to the social unrest. Because of the lack of consensus, new elections were due in mid-1991.

13 October 1991. In the first elections under a new constitution (postponed because of political squabbling), the UDF emerged the winner in a contest for 240 assembly seats. UDF took thirty-five percent (110 seats); BSP thirty-three percent (106 seats), MRP seven percent (twenty-four seats). UDF's Filip Dimitrov was named prime minister in a coalition with the MRP. The BSP retained more than a third of the seats, enough to block key legislative measures.

20 January 1992. Forced into a second round for the first direct election for president, incumbent Zhelev polled a majority of fifty-three percent with UDF and MRF support. Voter turnout was seventy-six percent.

7 May 1992. Bulgaria was admitted to the Council of Europe. A European Community association accord was projected for May 1993.

16 May 1992. Disagreement erupted between Premier Dimitrov and Defense Minister Dimitar Ludzhev over the export of armaments to Arab states. Under pressure, Dimitrov had promised the US it would cut off this trade, which Ludzhev favored. Dimitrov's rival, Zhelev, supported Ludzhev, who was then ousted during a cabinet reshuffle.[30]

20 November 1992. The assembly failed to agree on a government led by Dimitrov by a vote of 104 (for) to 124 (against). He had lost a vote of confidence in October because his MRF partners had denied their support in protest against the lack of consultation and lack of positions given to the MRF in a draft cabinet.

30 December 1992. The MRF won approval for President's Zhelev's economic advisor, Lyuben Berov, to form a "non-party" government. The vote was 125 (for) to twenty-four (against) with many UDF abstentions. Berov promised to push for privatization in the economic sector.

18 June 1993. UDF supporters pitched a tent "City of Protest" outside President Zhelev's office, alleging he was too cooperative with the BSP ex-communists and demanding his resignation. They tore up copies of Zhelev's dissident publication "Fascism" and littered the tomb of Georgi Dimitrov, using it as a urinal.

25 September 1993. The Bulgarian national assembly appealed to the United Nations for financial compensation, claiming that it was losing US$2.3 billion in trade annually because of the war in ex-Yugoslavia. Business continued to slow down and stagnate.

3 February 1994. Prime Minister Berov claimed that mid-1994 would see mass privatization. He stated that goals for 1993 had been fully met, citing forty-nine decisions to sell, of which thirteen were completed. This brought in 415 million leva, excluding employees' shares sold on a preferential basis. 893 million leva in debts were paid. 1,400 million leva of new owner investment over three years was expected. If one reads of 318 enterprises, 218 procedures, thirty-four transactions, and you wade through pages of legal details, you begin to get a glimmer of the complexities involved in privatization.

6 October 1994. Provoking critical comments from the European Union, Bulgaria restarted its controversial Kozloduy number one nuclear reactor, which had been shut down for safety reasons. The twenty-year-old power plant on the Danube produces forty percent of the country's power. EU urged checks by Western experts and offered a free supply of power. Sofia insisted its plant was now safe.[31]

17 October 1994. The assembly was dissolved after it failed to form a new government. Prime Minister Berov had resigned a month earlier out of frustration and exhaustion, stating only a new election could break the parliamentary deadlock. Renata Indzhova was named caretaker prime minister. Elections were scheduled for 18 December. Within days, Indzhova went on TV to cite the threat to democracy posed by the new mafia—"the infiltration of organized crime into state structures." She was the first to talk of "…brutal street racketeering touching the lives of people."

18 December 1994. The BSP swept the elections winning fifty-two percent (125 seats); UDF sixty-nine seats; Popular Union eighteen seats; MRF sixteen seats;

Bulgarian Better Business Block twelve seats. The BSP elected Zhan Videnov to head its parliamentary group until a cabinet could be voted on in late January. Ivan Kostov, a former finance minister, replaced Filip Dimitrov as head of a badly battered UDF.

26 January 1995. The assembly approved BSP Prime Minister Zhan Videnov's cabinet. It was also endorsed by former dictator Todor Zhivkov who stated from his granddaughter's villa that, while he didn't know the ex-communist youth leader personally, his cabinet looked solid and had able people appointed to it. The MRF objected to the inclusion of Ilcho Dimitrov who, as education minister under Zhivkov, had dismissed thousands of Turkish teachers who opposed the regime's campaign of forced assimilation.

28 February 1995. A BSP-led assembly overturned a ban on former communists taking top academic positions. It also called for new elections for the directors of state-run bodies and institutions.

26 April 1995. The head of the Bulgarian wrestling federation, Vassil Iliev (29), was shot dead in his car. Iliev ran the car insurance company, VIS-2; rumored to have mafia connections. A few days earlier, three security guards had been killed by a VIS-2 employee in northern Bulgaria. Police thought it was gang rivalry.

9 June 1995. The Council of Europe urged Bulgaria to sign its convention on the protection of minority rights, after many delays. An EU association agreement did better, as one third of the country's trade turnover was now oriented toward the EU.

10 June 1995. Bulgarian ships joined a NATO "Partnership for Peace" exercise along the Black Sea coast. President Zhelev had urged full membership in the face of the BSP's reluctance to apply. This has been his position from the outset. Moreover, he had gone out of his way to differ with the BSP since they regained power.

19 June 1995. The constitutional court backed President Zhelev's veto of BSP amendments to existing land laws, which would severely limit private ownership rights. The amendments required owners to offer their land first to their neighbors and then to the state, favoring also newly established cooperatives. The government was to have two months to decide whether to purchase. BSP asserts that farming land is too fragmented for modern methods following the return of seventy percent of state lands to its owners, pointing out that production had declined fifty-five percent over five years. Zhelev had earlier tried to block a BSP-drafted three-year ban on the return of homes, shops and offices to their original owners. His veto was overridden by the BSP's assembly majority.

20 June 1995. Prime Minister Videnov had talks in Athens with Pasok socialist Prime Minister Andreas Papandreou on topics, which included a Burgas-Alexandroupolis oil pipeline. This project had run into problems over financing and the share-out of transit fees. Due to be completed in 1997, it fell by the wayside along with plans for a Burgas to Brindisi pipeline; a para-Egnatia highway from Varna and Istanbul to Durres; and a gas pipeline from Iran-Turkmenistan. Bulgaria remained dependent on Russian natural gas.

15 June 1995. The assembly voted on BSP's privatization program for the year. With UDF-MRF opposed, the plan left the railroads, power, mining, military property, and free-trade zones public.

23 June 1995. The BSP pushed through the assembly the removal of the heads of state TV and radio and appointed replacements. BSP also replaced the head of the Bulgarian News Agency, who had died.

29 August 1995. An IMF team was due in Sofia to resume funding talks, which had been broken off in March because the government had failed to meet reform targets.

25 September 1995. At a final hearing of the Supreme Court, the defense lawyer for Todor Zhivkov argued that the accused couldn't be convicted of misusing state funds because he was the head of state at the time! Under the law, he could only be charged with treason. She said the old and new constitutions supported this.

10 November 1995. The assembly adopted the government's amendments to its privatization bill and projected a first round of mass sell-offs in March 1996.

20 December 1995. Bulgaria's chief prosecutor stated he would launch a probe over the shortage of wheat. The cabinet had said in September that there was a surplus of 500,000 tons. This was also followed by a very serious shortage of drinking water.

9 February 1996. Former dictator Todor Zhivkov was acquitted and released from house arrest. He immediately spoke to the press and crowed that he had been completely exonerated.[32]

9 February 1996. Over opposition objections, the BSP government passed its annual budget in the assembly. Its claimed projections were said to be unrealistic and incapable of implementation.

27 April 1996. The government admitted that without thoroughgoing economic reforms, Bulgaria was headed for collapse. They claimed they had promised the IMF and World Bank that they would shut down 106 lossmakers with 17,000 employees. They said they would attempt to stabilize fifty-eight others with 190,000 workers (sixty percent of total losses). If this failed, they would be shut by mid-1997.

1 June 1996. Bulgarians went to the polls in a US-style primary for the presidency. This placed incumbent President Zhelev and Petar Stoyanov, both of the right, against each other. To everyone's surprise, Stoyanov won sixty-six percent to Zhelev's thirty-four.

5 November 1996. After two rounds of voting, UDF Vice-Chairman Petar Stoyanov emerged the winner for Bulgaria's presidency over BSP candidate Ivan Marazov. The results shook the ruling BSP.

21 December 1996. Prime Minister Zhan Videnov stunned the BSP by resigning both the party leadership and his government post at the conclusion of a party congress. Videnov was thought to have been considering a cabinet reshuffle and possible early elections until he had run into a buzz saw of criticism by BSP reformers and old apparatchiks. Opposition demonstrations and strikes had picked up intensity. Bulgaria was close to economic collapse.

10 January 1997. UDF members of the assembly walked out to join thousands of demonstrators who had gathered outside. Protesters led by a gypsy band had poured into parliament to burn red flags and shout slogans. Angry scuffles erupted when a restraining line of students was broken and snowballs, stones and trashcans were thrown at policemen and BSP deputies. Dozens were injured.

11 January 1997. Outgoing President Zhelev met with BSP and UDF officials and security authorities in an effort to restore order. UDF head, Ivan Kostov, called for the demonstrations to continue, while his assembly leader, Yordan Sokolov, warned they might not be able to control protests unless early elections were agreed to.

14 January 1997. The BSP stood firm and insisted it would serve out its 20-month mandate under prime minister designate, Nikolai Dobrev. It said it would talk to the UDF, but not accept its program. Then later, BSP said that elections might be possible at the end of the year. Zhelev refused to ask the BSP to select its new cabinet.

18 January 1997. At Kardzhali, in the south, ethnic-Turks were bussed in from outlying villages to demonstrate against the BSP. Speakers recalled communist efforts to erase their Turkish names and suppress Islam—actions that drove thousands to Turkey.

31 January 1997. Following talks with President Petar Stoyanov, BSP Minister of the Interior Nikolai Dobrev suggested that a broad coalition might be the best solution. He continued to hold his mandate while frenzied discussions went on in the BSP and UDF camps.

3 February 1997. The BSP approved a draft cabinet, 150 to seven, as mass demonstrations and strikes swept the country. The Podkrepa trade union led by Konstantin Trenchev had shut down key sectors of the economy as truckers, and others, began to block roads leading to neighboring countries. Bulgaria became paralyzed.

4 February 1997. The BSP caved in and agreed to April elections. The announcement came hours before the expiry of their mandate. Under the constitution, Stoyanov had to dissolve parliament and appoint an interim cabinet by 20 February. This was done in days.

25 February 1997. The IMF's Anne McGuirk arrived in Sofia to begin talks on how to bail Bulgaria out of its financial problems. By 17 March, she had US$650 million in SDR standby loans, which included US$148 million to purchase grain. By April, the pledges from the international community totaled US$1.2 billion.

28 April 1997. The UDF won convincingly in national elections. It took 137 seats (fifty-nine percent); the BSP took fifty-seven; Euroleft, UNS, and BBB took fourteen seats, twenty seats, and thirteen seats respectively.

5 June 1997. An IMF-supervised "soft" (Argentine-type) currency board was ready to begin operations. The Bulgarian National Bank was to abide by the board's regulations as was the rest of the banking sector. The lev became pegged to the German deutsche mark at 1000 lev to 1 DM. The DM was designated as a reserve currency.

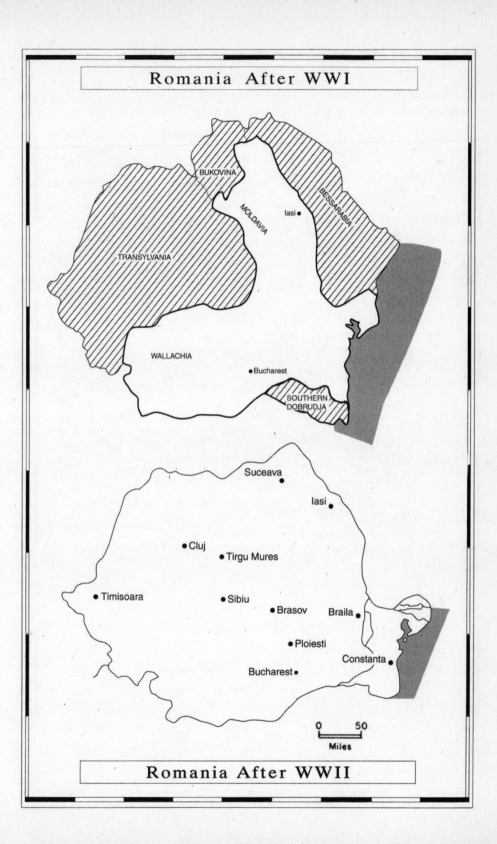

Romania After WWI

BUKOVINA

MOLDAVIA

BESSARABIA

Iasi

TRANSYLVANIA

WALLACHIA

Bucharest

SOUTHERN
DOBRUDJA

Suceava

Iasi

Cluj

Tirgu Mures

Timisoara

Sibiu

Brasov

Braila

Ploiesti

Constanta

Bucharest

0   50
Miles

Romania After WWII

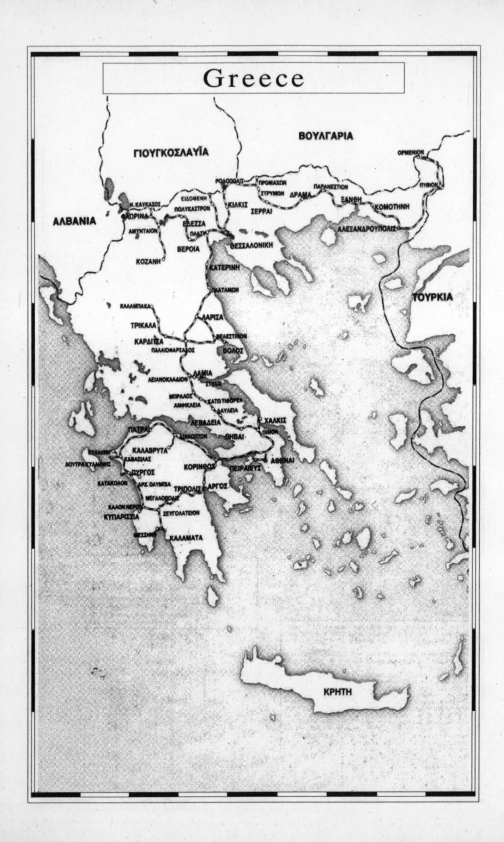

Greece

ΠΟΥΓΚΟΣΛΑΥΪΑ

ΒΟΥΛΓΑΡΙΑ

ΟΡΜΕΝΙΟΝ

ΑΛΒΑΝΙΑ

Ν. ΚΑΥΚΑΣΟΣ
ΦΛΩΡΙΝΑ
ΑΜΥΝΤΑΙΟΝ

ΕΙΔΟΜΕΝΗ
ΠΟΛΥΚΑΣΤΡΟΝ
ΕΔΕΣΣΑ
ΠΛΑΤΥ
ΒΕΡΟΙΑ

ΚΙΛΚΙΣ
ΣΕΡΡΑΙ

ΡΟΔΟΠΟΛΙ
ΠΡΟΜΑΧΩΝ
ΣΤΡΥΜΩΝ ΔΡΑΜΑ
ΠΑΡΑΝΕΣΤΙΟΝ

ΞΑΝΘΗ

ΠΥΘΙΟΝ

ΚΟΜΟΤΗΝΗ

ΑΛΕΞΑΝΔΡΟΥΠΟΛΙΣ

ΚΟΖΑΝΗ

ΘΕΣΣΑΛΟΝΙΚΗ

ΚΑΤΕΡΙΝΗ
ΠΛΑΤΑΜΩΝ

ΤΟΥΡΚΙΑ

ΚΑΛΑΜΠΑΚΑ
ΤΡΙΚΑΛΑ
ΚΑΡΔΙΤΣΑ
ΠΑΛΛΙΟΦΑΡΣΑΛΟΣ

ΛΑΡΙΣΑ
ΒΕΛΕΣΤΙΝΟΝ
ΒΟΛΟΣ

ΛΑΜΙΑ
ΛΕΙΑΝΟΚΛΑΔΙΟΝ
ΣΤΥΛΙΣ
ΜΠΡΑΛΟΣ ΚΑΤΩ ΤΙΘΟΡΕΑ
ΑΜΦΙΚΛΕΙΑ ΔΑΥΛΕΙΑ
ΛΕΒΑΔΕΙΑ
ΛΙΑΚΟΠΩΝ ΘΗΒΑΙ
ΟΙΝΟΗ

ΧΑΛΚΙΣ

ΠΑΤΡΑ
ΚΑΛΑΒΡΥΤΑ
ΧΥΛΛΗΝΗ ΚΑΒΑΣΙΛΑΣ
ΛΟΥΤΡΑ ΚΥΛΛΗΝΗΣ
ΠΥΡΓΟΣ
ΚΑΤΑΚΟΛΟΝ ΑΡΧ. ΟΛΥΜΠΙΑ
ΜΕΓΑΛΟΠΟΛΙΣ
ΚΑΛΟΝ ΝΕΡΟΝ
ΚΥΠΑΡΙΣΣΙΑ
ΜΕΣΣΗΝΗ
ΚΑΛΑΜΑΤΑ

ΚΟΡΙΝΘΟΣ
ΤΡΙΠΟΛΙΣ ΑΡΓΟΣ
ΖΕΥΓΟΛΑΤΕΙΟΝ

ΑΘΗΝΑΙ
ΠΕΙΡΑΙΕΥΣ

ΚΡΗΤΗ

Chapter 9

Exorcizing the Great Engineers

Romania: November 1998–February 1999

It was in the 1980s that Ceauşescu forced university students like myself and military conscripts to volunteer to work underground in the coal mines... without any previous training, or instruction. Naturally, the rate of accidents and fatalities was very high... even for the Jiu valley. Once, because of faulty technique, a section of the tunnel collapsed behind myself and several others. We were trapped for hours before being rescued.

Nicolae Craciun, mining engineer

Somehow something Romanian had always remained back there like a half-remembered dream, a faded memory from childhood. Mrs. Dangle, who lived behind us on Matilda, dug dandelions to use in her salads and for wine, and her kitchen always smelled good. Anna, her daughter, took care of me. With her long dark hair, I thought that she was very beautiful. The older neighborhood that we lived in included *booyahs* and *shivarees*... when, outside a church, the newly married groom would throw down coins for us children. We played by the Como railroad tracks and out past Larpentuer where gypsies occasionally camped. Near Rice Street was St. Bernard's Catholic church and school, set apart by tradition from our spare Lutheran rite and my Gorman grade school. We were Scandinavian on both sides of the family and somewhat sober-sided compared to south Europeans like my Aunt Seena's husband—my

Uncle Rom. Romulus was darkly handsome with a ready smile and readier words that always charmed. He looked Latin, played the piano and sang all of the popular songs. It's no wonder that my mother's sister fell in love with this lively Romanian on the make.

Romulus's father, Nicolae Bretoi, came from Teius in Transylvania near Alba Iulia. His wife, Elena, was from neighboring Stremti. Together, besides Rom, they raised Sylvia, Tiberius, Viorica, Remus, and another daughter, Elena, sustained by a gravel pit and a machine that made cement blocks. Earlier, they also had a bar-restaurant for a time. In the early 1920s, a cousin, Emil, came over to design and build St. Stefan's Romanian Orthodox church. Consequently, in 1926, when Queen Marie toured America and passed through St. Paul, the Bretois stood proudly up in front. Rom and Sylvia were given scholarships to Bucharest University. Rom did a year and Sylvia two. Remus was to do *liceu* there, but war intervened. However, he went on to become an engineer whose career spanned thirty years in the aircraft industry and the US National Aeronautics and Space Administration. Remus had a heavy dark overcoat and a black suitcase covered with travel stickers. He returned from Bucharest in late 1939. Maybe that was the time when Grandma Bretoi had us over for a family reunion. Then, I only knew that Romania was far away. But the war, and American bombing raids, taught me about a place called Ploiesti. I soon learned to find it on the map.

Many years later, in South Asia, I became friends with a Romanian diplomat who was enthralled with Italian, and Italian classical music, the operatic arias. If he had attained his ambition, he would have become the only one from Timisoara to own a brand-new white BMW automobile. He had ordered it from Germany and would drive it home before going on to another posting.

In the late 1960s, I was offered Bucharest, but I had accepted New Delhi the previous day. A friend served there later and told how he and his family drove to Thessaloniki to load up on food and escape from the constant surveillance of the Securitate. Another related how, in the mid-1980s, he and his wife spent their winter evenings in front of a fireplace, because Ceauşescu had reduced residential heating to almost nothing. It was a miserable time for everyone.

The Ceauşescus were bad beyond belief. Having made their country into a big Albania (even worse because Romania had past ties with the West) and having caused so much privation by their arbitrary abuses of power, it was not surprising that Nicolae and Elena, his wife, were executed within days of their arrest. Of course, those who had seized power wanted them well out of the way. But, if they hadn't done it, it's likely that the people would have demanded it. They wanted the "great engineers" dead—wanted to tear out their hearts! Today, almost ten years later, Romanians are still trying to exorcise their influence! I once read that Ceaușescu, to make people fear him even more than they did, had compared himself to the fifteenth-century tyrant, Vlad Dracul, who became known as Dracului, "the devil," and as Vlad Tepes, "The Impaler," because of how he executed his Turkish prisoners. When Nicolae's death was announced, Romanians fervently crossed themselves because they had difficulty believing that the "devil" was really dead. In their minds he had become evil incarnate.

Poor Romania. This potentially bountiful despoiled country has been ruled so badly for so much of its history. Divided geographically, it remained disunited and under the sway of stronger powers, struggling to survive and remain Romanian at the very place where the Ottoman, Austro-Hungarian and Russian empires all converged. It was forced to be so many things for the benefit of others. I half expected, after the Ceaușescus, to find its people suffering from an extreme form of multiple personality disorder! Their past has been such that they were always being torn between divided interests, false loyalties and conflicting passions.

However, to arrive in Bucharest, once dubbed the "Paris of the East," is to arrive in a city so unlike others in the Balkans you wonder if you have gone in the right direction after leaving Athens. Here, much has been done on a grand scale, with actual planning. The city is laid out with broad boulevards and avenues like spokes which radiate from Piata Victoria, Piata Revolutiei, Piata Unirii and a dozen other civic landmarks. Here is the Arcul de Triumf, which is modeled on its French cousin. Here is the exquisite Athenaeum music hall, a jewel of neo-classic design. Here is the impressive Cercul Militar, its interior Arch of Berlin being the largest in Bucharest. Here is the Athenee Palace Hotel, which has been a witness to so much history. Here then, one is tempted to believe, must also reside rationality and reason among the palaces, theatres, museums, opera houses, libraries—and, of course, my Uncle Rom's sprawling universitatea.

Without question, Romanians are trying to assimilate and overcome their past. They and well over one hundred political parties are exploring democracy, discussing concepts of "rights" and which group will best benefit them as their economy falls apart and unfathomed forces push them, not just below the poverty line, but to a level where, for some, sheer survival is at stake. Empty stomachs do not provide the best environment for rationality and reason. It's a sad fact. The tear-streaked face of an old woman huddled in the cold against the wall of my hotel, and the way a porter thanked me for the modest tip that I had given him after he had carried my bags, suggested that not everyone is dressing for the opera these days. Romanians expected that 1999 would be the worst year since the fall of Ceauşescu. Despite everything, however, the Grand Hotel Boulevard was attempting a comeback. The once-dignified lady, built in 1867 (the first "modern" hotel in Bucharest) had added the finishing touches to its refurbished Bistro cafe. It was trying. And to look out on Calea Victoria and Capsa's restaurant is to know you are in the heart of the city.

To get at the heart of Romanians is somewhat more difficult. I began at the national historical museum by carefully studying the replica sections of Trajan's column, which was erected in Rome by that emperor in the last decade of his life. I wanted to know how the Dacians had lived at the time they were being conquered and then assimilated into the empire circa AD 150. The reliefs depict a people, who built mostly with wood, being overrun by Romans who used stone. Amid scenes of slaughter and surrender, it is evident that the Romans were using heavy broadswords, while those of the Dacians were shorter and curved. Both used shields, but those of the Romans look superior, as do their helmets. Archers and cavalry were used by both. A striking difference are the trousers of the Dacians and the tunics and bare legs of Rome. Now, a fast-forward of nearly two thousand years to the Caru ce Bere down old Stavropoleus Street. An older man with a massive head of gray is dining with his friends. His speech is Latin-like. His facial expressions and gestures are Latin. He is singing to the chanteuse, a striking, tall, black-haired, gypsy. He caresses her with his eyes, with his intonation, as only Latins do. In his delight, he is up and down in his chair. Romanians are a "Latin" people!

I walk and walk for miles. There is so much to see. I try my best to imagine how Bucharest might have been when Olivia Manning was making the notes she would use in *Balkan Trilogy*; when, in the early days of World War Two, the American-Jewish-German journalist, Rosa Goldschmidt Waldeck, interviewed Nazis at the Athenee Palace hotel. The Athenee has been renovated and is now a Hilton. It's gorgeous; but it's a Hilton. The old ambience is gone. There is also an Inter-Continental Hotel—equally well appointed and equally antiseptic and sterile. If you didn't know where you were, you might be most any place. But, Capsa's remains, seemingly eternal. Its walls are covered with old photos of its staff—those who looked after writers, artists, poets, and politicians. There it is partially bombed out during the war, its facade down in the street. From Capsa's, Lipscani (the oldest remaining section of Bucharest) is but minutes away—a warren of shops, boutiques, and boites. Here also are old inns that are still in business—Hanul Gabroveni, Hanul Polonez, and Hanul lui

Manuc. The latter dates from a princely court in about the seventeenth century and converted to a caravansarai in 1808. Today, it also has a fine restaurant in its shady and partially covered interior courtyard. Much of old Bucharest still survives, but mostly in bits and pieces.

In 1984, Ceaușescu began to cut a huge swath out of the center of the city to build his monstrous "House of the People" on a rise south of the Dimbovita river, destroying an untold number of fine, old, nineteenth-century residential homes, buildings and churches where 40,000 people were living. The edifice (now used by parliament) is a white wedding cake affair, the third largest in the world after the Pentagon and the Potala. Some 7,000 workers were on the site daily until its exterior was completed in 1989. In addition, on either side of a double boulevard, which joins it to the Piata Unirii (replete with fountains, pools and Parisian lamp posts) were constructed huge art deco luxury apartment complexes for ranking communist party members and government officials. The Great Engineer planned to cram most of his party and government offices inside...whole ministries. It has twelve stories, four underground levels, and over one thousand rooms. Its interior has used astronomical amounts of marble and gold leaf, and innumerable chandeliers. Ornate, gilt-trimmed, rose-colored damask-covered sofas sit on a matching carpet in an enormous white-walled reception room. Other rooms for other functions are equally spectacular. It was indeed a palace to suit Ceaușescu's pharaonic megalomania and included a nuclear bomb shelter. It is still unfinished and a companion Centru Culturii remains a pile of raw concrete and rusting steel.

It is early February. The man I began to chase after last November is still not available. He is Dan Voiculescu who, in 1989, ran a Romanian state trading company on Cyprus. I had been told that when Ceaușescu fell, he cleaned out the company's accounts. He now has Antena TV, the tabloid *Jurnalal National*, an airline, and a small political party of "capitalists." His instant success is not untypical of many former communists. Everyone grabbed what he could. Anyhow, I gave up and went to a CFR office and booked myself on the train to Iasi in the northeast near the border with Moldova, or what to Romanians is still Bessarabia.

First class is a crowded compartment, but it is clean and heated. Second class might mean fighting for a seat, or standing in the passageway. It is all determined by the curious little cardboard tickets issued by CFR and some barely decipherable marks made by the agent. It works rather efficiently and it starts and ends at Gara de Nord. Exactly on schedule, a sharp, shrill whistle pierced the air as the train pulled out from the station.[1]

Ploiesti is only an hour or so north of Bucharest. Its refineries can be seen from the train—a jumble of cracking towers and miles of pipes, and gas being flared off day and night. In 1857, the first oil wells were drilled here. Bucharest became Europe's very first city to have lighting from oil lamps, a modernizing development that contributed to what became Romanian "exceptionalism"— the belief that Romania was not destined to remain mired in Balkan mud. By World War One there were ten foreign refineries. The British did their best to blow them in 1916 to deny their use to the Central Powers. They were repaired, however, only to be wrecked with more efficiency by the Germans in 1918. After the war was over, Royal Dutch Shell demanded reparations from the Romanian government and got them from a regime that was anxious to please the Allies. At the beginning of World War Two, British plans to sabotage Ploiesti failed to come off, as did a scheme to block the Danube at its "Iron Gates" so that oil barges couldn't get to Germany. To bomb the oil fields from Greece was impossible. Consequently, Germany gained control of Europe's second largest petroleum supply after the Soviet Union. Ploiesti produced one third of the Luftwaffe's gasoline. It became one of the most vital assets Germany had.

The range of bombers had improved by 1943 and US crews took off from North Africa on 1 August to plaster Ploiesti in Operation Tidal Wave—a massive, low altitude, daylight raid. Combined flak and fighter opposition proved murderous, so much so that the Allies had to wait nine more months to strike again. This time, in April 1944, the planes left from Bari and Foggia in Italy—with fighter escorts. The Americans bombed by day, the British by night. There were heavy losses but Ploiesti was taken out. As I looked from the window, I thought of my Greek friend Christos, a former fighter pilot. He said that during the Cold War, they were ready for one-way missions to Sofia and Bucharest, with a nuclear payload. I thought of my own days as a USAF gunner (when bombing was at 20,000 feet) and wondered what it had been like to come in over the rooftops. Today, most technology at Ploiesti has become semi-obsolete. Considerable sums are required for reinvestment.

To the east were some of Ceaușescu's (and his predecessor Gheorge Gheorghe-Dej's) worst economic catastrophes—enormous projects that made little sense economically. At Galati lies a steelworks complex that Ceaușescu sank hundreds of millions of dollars into in foreign funds. Unfortunately, Romania lacked iron ore, so it had to be imported. Additionally, its products found difficulty in the markets abroad. Consequently, Ceaușescu cut domestic food consumption to the bone, exporting as much as he could to pay off his debts. In the mid-1990s, some 30,000 were still employed producing a third of what they had in 1989. The Danube-Black Sea canal was another good idea that went wrong in execution. It was planned to cut a 400 km loop out of a river that first meanders north, and then east over through the delta to the sea. A canal large enough for ocean vessels from Cernavoda east to Constanta would save time and money and increase traffic to Western Europe. After all, it would be only 60 km long. Or so it was thought.

It was begun in 1949 with the slave labor of political detainees, common criminals and peasants who resisted collectivization, angling through 250-foot hills to Navodari north of Constanta. It is estimated that 100,000 people died working on what was known as the "Canalul Mortii" until it was admitted that the route was wrong. Abandoned in 1953, Ceausescu began work again in 1973 and finally completed it in 1984, running the route just south of Constanta. However, only twenty percent of the predicted amounts of tonnage use it as much depends on peace in Yugoslavia and opening up new trade to Western Europe.

At the Cernavoda nuclear power plant, Ceausescu personally insisted on reducing the amount of concrete used for foundations. Consequent settling has caused some welds to crack, so that only one of five reactors came on line in 1996. The countryside all the way up to Iasi is blighted by industrial pollution caused by factories that are at risk of falling apart.

Iasi ("Yash") is said to be the soul of Romania. Historically, it was the capital of Moldavia, which, with Wallachia to the south, formed the two Danubian Principalities that held to the "Romanian" idea through a thousand years of struggle. In 1916, Ferdinand and Marie fled there with their ministers and remnants of their army to fight on against Germany, the Austro-Hungarian Empire, and the Bulgarians. I stayed at the Traian Hotel, which was built in 1882 to the design of Gustave Eiffel near the square from where Alexandru Ioan Cuza raised his cry for liberty after his election as Prince of a United Moldavia and Wallachia in January 1859. Even in the dead of winter, Iasi has panache and elegance—palaces; a theatre built by the Austrians Helmer and Fellner; the homes of famous writers and artists; a renowned university done by Louis Le Blanc; and some of the most famous churches in Orthodoxy. It was also once the home of a virulent, popular anti-Semitism.

I tried to juggle generations of orientalized boyars; the Porte, the Phanariots, and the Patriarches of Constantinople, overlays of Austro-Hungarian and German influence, the threats of Tsarist Russia just beyond the Prut River, only kilometers away; and the audacity of an upstart Colonel Cuza to challenge the mighty of mid-nineteenth century Europe by upholding Romanian independence against all odds! In moments like these, wine helps. It came as a red Murfatlar from Dobrodgea, which sounded awful, but actually was quite acceptable. It, veal and pork *sarmale* and corn meal mush, the *mamaliguta* so beloved of Moldavians, helped me to come to grips with Cuza, the father of modern Romania.

To begin with, he had strong French backing. The French Consul in Iasi, Victor Place, stayed right at his elbow. Secondly, he was very handsome and cut a dashing figure in his splendid uniforms. And for a time, the liberal ideas he brought from Paris boosted his popularity. But, he was ill equipped to lead the country and he alienated almost everyone. It is said that when he was forced to resign seven years later, officers found him engaged in bed with his mistress, Marie Catargiu-Obrenovic, the mother of the Serbian Prince-Regent Milan. Apparently quick with his words, he pointed out that he had no pen. An officer whipped one out and another offered his back so that Cuza could scribble his resignation. With Prince Cuza out of the way, I ordered wine for the Traian's young musicians. And, because they were playing a familiar old Greek tune, I got up and danced a solo Syrtaki!

From Piata Unirii, one can walk straight on down Stefan the Great and experience successive phases of Romanian history. The ornate, carved-from-stone Three Heirarchs church, built by boyar Vasile Lupu (Wolf) in 1639, is truly unique. Its intricate exterior, and sumptuous interior icons, dazzle. Niches contain the remains of Princes Cantemir and Cuza, but what is most interesting are the portraits of Iasi's great boyars and their families, resplendent in their furs, silks and oriental turbans. They are amazingly lifelike. Nearby is the largest Orthodox cathedral in Romania, construction of which took a century of building and rebuilding. It contains the relic bones of St. Paraskevi (Saint Friday) of Epivat (circa 980–1050), who is Moldavia's patron saint. Here, on a bare stone floor, half a hundred Romanians were down on their knees. One young man repeatedly crossed himself and bowed for a half hour with a religious fervor I had only witnessed at the Wailing Wall, or the Temple Mount, in Jerusalem.

The Berindei-designed palatul at the end of the park would suit Prague or Berlin. Built 1906–25, the palace of 365 rooms contains four museums, a library, and old masters from Western Europe, as well as Romanian artists. Iasi, it turned out, has dozens of attractions and I was only scratching the surface. But I came as a writer, not a tourist, so I headed up one of Iasi's seven hills to Alexandru Ioan Cuza University. It was exam time and the students were wandering about preoccupied. They were almost all neatly dressed, many in heavy, Western-style jackets with the logos that are so desired in this celebrity designer age. A post-graduate was proud of his, explaining how he had blown his entire student stipend on it, knowing that his parents would rescue him. A mixed foursome that I talked to, all sophomores and all in computers at the economics faculty, voiced little or no optimism that jobs will await them when they finish school. They laughed, and said they were in the right field, but in the wrong country! Walking down the university's "Hall of Lost Footsteps," I listened for a distant echo of Professor A. C. Cuza.

Cuza, no relation to the colonel-prince, looks out from his photo with white whiskers, bald head, and glasses, ever so much like a Caspar Milquetoast character. He was anything but. In 1923, Cuza founded his League of National Christian Defense along strictly anti-Semitic lines. His most eager protégé and enthusiast was an anti-communist law student, Corneliu Zelea Codreanu, of whom much will be heard later. In 1935, with German financial support, the league merged with Octavian Goga's National Agrarian Party to form the National Christian Party (NCP). Rightist and extremist, it backed King Carol II's anti-democratic, anti-Jewish policies.

Iasi, the "Little Rome," was home to much of this. Nicolae Iorga came out of Cuza U in the 1890s and became a virtual Renaissance man of learning. However, his learning was rooted in nationalist politics of the right-wing variety. In 1910, he and A. C. Cuza set up a short-lived Democratic Nationalist Party. Later, as a world-renowned scholar, Iorga got into politics and supported Carol II. Even earlier, the romantic-nationalist poet, Mihai Eminescu, who had lived in Iasi and who had rocketed to fame and a premature death in the 1880s, tinged some of his poetry with anti-Semitic themes. Iasi, so rich in history and culture, so mesmerizingly beautiful, developed an inescapable aura of strident intolerance and hatred that eventually engulfed its Jewish community.

The sun sat low on the horizon, becoming dimmer by the minute. It was snowing, the wind blowing it into little drifts. And as it was Friday, and as Iasi left me with questions that could be answered only by trying to place myself in the past, I found myself at the city's only Jewish synagogue. The Great Synagogue is a small shabby, one-story affair opposite the old Golia monastery. I was puzzled why a synagogue dating from 1671 would be so ordinary. Shabbat had already begun when I slipped in and sat on one of the plain wooden benches, which resembled those from a country school. An elderly rabbi was giving a lesson in Hebrew. In rotation, everyone had his turn. I sat listening and read the names on memorial plaques and lights, thinking that, perhaps, the original building had been destroyed. After a while, the rabbi matter-of-factly made it known that now it was my turn. I was to stand up, explain who I was, and say what I wanted as simple as that.

Actually, expressions didn't change much when I said I was "goy" and an American journalist. But, there was more interest after I explained I had lived in Jerusalem and wanted to learn what had happened to them in Iasi. My few comments seemed to please them. When the service was over, a young man told me that before World War Two, 150,000 Jews had lived there. Today, there are barely 200 or so and many are now old and sick. He said it was hard to say if they were discriminated against or not as life is difficult and uncertain for everyone. I asked if he ever thought of *aliya*, of immigrating to Israel, adding that I once was told that the best pilots in the Israeli air force were the Romanians. He said he had been there and they had called him a "Romanian." Here, he said, Romanians call him a Jew. This tall, well-built boy, who was wearing a black leather, fringed jacket and looked just like a Neil Diamond double, said what he really wanted was to live in a country where to be a Jew, or a Romanian, didn't matter at all.

In 1940, even earlier, it mattered greatly. Given Nazi pressure, agitation by the Legionari and the machinations of nationalist business circles, Carol II had already framed laws that served notice on Jews that their dominant position as an owning, entrepreneurial class was over. The Iron Guard regime of General Ion Antonescu, especially in 1941–42, brought a holocaust down upon their heads. In 1941, some 8,000 Jews were killed in Iasi. Then, with the Romanian army as part of the German juggernaut sweeping east, 150,000 Jews (mostly from Moldavia and Bessarabia) were deported under horrific conditions in winter to Transnistria—across the Pruth out of Moldavia and across the Dniester out of Bessarabia, where they were ravaged by Romanian occupation forces assigned to the Odessa sector of the Ukraine. Only 50,000 lived to tell about it. That Romania's Jewry was spared a final solution lay more with the practical requirements of running an economy in wartime than in any humanitarian considerations.[2]

But I am getting ahead of myself, setting down strange names and events of almost sixty years ago, barely three generations. I wondered what has been passed on from father to son, from mother to daughter. The train rolled on hour after hour across black untilled earth. After 1989, much of it had been returned to those who had a pre-collectivization claim on it. Much of it has lain idle since, because when the collectives broke up, machinery and livestock, were scattered to the winds. What can a city dweller do with two cows, three pigs and twelve chickens except eat them? In many places, it is being worked under primitive conditions, actually by horse and plough. Production has plummeted. Rich farmland passed by my window. But the lack of financial resources and rational, large-scale production methods make it unlikely

Romania will reach its agricultural potential again any time soon. I sat back and read, waiting for Cluj to come into sight.[3]

Klausenburg to the Germans and Kolozsvar to the Hungarians, Cluj is where cultures collide. The city was founded by Germans in the twelfth century for the Hungarian King Geza and a succession of Magyar and Austro-Hungarian rulers kept Transylvania under their control until 1920 when it was united in a Greater Romania. Part was lost to Hungary in 1940 owing to Hitler's "Diktat." After World War Two had ended, the Russians returned it to Romania. Ceauşescu added Napoca to its name in recognition of the fact that the city has Dacian-Romanian roots that go back almost two thousand years. Hungarians claim Cluj as their own, looking with regret at the loss of their famed university town, so learned and literary. The Romanians give short shrift to all of this, pointing out that the Magyar landowners had kept the peasantry, the ethnic-Romanian majority, crushed beneath their heel until the bitter end. It was even worse during the wars. So Cluj-Napoca is how it reads today!

I was excited when I checked in at the Continental, for somewhere in the city were the relatives of my Uncle Rom. His brother, Remus, living in Palo Alto, California, had given me their names, phone numbers and apartment addresses down to the number of the *scara*—the stairway. He had left nothing to chance and had advised them that an American shirttail relative would look them up.

After breakfast, I taxied to an apartment complex a few minutes away. There, Gigi was waiting outside. Virgil (Gigi) Salantiu threw his arms around me with a broad smile and took me upstairs to meet his wife, "cousin" Sabina, who was known to her friends and family as Nina. Both were perhaps around sixty years old. Nina was a mechanical engineer and Gigi a professor of veterinary medicine. Gigi was also an accomplished artist of peasant scenes taken from life. He carved as well, had exhibited abroad and had been recognized by the American Biographical Institute. A dynamic, honey blonde daughter interpreted. Daniela Opruto, age 40, was a professor of mechanical engineering, who was also doing business with the US in computers. Their apartment might have been small and lacking in luxury, but their warmth and generosity—Gigi insisted on giving me two of his books—were recognizably rich. They were wonderful people.

After family talk over several cups of coffee, I asked what had happened in December 1989. At first, Gigi and Nina looked at each other and then Daniela coaxed Gigi out of his modesty. He said that, as news from Timisoara and Bucharest came in, Cluj became a scene of confusion. On the twenty-first, there was a demonstration in the square and some dozen people were shot.

The army and the Securitate then tried to clear the streets. The next day, both sides eyed each other uneasily. A large crowd gathered, despite the soldiers and the tanks. Everyone waited for the worst to happen. Then, as if by a miracle, they heard that Ceaușescu had fled Bucharest. And, just as quickly, the police and army disappeared from their positions.

Actually, that night, there was random shooting in the city. Gigi had joined others in the municipality building when shots came in through a window. One grazed the sleeve of his jacket. But, as he was intoxicated with excitement like everyone else, he stayed to help with security duties. Power, water, phone, and other facilities had to be protected. The city was charged with tension.

Gigi's job was to guard the Securitate files, which he carried by bicycle, box by box, for safekeeping to another location. He said it took all night to finish the job. Amazingly, it went off without incident, as few would ever have imagined he would take on such a dangerous task. However, later, some suggested that he had read the files of his fellow citizens. This, he said, was impossible as he was too busy getting them moved. Showing some embarrassment, he showed me a certificate from the Guvernul Romaniei, which thanked him for his contribution to the revolution. With a wry smile, he said that since 1989 all of the Securitate files had been kept secret and none had been made public. I sensed he disapproved. I asked him how he felt about the present situation. He said most people didn't want a return to communism, but one needed only to look around to realize the country had very serious problems. He thought that President Constantinescu was probably a good man and had good intentions, but was in over his head. He believed many would say the same. Gigi made a phone call to set up an appointment for me and then Daniela gave me a quick tour. Cluj-Napoca is both scenically impressive and ethnically interesting because it is here that the Romanians, Hungarians, Szeklers, and German Saxons have all come up against each other.

The Continental Hotel with its silver cupolas was comfortable and right off the main square. Gracing its fin de siècle dining room at breakfast was a raven-haired beauty from Stuttgart—a tall concert violinist. Her posters were up and Daniela's daughter was looking forward to an evening of Mozart at the Teatrul National. I had time before the ethnographic museum, so I walked around the square. Near the hotel, antiquities have been discovered, much to the glee of Cluj's mayor, Gheorghe Funar, who was something of a Romanian "fundamentalist" who never missed an opportunity to rub the Hungarians the wrong way. The antiquities were not so very important, but, as Roman-Dacian ruins, they predated anything that the Hungarians ever had. It's said that Funar was tempted to move a statue of the Hungarian king Matthias Corvinus to see what else he might find. Funar did erase the "Hungariae" from in front of "Matthias Rex," and flanked the statue with Romanian flags. He also changed Piata Libertatii to Unirii to re-emphasize Romania's reunion with Transylvania. It was a bit much![4]

Matthias Corvinus is a good starting point. He was the son of the famous commander, Janos Hunyadi (Iancu de Hunedoara to Romanians), of whom we spoke earlier and of whom we will speak more later. He became King of Hungary in the late fifteenth century. To Hungarians he is Matyas Corvinus or Hunyadi Matyas, or even Matei Corvin. Thus, a statue in the center of Cluj becomes a bone of contention. Even the name Cluj (from the Latin, meaning "closed," or "enclosed by the hills") bristles in keeping with the fact it was a fortress town.

I went inside St. Michael's church, which was built by the Saxons in the mid-fourteenth century and agree that its vaulting roof is what they say it is. Across the street, I admired the baroque Banffy Palace, which was completed in 1791 by Johann Eberhardt Blaumann. It is now an art museum said to display works once owned by the Banffy family and other former Magyar land-owning aristocrats.

I walked to the ethnological museum with more than just an inkling that this city of 300,000 people and 30,000 university students is the scene of an ongoing turf struggle. It was a struggle for possession of the past and the future. Tiberiu Graur, the director, was a giant of a man with an avuncular manner, a teaching professor in his own right. With an innate sense of protective decorum, he hesitated to face questions regarding ethnic animosity head on. He talked around the subject. Perhaps he thought that this was how the head of a museum dealing in tribes should act. He explained that, as had happened to many after the communists took over, his father was arrested in 1947 and was jailed for three years. This, he said, had clouded his growing up and conditioned him to move very warily through life. Then, Gheorghiu-Dej had brutally crushed and purged the Anna Pauker-led Jewish wing of the party and had sent many to prison, so that one had to be very circumspect on Jewish issues. The same was true regarding ethnic-Hungarians. After all, neighboring Hungary was a part of the socialist bloc. It was only when Ceauşescu himself pushed programs that disadvantaged the Hungarians that one could determine where one should stand. I tried again, throwing out the names of Eminescu, Cuza, Iorga, and the recent Hungarian anti-regime activist, Reverend Laszlo Toekes, who had sparked the December 1989 revolution. Graur eyed me with growing curiosity.

He said that I must read more and gave me two of his own books. I said, fine, but what I really wanted was his comments. Then, without more prodding, Tiberiu opened up. He retold a joke which was popular among Hungarians in the 1980s: with three Hungarians one has a revolution; with three Saxons, a business venture; and, alas, with three Romanians, a gang of thieves! "They really don't like us you know," he said with not a little conviction. "They exaggerate and make an issue out of every little grievance." He told of attending an academic conference in Budapest in 1975 where no sooner had they sat down at a restaurant whose walls were covered with the coats of arms of the great Magyar families (including many from Transylvania), when one of the Hungarians bluntly asked him if he, as a Romanian, knew what those families stood for and how deep the Hungarian roots were in Transylvania? Graur said an argument erupted immediately and he walked out. On the subject of Reverend Toekes, Graur said that he had lived in Cluj-Napoca for a time and was just as contentious then as he was in Timisoara. He implied he considered Toekes something of a pain.

I asked him about the Jews and Romanian anti-Semitism; about Eminescu's poetry; Cuza's Jew-baiting tirades; the streak of anti-Semitism that ran through Iorga's writings. Not exactly defending them, the director suggested ever so politely that I perhaps lacked perspective. He explained they had all written so much and had said so much on various subjects over many years. Whether he realized it or not, he sounded sympathetic to how too many had felt during the inter-war years. He continued, "The Jews owned so much, all of those thousands of shops—even out in the villages—jewelry shops, cloth shops, the taverns where peasants drank away their misery. And, if someone didn't have the money, it was all written down in a little book. The peasants became indebted to the Jews up to their necks." His words were a whisper from the past. They conjured up visions of pogroms, of the time when a morally bankrupt Carol II turned the Jews over to the savage thuggery of the Legionari, to those who hated the Jews for what they were, and more especially for what they owned.[5]

After December 1989, several rightist groups were established. A Vatra Romaneasca (Romanian Homeland) attracted over two million nominal members. Another was Romania Mare (Greater Romania) (PRM). Both were linked to the successor to the Securitate, the Romanian Intelligence Service, and both had Legionari overtones because of their strong nationalist and xenophobic views. Romania Mare had thirty seats in parliament and was led by Corneliu Vadim Tudor, a journalist who was Ceaușescu's favorite court poet and acolyte. Both had been involved in ethnic clashes between Romanians and

Hungarians and also expressed a strong dislike of Jews and gypsies. This was just as strongly denied by Romania Mare's deputy leader in Cluj, Muuteauu Viorel. Simply put, Viorel asserted that PRM was a party that emphasized the national good and patriotism. It was for the re-establishment of the Greater Romania of 1918, but openly and without the use of force. Thus, questions concerning Bessarabia; any changes in the Hungarian border; Bukovina; and the missing piece of Dobrodgea in Bulgaria, would be resolved by negotiations. He also mentioned a place I couldn't find on my map!

Although PRM was polling only around five percent, the rapid fall in living standards and its appeals for social justice made it a movement that cannot be easily dismissed. Tudor was a clever man who had skewered opponents with detailed information that probably came from security files. And although the party appealed mainly to average working people, Viorel cited the names of professors who also belonged. He said that PRM was strongest in Moldavia, but had good support in Transylvania as well. In keeping with Tudor's stock in trade when he was with Ceauşescu, PRM's high circulation weekly by the same name continued to run diatribes against ethnic minorities. PRM often targeted Hungarians, specifically, the same Reverend Toekes (now a Calvinist church bishop) who was elected chairman of the Magyar Democratic Union of Romania (UDMR), but who in fact heads the UDMR's radical faction. In February, Toekes was found attacking UDMR's leadership at their Magyar Forum for their lack of action. Demanding full autonomy, the resignation of UDMR members from their government posts, and government payments for "moral and material damages," Toekes hailed his faction's recent wins at Cluj-Napoca, Timisoara, and Tirgu Mures. He vowed, "Things cannot continue as they are... something must be done about it!"[6]

Stamped out under Ceauşescu, post-revolution Romania saw dozens upon dozens of ethnic-Hungarian publications and cultural groups come back to life—and the Germans, gypsies, and Ukrainians did the same. The Hungarians, however, predominated by dint of numbers and historical tradition. Initially, the ruling National Salvation Front (NSF) of Ion Iliescu supported all of this and Toekes and others were included on the NSF council. Romanian TV and radio began minority language broadcasts. Still, the countryside was in turmoil. Bands hunted down (and executed) Securitate members and the like. There was also widespread movement. Young Romanians drafted for Ceauşescu's work schemes in Transylvania up and quit and went back to Moldavia and Wallachia. Over 100,000 Saxons left for Germany, half of their entire community. Gypsies moved in as soon as the Germans moved out. Then, almost before the government had set down official guidelines, local committees of Hungarians began to restructure the school system where they were in a majority, or where they could point to past ownership. It amounted to a take-over of primary and secondary schools. Romanian students were, in many cases, forced into makeshift arrangements. Plans were afoot to again Magyarize the prestigious Babes-Bolyai University in Cluj and to split a medical school in Tirgu Mures. Romanian students took to the streets in angry protest.[7]

Into this unsettled situation in early 1990, came Vatra and even a wacko call for a new Legionari. The latter quickly faded, but Vatra, along with its respectable elements, attracted a rabble of poorly educated young workers. Soon, amid rabid, pro-Romanian rhetoric, came calls for Hungarian blood. At local levels, Vatra worked with the Romanian National Unity Party (PUNR) and soon infiltrated the NSF and the National Peasants Party (PNTCD). The word at the time was that Vatra's cadre comprised many ex-Securitate members. Interestingly, Vatra was well received by the press and political leaders who embraced Vatra's heavy emphasis on a unitary state. Thus encouraged, Vatra prepared for action.

As tensions mounted (there were incidents at monuments and more ugly was an attack on gypsies where homes were burned), 15 March arrived, which is Hungarian national day. Hundreds of flags were hoisted amid crowds of Hungarian demonstrators. Most passed off peaceably, but feelings were running especially high in Tirgu Mures because of the school situation in a city that was equally populated by Romanians and Hungarians. On 16 March, a Hungarian pharmacy owner added *gyogyszertar* to *farmacie* on his sign. A Vatra member nearby gathered his bravos, beat up the Hungarian and wrecked his shop. During the fracas, a Hungarian drove his car into the crowd, injuring several. A few days later, Vatra vowed to remove a lawyer friend of Toekes from the Provisional Council of National Unity (PCNU). On 19 March, Vatra men poured into town from outlying factories armed with pitchforks, wooden clubs and axes, escorted by local police and a few Orthodox priests. It was said they were also well fortified with *tuica* or plum brandy. They beat up Hungarian students and people at a UDMR office. The noted writer, Andras Suto, almost had his eyes torn out.

The next day, Romanians and Hungarians attempted to hold a unity demonstration, but that, too, was broken up by Vatra mobs after an ineffective effort by police and soldiers failed to stop them. In reaction, hundreds of armed Szeklers and gypsies arrived and took on Vatra well into the night. Now running out of reinforcements, Nistor Man (a Vatra leader on the PCNU), called on the army, which arrived in strength the next morning. When it was all over, four had died and some 300 were injured. The incident spilled over to some other towns where Catholic Armenian priest, Francisco Darian, died horribly and Calvinist pastor Ferenc Erosdi's home was sacked. It should have resulted in resolute action and a condemnation by the NSF, but it didn't. With national elections two months away, the Hungarians were blamed for what had happened. TV and radio ran an officially sponsored lie, which falsely claimed that troublemakers had entered from Hungary. In the weeks and months that followed, a steady trickle of Hungarians packed up and left for good.

Wherever one goes in Transylvania, one runs into Hungarian statement and Romanian counter-statement. Some are clearly provocative, such as an Orthodox fresco in Tigru Mures, which depicts Christ being tormented by Hungarian soldiers in traditional dress while Romanian peasants look on weeping. It was done in 1985. My train ride to Alba Iulia gave me additional time for thought as to the rights and wrongs of problems that still continue years after the revolution. I arrived in the late evening at the Parc Hotel only to find it full up. So I went over to the Transylvania escorted by a pack of whooping gypsy children who had appeared out of nowhere. My heart went out to these unfortunates who pester you for money, candy, or cigarettes ever so much like playful puppies. The latter might take off with your shoes, but gypsy youngsters might make off with all of your luggage! The Transylvania was definitely downmarket, but it had a lady at the reception who, while seemingly burdened with the worries of the world, spoke excellent English and ladled out good advice as though it was chicken soup for the flu. My hotel was in the lower town. In the morning, I would walk up to the upper town, or the citadel, which is the haunted soul of this city.

The citadel sits on a hill and is enormous. For twenty-eight years in the early eighteenth century, some 20,000 Romanian serfs labored under an Italian architect to build a star-shaped structure that came to be called Karlsburg. Under the Hungarians, virtually all of the Romanians were serfs. Fifty years later, the Romanians rose up in revolt and were crushed. Above an entry gate is the cell of Horea, who, with Closca, was tortured and then was torn apart on the wheel. A companion in their struggle for liberty, Crispin, managed to commit suicide. An obelisk stands to commemorate the deaths of Romania's national martyrs. Inside the Roman Catholic Cathedral of St. Michael, I looked at the tomb of Hunyadi, or Hunedoara, depending on your ethnic preference. It was defaced a century after his death by Turks still smarting from defeat at the hands of this brilliant tactician. At the Orthodox cathedral (built in 1921 for King Ferdinand and Queen Marie's coronation), a mass was in progress. Several hundred Romanians were present for the mystery amid choral music, shimmering candles and clouds of incense. Many were dressed poorly for the cold and knelt on the stone floor. Outside, on its steps, beggars sat motionless as the snow fell just as silently to the ground.

Nearby ruins attested to a Roman-Dacian presence. Here, in 1599, Michael the Brave had briefly united Transylvania with Wallachia and Moldavia. Somewhere, under the snow, were the foundations of his Coronation Church, which was razed by the Magyars upon their return. Over three hundred years later, a half-English, half-Russian fairytale queen and her Hohenzollern husband king were crowned in 1922 to rule over Greater Romania. It was but the briefest of moments in history, but it enshrined Alba Iulia in Romanian hearts forever. At only age sixteen, beautiful, tall, auburn-haired, Marie Alexandra Victoria was engaged to Crown Prince Ferdinand after protracted talks between Marie's grandmother, England's Queen Victoria, and Wilhelm II of Prussia, the German Kaiser and her first cousin. After marriage in 1892, she went native, learning Romanian, riding with her regiment, and rambling over the dusty roads of Romania far from England's salon society. In World War One, she worked as a Red Cross nurse, walking in the mud to attend the wounded and holding the hands of those dying of typhus. She was a regal heroine with a common touch. She has been called, by her many admirers, the "Warrior Queen," and also, most accurately, the "Last Romantic."

The train to Petrosani in the Transylvanian Alps twisted through wooded mountains and tunnels following small rivers close to the valley floor, home to European red deer, brown bear and the wolf. It was here where Ceaușescu had his specially arranged hunts followed by photo sessions and a big feast for his guests. My travel companions told me that it was here, also, where, through the years, thousands of political prisoners had worked on labor gangs to lay the tracks through this rugged terrain.

Perhaps because of the snow, I recalled another scene from Angelopoulos's *Ulysses' Gaze*. Harvey Keitel remembers a Christmas in Bucharest sometime after the communists took over. He is a small boy and his Greek family is having a party. Everyone is in a holiday mood and the grown-ups are waltzing around in a room all ablaze with lights, candles and a tall Christmas tree. A maid responds to a knock on the door and Securitate men step inside. Then, without a word, one of them detaches a man from his dancing partner and waltzes him out of the door. Family and friends stand in stunned silence. A few seconds later there is another knock. The Securitate enter again, and this time they carry off the piano.

Pitesti prison began to fill up in December 1949. A brutal effort was made to "re-educate" and to break inmates by starvation and by isolation and finally by forcing prisoners to torture each other. The latter practice was extended to other jails and to the canal project before it was stopped in 1952. Sighet was a VIP prison only in the sense that this old jail, built in 1898, was where high-ranking non-communist "old regime" officials were sent and where many of them died. Romania under communism had an extensive labor camp and prison system and one of the largest, most repressive, security organizations in the Soviet Bloc—the Securitate. It is estimated that by the late 1980s it had 20,000 employees and thousands of paid informers. Other accounts are higher, claiming 70,000 to 150,000 workers and as many as a million informers. Because military units were also attached, it is difficult to get an exact figure. However, it was huge and the fact that its files were liberated at the time of the revolution only to disappear is as mysterious as events surrounding the revolution itself.

All are agreed that it began in Timisoara in December after years of official harassment of Toekes who, as the one most activist-minded of a dynasty of Reformed Church clergy, had become a symbol of Hungarian protest and anti-regime dissidence. Matters came to a head at a time when other communist regimes were coming apart. By mid-December, many younger Romanians had literally linked arms with their Hungarian townspeople to protect Toekes and then, a few days later, began demonstrating to protest Toekes's arrest and to demand an end to rationing and privation. They surged through the streets shouting anti-Ceauşescu slogans, smashing shops to get at regime publications (which they burned) and to tear down Ceauşescu's photo, which had hung everywhere. Ceauşescu convinced his Political Executive Committee (Polexco) that what was afoot was a plot hatched by Washington and Moscow, which he intended to put down by force. Army, police and Securitate poured into town with their truncheons and arrested hundreds. On 17 December, the protestors were joined by the polytechnic and by factory workers. They now shouted for freedom, democracy and elections having torn the party symbol from the center of the national flag. They shouted that the army was with them. The party office was sacked.

The order to use utmost force had been disobeyed by the Polexco members responsible for security, Internal Affairs Minister Tudor Postelnicu and Defense Minister General Vasile Milea. Their reluctance has variously been explained by their belief that the situation was not so serious and that shooting would make it worse. On the afternoon of 17 December, Ceauşescu reamed them out at a Polexco meeting and told how he had put down demonstrators back in 1945, by killing them. By closed-circuit TV, he told county party leaders that an international plot was underway. Then, he did the inexplicable. He left on a three-day scheduled visit to Tehran, leaving control of the country in the hands of Elena and their close cohort Manea Manescu, with the expectation that his orders would be carried out. After all, he had sent some of his toughest men into Timisoara and they had begun to use deadly force. Army, Securitate, and the anti-terrorist USLA shot people, ran them over with armored vehicles and bayoneted bystanders. With some seventy dead, the regime had seemingly reimposed authority by 19 December. Bodies were taken from the morgue and incinerated in Bucharest. And, with the borders sealed, local cadres began to organize counter-demonstrations.

However, despite the bloodshed, a general strike got under way in Timisoara and ad hoc committees sprang up overnight. Protesters swarmed into the city center and many now wavering soldiers and even some Securitate began going over to the crowd. By evening on 20 December, 100,000 demonstrators were in the streets with T-55 tanks. Once back, Ceaușescu resumed command and spoke nationwide about "hooligans" and conspiracy abroad. He thanked his security forces for doing their job. By then, however, the army had backed off and was flying white flags. Commands were ignored. Infuriated workers threatened to blow up a petro-chemical plant. A baffled Ceaușescu learned that he had lost the city on the morning of 21 December. He ordered talks until he could ready a counterattack. At the same time, demonstrations were erupting elsewhere—in Tirgu Mures, Cluj, Arad, and Constanta—and feeding back into Bucharest by TV, radio, telephone and eyewitness reports. Still ignorant as to the mood of the people, Ceaușescu bussed thousands to hear him talk on that same day. By noon, 100,000 had gathered before the Central Committee building. Only minutes into a ration of canned remarks, shouts of, "Murderer... Timisoara," erupted and a nation saw the Dracului transfixed with a look of stupefaction and disbelief on his face. Then, stumbling along, he mumbled out some unconvincing promises. Shouts and booing continued. The same speech was rebroadcast later with voice-over sounds of adulation.[8]

But, by now, Bucharest had a huge crowd in the center of the city that refused to budge. Armored cars with water cannons and tear gas were brought in. When that failed, security personnel began to open up with their weapons. People broke up into small groups and began to throw up barricades. Again, Ceaușescu's books were burned and his pictures torn down. Reinforcements were ordered in and told to shoot. The Polexco Permanent Bureau met. Another TV talk to party bosses was laid on. Elena interrupted, telling her husband to be more forceful. They tried to tread water, but, in fact, they were drowning. Orders were being disobeyed, ignored. Confusion spread as the command structure broke down. Probably at this point, a number of regime officials realized that Ceauşescu and Elena would both have to go, but with luck and some needed reforms they could step into their shoes. The rapidity with which the NSF was established suggests this explanation despite efforts by those who took power to obscure the true facts. Subsequently, efforts were made to claim that a "resistance committee" had been set up earlier by some twenty or so Securitate and army generals. The names and details vary depending on who is telling the story.

However, great credit goes to Defense Minister Milea, who had crossed Ceauşescu earlier. He continued to disobey orders, telling his closest commanders not to crack down hard. Then, on the morning of 22 December, when Ceauşescu learned that the Central Committee was still lightly defended, Milea was taken out and shot. The Great Engineer probably thought that a military coup *was* under way as reports were coming in from the provinces that the army was no longer shooting, that it had adopted a passive posture. But, in Bucharest, Securitate and army units chased students through the center of the city. The latter lit candles beside the fallen. Milea's death caused additional confusion among his subordinates. Some Securitate had already quit. Some were seen trying to direct the demonstrators. USLA Securitate, which had responsibility for the Central Committee building's protection, permitted the enraged crowds to surge forward. Finally, at around noon, they broke into the ground floor and began to trash the lower levels of this huge symbol of party supremacy. Ceauşescu appeared on an upper balcony and then his wife pulled him inside. Within minutes, a military helicopter lifted off from the roof with the Ceauşescus, Manescu, and Emil Bobu. As the regime fell, the dictator and his wife were hunted down like dogs, given a summary trial and were executed.

In the chaos that followed, the younger people went wild with joy. Others cautiously wondered what to expect next. Dissident Mircea Dinescu made rousing speeches, formulated demands and announced the names of those that the students wanted to form a government. Some expected a Ceauşescu man to take over. Commanders and their troops stood by awaiting their orders. Amid great confusion, Ion Iliescu and General Nicholae Militaru immediately took matters into their own hands. Both were communists. Ceauşescu had forced Militaru out of the army and the Central Committee in the 1970s. Iliescu was sidelined from the Central Committee in 1984. Acting together, they contacted senior officers in command around the country while others coalesced around them in the capital. They appealed to people by name over national radio in the name of the revolution, in the name of an NSF. Generals responded by radio and by phone. By the evening of 22 December, a government of sorts was said to exist. They promised immediate reforms and asked a number of anti-regime personalities to join them until new elections.

The NSF was inaugurated by Generals Militaru and Chief of Staff Stefan Gusa. Vasile Ardeleanu, the commander of the USLA of the Securitate, was in. Experienced party leaders, besides Iliescu, included Alexandru Birladeanu and Silviu Brucan. Party reformer Petre Roman joined up. Also included was Ion Pircalebescu, head of the paramilitary Patriotic Guard. Vasile Nicolcioiu linked up the party cadres. Altogether, very early on, the NSF represented the most powerful groups in Romania. It immediately backed multiparty democracy, elections and reforms in industry, agriculture and education. Militaru's idea that NSF should remain within the framework of the party was rejected. A NSF Council was set up which named Toekes, Dinescu, Doina Cornea, and Ana Blandiana towards the top. Commanders and communists who had come over were listed further down. An appeal was made that all security organs should subordinate themselves to the front. Within a day, even hours, NSF was a fact.

The clapboard and plaster-sided shacks were squeezed up against the railway siding coming into Petrosani, and enclosed about with wire mesh and whatever else was available to protect the pitiful possessions and animals of gypsy families huddled under a heavy blanket of snow. Only a short drive away, one could see sculptures by that bearded genius, Constantin Brancusi. But Petrosani offered little for the creative imagination, for here in the Jiu valley generations of coal miners have dug their family's bread out from the earth in a dangerous, backbreaking struggle for survival. It had got underway in the mid-nineteenth century, at a time when barefoot miners dug lignite, the *huila*, for foreigners. Photos of the hovels they lived in resembled those of the gypsies just out of town. The miner's museum also has great grainy black and whites of early trade union meetings, demonstrations and strikes and of when, in the 1930s, miners worked under the bayonets and rifle butts of the gendarmerie. Depression, a disastrous war, political upheaval and years of communism did little to alter the tradition of valley men as tough, proud fighters. They claimed that they were the first dissidents, occupying the pits in 1977 in protest until Ceausescu came to talk. He lured them out with promises and then arrested the leaders and took them away. Miron Cosma was there.

I had come to meet the controversial unionist who had led his men to fight in the streets of Bucharest as Iliescu's "muscle" when Ion was on top and more lately to intimidate the ruling center-right coalition of Christian Democrats. As Cosma has flirted with Romania Mare as well, he was the paradigm of the rebellious man of action who cut across the political spectrum—a romantic hero to people in need of someone to stand up for their rights. Elegantly handsome at forty-five, Cosma at ease exuded controlled energy. His movements were fluid, cat-like. He had an amazing resemblance to the poet Mihai Eminescu, even to his long, dark hair. Some associated him with Mihai's "Luceafarul," not because of love, but because he was star-crossed, the planet Venus, the rebellious archangel, Satan himself. He was fated to violence. He tied his hair back like Steven Seagal. Maybe that was a clue. Built like a middleweight, Cosma had punched out policemen and journalists, and had wrecked a restaurant. Years ago, a woman dashed into the side of his car—an accident. He stayed by her side until she died, but people in power, those who hide behind power, held it over him. A Jiu valley man, he went underground at sixteen and then became an engineer. He collected music and had written about St. Varvara, the patron saint of miners. He played football and tennissoccer, where agility is everything. Married with children, Cosma lived in a simple apartment like so many others in Petrosani. But he was far from a simple personality. Daring and always out on the edge, Cosma spells danger... defies description. He is incandescent![9]

I found him late in the evening at his office after extended talks with the National Pitcoal Company, which were being conducted against a government deadline. He threw out unverifiable facts and figures that he said, after a five-year period, would see some twenty-two mines shut down. Meanwhile, however, he had prevented the company from closing two mines immediately and was on his way to winning an average seventeen percent wage increase for both workers and management.

Quite relaxed, Cosma didn't mention the fact that this had come about only a few weeks earlier after he had taken 10,000 men on a march on Bucharest. This latest round of collective bargaining Romanian-style had begun in early January when it was announced that two mines would close and 1,700 men would be sacked. In reaction, the Syndicated League of Jiului Valley Miners downed tools and Cosma appealed to Prime Minister Radu Vasile and Minister of Industries Radu Berceanu to come to Petrosani for talks. If they refused, Cosma had threatened to go to Bucharest. Just a week later, Cosma asked President Constantinescu to see their problems for himself. The government declared the strike "illegal" and vowed to force the miners back to work. They had already begun to position the police near Petrosani. After a vote, Cosma's men took to the road. With stones, clubs and bombs, they pushed past cement barricades and outfought the police in a five-day battle, which ended before cheering crowds. Humiliated after losing hostages and vehicles in round one, 3,500 riot police in full battle gear were readied for round two. During an uneasy truce, Cosma won his concessions from Vasile at a quiet monastery at Cozia. A rattled cabinet recalled parliament from its recess to vote more money. Alarmed, President Constantinescu's Supreme Defense Council came within an ace of declaring a state of emergency. The government was clearly shaken as the miners returned to their homes victorious.

I asked if he would march again if the current negotiations broke down. Confident, Cosma didn't think that would happen. He hinted if that occurred, others were capable of taking on the authorities again. Then he reasserted his role, stating that he had four more years to serve as union president. He claimed support from seven West European labor organizations and waved a Christmas card in the air that he had received from US President Bill Clinton. As to the eighteen-month sentence he had served for leading a riot in Bucharest that resulted in the ouster of Prime Minister Roman, he brushed it aside and said that he would never have been jailed if he had been involved with one of the larger political parties. He explained that in 1996 he had his sights set on a Senate seat as an Independent. He narrowly missed it, but, most certainly, he would have won had he chosen to run for the Chamber of Deputies. He bristled a bit when I asked if he regretted his role in even earlier incidents of June 1990 when the miners had bashed heads for Iliescu. He obviously had been asked that one before and was ready with a plausible explanation. He was smooth, smart and eager to burn a path through Romania's political firmament.

Company spokesman Valeriu Butulescu said that if the mines were located anywhere in the West, they would be closed as unsafe. He cited statistics indicating they were even worse than China's. And because Ceauşescu had refused to modernize them, average production per man per year was only 150 tons, much less than a Czech, or Polish mine. He explained how they had run at a loss for years producing low-grade coal. Even with complete industrial peace, he said they would still lose money. It cannot continue, he stated. I threw out Cosma's name, hoping to provoke him. He thought for a moment, and then said that they were more sad than angry over what has happened. He said, "In truth, Cosma has fought for all of us!"

As Cosma had complete disdain for those from Bucharest in their expensive suits who tried to tell them about coal, I wanted to see for myself. Dressed in hardhat and rubber boots, I trailed after engineers Nicolae Craciun and Constantine Dirnu down Dalja mine outside of Petrosani. Treading carefully on broken planks through mud and water in a maze of overhead pipes, pneumatic and electric cables, and machinery, we finally came to an antiquated elevator cage. Craciun crossed himself as Dirnu signaled for the descent and braced himself against the side in case of some surprise. The next level was full of twists and turns and railed for coal cars. Another elevator brought us to 500 meters. We met other workers and exchanged the traditional *noroc bun* good luck greeting! Now the gallery had a conveyor belt and the air was thick with dust. Workers were bent over sorting out cables for a demolitions charge. We continued on to a rock face where a four-man *brigada* had been working. They were drilling holes for "flashless" dynamite. They were all young, covered with grime and very intent on what they were doing. An air hammer chattered away in the arms of a worker who probably was in his late teens. Craciun said that there were few jokes at this point because the ten, or so, meters that they had made were still unbraced—and they were about to blast again! I longed to take a photograph, but couldn't because of the danger of methane gas. After some shop talk between the *brigada* and my guides, we shook hands all round and retraced our way back up to the surface. I was happy to see the light and breathe fresh air again. You can't really understand a mine until you go down one, and then words are inadequate. Because Dalja is one of the very oldest, I had had the uneasy feeling I was walking in the bowels of a mountain resembling Swiss cheese. A map confirmed this, and the unexpected does happen. It's possible that men must have some of the *dracului* in them to work and survive down there!

Dalja is one of thirty mines in the valley; and some 200 are to close nationwide, involving all of the extractive industries. The government had bought out 18,000 workers at Petrosani two years before, but because no job training was offered and jobs were scarce everywhere, many stayed on, gradually going through their money, remaining idle and, in frustration, marching with Cosma. He still had some 20,000 on the job, but time was running out for them. Constantine Dirnu was considering working on a North Sea oil rig, and he was professionally educated. The Retezat Mountains to the west have real possibilities for tourism if money somehow became available. A Bucharest bureaucrat had told them to grow mushrooms! It was talk like this that fuelled their rage when they followed Cosma to Bucharest. Often, those that packed up and left trashed their apartments in revenge against what they viewed as a rotten system. Meanwhile, those that were working earned about twice the national average of US$100 a month, raising their children in small, poorly constructed apartments badly in need of repair. Some lived in small cottages built over a century before. The young went out to the ubiquitous pizza parlors, discos and bars to dance, shoot pool, and drink. With short-term goals, they were into "the look" in apparel, pop culture, and the often unobtainable music system and car. Under Ceaușescu, there was money, but nothing to buy. Now, there are many things to buy, but not enough money!

The train back to Bucharest made a long loop through Tirgu Jiu and Craiova through the heart of Wallachia. I had hours to think about what had occurred over almost a decade and it was clear that Cosma and his men more than symbolized the problems of post-Ceauşescu Romania. In early 1990, when the NSF was establishing itself, state authority was still shaky. There were times when a police or military presence was needed, but they either had stood back from unruly crowds, or had failed to assume their responsibilities. Part of the explanation was that they were unsure of where they stood because they were being reorganized and partially purged. Cosma and his men, and many other workers, had filled the gap as almost all were supportive of the NSF, which had just given them sweeping pay increases, had put food into the marketplace, and had promised to guard the nation's wealth and not permit outside interests to take over. Iliescu was very popular, talked in terms of gradual privatization and was aware of the need to protect job security. What worker wouldn't volunteer his time in those heady days after NSF first came to power? Cosma's men did just that in January and February, promising to return if they were needed.[10]

Partly reformist and partly opportunist, with many of the same old faces still around, the NSF began to be viewed with suspicion and animosity by students, younger people and by politically minded professionals, especially so after it swept the national election of 20 May 1990, which was flawed in its execution and inflamed by Iliescu's nationalist rhetoric. Even earlier, dissidents such as Cornea and Blandiana had quit the NSF council because of heavy-handed treatment of oppositionists and the reversal of its stance not to contest elections. By late April, students and others had set up an "Anticommunist Zone" near the university, an island of protest and a precursor of Sofia's "City of Truth." It attracted hundreds daily led by university student league chairman Marian Munteanu. It also became the venue of gypsy vendors, who moved in to do their various *bizhnitsa*, and those the government called *golani* (hooligans). The activity spilled out into the streets, often disrupting traffic and provoking clashes with the police. A constant refrain was their call for a "real revolution," without the NSF and with an independent media and thoroughgoing democratic reforms. It was a combination of political catalyst and carnival.

Before dawn on 13 June, the police swept through the area and made many arrests. By late morning, they had sealed it off with police buses and vans. A large crowd gradually gathered in protest. Then fights erupted—stones and Molotov cocktails were aimed at the vehicles. Strangely, whereas the police had acted resolutely earlier, they now retreated. The mob marched on the main police station to demand the release of the detainees, damaging parked cars and other property along the way. They split, some rampaging towards the foreign ministry, others towards the ministry of the interior. Iliescu appealed to the public on TV to defend the government. The station was invaded by rioters who ransacked a few rooms and disrupted broadcasting for an hour. Soon after, a shaken Iliescu made a second appeal for help, blaming "extremist elements of a fascist nature" who were threatening to undo the revolution. He again made an emotional appeal to defend "democracy."

That night, Iliescu sent three trains to Petrosani and, sometime after midnight, Cosma and over 2,500 miners crowded aboard. They arrived in Bucharest in the morning and were taken to a stadium filling up with NSF supporters that had been bussed in from outlying factories—some 40–50,000 people. Cosma denied being given lists of people to hunt down, as has been alleged by others. Neither was it spontaneous. Iliescu and his aides had put out a call to clear the streets and to restore order. The miners, along with the others, swept through the center, beating anyone who was in their way. The offices of the Liberal and Peasant parties were smashed, as was *Romania Libera*, an outspoken independent newspaper. Cosma's men entered the university, beating students and damaging academic offices. Munteanu was beaten senseless before being arrested. Gypsies were also singled out. Thugs appeared at the doors of opposition MPs, who were roughed up and threatened. The police, almost to a man, stood by, or egged on the assailants. By the time it was over the next day, some 600 had been hurt and as many as twenty lay dead. Over TV, Iliescu draped his arms around Cosma's men and thanked them for their help. They left Bucharest as heroes after having been manipulated into acting as Iliescu's strong-arm bully boys. Cosma helped NSF to consolidate its grip on power following an election that was stacked against its rivals.

Even after an investigation, the events of 14–15 June 1990 remained unclear. Secrecy. Files. This in a country where a third of the adult population had joined the communist party; where thousands had collaborated with the security service; and where others remained silent. The files still existed, having been passed to the hands of the new SRI. And, because secret knowledge is power, Cosma had been busy in Bucharest. Thirty-four Bulevardul Republicii, the offices of the Peasant Party, were in the same building as the National Water Council where Iliescu was director from 1979–84. While Cosma had men breaking furniture, others were in Iliescu's old office breaking a wall to get at a safe. This was burned open and papers were removed of an undisclosed nature, only to disappear. It's hard to imagine Cosma being elsewhere when something so sensitive and politically explosive was happening. Did he hand them over to Iliescu? Did he make copies for himself? What were they that made them so important? Had Iliescu ordered it, or was it Cosma himself?

Over the next year, the NSF government remained in ferment. It was divided over the question of how best to make a transition from a state-owned command economy to something that would approximate a liberal free market. Privatization Minister Adrian Severin wanted a quick "shock" approach like Poland to shut down state-owned loss makers and to sell off the rest as soon as possible. Prime Minister Roman favored this also, but at a more measured pace. Iliescu was bothered by the question of social cost and how this might cut into his constituency of voters. He remained focused on keeping the NSF (himself) in power and also resented Roman's growing popularity, boosted by the latter's irresponsible and unproven accusation of "plots" by the Hungarian minority. Early September found Cosma engaged in negotiations over wages and conditions in the valley. By mid-month, agreement seemed near. However, just a week later, the miners struck to force deputies to come to them.

Cosma was in no mood to wait, however. He and his men hijacked two trains on the evening of 24 September and ordered the crews to take them to Bucharest. Arriving on the afternoon of the twenty-fifth with clubs and crowbars, the miners marched out of the Gara de Nord with the aim of forcing Roman out of office. Some tried to take over the TV station, others stormed towards parliament. They were soon joined by students by the hundreds. This time, Munteanu donned a miner's hat and called Cosma his "brother." By the twenty-seventh, the police and gendarmerie were on the losing end and a large mob pressed towards Cotroceni Palace, the president's residence. Roman had resigned on the previous day, but now the crowd chanted slogans against Iliescu. Again, Cosma somehow worked his sorcery and got them under control. He claimed he had met with Iliescu and had gained important concessions. He told them that they had won. By evening, calm was restored. With three dead, 500 injured and Roman removed, Cosma's name rocketed around the world. Again the question was asked whether Iliescu had brought Cosma and his men to Bucharest? Some wondered if Cosma's move on Cotroceni was intended to send Iliescu a message? There were more questions than answers.[11]

Headlines in Bucharest blared out the news in big, bold, type. I had arrived the previous night thinking that Romania, for me, was almost over. But, at breakfast, and in the street, everyone was talking about how the Supreme Court had met and had overturned a decision that had jailed Cosma for eighteen months for his part in the events of September 1991 and had sentenced him to eighteen years! I spoke to several journalists who were thunderstruck. They talked of upheaval and of a possible revolt against the government. In addition the court ordered seven years' loss of civil rights after his release and banishment for five years from Petrosani, or Bucharest. It was an attempt to crush Cosma as a man and ensure that he would never again participate in public life. As Cosma had already done his eighteen months, it appeared to be a case of double jeopardy. And, it was done under a so-called democratic reform government, one that was floundering in its own incompetence. The IMF and the World Bank were breathing down its neck threatening that unless reforms got underway, they would not provide any new loans. Aimed at Cosma, and indirectly at an opposition led by Iliescu, the sentence smacked of something from the Ceaușescu era.

With an arrest warrant out, Cosma stormed out of Petrosani with several thousand workers in cars, vans, trucks and buses in the direction of Bucharest. In the main square of Tigru Jiu, he wore a black Nike cap like his supporters and hurled out his defiance. By now, 4,000 men were on the move. The next day, 17 February, the miners, armed with clubs, chains and even axes, met a line of 1,000 riot police at Stoenesti armed with heavy plastic shields, tear-gas canisters and assault rifles equipped to fire a steel ball encased in hard rubber. They fought for three hours, with the police finally getting the best of it. One miner died of a heart attack and a hundred were injured. Dozens of police were hurt as well. Some 500 miners were arrested, including Cosma, who was found surrounded by his friends in a bus. Remanded in custody, he began an appeal, which President Constantinescu refused to respond to. *Luceafarul* remained ensnared.[12]

* * *

After thousands of years of pre-history, long before Herodotus wrote about them, a Thracian people lived east of the Morava and north of the Danube, a people that at the time of Christ were known as Dacians. Burebista had united the tribes and established a stronghold at Sarmizegetusa in the Carpathians. Shortly after, at the end of the first century, the Dacians under Decebal mounted successive military campaigns into Moesia, colliding with Roman commanders bent on extending their empire and trade eastwards. He won Rome's respect because of his military prowess and a peace treaty was written in AD 89 under Domitian, which even included a Roman military assistance program (military engineers, advice) if Decebal's Dacia would become a client state. Rome also offered to help build defensive fortifications along Dacia's boundary. It went well until Emperor Marcus Trianus, Trajan, appeared on the scene. Trajan, it seems, was planning war against the Parthians and wanted to ensure his Danubian flank was secure. He had also heard rumors of Dacian gold and toyed with the idea of colonization.[13]

In AD 101, Rome sent 150,000 men against Decebal, crossing the Danube on a bridge of boats in the Banat. A year of fighting brought Trajan close to Sarmizegetusa. In the spring, Decebal launched an offensive in Dobrodgea to relieve his capital, but it failed to carry as expected and he sued for peace. Trajan's terms weren't harsh. Decebal had to give up his siege machines and Rome was permitted to keep a garrison in the capital and at strategic points along the Danube. Decebal, however, failed to disarm and three years later, in AD 105, Trajan mounted an attack from the south. Again, a year of fighting saw the capital under siege and Dacian forces withdrawing into the mountains. A bearded Decebal, strongly handsome in a curious cloth cap, preferred to take his own life rather than surrender. Some followed his example. Others fought on, or fled elsewhere. But the vast majority surrendered and were assimilated into what, for the next 150 years, became a Roman colony. They even adopted a bastardized, or vulgar, Latin that Trajan's soldiers and settlers spoke. Dacia or Dacia Felix saw the imposition of a superior civilization. Laws, political organization and the tools of war and peace became Roman.

As the last of Rome's far-flung colonies, it required a very large garrison force to defend it from other barbarians. Consequently, following internal stress after the death of Emperor Severus, Aurelian decided to withdraw to defense lines south and west of the Danube, leaving Dacia's indigenous population and settlers to remain to fend for themselves. It did not happen overnight and there was no sudden collapse internally or in terms of trade. It did mean, however, that others gradually made inroads into the area and a people whose blood had mingled with the Romans saw the coming of the Huns, Avars, Slavs, Bulgarians, and, finally, the Hungarians. The record is unclear during this epoch of migrations from the east. Suffice to say that throughout this long period of turmoil, a people who had been formed ethnically into "Romanians" clung to their Latin-based language and their early Christianity. By AD 1000, Hungarians, beginning their conquest of Transylvania, acknowledged Romanian, or Vlach *voievods* (leaders). The latter remained Orthodox, true to Constantinople after the Great Schism.

In the next few centuries, the area was convulsed by the invasion of the Mongols and, more gradually, Hungarians under the successors of Arpad. Romanian *voievods* preserved princedoms here and there, but only Basarab I succeeded in defeating King Charles Robert I of Anjou at the battle of Posada in late 1330 to keep Wallachia. Caught in a narrow defile, masses of Romanians rained stones and arrows down upon the flower of the Hungarian nobility. Similarly, Roman I maintained his rule in Moldavia after being forced out of Maramures. Therefore, while the first Romanian states were becoming established, the Hungarian kings (mindful of their small numbers) induced Szeklers, Saxons, and even Teutonic and Johannite knights to settle Transylvania with the title and privileges of nobles and sworn to defend the eastern borders of the kingdom. Romanians under their rule became serfs whose condition was akin to slavery. The Slavs and Greeks had the Ottomans, just as the Romanians had the Hungarians, for over 600 years.

Moldavia was somewhat buffered from the west by the Carpathians, but a succession of boyar princes had to contend with the Poles and Russians. To the south, Wallachia had to fend off an Ottoman threat that swept westward. All attempted to play power against power in an effort to maintain their independence, even while they, themselves, fought each other. Ultimately, by 1400, Alexander the Good of Moldavia vassaled himself to the Poles for the benefit of both. In Wallachia, the German Emperor (and Hungarian King) Sigismund supported rival claimants who made common cause with the Serbs or Ottomans depending on the situation, so as to keep Hungarians out. Vlad Dracul II was one such who enjoyed a run of luck. More outstanding, of course, was the Transylvanian *voievod* Janos Hunyadi who was possibly the son of Sigismund and an Erzsebet Morsina, wife of Serba Vojk. After Sigismund gave Vojk Hunyadvar castle in Transylvania, the latter renamed himself Hunyadi and his "son" entered the fast track to advancement. Fortunately, Janos proved to be a great soldier, starting out as a mercenary condottiere in Italy. Many successful skirmishes with the Turks earned him a sobriquet, "Torokvero," Scourge of the Turks. In 1437, he was commander of southern Hungary. However, Sigismund died that same year and King Ladislas V assigned him Belgrade and Transylvania, literally the front line. Hunyadi fought brilliantly, taking on Beg Iszhak at Szendro, Mezid Pasha at Nagyszeben, and Sehabeddin at the Iron Gates. Hunyadi covered himself in glory. As leaders will, however, Ladislas interfered at Varna, a battle resulting in defeat, his own death, and Janos's capture by the Wallachian warlord *voievod*, Vlad Dracul II. Released, Hunyadi killed Dracul and his son but he had another close call at Kosovo. In 1456, Sultan Mehmet II moved on Belgrade (Nandorfehervak) with an army of 100,000 and 200 ships. Hunyadi had 10,000 veteran fighters of his own, volunteers from the armies of central Europe, and a mass of peasants collected by the Franciscan monk John Capistrano—perhaps 70,000 in all. Hunyadi broke the blockade of the Danube while Ottoman artillery pounded the walls of the city. The Turks mounted a night assault on 21 July, but hundreds of janissaries were incinerated inside the city. The next day, "crusader" serfs led by Capistrano took the Turks by surprise and wounded Mehmet. The Turks panicked and retreated, with a loss of 75,000 men.[14]

Hunyadi died of plague in August, followed by Capistrano, but his son, Matthias, went on to become one of Hungary's most famous kings and soldiers. Hunyadi-Hunedoara's fame, bolstered by rumors of his royal origins, strengthened Hungary's hold on Transylvania. Not even Vlad Dracula III (The Impaler) of Wallachia, who was in and out of favor with Matthias, even as he skewered thousands of Turks, presented a challenge. Although he was cut down in battle, Dracula would be remembered mostly for his cruelty. Also, Stefan the Great, a contemporary who regained Moldavia, variously allied himself with the Ottomans and Hungarians, or fought against them. In his last years, Stefan had to beat back the Poles. Both states, Wallachia and Moldavia, had too many external enemies and internal rivalries to think of liberating Transylvania. By the 1500s, they were increasingly under Ottoman influence, unable to take advantage of Hungary's disastrous defeat at Mohacs in 1526. Michael the Brave did briefly unite the three principalities in 1600 during this period of Hungarian weakness, but was unable to prevent the Magyars from retaking their "Erdely," their "over the mountains," a place apart from the broad plains of their Hungarian "Alfold." The Ottoman's confirmed Habsburg rule of Transylvania in 1699 by the Treaty of Karlowitz.

The 1700s was a century of suffering for Romanians. The Ottomans, now in slow decline, administered Wallachia and Moldavia through a rapacious clan of Greek tax collectors called the Phanariots because they came from the Phanar quarter of Constantinople. They lived in great luxury in Bucharest and Iasi, holding court and intriguing among a succession of Romanian "hospodar" princes. The first was Nicholae Mavrocordat who assumed his authority after a series of beheadings of the more prominent boyars by the Sultan. Some point to reforms under the Phanariots, but the fact remains that the types of taxes proliferated, as did the need for bribery at all levels of society. If Phanariot rule was more efficient, it was to better exploit the peasantry. Serfdom was ended, but most continued to live in abject poverty and ignorance. Peasants slept on the ground on a worn mat with a stone for a pillow and lived on corn porridge. In winter, a crude wooden hut of sticks and mud had to do. In Transylvania conditions were as bad, or worse.

Habsburg Empress Maria Theresa requested in a letter in 1773 to her Transylvanian governor, in advance of Joseph II's visit, that he "clear the road of corpses of those killed by hanging, impaling, or quartering, which the Hungarians, to the traveler's horror, have purposely let rot along these roads."

The Romanians exploded in revolt in 1784 led by Horea, Closca, and Crisan—peasants. As others had done, Horea attempted to petition the Imperial Court in Vienna, to no avail. That avenue blocked, he joined a group of peasants who were trying to escape from their lowly status by becoming frontier guards. When enlistments were arbitrarily suspended, their accumulated frustration turned to anger. After they had assembled in protest, three officials were killed trying to take Crisan. The peasants began to sack the houses of the Hungarian landed nobility, killing them, or forcing them to convert to Orthodoxy. They called for an end to the nobility, and the redistribution of land. It was brief, but very bloody![15]

The new emperor, Joseph II, had put down the revolt by February 1785. And although its leaders died horribly, Joseph abolished serfdom some months later and permitted freedom of movement. Later on, he tried to gain greater rights for the ethnic-Romanians, something that the Hungarian Diet resented and ignored. The Magyar nobility remained adamantly opposed to reforms right up to the end of the Austro-Hungarian empire in 1918. In Wallachia and Moldavia, however, change was ushered in by the end of the Phanariots in 1821 and Turkey's defeat by Russia in 1829. The Russians gave them a quasi-constitution in the form of the Organic Regulations, a development that gave rise to liberal thought. The church, first steps in education, and cultural trends were all affected for the better. A Romanian consciousness that had existed for centuries took on a national coloration. Great Power intervention by Habsburgs, Russians, and others, would both help and hinder.

Tudor Vladimirescu and 8,000 Oltenians beat the Greek Alexander Ypsilantis to Bucharest in February 1821 and the two upstarts did their best to outwit each other before the Ottoman army arrived. Vladimirescu was willing to make common cause up to a point, but wanted the Phanariots and the Greeks out of the principalities. Ypsilantis became aware of Vladimirescu's willingness to talk to the Turks, betrayed him and then had him shot. Ypsilantis's rabble was beaten by June and the one-armed, former Russian general fled to Austria to die in Mugats castle as a prisoner. Some blew themselves up inside a Moldavian monastery in Secu in a heroic gesture of defiance that sent sparks flying through the Balkans. Although the Ypsilantis episode failed miserably, it did serve to restore the rule of Romanians in the two principalities.

All of this was against the backdrop of the defeat of Napoleon's France and the Congress of Vienna in 1815, which attempted to restore stability and support to the conservative forces of Europe, including a resurgent Russia. At the same time, each of the Great Powers had their own interests in the Balkans and each attempted to influence events for their own benefit. Popular revolt in 1848 in Paris, Vienna, and Budapest reinforced this. When Iasi's boyars in April presented a reform petition, they were arrested by Prince Michael Sturza, exiled and scattered. That same month, some 4,000 gathered at Blaj, Transylvania, to voice their demands. By mid-May this was multiplied tenfold under Simion Barnutiu, who demanded Romanian rights and a real end to serfdom as had been announced more than fifty years earlier. Days later, the Hungarian Diet at Cluj voted for formal union with Hungary. This was agreed to by a frightened Ferdinand I in June. In Wallachia, armed rebellion got underway in Oltenia led by young men back from Paris. Justice and Brotherhood had conspired with militia commander George Magheru, who had the trust of Prince Bibescu. They announced their demands on 21 June, taking Bibescu and his Russian advisors by complete surprise. A broad-based provisional government was formed as the prince and the Russian Consul in Bucharest took to their heels. The reform-minded rebels lasted until late September when their 25,000 irregulars fell back before Ottoman-Russian intervention forces. With Hungarian troops taking over Transylvania in 1849, a Romania in the making was fitfully occupied for several years.

Out of 1848, and the Crimean War which followed, emerged leaders more experienced and sophisticated who kept the Romanian Question before the Great Powers. The French came around to see Wallachia and Moldavia as a convenient buffer state on the Danube. The idea was picked up by the French and British press and gained support at the Paris peace congress of February 1856. Although nominally still under the Porte, the principalities' status became viewed as an open subject to be decided in consultation with its people. And given that petroleum deposits were discovered in 1857, the circumstances that saw Prince Cuza come to power hardly surprise. With oil, efforts would be made to keep the Ottomans and Russians at bay and the need for internal stability would see a German, Karl of Hohenzollern-Sigmaringen, proclaimed Prince Carol I of Romania in 1866. Carol I was what Romania needed. Diligent, able and connected to Europe's royal families, he also proved capable of working with the two main streams of Liberal and Conservative politicians that would rotate in and out of government for many decades to come, particularly the Liberal Ion Bratianu.

A Catholic, Carol had seen service with the Prussian Royal Guard and took a keen interest in building a state, a serious military force and engaging in continental diplomacy. In 1877, he threw in with the Russians during the latter's war with the Turks, first declaring Romania's independence from the Ottomans and then sent in an army commanded by his own officers that in five months of fighting would finally take Plevna. 10,000 Romanians died in the campaign. However, independence was recognized, and Dobrodgea and the Danube delta were added at San Stefano even as Russia added the counties of Bolgrad, Cahul, and Ismail to their Bessarabian territories between the Pruth and the Dniester that they had grabbed in 1812. Within a few years, in 1881, Romania became a kingdom. Perhaps resentful of the Russians, who were rebuked by the Treaty of Berlin in 1878, King Carol signed on with the Central Powers of Germany and Austria-Hungary. This was done in secret, seemingly a safe thing to do in terms of existing circumstances at the time. After all, Carol was a German, and a major war seemed a distant prospect as Romania's upper classes developed a taste for the good life. In 1884, electric lighting was installed at Timisoara, the first in Europe. In 1885, a new bridge over the Danube at Cernavoda was the longest on the Continent. Romania appeared to be coming of age.[16]

However, widespread political corruption, a bloated bureaucracy, administrative inefficiency, government meddling and government half measures, particularly in agrarian reform, sapped Romania's promise and led to enormous debts. Costly public works and a costly celebration of forty years under Carol in 1906 were borne mostly by the peasantry. With their lands subdivided into patches incapable of supporting their families, contracts of a usurious nature, and the grain trade controlled by absentee landowners, the peasantry exploded in 1907. They destroyed records, public buildings and the homes of wealthy boyars, seized crops, and battled a mobilized military force of 120,000. Order was restored only after 10,000 peasants had died and again efforts to improve their lot was inadequate. They were considered to be no better than animals.

In the run-up to the Balkan Wars, party politics was dominated by another Bratianu, a son. Ion I. C. Bratianu was an intelligent technocrat (an engineer by education) and the natural leader of the Liberals, who favored economic development by and for Romanian businessmen. Nationalist and assertive, they tended to downplay traditional German and Austrian ties. The annexation of Bosnia by Austria only reinforced this. And, looking on at the carve-up of Ottoman territory in the first Balkan War, Romania jumped in to join the attack on Bulgaria in the second and took some of south Dobrodgea, land it had never possessed before. The same outlook held on the eve of World War One, when an ailing and elderly King Carol expected Romania to honor its pact with the Central Powers. Carol (a constitutional monarch) summoned a Crown Council on 3 August thinking he had sufficient support to carry the day. However, the Liberals and Conservatives argued that the treaty was defensive in nature and that Austria's attack on Serbia relieved them of their obligation. Bratianu asserted that Vienna and Berlin had failed to consult with them and underlined the nation's felt antagonism towards Hungary over Transylvania. It voted neutrality. In two months, Carol was dead of shock and disappointment.

Because Carol had produced no male heir and his daughter had died, a German nephew, Ferdinand I, ascended the throne. He had been long prepared and had a military background. His Princess, Marie, was the perfect counterpart. Pro-Entente, Bratianu convinced him to remain neutral until Romania was ready for war. Understandings were entered into secretly with Russia and Italy. Over the months some 20,000 officers and 800,000 soldiers were placed under arms. However the problem with Bratianu's policy was that Bucharest was being entreated by every side and, as the war ground on, Romania spun on its own diplomatic axis. Finally, in August 1916, it went with the Entente on the promise of Transylvania, the Banat, and Bucovina. But a more complete disaster could hardly be imagined. Advances turned into routs. Enormous quantities of both men and materiel were lost. Allied aid failed to arrive. In four months, Bucharest had fallen and Romania was surrounded on three sides by Austrian, Hungarian, German, and Bulgarian forces. It was a total catastrophe and the Russians were on the run as well![17]

Ferdinand, Marie, the court and Bratianu's cabinet went to Iasi and a line of defense finally stabilized in southern Moldavia. By mid-1917, a French military mission had organized twenty divisions of some half a million men. With German General August von Mackensen poised to smash through to Odessa and the Ukraine, the Romanians surprised everyone by advancing at Marasti and holding Maraseti in a month of furious fighting that cost the Germans 60,000 dead. However, the Russian revolution took that country out of the war in late 1917 leaving Romania in an untenable position. Amid German threats and Allied pleas, it kept some divisions in place, but stopped fighting. When events went against the Central Powers in 1918, Romania again declared war on 10 November. With a French expeditionary force by its side, they forced the Germans to withdraw to Transylvania. On 1 December, the king and queen were back in Bucharest. Bratianu went to the Paris peace talks and returned with Greater Romania—Bessarabia, Transylvania—everything.

Actually, the Allies had been presented with a fait accompli. When Tsarist Russia collapsed, a Moldavian national movement was soon in operation in Bessarabia. A republic was proclaimed in December 1917, which was initially disputed by Bolshevik detachments that occupied Chisinau in January 1918. A Romanian division permitted an ethnic-Romanian dominated assembly to declare its independence from Russia and enter into unification talks almost immediately. Bucovina was even easier, brokered by Romanian deputies from the old Vienna parliament. With Slovaks, Czechs, Croats, and Slovenes all forming national councils, no one cared when Bukovina united with Bucharest in November 1918. The Romanian National Party of Transylvania rose up as well. In October 1918, it separated from Hungary and called for an assembly. A national council backed by Romanian troops set up its administration everywhere and ignored Hungarian offers of autonomy. On 1 December 1918, delegates by the hundreds met in Alba Iulia and declared for unification. This was reaffirmed by King Ferdinand before the month was out. As Romania had helped to put down the communist revolt of Bela Kun in Budapest, and had joined the Allied effort against Lenin's revolution as well, it was welcomed into the circle of victors after World War One.

Unfortunately, its ruling classes, both monarchy and politicians, failed to sustain that promise. Ferdinand and Marie tried as much as possible to consolidate their gains, but party hacks, with the exception of the National Peasant Party of Iuliu Maniu, went back to their old ways of rigging elections and lining their pockets. In addition, the monarchy itself became unstable because a willful and thoroughly rotten Crown Prince, Carol II, had twice renounced his right to the throne and preferred to immerse himself in scandal. During the war, he deserted his post and ran over to the Russian lines to marry Hungarian commoner Zizi Lambrino. A few years later, he took up with the divorced Jewess, Magda Lupescu. The fact that he was married to Helen of the Greek royal family mattered not at all. When Ferdinand died in 1927, Carol II's six-year-old son, Michael, was in line to succeed. The Queen Mother was marginalized—immersed in her personal problems. Carol II, twice exiled, returned in June 1930 and reclaimed the crown with the help of a coterie of businessmen-politicians, who proved quite incapable of coping with an economic depression, mass discontent and the rise of communism and fascism. They proved disastrous.

First, there was an inordinate fear of socialism among Romania's landowning and commercial classes, aware as they were as to how they had unmercifully exploited the peasants and urban poor. And, as the Soviet Union gradually grew in strength under Stalin, they all feared the Comintern's call for independence for nationality groups. It was a threat to the Greater Romania just recently won. For this reason, they welcomed right-wing nationalists who opposed socialists and communists of any stripe and supported the rise of Corneliu Zelea Codreanu's strange, mystical Legionari movement of the Archangel Michael. It was created in 1927 by a Codreanu who had been influenced by A. C. Cuza in Iasi. By 1930, Codreanu was a popular hero, having once been acquitted of killing Iasi's police chief. Handsome, given to flamboyant peasant dress and claiming to be guided by God, Codreanu acquired a following of millions.

In 1930, the Legion (which advocated "holy" terror and emphasized national revival through redemption by the deed) set up an elite military wing called the Iron Guard. Whereas the Legion had often engaged in violence in the past (often surrendering themselves), the Guardists developed an ideology and a ritual directed towards terror based on extreme nationalism and anti-Semitism. They were taken with the idea of sacrifice, death and Romanian sacred soil. Their *cuibs* (nests) of three to thirteen members conducted an elaborate blood oath before setting out to do violence. Codreanu was the Captain, or *Capitanul*, and Carol II was his patron for several years. In 1933, Prime Minister Ion Duca cracked down. Guardists were arrested and several were killed. In retaliation, Duca was assassinated. In 1935, Codreanu and war hero, Gheorghe Cantacuzino-Granicerul, organized the All For The Country Party. Then, in 1936, Codreanu broke with the king because Carol II's camarilla was corrupt to the core. Now extremely jealous of the *Capitanul*'s popularity, and viewing him as a competitor instead of a tool, Carol II established a dictatorship in early 1938.[18]

Within weeks, Carol II had Codreanu and his lieutenants arrested. In May 1938, he was sentenced to ten years for treason and some months later, he and thirteen others were murdered during a prison transfer—strangled en route to Fort Jilava. In September 1939, the Guardists assassinated Prime Minister Armand Calinescu. Hours later, Carol II had 252 leading Guardists executed without trial. However, events were now closing in on a Romania that had seen eighteen premiers in ten years and a king with a lust for sex, wealth and power. In June 1940, after France had surrendered to Germany, Moscow demanded that Romania cede Bessarabia. This done, August saw Hitler order Carol II to return most of Transylvania to the Hungarians and south Dobrodgea to Bulgaria. A devastated Carol II released General Ion Antonescu from jail and asked him to form a government. Amidst a collapsed regime, an end to Greater Romania, and massive Guardist demonstrations demanding he quit, Antonescu forced an abdication in favor of Carol II's son, Michael. Furious at being out-maneuvered, his last outrage as king was to load up an enormous amount of gold and treasure into his private railway cars before fleeing with Lupescu to Switzerland.[19]

"Red Dog" Antonescu formed a Guardist regime with King Michael I as a figurehead. Queen Marie came back to Bucharest, but no one doubted that the military and the green-shirted Guardists were in control. With their rabid longhaired leader, Horia Sima, now vice-president of the Council of Ministers, the Legionaries went on a killing spree. First, some sixty-five cronies of Carol II were murdered. Guardists roamed through the Jewish quarter killing, looting, and burning. Old Iorga died, his beard yanked out, a liberal paper crammed down his throat and having been tortured. After a state funeral mass for Codreanu, which was attended by a crazed mob of 150,000, the Guardists set out again burning synagogues, raping women, and shooting hundreds stripped naked in the January snow. On the following evening, they rounded up some 200 Jews and took them to an abattoir where, naked, they were slaughtered like animals and hung on meat hooks. Sima attempted to take power with an orgy of death directed almost exclusively against the Jewish community.

Finally, Antonescu ordered the army into action: hundreds died in street fighting; 9,000 were arrested; some 1,000 sentenced; and twenty were actually executed. Many fled to Germany. However, others survived to collaborate in the take-over of Jewish businesses. A huge German military mission was in the country that constantly demanded ever-larger quantities of oil, grain and other products. Spring 1941 saw Yugoslavia and Greece fall to the Axis powers. A now all-powerful Antonescu (called the *Conducaturul* or leader) awaited Romania's opportunity. It came on 22 June, when Hitler sent 180 divisions into Russia. Having joined the Tripartite Pact the previous November and eager to take Bessarabia, thirty Romanian divisions of 400,000 men crossed the Pruth and drove towards Odessa. In the Ukraine, the Romanians demonstrated a bestiality towards civilians that was later revenged before Stalingrad.[20]

By late 1943, bombs had fallen on Bucharest and the Russians were pushing west. An opposition of sorts had emerged and Iuliu Maniu had Antonescu's permission to put out peace feelers, offering forty-two train wagons of gold, 400 of wheat, 300 of corn and twenty-two armed divisions if the Allies arrived before the Russians. This was all rejected and, when the Russians arrived in September 1944, they ordered Romania to turn on the Germans. Romania sent twenty-seven divisions west, taking heavy casualties fighting in Hungary-Czechoslovakia. Antonescu had already been arrested in August on the orders of King Michael I. Actually, Romania's position had collapsed. Antonescu was eventually shot as a war criminal and arrests and purges in 1946–47 ushered in communist rule. A pliant Petru Groza from the Ploughman's Front was controlled by a Romanian Workers' Party led by Gheorghe-Dej. Among his closest cohorts was a young man named Nicolae

Ceaușescu, a one-time cobbler's assistant with whom he had once shared a jail cell.[21]

In 1953, the front was abolished and the communist party became the only legal party. Widespread nationalization of the economy had already taken place and collectivization of agriculture was under way despite resistance by the peasantry. Gheorghe-Dej pushed through a program of industrialization including machine building and metals. A shift to urban life began under complete communist control, even though some Legionari supporters held out as late as 1959 in the Banat. However, the situation within the party was hardly smooth. Nationalist-minded Lucretiu Patrascanu was arrested in 1948 and shot in 1954. In 1952, the so-called "Moscow group" led by Anna Pauker and Vasile Luca was eliminated. The party was about power, total power, and although Romania did orbit around the Soviet Union, it remained Romanian in its personality. Only days after Gheorghe-Dej died, and Ceaușescu took over, reminders of the old leader literally disappeared. At the ninth party congress, the new general-secretary denounced Gheorghe-Dej's "Stalinist" ways. But after a period of liberalization and independence, which won approval by the West, the Ceaușescus reverted to building a cult of sycophants around themselves like the boyars of the past. Both this, and the projects the peasant engineers decreed, were much like those of despots of old. They measuring out food and rewards; sold exit permits to those who could purchase their escape; and misery to those who remained trapped within the system.[22]

* * *

3 January 1990. A decree signed by NSF president, Ion Iliescu, re-established a multiparty political system. A month later, following negotiations between the NSF and various political groups, a PCNU temporary government was formed. The situation was unsettled.

20 May 1990. Free elections were held with 86.2 percent of the eligible voters participating. The pre-war National Liberal Party (PNL) was reconstituted from elderly former youth league members. It chose Radu Campeanu, who had been jailed by the communists and then exiled to France, as secretary. A National Peasants Party (PNT) had the same composition—the elderly. It was soon taken over by a wealthy London property and shipping tycoon, Ion Ratiu, who had left Romania in 1940. Ratiu, Cambridge educated, had headed the World Union of Free Romanians during the Cold War years. When the final results were announced five days later, the NSF had won by a landslide: NSF 66.3 percent (263 chamber seats, ninety-two senate), PNT 2.6 percent (twelve chamber seats, one senate), PNL 6.4 percent (twenty-nine chamber seats, nine senate). The Hungarian UDMR started late, but won 7.2 percent (twenty-nine chamber seats, twelve senate). Ion Iliescu was elected president with eighty-five percent of the vote over Campeanu and Ratiu. All, except the NSF, complained of numerous campaign and election irregularities.

9 June 1990. The first session of the new parliament convened.

8 December 1991. A new Western-style constitution was adopted. A new election code had already been in place since early 1990. In parliament, there was much talk and little action amid political turmoil. Prime Minister Petre Roman was ousted in September. An Independent, Teodar Stolojan, became prime minister. He included some PNL members. The constitution was affirmed by a referendum.

27 September 1992. The people went to the polls again. Out of 151 registered parties, only thirteen made it past the three percent post. Since 1990, many parties had split or merged with others. Iliescu's own Social Democracy Party of Romania (PDSR) won 117 of 328 seats in the chamber and forty-nine of 143 seats in the senate. The Democratic Convention coalition of most of the opposition parties won eighty-two in the chamber and thirty-four in the senate. No one party had a majority. The UDMR held its position and Romania Mare won sixteen chamber and six senate seats. Untested Prime Minister Nicolae Vacaroiu brought communists and Romania Mare (two extremes) into his government. Iliescu was again elected president with sixty-one percent after two rounds of voting.

1 February 1993. In Brussels, Prime Minister Vacaroiu signed a European Community (EC) association agreement. Moving out of its isolation, in September, Romania joined the Council of Europe. The EC-EU agreement did not go into effect until February 1995. In reality, Romania continued to grope its way towards the West.

26 January 1994. Romania became the first East European country to join NATO's Partnership for Peace program.

16 September 1996. Romania and Hungary signed a mutual cooperation treaty concerning ethnic-cultural issues. It would help to smooth the way for both regarding EU-NATO membership, even if only symbolic.

3 November 1996. In general elections, the Democratic Convention (DC) won a plurality, followed by Iliescu's PDSR. For the presidency, Iliescu took thirty-two percent and DC leader Emil Constantinescu twenty-eight percent requiring a run-off. The results were welcomed in Western Europe.

17 November 1996. Constantinescu was elected president, winning fifty-five percent of the vote to Iliescu's forty-five.

29 November 1996. Professor Emil Constantinescu was sworn in as president with a shift in power to the center-right in Romania.

12 December 1996. A new government led by trade unionist Prime Minister Victor Ciorba was sworn in—a coalition of the DC, Social Democratic Union, and the UDMR. It promised reform and an orientation towards Western Europe. Support from the West was expected.

18 February 1997. International Monetary Fund (IMF) negotiator Poul Thomsen approved the new government's policies, but warned against continued subsidies. In a move towards a market economy, petrol costs increased by fifty-three percent and diesel fuel forty-one percent. The IMF was set to grant US$80 million of a US$400 million rescue package.

1 March 1997. King Michael I, age 75, returned to Romania for a visit. His citizenship was restored by the Ciorba government.

2 June 1997. Romania and Ukraine signed a friendship agreement designed to ease feelings over the loss of Romanian territories to the Ukraine during World War Two (north Bukovina and areas in the Danube delta) and the status of 500,000 Romanians living in that country.

13 April 1998. After weeks of argument and government paralysis, Ciorba resigned and Radu Vasile became prime minister. The 1998 budget was due to be reviewed as the IMF pressed the issue of stalled reforms. The government kept the same parties in its coalition.[23]

1 May 1998. With the government trying to get admitted to NATO, army and security officers were caught smuggling 3,000 cases of cigarettes in through a military airport in Bucharest. An officer who had fled and then was arrested claimed government officials and their parties were involved. This was hotly denied.

13 July 1998. Finance Minister Daniel Daianu attacked President Constantinescu on the eve of his trip to the US stating Romania could not afford a US$1.5 billion project to build ninety-six "Dracula" attack helicopters in collaboration with US Bell Helicopter. Bell would pay US$50 million to acquire seventy percent of Intreprinderea Aeronautica Romana to co-produce the AH-IRO. It had been approved in cabinet over Daianu's objections. The IMF had also questioned its wisdom. The issue continued into the autumn when the deal fell apart owing to lack of financing and strong political opposition.

8 November 1998. Thirty-five percent of Romtelcom was sold to the Greek state telephone organization (OTE) for US$675 million. The whole transaction was far from transparent with rumors of pay-offs.

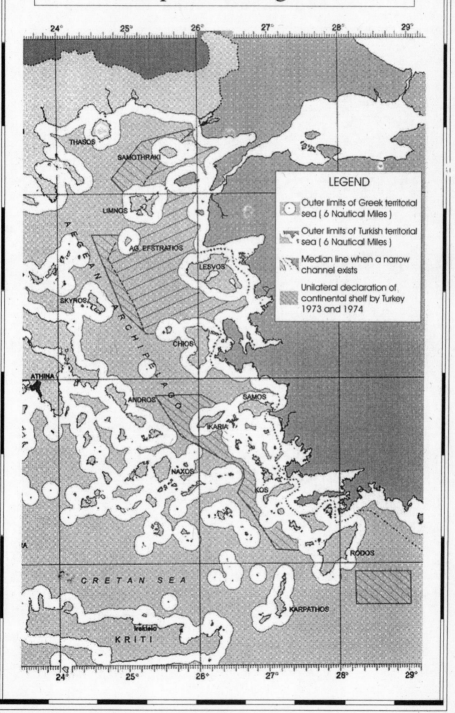

Disputed Aegean

LEGEND

- Outer limits of Greek territorial sea (6 Nautical Miles)
- Outer limits of Turkish territorial sea (6 Nautical Miles)
- Median line when a narrow channel exists
- Unilateral declaration of continental shelf by Turkey 1973 and 1974

THASOS

SAMOTHRAKI

LIMNOS

AG. EFSTRATIOS

LESVOS

SKYROS

AEGEAN ARCHIPELAGO

CHIOS

ATHINA

ANDROS

SAMOS

IKARIA

NAXOS

KOS

RODOS

CRETAN SEA

KARPATHOS

Iraklelo

KRITI

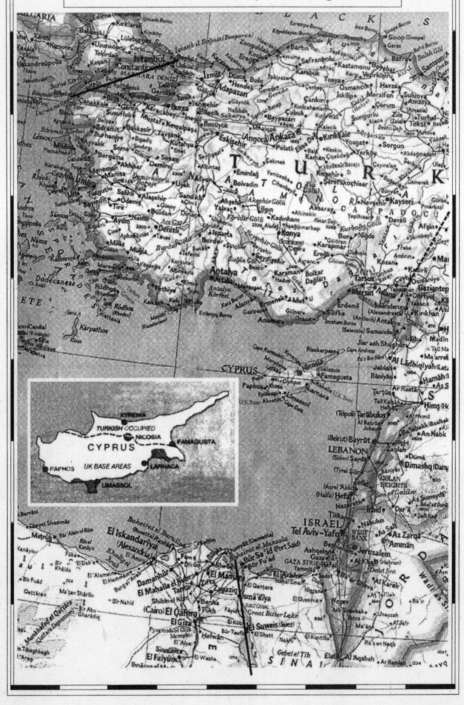

Strategic Mediterranean, Bosporus, Suez and Baku-Ceyhan Pipeline

Chapter 10

Robin Hood and His Merry Men

Greece Up for Grabs: June 1989–June 1999

On relations between the capitalist Metropolis (the US and other centers of finance and industry) and the Periphery (Greece and other developing nations): "The upper class, the big industrialists and entrepreneurs, exist in the country with anachronistic pre-capitalist forms of exploitation, while at the same time are dependent more and more on foreign monopoly capital, which determines the framework of their activity. The unequal distribution of national wealth and the national income becomes more and more intensive over time because it is promoted by structural institutions that use to the advantage of the economic oligarchy the mechanism of inflation of profits, which is a basic characteristic of monopoly capitalism in this phase. And, this also unavoidably pushes forward the sharpening of conflict between the economic oligarchy (native and foreign) and the large mass of workers…"

Panhellenic Socialist Movement,
leader Andreas Papandreou, 1977

Nineteen eighty-nine is not only significant for Greeks because of the collapse of communism in central and eastern Europe. It also was the year voters turned away from the Pasok party owing to allegations that Prime Minister Andreas Papandreou was involved in an unprecedented financial scandal involving some several hundred million dollars. It was both delicious as a story and sweet revenge for a New Democracy opposition now out of power for eight long years. I was then thinking of staying on in Athens, as I had become attached to the place and its constant round of goings-on. I was never bored. And, as I joked with my friends, I felt like a bit player in a Fellini film, as it seemed that Greece was more of a "happening" than a really serious country. And, when I added that if my Greek were good, I would have a better grip on the plot, they invariably laughed and assured me that there wasn't that much of a plot as such. But there was, actually. There were always plots being played out on different levels in a very Byzantine fashion. Greeks can be refreshingly direct. But at other times, when guile and wiliness are called for, events move by indirection. Greeks like to think that they can buy you, or sell you. They are really survivors who are in love with life, people who pinch themselves after the latest disaster and shout, "But, I'm still alive!" And then, as avid Pagan-Christians, they go at their days, and their nights, with a joy that non-Greeks can only envy and imitate.[1]

Americans assume that history is linear, something charted on an upward sloping line called "progress." Some Greeks do also, but because memory goes back many millennia, others hold to the ancient idea of "eternal return," that all history is circular or some sort of spiral. Greeks always remember something similar that happened a long time ago. And, because they are deservedly proud of the most powerful cultural heritage in the West, it's unsurprising that Andreas Papandreou resonated in the hearts of many as a modern day reincarnation of Homer's hero, Odysseus: he who went against the will of his ageing father who in the 1960s was a popular prime minister; he who rebelled against the junta of colonels; he who defied the gods by shaking his fists at the US and NATO; he who took women where he found them... spreading his seed as far north as Sweden; he whose nimble brain and tongue beguiled his friends and supporters—and confused his enemies. "Andreas," they shouted! Andreas, who brought socialism's fire down from the heavens and *allaghi*, "change" to Greece![2]

No one had seen anything like it. After the collapse of the junta in 1974, Andreas started a popular grass roots movement on the ethos of leftist resistance and protest. Anti-junta personalities such as Mikis Theodorakis, Melina Mercouri and dozens of others involved in the struggle against the dictatorship stood with him. Amalia Fleming lent her voice. In Rome, Oriana Fallaci kept Alekos Panagoulis's prison ordeal alive. By 1981, Andreas—Trotskyite in his youth; US navy corpsman in World War Two; Harvard graduate; professor of economics at Minnesota and Berkeley—had crushed a New Democracy party founded by Greece's foremost statesman and pillar of conservatism, Constantine Karamanlis. Pasok was more of a movement than a party, a merger of middle-class Greeks with organized labor. Vietnam, Chile, and Allende, the Sandinistas and the CIA became a constant diet in the press and Pasok's speeches. Andreas had even visited an Al Fatah training camp in Lebanon, squeezing off a few rounds with a Kalashnikov. A Fatah official told me, "He went to the PLO like a man goes to a woman!" He embraced the idea of revolution throughout the Third World![3]

One of the "happenings" that had taken place since mid-1974 was the December 1975 shooting of CIA Station Chief Richard Welch by 17 November ultra-leftist terrorists. Junta torturers Mallios and Petrou followed. Soon after my arrival in Athens, US Navy Captain George Tsantes, who liaised with the Greek military, was murdered in his car on one of Athens's main avenues in broad daylight. 17 November would go on to rack up twenty-two killings over some twenty-five years—along with attacks by bombs and rockets—without one arrest! Palestinians and Israelis were out reaping revenge, as Andreas's permissive attitude made Greece a crossroads for Arab groups. It was here, where border controls were lax and police were ineffective, that weapons, plastic explosives and false documents were stored. Col. Hawari and Abu Nidal operated freely. Both Yasir Arafat and Libya's Colonel Gaddafi funneled money into Pasok. Libyan exiles were killed with impunity. TWA, Pan Am, and other airliners were hijacked and bombed. In mid-1988, the *City of Poros* cruise ship was turned into a scene of death and destruction just days after "17" decapitated US Navy attaché William Nordeen with a car bomb.

While Karamanlis had attempted to integrate Greece with the EC and NATO, Papandreou tried to take it in the opposite direction. Instead of taking advantage of a historic opportunity to heal sharp divisions in society that had existed since the civil war, Andreas exacerbated class conflicts and talked vaguely of Greece becoming a bridge between Europe and the Middle East. Nothing of significance came of it except munitions sales to Iran and Iraq during their long conflict. Andreas angered NATO and Washington by citing a "New Defense Doctrine" that named Turkey as Greece's main military threat, not the forces of the Warsaw Pact. He had also supported General Wojciech Jaruzelski's martial law regime in Poland and was the only Western leader to back Moscow's claim that a Korean airliner they had shot down was on a "spy mission." Calling for a nuclear-free zone in the Balkans, Andreas alienated Greece from its potential friends and eroded its defense capabilities. In 1987, he inflated an incident with Ankara in the Aegean into a full-blown military crisis that served only to prove that Greece was in no position to take on Turkey. Troops rushing north to Thrace became lost and tank transporters went off the road. It was a shambles. And Andreas was now Western Europe's odd man out!

On the domestic front, Pasok did forge ahead with women's rights, some useful social programs such as childcare, and educational reform. However, they eventually backed off from a fight with the Orthodox Church over its vast land holdings, finding it easier to move against the properties of King Constantine who was exiled in London. They also talked a lot about the economy's commanding heights, but nationalized only Hercules cement. In fact, much of the economy was already state-owned and had been for years: railroads, an airline, telecommunications, electric power, and an oil refinery. What they did do was appoint Pasok members to positions of authority in these state bodies and try to weed out those who voted New Democracy. The more zealous were called "Green Guards." Government administrative bodies down to the municipality level and the military were affected as well. It was the usual "spoils system" that always occurred with a change of government, but never before had it been done in such an extensive and organized way. As part of the "socialization" process, labor laws gave workers such sweeping rights that increasingly employers found that their hands were tied. There was a great leveling out in society. The old days when workers went hat in hand to their bosses were over.[4]

What it did was to polarize society even more, as well as create a bloc of hundreds of thousands of loyalists who voted for Pasok because a son or a daughter had been given a job somewhere, or a father or brother somehow benefited from Pasok's patronage. It had a rippling multiplying effect at the polls. Undeniably the most powerful party, Pasok won heavily again in 1985 after four heady years in power. As a proliferation of Pasok-backed entities came into being (agro-cooperatives, small businesses, and dozens of quasipublic enterprises), the situation was repeated. Jobs were scarce and there was a large amount of underemployment. It was not unheard of for people to work at two jobs to make ends meet. No one, especially Papandreou and Pasok's leadership, cared that the state bureaucracy grew larger and larger with each successive year.

However, soon revolution and ideology meant less and less (Pasok began to talk to the much more moderate Socialist International) and opportunities to make money meant more and more. *Kobinas*, or shady deals, proliferated. My Pasok friend, Vassilis Anastasiadis, stopped talking about Nicaragua as soon as he was appointed head of an office controlling import licenses. A sharp lawyer, he also became governor of a newly created bank. It wasn't long before he had a new villa and was driving a Mercedes. He tried to take care of his relatives as well. To have power meant "to eat" in Greece. Another explained that one of the best jobs for a party member was to become a night "watchman" at some state storage depot for agriculture produce, like olive oil. Much of it disappeared and was sold. The secret of Pasok's popularity was that Andreas had something for everyone. By spreading the nation's wealth around, many people ended up "dirty." There were advantages in keeping it this way, because when ordinary people bent the law, they didn't complain when their politicians were caught out. Usually, that is, if it was kept within bounds. Andreas was a "Robin Hood" and his ministers, and ranking party cadres, soon became very Merry Men.

Odysseus, Robin Hood, would-be-Revolutionary, Andreas meant many things to many people, including his women. While his wife, Margaret (née Chant of Illinois), dedicated herself like Penelope to weaving a blanket of women's rights, Andreas was playing around. The last in a long string of conquests was a tall, buxom, blonde, thirty-four-year-old Olympic airline stewardess. In fact, it was Dimitra Liani who caught Andreas in her own honeytrap. When she learned that she would be on the same flight as the prime minister during a state visit to China, she was ecstatic. Cupping her full breasts with both hands, she confided to a girlfriend that she was going to put them right under his nose. She did just that, and, as the story goes, Andreas kept the curtains closed for most of the flight. Soon they had a love nest on a dead-end street in north Athens where unmarked cars from his security detail kept watch. Now distracted by Dimitra ("Mimi") and stressing a heart that would soon give him trouble, Andreas wasn't paying attention to what some of his people were up to, or so he later claimed!

Some had become involved with a youngish financial whiz named George Koskotas, a former house painter and janitorial service contractor out of Chicago. Initially only an employee at the Bank of Crete, Koskotas somehow was able to buy it from ship-owner John Karras in 1984 and immediately brought his Pasok friends inside. Things went well. State companies (including Olympic) later deposited enormous sums of money at the bank, whereupon some of the interest was skimmed off. But, trouble arose in late 1987 during a trip to the US. Koskotas was arrested by the Federal Bureau of Investigation on sixty-four counts of fraud and tax evasion just after he had attended a White House luncheon. This dark-haired, roly-poly Greek's name was already on everyone's lips in Athens as, by then, he also owned a publishing empire and a soccer team. Given a summons and deprived of his passport, Koskotas ran to the Greek embassy. He obtained another and immediately returned home. It wasn't long, however, before the whole squalid business began to leak to the press. Koskotas became a ticking time bomb.

The events that followed were bizarre, to say the least. As rumors of collusion and corruption swirled around several of Andreas's top aides (Dmitris Tsovolas, George Petsos, Panayotis Roumeliotis, and Agamemmnon Koutsoyiorgas or "Limping George"), pressure grew to arrest Koskotas. But while under surveillance by EYP security, this high-profile personality somehow slipped away to a friend's Lear jet where he was flown first to Reykjavik and then to Rio. In a few days, his whereabouts became known and the fugitive flew to Massachusetts where he surrendered himself to the federal authorities. He claimed he was in danger of being assassinated by the Greek government! In the following months, scandal engulfed Andreas as well, as the press went into a "feeding frenzy" over Koskotas and Mimi. A security guard had stolen photos of her cavorting semi-nude. One showed her hand on the crotch of a male friend. Undeterred (not even by triple bypass heart surgery in London), seventy-year-old Andreas headed for a messy divorce as Pasok was defeated in the election of June 1989, even after changing the election laws to his government's advantage.

With no decision at the polls that translated into a majority in parliament, Greece staggered through three national elections in ten months. Finally, with a court trial pending against Andreas and the others, New Democracy won with forty-seven percent in April 1990.

Constantine Mitsotakis (a World War Two officer and a resistance hero who had twice escaped death at the hands of the Nazis) became prime minister with a razor-thin majority of one vote. Mitsotakis was intensely disliked by Andreas because he and his "apostates" had quit the elder Papandreou's Center Union in 1966, hastening a coup by military officers the following year, which led to his father's arrest and subsequent death. Mitsotakis resented Andreas equally, viewing him as having been elevated to power because he was George Papandreou's son. The Greek political stage was almost too small for these two men who had been rivals for twenty years. If Andreas's main shortcoming was his lack of personal loyalty, "Mitso" was prone to the Cretan habit of relying only on his most intimate friends and immediate family.

During this unsettled period, however, Mitsotakis had reached out to the veteran leader of the Greek Communist Party (KKE), Harilaos Florakis, to form a coalition. The latter, an ex-Stalinist who had survived jail, Dachau, and exile, actually demonstrated moderation in office and pledged, along with New Democracy, an effort to clean up (*katharsis*) corruption and heal the old wounds of the past. Symbolic of a desire to put the bitter memories of the civil war and decades of anti-leftist repression behind the country was the solemn burning of thousands upon thousands of EYP security files that had been gathered on Greek citizens over the years. *Katharsis* was something else, however. Pasok hovered around forty percent in the polls, showing a staying power for Andreas and his party, which surprised many. In fact, the former prime minister called allegations against him a political witch-hunt and disdainfully refused to cooperate with the parliamentary commission charged with investigating the Koskotas affair's missing US$210 million. He claimed the allegations that he had ordered the skimming-off of interest to create a huge political slush fund were nothing but lies.[5]

Not only that, Andreas refused to accept defeat and vowed that if he could not govern, he would make it impossible for anyone else to do so. From mid-1990 onward, New Democracy was besieged by strikes and labor unrest. Constant mass demonstrations that went on into the night caused chaos. He shut down the power grid and public transportation, disrupting business and resulting in losses of millions of dollars. Garbage and trash often went uncollected, growing into gigantic, stinking heaps that resembled those of Beirut during its civil war. This was an all out Balkan-style political war with no holds barred!

In June 1991, Koskotas sat in court after being extradited from the US. I looked at him from the gallery, this pale, fat, thirty-something with two file folders in front of him. By January 1992, it was all over. Koskotas had failed to convince. Andreas was judged innocent on all counts by a split decision— seven to six. Petsos and Tsovolas got ten and thirty months each for petty misdemeanors. Koutsoyiorgas, perhaps the most guilty of the three, had collapsed in court and died of a heart attack. Koskotas went back to Korydallos prison. Andreas gloated over the verdict and egged on his followers!

ND was on the defensive because its austerity measures and moves to privatize had affected workers directly. Besides belt-tightening (Mitsotakis tried to stem ten percent inflation by clamping down on wages), privatization would mean the loss of many thousands of jobs and appointments. Also, destitute Albanians kept coming over the border in a steady stream, some engaging in acts of theft, rape, and murder. Their numbers grew to 200–300,000 and the army and police seemed powerless to stop them. Then, when Yugoslavia broke up, Greeks became angry when the former Yugoslav Republic of Macedonia simply shortened its name to Republic of Macedonia. Andreas took much comfort in this sitting in parliament sniping away, as the furor over his recent marriage and Koskotas faded from a jaded public's mind. He even began to relax a little. He really enjoyed Mimi and how heads turned when they entered their favorite *bouzouki* restaurant in Halandri. He felt young again when his long-legged wife chose stylish shirts and ties for him to wear. The pacemaker and pig's valve which had been inserted by an Egyptian surgeon worked like a charm.

Other factors worked to Andreas's advantage as well. People didn't like how Mitsotakis had built up his MP daughter Dora Bakoyannis to function almost as a super minister in charge of almost anything without having been appointed as such. She had a divisive effect on a lackluster cabinet, which demonstrated little imagination and drive. Also, Mitso had sacked his forty-two-year-old Harvard-educated foreign minister, Antonis Samaras (a personal protégé), after the latter went overboard on the "Macedonia" name issue. Samaras had gone public with demands that Greece close its border with this tiny, weak neighbor to the north to strangle it in its infancy. Samaras, whom Mitsotakis publicly embarrassed by calling him "his mistake," resigned from parliament in October 1992, but urged like-minded dissidents within ND to remain on until their mandate was completed in April 1994. In fact, what he was doing with his magnanimous-sounding advice was to lay plans to take his revenge.

After shaking hands up and down Greece, holding interviews where he milked "Macedonia" for all it was worth, and assembling some support staff, Samaras launched his Political Spring party in June 1993. Out of parliament, many thought he was just an added irritant to Mitsotakis. But, behind the scenes, events going on in the Greek business community (the forces that more often than not drive Greece's politics) were to provide the catalyst that would bring Mitso's government down. It all had to do with the simple telephone, something taken for granted in the West, but which was still unobtainable for many Greeks. People waited years for one. But now, new technology was about to usher in the cellular phone and its potential was enormous. Mitso's Cretan friends were aware of this also—the super-wealthy Vardinoyiannis boys who owned ships and oil refineries, whose interests ran from Saudi Arabia to Russia. And behind the Vardinoyiannis clan were Alcatel and France Telecom who wanted to take over Hellenic Telecommunications (OTE) as soon as its privatization permitted. If things went right, Alcatel would supplant Siemens of Germany as OTE's main supplier. Billions of dollars were at stake![6]

Other companies were looking at Greece as well including the American giant AT&T. But the most important player in all of this was Socratis Kokkalis, the owner of an expanding electronics firm called Intracom. Kokkalis's father had been a prominent politically active KKE professor of medicine who had left Greece during the civil war and ended up in East Germany. Kokkalis grew up and was educated there. He returned to Greece and later established a company that had close continuing business contacts with the East German regime. Under Pasok, Intracom sold cheap East German equipment to OTE and made high profits. Soon he was working with Siemens as well. In 1993, both he and Siemens stood to lose if OTE was privatized and if foreign "strategic" investors replaced what many people knew was a management on the take. OTE managers had been taken to court, fined and even forbidden to leave the country to no avail. Under Pasok, this sort of thing had flourished. Even Kokkalis had had problems, but his friendship with Andreas had kept him out of hot water.[7]

Things came to a head in August when ND finally pushed its landmark privatization bill through the summer session of parliament (the "Vouli" was then a big committee based on proportionality). It was not easy. To get the votes, ND had to replace two rebel pro-Samaras MPs with cabinet ministers and then hastily rewrite part of the bill to reduce the ability of an outside investor to control OTE. Even with this last-minute change, massive protest demonstrations filled the center of Athens and unions mounted a general strike. Samaras joined the opposition in accusing Mitso of a "sell-out." A few weeks later, OTE's chairman resigned when ND's economics minister cancelled a bid "won" the previous March by Intracom-Seimens for a million digital switches at a reported cost of US$200 million, arguing that OTE's anticipated foreign management team would probably be adverse to its long-term implications. Kokkalis asked ND to permit it to go forward, but this was denied. A few days later, Samaras appealed to his ND friends to withdraw their support. Within twenty-four hours, a pro-Samaras MP had quit and others followed. The Mitsotakis government collapsed.

New elections were set for October, seven months ahead of schedule. Everyone had to scramble, but ND found itself upstaged by an Andreas who immediately announced that, if Pasok won, he would annul all planned privatization as well as review a recently signed contract with Germany's Hochtief for construction and long-term management of a new US$2 billion airport. Mitso tried to exploit Pasok's past sins, but it had little effect as he himself was accused of misdeeds. At every rally, Andreas brought out his allegations: Mitso was conspiring with ex-king Constantine; he wanted to release jailed junta members; his point man for Macedonia, General Gryllakis, had organized phone taps of Pasok (as Andreas had with ND); Mitso's ex-personal security chief (now deputy police chief) was involved with antiquity smugglers. Also, a big scandal had erupted in Italy suggesting ND had received bribes from its recent sale of Hercules cement to the industrial giant Ferruzzi-Calcestruzzi. And, to top it all off, that July a London court had announced a settlement under which the American *Time* magazine paid Andreas an undisclosed sum in return for dropping slander charges arising out of its March 1989 cover story on the Koskotas affair. Papandreou and Pasok were on a roll!

When votes were counted, Pasok had won with forty-seven percent and had 170 seats to ND's 111. The latter had fallen to thirty-nine percent, largely because Samaras's Political Spring had taken five percent—mostly ND voters. As the results came in, a noisy crowd of well-wishers gathered at Andreas's house to get a glimpse of the Papandreous. Never one to disappoint a crowd, the couple that some compared to Juan and Evita Peron waved back in triumph. It was a sensational comeback for a seventy-four-year-old whom many thought was politically over the hill.

In retrospect, Mitso had had a very bad run of luck. And there was Samaras and Kokkalis. The latter had always been close to Pasok, as his lines into OTE continued under ND. The connection of Kokkalis to Samaras is less clear. However, Kokkalis and Samaras subsequently issued almost identical denials that the latter had conspired with him to bring down Mitsotakis. Also, when ND's pro-Samaras MPs resigned from parliament (which permitted ND to name replacements), or became "independents" (ND lost their vote), all of the persons so involved immediately gave explanations for their actions over Kokkalis's popular "Flash" radio station.

A well-connected journalist offered this explanation: back in the late 1980s, rumors were circulating concerning Intracom-Siemens's shady dealings with OTE. Some OTE managers in a position to know didn't like it. One such person showed a few journalists a copy of a contract that was illegally executed and they got it before a judge. Kokkalis was called to appear any number of times, but his lawyers were always able to arrange a postponement on some technicality. It dragged on for years, with the case passing from one to another. Reportedly, bribes were being passed out to keep it from being prosecuted. Then, in the summer of 1993, with Samaras's Political Spring on the scene and Mitso pushing OTE's privatization with a shaky two-vote majority, Kokkalis saw his opportunity and took it. After Papandreou's victory, he allegedly bragged to intimates that he had finally decided that it would be cheaper to just pay off a few MPs rather than continue to bribe judges!

It had been vicious. Mitsotakis's son-in-law, Pavlos Bakoyannis, had been gunned down by 17 November. A "17" rocket had glanced off Vardis Vardinoyiannis's armor-plated car. Another was aimed at the Greek finance minister near his office and accidentally killed a young man. Very tellingly,

Papandreou's election had a calming effect. The constant waves of strikes stopped as Pasok's familiar faces took up their ministerial portfolios. Andreas's first act in mid-October was to announce that OTE would not be privatized. His second step was to make Mimi head of his personal office staff. His third began the process of laying charges against Mitsotakis. By year's end, he had replaced the military chiefs with Pasok men and plugged holes in a new budget by using creative accounting. As usual, he promised bold new projects and progress, stating ever so fatuously for an economist that while Greece had not made the grade during the industrial age, the country would enter an era of prosperity in the age of high technology. It was all pure Papandreou at its worst. With Greece due to receive billions from the EU's Delors II cohesion fund for Europe's poorer countries, he showed his appreciation by blockading Macedonia. Always lucky, the EU's response was predictably limp as Andreas held the EU six-month rotating presidency. He was further rewarded by finally being invited to Washington to meet a US president—Bill Clinton.

But, inevitably, time took its toll. The drachma sank lower on the international market and an ailing Andreas shrank inside of his suits. He was able to work less and less despite efforts by his doctors. He had always popped pills and taken injections to get himself "up," but now his heart was beginning to give out. He nervously reshuffled his cabinet. In the autumn of 1994, Greece won an EU-approved financial bail-out for Olympic airlines (debt write-off premised on a reform plan that would never fly), and it decided (under EU pressure) to float twenty-five percent of OTE internationally. The first would keep Olympic in the air while its debts mounted. The second flopped and was withdrawn. Foreign investors were leery of OTE with its hidden dealings. What did appeal were plans to sell Greece's ten gambling casinos, a project pushed by Pasok's pseudo-socialists. The US Hyatt Hotels, Lady Luck, and Magic Corporation jumped in. And, predictably, a Pasok-controlled parliament placed charges against Mitsotakis and some of his former ministers and aides concerning the sale of Hercules and wire-tapping.

But, in January 1995, amid heated debate, Andreas pushed Pasok into agreeing to drop the matter, arguing that it was time to forget the past. Hardly was that said when the press was buzzing with questions concerning an enormous pink mansion that Andreas and Mimi were building in the luxury Athens suburb of Ekali. It had fifteen bathrooms and was estimated to cost around US$2 million. It didn't fit Andreas's supposed financial status, but he claimed that he had borrowed from cabinet members and friends, including George Hallaq, a Lebanese wheeler-dealer specializing in arms and aircraft sales. Hallaq had once sold aircraft to the PLO and the Sandinistas and had carried a Nicaraguan diplomatic passport. By April, a public prosecutor was probing into alleged construction violations and the legitimacy of the so-called loans.

In much of this, particularly the "pink villa" affair, was found Mimi. It angered movers and shakers in Pasok that their access to Andreas often had to go through his new wife and that she had not only brought in her own circle of friends and relatives, but was interfering with governmental and party business. Pasok began to break up into competing centers of power, all looking at the post-Papandreou succession. In the autumn of 1995, Andreas shuffled his cabinet again. He also pushed EU-funded infrastructure projects knowing that there was nothing like fat contracts to make his once merry men content. As the deals were drawn up, Greece's fragile, endangered ecology was of far less concern than the new casinos that were being planned. Besides the usual circulation of "black" money, newly rich Russians were expanding operations. The action included furs, property, protection and prostitution. Hundreds of desperate young women were imported from Russia, the Ukraine, Bulgaria and Romania to work in clubs and whorehouses. But Andreas was oblivious to all this by now having been admitted to the Onassis Heart Center in November. Time was running out.[8]

The all-too-mortal Andreas resigned in mid-January 1996; went to his pink villa; and passed into a slowly fading twilight that lasted until June. The new prime minister, Costas Simitis, tried to exclude Papandreou's widow from public and party functions leaving her exposed to vicious gossip and innuendo. There was no love lost between this ambitious woman and the new party lineup. Actually, Simitis had his hands full holding onto the leadership at a hotly contested party congress that followed. But, he not only emerged on top, he immediately wrong-footed ND, and some of his own people, by holding snap elections in late September. There is nothing like the selection of candidates for an election to keep party members in line. And, despite doubts from within Pasok, Simitis brought them all home safe with 162 seats. ND was reduced to 108 and Samaras's New Spring failed to make it into parliament. Mitsotakis no doubt took a little comfort in that as he slid into his seat in the "Vouli" that might just as well have had his initials carved on it.

The task before Simitis was formidable. He was faced with putting right an economic situation where most of the numbers were wrong and re-energizing a party which now tended to run on its institutionalized inertia. There had been little creative thinking. Old slogans had been repeated endlessly. Few ever thought of Pasok as a movement (*kinesis*). It had become a machine to get out votes, an organization that allocated power and patronage. And, the old problems remained. That past May, *Kathimerini* newspaper, owned by wealthy ship-owner Aristidis Alafouzos, had re-raised the issue of Intracom-Seimens's old US$200 million contract, which had gone through after all, alleging that eight OTE officials had taken bribes totaling US$6 million. And there were details. Money had allegedly been traced back to Kokkalis's account at Handelsbank in Germany.[9]

Simitis and his justice minister vowed action and yet another prosecutor was poised to dig into the case. Kokkalis lashed back, accusing Alafouzos, Mitsotakis and "foreign interests" of trying to wreck Greece's high-technology industry. On 20 May, the affair was expected to go forward, but stalled when a former prosecutor failed to appear. The matter then dropped from public view. That autumn, it was announced that NATO had selected Intracom to build a component of the Sea Sparrow missile system and Kokkalis was visited by the former US Defense Secretary, Caspar Weinberger (now president of *Forbes* magazine). Skillfully, Kokkalis demonstrated keen PR instincts by setting up scholarships and a study program at Harvard University in America. He took care of the Greek side of things by buying both a football and a basketball team. In retrospect, Andreas must have had Kokkalis in mind when he had spoken of Greek prosperity and its prospects for high technology.

But not all like technology. Almost every year, at the annual 17 November demonstration, Athens's large Polytechnical University is trashed by so-called "anarchists" with its laboratories and classrooms ending up being ruined in an orgy of thuggish fun. Like others before him, the soft-spoken Simitis has failed to take effective action against hoodlums who surged into the streets, smashing shops and burning cars. The police were rarely around, and when they did arrive, they were inevitably late. I have walked along and watched toughs in tight jeans and boots break tree limbs to use as staves. They were great for breaking windows, as were rocks and rubble. They also tossed Molotov cocktails. One young punk went over to a kiosk and commandeered all of the lighter fluid from a frightened owner. When the police finally did move into position, projectiles of every description were hurled into their ranks of heavy plastic shields. The police usually gave way. Once a metal folding chair missed an old man's head by inches. Innocent people had been incinerated while defending their own property!

Greece's police were poorly paid, poorly trained and subject to pressures from their politicians and the street. There were many good, brave men who had been transferred for being too good at their job. The upper echelons have been periodically purged, counter-terrorist staffs broken up, elite units disbanded. Policemen at the lower levels had little incentive to put their lives on the line.

In February 1997, Russian contract killer Aleksander Solonik was found strangled in Varibobi forest outside Athens. "Sasha the Macedonian," *aka* the "Kurgan Rambo," had killed four Russian policemen and was the boss of a gang in Greece. He had three luxury homes with swimming pools and gyms. In one, police found a collection of firearms—Kalashnikovs and 9mm pistols. That same month, on Crete, a tough, hard-charging investigator's wife had her leg blown off when she started their expertly booby-trapped Citroën; she had been taking her children to school. Officer Costas Soldatos was working against gunrunners, drug smugglers, loan sharks, kidnappers and protection gangs. His car had been bombed three years earlier. His wife, Georgia, had hung tough with him. Solonik's girlfriend (a former Miss Russia) had less luck. In May, she was found dismembered south of Athens at Lagonissi. Greeks now felt insecure. Break-ins and robberies were reaching epidemic proportions. Banks were robbed with regularity. Police sworn to protect have been found involved in protection rackets, procure-for-pay residence permits for illegals or, failing that, shakedowns, most often of struggling Albanian workers.[10]

Slight of build, smiling, Prime Minister Simitis concentrated almost exclusively on number crunching—how to get Greece into the European Monetary Union (EMU) at least by the second wave. In this, he showed singular dedication, refusing to take risks regarding Turkey, Cyprus, the Aegean, and ex-Yugoslavia (particularly Macedonia and Albania), areas where Andreas had always made waves. He is probably the most European of Greece's recent prime ministers. Educated in Germany, ever cautious and low-key, his steadying influence controlled the broad center of what today is a sprawling party apparatus which he must wean away from personal rivalries and parochial interests and convert to Clinton's now-famous mantra: "But, it's the economy...stupid." However, many remain wedded to personal advantage, not the national welfare. In this context, Greece has the largest per capita black economy involving hidden income in the world, some thirty to forty percent more (some think even higher) than that which is declared. Ninety percent of it is ploughed into property. This situation results in an estimated US$8 billion loss in tax revenue annually.[11]

Greece under Simitis had done better, but continued to struggle to reach the EMU criteria for conversion to the Euro currency of a budget deficit of three percent or less; a total debt of under sixty percent of gross domestic product; and three percent inflation, or less. Adding to the economic imbalance, Greece is saddled with a heavy bill for armaments, heavier percentage-wise (4.6 percent of GNP) than anyone else in NATO. High spending was driven by the need to defend a rugged northern border during the Cold War, but more and more in recent years against a Turkey that seeks to expand its influence into the Balkans and eastern Mediterranean. It was once Greek defense doctrine to be able to fight flat out for two weeks with theatre superiority against the Turks until NATO intervened. This edge, particularly in air power, has been lost. A US military aid ratio of 10:7 in favor of Ankara has contributed to this, but it is more the result of a massive Turkish military modernization program than anything else.

After almost a three-year delay, Greece is going forward with a US$17 billion procurement program which will include fifty F-16Fs, fifteen French Mirage 2000-5s, AWACs airborne surveillance, Patriot antiaircraft missile systems, US Apache attack and heavy lift helicopters, submarines and various surface ships, 170 Leopard German tanks (used), 200 new main battle tanks (type undecided), and some 1,300 shoulder-fired Stinger missiles. Greece plans to participate in the Eurofighter program and talks of buying sixty to ninety fourth generation fighters after the year 2005. Turkey, however, pulled ahead a decade ago and will spend US$150 billion through the first quarter of the century. Ankara is already co-producing US F-16s and other NATO weaponry and has a much larger economy (even allowing for distortions of inflation) that Greece cannot match. This uneven rivalry has been exacerbated by fallout from the Conventional Forces in Europe (CFE) treaty, whereby NATO's northern members have shed excess armaments, but were permitted to give them to Greece and Turkey. Greece received 1,000 tanks—and Turkey 1,500. Thus under NATO's Cascade Program, these most uneasy of allies improved their capabilities to fight each other.

The two are often poised on the edge of conflict and some believe it is just a question of time before (through miscalculation, or otherwise) there will be another incident that could lead to war. The crux of the matter is divided Cyprus, Turkey having invaded and occupied the northern thirty-eight percent of the island republic in 1974. As we will get into later, Greece's ruling junta provided a pretext for Ankara's action. But after democracy was restored in Greece, the Turks stayed on, later establishing a Turkish Republic of Northern Cyprus (TRNC), which remains unrecognized internationally and which has been virtually annexed by Ankara. Thus two governments and two, old, rival lawyers run Cyprus, the northern Turkish-Cypriot part by President Rauf Denktash, who had studied law in the UK with President Glafcos Clerides, leader of the majority Greek-Cypriot community. They were then friends. Over the years, both took on the burden of their respective community's problems while adding to their own girth. Clerides would have to squeeze into the fighters he flew in the western desert of North Africa with the RAF during World War Two. Denktash is even more rotund.[12]

Enter Andreas after re-election. To counter Turkey's build-up of troops and weaponry on the island (30,000 to 15,000 Cypriot National Guards), Greece and Cyprus agreed to a joint-defense pact, which means, in effect, that any Turkish attack on Cyprus would be considered by Athens as an attack on itself. Greece has tried to flesh this out with joint planning and maneuvers and by giving Cyprus some hand-me-down US military equipment. This took an even more serious turn when Greece and Cyprus decided to buy the Russian-made S-300 surface-to-air missile system to help offset Turkey's air superiority. Simitis took the project over in the face of repeated threats by Ankara that were translated into repeated violations of Cypriot and Greek airspace, provocative naval incidents in the Aegean, and a build-up of Turkish arms on Cyprus. Ankara vowed to "take the missiles out" if they were ever installed, saying they would threaten the Turkish mainland.[13]

If Greece and Cyprus thought to use the S-300s as a bargaining chip, as some said, it failed to work. Both came under intense pressure to abandon deployment from Washington and the EU. With regard to the former, US officials sometimes strayed from the accepted UN formulation of a bi-zonal, bi-communal, federation for the island—of shared and rotating executive responsibility. At times, the Clinton administration skirted close to the US government's unstated pre-1974 preference for partition. And, as for the EU, hints were made that if tension continued Cyprus's candidacy to join the EU would be suspended. As always, US, EU, and UK envoys orbit Athens, Ankara, and Nicosia to provide the appearance of deep concern. But no one has ever told Turkey that its occupation of northern Cyprus is an anomaly that has to end. Finally, in sheer frustration and anger, Greek Foreign Minister Theodoros Pangalos blurted out that US President Clinton had "lied" about Cyprus. As a result, US pressure increased even more and finally, in January 1999, Athens and Nicosia announced that the S-300s would be sent to Crete instead. They are there now, incapable of providing any protection to Cyprus and hardly able to cover the island of Rhodes. And, Ankara wants them out!

In Thrace, Greek and Turk border units periodically fire at each other across the Evros River. And Turkey, which drove virtually all of the Greeks out of its country decades ago, agitates on behalf of 150,000 ethnic-Turks who, in some ways, are second-class citizens. However, they do have their own language, schools and mosques and their elected members sit in parliament. In Turkey, about the only reminder of a once proud and prosperous Greek community is the poorly protected Orthodox Patriarchate and the many thousands of homes and businesses left long ago by the fleeing Greeks. A few are still empty, standing near the Bosphorus, or up on the hill at Izmir (Smyrna) in mute testimony of what once was. Athens is still dotted with refugee neighborhoods where second and third generation Greeks live in the same tiny houses as their grandparents. Émigré associations of those who came from Smyrna, Trabzon, and the interior of Anatolia remain active. The same goes for those from Greek islands lying close to the Turkish mainland. Lesvos, Chios, Samos, and others are viewed as the most sacred ramparts of the Hellenic republic. Greek blood has stained their rocky slopes and the waters around them.

Greeks passionately love and, at the same time, agonize over their islands. Besides their unquestioned beauty (Greeks endlessly debate the virtues of this, or that island, and brag about how many they have visited), some see them as a dagger aimed at the throat of the Turks. Others view them as hostages, territory to be easily overrun by Ankara. Both have their arguments. What they do agree upon, however, is that not one more stone will be lost. In fact, in January 1996, Greece and Turkey almost went to war over what amounted to a large barren rock inhabited by goats. In December, a Turkish freighter ran aground on Imia and refused assistance from the Greeks, claiming it was Turkey's "Kardak." Ankara's foreign ministry backed up the assertion, which Athens immediately rejected. A few days later, an irate mayor of Kalymnos planted a Greek flag on the islet. Next, a group of Turkish journalists took the Greek flag down and replaced it with their own in front of the TV cameras. It was seen immediately in both countries and provoked an uproar from politicians of all stripes. Soon naval ships, helicopters and commandos converged on the now famous rock. The situation was defused only by frantic midnight phone calls by US President Bill Clinton and Dick Holbrooke!

While this might seem ridiculous, it is not. Turkey is testing Greece's determination to hold on to islands just off Turkey's coast and dozens of islets scattered in the Aegean. These were awarded to Greece by the Treaty of Lausanne in 1923; the Montreux Convention of 1936; and the Treaty of Paris of 1947. Ankara is concerned should Greece avail itself of the Law of the Sea and extend its territorial waters from six to twelve miles, an act that would have profound military and economic implications. Besides blocking Turkish access to certain sea channels, Greece could extend its claims to the oil and mineral wealth on the seabed. The Aegean would become a Greek lake. Athens has given absolutely no indication that it intends to do this. Nonetheless, the Turks view it as a serious problem. Both sides react to any and all naval or air incursions, playing armed games of "chicken"!

Sometimes even the US pretends not to know what belongs to whom, even though all of the Greek islands and islets are printed on the US navy's maps. This encourages Ankara, which has repeatedly urged that the Aegean be renegotiated. Washington has verbally supported aspects of this as well. Thus, Turkey speaks with the power of a population six times that of Greece (approximately sixty-five million and growing to ten million and declining); a larger economy; and with the sure knowledge that the US judges it to be of greater strategic importance. This, and the constant stream of threats from Ankara, works many Greeks up into such a state that they often react emotionally and try to punch above their weight. Greece has often vetoed EU funds allocated to Ankara. It keeps Turkey's poor human rights record before the European parliament and the UN. And, importantly, it had provided moral and political support to Turkey's Kurdish minority, particularly to the PKK.[14]

With Turkey (backed by the US and Israel) having ordered Syria to deny PKK leader, Abdullah Ocalan, safe haven in Damascus and close a guerrilla training camp in the Bekaa Valley of Lebanon, or else, in November 1998, 109 Pasok deputies invited Ocalan to Athens. He didn't come just then, but wandered around trying to figure out what to do next. He had flown from Damascus in a hired aircraft in October for Russia. Denied refuge there, he went to Italy, was arrested, but was granted temporary asylum. Unhappy with his situation, in mid-January 1999 he went back to Russia. By the end of the month, he was in Greek hands and arrived in Athens, having been invited by his "friends." The latter included a former naval officer who got Ocalan through the Athens airport VIP lounge to a safe house by the sea. They flew to Minsk, tried The Netherlands, but then returned again to Athens. With key Greek government officials involved, Ocalan went next to Corfu and then to Nairobi, where he stayed at the Greek embassy. Ocalan was now a "disposal problem" because by mid-February his pursuers knew his exact whereabouts.

It seems that Ocalan and his Greek hosts used the telephone in a most insecure and amateurish fashion. Almost immediately, groups of surveillants were eyeing each other outside the Greek embassy compound. The press claimed that the CIA, Mossad, and the Turks were all working together. And soon Kenyan authorities were at the door of the embassy demanding that Ocalan be handed over. What happened next is not fully understood. But it appears Ocalan was induced to go to the airport with the expectation he would be taken to a safe destination. En route, his Greek protectors "lost" him and the Kenyans gave him to the Turks. The Kurdish community in Europe went wild. Greek embassies were overrun amidst violent protest demonstrations. A Kurd tried to immolate himself. When a blindfolded, handcuffed Ocalan was seen on TV, Greeks could not contain their shame over how his situation had been mishandled. It hit their inner sense of honor, their personal *philotimos*. Faced with a first-class fiasco, a political firestorm, Simitis fired his foreign minister, his interior minister, the minister of public order and the chief of EYP. The Greeks have a much-loved children's puppet show called *karagkiosi* wherein the oh-so-clever Greek always manages to outsmart the Turk. In the real-life case of Ocalan, however, the roles were reversed![15]

Then, within only weeks, NATO went to war against Yugoslavia and Greece was expected to contribute its full support. Simitis, already on the defensive because of his S-300 missile climb down and Ocalan and under heavy pressure from Washington (the US Departments of State and Defense took the opportunity to suspend arms sales and deliveries while spokesmen accused Greece of being soft on terrorism and illegally delivering US-manufactured arms to Cyprus was forced to take a stance against Yugoslavia counter to the feelings of the overwhelming majority of the Greek public. Besides the fact that the Serbs are Orthodox like themselves, a history of common struggle in this century binds the two peoples together emotionally. Thus, while Greece gave transit facilities to NATO through its port of Thessaloniki, and related support as required, thousands of Greeks demonstrated outside the American embassy in Athens, the huge US naval base at Souda Bay in Crete, and at Araxos in the Peloponnese near Patras where the US reportedly stored nuclear weapons.

The Greek news media was welcomed by Belgrade because it showed a side of the bombing campaign that was not focused on by US and UK TV: death and injury to Yugoslav civilians and the destruction of civilian targets. The normally pro-US leader of ND, Constantine Karamanlis (the nephew of the former president), opposed the war, as did the rest of the political opposition including Mitsotakis. It was not just leftists who had demonstrated, but a broad cross-section of the Greek public including prominent churchmen. NATO vehicles were pelted with eggs and sprayed with red paint. As the flatbed trailers, trucks and vans lined up, angry slogans were smeared on their sides by irate, placard-waving demonstrators. UK troopers huddled behind the windows of their railway cars as they left for Skopje, knowing they were the object of scorn. The US marines who waded ashore with their Stars and Stripes were met with hoots and jeers. Road signs were removed, or turned around. One convoy ended up in a farmer's market. A British soldier drove six hours to

Piraeus outside of Athens and asked if it was Pristina. Drunk or sober, his evident confusion was symbolic of yet another Balkan catastrophe!

Greeks do not sympathize much with the Kosovo Albanians. They saw the war as Greater Albania-in-the-making, as trouble on the way. The rapidly multiplying Albanians were everywhere. And, too many, as far as the Greeks were concerned, were into crime. They roamed the neighborhoods. They were at the construction site down the street. They broke into shops, houses, cars and churches. They were daring and innovative and violent. Just days before, one hijacked a bus and took eight hostages across the Albanian border for ransom. During a botched rescue, a young man was shot dead. Another kidnapped a child and threatened to cut her up for body parts if his demands were not met. Businessmen have had similar experiences. One with US$250,000 in goods, hired two Albanians armed with Kalashnikovs to guard his warehouse. Both were killed and he was cleaned out. The Kosovo Albanians, who have suffered horribly from a tragic war, should be viewed differently from common criminals. However, this distinction is made by too few.

In June 1999, the Greeks were experiencing a summer of discontent. Gloom hung in the air like *nefos*, like smog. The Balkans had suddenly become a much more dangerous place. Humiliated over the S-300 and Ocalan affairs, they saw the time for a settlement on Cyprus passing. The initiative had again gone over to Ankara. The Greeks had had almost seven years of expressions of concern by the Clinton administration, the only power that could have fixed it. When George Stephanopolous made his exit, hope went with him. They saw in Turkey how the military openly manipulated the political process with impunity, working with extreme nationalists—the "Grey Wolves"—and crime bosses who were on the payroll of the security police. Bulent Ecevit, the architect of the invasion of Cyprus and leader of the Democratic Left Party (DLP), was again Prime Minister, this time in coalition with Nationalist Movement Party (NMP) head, Devlet Bahceli, and Mesut Yilmaz of Motherland. Center-left to extreme right, what they had in common was strong opposition to the UN's approach to Cyprus; opposition to real normalization with Greece; and opposition to Turkey's growing Islamic movement. All had systematically violated the rights of activist critics, leftist parties, and millions of Kurdish citizens. And, Greeks had watched as NATO methodically destroyed a neighboring country's industries and its infrastructure in the name of those very same human rights. It jarred on their feelings of fair play and reminded them of Thrasymacus—that justice favors the stronger. In that same sense, the cynics have it for now.[16]

And the cynics were ready to grab. After World War Two, members of the *Vouli* appropriated land for themselves in Athens in what is now the exclusive suburb of Politia. The military and police were awarded land in Papago. The judges selected sites by the sea. Doctors and lawyers have acquired large tracts in a mountainous, wooded area west of Athens behind Kiorka. Poor squatters and the rich have built without permits everywhere. Land grabbers put up fences where they could and planted a few trees. Developers burnt-off wooded hillsides and waited. This year, 160 years on, Greece began to compile a central land and property registry, and recorded titles. Finally, Greece's beautiful mountains will be mapped. But the best of intentions failed to take into account the ubiquitous envelope, the *fakellos*. It was even common in hospitals, almost customary. So no one should be surprised when EU-funded infrastructure projects are found to be substandard. And no one should be surprised that Socratis Kokkalis is still in tight with OTE.

Kokkalis, who looked a bit like an older, shaggier Bill Gates, was now the object of an EU Commission inquiry as to why Intracom was awarded twenty-two OTE program contracts without an open-bid process. He and OTE will probably get off the hook through a loophole whereby state enterprises were encouraged to do business with Greek firms. Meanwhile, OTE has plunged into the Balkan phone business, buying thirty-five percent of the Romanian, twenty percent of the Serbian and ninety percent of the Armenian telecommunication companies. Moldova was now on hold because OTE's negotiator, a Kokkalis man, had boosted the price that OTE was to pay! All of the purchases involving several billion US dollars were conducted under conditions that were far from transparent.[17]

But even the cynics cannot spoil the 2004 Olympics! Miffed at not getting the 1996 Centenary games, Greece is thrilled and proud to have been chosen to host the games three years hence. Seventy percent of the facilities already exist and a big push towards completion will take place after 2001. By that time, a new airport and metro will be in operation. The Olympics, in fact, will be the biggest happening in recent times. Contractors are salivating over the estimated US$1.6 billion required to produce the games (US$700 million to be provided by the international committee) and eager businessmen anticipate the invasion of tourists that will come with it. But they promise to be great games because they will be less commercialized and take place in their original setting. The Greeks will stop all of their feuds as in ancient times. We will be taken back to 1896 in Monistaraki and Plaka. We'll all drink retsina and ouzo into the night. We'll dance on tables and break plates. Athens pulsates like a strong *bouzouki* beat with unrivaled authenticity. The games will be unforgettable, unique. The

Greeks are generous and hospitable to a fault in celebration, and the Olympics will be one big celebration! We will all try to become Greek!

But until then, we will have (as one author put it) Greece without the "columns." We have Pasok and ND, Socratis Kokkalis and the Vardinoyiannis clan. Rivals in politics and business, they have taken their competition to the sports stadium and their fans love it! The red and white stripes of Olympiakos of Piraeus flies over Kokkalis's well-guarded residence in north Athens. The soccer team founded in 1925 (previous owner George Koskotas) has a following of thousands, which its rivals refer to as *gavros*—sardines, because the Piraeus fans are poorer and absolutely fanatical in their devotion, like minnows trailing after their leader. The green machine of Panathinaikos is older, dating from 1908. Its symbol is the three-leaf clover, which its opponents associate with a brand of Vaseline from the same period. The supposedly wealthier, effete Panathinaikos fans from Athens are called *vazelos*, a crude slur on their manhood. To prove who is tougher, the sides riot at every match, breaking and burning seats and causing mayhem. Less flamboyant, other super-wealthy Greeks fight their battles out of the glare of publicity. *Forbes* magazine has listed Spiro Latsis with a fortune of US$5.4 billion. The money comes from his father Yannis ("John") who was once dirt poor on the island of Peloponnese. He went around selling olive oil. He worked on the docks of Piraeus during World War Two, some say in the black market. With great energy, he continued his rise, moving his interests to Saudi Arabia under the junta. Down there, in the "sandbox," Latsis cleaned up, making millions in construction and engineering. Back in Greece, he built a refinery and now owns one of the largest private stocks of oil in the world. He is also in banking. Now in his eighties, he is still at work by 7.30 and expects his executives to be ready with the answers. A friend of ex-King Constantine, former President George Bush and a backer of British Prime Ministers Thatcher and Major, he quit school when he was a boy, like the kid who wants to wipe my windshield. Someday, even he might be wealthy. But, the odds are against it.

In 1998, Greeks worked more hours annually than all others in the EU and they had to work over eighteen hours to buy the same food a German can earn in nine hours and a British worker in eleven. Twenty percent of the men have more than one job and many women (both single and married) now work. Twenty percent are in agriculture and an amazing one in two Greeks is self-employed in some way. Twenty percent earn less than half of the national average and are classified "poor." Nonetheless, Greeks are very independent and prefer to have their own not-very-profitable business than work for someone else. It's a nation of small shopkeepers par excellence. They are savers in a country where credit, or financing, is very limited. Greeks must pay cash, but more own their own homes than any others in the EU. Many also have a little piece of land somewhere, or a small house by the sea. Some middle class families now have two cars, but you can be sure that it was a struggle. Men put off marriage because rents and furniture are costly. But basically the extended family works hard together and is much closer than most West Europeans. Church has a real place as Greeks are believing belongers. Again, to be Orthodox is to be Greek and to be Greek, is to be Orthodox!

Opinion is informed by experience and storied tradition, written, or verbal. One of the first Greeks I met was "Dino" the spy, a police surveillant. We started chatting at a pizza parlor. It was 1978, and I was passing through Athens after Beirut. When he found out I was an American, he told me he loved California and had once visited it. Over beer, I asked what he did for a living. That's when he told me he was on-duty, a security man. I was incredulous to learn he was following a teenaged boy and girl holding hands across the room. To prove it, Dino flashed his ID and showed me a pistol he had under his belt. He wasn't kidding! I knew that Greece had had a dictatorship from 1967 to 1974, but I had assumed that that kind of thing was over. I asked myself what kind of democracy it was that followed children around? Later, I learned that KYP, now EYP, had been around since the CIA set it up after World War Two. After the Cold War, after the junta, and after a brutal civil war, thousands had a file that still dogged their footsteps.

My brother-in-law Nikos probably did also. Long before the knock on the door on the first night of the junta, and unwanted visits of security police, was his ordeal on Makronisos. It was typical of what had happened during the civil war. His father had died and a scheming relative used a former Gestapo informant (a drunken, ignorant municipal gardener) to denounce him to the police as a "communist." Nikos was interned on the barren, dry island of Makronisos with thousands of KKE party members and suspects—men, women, and children. It was summer and boiling hot. Under guard, Nikos made small rocks from big ones day after day in the sun. Many inmates collapsed and died. There were beatings and re-education sessions. Men and women were held underwater, nearly drowned, in an effort to extract a confession. Some were kept in wire cages too small to stand up in. Water was denied, as was food and medical care. After four months, Nikos was sent up north to fight at the front. Some, like him, were shot in the back during their first battle. Nikos was lucky to be finally released through the efforts of his friends. From 1947–53, 50,000 Greeks were sent to this hell-hole.

It was difficult to remain neutral, as the hatred and fear was so intense. My Sophia's father had tried. A family photographer, the communists nevertheless sought him out and wanted him to go with them outside of Athens to take photos of an atrocity committed by the royalists. He refused, but he became so frightened because of the possibility that some might consider him to be sympathetic to the rebel *andartes* that he suffered a stroke. Just three years earlier had been the war and the German occupation. The memories were still raw: air raid sirens, Piraeus on fire, people dying of starvation. The Germans had had the house and he and his three girls had lived in a garden cottage that became home for more than three years. Sophia was a child and remembers the Germans as cruel and kind by turns. She sat in their laps and stuffed soup packages under her skirt. She speared soap through a barred window using a nail on a stick. They ate greens, snails and caught birds in a trap. Once a piece of fruit went missing and an officer emptied his pistol next to her ear. When an officer's girlfriend's pet goat was shot, a full investigation followed, children included.

Down in Piraeus, in Nikaia ("Victory"), things were much worse. Food was very scarce, the harbor area was frequently bombed, and an active communist-led resistance meant that the collaborationist Greek Security Battalions and the Germans were active also. In 1943, Sophia's aunt's husband (a skilled worker) was swept up in a round-up ("blocco"). Marianthi spoke to him through the wire a few times and then he and hundreds more were sent to Germany as slave laborers. A letter that she received later from one of his friends explained how he had died from disease and exhaustion a few weeks before the end of the war. Sophia had lived in Nikaia before the war in a small low house that still exists. Thousands of refugees lived there who had come out of Turkey in 1922–24 after the Greek army was defeated by Ataturk. Sophia's aunt and grandmother were among them. At first, it was muddy and dusty with no water taps. The grandmother wore black to mourn the death of her husband, a college professor who was cut down at some nameless roadside by some nameless Turkish cavalryman.

Greeks have known wars and upheaval and tragedy. It is part of their persona as much as love, love lost, and their lust for life. But, most are as strong and resilient as that slim, erect, young man who visits Petran's taverna in Kifissia. He must be in his eighties. When it's late at night and he's found his *kefi*, he smoothes his short gray hair, steps out, and does a turn—flipping his tie over his shoulder—running his hand along his sharply creased trouser leg. His eyes are like a hawk's—and turning again, arms outstretched, he is locked in memory. He does a jump half squat, slapping his shoe as he spins—never missing a beat! "Oopa!" He continues. This is his time—his solo. He steps, spins—and others begin to clap to lend their encouragement, to show him their approval. I kneel down on one knee and clap with the beat. He is into his moment now. He is young again—flying. He is a bird—free, soaring. An eagle. "Zito! Zoi!"—"Up with life!" He cannot stop. The music possesses him. He possesses the music. They are one. "Oopa!... Oopa!" Greece is where the ego originated. "Ego!," "I am!" Never underestimate a Greek!

* * *

In the 1820s, the odds against the Greeks achieving independence from the Ottoman empire were daunting indeed. There had been many spontaneous revolts that were quickly snuffed out by the Turks. But the whole of the Balkans was in ferment and educated Greeks had taken the lead in advocating change. They were all influenced by the French Revolution. Regas Pheraios, an aide to Phanariots in the Danubian Principalities, was for armed revolt and traveled between Constantinople and Vienna in the 1790s to distribute his secret news sheet, *Ephimeris*. He worked out a constitutional order of citizens' rights and duties based on the French model. He was betrayed by a fellow-Greek in Trieste and was arrested by the Habsburg authorities who gave him to the Turks. He and eighteen others were executed by strangulation in Belgrade. But change edged closer. The Ionian Islands went to the French in 1797 following the successful military campaign of Napoleon Bonaparte in Italy. The island of Corfu was awoken from its Venetian slumber. Contact was made with Ali Pasha across the narrow channel over in Epirus.[18]

Alarmed, the Ottomans (out of sheer expediency) made a pact with their Russian enemies and the two sent a joint naval force into the Ionian to dislodge the French. A Russian-Ottoman condominium was set up which turned into a Russian protectorate. They went to France again in 1807, but became British in 1814 and, in a display of diplomatic fiction, were declared a free, independent state under His Britannic Majesty's protection. Under "King Tom" Maitland's constitutional rule, by 1820, the island of Corfu was a haven for scholarly English eccentrics, who walked around in togas, and *klepht* brigands from Rumeli and the Peloponnese. One such, Theodoros Kolokotronis, became a captain in the Duke of York's Greek Light Infantry under Major Richard Church. He, and others, became fired by the revolutionary ideas of the *Philiki Etairia* (Friendly Society), which had spread from Odessa and the Greeks rose up at about the same time as Ypsilantis in Romania. On 25 March 1821, Germanos, the metropolitan of Old Patras, raised a flag over the monastery of Aghia Lavra near Kalavryta. Shipowners from the Three Islands of Hydra, Spetses, and Psara joined in.

In the south, in Peloponnese, the Turkish soldiers and civilians (some ten percent of the population) were driven back into their citadels after bitter fighting and great brutality by both sides. Tripolis fell in October, the Turks slaughtered and the town sacked for its spoils. The insurgents were joined by Ypsilantis's brother Dimitrios and Alexander Mavrokordatos. In Constantinople, Patriarch Gregory V and his ranking clergy were executed and his body thrown to a Jewish mob, which dragged it to the Golden Horn. The Great Powers, then meeting in Laibach (Ljubljana), took a dim view of the Greek affair, especially the Austrian Metternich who wanted stability above all else in Europe. Idealists and intellectuals, however, saw it as an opportunity to restore Hellenism to Greece and to raise the banner of Western civilization against the Ottoman menace. Money and volunteers from many countries were forthcoming. Many philhellenes were appalled at the motley bands of bandits, peasant farmers and adventurers who had taken up the fight. Some left, but most stayed on, including the now General Sir Richard Church, the American Samuel Gridley Howe, and Byron.

The Turks were in a quandary—the ever-assertive Ali Pasha, or the Greeks? They tried coming down the eastern and western coasts to Corinth from where they hoped to subdue the Peloponnese. Greek guerrilla fighters harassed them all the way and the Porte's lack of control of the sea prevented reinforcements and supplies from arriving, causing the whole offensive to bog down. The Greek success in gaining a stalemate gave rise to quarrels over leadership. By 1823, there were two rival governments, who had taken up arms against each other. Kolokotronis was almost executed, then put in jail. Regional rivalries erupted. Sultan Mahmud II and Mehmet Ali of Egypt took advantage of the dissension, first taking Crete and then pushing forward in the Peloponnese. Fortunately for the Greeks, trade to the Levant and Russia had been adversely affected and Britain, France, and Russia suspected that their rivals wanted to exploit the situation to their own advantage. Thus, all sides began to support the Greeks in one way or another. British, French, and Russian factions or parties came into existence and their respective foreign principals began to discuss the size and shape of a future Greek political entity. By 1827, despite Greek defeats—the massacre at Mesolonghi and the fall of Athens—the Great Powers moved towards mediation or what British Foreign Secretary George Canning called "peaceful intervention."

As the Porte evinced little inclination to negotiate just then (it was winning), and continued to put men into the Peloponnese, a combined British,

French, and Russian flotilla commanded by an Admiral Codrington found the Turkish-Egyptian fleet at Navarino Bay (present day Pilos) on 20 October 1827 and sent it to the bottom. After that, independence backed by the Great Powers was virtually certain. John Capodistrias, a Corfiot who had served in the Ionian republic and with Tsar Alexandria, was brought in as the president for a seven-year term. Having experienced chaotic, but essentially free assembly debate, Capodistrias's centralizing authoritarian bent didn't go down well. But he did realize that the extent of a Greek state would depend on how much territory they held. Consequently, he pushed General Church and Ypsilantis to the utmost while a Conference of London, consisting of senior British, French, and Russians officials, met repeatedly in search of a solution based on a proposed Arta-Volos demarcation line.

Capodistrias had a thinly veiled contempt for Greece's prelates, military *kapetanioi*, intellectuals and Phanariots combined with a very high opinion of his own abilities. He began to build a national army, a state bureaucracy and an educational system, and the most difficult task of all, to organize the distribution of lands that had been won by conquest. He wanted to share them out with the nation's peasantry, but found that much of it was already in the hands of the chiefs of armed bands and the clergy. But if he had good intentions, his manner offended many, including many Western philhellenes, who disliked his dictatorial attitude. Not surprisingly, it ended in tragedy, with him being assassinated in October 1831 by George and Constantine Mavromichalis (Mani clan leaders) outside a church in Nafplion. Anarchy and fighting again erupted and continued until May 1832 when the conference powers induced a seventeen-year-old Otto of Bavaria to rule the Greeks.

Prince Frederich Otto of Wittelsbach was the second son of King Ludwig of Bavaria and a second choice. The job had been offered two years earlier to Prince Leopold of Saxe-Coburg. Otto arrived to a Greece shattered by war, and poor. For a time, he preferred to live on a ship anchored in Nafplion harbor rather than take up residence in town. Still under age, Otto had to take a backseat to a three-man regency council of Bavarians bolstered by an army of 3,500 from home. Britain, France, and Russia stood as guarantors and agreed to pay out a sixty million franc loan over several years. The Porte would receive an indemnity once the frontier was fixed. However, because many Greeks still remained under Ottoman rule, it was natural that irredentism arose at every opportunity. They saw it as their duty to expand into Ottoman land despite the perilous state of their economy, large foreign debts and internal discord. Hellenism was on the march!

Corfu in 1864; a large swath of present-day central Greece in 1881; Northern Greece and Crete in 1913; Thrace in 1920; even beyond. The Greeks accomplished this, you could almost say, in spite of themselves, because they were always broke; saddled with foreign advisers and onerous taxes; and ruled by kings who were slow to usher in constitutional change and real democracy. None of the monarchs had a drop of Greek blood in them, and, more often than not, they were more interested in promoting their own prerogatives than the development of the country and the welfare of their subjects. Otto did talk up the "Megali Idea" (Great Idea), the belief that Greece was destined to encompass in its borders all Greeks living under the Ottomans. With banditry rife, irregulars and student romantic nationalists made repeated armed forays into the north. To keep Greece out of yet another Turko-Russian war, France and England occupied Piraeus in 1854 and remained for three years, finding it opportune as well to dig into Greece's murky finances. Finally, fed up with Otto's Bavarians and his refusal to promote reform, a group of Greek officers sent him packing in 1862. Next, Prince Christian William Ferdinand Adolphus George came out from Denmark. A constitutional convention produced a wider franchise in 1864, but King George I's powers and his ability to bend the election results remained considerable. In the last two decades of the nineteenth century, the Trikoupis and Deliyannis factions ruled over the ballot box. Bribery, patronage, and fraud were rampant.

But, by the turn of the century, Athens had touches of elegance: neoclassical buildings, Ottoman-style balconies with swirls of wrought iron, and lampposts inspired by Paris. There were a few broad avenues for horse carriages, several parks and squares, and an unobstructed view of the Acropolis. There were some 700 miles of railway and telegraph lines. Greek steamships plied the seas. Under French tutelage, an army and navy were being built after two rebellions on Crete and a Thessaly campaign had failed. Somehow, it seemed not to matter that Greece had gone bankrupt in 1893, the year the Corinth canal was finished. Three years later, it held the first modern Olympics and Spiro Loues won a gold medal. Wealthy Greeks from abroad bestowed large financial gifts used to construct public buildings and to promote education and the arts. Greece might be wobbly, but it was now an established state.[19]

Nationalist ferment continued because of Crete and the turmoil in Macedonia. Clandestine groups within the army coalesced in 1909, forming a powerful Military League of over 1,000 junior officers. Under Colonel Nicholas Zorbas, they vented their professional and political grievances at Goudi outside Athens in August, threatening to march on the capital. A prime minister resigned and his replacement and the king promised to enact reform measures that would end the royal family's involvement in military matters, among other concessions. Soon, however, the league's reform program became watered down in the *Vouli*, and the military turned to a Cretan, Eleftherios Venizelos, who was an incorruptible reformist and a believer in the "Megali Idea." Reluctantly, George I agreed to new elections and the revision of the 1864 constitution. The Venizelists won by stages, with Eleftherios first becoming a minority prime minister. After a second round in December 1910, he had a resounding majority because the opposition abstained. He made liberal and progressive changes in many areas, including land reform, the civil service, education and labor. Furthermore, he pushed the building of an army that, by 1912, stood at 150,000, and a navy that had several ships equal to the top of the line.[20]

Greece's gains in the Balkan Wars (both conducted with brutal atrocities) have been discussed previously. Suffice it to say that its territory grew by seventy percent and population from three to five million—including Slavs, Turks and Jews. There was general elation despite the death of King George I, who was killed by a madman in Salonika in March 1913. Crown Prince Constantine became king just as Austria-Hungary began to view Serbia's enlargement with utmost displeasure and events began their precipitous slide towards June 1914. From the outset, Venizelos was pro-Entente, although Greece was not obliged by treaty to help Serbia. England demurred on his offer out of concern that Greece's entry would bring Bulgaria and the Ottomans in on the side of the Central Powers. In fact, there wasn't a consensus regarding Greece's position, as King Constantine I had been schooled at the Prussian military academy and his wife, Queen Sophia, was the sister of the German Kaiser Wilhelm II. The royal family's anti-Entente views become clear later on.

The Balkans became a cockpit of contention with offer and counter-offer being proposed by the major powers. When Turkey unexpectedly joined the Central Powers in November, Lord Grey proposed that Greece might cede the Seres, Drama, and Kavalla block to Bulgaria (to keep Bulgaria neutral) in return for certain lands in Asia Minor (unspecified, and similarly offered to Italy as an inducement to join the Entente). Venizelos was tempted, but the Greek General Staff and Constantine thought it was all too vague. Venizelos kept his hand in during the Entente's ill-fated Dardanelles campaign, hoping that Greece might somehow fall heir to Constantinople and the Straits. He thought he had won the king's agreement to open a front against the Turks when the acting chief-of-staff, Colonel John Metaxas, resigned arguing that an attack on

Turkey would bring Bulgaria in, and, additionally, that Asia Minor would be hard to hold. Constantine reversed his stance, causing Venizelos to resign in March 1915. This led to the National Schism, a split into two camps amidst confusion, and foreign intervention.

Much depended on whether Bulgaria would remain neutral, or go to war. Constantine looked to the Entente for answers, but none were forthcoming. He called new elections, only to have Venizelos win and become prime minister again. Then, in late September 1915, the Bulgarians mobilized against Serbia and again Venizelos argued that Greece should fight. The opposition stood firmly against, with Constantine opting for armed neutrality. Initially, the king went a step further and agreed with Venizelos's invitation to the Entente to land forces at Salonika in support of Serbia (while at the same time opposing a vote in the *Vouli* that Greece should join in). Then Constantine reversed course regarding intervention by the Allies and asked for Venizelos's resignation. This caused a constitutional crisis, the appointment of minority premiers and a boycott of the political process by Venizelos. The Entente took up positions in Salonika in October 1915; Corfu in January 1916; and later, in Athens-Piraeus in December 1916.

On 30 August 1916 a group of pro-Venizelos officers staged a coup against the official royalist government, setting themselves up in Salonika. Venizelos, having quit parliament, visited Crete, the Aegean islands and arrived in Salonika to much fanfare. He thereupon established a provisional government and took steps to transform a popular organization called National Defense into an army. After initial hesitancy and caution, the British and French threw their weight behind Venizelos and blockaded the royalists, putting pressure on Constantine, who is said to have been paid forty million gold marks by the Kaiser to keep Greece neutral. Finally, he went into exile in June 1917, taking his eldest son George with him and turning the throne over to his second son Alexander. Venizelos immediately moved his government to Athens, became prime minister and reconvened the parliament of June 1915. This time, the oppositionist royalists who had been in power boycotted. Some thirty pro-Germans were exiled to Corsica and the Venizelists purged the civil service, the judiciary, the army, and even the Orthodox Church in a way that later caused serious repercussions.

Greece's contribution of nine divisions to the Salonika offensive in September 1918 has already been cited as well as its commitment of two divisions after the armistice against bolshevism. Venizelist thinking was that Greece was well positioned to pursue claims at the Paris peace talks, especially with regards to Constantinople and western Turkey. However, he soon learned that Italy had been given the Antalya area in the London Treaty of 1915. As a result, he was willing to be flexible over Epirus, Bulgaria, and the Dodecanese islands if Greece's "Megali Idea" aspirations could reach fulfillment. There was talk of internationalizing the Straits and Constantinople. An autonomous Armenia was discussed. It was clear that Greek and Italian claims clashed as the latter's interests had even been widened in April 1917 to include Smyrna, the very heart of Greece's desires. The Turks might have a million people in the vilayet of Adyin to some 650,000 Greeks, but Venizelos felt sure that Greeks would flock in from Asia Minor and elsewhere to tip the balance in their favor. Already, Turkish persecution of the Armenians was causing concern among ethnic-Greeks. They were all looking for protection from Athens and the victorious Allies.

Then, unexpectedly, Italy began disembarking troops in Antalya in March 1919 before anything was settled. Soon they began to move towards Smyrna. Now somewhat alarmed, the British, French, and the Americans approved Venizelos's request to send troops to Smyrna to protect the Greek population. Allied ships even brought them into the harbor on 15 May. Thus, in the most offhand way, Greece began its occupation of what would become a large piece of the Turkish mainland. Troy, Bergama's amphitheatre, the ruins of Ephesus and centuries of continuity seemed to attest to Greece's claims. However, the landings were opposed by the local Turks who suffered casualties. Even an even-handed Greek High Commissioner failed to ease Turkish feelings. Soon irregulars on both sides had taken up arms and nationalist fervor against the Allies swept Anatolia. In February 1920, Mustafa Kemal (Ataturk) proclaimed his National Pact, breaking with the tame, Allied-controlled, government in "Stamboul" and announcing his opposition to foreign occupation and the threatened division of Turkey.

As Ataturk began to assemble an army, first the Italians and then the French (who had planned to take Cilicia) began to have second thoughts. Not the Greeks, however, who, by the Treaty of Sevres in August 1920, were granted the right to govern Smyrna and its interior for five years, after which time it might unite with Greece through a plebiscite or a vote of an assembly. Greece was carried away with emotion and nationalist élan. Furthermore, its control over Aegean islands won in the Balkan Wars was recognized, as was west and eastern Thrace. Italy even agreed to return the Dodecanese, less Rhodes. As if to signify its coming of age, the British and French formally ceased being guarantors to Greece. It seemed to some that nothing was impossible. Then, as luck would have it, King Alexander was bitten by a pet monkey and died. With none of his brothers willing to become king, the elections of November 1920 were translated into a contest between Venizelos and Constantine. Incredibly (or predictably), all the old issues came to the fore (representing royalist resentment of Venizelos) and Venizelos was soundly beaten. This unexpected turnabout took place within the space of only three short months!

Constantine returned as king in December 1920 despite statements by Britain and France, which attempted to prevent it. An obviously manipulated referendum recorded overwhelming approval. Almost immediately, the anti-Venizelist military officers were restored to rank and the anti-royalists transferred, or encouraged to resign. It had a very unsettling effect on an army of some 200,000, which was stretched to the limits after having been mobilized for eight years. More germane to Greece's extended position in Turkey, both France and Italy used Constantine's return as an excuse to make a deal with Ataturk that went a long ways towards relinquishing all territorial claims. With France and Italy withdrawing, Greece was of a mind to press forward, believing Britain was still in its corner.

In March 1921, the Greeks launched a major offensive that took them to the Sakara River only 100 kilometers from Ankara. By autumn, Ataturk had pushed back to the Afyon Karahisar railhead. A stalemate of sorts settled in, although the Greeks were now vulnerable on their far flanks. The armies remained there all that winter.

In Paris in March 1922, Britain's Lord Curzon proposed that Greece withdraw and that the ethnic-Greeks in Turkey be protected by the League of Nations. Athens agreed. Ataturk, however, sensing that this was the time to tear up the Treaty of Sevres, turned it down. Encouraged by ambivalent comments by Prime Minister Lloyd George, in July, Greece unsuccessfully attempted to enter Istanbul as an Allied occupier. In fact, Greece's position was weakening as Ataturk grew stronger. He struck in late August at Afyon Karahisar with such force that the 200-mile-long front was broken. A defeat that quickly turned into a rout could have been avoided if an able commander-in-chief had not been replaced by an elderly general who had not fought since the Balkan Wars. The Greeks fell back on Smyrna in disarray and re-embarked on 8 September. The Turks entered the next day. That evening, shooting and looting began and within hours the Greek, Armenian, and European quarters were aflame. Before it was over, 30,000 Christians had died, either in the fire, or by uncontrolled slaughter. Quarter of a million people stood at the water's edge, with an inferno behind them and the Allied ships just out of reach before their eyes. Greeks called it "The Catastrophe"![21]

In October, correspondent Ernest Hemingway saw it as a "ghastly, shambling procession of people being driven from their homes"—250,000 people moved west out of eastern Thrace. Somewhere east, Greek soldiers had broken the forelegs of their pack mules and drowned them. It was sheer chaos as Greek and Turk peasants tangled along the rutted roadways, trying to carry away what they could of their possessions. A million or more destitute people were about to descend on Athens. A group of angry army and naval officers (backed by a battleship) demanded that Constantine abdicate and that his government resign as well. A "revolutionary committee," led by Colonels Plastiras and Gonatas, dropped leaflets over the city by airplane. Disgruntled soldiers took up positions in the streets. A hastily assembled commission inquired into the disaster in Asia Minor, naming eight who were subsequently court-martialed on spurious charges of treason. Six, including the old commander-in-chief, were executed by firing squad. It was the end of the "Megali Idea" and the 2,500-year presence by Greeks along the coast of western Turkey.

In January 1923, an exchange of populations was agreed to between Athens and Ataturk. 1,100,000 Greeks for 380,000 Turks. This was formalized by the Treaty of Lausanne in July whereby Greece ceded claims to Smyrna, gave up the islands of Imvros and Tenados close to the Dardanelles, and all of eastern Thrace. And, adding insult to injury, Italy reneged on returning the Dodecanese. Also, many thousands of Greeks staggered across the border from Bulgaria and Russia with a few bags of clothing and their family icons. Greece fell into a period of confusion beyond description: an attempted counter-coup in October 1923; a royalist boycott of elections in December, giving the Venizelists 401 seats to seven! The new king, George, went away on a "leave of absence." Venizelos returned, was premier for a month, and then relinquished power to others. April 1924 saw an overwhelming referendum for a republic. The newcomers from Turkey were pro-republican. Some were socialists, or communists, active in Greece's first trade unions. One General Pangalos seized power and was overthrown by Admiral Koundouriotis. Leaders with forgettable names alternated in power, claiming republican or military support. Finally, Venizelos took over again from 1928–32.

By this time, severe economic depression was sweeping Europe and fascists and communists were claiming that parliamentary rule and capitalism were only a scheme by which the rich robbed the poor. A Greece that was poor (the prices for its exports had plunged—tobacco, currants and olive oil—and remittances from abroad were down), unstable and buffeted by big power politics was not an exception. Venizelos enjoyed some success at mending relations with Turkey and promoting cooperation among Balkan countries. But domestically, it was the same old mess—political infighting and one government after another. When the Populists (royalists) came out on top in the election of March 1933, the same Plastiras (now a general) attempted another coup, which many believed was backed by Venizelos. All of the bitter resentments of the National Schism resurfaced. An attempt was made on Venizelos in a gangland-style car chase down Kifissia Avenue. Pro-republican officers attempted another coup and failed. After this latest episode three officers were executed, over 1,000 were purged from the military, and many were fired from the civil service and universities. Venizelos and Plastiras fled to France and were sentenced to death in absentia.

In the wake of this, the Populists demonstrated no more ability to govern than the Venizelist Liberals. With martial law, press censorship and the opposition boycotting, the Populists held all but thirteen seats in a 300-seat *Vouli*. John Metaxas's Royalist Union had seven. Prime Minister Panayis Tsaldaris rigged yet another referendum regarding the monarchy, which produced predictable results. King George II returned from years of exile in London to a scene almost beyond repair. Moving towards an amnesty, an inconclusive election in January 1936 only confused the situation even more. After months of indecision and political uncertainty, George II appointed the little-known Metaxas as prime minister while talks between the main parties and the newly established communist-led Popular Front continued. In a moment of fatigue, the deputies accepted Metaxas's proposal that parliament be suspended for five months until September, with an all-party commission standing in the interim. That ended parliamentary politics in Greece, for, together, George II and Metaxas took over as a matter of course.

The summer saw labor unrest and strikes, a protest against poor pay and conditions of work. Twelve tobacco workers had been shot and killed by police and conscripts in Salonika. A general strike was called for 5 August in opposition to a legislative proposal to impose compulsory arbitration in labor disputes. In response, Metaxas, with George's approval, suspended several key articles of the constitution, including freedom of the press. For years on the political margins, Metaxas now had the opportunity to fashion a regime according to his own authoritarian bent. What followed was the Third Hellenic Civilization, a grandiose conception on the fascist model that fell short in its implementation although it is remembered mostly for its antidemocratic excesses as well as for its somewhat comic pretensions. Metaxas became the Leader, First Peasant and First Worker, surrounded by a youth organization that marched and paraded and wore blue neck scarves and white shirts and blouses with shorts and skirts. The dark side of it was its ruthless persecution and arrests of leftists and trade union leaders and the use of torture to induce coerced denunciations of the KKE.

Under Metaxas, various politicians were sent off to reside on this or that island. The KKE was largely broken up as an organization, although some clandestine elements managed to remain at liberty. The public, without enthusiasm, grudgingly accepted it as a sign of the times. Additionally, most Greeks were poor and uneducated. There was little the public could do on its own with the parties repressed and a king who was cooperating closely with the regime. By the late 1930s, Hitler's Germany was fast gaining in influence through economic penetration, while Italy, for reasons better known to the vainglorious Mussolini, had engaged in provocations for years. Neither dictator took the Third Hellenic Civilization seriously. Britain, now concerned about its sea lanes to the east, exerted leverage as best it could through George II and the royal family. In April 1939, after Italy's occupation of Albania, both Britain and France extended their guarantee of Greece's territorial integrity should it choose to fight. The outbreak of World War Two that September cast doubts on their ability to deliver.

Greece witnessed the first year of the war with growing unease as to its ability to remain neutral as Italy's military build-up in Albania clearly exceeded its occupation needs. Then, on 15 August 1940 (the Feast of the Assumption of the Virgin Mary, a big Greek holiday) at Tinos Island, an Italian submarine sank the cruiser *Elli* with heavy loss of life. Metaxas swallowed it. Then, at 3 a.m. on 28 October, an Italian minister got Metaxas out of bed and handed him an ultimatum that demanded permission for the entry of Italian troops into Greece. Moreover, a reply was demanded by 6 a.m.—in three hours. To the ambassador's surprise, Metaxas gave him a blunt, *"Oxi!"* ("No!") on the spot and added that it meant war! In fact, Italian shelling of Greek soil began at 5:30 a.m., and, at 10 a.m., its aircraft bombed Tatoi airfield outside Athens. Church bells had already been pealing since morning as Greece mobilized.

Contrary to Italian expectations, Greece did not collapse. Italy's first forays across the border met with stiff resistance. Then, as thousands of Greeks flocked to the colors, an army that had been rebuilt by Metaxas went on the offensive. Korce (Korysta) fell on 22 November; Sarande (Ayioi Saranda) on 6 December; and Gjirokaster (old Argyrokastro) on 8 December. Only bad weather and difficult supply lines kept Greece from taking Vlore and cutting Albania in half. Church bells again rang out the news of the capture of many ethnic-Greek villages in Albania (north Epirus). Greek women made bandages, knitted socks and mittens, and, in the north, even lugged ammunition boxes to the front. Priests and old men joined in, carrying weapons, equipment and food over narrow mountain trails. Greece's initial success as Britain's only active ally was heart-warming to a nation then undergoing the Blitz by the German Luftwaffe. Prime Minister Winston Churchill had sent a few air squadrons over and later offered ground troops, which Metaxas declined to accept.[22]

However, within weeks, Metaxas was dead and Greece became even more dependent on Britain for guidance and material assistance. A high-level staff came out from London and sought assurance that Athens would fight on. A British expeditionary force of some size was on the way. Somehow, however, a fatal misunderstanding existed as to the deployment of Greek forces on the Bulgarian border, which, when the German invasion of Greece from Bulgaria (Operation Marita) began on 6 April, doomed British units in north-central Greece. A futile attempt was made to fall back and regroup, but the Germans had overwhelming superiority. Salonika fell in three days and the Germans entered Athens on 27 April. Hitler sent a message of mock congratulations to the Greek forces for having fought to the last man at Fort Rupel. Prime Minister Alexander Koryzis had already shot himself in shame. King George and his family were evacuated to Crete. British soldiers, now separated from their units, made their way to southern fishing villages where they hoped to find some small boat to take them to safety.

Despite the defeat, 42,000 of 58,000 British and Commonwealth men had survived, and an attempt was made to hold Crete. This failed in the face of a swift, bold German airborne operation on 20 May by paratroops and glider forces, which succeeded after seven days of hard fighting. King George and his ministers flew to Cairo. In the aftermath of the Nazi victory, collaborators and pro-Germans came forward to assist in the task of what would prove to be one of the harshest occupations in all of Europe. Defeatist General Georgios Tsolakoglou became prime minister and stood by while the Germans set about to organize the plundering of the country. The Bulgarians had Thrace, the Italians most of the mainland, and the Germans more critical areas like Athens, a Salonika salient, some strategic islands (including most of Crete), and a strip bordering Turkey. All food stocks and grains were seized, as was any machinery and dry goods that might be useful. The output of mines was contracted for on terms that meant confiscation. Tsolakoglou was told that Greece must pay for its "reconstruction." The banks were looted of hard currency and gold bullion. The drachma became worthless amidst soaring inflation. Food distribution broke down and disappeared from the market—hoarded. During the winter of 1941–42, some 100,000 died in Athens-Piraeus alone of starvation.[23]

After dictatorship and repression under Metaxas, a heroic popular effort against Italy, and the discrediting of the old political order, the traumatic conditions of occupation became the catalyst for a new effort by a communist leadership bent on resistance, a social revolution and the seizure of power. In just a year or more, those who survived Metaxas had rebuilt some of the KKE's old capabilities. The invasion of the Soviet Union by the Germans turned an imperialist war into one of national patriotism in the eyes of the party, helping it to enlist the efforts of thousands. Begun in 1918, the KKE was led by an Anatolian, Nikos Zakhariadis, in the 1930s until his arrest by Metaxas and his subsequent transfer to Dachau by the Germans. He was replaced as secretary-general in November 1941 by Giorges Siantos, a tobacco worker, backed by Giannis Ioannidis, a Bulgarian-born barber. Together, they and their party colleagues built a broad-based movement from the bottom up, an organization that eventually had the active participation of hundreds of thousands of Greeks, who viewed it as a democratic expression of their yearning for a new way of life. Many, if not most, remained unaware, or uncaring, of the fact that a KKE leadership was at the core of things.[24]

A National Liberation Front (EAM) became an umbrella for National Solidarity (EA) (relief work), National Workers' Liberation Front (EEAM) (trade unions), youth and women's organizations, a network of village councils and courts, urban neighborhood committees and ELAS—the National Popular Liberation Army. The latter became the most effective guerrilla force in the country and came to be supported by the British Special Operations Executive (SOE) and the American OSS. ELAS also fought to eliminate its smaller right wing and royalist rivals. It fell heir to thousands of Italian weapons when Italy left the war in 1943 and was well positioned to step up the pace against the remaining Germans and to prepare for a post-war takeover. Regrettably, space does not permit me to detail British efforts to work with King George's government-in-exile, or to control the communists who cooperated or reacted with defiance and revolt. Suffice it to say that a power struggle was in the offing when the Germans pulled out on 12 October 1944.[25]

By the war's end, upwards of 1,300 rural villages had been laid waste by the Germans. Some 150,000 had been executed. Some 300,000 had starved to death. Seventy-five thousand Jews from Salonika had been sent north to concentration camps. Virtually all died, as did many chosen as slave labor. The economic life of the country was at a low ebb, a maritime fleet in ruins. The atrocities at Distomo, Kalavryta, Kondomari, and Komeno, and the horrors of Auschwitz, Birkenau, and Mauthausen were burned into the minds of those who had survived. As a matter of mixed pride and calculation, the men and women of EAM-ELAS had surmounted it all and now expected to build a different Greece. The British, with Stalin's agreement that the country was in their sphere of influence, planned to bring back King George and pick up again on pre-war politics. They appointed one George Papandreou head of a Government of National Unity in exile, and then had brought him in when Athens was liberated. Besides last-minute demolitions by the Germans, what greeted the arriving British tommies, a battalion of Greeks who had fought in Italy, a few RAF pilots and planes, and dozens of British military officers with their Greek ministers in tow, were not only crowds of cheering Greeks, but a city where ELAS had not only taken up positions, but the KKE was holding massive rallies and erecting huge banners proclaiming power to the communists and victory. Tension mounted as Lt. General Scobie entered into talks with Siantos over arrangements for demobilization, only to have a previous understanding fall apart amidst confusion, suspicion and blunders by all sides. In protest, KKE-EAM called for a rally at Syntagma (Constitution) Square on Sunday, 3 December. Demonstrators were walking peacefully with their placards when city police opened fire, killing fifteen and wounding dozens more. The large crowd scattered in panic in full view of foreign journalists staying at the Grande Bretagne Hotel. The Greek civil war, round two, had just begun.[26]

Calling for a general strike, KKE also ordered ELAS into action. That night armed units took over police posts, Special Security and Gendarmerie headquarters, prisons, and several extreme right-wing camps of National Action—"X"ists (Chi) of Colonel Grivas. Within a few days, KKE-EAM-ELAS had perhaps 20,000 men in Athens, twice those of the combined British-Greek force. Having advised London of the deteriorating situation, Scobie was told by Prime Minister Winston Churchill to deal with it as he would an enemy. Outnumbered, but with heavy weapons and aircraft, the government side secured the strategic heights in Athens and took back some key buildings. ELAS's tactics in the city lacked the effectiveness they had had when mounting mountain ambushes. Nonetheless, Churchill considered the situation so serious that he arrived at Christmas to see things first hand and stiffen his government's spine. In just days, he had 75,000 British soldiers in the city, backed by rightists and collaborators who felt it now opportune to join in with the anti-communists and royalists.

By 15 January, the two sides had entered into a truce. In Athens, the communists had been beaten, suffering 3,000 dead, 7,000 taken prisoner and innumerable wounded. The government had 3,500 dead and several thousand captured. British casualties ran to 250 dead and missing and 1,000 taken prisoner. EAM members fled Athens. Those who felt threatened by EAM left the countryside for the city. In fact, KKE-ELAS cleaned up on what remained of the rightist forces in the rural areas and increased its authority in mountain Greece. But the British could play the card of aid (food, medicine, and clothing) to a population on the verge of starvation and denied it to communist-held areas. A stalemate of sorts settled in. The British also replaced Papandreou with General Plastiras and said that a plebiscite would decide the question of the king's return. ELAS was finally induced to surrender a large quantity of arms on the promise of free elections and a new government.

But hardly had the ink dried on the Varkiza Agreement when it became known that KKE-ELAS had committed atrocities during the disorders—executions and the settling of old scores. Detainees had been maltreated and many had died. Under the eyes of, or encouraged by the British, a reorganized national guard, gendarmerie and police (rightists and ex-members of the Security Battalions were included in their ranks) instituted what some have called a "white terror" on known, or suspect KKE-EAM-ELAS members or anyone who had been associated with the political left. Arrests and summary executions, assassinations and kidnappings went on month after month in the year before Greece's elections in March 1946, the first since 1936. In such a climate, the KKE (now again led by Zakhariadis) opted to boycott, giving a rightist coalition led by the People's Party almost total power. The plebiscite over the king was advanced eighteen months with similar results. That same month, September, a pasty-faced George II arrived at Piraeus. The KKE had been in a quandary whether to again take up arms or to try to gain power through the ballot box. Finally, in October, it announced the formation of a Democratic Army (DA) under "Markos" Vafiadis. Ominously, the government of Constantine Tsaldaris had claimed two months earlier that the KKE had Yugoslav and Bulgarian backing.[27]

By the spring of 1947, Athens was on the defensive and steadily losing territory to the communists. An exhausted Britain appealed for American assistance. US President Harry Truman responded by going before Congress to request US$400 million (an enormous sum in those days) in military and material aid for Greece and Turkey to prevent a communist victory. Most of the funds were earmarked for Greek military equipment and supplies. US military advisors went into the field with the royal Greek army and American aid and economic officials assumed unprecedented power. However, it took many months before US intervention was felt in what was a successful DA hit-and-run campaign. Emboldened, but increasingly over-stretched, Markos attempted and failed to make Konitsa the capital of a provisional government as announced at the end of 1947. Then, Zakhariadis made the fatal error of ordering the DA to adopt conventional tactics, exposing it to air strikes and artillery and, ultimately, to a better trained and equipped army.[28]

By late 1948, the DA was relying on forced conscription in its areas of control, drawing more and more on women and Slav Macedonians from the border regions. It had already evacuated some 25,000 children and had sent them north to several communist countries. Yugoslavia's dramatic break with Stalin denied it support from that quarter. Now hungry and ragged and increasingly isolated, the DA courageously, but foolishly, tried to stand and fight in pitched battles in the Grammos and Vitsi mountains in the summer of 1949. Its troops were dive-bombed and napalmed into a footsore retreat into Albania. Greece was now to know the peace of the exhausted five years after World War Two had ended! Much had happened, including the succession of King Paul and an iron-willed Queen Frederika to the throne. Both were anticommunist to the core and eager to place Greece in the front ranks of the Cold War. Greeks went off to fight in Korea and, at home, Greece became a US-controlled client state.[29]

Washington's clients were the crown, compliant (often compromised and corrupt) politicians, cooperative security-police officials, and senior officers in the armed forces. The American embassy in Athens pulled the strings in governmental ministries and over at the military's huge "Pentagonal." Martial law ended in early 1950 and elections followed. Greece's bourgeois politicians seemingly had learned nothing after decades of disaster and served up one weak government after another. Finally, American arm-twisting and threats brought needed constitutional change in a simple majority system. The result was that General Alexandros Papagos's rightist Greek Rally, with less than half of the popular vote, gained five sixths of the seats in parliament. Papagos worked well with Paul and Frederika until his death in 1955, whereupon Paul passed over his successor and brought in Constantine Karamanlis. He soon tailored a renamed National Radical Union to his liking and made more constitutional changes to his party's advantage.[30]

Now outwardly stable, and a member of NATO, Greece retained emergency laws not befitting a democracy, but helpful to a large domestic security apparatus. Set up by the CIA, KYP had widespread intrusive police powers. Phone taps, mail intercepts and entries were common. Also, a certificate attesting to "sound social views" (no leftist connections) was required for state employment, a driving permit, a passport, and, for a time, university entrance. Out of this miasma came the murder in 1963 of Gregory Lambrakis at an anti-NATO peace rally in Thessaloniki. A United Democratic

Left MP, Lambrakis was killed by right-wing extremists connected with senior gendarmerie officers. Karamanlis did not survive this, as it was combined with serious friction with Paul and Frederika. The royal couple stretched the constitution to the limit and had the ear of American ambassadors and CIA station chiefs, playing them as only royals can. They then received US$567,000 a year in salary. They had a city palace, a country estate, a large villa in Paleo Psychiko, a palace on Corfu, two island homes, a farm and forest land, a hunting lodge, two DC-3 aircraft, a jet aircraft, a helicopter, several large yachts, and eighteen automobiles (two Rolls Royces), all tax free in one of Europe's poorest countries. Plus, Frederika had a "foundation" which placed an added tax on cigarettes and cinema tickets. Thus, while living very luxuriously, a King Paul who admitted that he had little feeling for the Greeks died of cancer and was succeeded by his son, Constantine II.[31]

In early 1967, Constantine and his mother were waiting for a coup to come along, something acceptably predictable, run by some of their close senior officer friends in the armed forces. Rumors of who would do it—this, or that general—were making the rounds as many opposed populist George Papandreou's Center Union (with his radical son Andreas) winning an election set for 28 May. They had already had several years of Papandreou after Karamanlis—the rise of the United Democratic Left, short-lived coalitions, and Andreas's attempt to form a secret organization of junior army officers (*Aspida*, or "Shield")—forgetting the fact that the army had its own vote-rigging capability in Operation Pericles. No, they could not have the Papandreous! It finally took place at midnight on 20 April when special forces took over the Pentagonal and then tanks rolled out of Goudi barracks. But to the amazement of almost everyone, the coup was being led by a relatively obscure Colonel George Papadopoulos, who had been on the CIA's payroll for years! It was what everyone called the "wrong coup!"[32]

The conspirators, almost immediately called the Colonels' junta, had simply taken an off-the-shelf NATO plan named Prometheus—an operation that was to be put into action if civil unrest erupted—and used it to take over the nation. Constantine was at the royal estate at Tatoi at the foot of Parnitha Mountain outside Athens. At about 1 a.m., an aide rang him with a report of gunfire. Just then, throughout the city, the prime minister, ministers, and all key government officials and politicians were being arrested, or taken into "protective custody." Within a few hours, while it was still dark, 10,000 people were rounded up. At 6 a.m., the state radio announced a decree in the name of the king suspending civil liberties (eleven articles of the constitution) and putting draconian search and arrest powers in force. Just after 7 a.m.,

Papadopoulos, Brigadier Stylianos Pattakos and Colonel Nikos Makarezos arrived at Tatoi and asked for the king's cooperation. In a huff, Constantine demanded to see their superior, not realizing that they were the leaders. Prime Minister Kanellopoulos urged that he oppose them, but Constantine was hesitant and confused.[33]

Before the day was out, Constantine (in dress uniform) signed a royal decree for the puppet regime backed by Papadopoulos and his men to avoid bloodshed, or so he said. He signed seventy, or more, laws until his amateurish counter-coup fell apart that December. Again, he said that he didn't want fighting. Giving up, he and his family flew to Rome and then on to London. If the actual coup was virtually bloodless, its aftermath was anything but. After he had purged the military of royalists, Papadopoulos became a ruthless, dictatorial prime minister. His eager subordinates restructured the school system, courts, judiciary and ministries. They rigged a referendum and served up a new constitution. All the while, his security and ESA military police began putting political suspects through weeks and months of interrogation and torture. Convinced that their detainees threatened their twisted idea of a "Helleno-Christian Civilization," they, themselves, showed no mercy, and tortured their victims in the most bestial fashion.[34]

Some, however, particularly the young, began to resist. Alekos Panagoulis, a Center Union youth activist, tried to blow up the dictator's motorcade on a mountain road south of Athens, but was caught. He became the man that Papadopoulos couldn't break as he passed through the expert hands of Babalas, Mallios, and Major Theophyloyannakos. He became a cause célèbre when people abroad appealed for his life. Still, there were others who were unmoved that the jails were full. Greece's standing with NATO remained unimpaired, with Washington ready to run interference if someone asked embarrassing questions. In 1968, through KYP and US-Greek businessman Tom Pappas, the junta gave US$549,000 to the Nixon presidential campaign. US Vice-President Spiro Agnew (who later ran afoul of corruption charges) in 1971 was wined and dined by the junta. Other senior US officials visited Greece as well. In 1972, the US navy acquired homeport basing at Souda Bay without any reference to the Greek people. The Soviets were then trying to move into the Mediterranean and, in October 1973, Israel was attacked in the Yom Kippur war. Because of Greece's strategic location, it became paired with Israel in US policy concerns.[35]

But despite aspects of international acceptance, the situation at home had begun to become shaky. The law faculty at Athens University was occupied by protestors in March. In May, navy officers mutinied and took a destroyer to

Italy. Papadopoulos, seemingly removed from reality, declared Greece a "republic" and rigged yet another referendum in which he promised elections and reforms. It was not enough, even after he had lifted martial law and announced an amnesty for political prisoners. That November, after a memorial for George Papandreou, demonstrators and police clashed. Then, a few days later, students began occupying the Athens Polytechnical University, as well as university buildings in Thessaloniki and Patras. At first, the regime acted with restraint. But after a clandestine student radio station urged revolt, the tanks were sent in. On 17 November, using automatic weapons, tear gas and truncheons, the army and riot police burst into, the polytechnic's compound. At least thirty-four protestors were killed and several hundred were wounded. Mass arrests and martial law followed, even as Papadopoulos continued to prattle about elections.[36]

Such talk unnerved his cohorts and Papadopoulos was removed by Brigadier Dimitrios Ioannidis chief of the dreaded ESA. This, and the repression that followed, gave a boost to various Greek resistance groups abroad. But finally it was Cyprus, and efforts by the junta to intrigue on that island of Greeks and Turks, that led to their demise and downfall.

It had gone on a long time. The Greek Cypriots had fought a guerrilla war against the British to gain independence. Colonel Grivas, the former head of "X," had led EOKA-Alpha and fought for *enosis* (union with Greece). But Cyprus was saddled with constitutional arrangements unsatisfactory to both sides. A UN peacekeeping force went in after months of sporadic fighting. Grivas returned to the island in 1964 and clashed with President and Archbishop Makarios over control of the National Guard and armed Greek-Cypriot groups. Grivas then left. Britain's interest remained restricted to keeping two sovereign bases that exist today—an air base and very important electronic facilities.

When the Colonels took power, they too insisted on *enosis*, but were rebuffed by Ankara. Inconclusive communal talks continued. There were plots against Makarios, tension and instability. In 1971, Grivas came back and after a year launched attacks against government installations, having formed EOKA-Beta. The Greek-Cypriots divided over *enosis*, or independence, under Makarios. In February 1973, Makarios was re-elected. EOKA-Beta stepped up its attacks and bombings, even kidnapping a minister. Makarios took decisive action against Grivas and pro-*enosis* bishops, mounting an effective operation that uncovered arms stockpiles and led to the arrests of many EOKA-Beta members. Grivas died in January 1974, allowing Makarios to grant an amnesty. But by July, when Makarios attempted to purge his National Guard, police and civil service of Grivas's men (Makarios wrote to Greek President Ghizikis accusing Athens of subversion and demanding also that Greek officers be withdrawn), Athens ordered them to stage a coup. EOKA-Beta gunman Nikos Sampson became "president" after loyalist resistance ceased and Makarios took refuge with the British. The Colonels sent more officers over to reinforce the National Guard.

Turkey didn't wait long. After its appeals to the British (as a guarantor power) for joint action failed to get a response, on 20 July its military landed at Kyrenia in the north and pushed a corridor through to the Turkish-Cypriot sector of Nicosia. A UN ceasefire was ignored and its peacekeepers were of little help. There was sharp fighting and civilian casualties on both sides. The Colonels failed to get Greek reinforcements to the island and, in a second invasion in August, Turkey seized all of the northern part as it remains today. With its attempt at *enosis* having failed, the junta resigned on 23 July. They made a phone call to Karamanlis in Paris, where he had lived since 1963, and asked him to return to Athens to restore civilian rule. He flew in the next morning to a huge crowd of well-wishers. Athens went wild. Car horns hooted. Crowds spilled into the street. However, the return to democracy was a difficult task as the government was full of pro-junta people—officials, military men, judges, police, and security officers. Some trials were held, but most went unpunished. Many remained on for years… even until today.

* * *

18 June 1989. In national elections, New Democracy won 44.3 percent, or 145 seats; Pasok 39.1, or 125 seats; Left Coalition 13.1 percent, or 28 seats. Because no party won a majority, a caretaker government was set up until new elections. *5 November 1989.* New Democracy won 46.1 percent or 148 seats; Pasok 40.6, or 128 seats; Left Coalition 10.9 or 21 seats. Again, no one won a majority. An all-party caretaker government was established under octogenarian Prime Minister Xenophon Zolotas. *8 April 1990.* New Democracy won 47 percent or 150 seats; Pasok 38.5 or 125 seats; Left Coalition 10.3 or 21 seats. In July, a Democratic Renewal member joined ND. In November, a court ruling gave ND a contested seat on Corfu. It now had 152 votes in parliament. ND would have come to power in June 1989 if Pasok had not amended the electoral law to a weighted proportional representation.

10 October 1993. Pasok won 47 percent or 170 seats; New Democracy 39 percent, or 111 seats; Political Spring 5 percent, or ten seats. Communist Party of Greece 4.5, or nine seats. Again, the election was run by different rules.

9 March 1995. A Pasok-dominated parliament elected a compromise national president in Costis Stephanopoulos. The new president, the former head of the failed center-right Democratic Renewal, replaced Constantine Karamanlis who had been president twice, most recently from May 1990. If anything, the new president would strictly adhere to his limited constitutional role and not take up controversial issues, or take initiatives.

15 January 1996. Suffering from failing health, Andreas Papandreou resigned as prime minister. He was to remain titular Pasok party chairman.

18 January 1996. After a two-day intra-party campaign, Costas Simitis was elected as the new prime minister in two rounds of voting. He was a moderate, reform-minded, consensus builder.

30 January 1996. Greek and Turkish military forces maneuvered off Imia islet in the Aegean in an argument over ownership. US President Bill Clinton made phone calls to avert a clash. Simitis was soon invited to the White House for bilateral talks in April.

23 June 1996. Andreas Papandreou died after a long illness.

14 August 1996. Greek-Cypriot Solomos Solomou was shot dead by a Turkish security man at close range in the buffer zone when he was climbing a flagpole intent on pulling down the Turkish flag. Three days earlier, his cousin, Tassos Issac, had been clubbed to death by Grey Wolves during a similar fracas.

22 September 1996. Prime Minister Costas Simitis called a snap early election (announced in August) and managed a Pasok win with 41.5 percent, or 162 seats; New Democracy thirty-eight percent, or 108 seats; Greek Communist Party 5.5 percent, or eleven seats; Left Coalition five percent, or ten seats.

28 February 1997. While visiting Athens, NATO Secretary General Javier Solana urged Greece and Turkey to accept installation of a "hot line" between Athens, Turkey, and NATO headquarters. NATO was to review Greek and Turkish radar images of military incursions. He also urged that military aircraft fly unarmed (not accepted).

1 June 1997. Due to higher costs, some 135 Greek ships sought a flag of convenience in 1996. The remaining 2,000 ships still constituted the largest merchant shipping fleet in the world.

25 July 1997. Prime Minister Simitis threatened to veto EU expansion in central-eastern Europe if Cyprus's admission was left out.

14 March 1998. After France dropped its objection, EU foreign ministers agreed at Edinburgh that Cyprus's accession could begin on 31 March. Cyprus

President Glafcos Clerides had urged the Cypriot Turks to form a delegation and join the talks. This was not accepted by their leader Rauf Denktash.

15 March 1998. In a surprise move, the Simitis government permitted the drachma to float, entering the European Exchange Rate Mechanism. The drachma dropped a little, but proved stable. The Athens stock exchange rose sharply.

23 April 1998. Former president and prime minister Constantine Karamanlis dies.

22 June 1998. Amid escalating tensions over Cyprus, US special envoy Richard Holbrooke arrived in Athens for talks with Prime Minister Simitis and Foreign Minister Theodoros Pangalos. Ankara talked of war after Greek military planes landed at Paphos (S-300 site). Turkey responded by sending its ships to northern Cyprus.

24 July 1998. On the eve of a visit to northern Cyprus, Turkish President Suleyman Demirel stated that Cyprus would never become a "second Crete." He warned of Turkish military action. Athens said that a White House spokesman's comments that depicted the Cyprus problem as one of communal tension, not occupation, was in error.

28 July 1998. Prime Minister Simitis moved to end a war of words after Foreign Minister Pangalos accused US President Clinton of having lied about his willingness to resolve the Cyprus issue.

10 November 1998. EU enlargement talks went forward in Brussels, but France, Germany, Italy and the Netherlands expressed doubts that a divided Cyprus should be admitted. Greece again voiced its objection and again threatened to use its veto power.

27 February 1999. In a foreign policy speech, President Clinton admits that he had been unable to improve Greek-Turkish relations.

27 June 1999. George Papadopoulos, the leader of the Colonel's junta, died unrepentant in prison. His past was negatively noted by the Greek press. His death predated the twenty-fifth anniversary of an ill-fated coup on Cyprus which then led to the island's division.

Caspian Oil Pipelines

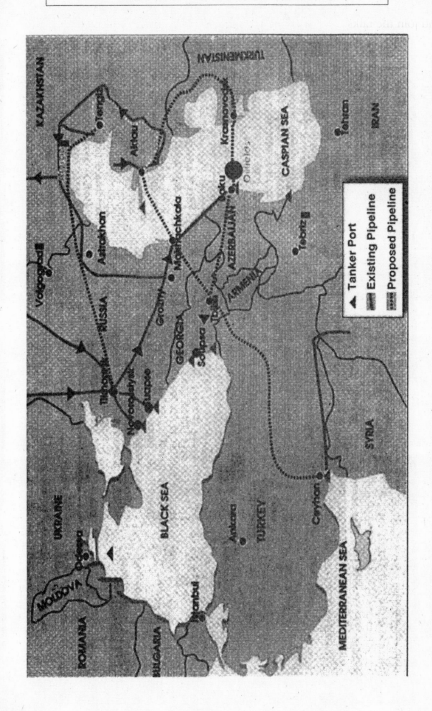

Islamic Expansion and Narcotics Routes

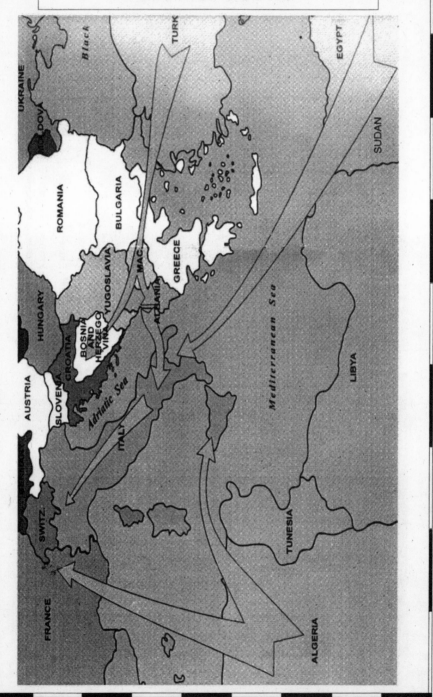

Chapter 11

Kosovo: The Bartered Bride

July 1998–December 2000

Unlike the opera by the Czech composer Bedrich Smetana, the story of the Balkan bartered bride does not end happily. Dressed in her wedding finery over which she has labored for many months, she is abducted en route to the ceremony by a jealous suitor. Assaulted and raped, she emerges from an ensuing shoot-out defiled and in a state of hysteria, for her intended husband, her true love, is killed in the rescue. She is totally incapable of explaining the sequence of events and is soon heaped over with lies and blame—dishonored. Fleeing from her family, she naively trusts an older "gentleman" who promises to help her establish a new life in the big city where no one will know her. Instead, she is raped again and sold to the owner of a whorehouse frequented by foreigners. There enters a dashing man of affairs from London. Enamored of her beauty, and seemingly sympathetic to her plight, he proposes to buy her freedom. But, once aware of the plot, the chief of police and the town mayor (both favored customers) send an intermediary to the Englishman and persuade him that his money will be better spent used as a bribe, which will enable him to win the contract he's been seeking. He agrees, gains the business deal that he desires, and departs. The "bartered bride" is abandoned to her fate, now worse off than ever.

All in the Balkans have played the role. In the summer of 1998, it was a question of whether the West and NATO would permit the Serbs to mop up the floor with the Kosovo Liberation Army (KLA), or whether Washington would intervene on behalf of the Albanians. Each week that went by without NATO air strikes meant that the KLA was being driven back. In mid-August, I decided to add Kosovo to Belgrade and Zagreb. An improbable Avioimprex flight from Zagreb to Skopje in an old twin-engine Tupolev made it easy. From there, all I had to do was grab a bus. On the road to Pristina, heavily barricaded police posts ringed with sand bags and rubber tires had been established at the major intersections. From the bus station I taxied over to the Grand. It had actually improved. It had been spruced up some and the elevators worked. I was told that a Serb Media Center had been set up as well. There, I learned that an old acquaintance, Radovan Urosevic, was in charge and that, if I hurried over to the Democratic League of Kosovo (LDK), I would be able to hear American ambassador Christopher Hill and the Kosovo Albanian leader Ibrahim Rugova making statements to the press.

I joined the crowd pressing up against the ropes and waited. Hill was trying to put together a unified delegation and an agreed upon position to represent the Kosovar Albanians. He obviously had his hands full. The meeting was running late. Then, a shiny, late-model BMW pulled up in a cloud of dust. Its driver exited to assist a lone passenger in the back seat. While being eased into a blue blazer, the man looked around expectantly to see if he was being observed, or photographed. After adjusting his blue tie up against his white-collared light-blue shirt, he strode inside. Finally, Hill and Rugova emerged and offered the predictable. Hill expressed hope that substantive negotiations would get underway, while Rugova straddled the issues as best he could. Then, the BMW's owner, Austrian ambassador to Belgrade Wolfgang Petritsch, spoke. His words were surreal. "The Austrian government," he intoned importantly before correcting himself to say, "the presidency of the European Union." Yes, tiny Austria is again back in the Balkans. And, with Vienna's military attaché in Tirana being billed as the resident expert on Albania, and the Contact Group now fully seized with the Kosovo question, echoes of 1912 could be heard all over again: "Which territories ought to be Albanian?"

As things stood, a weak Kosovar negotiating team was the best that Hill could do. Fehmi Agani, Fatmir Sejdiu, and Edita Tahira of the LDK had stood in Rugova's shadow. The same went for Tadej Rodiqi of the Christian Democratic Party and Ilas Kurteshi of the Social Democrats. The fiery nationalist Adem Demaci refused to join, as did the popular intellectual Rexhep Oosja. Barjam Kosumi of the Parliamentary Party and Mehmet Hajrizi of the

Albanian Democratic Movement had also declined. Most importantly, Rugova was the Kosovars' recognized leader, but he refused to take the helm. Perhaps this was to avoid a power struggle with the KLA, or because he didn't want to risk a failure. In any case, his usual tactic was to refuse to talk while the Yugoslav Army (VJ) was on the offensive. Since early March, Belgrade had extended repeated written invitations to the Albanians and had sent a high-level delegation to Pristina headed by the President of Serbia, Milan Milutinovic. As the Serb side was left cooling its heels, Ratko Markovic had taken over. And, with no talks, and no ceasefire, the VJ and special police went into action with a vengeance!

Because Kosovo's "emergency" was now very real, the next morning I walked over to introduce myself to the Ministry of Information to obtain a press permit. Then, I went to look up Radovan. He's an amazing guy, lean, athletic and addicted to speed, whether downhill skiing or driving his car. With great good humor, he once told me how at Pristina University his Albanian professor had flunked him seven times in a row in English. Radovan doggedly re-enrolled each time and finally the teacher gave up and passed him. Whatever the case, he is fluent with little, or no trace of an accent. Unaware of coming events, I jokingly said that he should have joined his uncle in New York as he once mentioned. He laughed and then became serious. He said that he thought that things were going to be "okay" in Kosovo once the KLA was finished as an effective fighting force. He said that they knew that the Kosovars must be given autonomy. It was just a question of how much, and they needed talks to determine that. He showed me around the center of which he was justifiably proud. It wasn't a blatant propaganda operation as he included all source information, including Albanian news. After a while, he asked if I wanted to go for a ride. Lacking any transportation of my own, I readily agreed.

We drove out of town at breakneck speed in a new Land Rover that Belgrade had provided him. He winced as he pointed to a fender that had been dented by a brick thrown by an irate Serb. He had been caught in a demonstration. Radovan was always quick to admit mistakes on the part of the Yugoslav authorities, occasions he usually prefaced by exclaiming, "We stupid Serbs!" To me, at least, he had never expressed hatred for the Albanians. He and another Serbian family lived in an apartment building with eight Albanian families. He said that he liked them as neighbors. That they got along "okay." He added that for themselves (as opposed to government employment) they worked hard and were good businessmen. We continued along at the same pace. Radovan pointed out a low range of wooded hills to the southwest. He said that the airport was on the other side, as well as TV and radio transmitters.

The KLA, he said, had almost taken them before being driven off. This, he said, had been their high-water mark, when they had controlled almost half of the province. Passing a pile of twisted metal and debris, he showed me where the KLA had cut the road to Pec, a historically important town to the west near the border with Albania.

Once off the main road, we arrived at Belacevic adjacent to one of the largest open-pit soft-coal mines in Europe. Most importantly, it fueled Kosovo's electric power generating plants. The KLA had actually taken the mine. But today, there in the bright sunshine, blue-uniformed police were guarding Albanian farmers as they harvested wheat. What Radovan was displaying was an obvious "show and tell," but his story of how the land belonged to the state mine, how it was used rent free by the Albanian villagers, and how, unlike the mineworkers, they had refused to evacuate with the KLA when they had had to pull out, had a ring of truth to it. He pointed to a burned patch where the KLA had infiltrated one night and set the hillside on fire. We retraced our route and turned right again on the main road and drove to Komorane, twenty-five kilometers west of Pristina. We stopped at a checkpoint, and I shot a few photos. The police invited us inside their position for a glass of slivovitz. I asked how things were going. They said it was quiet and very boring monitoring traffic, but then jokingly added that it was better than fighting. Only two weeks later, twenty-three-year-old Goran Andric, a policeman, would be killed there in a KLA attack.

They suggested that we visit an Albanian family who lived in the village. There we found seventy-five-year-old Mehmet Gasji, his wife, a daughter, and her young children. Over cigarettes and cola, Gasji explained how the KLA had ordered all of them out when they were forced to retreat and said they had lived rough some distance to the south for two weeks. Mehmet, however, returned to see if his house was still standing after being told by the KLA that the village would be torched. To his surprise, it was untouched, and, when the Serbs found him there, they repaired a power line as an inducement to get others to return. It seems that only his family had come back, for the village was deserted. But, there we sat on the ground chatting, looking at photographs of two sons who were working in Germany. It was impossible to determine the details of what had happened, but the visible damage consisted of broken window glass and two burned-out shops close to the main road.

At lunchtime, we downed enormous hamburger steaks and chips with *pivo*. I asked Radovan why he didn't carry a pistol when he drove out into the countryside as the KLA were still holed up in small numbers in deserted villages. He just shook his head and said that he wasn't afraid, and that he had nothing to fear from the Albanians. I suggested maybe not from his neighbors, who knew him, but from others. Then I asked him what it had been like before Milosevic and 1989. He thought for a bit and said that apart from the corruption and mismanagement, it was how the Serbs were always given the run-around that angered most. He said that Albanian officials went out of their way to find something wrong with their papers—an application, or whatever— so that they were sent away for no valid reason and told to come back another time. Often, they were just not at their offices when they should have been. It really did irritate, he admitted. He said that, in a private capacity, most Serbs have no problem with the Kosovars. "We do deal with them," he said, "as they own most of the businesses." For example, he claimed that he could never dream of running a gas station like the Albanians do. To me, it seemed like such a modest ambition.[1]

Back in Pristina, I talked with Radovan's young secretary while waiting for Sinisa Ljepojevic. She and her family had fled from Krajina in 1995. She plied me with questions about the US as she had been approved for admission and was soon to leave for Chicago. She was very excited over the idea of life in America, but didn't know how, or when, she would see her parents again. I commented, inanely, how everyone had been through so much. She gave me her best smile and said, "Well it's good that we Serbs are strong." Her mother had been born in a cave in Bosnia during World War Two, as some had taken to the mountains to escape the Croat Ustashe. I advised her to go to the States and to never change her mind. Sinisa had no premonition of the future either. He said that the VJ was getting things under control. I asked how the effort was being organized. Most of the army, he said, belonged to Pristina Corps, commanded from Nis. A special border unit was linked to the VJ General Staff in Belgrade. Also, there were at least 10,000 regular and special police from the Ministry of the Interior—MUPs as they are called—up from 7,000 in July. In addition, Ministry special paramilitary forces, the "red berets" had arrived, whom, Sinisa said were "very tough guys sent to do a very tough job." He said that Milosevic would succeed in keeping Kosovo and deal with the Albanians from a position of strength after eliminating the KLA.

I asked what had been learned about the KLA since they had surfaced as a serious force. He said that some had been left-leaning activists at Pristina University, but were essentially nationalists. The same went for some who had once been officers in the JNA. In recent months, he added, local LDK leaders had gone over to them. Jakup Krasniqi, the KLA spokesman, had run the LDK office at Glogovac. When they took the offensive last spring, Sinisa explained, many villagers had joined up, either voluntarily or under duress.

Their families were now compromised, he added, forcing them to go with the KLA. He claimed that the latter had killed some who tried to remain loyal, had mortared villages, or otherwise intimidated those who were on the fence. Also, now, he added, fighters were coming in from Albania. I asked about the rumors of foreign volunteers. He agreed there were rumors, but none had been found, dead or alive. He did cite evidence from hastily evacuated strongholds—paper litter that pointed to Saudi Arabia, Germany, and, of all places, Scotland. A newspaper in Yemen supposedly cited the deaths of five Arab fighters in Kosovo. More likely, he thought, most were Albanians who had been working in Western Europe. Later, we would hear of those who came over from the US.

Much remained unclear, especially the KLA's command structure. It seemed that some political direction came from the Kosovar "prime minister" Buyar Bukoshi (formerly close to Rugova) who moved around Western Europe to promote the People's Movement of Kosovo and KLA fundraising through a three percent "tax" on the incomes of 600,000 Albanians living there. Bank accounts were established in Switzerland and Germany, some under an umbrella Homeland Calling (*Vendlindja Therret*) fund. Berisha in northern Albania was involved, as was Tirana through its training camps. But inside, not much was known apart from the Jasharis who had been killed in a shoot-out at Prekas the previous March. The Jashari clan had long been involved in black-marketeering, and other crimes. Its leader, a young tough in the *kacak* brigand tradition, Adem Jashari, was wanted for rape and extortion, as well as smuggling military arms in from Albania as early as 1991. He eluded capture and became a legend. By 1997, he had induced other clan leaders to cooperate with the KLA. In early 1998, he and a brother led several attacks in the Dreneca area. After another such incident, the police surrounded their village on 5 March, and in two days of fighting, fifty-one Kosovars were killed, thirty from the Jashari clan.[2]

Yugoslav sources say that, from January to July, 887 actions took place during which forty-four policemen and sixty-six civilians died. Some ninety-six policemen and thirty-eight civilians were seriously wounded. And, 171 civilians had been kidnapped—125 Serbs and Montenegrins, thirty-seven Albanians, six Roma, one Yugoslav Muslim, and one each from Bulgaria and Macedonia. Of these, fifteen were killed, seven escaped, thirty-two were released, and 118 remain missing. At that time, the US still labeled the KLA a terrorist organization. One factor, among others, which would change Washington's stance, was the mounting toll in civilian casualties. Much of the fighting took place in village or family compounds where thick-walled stone dwellings were traditionally built for defense. Not wanting to take casualties themselves, the VJ and police blasted away with heavy weapons. And, because some were involved with, or supported the insurgents, family members stayed with the KLA fighters and were killed—men, women, and children—both the young and the very old.[3]

Without air support or heavy weapons, the KLA was losing ground. Also, it lacked a long-established logistical infrastructure. The many goat paths over the mountains into Albania weren't a Ho Chi Minh trail. Still, they were often well dug into the ground they held: deep trenches, spider holes, caves and rocky crevasses where it's hard to dislodge determined fighters. It often had fixed medical support, which suggested that it planned to stand and fight. Some of its weapons were foreign—including Ambrust anti-tank weapons as were used in Bosnia and interestingly the Barrett semiautomatic sniper rifle, which is new to the US inventory. Fitted with a telescopic sight, it fires a .50 caliber round that can pierce the side of an automobile at 1,200 yards. At US$3,000 a copy, the Yugoslav military was of the opinion that it would more likely be "given," rather than "purchased." Whatever, my talks with journalists who had traveled farther a field than I had indicated that the KLA was increasingly on the run. That also meant that those civilians who had provided them with any kind of assistance, or support, were increasingly at risk of reprisals.[4]

Without question, many Kosovar civilians had already been killed, or driven from their villages, either by the Yugoslavs or KLA. Still, I had the impression that Belgrade was seeking a political solution. Certainly, it would be on their terms after the KLA was beaten and Rugova was reined in after having promised so much and having delivered so little. I felt this way as most of the Kosovar political elite was free to go where they pleased and say what they wanted. They lambasted Milosevic day and night and had foreign representatives hanging on their every word. But, the question was whether they would be willing to compromise after ten harsh years of struggle and repression? Still, there were people like Besim Latifi. I had met him quite by accident while walking around Pristina a few years earlier. He had studied business and economics at Pristina University and wanted no part of Rugova. An Albanian, he wanted a degree, a job, and a normal life. He had no problem with the Serbian people, or with using their language when required. He asked me to come to his apartment to meet others who thought like he did. I've since regretted not doing so, as ordinary people are never ordinary.

After ten days on the road, I returned to Skopje thinking I would take the train home. But, the schedule had changed and I faced an overnight stay. I asked a taxi driver to check the tour agencies. He kept muttering, "Balkan catastrophe" over and over. Miraculously, he found a bus leaving for the Greek border, to Gevgelija. I was happy until the driver put me down in the dark, not at a bus station, but by a worn footpath through the bushes outside of town. It led to a wire mesh fence beside the main highway, which was still some distance from the border. But, I got my bags over and walked to a petrol station up the road. There, my one remaining US dollar bill convinced a driver to take me to the check post. Puzzled, the Macedonians chopped me through. Then, I was rescued by a Serbian driving for Venus Van Company who took me over to the Greek side. Amazingly, he had a copy of Kissinger's *Diplomacy* in translation in his cab! He was reluctant to take me on to Thessaloniki, but dropped me at a café where I could use my drachmas. A taxi got me to "Thess" just before midnight, and I made the last KTEL bus for Athens. It put me out on the "National Road" near Kifissia at around 7 a.m. A taxi had me home in minutes. A Balkan "catastrophe" followed by a minor miracle!

While I was in Belgrade, a miracle of another kind had occurred. An impoverished and ostracized Yugoslavia won the world basketball championship in a final against Greece. The city went wild with joy for two days. People poured into the parks to celebrate their victory. Flags waved and sound boxes boomed out a rock beat "Yugo-slav-ia!" Kids daubed their cheeks with the blue, white, and red of the national colors. It was the first time that I had seen them as they would prefer to be—happy and carefree. Many had no jobs to go to and probably welcomed the diversion. I stayed at the Excelsior and was having dinner with Dragomir when the final basket went in. The whole staff was in front of the TV set cheering. However, a waiter with grim black humor told another, "Well, I suppose that NATO will have to bomb us now!" Although I laughed when Dragomir translated his remarks, it remained like a dark cloud in my mind that grew ever larger in the days to come.

By September, Washington was insistently calling for a "in place" ceasefire—a situation that would permit the KLA to keep whatever territory it still controlled. It also legitimized them as a recognized party to the conflict. The KLA itself was unwilling to stop fighting, or change its policy to accept anything less than full independence. Milosevic, in turn, mounted a stepped-up offensive, despite opposition from the Contract Group and a drumbeat of criticism from the foreign media. Many western print and TV journalists began to depict the conflict in terms of David and Goliath. KLA guerrilla commanders with dramatic war names were romanticized and described in heroic terms, in contrast to the "thuggish" Serbs. It made for good copy. By early October, US special envoy Richard Holbrooke had reinforced Chris Hill in Belgrade. Holbrooke, who had already met with the rebels, obtained an agreement with Milosevic calling for an end to violence by both sides, a political settlement that recognized: that Kosovo would remain within the borders of Yugoslavia; the equality of ethnic communities in religion, culture, and heritage; Kosovo as an integrated society; that Kosovo's legal system, under self-government, would conform with that of Serbia and the FRY; that elections to parliamentary, executive, and judicial bodies would take place within nine months; and that a large OSCE contingent would monitor events and supervise fulfillment of the obligations to be undertaken by both sides.[5]

Moreover, a rigid timeframe, which specified what was to be done and when, was imposed almost before a beefed-up OSCE group was organized and on the ground. Demaci, now speaking on behalf of the KLA, rejected the agreement out of hand. The more moderate figures like Rugova also criticized it and continued to demand independence. The Contact Group ignored this, but began to rant about a new press law that Belgrade had instituted to gain greater control over its media at a time of a worsening crisis. And, in the face of the KLA's refusal to stop fighting, it, and more importantly, Washington, insisted that the VJ reduce its forces. In fact, fighting continued, fueled by both sides. Another serious complication was that US envoy Chris Hill's changed constitutional structure for Kosovo required that Serbia and FRY recast their constitutions. Instead of Kosovo conforming to extant FRY legal structures, the reverse would obtain. Clearly autonomy, plus, was being planned—virtually that of a state entity. Also, certain important questions would be decided solely by the Chief of the Verification Mission, an OSCE appointee.[6]

By December, the atmospherics were ominous. That black cloud had become a thunderhead. Milosevic turned east in an effort to gain more leverage. On 17 December, his defense minister signed an open agreement with Russian Minister of Defense Marshal Igor Sergeyev, which may have also included promises of arms supplies. Future historians will determine if this act alone in Washington's mind constituted crossing a "red line" by raising the threat of a return of Russian influence to the Balkans through a power (Yugoslavia) which refused to knuckle under. Although one can understand Milosevic's motives, it was probably a mistake. He had sufficient wherewithal to deal with the KLA, but he was now attempting to involve Moscow militarily. It immediately changed the nature of the situation. This must be juxtaposed with a steady drumbeat of commentary from US columnists and others to the effect that Milosevic was part of the problem, not the solution, and would have to go.[7]

As the year began, things were at an impasse. The fighting wasn't very heavy, but clashes were continuing. And, nearly three months after the Holbrooke-Milosevic talks, only some 700 OSCE monitors were in Kosovo, not the 2,000 agreed upon. Neither Belgrade nor the KLA were willing to back down in the absence of negotiations. Rugova and Pristina's politicians continued to squabble. And, the OSCE had no real role other than get to the scene of the latest incident. On January 15, a firefight took place that tilted international opinion against Yugoslavia even further. Following the deaths by shooting of four policemen, the village of Racak was surrounded, and, in the early morning hours, security forces began to move in against armed opposition. After the KLA pulled out, journalists and a TV crew observed bodies scattered about. Some OSCE personnel had also arrived to begin an investigation along with a magistrate and her police escort. However, by late afternoon sporadic gunfire was still heard. The next day, Kosovo Verification Mission head William Walker was unable to convince the Yugoslavs to return with him. Angered, he went himself with Albanian journalists. Villagers took them up a hill to a ditch where twenty-three bodies—almost all men were sprawled on the ground. With forty-five dead, including nine KLA, Walker immediately announced that it was a "blatant massacre of civilians" and asked the Hague tribunal to step in. Denying the accusation, Belgrade declared Walker (a senior US diplomat) persona non grata and prevented tribunal chief prosecutor Louise Arbour from entering Kosovo. The already strained relations between the Contact Group and Belgrade became poisonous.[8]

Amid general recognition that the Holbrooke mission had failed—although the many reasons for its failure were never explained by the US administration except in terms of Belgrade's belligerence—the Contact Group called upon the parties to the conflict to meet at Rambouillet outside Paris in early February in a last ditch effort to reach a solution. Now quite frustrated, the US reworked versions of the Hill plan into a draft paper which later came to be called the "Interim Agreement for Peace and Self-Government in Kosovo"—replete with extensive annexes. There were to be no substantive revisions, or prolonged negotiations. It was served up on a take-it-or-leave-it basis, with what would happen if it was rejected left for NATO to decide. To stress its seriousness, a NATO-OSCE extraction force of 1,800 men formed up in Macedonia and NATO Secretary-General Solana was authorized to take action if positive results were not forthcoming within just three weeks: a week to get down to business and two weeks to reach an agreement.

Again threatened by war, the Serbs slouched into Rambouillet. The Kosovar Albanians (including KLA members) were also suspicious, but in a more open frame of mind. Now enjoying virtually official recognition, the KLA became almost cocky, knowing that their rag-tag, will-o'-the-wisp military force which mingled with the populace would never be a target of NATO's bombs. Moreover, NATO (principally the US, Britain, France, and Germany) began the task of gathering upwards of 30,000 troops for the deployment of a peacekeeping force. It seemed that after struggling for decades, and after being ignored at Dayton, that the hour of the Kosovars had finally arrived. Although an unofficial ceasefire was in place, the KLA did not hide its expectation that all out fighting would resume when warmer weather arrived. Furthermore, it indicated that they would fight until they obtained independence. The Yugoslavs, led by Milutinovic and aware that the cards were stacked against them, held to a ten-point statement that the Contact Group had issued in January, stating as it did that Kosovo would remain an integral part of Serbia in Yugoslavia. With both sides in total opposition, the first week was wasted in argument over who was to blame. It was hardly an auspicious start.

However, US delegates felt from the outset that they could surely bring the Kosovars around. From all accounts, there was much arm around the shoulders friendly conversation and even jogging time together, even as the Albanians (particularly the KLA) made it clear that should they come to accept a deal, they would demand a referendum after three years of transitional rule. US Secretary of State Madeleine Albright arrived to help push things toward a conclusion. At a minimum, Washington wanted an agreement with the Kosovars so that Belgrade could be blamed for the failure as NATO readied itself and talked of impending massive air strikes. Solana said that he wouldn't wait long before going into action. Reports of some 430 NATO strike aircraft, US F-117 stealth jets, and B-52 bombers filled television screens. In Belgrade, Milosevic repeated his opposition to giving NATO unimpeded access to all of Yugoslavia. He cited Yugoslavia's sovereignty and then, with the clock ticking towards the 27 February deadline, he "stiffed" Chris Hill who had requested a meeting. Secretary Albright bore down on the Albanians, expecting them to get in line. However, none on the US side had expected that twenty-nine-year old Hashim Thaci, the KLA's political chief would remain so tough-minded. Claiming he had talked over the phone with his field commanders, Thaci stuck to his initial position that a promise of a referendum was their price for an agreement. Additionally, he also said that the KLA would be against disarming and that it would remain "their army." His words carried extra weight as it had become clear in recent weeks that the KLA overshadowed the entire delegation, including Rugova. Facing a total fiasco, Albright stopped the negotiating clock on 23 February after the Albanians refused to sign. The KLA, however, finally agreed to consult among themselves and return on 15 March. Albright called it a success, a conditional agreement.[9]

By the end of the week, NATO forces were pouring into Macedonia as heavy equipment landed at Thessaloniki. Milosevic matched the build-up by positioning some 7,500 troops and 200 tanks close to the border of Kosovo. He already had approximately 25,000 men in the province, only slightly more than what had been agreed upon in October. NATO Supreme Allied Commander in Europe General Wesley Clark flew to Belgrade and had a long and testy exchange with him. Clark had already measured President Milosevic with a jaundiced eye when trying to get him to reduce force levels and he personally believed that Milosevic was to blame—that the KLA was justified in fighting given Yugoslavia's practices in Kosovo. A US reporter in conversation with the general was left with the assessment that NATO's aircraft, once the order was given, would rapidly destroy Milosevic's ability to wage war in Kosovo, thereby preventing any repeat of Racak. This, and other optimistic assumptions, would come back to haunt Western leaders in the weeks ahead.[10]

For the moment, however, an almost palpable enthusiasm held sway as US Defense Department spokesmen and NATO briefers ticked-off the impressive array of land, sea, and air power that was converging on Kosovo. And, given the gravity of the situation, it soon became obvious that General Clark would be central to the success or failure of NATO's greatest undertaking since its founding. Assuming command in 1997, he had participated at Dayton and was deeply involved with SFOR Bosnia. He had been first in his class at West Point and had been decorated in Vietnam for bravery. And, like his president, he was from Arkansas and had been a Rhodes Scholar at Oxford. Intense and driven, and highly competitive, Clark shared the view of many that NATO's entire credibility was at stake in Kosovo. And, while displaying distain for the semi-obsolete Yugoslav army, the slim, cerebral Clark would come to ask for, and receive, the most sophisticated weapons in the US inventory: Tomahawk cruise missiles; Nighthawk F-117 stealth fighters; B-2 bombers; AWACs electronic support aircraft; lumbering old B-52 bombers; A-10 Warthog tank busters; and squadrons of Apache attack helicopters. Although US navy and air force fighters and bombers would come to handle upwards of eighty percent of the total missions flown, the political and military might of over half a billion people had lined up against a small, poor country of ten million. Almost personalizing the conflict, Clark vowed that he would soon smash Milosevic!

After almost a year of on-again, off-again, threats by NATO and the Contact Group, the credibility of the West *was* at stake. If really effective diplomacy had been used, force may not have been necessary. But it had been a year of ultimatums and legitimization of the KLA—despite kidnappings, assassinations, atrocities, and outright armed revolt—all aimed at Milosevic. Had anyone given him any incentives like reducing sanctions and Yugoslavia's isolation? Had anyone talked seriously with him about a Yugoslav plan for autonomy? No. He had been pushed more and more into a corner. Even after Rambouillet broke up, Belgrade talked of a need for UN involvement, a larger OSCE and of a peacekeeping role for the Russians. However, it was very late in the day. The Contact Group (and especially the US) faced the dire prospect of failure on the eve of NATO's fiftieth birthday bash in Washington. Policy pundits and talking heads were questioning its purpose and worth.[11]

There shouldn't have been any question in anyone's mind, no matter how muddled his response in Kosovo might have been, that Clinton could not be seen to have been made a fool of by Milosevic. Some would argue that the US president might even welcome a foreign crisis just then so that he could be seen standing tall and asserting leadership. Certainly, the US was again demonstrating that the Europeans were unable to deal with their own security problems. This was, after all, the main reason for a US effort to continue its dominance of NATO, and through it, to extend its influence in Europe. And, just how muddled was this policy after all? As in Bosnia, intervention in Kosovo pleased many Islamic powers. This and SFOR's involvement in Bosnia had shifted NATO's focus to southeast Europe where Washington traditionally had ties with NATO members Turkey and Greece, thereby putting pressure on them to resolve their differences. Now, also, Albania and Macedonia had become US client states. And, there was Romania and Bulgaria. With the importance Washington had assigned to Caspian oil and gas and new energy avenues westward, particularly its insistence on building a new pipeline through Turkey, the need to assure stability and control from the Balkans over to Central Asia—including the Aegean and the eastern Mediterranean—could increasingly be argued as a strategic necessity. What was expected to be a brief bombing campaign was a small price to pay for knocking Milosevic off his high horse and putting the Serbs in their place.[12]

As for the Britain of Prime Minister Tony Blair, the very close personal relationship between the occupants of 10 Downing Street and the White House was well known. Clinton had helped Blair on Northern Ireland. The similarly youthful Blair, who had once worn a Beatles haircut, but who now envied Conservative Party ex-prime ministers Thatcher and Major for their splendid little wars in the Falklands and Iraq, was more than ready to reassert the UK's special relationship with the US. He had been railing against Milosevic for months. France had emotional ties with Serbia going back to

World War One. They had fought side by side, and a Yugoslav king had been assassinated on French soil. But, President Jacques Chirac pushed that aside and thought of his soldiers who had died in Bosnia under Serbian gunfire. He felt that his patience had been tried enough. A blood debt was owed. German Chancellor Gerhard Schroeder was relatively new to his responsibilities and was aware that there was reluctance within his coalition among the Greens and even in his own party towards the idea of waging war on Belgrade. Germany's hands had been bloodied there. But, as his advisors probably explained, to do so was in keeping with Bonn's previous policy of dismantling Yugoslavia. And, equally important, it was looked upon as a historic opportunity to engage Germany militarily outside of its borders for the first time since World War Two. Thus, all were ready to respond militarily, especially Washington, where there was an intense, stoked up prejudice against everything Serbian.

Signals of KLA acceptance of Rambouillet were soon in coming. Demaci, who opposed signing the accords, resigned from the KLA leadership. It is a moot point whether he was aware that Thaci had received implicit assurances from Albright (probably through her spokesman James Rubin) that there would be a referendum before leaving Rambouillet. Reportedly, Albright also conveyed the message that once the KLA agreed and Milosevic refused, the NATO bombing campaign would begin. The KLA had judged correctly over the previous year that their attacks would be met by Belgrade with reprisals against its civilian supporters and that, viewing the resultant carnage, the US and NATO would ultimately intervene on its behalf. What Thaci was told in effect, contrary to repeated earlier denials, was that NATO would become the KLA's air force.[13]

Thaci returned to Paris as the head of a self-proclaimed provisional government. He also had an official invitation from Washington for himself, and an Albanian delegation. Former Senator Robert Dole, an influential advocate for the Kosovars, had flown out to Skopje at Clinton's request to smooth things in advance. The young KLA commander also consulted with Tirana, which voiced its assurance of acceptance. To keep the pressure on the Serbs, Holbrooke returned to Belgrade to remind Milosevic what a rejection would mean. In fact, he was but one of many envoys who beat a path to his door to urge him to agree. However, despite this, and a personal liking for Holbrooke, he continued to object to the fact that it would be NATO that would occupy Kosovo. And, it angered him that Russia would not be allowed to play a peacekeeping role. Washington had made sure to keep them out. His delegation, again headed by Milutinovic, again objected to NATO's complete control (instead of the UN, or OSCE) and demanded several changes—even as

Milosevic massed his forces. Given Belgrade's refusal, the British and French co-chairman suspended talks on 18 March. Thaci signed the draft agreement. The Serbs packed their bags and left.

Others packed their bags as well. The OSCE mission in Kosovo, now up to full strength, was ordered out by Washington. Western diplomats in Belgrade also began to close the doors of their embassies and take their dependents to safety. Over the weekend, NATO officials met to fine-tune their latest, and last, threat, while Holbrooke prepared to meet for one last time with Milosevic. The Austrian, Petritsch, also made another attempt, but came away empty-handed. Then, US President Clinton spoke in unmistakable terms. Milosevic had to pull back or face bombing. Equally adamant, Milosevic had told the British and French foreign ministers that Yugoslavia was defending its territory from separatism, and its citizens and their "historic dignity from hooligans who don't know what history and dignity means." Holbrooke, who was not authorized to conduct negotiations, only to accept compliance, found Milosevic resigned to war with NATO. In two sessions, there was no meeting of minds, only meandering conversation tinged with regret. Clinton added that if NATO ignored Milosevic's actions, "It will be interpreted as a license to continue to kill. There will be more massacres, more refugees, more victims." An attack by NATO, he said, "was morally right, and in the vital interests of the United States!"

Milosevic's comment about the Kosovo Albanians was no doubt full of bitterness, for, from the day that they came out of Trepca mine in February 1989 to strike and demonstrate, his national project for Serbia had been in jeopardy. His words were dismissive of the Albanians and their aspirations. True, according to many reports, the KLA has its roots in organized criminal activity—drugs, smuggling, prostitution and the like. But could that describe an entire people? His remarks were similar to those of Krajisnik over in Bosnia— that the Muslims only knew to live as masters, or slaves. They spoke with an attitude, a certainty of Serbian superiority exactly the same as that expressed by Israelis when speaking of Palestinians, or other Arabs. Serbs and Albanians alike were molded by their experiences. Between 1912 until today, Kosovo has been periodically drenched in blood, with both power and control alternating between Turks, Serbians, and Albanians. Pogroms and expulsions have affected all. For President Clinton to moralize about integration and racial harmony in America was a poor example. It is necessary to read Milovan Djilas's masterful epic novel *Under the Colors*, which describes the ordeal of the Radak clan living under the Ottoman Turks in the latter part of the nineteenth century in western Kosovo, to get some idea of the brutality, violence, and constant struggle that had been life itself. And, if some like Radovan and Besim had made a transition to a better way of thinking, most had not. It was always a case of "us against them!"

Milosevic knew well what Serbian blood had been shed for Kosovo, and his political career had been built upon it. He would never give up Kosovo without a fight, even against the might of NATO. And, many Serbs felt the same way when they reported to their units. There were others who didn't care that much for Kosovo. But, when the bombs began to fall and NATO began to build up big in Albania and Macedonia, they rallied around their flag. The West was wrong to think that they would immediately turn on Milosevic. We also know now that US Secretary of State Albright strongly backed the bombing and erroneously believed that Milosevic would come to terms after a few days of air strikes. NATO's "green light" had come when Russian Prime Minister Yevgeni Primakov was en route to Washington. A phone call from US Vice-President Al Gore caused him to abruptly turn around in mid-air and return to Moscow—angered, prevented from presenting any arguments on Belgrade's behalf. Apart from Slavic solidarity, Moscow registered its strong objection to NATO action without the approval of the UN Security Council. Also, Yugoslavia was dealing with a separatist struggle within its own recognized borders. It was not a case of external aggression. Washington, it seems, didn't want to hear any of this. It wanted its war—now!

The cruise missiles didn't drop silently out of the night sky, but roared hundreds of miles at low altitudes before homing-in on their pre-selected targets. On impact, the detonation's shock wave broke the eardrums of those who had miraculously survived the blast itself. On the night of Wednesday, 24 March, some forty targets were bombed: airports, barracks, command communications, and storage depots. Belgrade and Pristina were particularly hard hit and civilian casualties resulted. General Clark, in the toughest of language that he often repeated in the weeks ahead said, "We're going to systematically and progressively attack, disrupt, degrade, devastate, and ultimately—unless President Milosevic complies with the demands of the international community—we're going to destroy his forces." This was yet another statement that would come back to haunt NATO's planners.

When it was over, seventy-eight days later, NATO had flown 37,200 missions (500 to 600 a day) and had dropped some 25,000 tons of ordnance, including 1,100 cluster bomb units containing 200,000 "bomblets" scattered about in civilian populated areas—often unexploded. Offshore, in the Adriatic, the US navy had launched hundreds of cruise missiles. Dissatisfied with the results, General Clark increased his striking power to over 1,200 combat aircraft, which attacked so-called "dual-use" targets in an effort to break civilian morale. Upwards of 1,000 civilians were killed and many more were wounded. Thirty-two road and railway bridges were destroyed or heavily damaged, including those over the Danube, which reduced traffic on that important waterway to a mere trickle. Railroad tracks and tunnels were cut at 16 places. Rail and bus stations, and civil airports, were hit, as were highways and road junctions. Factories, including those producing pharmaceuticals, foodstuffs, and clothing were bombed, not to mention machine tool, machine building and automobile factories. Petroleum refineries and power plants were taken out. Laser guided "smart bombs," graphite bombs, depleted uranium ordnance, and "dumb," old-style gravity bombs were used with devastating effect. In addition to power transmission lines, television and radio communications, and government buildings—civilian-related buildings in the hundreds were damaged, or totally destroyed. Decades of work and social investment were wiped out in a matter of weeks![14]

At the same time, the military structure that Clark had vowed to destroy went into action with telling effect. The VJ had formed up in the un-dramatic, methodical fashion as is customary with the Serbs when they go to war. It was not enough for NATO to get overly excited, but they had the men and materiel ready when NATO began its bombing campaign. They moved immediately with the first bombs and rounded on the KLA and the villages where they had been living with little mercy. The KLA fell back, fighting where it could, and running when it had to. The civilian population was left defenseless, and, as the death toll mounted, two-thirds of Kosovo's Albanians both fled and were driven into Macedonia and Albania proper. It was a repetition of 1944–45, a gigantic repetition of 1924–25. Given the horrors of the Bosnian war, NATO should have expected the worst once the bombing began. Until March, some 2,500 Albanians (including KLA) and two hundred Serbs had died in Kosovo, and a large number of Albanians and Serbs had been displaced and were living in the woods, or in different villages. But what happened after 24 March came as a complete surprise. Both Washington and NATO groped for explanations as 800,000 Albanians left Kosovo. And, in the process, the VJ, MUPs, specials and paramilitary killed several thousand more civilians—sometimes brutally. NATO's oft-repeated premise for waging the war, the prevention of a human catastrophe, had come to pass.[15]

It proved to be a strange war. The KLA was bloodied for sure, but the Kosovar civilians suffered much more. The VJ and others certainly took casualties, but more civilian damage was done. The rules of engagement for US-NATO were complex and were designed to reduce Allied casualties. Strike aircraft operated at high altitudes with very limited visual contact with their ground targets. Consequently, there were tragic mistakes—refugee columns mistaken for army convoys, passenger trains and buses in the wrong place at the wrong time, and misidentified buildings like the Chinese embassy in Belgrade. Only a few Allied aircraft were downed and their pilots were extracted. In the beginning, defiant Serbs wore targets to rock concerts in the center of Belgrade. They formed human chains on their bridges, day and night. Men slept in their factories and some died in the bombing. But it was the unending tide of Albanian refugees that filled television screens with tales of disaster. There were many young men among them, but the cameras tended to focus on children, the women, the old and the infirm. It was all as heart-wrenchingly appalling as it was unnecessary.

To President Clinton and Prime Minister Blair, it had been totally justified and necessary. In a real sense, they imposed a Balkan-style "truth" on the situation—their own. However, after weeks with no end in sight, other allies (the Italians, the Greeks, and even the Germans) began to urge that the Contact Group return to the diplomatic track. President Clinton had wrongly stated from the outset that a ground attack would not be launched. But, as events were unfolding, it appeared that this would be necessary if the Allies were to prevail. In fact, General Clark, on his own, began to push the planning for this eventuality early in the bombing campaign. At the same time, it was felt by some that NATO solidarity would shatter over this issue. No one, especially Washington, wanted to slug it out with the Serbs on the ground. The invasion routes into Kosovo were over very rough terrain, which favored "low-tech" defenders. And, it would have been close to impossible to get the numbers of troops and equipment in place to undertake an offensive that could have been successfully completed before winter. Even the US Apaches were having their problems, as two had crashed in training. Finally, and with great reluctance, Washington gave in and asked Russia to talk terms with Milosevic—now an indicted war criminal.[16]

Milosevic had tried to play the card of pan-Slavism earlier in the war, a ridiculous trial balloon proposing union with Russia and Belarus. Needless to say, it didn't fly. Nor did the Russian envoy Viktor Chernomyrdin, working with Finnish President Martti Ahtisaari, depart from the Contact Group's brief as to how the conflict could be ended. Milosevic, however, was able to win two important concessions from the Contact Group that were finally finessed into a G-7 formulation during meetings in Bonn. The first was that all NATO peacekeeping forces, now to include a Russian contingent, would come under the UN following the approval of the UN Security Council. The second was that Kosovo would remain within Yugoslavia as part of Serbia and the Contact Group (US) plan for a referendum after three years was to be dropped. While these end-game talks were going on, NATO eased off on Belgrade, but cooperated openly with the KLA by trying to wipe out a force of VJ at the Albanian border that had blocked a KLA counter-offensive. Called in quickly, B-52 bombers from Britain unloaded cluster bombs near Mount Pastrik. However, when KLA spotters combed the impact area no VJ bodies were found. As confirmed by many sources, almost the entire VJ pulled out of Kosovo on schedule along agreed upon exit routes in good order with relatively limited losses. Upon leaving, some displayed their three-fingered victory sign—still undaunted.[17]

But, if the Serbs had displayed their usual disdain of danger in adversity to win concessions on paper, the deal done under duress had an enormous downside, in fact, on the ground in Kosovo. Rambouillet had made provisions for a staged withdrawal of the VJ and the police from the province down to minimal levels as NATO peacekeeping forces took over in a transition of several months. Yugoslav flags and symbols would remain along with a small border force and a customs unit. However, after a war from which the UN had been excluded, no real preparations had been made to set up a functional civil administration. The various multinational peacekeeping components (mainly the US, British, and French) had an idea of what their duties would be as an occupation force. But the UN Mission in Kosovo (UNMIK) had to be created overnight, thrown together after the Security Council approved what NATO had allegedly done in the name of the international community. Kosovo was a power vacuum. And, as fast as NATO arrived, the KLA came out of their villages and out of the woods to set up their own administration. Closer to the point, as the many thousands of Kosovars returned from Macedonia and Albania, the KLA installed itself as a "government" simply by taking over offices and buildings at gun point. Its Interim Government of Kosovo (IGK) fast became a fact of life that UNMIK found itself forced to deal with.

NATO's entry into Kosovo was not without problems and had the drama of crisis. Not, as one would suppose, from the Yugoslavs, but from the Russians who had helped to strike the deal with Milosevic. To insure that they were not pushed out of the game, two hundred Russian soldiers assigned to peacekeeping duties in Bosnia made an unexpected dash for Pristina and took control of the airport before NATO had arrived. When he was informed, General Clark's visceral and angry reaction was to order British Kosovo Force (KFOR) commander General Michael Jackson to use his British and French troopers stationed in Macedonia to expel the Russians from the airport.

Confronted with an unexpected dilemma, Jackson refused—famously shouting down the phone to his superior officer, "I'm not about to start World War Three for you!" According to NATO procedures, the issue was reported up the chain of command of each country. British Prime Minister Blair backed up Jackson. The US Chairman of the Joint Chiefs of State, General Hugh Shelton, and President Clinton agreed that the risk of an armed clash with the Russians and an angry British ally was too high a price to pay to try to force Jackson to comply with Clark's decision. Russia's role, it was felt, could be kept to a minimum and its symbolic presence politically useful after weeks of seriously strained relations. However, it did demonstrate that the US military commander of NATO was prepared to use force, or the threat of force, to prevent Russia from playing a real role in Kosovo. And, it was not just one man's whim. The US immediately prevailed on Hungary, Romania, and Bulgaria to deny Russia's urgent over-flight requests, which, if granted, would have enabled Russia to bring in men, equipment, and supplies in quantity—a prospect opposed by Washington.[18]

Almost immediately, as well, the KLA directed its hatred of Belgrade against the Serbs who had remained and to a lesser extent against other minorities, such as the Roma gypsies. It's likely that anyone who had participated in war crimes against the Kosovars would have left with the VJ or before. Those who stayed probably had nowhere else to go, or felt they could somehow live with the victors. Either way, the Serbs began to be murdered with a sickening regularity as the Albanians took their revenge—even as they celebrated victory. And it *was* victory for the KLA and its increasingly unabashed US sponsors. Madeleine Albright came out to do her victory lap. A very determined and elated General Clark was idolized by cheering crowds of Albanians in Pristina who, in front of the TV cameras, were given tiny US flags to wave. There was Thaci, also, shaking hands as well, dressed in a new three-button suit and looking very much like a winner. Even reports in the US press that he had ordered the execution of several of his rivals within the KLA did not remove any of the gloss, or reduce his stature. The fact that he was being groomed by Albright and was often seen at the US military base near Urosevac was proof enough that he was Washington's man. Not long afterward, the KLA claimed it had been promised that they would be permitted to turn their small army into a "national guard"—their own defense force, as they put it. Additionally, as if that weren't enough, they were given additional time to turn in their weapons.[19]

* * *

It had now been a year since I had been in Belgrade and Kosovo, a year which saw the final catastrophe. So much had happened that there was no question of not going. But getting there was now very difficult. Olympic, or any other airline could no longer fly to Belgrade. Even the train no longer went because the main north-south rail line had been cut in several places by NATO bombing. I had to overnight in "Thess," get down at the Macedonian border, and then continue on only to Skopje. From there, I took a bus routed east through Kumanovo. Then, when we reached the Yugoslav border, I was told I had to get off, as they had to check my visa with Belgrade. The bus left and I was told to wait in a small room. As it was late Sunday afternoon, I thought I might have to wait until Monday before they could find someone to talk to. I sat, paced back and forth, and vented my anger, all to no avail. No one was hostile. They just ignored me until two hours later when I was told that everything was "okay." I was free to go. The police were all smiles now and jokingly suggested that I write about their good security. I shared their humor as best as I could, but I needed a bus. "No problem," they assured me and after an hour, one came through for Leskovac. I finally arrived at the Excelsior after midnight, tired and hungry. "No problem." A *pivo* and an omelet appeared in only minutes.

Over breakfast, I tried to retrace my bus route on my map. We had left the highway at several places to get around downed bridges, caved-in sections and bomb craters. We had detoured at slow speed on country roads. Even there, near a small bent bridge, I had seen bomb damage to homes. Nis had been hit hard—official buildings and factories, and again, houses and apartments. At night, I was unable to tell what might have been used by the VJ, or police. Most, however, had a civilian look to them. In some places the damage was very extensive. Of course, I immediately phoned Dragomir. He had refused to take shelter during the raids and had stayed in his apartment to write an account of the bombing. When we met, he was still all smiles. "See," he said, stretching out his big arms, "I am still alive. NATO can't destroy me, or our society!" He was very philosophical in his tender, tough Serbian way. His family, altogether, had sent fifteen reservists to fight with the VJ. "Yes, things happened down there. But, it's part of our country. We're ready to fight for it, even now." There was nothing I could say.

NATO might not be able to destroy Dragomir, but downtown Belgrade had taken some heavy hits. On Knez Milosa, the mammoth very modern Ministry of Defense building was shattered, its insides a burned out shell. The beautiful nineteenth-century Serbian Ministry of Information was badly damaged. A bomb had hit about where I had visited from time to time. Its twin Foreign Ministry building was boarded up, its windows blown in. A police building was gutted. And, there was the American embassy. All it had suffered was some angry graffiti and a few thrown eggs. I took a taxi to see the Serbian radio-TV station where fifteen journalists had died at their work. The tower block across the Sava where Milosevic had his SPS offices was blackened. The Chinese embassy, standing isolated and clearly identifiable, had taken several hits. Over in Topcider, Arkan's new villa stood on a corner untouched. It had satellite dishes and an antenna array on its roof, suggesting that it was more than just a residence. Instead, NATO had bombed a hotel and had killed an innocent man. Over on Knez Mihaila, the US Cultural Center was trashed and being used as a hangout for kid capitalists who all had their wares spread out on the sidewalk. I took in the slogans scrawled on the walls: "NATO Killers," "Death To Sadism," and "Damn You Columbus For Your Curiosity!"

I was curious how the people of Belgrade were holding up after an intensive bombing campaign that had smashed much of Yugoslavia's infrastructure and had flattened dozens of its factories—a war Washington had assured the world was not directed at the people. Another 500,000 workers were now unemployed. Grown men broke down and cried when they found their workplaces in ruins. Some experts estimated the losses at US$30–60 billion. After this blow, and Kosovo, it was doubly foolish to expect them to rise up against Milosevic, especially when the opposition was so disorganized. Now, when thousands more were struggling just to survive, most had no time for politics. They might attend rallies occasionally out of curiosity, but real active involvement required time and energy. The students had both, but I saw them distributing leaflets that most adults just looked at and handed back. Dragomir and David had dropped out. And, because the institutes didn't have money to fund research, very few were publishing or attending conferences abroad. The country had, intellectually imploded. Such professionals who still remained, who had not gone abroad, searched for some sideline to get into.[20]

Dragomir, it seemed, had become a minor celebrity. He had learned to cook meat-less meals while doing his research at Serbian and Greek monasteries. Now, with the sharp drop in incomes, people ate less meat and he had cooked dozens of dishes on TV at the Hyatt Hotel. His endless varieties of vegetables and soups were a big hit. He now supervised the kitchen of a popular restaurant in Terazije. Once he took me home for bean soup, which he lovingly watched over with glasses of slivovitz—while talking about his royalist father ("Wes, you must move your body when you mention the dead!") and of a grandfather who had been a wealthy landowner. After the soup, and more slivovitz, he talked about what it meant to him to be a Serb, to believe in their special destiny under God. He removed a gold-covered bible from its hiding place, unwrapped it, and then kissed it. He said they would starve to death before ever parting with it. Very simply put, "Serbdom" means to stand up for God and country—for their Serbia![21]

But, Belgrade wasn't coming together. UNHCR was always good, but other offices had moved. People weren't answering the phone. The war had disrupted the lives of millions. When I tried to set up an appointment with Vojislav Kostunica, I was politely rebuffed. After two days of this, I finally decided to get down to Kosovo.

The bus situation was uncertain. Pristina was still in the schedule, but the drivers (for reasons of safety) were going only as far as the Serbian-controlled side of Mitrovica. And, to travel alone into an area where emotions were running so high, didn't seem wise. It was one of the few times in eight years that I felt uneasy. So, I returned to Skopje to enter from the south. Luckily, as it turned out, UNMIK had a shuttle to Pristina every morning and it took others like myself. It was an odd experience to get waved through at the border with no Yugoslav flag, police or passport check. Likewise, I was amazed to see KFOR troops of all descriptions—US, UK, French, Italian, Polish, Norwegian, and others in trucks and armored vehicles. Helicopters chuttered overhead to investigate distant columns of smoke, which might be a field being burned off, or a Serbian or Roma home going up in flames.

I checked into the Grand Hotel, which, like everything else, was now under new management. Its Serbian staff had left, or had been run off. It was now all Albanian. The German deutsche mark had replaced the dinar. The reception counter knew its job and a young, female "meeter-greeter" was at the entrance. I wondered how many had worked there ten years earlier. They were all very friendly and urged me, a "very welcome American," to use their press center. It was exactly where Radovan's had been, if only more modest. Very immodest had been the attractive, long-legged young lady, wearing a peach-colored pantsuit, who had preceded me up the stairs. She settled herself into a chair and immediately became the center of attention. It wasn't her gauzy, see-through blouse that caused so much commotion among the men. It was because she was Thaci's personal secretary. She very proudly announced they had received an invitation from Albright to travel to Washington and it was obvious that the prospect pleased her immensely. She added that Thaci was now in Tirana and would return after the weekend. I introduced myself and asked if she would help me meet him. "But everyone is trying to see the 'prime minister,'" she exclaimed—acting not a little put upon. "It will require days!" I told her that "President" Rugova had not been as difficult and left. It was clear that Thaci had slipped on the mantle of power just as easily as his new suit.[22]

UNMIK headquarters was a scene of confusion and staffed by young Albanian men and women. It took over an hour to get through to the secretary of Jock Covey, who was now deputy to UNMIK Special Representative of the Secretary (SRSG) Bernard Kouchner. Covey was out of the country, so that closed off that avenue. I did pick up a press release, which stated that the second session of the Kosovo Transition Council would be held the next day with Thaci in attendance for the first time. Apparently, UNMIK was unaware he was in Albania. A Voice of America radio correspondent complained that he hadn't been able to see the UNMIK press officer. I went over to where NATO had taken over the sports complex to get a KFOR identity badge, and then looked for something to eat. Again, I was amazed at the many nationalities: blacks from Africa shuffled by with UN badges dangling from their necks; Asians from Bangladesh and Malaysia; beefy, red-faced German policemen sat at a sidewalk café drinking beer. I met three blue-uniformed US cops who were there to open a police academy. They were all retired and expected to be there for six months teaching "democratic" police methods, whatever that means. Over a burger, an exhausted German aid worker from Prizren expressed her anger and frustration. "We are mostly making people fill in forms. I don't feel like I've helped at all." She said that Serbs there were being murdered every night.

That afternoon, I hung around the press center and spoke with its director Bekim Collaku. He was a young man who declined to talk much about himself. He said that the KLA and its Interim Government of Kosovo (IGK) controlled most of the province, except for the north and some Serbian enclaves; that they were trying hard not to antagonize UNMIK; but that they were a fact of life and acted in accordance with their peoples' wishes and expectations. He explained how, recently, IGK "finance minister" Adem Grabovci had met Paul Davis, and "deputy local government minister" Sokul Dobruna, Michael Cox—both of USAID, which suggested that Washington had no reluctance in dealing with them. He also took satisfaction in the fact that the KLA was declared "in compliance" by KFOR with regard to handing in weapons. He pointed out that many KLA officers and IGK officials could wear side arms, accompanied by armed bodyguards. In other words, the persons responsible for the routine murder of helpless civilians were being well protected.

That night, random gunshots could be heard from my room. The next morning, I went out to Gracanica to deliver some food items. Two British troopers guarded its entrance. To my surprise, Sister Katerina, whom I had met years earlier, was there in her habit looking just as I had remembered. Even though the compound was crammed with refugees, she insisted on making coffee. She told how she had had to flee from another monastery some days earlier and that close to thirty churches had been destroyed or damaged since NATO's entry into Kosovo. The worst part of it, she said, was that they felt it would continue. Knowing that what she said was most likely true, words failed me. On impulse, I taxied over to Gazimestan to the "Field of Blackbirds." The place was empty, its memorial tower still standing, but unguarded. Gazi or *Ghazi* is Turkish for a hero or conqueror. Mestan is the name of a standard bearer who was killed in the battle of Kosovo in 1389. It was overcast and cloudy. I stood in the brooding silence and listened. Out there, under the mounds of earth, the bones of men of two faiths lay amidst the debris of battle. And now, Kosovo and the ancient church lands of Metohia were threatened with the return of Muslim rule.

That afternoon, a crowd of journalists (myself included) had an interminable wait for the council meeting to break up. Inside were Kouchner, the LDK's Rugova, Bilal Sherif of the KLA, Mehmet Hajrizi and Rexhep Oosja of the LBD, Sezar Shaipi of the Turkish People's Party, Numan Balic of SDA, and independents Blerim Shala and Veton Surroi. The Serbs had Momcilo Trajkovic of the Serbian Resistance Movement and Bishop Artemije from the Serbian Orthodox Church. KFOR's commander, General Jackson, his aides, and UNMIK deputies, sat in as observers. When they came out, all that Kouchner said was that it had focused on security, and that he hoped that the next such session would be conducted in a more businesslike fashion. In fact, it had been stormier than he had let on, as Trajkovic had proposed that Kosovo be partitioned. I asked Kouchner if Albright's invitation to Thaci would unduly influence the political situation—given that elections were expected the following spring. Smirking, he deflected it, stating that he thought that the exposure would be beneficial. When I put the same question to Surroi (the editor of *Koha Ditore*), he just laughed and said that I should check with Thaci's travel agent. It was as if he was referring to Madame Albright. After a few minutes, it ended, and the KFOR officers came past—the Brits in battle jackets and berets, the Americans in heavy armored vests and helmets.

That evening, the *korzo* near the Grand Hotel teemed with young people in a holiday mood—eating roasted corn, candy, ice cream sticks, and sipping soft drinks. Lights had been strung up and Albanian music blared out into the night. American and Albanian flags were everywhere. Kiosks offered Adem Jashari and Skanderbeg T-shirts. Others the double eagle on outline maps of

Greater Albania. There were khaki camouflage KLA army uniforms for kids! Up at the end of the street I found two British soldiers bargaining for imitation Nike running shoes. They were from Scotland and would rotate home in October. I walked to my favorite Serb-Roma restaurant and found that it was now an Albanian café. I was bluntly told that it had never been a restaurant— ever. I ran into a young American high school teacher from Los Angeles who had spent several weeks wandering around Kosovo. He was staying in an apartment that had once been owned by a Serb for US$5 a day. It had water and lights and had been set up by its Albanian "owner" with a mattress and a new lock on the door. This was being repeated all over.

On Sunday, I walked around taking photos of bomb damage. As in Belgrade, it was extensive in places and not in others. UNMIK's building had been government, but was untouched. Others were hit hard. My favorite photo was what looked like a theatre that had "Adem Jashari" boldly painted over its entrance. On one wall was a statement likely put there by the KLA (*Ushtria Clirimtare e Kosoves,* or UCK as the KLA is more properly known): "2 Korrik 1999 NATO! Toni Bler Klinton Shroder Shirak Prodi Robin Kuk Sollana Klark Xh. Shea" and a very large "Olbright" at the end, with a "Thank You!" underneath. The message couldn't have been clearer. It was obvious that either by NATO's acquiescence, or intent, that the KLA was gaining control over Kosovo and the Serbs were being driven out. An irrevocable fundamental change was under way.

Bekim was still at the press center, working on the IGK bulletins that he churned out. He looked tired, had a growth of stubble, and was wearing the same clothes for the third day. Nonetheless, his bulletins were reasonably well written in English and I told him so. As he warmed to that, I asked him to explain the origins of the KLA and repeated Rugova's ridiculous assertion that the KLA didn't exist—that it was a provocation by the Yugoslav authorities. He just laughed and said that everyone knew that an army was being formed. He explained the involvement of the Jasharis and the other clans, and then told of fundraising abroad. He said large amounts of money came from the US-Albanian community. I mentioned that I had seen Americans on TV who were preparing to go to Kosovo and asked him if they actually had made it over. He said that about seventy had arrived and were formed into what was called the "Atlantic Brigade." And, they did fight, he said, but thought that they were now back in the States. It was an incredible reversal of fortune for the KLA— and all because of US and NATO intervention.

I shuttled out on Monday morning. Gutted houses passed by. One was flying a tiny red Albanian flag. Up on a hillside, a mass grave was being uncovered. Even small factory buildings had been bombed. I asked an Irish army officer what he thought of the situation. He was very blunt. "This is a first class cock-up! Neither KFOR, nor UNMIK, know what they're doing. This place is in chaos, with no laws or police. It's being taken over by the KLA and the Albanian mafia!" As he had once served in Beirut, I assumed he knew what he was talking about. His comments certainly bore out my own impressions. He said two or three Serbs were murdered each night in Pristina and elsewhere, often shot through their apartment doors. An elderly woman was physically drowned in her own bathtub. At Crkvena Vodica, there was a drive-by shooting of a Serb café that wounded four. The same car threw a live grenade into a children's playground. An Irish aid worker was with us as well. She was from Pec where she said Serbs were being murdered so frequently that KFOR had to put them inside guarded compounds until they could be evacuated. A large black Mercedes passed us in the opposite direction. It had Albanian plates. I had seen several around Pristina. They might have been criminals over to set up protection and prostitution, or just businessmen out to purchase Serbian property at bargain prices.[23]

UNMIK's assertion that the security situation was stabilizing was quite untrue. In fact, NATO-UNMIK's presence to date didn't begin to translate into a protective force, or a civil administration worthy of the name. By mid-August, only 736 of an authorized international police force of 3,100 had arrived. And, it would be months before any new trainees would be ready for duty. Also, there was no code of law. UNMIK had wanted to use those Yugoslav laws that met international standards. However, the Kosovars refused, and insisted on their pre-1989 legal code. When the members on the legislative council all threatened to resign, Kouchner proposed that new laws be drafted. Panels of lawyers and jurists were assembled and they began the long task of working on new laws, one by one. Meanwhile, the IGK issued its own laws dealing with the key questions of residency and citizenship. It attempted to project an image of legality, but, in reality it was backed by the KLA and "the gun." Political moderates like Rugova, and others, were being pushed aside. Thaci and the KLA represented the face of Kosovo's coming rulers.[24]

Since I had left Kosovo, things had only gotten worse. Now, Kouchner openly displayed his sympathies by paying tribute to the Jasharis as "freedom fighters" and by participating in pro-Albanian demonstrations. Developments were occurring that impacted very heavily on Kosovo's future status. Supposedly to avoid a clash with Thaci's IGK, but perhaps as intended all along, KLA cadre and ordinary members were being converted into a Kosovo

Protection Corps commanded by Agim Ceku. In 1998–99, he became military chief of staff after having made a bloodstained odyssey from the ZNG and Croatian army to the KLA. The new "corps" was being advertised as only a civilian organization for civil emergencies such as natural disasters—floods, forest fires and the like. However, no one, not even UNMIK, believed that the KLA had turned in the bulk of its weapons. The KLA, itself, said it was the foundation for its future army.

As for the new police, many KLA members were being recruited into its ranks. Almost no Serbs, or men of other ethnic origins, were being trained. Some applied, but dropped out after being threatened by the Albanians. The situation had become so bad that the target numbers of international police was raised to 6,000. Then, in mid-December, UNMIK was forced to admit that it and NATO were unable to administer Kosovo alone. Kouchner brought Thaci, Rugova, and Oosja into a power sharing arrangement that was to run from 31 January 2000 until elections later in the year. KFOR's new German commander, General Klaus Reinhardt, was soon to order more patrolling, more roadblocks, and more vehicle checks in order to stem the rising tide of crime and anti-Serbian violence. Possibly as a hint, he sent an extra battalion over to the US zone. Finally, there remained the fact that close to 250,000 Serbs and other nationalities had left the Albanian-dominated areas.[25]

If Kosovo and NATO's ill-thought out intervention had turned into a human catastrophe in terms of the suffering and the numbers of Albanians killed after the bombs began to fall, and the numbers of Serbs and others killed and driven out after the bombing ended (not to mention the toll of death and destruction elsewhere in Yugoslavia), it was, in narrow national terms, being described as a US strategic success. In a Balkan "bartered bride" situation, NATO had been preserved and even expanded, and the world had been given a massive demonstration of US air power—against a small country that could offer little resistance to the bombing. Its aircraft, weaponry, and heavy lift capacity were shown to be unrivaled. Through NATO, the US had projected its power to the south and east—into the Balkans. And, not one man had been lost in combat. Some said that the military textbooks had been rewritten. Albania and Macedonia were added to a long list of client states. And, it appeared that another was in the making—Kosovo. US Army men and women were now on duty at a new base in southern Kosovo—one with a made-for-TV name, Camp Bondsteel. From there, troopers resembling robots with their body armor went on patrol without interpreters, without any way to talk to the local population. But, in reality, there wasn't much desire to know what was going on in the back alleys of Gnjilane. It was enough for US Secretary of

Defense William Cohen to visit at Christmas to praise them for their peacekeeping role. Also along were former football stars Terry Bradshaw of the Pittsburgh Steelers and Mike Singletary of the Chicago Bears. Other NATO members soldiering in less Baskin-Robbins surroundings derisively referred to the facility as "Disneyland East."[26]

* * *

And, the effort to remove Milosevic continued. As soon as the bombing stopped, US officials showed up in Montenegro to talk to Djukanovic. Having grown wary of Draskovic and Djindjic, Washington (without any sense of restraint) went all out to win Milo over to its side. US special envoy Robert Gelbard held what amounted to a war council with Yugoslav oppositionists in Podgorica, backed up by US$9 million to pay for Milosevic's ouster. In late June, Djukanovic flew to Ljubljana and met US President Clinton for the first time. Then, in August, Montenegro announced its demands to recast the relationship between the two federal entities, which, if adopted, would make it independent in everything, but name. Should Belgrade refuse, Milo said he would go to a referendum. Milosevic proposed talks, but also began to line up the support of some of the larger clans through Momir Bulatovic and his own political "mafia." Milosevic also took steps to ensure the loyalty of his VJ commanders serving there. The Clinton administration had all but stated that it would welcome a civil war in what remained of Yugoslavia to get rid of Milosevic. If it continued as it had, pitting Milo and his police against Milosevic and his VJ, a blow up in beautiful little Montenegro was indeed possible.

Whatever the disaster, however imperfect the response, US interventionist policy has slowly taken shape in Slovenia, Croatia, Bosnia, Macedonia, Albania, and now Kosovo. It was anti-Milosevic and anti-Serb (and, anti-Russian as well) in an effort to remove an obstacle to its hegemony in southeastern Europe. And, after having successfully ended the decades old dream of the Kurds in Turkey by colluding in the capture by Ankara of PKK leader Ocalan, it finally focused on reducing tensions between Greece and Turkey over divided Cyprus and control of the Aegean. Athens soon came under tremendous US pressure to drop its veto of Turkey's candidacy to EU membership. However, to his credit, Clinton also exerted pressure on Turkey to allow UN-sponsored talks to begin between Clerides and Denktash. And, he said all the right things during his well-timed November visits to Greece and Turkey, which helped to improve the atmosphere between the two antagonists. Then, with Turkey seemingly acquiescing to Nicosia's EU entry, a EU Summit at Helsinki in December agreed in principle to begin the process for Ankara's own accession.

It was during a first ever visit by a US President to Turkey that Clinton pledged "... a Europe that includes Turkey... and a (US) partnership." Turkey's president, Suleyman Demiral, provided much greater detail when he stated, "We are working together for peace, stability, welfare, and security of a vast geography, from the Balkans to the Caucasus, from Central Asia to the Middle East and Europe, and developing together a political agenda in accordance with the new political conditions of the world." His remarks accurately reflected the reality of the situation. In Istanbul, on the margins of an OSCE meeting attended by Clinton on 18 November, the presidents of the US, Turkey, Azerbaijan, Turkmenistan, and Georgia signed documents setting into motion the construction of a controversial US$2.4 billion Baku-Ceyhan pipeline for which Washington had lobbied for years. The deal, which was described by Clinton as simply filling the need for alternative routes, effectively locks Russia and Iran out of the transport of Caspian oil.

At that meeting, Clinton aimed sharp words at Russian President Boris Yeltsin over human rights and the latter's military campaign against Islamic separatists in Chechnya—pointedly suggesting a strong similarity with Kosovo. Obviously angry, Yeltsin left abruptly. His defense boss, General Sergeyev, went so far as to accuse the US of stirring up trouble in Chechnya and the Caucasus. Supportive of Russia's own views, even Western observers said that the pipeline project was but one part of a US effort to supplant Russian influence in Central Asia by promoting the independence of those oil and gas wealthy states from Moscow—a region Russia regards as its own "Near Abroad." Clinton himself said that the pipeline deal was one of his biggest foreign policy successes. Links between the Balkans, Turkey, the Caucasus, the Middle East, and Central Asia became more and more evident with each new development.[27]

The other side of the coin to the US thrust into the Balkans, the Caucasus, and on into Central Asia, is the resurgence of Islam in those three regions. Hardly a decade earlier, hundreds of mujahideen volunteers, who had fought in Afghanistan against the Soviet Union's occupation force (many trained and equipped by the American CIA and Pakistan security), were ready to continue their jihad elsewhere. Some of them went to Bosnia. And, when the Sarajevo side needed arms, Washington winked at their supply by Iran and even facilitated deliveries by the Turkish air force. Saudi Arabia, Malaysia, and other Muslim states had helped as well. When that conflict ended, Iran had by then attached hundreds of "special advisors" to the Bosniak military and security forces. Washington protested, but friendships forged in adversity continued. Next, the US and NATO agreed that Turkey would play a key role training and supplying the Bosniak army, a situation which continues to today. Turkey, the Saudis, the Gulf States, and even Jordan provide project aid. However, the US never expected that Bosnia would become a haven for terrorists. An arrest was made in Germany, and Algerians linked to the Armed Islamic Group (GIA), the Afghan war, and Osama bin Laden were arrested in the US with bomb-making materials. Fellow conspirators in France had earlier planned to bomb a G-7 meeting in Lille. Several of those involved carried Bosnian passports.[28]

Albania opened its doors to Islam after the downfall of Hoxha. Its mosques and religious schools were rebuilt and hundreds of young men are awarded scholarships each year to study in Kuwait, Jordan, Egypt, Libya, Syria, and especially Saudi Arabia. There, they are deeply indoctrinated in Wahabism, the most radically fundamentalist interpretation of Islam amongst the Sunni majority within the Muslim world. Wahabism has taken a strong hold in Pakistan, Afghanistan and in Chechnya. Saudi-trained Albanian mullahs became active in Kosovo from 1995 on. Islamic institutions were active as well: the Islamic Development Bank, the Islamic Charity Project International, the World Assembly of Islamic Youth, and, of course, OIC. Among them were Egyptian extremists suspected of targeting the US embassy in Tirana. A few were arrested and extradited back to Cairo, but not before a shoot-out had occurred. It was believed that they had ties to bin Laden.[29]

Regarding Kosovo, the Saudi connection has already been cited. And, as happened in Bosnia, there were of Iranian efforts to influence and penetrate the KLA—its Shi'ite orientation notwithstanding. And, beyond dispute, is Turkey's return to the area. It provided air bases during NATO's air campaign and 1,000 men from the Turkish army operate in the German sector near Prizren. Their presence is far more than symbolic because Turkey has one of the largest Albanian communities in Europe, and it had provided military training to the KLA. Old historic ties are now being renewed and even reinforced. However, a looming issue is what KLA veterans will do in a war-wracked economy to survive. Jobs were always scarce and will now be even more difficult to find. It will be tempting, especially for those who join the police and local administration, to return to criminal activities. This is particularly worrisome because the Kosovo trade drug to Europe has been established for many years and Turkish-Albanian-Italian mafia ties have become even closer. Now, given what some are calling the "Green Transversal"—that arc of Islamic influence from Islamabad to Sarajevo—we may see the flow of heroin base from poppy fields in Afghanistan to drug refineries in Turkey and on to Europe and the US through a KLA that requires large amounts of money to prepare for its push for full independence. After NATO's war, no one can believe that the Kosovars will ever accept autonomy under Yugoslavia. Too much has happened for that to be possible. And, after all, the KLA is bent on creating its Greater Albania.[30]

As for NATO, Kosovo proved beyond doubt that it's an alliance for war, not just a nice civil institution that spreads democracy and stability around Europe. Pushed by US strategic interests, it had come close to a clash with Russia. That caused a rift within NATO's high command that was eventually smoothed over, although the US and the Europeans remained as divided as ever over how the EU will upgrade its own strike capabilities. The admission of the Czech Republic, Hungary, and Poland into NATO was advanced over protests by Moscow as the Kosovo crisis deepened. Their first act as new NATO members was to participate in a war against a neighboring country. Although all were expected to be politically correct and toe the line, this particularly bothered Prague and it refused for weeks to agree to land and over-flight passage. Poland, it seems, only agreed to join in on "peacekeeping" tasks after the war was over. Hungary found itself right on the front line. Although it had lined up against Yugoslavia almost a full decade earlier, it strenuously resisted the idea of being used as a route for a land invasion and only agreed to NATO's use of Taszar air base. But, as expected, its center-right nationalist government began to make demands for the return to autonomy for its 300,000-minority community in Vojvodina. That it should play such a role after the atrocities it had committed there during World War Two is outrageous.[31]

And, if NATO's credibility was at stake before the bombing began, some were arguing that the issue was still open. The question was whether European members were willing to take casualties in out-of-theater operations. The US had stated at the outset that it was not contemplating a land invasion of Kosovo, a position shared by all except the UK. Even its Apache helicopters never saw action because it meant escalation and casualties. However, with Prime Minister Blair pushing the issue, and with the bombing campaign dragging on, it's likely that invasion options were being explored and that a final decision would have had to be made by early July. We know that NATO Supreme Allied Commander in Europe, General Wesley Clark, was making preparations. If Milosevic had remained defiant, and NATO's limited war faced failure, Clinton surely would have had to reverse course. A land invasion, even if ultimately successful, would have been very unpopular with Europeans and most Americans. The war, in fact, was a close run affair, both for Milosevic and the NATO alliance. In a moment of candor, German Chancellor

Schroeder expressed his doubts that NATO would want to run a repeat of Kosovo.[32]

The US had marginalized the UN before the bombing began and NATO went to war without a vote by the UN Security Council. This, the fact that Yugoslavia was not engaged in external aggression, and NATO's violation of that country's border, effectively destroyed a body of international law that had applied for fifty years. While it's true that the UN Secretary-General was reinvested with authority after the fact, the damage has been done. And, now, a cash-strapped UNMIK lacks the money to do the job given it—the cost of two days of NATO bombing. Efforts to contain nuclear proliferation have been damaged as well, as some countries will conclude that only the possession of the bomb will prevent being shoved around on the world stage. Ominously, Russia soon reversed its long-standing policy of "no first use" of nuclear weapons and, pushed by NATO expansion and US plans to set up a "missile shield," is now developing new generation weaponry of its own. The world has become a much more dangerous place than it was just one short year ago.

In the face of that, perhaps in a reflective, even guilty mood while NATO bombs were falling, Germany's "Green" Foreign Minister, Joschka Fischer, proposed that, after the dust had settled, that the EU come forward with what he called a "Balkan Stability Pact." He sketched out the idea with a fine feeling for history, stating as he did that the goal of the pact would be to rebuild the Balkans, uplift it, and do what is needed to bring its countries into the EU as full members by 2014—the hundredth anniversary of the beginning of World War One. The Balkans, he argued, must be finally integrated with Western Europe's advanced economy and its institutions. It was a wise and farseeing proposal, one that would do much to develop the region and encourage it to outgrow the disastrous nationalist causes, which have always led to equally disastrous foreign interventions. Most immediately, it would help to ease the loss, pain, and disruption that the war had caused. With unusual enthusiasm, the EU decided to work on it in cooperation with Washington.

With the EU initially talking of putting over US$30 billion into the program over five years, US President Clinton insisted at the pact "summit" at Sarajevo that no help would go to Yugoslavia as long as Milosevic remained in power, effectively doing much to emasculate the project before it even got started. Like it or not, Serbia has traditionally been a hub, or center, of much of the Balkan's commerce. Greece, and its maritime trade, is something apart. But, Albania, Bulgaria, Romania, and the other countries of ex-Yugoslavia had sought out markets over Serbia's roadways and up and down the Danube. When Sarajevo ended after only a few hours, US$2 billion (some US$700 million from Washington) was promised in directed aid to Kosovo. But the Clinton administration had made it clear that it had no deep pockets for economic assistance, asserting as it did, that it had done the bombing and that others would have to do the rebuilding.

At the outset, before even one Euro had arrived, the Balkans was estimated to have lost US$8 billion in business in 1999, directly due to the war. Their economies contracted almost four percent instead of experiencing an expected modest gain. It also lost US$1.5 billion in foreign investment. And the Balkans needed an additional US$1.3 billion in financial aid (bail out money) just to stay afloat. Kosovo was said to need an estimated US$5 billion, and, Yugoslavia, whose production dropped another forty percent from previous lows, and which was said to be about at the level of 1900, was said to need an estimated US$30–60 billion. No one knew for sure because the damage was so extensive and so much remained un-surveyed, semi-inaccessible with the outer wall of economic and financial sanctions still in place. However, the Austrian Petritsch became High Representative in Bosnia and Bodo Hombach, Schroeder's key political advisor, was chosen to coordinate the stability pact. As Germany had proposed it, and Schroeder's own man was put in charge, one would assume that things would happen. But, they didn't. Less and less was said about the pact—as if it had a "shelf life" that had already expired. By the end of the year, Hombach was criticized by the EU for failing to have any plans to bring it to a reality. To the people of the Balkans, the pact had become a cynical PR hoax—a cruel joke!

Chancellor Schroeder, himself, was suspect. His government was cash-strapped, and, as the largest contributor to the EU, many viewed Germany as a cash cow to be milked. As the leader of the SPD, he is obliged to back EU expansion eastward. But, he has often waffled on this and talked about the need to "deepen" EU structures, rather than "broadening" them geographically. And, he had Germany's central bank on his back. One might conclude that he agreed with Fischer at a time when his coalition was in trouble. Then, when Germany had completed its six-month EU presidency, he put Hombach in a position to scuttle it. What did survive, however, was the promise of future EU membership. This had always existed in a vague sort of way, but was reaffirmed at the Helsinki Summit. Having been told that there would be no shortcuts in the accession process, Bulgaria and Romania joined the back of the queue, similar to the cigarette and bread lines in their own country—yet another case of the "bartered bride" syndrome all over again.

Ten years after the collapse of communism, the various peoples of the Balkans and the many western interventionists—diplomats, officials, soldiers, humanitarian workers, and others—are all in a most sober frame of mind. For the fighting and upheaval in what was Yugoslavia has not only been a tragedy that staggers the imagination, but the wars, and many of the consequences of intervention itself, have had an adverse affect on economic, political, and social developments, slowed growth, and made the transition to democracy much more difficult. In straitened circumstances, many resisted change and the former communists hung on to power, or made a comeback when advocates of pluralistic politics and open markets faltered. Criminal organizations with para-state power have fixed themselves upon the populace as they face the future with foreign roadmaps.

If the Slovenes had once thought that breaking away would be easy, they now know better. They have remained in a "twilight zone," neither of Western Europe (the Osterreich of dreams), nor of the crisis-ridden states to the south, which are the stuff of nightmares. Still, agreements with the EU are working for them and early membership is assured. Their territorial issues with Italy have eased off and near normalcy can be gauged by the Austrian nationalist Joerg Haider's insistence that the famous Lipizzaner horses (originally from Lipica in Slovenia) are Vienna's alone. Their economy is down, but both Clinton and Schroeder assured them during state visits that they're on the right track. Judged by Ljubljana's objectives of more than ten years ago, it seems that they are.

Croatia is something else. It is still locked into the question of its territorial extent and its ethnic composition. Nationalism dies very hard and its leading proponent, President Tudjman, died by degrees in the final days of 1999. Surprisingly, there was not the outpouring of grief on a massive scale that was expected. And, his funeral was attended by few heads of state, notably only from Hungary. Croats, perhaps, had grown tired of the pomposity of it all—the endless pageantry and posturing. Nationalists they are, but who needs a white "Tito" uniform and a big limousine when there is twenty percent unemployment? Living standards are below those of ten years ago and a corrupt HDZ has kept control of the main levers of the economy. Tudjman and his cronies had maintained a system of authoritarianism and rabid nationalism that was racism and inefficient socialism combined. Even Washington got tired of Tudjman—his constant meddling in Bosnia, his paranoiac police and intelligence service, and his efforts to prevent the return of Serbians who had been driven out over the years. Parliamentary elections, and those for the presidency, were now scheduled for early in the year. Many were crossing their fingers and hoping for change.

It is difficult to talk about Bosnia as a state when it doesn't exist as such. Bosnia is more a geographical term—a location. The Bosniak-Croatian and Serbian government created at Dayton doesn't work and the only things that get done are those imposed by the High Representative. The whole affair would collapse if aid were withdrawn. Bosnia has already soaked up some US$3 billion of the US$4.5 billion promised to rebuild. And, as some have noted, its economy is only marginally better than at the end of the war. When aid is exhausted, Bosnia may well implode and fall back on subsistence farming and its booming black market. Serbs, of course, look across the Sava to Belgrade, but how to merge their unwieldy and politically divided entity with the mess made by Milosevic? The same can be said for the Croats. All, it seems, are playing the waiting game. But, Sarajevo is a city. And, while Izetbegovic might be absent from the international media, Bosniaks have established themselves in the minds of Muslims abroad with Islam. A walk around town will tell you that. What it would do with its US-backed army if the Serbs and Croats became restive is hard to say. Now it can also look to Ankara, Riyadh, and to the other OIC countries with their petrodollars. If it felt endangered, it might even resort to force to re-engage the attention of the international and Islamic communities.[33]

Now, with the Danube blocked, Romanians and Bulgarians have been denied a vital transportation artery that they both need desperately. The US has demanded the impossible—that Belgrade both clear it and rebuild its bridges. The latter does give the Russians and Ukrainians access to a narrow bypass channel, but not to others. Clinton publicly thanked Bucharest and Sofia for cooperating with NATO during the Kosovo crisis (both are seeking membership, even now) and he has added incrementally to their very modest, actually stingy, aid programs. The Romanians were saying that this had been the worst year since Ceauşescu was overthrown and meant it. Prime Minister Vasile staggered along, month after month, contending with strikes and protests until Bucharest called it quits. Actually, the government collapsed with the resignation of a clutch of ministers who wanted Vasile out. After he finally gave up, the president named a short-term technocrat to stand-in until elections. Vasile will be best remembered for passing a law that will finally permit Romania's citizens to examine their Securitate files, some 125 million in all. Because of the many prominent personalities who have thick dossiers, and the sensitive information they contain, one should not expect this to go smoothly.

In Sofia, Bulgarians looked on with dismay as NATO blasted Yugoslavia and shut off its own road, rail, and river links to Western markets. Not that

Bulgars cared much about the Serbs, but their own pocketbooks were being hurt. The only good to come out of the war was Brussels's decision to allow them to apply for EU membership, with no fixed entry date. Only half in jest, Prime Minister Kostov said that Bulgaria now felt like an adopted child who knows little about his new parents. Perhaps out of frustration, or to demonstrate its new orientation, the government decided to demolish Georgy Dimitrov's old tomb. Symbolic of the "old guard" party elite's staying power, it took three attempts to bring the marble edifice down. Onlookers jeered. Then, in November, Clinton stood in Nevski Square and told thousands that the pain of reform was worth it and that the US will smooth Bulgaria's way to the West. It was pure Clinton. Perhaps he even believed the history lesson he served up, one of selective truth. Before the year ended, Kostov reshuffled an exhausted cabinet—one surrounded by rumors of corruption.[34]

Europe's original orphan, the Albanians, survived the war and almost thrived on the chaos of hundreds of thousands of refugees, NATO troops clogging its pot-holed roads, hordes of humanitarian workers, and throngs of officials from the international community. They all threw money at Albania. Kosovo refugees were robbed of what little they had, NATO paid its bills generously and on time, and aid officials provided jobs and money and whatever goods that were not nailed down and which could be carried off. Albania's mafia moved into Kosovo big time. Socialist Prime Minister, thirty-two-year-old Pandelj Maiko, was forced out in a power struggle and replaced by thirty-year-old Ilier Meta. After two years of auditing, the bogus pyramid accounts were closed with virtually no money left for their investors. But new horizons beckon—Italy, Turkey, possibly Chechnya. The Albanian Minister for Security was stopped at the Greek border in a BMW stolen in Italy, the fifth such luxury auto obtained illegally from a gang abroad for use by a senior government official. It become a make it, or break it sort of a game for most: the politicians, the businessmen and tough, jobless, young men. Albania is pleased with its new status. Ten years ago, it was walled off, unknown. Today, it's almost a tourist destination!

Next door, in that fragile Macedonian house of mirrors, there are cracks everywhere from the seismic shocks that the war has caused. NATO turned the country into a military base and the refugees did the rest. Macedonians were wondering what and who they were. The Albanians knew, for they had agitated for years—Kosovo style. The Bulgarians reappeared and ran a refugee camp. The Serbs took out their fury on American embassy window glass. The government of, yes, you guessed it, Ljupco Georgievski, a shaky coalition, tried to cope as best it could. In its inexperience and eagerness to please, it permitted

NATO to do what it wanted. Actually, it had no choice. NATO forces and refugees arrived daily from every direction. Macedonia's "grandfather," President Gligorov, did take exception, but after years of struggling to save the center, after an attempt to kill him, it was time to step down. But, there are pipeline plans in store for FYROM, Caspian oil piped from Burgas, Bulgaria, through Skopje, and on to Vlore in Albania. If new investment comes in from Greece, things could improve. But, if its Albanians copy the playbook of the KLA in Kosovo, this small country could be shattered.[35]

So much has happened in the Balkans in this past century. And, what one takes for the truth is sure to be attacked on every side. A young Skopje journalist once told me that the "truth" about the Balkans would never be known because the exercise of power, and its "truth," buries every other truth that might have ever existed. In Kosovo, the graves of Albanians killed by the Serbs are now being uncovered. It's sad, but true. However, if people dig deep enough, and long enough, they'll likely find an equal number, or perhaps even more, of Serbians killed by the Albanians in times past. It is this kind of Balkan bookkeeping that renders the moralizing efforts by outside interventionists very suspect.

* * *

3 August 1998. After a month of steady advances by the VJ, the LDK Kosovo Information Center controlled by Rugova released a statement criticizing the KLA leadership for "careerism" and a lack of respect for the "institutions" created by Rugova's LDK. This was the first expression of serious political differences among the Albanians.

3 August 1998. Republic authorities in Montenegro announced that they were suspending all political communications with Belgrade.

17 August 1998. As the KLA was pushed out of the villages still under their control near the Albanian border, US ambassador Chris Hill told all sides that peace talks must begin without delay. US marines and aircraft exercised in Albania as NATO's US commander, General Wesley Clark, and the Contact Group began to tally up the numbers of troop contributions that could then be made available.

8 October 1998. To pressure Belgrade, NATO warned it was ready to mount air strikes. US special envoy Richard Holbrooke engaged in intensive talks with Yugoslav President Slobodan Milosevic. This followed a UN Security Council resolution demanding a ceasefire and negotiations. Belgrade claimed the KLA was virtually defeated, and that it would reduce its forces in Kosovo. Russia

430

and China indicated they would likely veto any UN resolution authorizing the use of force against Yugoslavia.

13 October 1998. Holbrooke announced an agreement in Belgrade. NATO officials rushed signatures on compliance documents. NATO was given an "activation order" to force Yugoslavia to withdraw its VJ and police within ten days. The Kosovar Albanians sat on the sidelines without participating, split between Rugova and the KLA. Rebel fighters immediately took advantage of the Yugoslav draw down in Kosovo.

6 November 1998. After being denied visas to enter Yugoslavia, the UN war crimes tribunal at The Hague called Belgrade "a rogue state," angered that its investigations in Kosovo were being blocked.

30 November 1998. VJ commander General Momcilo Persic, air force chief General Lbubisa Velickovic, and state security boss Jovica Stanisic are sacked by Milosevic. Others believed to be shaky in their loyalty were removed as well. US officials begin to mount a press campaign calling for Milosevic's removal from power.

15 December 1998. After thirty-one KLA fighters were ambushed and killed near the Albanian border, six Serbs were gunned down in a café. Tensions escalated and Holbrooke issued a warning, accusing both sides of playing with "dynamite." Milosevic claimed the US was supporting terrorism. Chief OSCE monitor William Walker visited the scene of recent clashes.

13 January 1999. Eight VJ hostages held captive by the KLA are released unharmed after negotiations with the OSCE.

15 January 1999. Two OSCE monitors are wounded amid continuing clashes. Forty-five ethnic-Albanians are killed at Racak—an incident Washington calls an outrage. Subsequent to this, UN war crimes tribunal chief prosecutor Louise Arbour was denied entry into Kosovo by Belgrade at the Macedonian border.

15 January 1999. US judge Gabrielle Kirk McDonald becomes head of the UN war crimes tribunal.

31 January 1999. The Contact Group approves a US plan to compel Belgrade and the Kosovar Albanians to accept peace terms. At the same time, NATO military committee head, German General Klaus Naumann, said that plans for intervention have been completed. On the ground, incidents occurred on almost a daily basis.

6 February 1999. Contact Group sponsors, Kosovar Albanians, and Yugoslavian negotiators arrive at Rambouillet outside Paris.

19 February 1999. Yugoslav President Slobodan Milosevic refuses to meet with US ambassador Chris Hill who sought acquiescence for the entrance of some 23,000 NATO troops into Kosovo.

23 February 1999. Rambouillet talks are suspended when both sides balked at the terms. At the last minute, KLA-led Albanians agreed to return after consultations, suggesting a willingness to sign.

1 March 1999. KLA mark first year anniversary of their war of independence. KLA leader Hashim Thaci is chosen to head a provisional government.

9 March 1999. US special envoy Richard Holbrooke returns to Belgrade for talks with Yugoslav President Slobodan Milosevic who remains adamantly opposed to NATO's intervention plan. Fighting intensifies.

15 March 1999. Peace talks resume in Paris. Kosovar Albanians indicate that they are ready to sign. US President Clinton states that NATO will strike if Belgrade still refuses to accept the agreement.

17 March 1999. EU Finnish forensic team concludes that Racak victims were mostly civilians shot at close range. Belgrade's build-up in and around Kosovo continues as VJ steps up its attacks. Talks in Paris are ended after the Albanians sign the accord.

19 March 1999. All OSCE monitors are ordered out of Kosovo.

21 March 1999. US special envoy Richard Holbrooke returns to Belgrade in final attempt to get President Milosevic to agree with Contact Group demands. After three days, the talks end in failure.

24 March 1999. In the late evening, NATO begins air bombardment of Yugoslavia.

1 April 1999. LDK head Ibrahim Rugova met in Belgrade with President Milosevic. Jointly, they called for renewed negotiations and a bombing halt.

14 April 1999. UN-EU initiatives to curtail the bombing campaign begin to surface. The Germans urged a twenty-four-hour halt and a Serb pull back.

23 April 1999. NATO Summit is held in Washington as UK pressure begins to build for a ground invasion of Kosovo.

27 April 1999. US Deputy Secretary of State Strobe Talbott meets in Moscow with Victor Chernomyrdin to engage Russia's help as a mediator with Belgrade. This followed a Clinton-Yeltsin exchange. Chernomyrdin traveled to Washington for talks at the White House.

2 May 1999. Five US soldiers captured along Macedonian border were released by Belgrade in a peace effort by US pastor Jesse Jackson.

6 May 1999. In Bonn, G-7 and Russia issue a statement that sets out the terms for ending the war. In the statement, a UN role is foreseen.

10 May 1999. Belgrade claims it has completed its military phase in Kosovo and would begin a partial pull back. This fell short of NATO's demands.

18 May 1999. US President Clinton states that NATO must prevail and all options are open, hinting at a possible shift in policy and the use of ground forces. At the same time, an *ABC-Washington Post* poll suggested that US public support for the air war was ebbing and that many preferred negotiations.

19 May 1999. Chernomyrdin and Milosevic discuss G-7 peace terms in Belgrade.

27 May 1999. Hague war crimes tribunal indicts Milosevic and four other leaders. Finnish President Martti Ahtisaari is to join Chernomyrdin-Milosevic talks as the representative of the EU.

29 May 1999. Milosevic's office announced acceptance of general principles of G-7 plan. NATO bombing continues, but eases off in and around Belgrade. Air strikes were now intensified in Kosovo.

3 June 1999. Milosevic accepts NATO's entry into Kosovo under UN auspices. VJ and NATO officers begin to discuss implementation details.

8 June 1999. Contact Group and Russia agree to wording of draft UN Security Council resolution based on G-7 agreement.

9 June 1999. VJ pull out arrangements are finalized and signed.

13 June 1999. NATO forces enter Kosovo, preceded by the Russians. VJ forces comply with withdrawal instructions on schedule, according to agreement. NATO bombing is suspended to facilitate troop-refugee movements.

18 June 1999. US and Moscow agree on minimal role for Russian peacekeepers who are not given their own security zone. They have a presence, but few responsibilities. A few days later, at a G-7 meeting at Cologne, an ailing Yeltsin is given a "pat on the back" by the Allies. NATO's war is declared officially over and "won."

21 June 1999. After ordering the KLA to disarm, NATO stated it would consider the formation of a Kosovar force similar to the state-level US National Guard. This was clearly a US-KLA initiative.

23 June 1999. Yugoslavia officially ends its state of war.

14 July 1999. Montenegrin representatives return to Belgrade and insist on looser, more confederal ties between itself and Serbia.

30 July 1999. Representatives of forty countries met in Sarajevo, Bosnia, at Stability Pact summit and pledged US$2 billion in reconstruction aid for Kosovo.

25 September 1999. A NATO-KLA agreement, which will convert the KLA into a Kosovo Protection Corps, is widely interpreted by the EU as a significant US tilt towards Kosovar independence. The disuse of the Yugoslav dinar; an all-Albanian customs service; and a new cellular phone system separate from Yugoslavia are all indications that the province is being separated from Belgrade contrary to UN Resolution 1244. The steps had the support of UNMIK SRSG Bernard Kouchner, and NATO commander General Wesley

Clark who personally negotiated with the KLA over its future. The latter pressed to maintain its operational capabilities.

30 September 1999. Police block Serbian Renewal Movement and Alliance for Change demonstrators marching on President Milosevic's residence in Belgrade. Vuk Draskovic said he opposes mass protest activities, indicating a serious split in the leadership ranks of the opposition. The number of demonstrators over the course of more a month dwindled. Sure of his grip on power, Milosevic said that he might agree to early elections.

4 October 1999. At the conclusion of his trial that began in March, World War Two Ustashe commander of Jasenovac concentration camp, Dinko Sakic, is sentenced in Zagreb to twenty years. He was held responsible for the deaths of some 2,000 camp inmates. Suggestive of leniency, the court decided not to try his accomplice wife.

1 November 1999. UNHCR estimated that 240,000 Serbs and other non-Albanians had left Kosovo and were now living elsewhere as refugees.

23 November 1999. Finishing a ten-day European trip, US President Clinton visited the newly built US military base, Camp Bondsteel, in Kosovo and then greeted joyous ethnic-Albanians at Urosevac.

26 November 1999. Franjo Tudjman's official powers are transferred to the speaker of parliament because of the Croatian president's seriously deteriorating health.

13 December 1999. Croatian President Tudjman dies in Zagreb.

16 December 1999. SRSG Bernard Kouchner complains that UNMIK is seriously under-funded. He said that he requested 6,000 foreign police officers and received only 1,800. He had also announced that Hashim Thaci, Ibrahim Rugova and Rexhep Oosja will participate in a joint-administrative council to help run Kosovo until the elections. Thaci had boosted his status by boycotting the Kosovo Transition Council, rendering it virtually ineffective. A photo shows a most unhappy Rugova shaking hands with Thaci who is all smiles. Momcilo Trajkovic of Serbian Resistance was also invited, but declined to attend.

21 December 1999. Admitting that the UN is unable to cope with rampant robbery and murder, KFOR's commander General Klaus Reinhardt ordered an increase in roadblocks, checks, and patrols.[36]

29 December 1999. The Hague tribunal said it would review claims that NATO had committed "war crimes." The Yugoslav government filed charges against NATO and political leaders in its own court system. Others forwarded charges to The Hague.

Epilogue

2000–2005

Democratization and secession do not blend.

Emir Kusturica, director of *Underground*

The following autumn, more than a year after the end of the war in Kosovo, after a winter of fuel shortages, power cuts, and worry about contaminated water; a spring that saw refugees from Kosovo arriving daily, adding their numbers to the hundreds of thousands from Croatia and Bosnia, and, to others long unemployed; and a summer of spiraling inflation and continued international isolation, with hardly a hope in sight, the bonds between the rulers and the ruled in what remained of Yugoslavia finally snapped. It would come to be called the "October Surprise," the culmination of US interventionist efforts towards that beleaguered country. It began in earnest a year earlier in a luxury hotel suite in Budapest, and, in the end, Slobodan Milosevic was ousted from power.

Legally barred from running again for the office of president of Serbia, Milosevic had carefully planned to shift his authority to the federal presidency through direct popular ballot, a change he had favored for years. He made no secret of this, had pushed through amendments to the constitution, and made his intentions clear when announcing the elections earlier in July.[1] They were set for 24 September. However, when the stark implications of more years of "Slobo" finally sank in, even in the heartland of his supporters, people from all across the political spectrum began to rally around Vojislav Kostunica, a moderate nationalist and a respected professor of constitutional law. The election would also select members of a federal parliament and local officials, but all attention was on Milosevic and Kostunica—the candidate for an eighteen party coalition called the Democratic Opposition of Serbia (DOS).

When election Sunday arrived, the turnout was heavy, but essentially peaceful. As always, there were minor irregularities at the polling stations, but it all seemed very normal. The results were expected out Tuesday, but already, on Monday, Kostunica claimed a DOS victory based on carefully compiled information taken at the polling stations. Spokesmen from the ruling SPS-JUL coalition questioned this, claiming that an uncompleted count indicated that Milosevic was ahead. Crowds of pro-DOS supporters began to gather outside the election commission's offices amid rumors that the commission had suspended their count. Then, on Tuesday night, the office announced its "official" tally, that Kostunica had forty-eight percent, and Milosevic forty—a situation requiring a second round run-off on Sunday, 8 October. A winner needed at least fifty percent. Kostunica and DOS rejected this, claiming an outright win. He and DOS leader Zoran Djindjic asked the people to rally to their side.

By Wednesday night, DOS had 200,000 demonstrators in central Belgrade, many holding a placard that said, *"Gotov Je,"* "He's Finished!" The government was said to be examining its options, including a careful weighing up of the loyalties of the army and police, a recount, anything that would give Milosevic more time. However, in a few days, pro-DOS demonstrations gathered strength and the country began to slide into a nationwide general strike. Milosevic came on television and appealed for calm—to their sense of patriotism. Kostunica visited striking coal miners whose action threatened to paralyze central Serbia's power grid. Roadblocks went up as towns joined in— Nis, Novi Sad, Cacak, Pancevo, and Uzice. VJ chief General Nebojsa Pavkovic promised more pay and told the miners to take up their tools. A former general who was fired by Milosevic, Momcilo Perisic, urged the miners to continue their strike. Ominously, in Belgrade, and elsewhere, police began arresting people barricading roadways. The rail line between Serbia and Montenegro was blocked. The copper complex at Majdanpek struck. DOS lodged its request for a recount before the constitutional court. Then, with the government insisting that Kostunica must go into a second round, DOS announced it had software evidence from the federal statistical bureau that proved that it had won—that the government had falsified the results. Finally, on 4 October, the constitutional court ruled the election invalid—stating that Milosevic would remain in power until his term of office expired in July, at which time new elections would be held.

That did it! On 5 October, oppositionists and supporters poured into Belgrade in response to Kostunica's urging—a half million people. Miners in working clothes, farmers in muddy boots, students, office workers and housewives gathered in front of parliament and edged towards a police barrier set up to protect the building. By afternoon, tear gas was in the air and the police had fired rubber bullets. But DOS and Otpor, the students federation, had planned the uprising well. Vuk Obradovic, a former VJ general, appealed to Pavkovic to come over to the side of the people. Momcilo Perisic talked to other commanders. And, some "red beret" special forces and paratroopers lent their muscle. Others, following a bulldozer, barged into the state television building, taking it off the air. Police stations were invaded, as was the state-run *Politika* newspaper. But, the response of the police at the barriers was only half-hearted. They didn't even shoot when windows were broken and rampaging youths intent on vandalism broke into parliament and started a fire. By early evening, it was realized that the crowd couldn't be contained, and the order was given for the police to quit. Milosevic had decided not to try to use force. It was essentially all over and not one life had been lost.[2]

The DOS had Doug Schoen to thank. As elsewhere in the Balkans in the 1990s, US administrations had decided that any important election was very much its affair. Consequently, the Department of State and Agency for International Development—through the National Endowment for Democracy and its sister organizations, the National Democratic Institute and International Republican Institute, were there to "help." And, they had money, US$10 million for fiscal 1999 and US$31 million for 2000. Funds were channeled directly and to private contractors and interested non-profit groups. Doug Schoen was a pollster, a senior member of the US firm Penn, Schoen, and Berland Associates. And, in October 1999, he was in Budapest advising eager opposition members how they could beat Milosevic. It seems he was not a newcomer to Yugoslavian politics, as he had also advised Milan Panic back in 1992. The key to victory, he insisted, was "unity"—and, he showed them data from a poll he had commissioned that suggested that Vojislav Kostunica was the best candidate. This scene was repeated dozens of times over the following year with other participants at different locations at seminars and training sessions run by US-paid "consultants"—even a retired US Army colonel. The "Republicans," by way of contrast, concentrated on the Otpor student organization. The end result was tons of printed political material; computers, fax machines, cellular phones, and office equipment; and repeated private tracking polls that confirmed that Kostunica was "the man"; and hundreds of trained people who had soaked-up campaign know-how, especially exit poll techniques; and even rock bands and thousands of cans of spray paint. The US support wasn't even secret. Milosevic knew it was happening, grumbled about foreign interference, but did little to stop it—unusual behavior for a "ruthless dictator." And, after his "Mayor Daley"-style rigged vote was exposed and he and Mira realized they couldn't annul the election without using force, they simply gave up. The election commission even conceded Kostunica his previously announced fifty-five percent of the vote to thirty-five for Milosevic.[3]

Weeks of tension followed. However, DOS and the SPS-JUL coalition agreed on a peaceful transfer of power. New elections for Serbia were held on 23 December, further consolidating a DOS victory—with sixty-five percent, or some 175 seats in a 250-member assembly, to only 37 for SPS. Djindjic, as prime minister, appointed a reform government that began to take over a state that was near financial collapse. And, if that wasn't challenging enough, William Montgomery, who had set himself up in Budapest in September, arrived as the new US ambassador and handed the government a three-page list of demands—headed by a request that Milosevic be delivered to the Hague tribunal. Should Belgrade not comply, US$100 million in aid would be cut off, and the US would block any financial support from the IMF and World Bank. It was also confronted by a deteriorating security situation in southern Serbia and renewed threats by Djukanovic to take Montenegro to independence. As for "Slobo," he remained secluded in one of the Tito-era presidential villas, but was essentially free to talk to his party leaders, friends, and supporters.

Given all the problems, serious differences between Kostunica and Djindjic soon broke out into the open. Djindjic wanted to purge the military, police, and security services. Kostunica believed this would destabilize a state still very much in crisis. Djindjic wanted Milosevic arrested. Kostunica wanted an investigation, proof of his law breaking—and was against giving Milosevic to the tribunal. If there were charges, he could be tried by their own courts. Having already met Clinton, Djindjic wanted to get in bed with Washington. Kostunica didn't even want to meet Madeleine Albright. Also, there were differences in style. Writer Aleksandar Tijanic accurately stated that Djindjic looked at parliament as a "casino," while Kostunica considered it to be a "cathedral." The former, as prime minister, actually had more power and he used it. Milosevic was arrested on 1 April and was spirited away to the Hague tribunal on, of all days, 28 June—Vidovdan Day![4]

While all this high level maneuvering to get rid of Milosevic was going on, KFOR and NATO ignored a new outbreak of armed Albanian insurgency that was hatched right under their nose. A year after the end of the war in Kosovo, a new armed group called the Liberation Army of Presevo, Medvedja, and Bujanovac (UCPMB) had made its appearance and had clashed with FRY police and VJ along the border area of eastern Kosovo—in Serbia proper. Dotted with Albanian villages, the north-south Presevo valley consists of 200 square kilometers inhabited by 100,000 people, mostly ethnic-Albanians. The main highway and rail line to Greece and the port city of Thessaloniki also threaded their way through its hills—making it of vital strategic importance not only to FRY, but also to other countries to the north. By the first of the year, there were dead on both sides, a carbon copy of Kosovo. On 16 February, British and Swedish KFOR troopers met a convoy of seven buses from Nis, Serbian refugees returning to Kosovo for their Orthodox *zadusnica*— commemoration of the dead. A few kilometers inside Kosovo, while escorted by KFOR armored vehicles, a command detonated explosive tore the lead bus apart—killing eleven (including a two-year-old boy) and injuring twenty, eight critically.[5]

Earlier, Belgrade had given KFOR twenty days to remove Albanian fighters from the five-kilometer wide buffer zone bordering Kosovo. But, even after the situation worsened, NATO took weeks and months to act. Finally, in mid-March, it gave Djindjic the "green light" and VJ and police units entered the zone over Albanian protests. This time, under the watchful eye of NATO observers, the UCPMB faded back into the hills after losing several firefights. However, they simply joined forces with other KLA fighters that, in late February, had opened up a completely new front—this time in northern and western Macedonia. The names were all familiar: Ali Ahmeti, Xhavit Hasani, Fazli Veliu, Emrush Xhemajli—all Albanians from Macedonia and all veterans of Kosovo. Ahmeti was the political leader of what they were now calling the National Liberation Army (NLA)—a force of several thousand that threatened to take the second city of Tetovo. As a first step, they demanded constitutional changes that would provide special status for Albanian majority areas—dual political power. Kosovo activist Fadil Suliemani made similar demands, as did leading Albanian politicians. As the fighting increased, the US-EU worked to achieve a cease-fire and then pressured Skopje into a compromise agreement with the rebels, granting them semi-autonomy—greater use of their own language, and more representation in the government and police. The NLA, which didn't join the talks, was granted amnesty. As reasonable as this may sound to outsiders, majority-Macedonians were of the opinion that the "Ohrid accord" will ultimately divide the country. There was also anger over press reports that MPRI, on official US contract to train the Macedonian military, was also training the rebels. Tempers flared when US troops extracted three hundred NLA rebels from the village of Aracinovo (only ten km from Skopje) and dropped them off back in the hills to fight another day. In late August, a mixed-NATO force of 3,500 was deployed to collect "token" arms laid down by the NLA. Not surprisingly, NATO called it another "success." Obviously very unhappy, Prime Minister Georgievski sharply criticized KFOR for failing to prevent fighters from arriving from Kosovo—warning that a "Greater Albania" will lead to a "new Taliban in Europe."[6]

In point of fact, after 11 September 2001, the US and other NATO powers began to look differently at the rapid rise of nationalist-cum-Islamic power in the Balkans. Whereas, in the past, it had been actively encouraged and aimed at Belgrade, what had developed into armed insurgencies were, overnight, viewed as potential terrorist threats. US security and military authorities in Bosnia soon uncovered plots against its diplomatic presence in Sarajevo and its SFOR personnel stationed at Tuzla. Arrests were made and several Islamic foundations were shut down. Seized records disclosed links to Al Qaeda's foundations elsewhere. By mid-2003, Muhammed al-Zawahiri, a brother of Osama bin Laden's deputy, Ayman al-Zawahiri, was reportedly attempting to set up an Al Qaeda network in the area.[7] US investigations led back to Tirana where Yasin al-Qadi, a fugitive Saudi businessman, ran eight companies in addition to his Muwafaq Foundation. Al-Qadi had collected millions from wealthy Saudis and was suspected of channeling money to bin Laden.[8]

The US began to feel uneasy. Although the imperium it had established through Balkanization, the creation of small, weak, dependent states remained unchallenged, it was now finding out that it could not control the political turbulence that this policy engendered.[9] The assassin's bullet tore through Zoran Djindjic's body with an impact that blew his heart apart. A second round cut down his bodyguard. Djindjic died without uttering a word. A few days later in mid-March 2003 Belgrade saw a massive outpouring of grief. Even Djindjic's detractors were stunned, angry—asking themselves was it not possible to escape from the cycle of violence that had destroyed so many lives. Some knew the reasons, for even Zoran the reformer had made his pact with the devil. To help oust Milosevic, he had conspired with Milorad Lukovic, *"Legija"* (Legionnaire), head of the "red berets" (JSO Special Operations Unit) and his predecessor Franko "Frenkie" Simatovic. The idea, which had in fact succeeded, was to neutralize Milosevic's praetorian guard—1,200 men who were superbly trained and equipped and very tough. Later, they had arrested Milosevic, and finally, they had even helped to deliver him to the Hague tribunal.

At some point, Lukovic left the JSO and took over the Zemun gang—a powerful "mafia" organization in Belgrade that had helped Milosevic circumvent international trade sanctions and finance paramilitary groups. Djindjic, to credit his motives, had declared war on organized crime, had sacked officials, and had gone after businesses linked to the previous regime. However, a cynic might accuse him of getting rid of Lukovic's competition—and that of some others. The relationship was sure to be problematic as Djindjic felt increased US pressure to send wanted suspects to the tribunal, or forego financial aid. Hague tribunal chief prosecutor Carla del Ponte was often in Belgrade to read the riot act to the young prime minister—to deliver up Radovan Karadzic, General Ratko Mladic and others whose names remained secret. It's said that Lukovic's name was on the list. And, immediately after Djindjic's death, his DS party successor, Prime Minister Zoran Zivkovic, arrested thousands and came up with the killer. And, within just weeks, former Serbian state security boss Jovica Stanisic, his deputy Franko Simatovic and Colonel Veselin Sljivcanin—all three accused of war crimes at Vukovar in 1991 were also sent to the tribunal. These actions by premier Zivkovic and his security minister Dusan Mihajlovic won the government a little time, a little western aid money, but very little else.[10]

Even the name "Serbia and Montenegro" stuck in everyone's throats! To help pacify Podgorica in order to stave off a referendum for independence, the US and the EU had foisted another constitutional conundrum on another Balkan country. That's what was said, but everyone knew that the real reason was that a "yes" vote in Montenegro would make Kosovo independence a certainty. So, the Yugoslavia of dreams died in the weeks before Djindjic's own death—virtually unnoticed by the international community and unlamented, except by some, who later adduced that it was "another good reason." Its founding document cited "one state" formed by "two member states." Approval of the arrangement, nothing more than a loose union with a figurehead president and a single army, was the EU's pre-condition for beginning talks on a Stabilization and Association Agreement (SAA). The constitutional form of the union came in for criticism in both republics as being unwieldy and unlikely to survive beyond 2005—when Montenegro can choose to opt-out. Additional pressure on Djukanovic to not bolt was exerted by Italy, which had threatened to bring smuggling charges against the young Montenegrin president. An Italian minister of finance had officially accused Djukanovic of harboring Francesco Prudentino "... the most powerful and most dangerous trafficking boss in the Mediterranean ... not only in cigarettes, but weapons, drugs, and people, above all children and women." Milo, of course, denied all, including accusations he was taking a cut of the action. At the end of 2003, however, Djukanovic was immersed in a sex-trafficking scandal that had erupted when a Moldovian woman said she had been "tortured, raped, and held as a sex slave in a brothel...where her clients included government officials."[11]

UNHCR, a very decent organization, likes to cite what they say is a success story—that, of 2.2 million people uprooted during the Bosnian war of 1992–95, 980,000 have returned to their villages by the end of 2003. Udo Janz, in Sarajevo, said that almost half were "minority returns"—Muslims, Croats, and Serbs. However, he explained that foreign aid money is drying up and local authorities will find it difficult to find money needed to rebuild houses and lives, including badly needed jobs and schools. In other words, people who were driven out during the war have returned to places where poverty and lack of opportunity rule. Perhaps that is why Paddy Ashdown is in a hurry, because he recognizes a "time fuse" when he sees it. As High Representative for Bosnia, he was scathingly criticized by a European think-tank for "running Bosnia like a raj."[12] Bosnia has been told to meet sixteen criteria by mid-2004 if it is begin talks on a SAA. Ashdown doubts this can be done in time and imposes his will when need be—which is most of the time. Economic reform has stalled, with un-employment at forty percent. Foreign investment is not coming in because of high corruption. In short, Bosnia is dysfunctional. The Dayton Agreement is not working. It stopped a war, but it cannot rebuild a country.[13] Every so often, the Croats try to break out of the federation. The Serbs limit their cooperation with Sarajevo to a minimum. The Bosniak Muslims, themselves, are inept and corrupt by turns. Crime flourishes. The veteran American journalist Flora Lewis will be remembered for her comments after her final visit: "... I toured the area and came away convinced that the minute foreign troops were pulled out war would break out again. I found that this is the common view of every observer who has made a serious effort to assess the situation not only in Bosnia but also in Kosovo and Macedonia."

The Slovenes, one assumes, are breathing a sigh of satisfaction, and great relief. For by being the first to secede, they were the ones who began the break-up and then were able to watch the slaughter from a position of safety. They could also take advantage of the money to be made from the war while preparing, ever so diligently, to enter NATO and the EU. The world's leader in ski technology might be selfish, but they are far from dumb. The same can be said for the Croats. The center-left reformist government that came to power after the death of Tudjman made progress in its relations with the US and the EU at the price of cooperating with the Hague tribunal. There was little said when a few low-level individuals were fed to the court for form's sake. This was how they thought it was to be—stacked against the Serbs. But, they went into a state of shock when their elderly former chief of staff General Janko

Bobetko was indicted. Bobetko was sheltered by Zagreb, which insisted that he was too ill to travel. That may be true, as he did die in a matter of months. And, the same was true when the tribunal asked for General Ante Gotovina, one of the commanders of the Krajina campaign of August 1995. In the latter case, however, he went into hiding in July 2001 and Zagreb claims not to know his whereabouts. Visnja Staresina, a columnist for *Vecernji List*, is of the opinion that Gotovina may well be sheltered by those who planned the operation—MPRI, the US organization of former generals and military men who act only on US government instructions. She argues that what Gotovina would have to say would be highly embarrassing and damaging to Washington.[14]

Whatever the case, the demands of the tribunal caused such a surge of popular anger that in November 2003, the nationalist HDZ was again returned to power. Prime Minister Ivo Sanader, head of a three party coalition, won handily and sent the social democrat SDP into the opposition. Predictably, President Stipe Mesic and Sanader announced pro-US, pro-NATO, and pro-EU views as Croatia's guidelines. How those policies will square with that country's poor record on human rights and the non-return of refugees remains to be seen. As in Croatia, dissatisfaction with the results of economic reform in Serbia was eventually expressed at the polls. Djindjic had become almost more popular in death than when prime minister. Zivkovic had inherited this deep discontent. And then, when the Hague tribunal served up a new list of names, popular feeling swung to the nationalist right. By late December 2003, Vojislav Kostunica head of the Democrat Party of Serbia (DSS) was likely to become the next prime minister. But the voting had been such as to rule out any reasons for optimism. Vojislav Seselj, leading his ultra-nationalist SRS from his cell at the Hague tribunal, came in first with twenty-eight percent! The others, parties of all stripes, were splintered all over the political landscape. Serbs had become tired of being told to hand over people to the court, at the pain of not receiving aid money, and gave the west an "in your face" sort of vote. Milosevic was on the list of the SPS and won. Two others indicted by the tribunal were elected as well! One is forced to doubt whether this wrecked republic, beset with economic dislocation and unemployment, crime and corruption, and its seeming inability to come to terms with its present situation, will prove capable of addressing its future—particularly the future of Kosovo. They were only agreed in their disappointment with the DS reformers who, in their eyes, failed to clean up the mess left by Milosevic; and, consequently, they lashed back in the only way they knew how.[15]

Aleksa Djilas, the son of Milovan and an acute observer of events, comes down hard on the tribunal and believes it is biased. He asks why it is that only political leaders from the FRY were sent to The Hague and not Tudjman and Izetbegovic—and some of their underlings. He believes it's a club to punish the Serbs and, at the same time, justify the US-led war by NATO in Kosovo. He argued that all sides had committed war crimes, but the Serbs are getting most of the blame. He said that few believe that the tribunal is concerned with "the whole truth." Another Croat, Petar Mlinovic, an HDZ survivor of Vukovar, believes that the tribunal is soft on the Serbs—that they, the Croats, were only defending themselves from the very beginning. You could go anywhere in former Yugoslavia and the pattern would be repeated by the Slovenes, Bosnians, Albanians, and the Macedonians.[16]

Apocryphal, or not, it's said that German Chancellor Otto von Bismarck, on his deathbed, with his last dying breath, uttered but one word, "Serbia!" Today, Western diplomats and officials seized with the problem all mutter "Kosovo" in their sleep. The question, according to Washington, is to be settled in 2006. And yet, it seems to defy solution. Partition comes to mind, but how to do it? If the province is divided at Kosovska Mitrovica, leaving the Serbs their majority areas and the Trepca mines—all to the north—most of its historic Orthodox churches and monasteries and its minority enclaves would remain with the Albanians. And, the south without Trepca would be very poor indeed. At the same time, four years as a UN protectorate garrisoned by NATO has proven that the two communities can no longer live with each other. UNMIK and KFOR officers curse Kosovo under their breath and ask how did it ever come to happen that a million Albanians and less than half that many Serbs should absorb so much money and attention from the international community—given that it's a cesspool of crime and violence, an actual menace?

One explanation was given to me at an Athens cocktail party. It was the fall of 2003. I was talking to an engaging young officer from the US embassy and I said that I had covered the Balkans as a journalist. Of course, I also mentioned that I had served at the embassy as my last post. He went on to say that his first assignment, in 1993–4, had been Tirana, and allowed how much he had enjoyed it. "It was just great!" he said. "We could do anything we wanted. In fact, they would like to be our fifty-first state." When I commented how "we" (the US) had really "gotten in bed" with the KLA, he became effusive with enthusiasm. "Yeah," he blurted out, "All the stuff was coming in right out at the international airport." The "stuff" he was referring to, I knew, was shorthand for military equipment. Then, he quickly moved to another subject while I took in the breathtaking implications of his remarks. It meant that long before Kosovo had gotten out of hand, and had broken into armed conflict, that the US was fomenting and actively supporting revolt in the province—that the US bears major responsibility for much of what followed, including the war and its unending tragic aftermath. I had, of course, heard rumors and comments that the CIA was involved with the KLA, and there were articles written by reliable journalists, but they concerned the latter phase of struggle of the Kosovar Albanians—1998–1999. Never had anyone suggested that the US government had become involved with the KLA from almost the beginning. But, there it was. The embassy officer had openly admitted it.[17]

At high cost in terms of Serbs and Albanians killed and tremendous destruction to a poor country for the purpose of ridding it of Milosevic, the US military now bosses the province of Kosovo and is, at the opening of a new century, comfortably bedded down at Camp Bondsteel. Its reach stretches from the Balkans over to the border of China, taking in the Caucasus, Middle East, and Central Asia. In Georgia, the US and Russia joust over local politics, ethnic minorities, and fragments of real estate—especially for control over the route of the Baku-Ceyhan pipeline now under construction.[18] And, moves are afoot to cut the US's military presence in Germany and relocate quick reaction forces to Romania-Bulgaria. Both hosted US military support teams during the Iraq invasion of 2003 and both will join NATO in 2004. By way of emphasis while visiting Europe in late 2003, US secretary of defense Donald Rumsfeld bluntly warned EU leaders not to undermine NATO's (read US) interests in Bosnia when they take over SFOR peacekeeping at the end of 2004.[19]

This past fifteen years in the Balkans has seen a succession of seismic events, some of a conclusive nature, while others were more tentative and still subject to change. The downfall of Soviet-style "communism" is final, never to be reversed. Yugoslavia broke up, or *was broken up*, and it's difficult to see it ever coming together again, except perhaps as a common economic zone. Eventually, the countries will enter the European Union. But, until that happens, political discontent over borders and the share out of ethnic power will be the norm, for nothing has been really resolved. In the Balkans, people are "nations" and nationalism dies very hard. And, when ethnic-cum-religious conflict takes place, all sides believe they are right.

The US and the EC failed to step in with forceful focused diplomacy at a time when armed conflict could have been avoided. Even before, but especially later, the various European countries saw the conflict in differing ways. When the US entered the fray, at first its actions tailed along after the members of the

Atlantic alliance. Soon, however, as stated by Lord David Owen, it was working to undermine a UN solution. Then, when the UN's effort was close to collapse; the US intervened overtly and covertly in support of the Bosniak Muslims and Croats.

We had the Dayton Agreement. And, that was supposed to solve the problem. But, apparently, what the US had begun with the Albanians earlier had developed a momentum of its own. NATO's war over Kosovo now places a broad question mark across much of the region. A comprehensive settlement is required, but where is the will and the wisdom? Whether the hegemony of the US, itself, will prove capable of preserving peace and engendering ethnic harmony remains very much open to question. During that crisis, we saw the beginnings of the unilateral interventionism that is the hallmark of the present administration of President George W. Bush—of a nation waging war for reasons beyond the stated *casus belli*. This is unsurprising since from the early 1990s onward US military schools and think tanks have adopted the doctrine of the desirability of a militarily backed "*Pax Americana*."

In 1999, Emir Kusturica, the Sarajevo-born director of *Underground,* had this to say about the situation in his homeland: "It's just a rerun of the same old story. [Ivo] Andric said, 'Wars in our region never solve the problems that spark them, they just create new ones which will never be solved.'" Regarding Yugoslavia, he said that it had been a democracy of a little known type, having no name. "In the foundations of this democracy there lie its Titoist past, the nationality conflicts and territorial issues, yet unresolved. The peoples that confronted each other are not to blame. It is the fault of world powers that could have averted this disintegration, although they chose not to. If someone, that is, a western politician, calls Tudjman "a democrat" it makes no sense to us. Democratization and secession don't blend."[20]

Selected Bibliography

Andric, Ivo, *The Bridge Over the Drina*, London, Harvill, 1994

Applebaum, Anne, *Between East and West: Across the Borderlands of Europe*, London, Papermac, 1995

Arendt, Hannah, *The Origins of Totalitarianism*, New York, Meridian, 1958

Avramov, Smilja, *Genocide in Yugoslavia*, Belgrade, BIGZ, 1995

Baerentzen, Lars, ed., *British Reports on Greece 1943–44*, Copenhagen, The Museum Tusculanium Press, 1982, In association with The Modern Greek Studies Association, New Haven, and The Center of Contemporary Greek Studies, King's College, London

Banac, Ivo, ed., *Eastern European Revolution*, Ithaca, New York, Cornell University Press, 1992

Basset, Richard, *Waldheim and Austria*, New York, Penguin, 1988

Bojic, Dusica, *Suffering of the Serbs in Sarajevo*, Belgrade, Commissariat for Refugees of the Republic of Serbia, Documentation Center, 1996

Boll, Michael, *Cold War in the Balkans: American Foreign Policy and the Emergence of Communist Bulgaria 1943–47*, University Press of Kentucky, 1984

Bower, Tom, *Blind Eye to Murder*, London, Warner Books, 1997

Bulgarian Academy of Science, Documents/Materials on the History of the Bulgarian People, Sofia, 1969

Bulgarian Academy of Science, Macedonia, Documents/Materials, Sofia, 1979

Churchill, Winston S., *The Second World War* (6 vols.), Boston, Houghton Mifflin, 1953

Carnegie Endowment, *The Other Balkan Wars*, Washington, D.C., 1993

Chaliand, Gerard, *The Kurdish Tragedy*, London, Zed Books, 1994

Clogg, Richard, *A Short History of Modern Greece*, Cambridge, Cambridge University Press, 1979

——, *A Concise History of Greece*, Cambridge, Cambridge University Press, 1992

Close, David, *The Origins of the Greek Civil War*, New York, Longman, 1995

Cooley, John K., *Unholy Wars: Afghanistan, America and International Terrorism*, London, Pluto Press, 1999

Croutier, Alev Lytle, *Harem: The World Behind the Veil*, New York, Abbeville Press, 1989

Deacon, Richard, *The Israeli Secret Service*, London, Sphere, 1979

Djilas, Aleksa, *The Contested Country: Yugoslav Unity and Communist Revolution 1919–1953*, Cambridge, Harvard University, 1991

Djilas, Milovan, *Land Without Justice*, New York, Harcourt, Brace, Jovanovich, n.d.

——, *Memoir of a Revolutionary*, New York, Harcourt, Brace, Jovanovich, 1973

——, *Wartime*, New York, Harcourt, Brace, Jovanovich, 1977

——, *Rise and Fall*, New York, Harcourt, Brace, Jovanovich, 1985

——, *Under the Colors*, New York, Harcourt, Brace, Jovanovich, 1971

Drakulic, Slavenka, *Cafe Europa*, Great Britain, Abacus, 1996

Echikson, William, *Lighting the Night: Revolution in Eastern Europe*, London, Pan Books, 1990

Fallaci, Oriana, *A Man*, New York, Simon and Schuster, 1980

Fleming, Amalia, *A Piece of the Truth*, Boston, Houghton Mifflin, 1971

Floyd, David, *Rumania. Russia's Dissident Ally*, New York, Praeger, 1965

Fourtouni, Eleni, *Greek Women in Resistance*, New Haven, Thelphini Press, 1986

Friedrich, Carl J., and Brzezinski, Zbigniew K., *Totalitarian Dictatorship and Autocracy*, Cambridge, Harvard University, 1956

Gage, Nicholas, *Eleni*, New York, Random House, 1983

Gilbert, Martin, *The First World War*, New York, Henry Holt, 1994

Glenny, Misha, *The Rebirth of History: Eastern Europe in the Age of Democracy*, London, Penguin, 1990

——, *The Fall of Yugoslavia: The Third Balkan War*, London, Penguin, 1992

Griffith, William, *Albania and the Sino-Soviet Rift*, Cambridge, The M.I.T. Press, 1963

Hall, Brian, *The Impossible Country*, Great Britain, Secker & Warburg, 1994

Harel, Isser, *The House on Garibaldi Street*, New York, Bantam, n.d.

Herman, Edward S., and Chomsky, Noam, *Manufacturing Consent: The Political Economy of the Mass Media*, London, Vintage, 1994

Hersh, Burton, *The American Elite and the Origins of the CIA*, New York, Scribner's, 1992

Honig, Jan Willem, and Both, Norbert, *Srebrenica: Record of a War Crime*, London, Penguin, 1996

Housepian, Marjorie, *The Smyrna Affair*, New York, Harcourt, Brace, Jovanovich, 1966

Iatrides, John, ed., *Ambassador MacVeagh Reports: Greece 1933–1947*, Princeton University, 1980

Jelavich, Barbara, *History of the Balkans* (2 vols.), New York, Cambridge University, 1983

Kosovo and the Albanian Dimension in Southeast Europe, Hellenic Foundation for European and Foreign Policy (ELIAMEP), 1999

Macedoine, *Institute of National History*, Skopje, 1981

Kazantzakis, Nikos, *The Fratricides*, London, Faber and Faber, 1974

Kaplan, Robert, *Balkan Ghosts*, New York, Vintage, 1994

Kinross, Lord, *The Ottoman Centuries*, New York, Morrow, 1977

Laffan, R. G. D., *The Serbs*, New York, Dorset Press, 1989

Lehrer, Milton and Martin, David, eds., *Transylvania: History and Reality*, Silver Springs, Maryland, Bartleby Press, 1986

London, Kurt, *Backgrounds of Conflict*, New York, Macmillan, 1947

Maclean, Fitzroy, *Eastern Approaches*, London, Mayflower 1961

Magas, Branka, *The Destruction of Yugoslavia*, London, Verso, 1993

Malcolm, Noel, *Bosnia, A Short History*, New York University, 1994

Manning, Olivia, *The Balkan Trilogy*, London, Mandarin, 1990

Marton, Kati, *The Polk Conspiracy*, New York, Farrar, Straus and Giroux, 1990

Mass, Peter, *Love Thy Neighbor: A Story of War*, London, Papermac 1996

Mozower, Mark, *Inside Hitler's Greece*, New Haven, Yale University, 1993

Murtagh, Peter, *The Rape of Greece: The King, The Colonels, and The Resistance*, London, Simon and Schuster, 1994

Pettifer, James, *The Turkish Labyrinth*, London, Penguin, 1998

Prodan, David, *Transylvania and Again Transylvania, The Cultural Foundation of Romania*, Cluj-Napoca, 1996

Rady, Martin, *Romania in Turmoil*, London, I. B. Tauris, 1992

Rieff, David, *Slaughterhouse: Bosnia and the Failure of the West*, London, Vintage, 1995

Ryan, Allan, *Quiet Neighbors*, New York, Harcourt, Brace, Jovanovich, 1984

Silber, Laura and Little, Allan, *The Death of Yugoslavia*, London, BBC-Penguin, 1995

Stavrou, Nicolas, ed., *Greece under Socialism: A NATO Ally Adrift*, New York, Rochelle, 1988

Sterling, Clair, *The Terror Network*, New York, Berkley, 1982

Sulzberger, C. L., *A Long Row of Candles*, New York, Macmillan, 1969

Torry, Glenn E., *Romania and World War One*, Iasi, Center of Romania Studies, 1998

Treptow, Kurt, ed., *A History of Romania* (Third Edition), Iasi, Center of Romania Studies, 1997

——, *Romania and World War Two*, Iasi, Center of Romania Studies, 1996

Tuchman, Barbara, *The Proud Tower*, New York, Bantam, 1967

——, *The Guns of August*, New York, Bantam, 1976

Vassilikos, Vassilis, *Z*, New York, Ballantine, 1969

Vickers, Miranda and Pettifer, James, *Albania: From Anarchy to a Balkan Identity*, London, Hurst, 1997

Vulliamy, Edward, *Seasons in Hell: Understanding Bosnia's War*, London, Simon and Schuster, 1994

Waldeck, R. G., *Athene Palace*, Garden City, NY, Blue Ribbon, 1942

West, Rebecca, *Black Lamb and Grey Falcon*, New York, Viking, 1941

Wheatcroft, Andrew, *The Ottomans*, London, Viking Penguin, 1993

White, William, *By-Line Ernest Hemingway*, New York, Scribner's, 1967

Woodhouse, C. M., *Apple of Discord*, London, Hutchinson, 1948

Woodward, Susan, *Balkan Tragedy: Chaos and Dissolution After the Cold War*, Washington, D.C., The Brookings Institution, 1995

Yugoslavia, Federal Republic of, Ministry of Foreign Affairs, *NATO Crimes in Yugoslavia*, Documentary White Paper (2 vols.), Belgrade, 1999

Notes

Chapter 1 – Back to the Future

1. Woodward, Susan L., *Balkan Tragedy: Chaos and Dissolution after the Cold War* (Washington D.C.: The Brookings Institution, 1995), pp. 114–117.
2. Op. cit. pp. 102–103, 133. Silber, Laura and Little, Allan, *The Death of Yugoslavia* (London: Penguin, 1995), pp. 90–92.
3. Woodward, *Balkan Tragedy*, p. 116.
4. Op. cit., p. 120.
5. Ibid. Also see Silber and Little, *Death of Yugoslavia*, pp. 100–105.
6. Silber and Little, *Death of Yugoslavia*, pp. 105–111.
7. Woodward, *Balkan Tragedy*, pp. 90–93; Silber and Little, *Death of Yugoslavia*, pp. 29–35.
8. Silber and Little, *Death of Yugoslavia*, pp. 113–128; Woodward, *Balkan Tragedy*, p. 139.
9. Op. cit., p. 133. Further to this, it should be noted that, between 1918 and 1974, the internal borders of Yugoslavia were readjusted four times. These changes had a political impact, but were regarded as lines of administrative demarcation by indigenous citizens and foreign countries. Only after the break-up of Yugoslavia and the recognition of the separate entities in 1991–92 were these boundaries given the status of international frontiers, in this instance by foreign powers supportive of Slovenia, Croatia, and Bosnia-Herzegovina.
10. Silber and Little, *Death of Yugoslavia*, pp. 113–128. The leadership of the federal army had developed operational plans to disarm illegal paramilitary forces and to reassert its authority, but it would do so only within the constitution. This plan failed to obtain a majority within the federal presidency and was never implemented.
11. Op. cit. pp. 152–160. Also see Glenny, Misha, *The Fall of Yugoslavia: the Third Balkan War*, n.p. (Penguin, 1992), pp. 75–78.
12. Glenny, *Fall of Yugoslavia*, pp. 105–110. Glenny provides an account of events at Tenja village just before my own visit. It is indeed possible that some Croats and some Serbs lived on either side of the line dividing "old" and "new" Tenja.
13. Doder, Dusko, "Villages Learn How to Hate" in *The European*, n.p., 26–28 July 1991.
14. Jelavich, Barbara, *History of the Balkans* (New York: Cambridge University Press, 1983), vol. 1, pp. 10–13, 27–29. I have depended heavily on Jelavich for a depiction of historical events in the Balkans. I am totally unaware of any ethnic bias on her part and prefer to assume that she was simply a very eminent American historian. Regarding language issues, which have assumed great importance, it should be noted that Slovenes have their own tongue, but understand Serbo-Croatian. Macedonian is closest to Bulgarian, but Macedonians claim it as a separate language.
15. Op. cit. pp. 306–308.
16. Op. cit. vol. 2, pp. 59–63.
17. Op. cit. pp. 60–62.
18. Op. cit. pp. 62, 65–68.
19. Op. cit. pp. 95–96. Also, Bulajic, Milan, *The Role of the Vatican in the Break-up of the Yugoslav State* (Belgrade: Strucna Knjiga, 1994), pp. 20–35. This documented work is a useful compilation of information on the relationship of the Vatican to the Croatian Catholic church before, during, and after the NDH. It also deals with Vatican support for the creation of the new Croatian state.
20. Jelavich, *History of the Balkans*, vol. 2, pp. 95–100; Tuchman, Barbara, *The Proud Tower* (Bantam, 1967). On p. 536, Trotsky is said to have watched Serbs march off to war in bark sandals and with a sprig of green in their hats, which gave them the look of "men doomed for sacrifice." Op. cit. pp. 536–537 Tuchman cites "capitalist" intervention before the war spread to involve Austria and Russia. *The Other Balkan Wars* (Carnegie Endowment, Washington, D.C., 1993), for graphic descriptions of the war's brutality.
21. Jelavich, *History of the Balkans*, vol. 2, pp. 106–114; Gilbert, Martin, *The First World War* (New York: Henry Holt, 1994), pp. 16–17.
22. Jelavich, *History of the Balkans*, vol. 2, pp. 112–114. Tuchman, *Proud Tower*, p. 538, states that the murder of Archduke Franz Ferdinand did not cause a great stir in much of Europe, while Gilbert, p. 18, cites the British Consul-General in Budapest as saying that, "A wave of blind hatred for Serbia and everything Serbian is sweeping over the country." Extensive archival material and photographs from

the National Library of Serbia attest to widespread acts of violence against the Serbian civilian population during World War One.

23. Jelavich, *History of the Balkans*, vol. 2, pp. 114–125. World War One casualties cited in Serbia, Ministry of Information of the Republic of Serbia, 1995.

24. Jelavich, *History of the Balkans*, vol. 2, pp. 143–157, 200–204.

25. Op. cit. pp. 235–237; Churchill, Winston, *The Second World War* (Boston: Houghton Mifflin Co., 1953), vol. 3, pp. 156–175. The statistics for the bombing of Belgrade are Churchill's.

26. Jelavich, *History of the Balkans*, vol. 2, pp. 262–273.

27. Ibid, "Never Again: Ustashi Genocide in the Independent State of Croatia 1941–45," Ministry of Information of the Republic of Serbia, 1995. Bulajic, *Role of the Vatican*, pp. 91–92, credits Dr. Mile Budak (Minister of Religion and Education) with the Ustashe formula to rid Croatia of its Serbs. Budak has been rehabilitated by Tudjman and honored by having a street named after him. Dr. Andrika Artukovic (Minister of Internal Affairs) was extradited from the US in 1986 to Yugoslavia and died in prison in 1988.

28. Avramov, Smila, *Genocide in Yugoslavia*, Belgrade, BIZG, 1995. This work details Ustashe atrocities generally cited in the above publications and is amply footnoted from documentary sources. With regard to the forty pounds of eyes, this was witnessed by the Italian diplomat, Curzio Malaparte, and Italian minister Raffaele Casertano, and cited in a book written by the former. The incident is also mentioned in Bar-Zohar, Michael, *The Avengers*, n.p., p. 126. It is unseemly to dispute Serbian deaths at the hands of the NDH as figures have ranged from 350,000 to 750,000 or more. What we do know is that Croatian President Franjo Tudjman's claim in his book *The Wasteland of Historical Reality* that the total number of deaths at Jasenovac numbered "only around 30–40,000" is typical of Croatian efforts to minimize the attempted genocide.

29. Jelavich, *History of the Balkans*, vol. 2, p. 265 cites 200,000–300,000 forced conversions. Avramov, *Genocide in Yugoslavia*, uses Ante Pavelic's statement that 250,000 had been converted on p. 353. Bulajic, *Role of the Vatican*, p. 99, has Archbishop Alojzije Stepinac reporting to the Vatican that 244,000 conversions had taken place by May 1944.

30. Hersh, Burton, *The Old Boys: The American Elite and the Origins of the CIA* (New York: Charles Scribner and Sons, 1992), p. 183. Avramov, *Genocide in Yugoslavia*, pp. 243–244, has Pavelic delivering crates of jewelry, gold, and other valuables to the Zagreb archbishopric on 4 May 1945 and leaving the next day disguised as a priest with Archbishop Saric of Sarajevo and some 500 other clerics. Pavelic hid in St. Gilgen monastery near Salzburg under the name Father Gomez. He then went to Rome, and then to Argentina in 1948. After an assassination attempt, he went to a monastery in Spain. He is said to have died in a German hospital in Madrid on 26 December 1954, with the personal blessing of Pope Pius XII. Further to Pavelic's time in Argentina, Richard Deacon's *The Israeli Secret Service*, n.p., p. 117, states that Adolf Eichmann was protected for a time by Pavelic.

31. Jelavich, *History of the Balkans*, p. 397, quotes Tito in July 1971 as expressing his concern over rising Croat nationalism, warning that it had "run wild" and "in some villages, because of nervousness, the Serbs are drilling and arming themselves. Do you want 1941 all over again?" Unfortunately, this prophecy was to fulfill itself twenty years later.

Chapter 2 – Embattled Borderlands

1. Zimmerman, Warren, "Origins of a Catastrophe: Memoirs of the Last American Ambassador to Yugoslavia," in *Foreign Affairs*, March–April 1995. Woodward, *Balkan Tragedy*, p. 104, states that for forty years Yugoslavia had enjoyed a special status with the US that guaranteed it access to Western credits to handle its foreign debt in return for its neutrality and its maintenance of a military establishment capable of deterring an attack by the Warsaw Pact. She notes that Zimmerman arrived in Belgrade after serving as ambassador to CSCE, and, therefore, was ready to exert pressure about human rights.

2. Silber and Little, *Death of Yugoslavia*, p. 121. See also pp. 165–66 for an account of Baker's meeting with Bulatovic. Zimmerman, "Origins of a Catastrophe," warned Borisav Jovic against using force when, in January 1991, the JNA was planning to use the army and police to disarm illegal militias. The warning

was made public by the US. Woodward, *Balkan Tragedy*, suggests, p. 151–157, that the US had, in effect, told the JNA that its international role was over, and that the US would not even condone the use of the JNA to put down internal threats to the constitutional order. In fact, by 1990–91, various US Congressmen wanted to cut off Yugoslavia from aid and credit because of the turmoil in Kosovo.

3. Bosnian Serb army and militia operations will be discussed subsequently. Suffice it to say, that apart from cooperation in military matters, the Krajina and Bosnian Serbs failed to forge any kind of political alliance. This was to weaken them later.

4. The mass gravesite is located at Ovcara outside of Vukovar. Serbian ex-mayor Dukmanovic was arrested by the Hague tribunal for his alleged role in the deaths of Croat prisoners. He took his own life before being tried.

5. Vojislav Seselj is the leader of the SRS and is Serbia's most rabid ultra-nationalist. A political science professor from Sarajevo, Seselj was jailed in the 1980s for anti-communist agitation. Seselj seized on the Chetnik tradition of irregular fighters from Serbian history (he supposedly received the title of "Duke" from Momcilo Dujic in the US in 1990). He established a militia of several thousands that has engaged in ethnic cleansing and atrocities against civilians. An advocate of "Greater Serbia," Seselj has long wanted to expel rump-Yugoslavia's Albanians and Croats. A member of parliament, Seselj was used by Milosevic and then was later jailed for his extremism and attempts to undermine the latter. More recently, they cooperated again.

6. "Knocking On Europe's Conscience," Prishtina, Council for the Defense of Human Rights and Freedoms in Prishtina, 1992. See Ilaz Bylykbashi's *Chronicle (1981–95)* (Prishtina: Rilindja, 1996), for a gripping documentary photo record of repression in Kosovo.

7. "Arkan" Raznatovic was elected to the Serbian assembly in December 1992 from Kosovo, but he failed to gain re-election. He was assassinated in Belgrade in January 2000.

8. While SFRY President, Stipe Mesic, was invited to Washington to meet with members of Congress to discuss the growing conflict. He helped to convince his listeners that the Serbs were aggressors.

9. In effect, Carrington and Vance were attempting to contain the conflict, yet the decision of the EC foreign ministers on 17 December rushed the recognition question for all ex-Yugoslavia.

10. Not much later, former US secretaries of state, Cyrus Vance and James Baker, singled out Germany's premature recognition of Slovenia and Croatia as the main cause for the spread of war to Bosnia.

11. Many think Cossiga's dramatic action was aimed at deflecting German influence while reasserting traditional Italian interests in the Adriatic. In 1918, Slovenia joined Yugoslavia to avoid being absorbed by either Austria or Italy. Since independence in 1991, Slovenia has had to fend off Italian territorial claims related to its small Italian minority in that country.

12. Silber and Little, *Death of Yugoslavia*, pp. 122–25. Babic opposed the Vance Plan because it meant the withdrawal of the JNA, which he believed should have stayed to secure Serbian control of the Krajina and Slavonia. After long arguments in Belgrade (during which Babic attempted to obtain assurances from the Bosnian Serbs who were also present), Milosevic split the Krajina leadership, worked to remove Babic from power and then denounced him publicly. Serbian President Milan Milutinovic once cited Belgrade's control problems to the author. Referring to the Serb minorities in Bosnia, and in the Krajina, he said, "They are our Palestinians. We must support them even if we don't always approve of their actions."

13. Op. cit., p. 226. The shooting immediately caused Serbs to take up arms and erect barricades. It is customary for Serbs to fly their flag at weddings. In this case, however, the church was located in an old Turkish bazaar neighborhood dominated by Moslems. A priest was also wounded. The incident, identical to an attack on a Maronite Catholic church in the Christian East Beirut suburb of Ain Rammanah in April 1975, might similarly be called the first shot of the civil war in Bosnia, as in Lebanon.

14. Woodward, *Balkan Tragedy*, p. 281. The "Lisbon Agreement" was signed by the three sides on 18 March. Within a week, Bosniak leader Izetbegovic went back on his word. The Croat Mate Boban then did the same, hoping to hold out for more territory. It was reported (*New York Times*) that Zimmerman had advised Izetbegovic not to sign the agreement in favor of immediate US recognition. Zimmerman denied it, but allows it was one of the "options." Serbs cite Lisbon as the last best chance for peace. It died over the next few months.

15. See Woodward, *Balkan Tragedy*, pp. 196–97. At the time of Lisbon, Washington was exerting pressure on the EC to recognize Bosnia. This was being done, in part, to reassert US authority vis-à-vis Germany. Izetbegovic probably assumed that recognition would assure Bosniak dominance at a settlement. Thus, the US undermined Lisbon by becoming the leader of the recognition bandwagon. The EC complied, and the US followed the next day, recognizing Croatia, Slovenia, and Bosnia. This came on the fiftieth anniversary of Hitler's bombing of Belgrade. Amid a new outbreak of fighting, Serb militias began operating in Bosnia.

16. The breadline "massacre" brought immediate international sanctions against the Serbs, even though it remains unproven who caused it. The UN commander in Sarajevo, General MacKenzie, voiced his suspicion that the Bosniak side staged it to get greater Western support. He said Bosniak TV crews were present. The street was closed. It reopened. People queued up and then there was an explosion. The ballistics, the lack of an impact crater and the wounds all suggested a command-detonated device.

17. By late spring, there were upwards of 100,000 armed Croats in Bosnia-Herzegovina. Woodward, *Balkan Tragedy*, p. 472, footnote 138. The subsequent "alliance" between Croatia and the Bosniaks legitimized Zagreb's presence, even though the Croats were busy carving out their own territory and would later turn against the Moslems.

18. The Sandzak is a politically important Moslem corridor that straddles the border of Serbia and Montenegro on two sides, and Bosnia-Herzegovina and Kosovo on its other two sides. In 1990–91, Moslems from the Sandzak flooded into Sarajevo to support Izetbegovic's SDA.

19. Vilic, Dusan, and Todorovic, Bosko, *The Vukovar War Drama* (Belgrade: DIK Knjizevne Novine Enciklopedija, 1995), pp. 16–22.

20. Op. cit., pp. 23–41. An account of Croat atrocities is taken from the interrogation of Miladin Miljkovic. The JNA states that many of Mercep's men were criminals, persons with "anti-social" backgrounds, alcoholics and mental deviates. Mercep left Vukovar before its capture, and went to Zagreb where he was feted as a hero. He later operated around Gospic. The Split newspaper, *Feral Tribune*, in January 1994, accused him of mass crimes against the Serbs. A Zagreb court defended him as a fatherland war fighter, and sued the newspaper for slander. Glenny, *Fall of Yugoslavia*, p. 113, states that Tudjmen removed Mercep because his notorious brutality was damaging Croatia's international reputation.

21. Woodward, *Balkan Tragedy*, p. 178, puts the number of dead at 2,300 and the wounded in the thousands; Silber and Little, *Death of Yugoslavia*, pp. 193–206. In the latter, p. 206, JNA General Panic is quoted as saying that, after Vukovar fell, there was nothing to stop him from going on to Zagreb. He claims he was reined in by Milosevic, who said that he wanted to gain control only of the Serbian-populated areas.

22. On the Croat side, Woodward, *Balkan Tragedy*, p. 266, cites renegade ZNG elements, called the Wolves of Vukovar, and neo-fascist bands, called the Zebras, who were loyal to Mercep. On p. 356 is cited Tudjman's use of extreme right-wing organizations such as the Croatian Party of Rights and its paramilitary wing, the Croatian Defense League (HOS), Mercep's Association of Croatian Volunteers for Defense of the Fatherland, and elements in the HDZ, in ethnic cleansing in Croatia and in Bosnia-Herzegovina, as well as in terrorist, semi-legal, and criminal activities. Black-market activity and the sale of plundered goods proved profitable to all sides.

23. Regarding Yugoslavia, the actions of Bonn, Vienna, and the Vatican were not taken in concert. Rather, they had overlapping interests. Vienna and the Vatican were sometimes ahead of Bonn. In mid-1991, Germany took the lead. Vilic, Dusan and Todorovic, Bosko, *Breaking of Yugoslavia and Armed Secession of Croatia* (Beli Manaster: Vuk Karadzic Culture Center, 1996), p. 21, cites contact between Tudjman and the BND. P. 24 cites a conversation of Zagreb's interior minister, Josip Boljkovac, who referred to BND support for Croatian independence. Boljkovac claimed his deputy, Perica Juric, entered the ministry at the BND's urging and that he attended the intelligence school at Baden-Baden. He expressed concern that Juric was setting-up a "parallel structure" within the ministry of people from the Croatian Statehood Movement.

24. See Caracciolo, Lucio, *What's Germany Looking For In Yugoslavia?* (Rome, in Limes, 1994), for a detailed treatment of German, Austrian and Vatican politics leading up to recognition in 1992. Besides Reismuller (who is also cited by Woodward), Caracciolo mentions Reismuller's Balkan specialist Victor

Meyer, Carl-Gustav Strohmm of *Die Welt*, *Bild Zeitung*, *Der Spiegel* and *Die Tageszeitung* as dominating the print media on the subject of Yugoslavia.

25. Pope John Paul II demonstrated a lack of sensitivity when, in 1986, he received Austrian president Kurt Waldheim at the Vatican at a time the latter was immersed in controversy over his wartime role in Yugoslavia. Although the US Justice Department labeled Waldheim a war criminal and barred his entry into the US, John Paul II chose to decorate him with a medal. When the Pope visited Zagreb, he made repeated flattering references to Stepinac and permitted himself to be photographed with President Tudjman, his entourage, and his family, including some of the most extreme Croat nationalists, such as Defense Minister Gojko Susak, Vice-Premier Vladimir Seks, and national security boss Hrvoje Sarinic.

26. Woodward, *Balkan Tragedy*, pp. 183–89. P. 149 cites the effect of Vatican-led lobbying through the Catholic church in Germany.

27. Caracciolo, op. cit.; Woodward, *Balkan Tragedy*, pp. 72, 159, 267–68 describes Croatia and Slovenia's involvement with the Alpe-Adria economic, tourism and cultural grouping of Italy and Austria that lobbied actively on behalf of the two breakaway countries.

28. Caracciolo, op. cit.; Woodward, *Balkan Tragedy*, pp. 183–89.

29. Regarding German arms assistance to Croatia, see Defense and Foreign Affairs Arms Transfer Tables for 1993: seventeen MIG-21 aircraft complete and twenty in knock down kits; 150 T-55 main battle tanks. The Federal Republic of Yugoslavia's thirty-seven-page 1992 aide memoire to the UN is an interesting example of illegal purchasing efforts by Croatia during 1991.

30. Lewis, Flora, "Stop This Assault on People and Old Stone," *International Herald Tribune*, 4–5 January 1992; Woodward, *Balkan Tragedy*, p. 182, states that Croat sharpshooters often provoked JNA shelling of Dubrovnik knowing that a Serb attack on this famous city would cause strong international protest. There was damage, deaths, and wounded. Its extent was exaggerated by the media, however.

Chapter 3 – Crossroads of Conflict

1. Kiro Gligorov was born in Shtip on 3 May 1917. He graduated in law from the University of Belgrade. During World War Two, he joined Tito and, in 1944, was a member of ASNOM responsible for finance. He has been secretary for finance of the SFRY executive council, vice-president of the executive council, a member of the SFRY presidency, and chairman of the SFRY assembly (parliament). Now a grandfather, he lives a quiet life. He is careful and calculating and not given to rhetorical excess. A political moderate.

   In 1993, there were about sixty political parties, seventeen of which were represented in the assembly. Several parties had factions allied to other parties, or functioning on their own. In 1996, there were thirty-one legally registered parties. Only five hundred citizens are required to form a party.

2. In 1992–3, leading newspaper columnists, editorial writers and politicians were predicting that the war in Bosnia would soon spread to Kosovo and engulf Macedonia pulling in Greece, Turkey, Bulgaria, and Albania. Such fears were fed by Vojislav Seselj's calls for the expulsion of Albanians from Kosovo and the fact that Arkan Raznatovic was elected to the assembly from there.

3. The NDP is sometimes confusingly referred to as the People's Democratic Party. In early 1997, Halimi was still president. In 1993–4, the NDP was linked to the PDP as part of the ruling coalition. By early 1995, only the PDP held cabinet positions. In 1996, Abdurahman Haliti was the PDP president.

4. The bridge's foundations are said to date from Roman times and could go back 2,000 years. However, since Skopje (Skupi) suffered quakes in 518 and 1555, it is safer to say it is Ottoman. Skopje has been in many hands over the centuries: Roman, Slavic tribes, Bulgarians, Byzantines, Normans, Serbs, Greeks, Turks, and Austrians. It was repeatedly pillaged and burned. It caught fire several times. It has been flooded, and has suffered from cholera.

5. It was the objections of the Greek government, which had been accepted by the Badinter commission in December 1991, that ruled out early recognition of Macedonia. VMRO-DPMNE's immature acclaim for the length and breadth of Macedonia as it existed under the Ottomans played into the hands of Greek politicians.

6. Woodward, *Balkan Tragedy*, p.151, cites US concern over Kosovo in 1991–2, led by Republican senator Robert Dole. P. 197 cites Kosovo as part of the US anti-Serb sanctions policy and the fear of war there

and in Macedonia. pp. 398–99 cite US "warnings" that were reported in the press concerning the displacement of the Albanians as well as the continued abuse of the Albanian population. p. 295 cites the UN's positive response to a request made by Macedonia in late 1992 for protection, which led to the deployment of UNPREDEP.

7. The Greek government did permit a few small shipments of oil for heating to go through for humanitarian purposes.

8. The main point of contact for Greek businessmen in Macedonia was Stoyan Andov who has been referred to as "the fixer." Andov became wealthy in post-communist Macedonia. His wife was said to be well placed in the state MAK petroleum company, which in turn collaborated with the Greek Jet and Mamadakis oil companies to supply Macedonia and to run petroleum into Serbia. People close to Mitsotakis were involved, presumably with the latter's knowledge. Former Greek security official, General Nikos Gyllakis (then aide to Mitsotakis), served as a political intermediary to Gligorov.

9. From May 1992–June 1994, Macedonia estimated its economic losses due to sanctions against Yugoslavia as US$3.1 billion. It stated that the Greek blockade cost an additional US$500 million annually, due to increased transportation and port charges. Oil cost an added US$57 a ton on average. 185,000 were unemployed. 60,000 had been laid off. 130,000 received partial salaries and 70,000 had not been paid for months. An estimated seventy percent of industry used 30–50 percent of its capacity. By 1994, its gross national product per capita was US$771—one-half the pre-war level.

10. Besides the major political objections cited, Albanian complaints were many: they said they were not fairly represented at the census institute, that, unlike others, census forms had not been delivered to their houses, that their applications for new identity and citizenship papers were delayed by the government. Unsophisticated attitudes surfaced as well: some thought the census would require them to spend money to purchase tax stamps. Others wrongly thought they had to validate their citizenship. Many Albanians in Macedonia are Albanian citizens, or only possess SFRY documents.

11. The government claimed that 20,000 Albanians were listed as members of an illegal paramilitary organization. They said they had confiscated 300 weapons. The defendants claimed that that the group had been formed for self-defense should events threaten the Albanian community. Ten persons were sentenced for up to eight years.

12. A document distributed by VMRO-DPMNE purports to describe the government's "Operation Raskol," which means "to split." In part, it is an alleged transcript of a phone conversation dealing with efforts to subvert VMRO-DPMNE. It has been published in the press in Skopje.

13. Dimovska overstates her case somewhat as, after the Kljusev resignation, Gligorov gave VMRO-DPMNE head Georgievski a mandate to form a government, which he was unable to do. It is possible, however, that Gligorov went through the required motions amidst an "agreement" not to work with VMRO-DPMNE's young leader. It is said that Georgievski's father was a Bulgarian communist. If it were true, it would not help his standing with some. By 1996, VMRO had five different groups. Dimovska defended this, saying they represent only tendencies, like the ruling coalition in Slovenia. For simplicity's sake, we will refer only to VMRO-DPMNE.

14. At the outset, it must be noted that most Bulgarians claim Macedonians are Bulgarian, including Delchev. If the weight of words alone counts, they might win the argument, for they have produced massive books to argue their case. It is more to the point to accept the fact that there were two Macedonian organizations: one under Delchev, the other established two years later which was under the control of the Bulgarian government and military. They fought each other savagely. It is logical to assume that Delchev's internal organization represented different, strictly Macedonian interests and is, therefore, the authentic movement.

15. Jelavich, *History of the Balkans*, vol. 2, pp. 89–95 supports the above contention. She also points out Austria's interests in an Aegean port.

16. Laffan, R. G. D., *The Serbs: The Guardians of the Gate* (1917). Lectures reprinted by Dorset Press, New York, 1989. Pp. 56–69 cover the pre-Balkan Wars turbulence in Macedonia. He usefully points out that, in 1870, the Sultan permitted the establishment of a Bulgarian Exarchate church in Constantinople only loosely connected to the Patriarchate to counter the Greeks and Serbs. Clause 10 of the Sultans *firman*, or edict, stated that, if two-thirds of the population in any district wished to be

Exarchate, they could do so. This led MRO-External to coerce, by threat of arms, villages over to their side in support of their plans to annex the entire area.

17. Kaplan, Robert D., *Balkan Ghosts: A Journey Through History* (New York: Vintage, 1994). Quoting a pro-Bulgarian hagiographer, Mercia MacDermott, Kaplan on p. 59 has Delchev die heroically in a firefight with the Turks. Jelavich, *History of the Balkans*, p. 94 says he was captured and executed. She adds that the uprising was poorly organized.

18. *Macedonia* (Skopje: Institute of National History, 1981), Pandevski, Manol, *Yane Sandanski and the Macedonian National Liberation Movement*, pp. 243–264. Sandanski's life is illustrative of the tragic, violent struggle waged by VMRO's leaders and members. He was associated with VMRO's top leaders, Delchev, Dame Gruev, Gjorche Petrov, Pere Toshev, and Nikola Karev, and played a leading role in trying to sustain VMRO after the failure of the revolt. Like Delchev, he had some military training. Interestingly, it was his idea to abduct the American Ellen Stone for ransom. Like many, he first attempted to cooperate with the Vrhovists and then fell out with them, striving to keep VMRO (sometimes referred to as VMRO-Odrin) independent. In early 1903, he expressed his opposition to mounting a revolt that year, as well as to Delchev's decision to admit Boris Sarafov (a Vrhovist) into VMRO. After Ilinden and VMRO's collapse, Sandanski worked for social reform with some of the survivors. A Vrhovist detachment unsuccessfully attempted to hunt him down in 1905. Sandanski laid an ambush, killing some, capturing forty-three. He executed four who were judged to have committed crimes. Another attempt to kill him was foiled by the ordered assassination of Sarafov by Todor Panitsa. By autumn 1908, a revived VMRO began to have contact with the Young Turks. Sandanski supported federalism within a democratically reformed, decentralized Turkey. Just before a VMRO unity congress set out for Salonika, another assassination attempt wounded him slightly, but broke up the meeting. Efforts to work with the Young Turks failed within three years. In the First Balkan War, he and his fighters sided with Bulgaria. When toasting a "free Macedonia" at a victory banquet in Salonika, Bulgarian officers tried to attack him with their sabers. At the outset of World War One, Sandanski and Alexander Stamboliski attempted to dissuade Sofia from becoming an ally of the Central Powers. In April 1915, Vrhovists, acting under Todor Alexandrov intercepted him along a road in Pirin Macedonia and killed him.

19. Jelavich, *History of the Balkans*, vol. 2, pp. 95–100.

20. Ibid. Lord Kinross, *The Ottoman Centuries: The Rise and Fall of the Turkish Empire* (New York: Morrow Quill, 1977), pp. 565–609.

21. Gilbert, *The First World War*, pp. 460–462, 466, 468, 474, 477, 489–490.

22. *Macedonian Times*, Sept. 1995; Minoski, Mihaljo, *The US and the Macedonian Issue in 1919*, n.p., pp. 15–18.

23. Ibid; Mihailov, Mile, *The Macedonian Association in the US and Canada During the Period from 1928–35*, n.p., pp. 443–462. At the third congress of the Balkan Communist Federation in Moscow in July 1921, Bulgarian delegate Kolarov advocated joining Vardar, Pirin, and Aegean Macedonia. Three years later, at the sixth congress, the Federation voted autonomy for a "Republic of Macedonia and Thrace" within a Balkan federation. This decision was ratified by the third congress of the Greek Communist Party.

24. Hristov, Alexandar, *The Formation of the New Macedonian State* (Skopje: Macedonian Review Editions, 1984), pp. 38, 42. Although written in communist jargon, this is a useful explanation of the relationship between AVNOJ and ASNOM. Also, it helpfully refers to the formation of Partisan units, and of commands at the corps and division level (the 16th brigade was formed in October 1944). It therefore suggests that considerable fighting went on apart from the main struggle in Bosnia. It also depicts a historic union of communist and nationalist aspirations. In late 1944, the US State Department stated its opposition to the establishment of an autonomous Macedonia that would include part of Greece. It described Yugoslav and Bulgarian efforts to reraise the Macedonian issue as a communist ploy aimed at gaining Greek territory.

25. Close, David H., *The Origins of the Greek Civil War* (London and New York: Longman, 1995), pp. 193–223. The larger communist guerrilla forces were called the Democratic Army of Greece (DSE). Tito began to break with Stalin in 1948 and finally closed the border with Greece in July 1949, sealing off the DSE from further support. Stalin always had doubts about the success of the Greek communists and limited his assistance. Greece was considered to be in the British sphere of influence according to the deal that Stalin had struck with Churchill.

26. Woodward, *Balkan Tragedy*, p. 161. The idea was to form a confederation out of federal Yugoslavia (SFRY).

27. In May 1994, Amnesty International expressed concern over the beating of Greek cleric, Nikodimos Tsarknias, and his sister, Maria, by Greek border guards after they had crossed at Nikis from Bitola. The two supported Macedonian minority rights. Amnesty also noted that Christos Sideropoulos was to stand trial for statements made at a conference in Copenhagen alleging the violation of minority rights of Macedonians living in Greece. The US State Department estimates there are upwards of 50,000 Slavs in Greece who remain unrecognized. The department's 1994 human rights report described the minority as suffering "harassment." In 1996, Greece protested a Carnegie Endowment-Aspen Institute study on their minorities. A Greek-born scholar, Anastasia Karakasidou, has studied the ethnic composition of northern villages in a work entitled, *Fields of Wheat, Hills of Blood*, concluding that a significant Slavophone minority exists.

28. The issue before the European Court was whether a country has the right to close its border if there exists a credible threat to its internal stability. Greece argued successfully that it had acted in defense of its national sovereignty.

29. Gligorov won a first round victory for president with 52.4 percent to VMRO-DPMNE leader Georgievsk's 14.4 percent. Claims of fraud were made most vigorously by younger, under-thirty-five, voters. The "results" of the second round gave the SDSM-led coalition a two-thirds majority in the assembly, enough to deal with its Greek problem and amend the constitution if need be.

30. It appears that the Macedonian government is demonstrating sensitivity on the Bulgarian language issue, as does Sofia, by not permitting people to assert any suggestion of a Bulgarian identity, should it exist for some. One suspects a minority overlap along Macedonia's eastern border.

31. Fadil Suleimani is one of a number of Albanian activists who have entered Macedonia from Kosovo. As rector of a non-government approved university set up in private homes and offices, he used the same tactics as the Kosovars against the Serbian authorities. He had appealed to his supporters to defend the school… and a few weapons turned up. Suleimani was charged with inciting a mass rebellion. Article 45 of the constitution states, "Citizens have the right to establish private schools at all levels of education under conditions determined by law." Article 46 states, "…The conditions of establishment, performance, and termination of the activities of a university are regulated by law." Hence, under *Catch-22* wording, university operations fall under the law.

32. After the announcement of the agreement with Greece, unsigned leaflets accusing Gligorov of betrayal were found scattered about Skopje. The bomb vehicle was traced to an outlying town and had been recently purchased by a person of Slavic origin who has not been identified. Gligorov underwent lengthy head surgery, losing one eye. Offers of medical assistance poured in from a number of countries. Allegations of Mafia involvement, including a large Bulgarian business group, remain unproven. No one has claimed responsibility.

33. The tally to drop the disputed flag and Article 49 was 110–1. Unfortunately, the new flag—eight broad sunrays emanating from a gold disk on a red field—resembles a Japanese naval flag from World War Two. So far, the Japanese have not protested.

34. Gligorov made strenuous attempts to keep the Liberals in the coalition. The new cabinet had ten ministers from SDSM, five PDP, and three SPM members. In May 1995, Andov had accused the SDSM finance minister of awarding the SDSM with US$212,000 in government funds for party work that he claimed should have gone to the Liberal Party. The minister brushed aside the accusation, stating that such allocations were irregular and not regulated by law. For its part, SDSM was irritated that Andov had invited he VMRO-DPMNE-DP opposition to attend a LP congress to "re-examine the existence of the coalition," according to LP party spokesman Ace Kocevski.

35. Albanian nationalism is an unsolved problem in Macedonia. The moderate PDP is led by politicians once kept content by ministerial portfolios and their share of patronage. However, today, they are pushed by their community to do more and get more. The PDP is not immune to influence from Tirana and Kosovo. This is doubly so for the NDP and the Party for Democratic Prosperity for Albanians (PDPA) led by Arben Xhafferi which split from the PDP in 1995. A triangular relationship exists between the activists in Macedonia, Tirana, and Kosovo. Just under the surface lies a network of trafficking in heroin and hashish that runs from Turkey, Bulgaria, Macedonia, and Albania to Italy and

northern Europe. Albanians from Macedonia and Kosovo are involved. Traffic is estimated at US$20 million a year in Macedonia alone. This problem has been cited by the Paris Observatoire Geopolitique des Drougues, the International Bulletin of Narcotics and the US Drug Enforcement Agency.

36. Upon ending his responsibilities for negotiations between Greece and Macedonia, US special envoy Matthew Nimitz stated that he was not pleased to use the name FYROM. He explained, "It is the same as if you call the USA a former British Colony in America... It is a reference, not a name." He made clear his personal preference for the Republic of Macedonia.

37. By 1996, inflation had been brought under control from 2,000 percent to about ten percent annually. Its currency has been stabilized. Some 600 state companies had been sold off and 400 more were in the pipeline (almost all from management/employee buy-outs). Its US$2 billion in annual exports were expected to improve. 18,000 private businesses had opened over the previous five years. Unemployment was estimated at thirty percent (200,000 persons of working age) with 25,000 jobs having been cut from loss-making industries. Stop-gap aid from the World Bank and EU was around US$240 million in 1995. 200,000 persons were pensioners (roughly ten percent). Wages were an average US$200 a month.

38. Cupino Brdo is a mountain on the border with Yugoslavia that overlooks an important east-west highway. Under protest, the JNA established an observation post some hundred meters or so inside Macedonian territory. This was subject to discussion between the two countries. After several months, the JNA pulled out without explanation. This was the only known Yugoslav intrusion during the five-year emergency.

39. Crvenkovski's cabinet changes increased the SDSM to ten, PDP five, and SPM three.

40. One must wonder what will take place in Macedonia in a post-Gligorov era. The SDSM is an alliance or union of groups with upwards of 50,000 members/supporters. As the major component of the ruling coalition, it has attempted to form a broad-based government with relatively wide appeal and, importantly, to include the PDP. The LP, a party representing significant business interests is now in opposition. The PDP has split with the PDPA now constituting the larger and more nationalistically assertive Albanian party. It is doubtful that VMRO-DPMNE is inclined to accommodate Albanian demands. Increasingly, young people supportive of VMRO-DPMNE/MAAK have clashed with Albanian activists. According to John Pomfret of the *Washington Post*, Gligorov learned to mistrust nationalism from Josip Broz (Tito). He quotes him as saying, "The nationalism others are pursuing makes them blind... The goals they have were important in the eighteenth and nineteenth centuries, but are not important now." Macedonia needs leaders who, with skill and wisdom, can get its people to pull together to achieve their rightful place in the European community.

Chapter 4 – Europe's Orphan

1. McGann, Jerome J., ed., *Byron: The Complete Poetical Works*, vol. 2 (Oxford University, 1980); Longford, Elizabeth, *Byron's Greece* (UK: Harper and Row, 1975); Cheetham, Simon, *Byron in Europe: In Childe Harold's Footsteps* (UK: Thorson Publishing Group, 1988).

2. Fan Noli established an independent (autocephalous) Albanian Orthodox church in Boston in 1908. Its status is questioned by the Greek Orthodox Church in Istanbul even today.

3. Jelavich, *History of the Balkans*, vols. 1 and 2. I relied heavily on Jelavich for historical background. A cautious use of *Albania, General Information* (Tirana: 8 Nentori Publishing House, 1984), was helpful. Griffith, William E., *Albania and the Sino-Soviet Rift* (Cambridge, MA: The MIT Press, 1963), proved extremely good for political background before and after World War Two.

4. Vickers, Miranda and Pettifer, James, *Albania: From Anarchy to a Balkan Identity* (London: Hurst and Company, 1997), pp. 25–29. What began in the winter of 1990 as a few Albanians attempting to seek refuge in foreign embassies had, by July, become 4–5,000 who demanded visas after Alia permitted them to have a passport. There were riots and the German embassy was gutted. The occupation of embassy premises involved a wide spectrum of people, but mainly unemployed youth. The regime blamed "hoodlum elements."

5. Initially, northern Greek communities gave food and clothing to hundreds of refugees. When the situation got out of control, Greek public opinion turned against them. Some 200,000 work in Greece

today. Many illegals are preyed upon by the Greek police who shake them down for regular payments in order to remain.

6. Stamos's activity was part of a concerted effort to deny legitimacy to the Albanian Orthodox Church and to assert territorial claims dating back to 1912–20. Seraphim told the author that all Epirus had been Greek for a thousand years, a gross exaggeration.

7. Qiriazati's open letter to Mitsotakis is clearly separatist. It was widely publicized in the Albanian press and undoubtedly provided welcome ammunition to the newly elected nationalist DP government of President Sali Berisha against Omonia and Athens.

8. Vickers and Pettifer, *Albania*, p. 14. The Elbasan metallurgical plant was built by the Chinese for which they are owed an enormous sum. The same goes for the Soviet-built Drin Valley hydroelectric scheme and other projects. In 1995, some US$3 billion was outstanding.
   An estimated 700,000 pillboxes were built from 1978 onward.

9. Robinson, Charles, *Ancient History* (New York: Macmillan, 1951), pp. 475, 562, 641, 643–48.
   Jelavich, *History of the Balkans*, vol. 1, pp. 4, 9, 25–26.

10. Op. cit., p. 31.
    Op. cit. pp. 34–35.

11. Vickers and Pettifer, *Albania*, pp. 22–23.
    Giovania, Christos, *Albania and Albanians in World Art* (Athens: Ferid Hudhri, 1990), pp. 22–37. A very nicely done book.

12. Kinross, *The Ottoman Centuries*, pp. 474–76, 502.

13. Jelavich, *History of the Balkans*, vol. 1, pp. 363–66.

14. *Kosova, Review No. 2*, Tirana, n.p., 1993. P.5 quotes Sir Edward Grey.
    Sulzberger, C. L., *A Long Row of Candles*, n.p. (Macmillan, 1969), pp. 45–61. Very interesting comments about a corrupt king.

15. Griffith, *Albania*, pp. 3–34. I have used Griffith and Jelavich also in the following paragraphs. The Albanian communists received US$26 million in UNRRA relief and also small amounts from the UK and US. However, UK–US missions were withdrawn after October 1946 when two British destroyers struck Albanian mines in disputed waters in Corfu channel. Forty-four men were killed. Later, in 1949–52, the US-UK infiltrated guerrillas into Albania in an effort to overthrow the communists and restore King Zogu. The operation failed when a British MI6 officer, Kim Philby, passed information to the Soviets. Three hundred Albanians died; Jelavich, *History of the Balkans*, vol. 2, p. 331, 378.

16. Op. cit. pp. 319–20.

17. Vickers and Pettifer, *Albania*, pp. 33–40. The authors suggest that Alia believed that Berisha and his DP associates would cooperate with the regime and even follow the lead of a shaky APL.

18. Alia's move to reduce personal customs duty indicated how far removed he was from the mood of the people. His timidity led the opposition to accelerate its drive for total political reform. APL never upheld human rights or legality, only Hoxha's rule.

19. Banac, Ivo, ed., *Eastern Europe in Revolution* (Cornell University, 1992); Biberaj, Elez, *Albania: The Last Domino*, n.p., pp. 188–206. Foto Cami, who attacked Gorbachev, is cited as the most liberal-minded member of the APL politbureau. Fatos Nano is not mentioned among reform-minded intellectuals and technocrats who included writer Ismail Kadare, Sali Berisha, scientist Ylli Popa, and economist Gramoz Pashko. When, on 20 February 1991 100,000 people tore down Hoxha's statute in the center of Tirana, Alia formed a new government and replaced Prime Minister Adil Carcani with Nano, whom Biberaj describes only as "a prominent thirty-nine-year-old economist." She states that Nano rejected comprehensive economic overhaul. Misha Glenny's *The Rebirth of History: Eastern Europe in the Age of Democracy* (London: Penguin, 1990), does not mention him. Neither does William Echikson's *Lighting the Night: Revolution in Eastern Europe* (London: Pan Books, 1990). It seems that Nano was a mid-level economist who was expected not to make waves. He was reappointed by Alia after the APL's win on 31 March. Vickers and Pettifer, Albania, pp. 52–53, state that Nano was included in Alia's advisory group and urged "Gorbachev-type reforms."

20. Vickers and Pettifer, *Albania*, pp. 53, 72. Following a delivery of 1,000 tons of Italian food and medicine in March, the G-24 gave over US$150 million in emergency food aid, which, in December, began to be distributed by 500 Italian soldiers in "Operation Pelican." Despite Mafia involvement

during the then socialist government of Benedetto Craxi, which resulted in wholesale theft, the aid is credited with preventing thousands from starving. It later also led to criminal charges against Nano.

21. Op. cit., pp. 52–80. Alia was intent on containing and capturing the uprising as had been done in Romania, relying on the army and a new National Information Service (NIS re-employed many Sigurimi members under Irakli Kocollari). Nano's government of National Unity collapsed amid a general strike in June. Ylli Bufi (*bufi* means "stupid" in Albanian), food minister, became the prime minister of an all-party government of National Stability. Gramoz Pashko (son of Hoxha cohort Josif Pashko) had been playing an important role negotiating foreign aid and putting together an economic program. When Berisha pulled the plug on Bufi, Pashko was in London talking to the IMF. He was furious with Berisha at the time and subsequently left DP. The mainly ethnic-Greek Union of Human Rights had several of its candidates disqualified owing to technical reasons. They claimed they were discriminated against.

22. Berisha's defense minister, Safet Zhulali (a school teacher, whom many say didn't know the front of a tank from its rear), made a practice of disclaiming Albania's Warsaw Pact participation. In fact, Tirana was a founder member and gave the Soviets a valuable submarine base in the Adriatic Sea on Sazan Island off Vlore.

23. According to information provided by the Albanian Ministry of Foreign Affairs Diaspora Department, 20,643 workers were ejected, 3,401 of whom had valid visas. Twelve were "gravely maltreated."

24. Vickers and Pettifer, *Albania*, pp. 239–40. Nano authorized food to be purchased with Italian credits using the Bari-based Levante firm at three times the world market price (much of it never arrived). Also arrested was former Prime Minister Vilson Ahmeti (1991–92 four month transitional government), accused of wasting US$1.6 million trying to reschedule Albania's US$450 million foreign debt. This was known as the "Arsidi affair" as two arrested bank officials paid Frenchman, Nicola Arsidi, a huge sum to fix the debt problem. He fled Albania with his fee, but failed to reschedule the debt.

25. A senior Greek journalist told the author that during 1991–94, dozens of ethnic-Greek Albanians were passing in and out of the office of the Greek National Intelligence Agency (EYP) in the city of Ioannia. It was like a revolving door. Undoubtedly, the Albanian government became aware of this activity.

26. In July 1995, the MAVI members were charged with murder and illegal possession of firearms. Subsequently, the murder charges were dropped when the prosecution failed to conclusively link them with the Peshkepia (Episkopi) raid. In February 1997, they were charged with planning a terrorist raid. They were sentenced to four and a half years. The sentence was appealed.

27. Vickers and Pettifer, *Albania*, p. 249. UN sanctions-busting across Lake Shkodra and the Bojana River was organized by Albanian gangs with the alleged involvement of the police. Most of the gangs had supported Berisha who, himself, is a northern Gheg from Tropoja.

28. In the spring of 1993, the US CIA began to operate pilotless drone observation aircraft from a field at Lezha for flights over Bosnia, Serbia, and Montenegro. There have been persistent rumors that US personnel are using Sazan Island as well.

29. No one has explained how the schemes operated for as long as they did. Money from the Italian-cum-local Mafia from criminal activity (UN sanctions-busting and narcotics trafficking) could have been laundered at discount rates, which could have augmented money brought in by ordinary investors. Apparently the schemes engaged in banking business activity, which lent credibility. Many believed that when the war in Bosnia ended, the schemes developed a liquidity problem, a shortage of ready cash. In June 1997, the IMF, World Bank and others, met with Albanian officials in Rome to assess the problem. In late August, the Nano government chose auditors to investigate to determine what money or assets could be salvaged. Mrs. Kadena's Sude was said to owe some US$60 million. Possibly the first pyramid was Illyria, which operated briefly in 1992. It, and the others that followed, reflected the urgent need for capital to finance imports, domestic enterprise, and public gullibility. Loan interest ran at twelve to twenty percent monthly (profits on imports were also high), while depositors received four to five percent. By 1994, demand for capital became extreme. "Black" money from corruption and graft and from crime filled the gap (est. US$600 million by mid-1996). While most of it was in lekes, Italian lira and hard currencies also were circulating. A lack of government transparency encouraged bribes, kickbacks and insider deals—especially concerning privatization. It snowballed. From US$500,000 a day, some pushed higher amounts before the collapse.

30. Dr. Sali Berisha, a cardiologist educated in France, headed a physician's organization under the communists and was a member of the APL. However, he had good reformist credentials and possessed a strong, charismatic personality. He went over to the democrats early on, demonstrated personal courage and his government was pro-West and pro-free market. If it had not been for the collapse of the investment schemes and his dictatorial traits, he would probably be in power today.

31. The so-called rebel "committees of national salvation" turned out to be largely leaderless, or led by criminal gangs. Jonathan Randal in the *Washington Post* of 27 April 1997 described the almost total breakdown in authority in Vlore, which had come under the control of Mafia elements, and now was being "policed" by a gang of ruffians with AK-47s led by a former jailbird.

32. Leka arrived wearing a camouflage uniform, a beret and carrying two side arms. Just before elections and the referendum, one of his rallies erupted in gunfire and a youth was killed. Leka's Legaliteti (one of two) advocated a constitutional monarchy, but lacked both a program and much of a following in Albania. Some of its diaspora members consist of pre-Hoxha land-owning interests.

33. Money laundering and other illegal business schemes require front companies, no doubt many of which in Albania are Italian.

34. In September 1997, Greek police in Athens seized forty-four AK-47s and 135 pounds of marijuana after a shootout with five Greeks and Albanians who had moved their wares south from Konitsa. A week earlier, two Greeks and two Albanians were caught in Athens with 315 pounds of marijuana, which had been brought to Corfu by boat. A sad example of the lawlessness that has seized this shattered society was the shooting on 18 September of DP MP Azem Hajdari by fellow Socialist MP Gafur Mazreku just outside the assembly's chamber. Two days earlier, the two had argued and traded punches over who had the right to address the assembly. Both came from the north where the Canun law of Lek Dukagjeni operated, where any insult can lead to revenge through bloodshed, the same as in Sicily and southern Italy. However, though Mazreku pumped four bullets into Hajdari, he somehow survived. Hajdari was a prominent anti-regime student leader in the early 1990s.

35. Reuters from Rome reported comments by Italian anti-Mafia chief prosecutor, Pier Luigi Vigna, that the Mafia was involved in the Albanian pyramid schemes. Organized crime squad head, Alessandro Pansa, added that criminals from Puglia-Calabria-Campania have linked up with Albanians to traffic in narcotics, arms, illegal immigration and prostitution. Quantities of marijuana were now grown in the south, even just outside Saranda, and production of cocaine is reportedly being attempted. Narcotics from Turkey transit Macedonia and Albania and are handled by the Kosovo mafia. It is widely assumed that Albanian police and security officials had their hands in this business. In any case, the following fled to escape charges or attempts on their lives: Bashkim Gazidede, the director of the now disbanded SHIK; Xhahit Xhaferi, commander of the presidential guard; Agin Shehu, national police director—all to Italy.

    The EU, and to a lesser extent, the US, had provided Albania with around US$260 million a year in aid, a not inconsiderable amount of money. One would have thought that the financial community would have insisted that the pyramids be shut down and that a proper banking-securities system be established.

36. The age of mandates is over. Nevertheless, the EU should use its existing machinery to exercise supervision, or oversight, of Albania's governments to insist that they establish needed institutions and an administration according to EU guidelines. The fact that a majority of Albanians are nominally Moslem should not influence any decision concerning its eligibility for admission to the EU.

37. For nostalgia's sake, the author suggests that an annual Lord Byron poetry reading be held at the John Belushi bar in Tirana.

Chapter 5 – The Heart of Darkness

1. Zeljko Raznatovic (Arkan) led the Serbian Volunteer Guards, also known as Tigers. The spoiled son of a senior JNA officer, Arkan was a delinquent who got into crime while organizing strong-arm supporters for Belgrade's Red Star soccer team. He became an agent for Yugoslav security and was sent abroad to work against émigré terrorist Ustashe who had attacked Yugoslav embassies. He continued his criminal activity and was wanted by Interpol. He acquired a string of cafes in Belgrade

and, with money made from ethnic cleansing and the sale of gasoline in east Slavonia, he became quite wealthy. He entered parliament briefly from Kosovo in 1992. Tall and boyishly handsome, he married a Serb beauty, had a son and lent his presence to flamboyant nationalist affairs. A photo of October 1995 shows a Tiger at Erdut during their fifth anniversary celebration. Another photo, of November 1995 (credit to Robert Rajtic) shows soldiers of Croatia's Tiger brigade parading in Zagreb on their fifth anniversary. It suggests that in late 1990, Serbia and Croatia were both getting their Tigers ready.

2. *American Photo*, Sept/Oct 1993, pp. 66–68, 76–77.

3. The main victims of conflict that aims to establish ethnic states are civilian. Carnegie Endowment, *The Other Balkan Wars* (introduced by George Kennan) (Washington D.C., 1993), contains the official Carnegie Peace Commission report on the Balkan wars of 1912–13. Then, what we now call ethnic cleansing was widely practiced by all sides: Serbian, Bulgarian, and Greek. It was accompanied by looting; the destruction of villages; rape; discriminate and indiscriminate executions; the mistreatment of prisoners of war; the internment of civilians for subsequent prisoner exchanges; and the murder of community leaders. The destruction of churches, monuments, books and artifacts attesting to the worth of a people was also common. David Rieff's *Slaughterhouse: Bosnia and the failure of the West*, London, Vantage, 1995; Peter Maas's *Love Thy Neighbor: A Story of War* (London: Papermac, 1996) and Edward Vulliamy's *Seasons in Hell: Understanding Bosnia's War* (London: Simon and Schuster, 1994), give searing accounts of Serbian misdeeds, mostly from secondary sources. However, many reports of death camps and rape camps were overblown. Deaths and rapes did occur, but not to the extent reported. Evidence was often in error as when a skinny Serb thief (who was thin because he had TB) was labeled a Bosnian Moslem. Another was an emaciated retired Serb JNA officer, Branko Velac, who, while he was in a Bosniak camp, was described by BBC TV as a Moslem captive of the Serbs. A great furor was made over the alleged Serb rape campaign against Moslem women. The ICRC and UNHCR found no evidence of systematic rape. Amnesty International did report in January 1993 that women from all three sides were victims of rape, but that Moslem women had suffered most and that Serbs were the main perpetrators. Arkan's men murdered some two dozen Moslems at Bijeljina. According to research conducted by Louise Branson of the British *Sunday Times*, it appears that about 150 Serbs died at Sijekovac. In May, some thirty-five Serbs (identified) were killed at Bradina with many more simply missing. By mid-1993, she had catalogued nine massacres—four by Serbs, two by Croats, one by Moslems, and two by Croats and Moslems combined. She stated that so far, only the Serbs were getting the blame when all were guilty and the Croats were getting away with murder. No doubt there were other atrocities as well.

4. Sefer Halilovic quit the JNA in 1991 to form the SDA Patriotic League. Made a general, he was the Bosniak army's first Chief of Staff. His book, *The Cunning Strategy*, Sarajevo, Marsal, 1997, which contains voluminous official documentation, suggests Izetbegovic was inclined towards ethnic division. This, and Halilovic's opposition to incompetence and corruption at the top led to his ouster in 1993 (Svarm, Filip, "Kill Then Tell," *Transitions*, Feb. 1998, pp. 22–29). Sarajevo's most infamous criminal leader during the early part of the war was Musan Toplovic Caco, who commanded the 10th Brigade in 1992–93. Caco's men were armed by the SDA with the full approval of Izetbegovic. Fighting by day and stealing and murdering by night, Caco cleansed hundreds of Serbs from their apartments, subjecting them to beatings, torture and murder. The authorities were aware of this and condoned it. Caco was killed in late 1993 because he was intimidating the regime's leadership. Senior police official, Munib Alibabic Munja, believes he was killed because he was living proof of atrocities committed against Serbs and of those in SDA who wanted a purely Islamic state. Of Caco's men, four have been given light sentences. Bajazit Tuzvic is Izetbegovic's bodyguard. Timur Numic is a top official at SDA headquarters. Caco was given a hero's burial in 1996. Estimates of Serb deaths range from 500 to 1,500. (Igric, Gordana, "Not Just the Victim," *War Report: Bulletin of the Institute for War and Peace Reporting*, n.p., Dec. 1997–Jan. 1998, pp. 9–10.)

    Commissariat for Refugees of the Republic of Serbia, *Suffering of the Serbs in Sarajevo* (Belgrade, 1996), (an 800-page collection of testimony by Serbs from Sarajevo in English and Serbo-Croat). The book contains documentary accounts with ICRC corroboration. Serb civilians who remained in Sarajevo were harried from their jobs and apartments, robbed and were kept at various locations where they were brutalized and murdered. Forced to dig trenches at the front, many were killed or wounded, or were shot by Moslem snipers as they were working. It appears it was nearly impossible for Serbs to remain neutral. One would have to prove loyalty by taking up arms, or performing some other service. However, some Serb and Croat officers willingly served in the army.

5. Izetbegovic worked two tracks politically. Through the first half of 1991, he proposed reorganizing SFRY as a confederation. After war broke out, he worked to take Bosnia-Herzegovina to independence. He began military preparations, went to Saudi Arabia, Pakistan, and Turkey, and sent SDA envoys to other Moslem countries. He later applied to join the OIC while he was a rotating president of Bosnia-Herzegovina. On 27 February 1991 he had told the assembly, "I would sacrifice peace for a sovereign Bosnia-Herzegovina, but for that peace in Bosnia-Herzegovina I would not sacrifice sovereignty." Put simply, he would fight for independence. Silber and Little, *Death of Yugoslavia*, p. 233. Another critical moment came during the Lisbon talks. After he had signed the agreement of 18 March 1992, which proposed having a canonized Bosnia-Herzegovina, Izetbegovic reversed himself in the knowledge that US recognition of an integral Bosnia-Herzegovina would be forthcoming. See Woodward, *Balkan Tragedy*, pp. 281, 495. The die was cast when he ordered full mobilization on 4 April (US recognition came 6 April). He then turned his forces against the JNA, which had tried to be neutral.

6. Iran provided arms aid to Sarajevo only a few months after war began. An Iranian Boeing 747, purportedly carrying humanitarian aid, arrived at Zagreb airport with tons of guns and ammunition, plus forty volunteers. Askold Kruscheinycky of the *European* reported in January 1993 that arms were entering via Split and Hungary. Iran used foreign ships, false end-user certificates and the Hezbollah in Lebanon for cover. In return, Zagreb (besides its cut of arms) obtained favorable terms for loans and oil. This arrangement went on despite Croat-Moslem fighting (Stepe Mesic once went to Tehran to smooth things over). He also reported the arrival of fighters from Moslem countries. In April 1996, it was revealed that the US administration had condoned Iranian arms via Croatia in 1994–95. In November 1994, *Le Monde*'s Remy Ourdan reported that arms from Moslem countries (Turkey, Iran, Pakistan, and Saudi Arabia) were entering Bosnia-Herzegovina in quantity via Croatia. He cited the port of Ploce, Krk Island and Zagreb's airport as transit points. As an example of diversification, he even noted the appearance of the Chinese-made Norinco Red Arrow 8 anti-tank missile by the Bosniak army. In February 1997, it was similarly reported that the government of Saudi Arabia had shipped large amounts of arms to Bosnia-Herzegovina (besides US$500 million in humanitarian aid) with the full knowledge of the US administration. Michael Dobbs, *Washington Post Service*, reported official Saudi sources as saying that the program ran for some three years. John Pomfret and David B. Ottaway of WPS state that Iran's effort began in 1992 with Turkish assistance and that by 1993 Ankara's effort involved Saudi Arabia, Malaysia, Brunei, and Pakistan. WPS reported that other shipments came from Hungary and Argentina, presumably destined for Croatia. Zagreb normalized relations with Tehran in April 1992 and sent a Moslem Croat, Osman Muftic, as ambassador. Sarajevo sent an arms dealer, Hasan Cengic. Cengic subsequently became Bosnia-Herzegovina Minister of Defense.

7. Silber and Little, *Death of Yugoslavia*, p. 333. By mid-August of 1993, the ICRC had gained access to 6,474 detainees in fifty-one detention centers or camps. 4,400 were Moslems held by Bosnian Croats; 1,400 were held by Bosnia-Herzegovina; 674 by the Serbs. Detention could be a matter of days, weeks, or months. Some Serbs in Sarajevo were in Central Prison for years. In late 1997, SFOR entered Central Prison and seized its records.

8. In 1993, Ruder-Finn was awarded the Silver Anvil by the Public Relations Society of America for its work on the Bosnian war. In an April 1993 interview by Jacques Merlino of TV 2, Paris, Ruder-Finn's director, James Harff, said that they had been working for Croatia, Bosnia-Herzegovina and the Albanians of Kosovo. He candidly admitted that when mounting a PR blitz, their job was not to verify facts. He said they did not claim there were Serb death camps in Bosnia, but simply made the *Newsday* articles widely known. By conjuring up Nazi Germany and Auschwitz, B'nai B'rith, the American Jewish Committee and the American Jewish Congress were won over (despite Tudjman's known anti-Semitism and Izetbegovic's Islamic views). By bombarding the media, administration officials, Congress and leading religious groups, public support for air strikes jumped dramatically, with two-thirds favoring US involvement.

Yossef Bodansky (Director of Research, International Strategic Studies Association) and Vaughn S. Forrest detailed Bosniak army use of Goradze. They also cited operations by special/mujahideen units against the BSA. "The Truth About Goradze," *Task Force On Terrorism and Unconventional Warfare* (House Republican Research Committee, US House of Representatives: Washington, D.C., 4 May 1994).

9. The question of how to get arms to Bosnia-Herzegovina made the rounds within the Clinton administration and in Zagreb and Sarajevo. With arms already flowing in via Croatia, Zagreb asked Washington for its approval. Zagreb was given a non-answer. This policy was defended before the US Congress by Assistant Secretary of State, Richard C. Holbrooke, and ambassador to Croatia, Peter Galbraith. Following a seven-month investigation in 1996, the Senate Intelligence Committee cleared the administration of charges of violating the arms embargo and of misleading Congress and the CIA. Citing executive privilege, President Clinton refused to disclose the findings of his Intelligence Advisory Board with Congress.

10. US experts reportedly set up radio equipment at an airstrip at Zivince south of Tuzla (the *Guardian* and several other newspapers reported eyewitness accounts, including UNPROFOR, of landings in late 1994–early 1995 of C-130 aircraft believed to be Turkish that delivered arms). US personnel repaired a strip at Visoko in central Bosnia to permit night landings. Americans were seen near Bosniak bases and were said to be involved in training. With US General John Galvin (ret.) visiting Sarajevo, US support was said to be an open secret. By late 1994, the US had drawn-up a "heavy option" of US$5 billion for Bosnian military aid and a "light option" of US$500 million. Covert amounts remain secret. See Silverstein, Ken, "Privatizing War," *Nation*, Jul.–Aug. 1997.

    By 1995, Bosniak forces totaled upwards of 150,000, depending on the state of mobilization. The Croat HVO had 100,000 with 50,000 more in Bosnia. The BSA was down to 80,000. The Krajina Serbs had 50,000 on paper, but probably less. The Serbs still had more tanks, APCs and artillery, but deficiencies in maintenance took a toll. In Bosnia, six arms factories were held by Bosnia-Herzegovina; five by the Serbs; and two by the Croats. Zagreb had a number of arms factories.

11. Thompson, Mark, "Generals for Hire," *Time*, 15 January 1996; Silverstein, op. cit. cites the use of Glatt by the CIA and the US Defense Intelligence Agency. Silverstein claims that MPRI's General Carl Vuono (ret.) held a series of secret meetings with Croat General Varimar Cervenko and his HVO staff on Brioni Island just before Operation "Storm." Operation "Flash" in May was just a prelude.

12. Honig, Jan Willem and Both, Norbert, *Srebrenica, Record of a War Crime* (London: Penguin, 1996). 6,546 Moslems, almost all men, disappeared at Srebrenica. Approximately 4,000 Bosniak fighters operated out of the enclave against Serb-held villages. By 1995, the enclaves posed a clear threat to BSA communications and rear areas (pp. 144–145). However, when Srebrenica came under attack, a majority of the fighters slipped through Serb lines at night and escaped. Mass executions went on under the nose of Dutch UNPROFOR troops.

13. The fighting effectiveness of the RSK army had badly eroded. In the weeks before the attack, a massive build-up of the HVO had been noted. Knin tried desperately to negotiate with Zagreb amid indications that Milosevic was willing to see Krajina fall. RSK communications, command and control were shaky, and some leaders were off in Belgrade.

14. John Zametica, Professor of European Security at Westminster University and author of *The Yugoslav Conflict* (IISS) Brassey's, 1992, states that sixty-four percent of pre-war Bosnia was registered to Serb ownership. When Karadzic said this, he was never believed.

15. In the autumn of 1994, Bosnian Serb demands remained incompatible with those of Bosnia-Herzegovina and Zagreb, not to mention those of the Contact Group. With the Krajina still in Serb hands, it would seem that the optimum time for Pale to show greater flexibility regarding the Contact Group plan would have been after Bihac in November.

16. Although the BSA had an unquestioned advantage in artillery around Sarajevo (although they also had to respond to UN demands in the exclusion zone), UNPROFOR observers noted that oftentimes the outgoing rounds were as numerous as the incoming. UNPROFOR also noted the activity of Bosniak snipers and threatened to shoot them. And, Bosniak fighters often took positions in schools and hospitals. In this kind of war, rules of conduct were ignored.

17. Karadzic drew former US President Jimmy Carter into the talks in the hope he could erode the stance of the Contact Group and upstage Milosevic. The US administration was unenthusiastic over his involvement, but did provide transportation and some support. The UN was more receptive to the resulting ceasefire, immediate evidence of BSA cooperation with UNPROFOR, and prospects of talks around the Contact Group plan. Carter also met Izetbegovic and Milosevic, but not Tudjman, a fact that may have detracted from his overall effort. After the ceasefire, he was out of the loop.

18. During three years of conflict, the Bosnian Serbs and the RSK talked unification, held joint meetings, drafted proposals for constitutional arrangements, but in the end did nothing. Unity, it seems, would have cut people out of official positions and out of the action. While RSK voiced concern that unification might end its ceasefire with Zagreb, many politicians were concerned that lucrative cross-border business deals might also end, e.g., the Bosnian Serbs furnished electric power to Dubrovnik in exchange for Croat petroleum. There were undoubtedly many deals going on. However, in addition to not solving political problems, military cooperation remained on an ad hoc basis. Even the vaunted BSA failed to push the Croats north of the Sava in order to widen the Brcko corridor.

19. Bogomilism was a dualistic belief akin to the Manichaeanism that worked its way into early Christianity. The latter favored asceticism to release the spirit in a fight of good against evil. The former believed that God had two sons, rebellious Satan and an obedient Jesus. The Albigenses, or Cathari, in France departed even further from orthodoxy and were slaughtered by the popes.

20. Jelavich, *History of the Balkans*, vol. 1, pp. 351–52.

21. Andric's friend, Dr. Max Loewenfeld, served as a doctor on the Republican side during the Spanish Civil War. He died in an air attack on his hospital in 1938. Andric's statue in Sarajevo was toppled in mid-1991.

22. Malcolm, Noel, *Bosnia, A Short History* (New York University Press, 1994), pp. 156–165.

23. Op. cit., pp. 165–173.

24. Op. cit., pp. 174–192. Malcolm cites the Bileca and Visegrad incidents as examples of Moslem acquiescence to NDH being viewed as collaboration. In *Wartime* (New York: Harcourt, Brace, Jovanovich, 1977), Milovan Djilas tells of meeting survivors of an Ustashe-Moslem attack on Serbs at Bileca. This was in early July 1941 en route to Montenegro by train (p. 11). It may have been in retaliation for the incident cited by Malcolm or vice versa. The point is that, as in the recent war, all sides took up arms. Given the history of the Moslem SS Handzar division during World War Two, and the lesser known SS 23rd Kama division, it is appalling that Izetbegovic gave his presidential guard unit the same name.

25. Malcolm, Noel, *Bosnia*, pp. 193–212.

26. Op. cit., pp. 213–233. Izetbegovic said from the outset that the SDA was a sectarian party, and although he received fewer votes than Fikret Abdic, he became the first rotating president of Bosnia-Herzegovina, as well as being party head (the separation is now blurred). He arrived on the scene with the reputation of having been a martyr for Islam. He had been jailed for three years as a youth for his membership in the Young Moslems. He had suffered police harassment. He was jailed for another five years after his 1983 trial. He had the reputation of an Islamist thinker. In 1990, he became a doer as well. His Islamic Declaration is a carefully written wake-up call to Bosnia's Moslems. It is not a radical, fundamentalist tract as might come from Iran. However, it does have a militant message. His program is the "Islamization of Moslems and Moslem people." His motto is "Believe and fight!" He speaks in the name of the "Almighty Merciful Benefactor." He instructs Moslems to return to their religious roots, to establish, when possible, an Islamic society. He speaks to those who have become secularized.

27. Vance-Owen got off to a very shaky start. In early January, Bosnia-Herzegovina Deputy Prime Minister Hakija Turajlic was shot at point-blank range while passing through a checkpoint while inside a UNPROFOR armored vehicle. Five years later, in February 1998, Serb Goran Vasic was arrested by Bosnia-Herzegovina authorities and charged with murder.

28. Bosnia-Herzegovina President Izetbegovic became a master at playing to the Western world. He made beautiful pro-pluralism speeches in public while hanging in with the hard-liners who favored an SDA dominated Bosnia-Herzegovina. Moderate former Prime Minister Haris Silajdzic eventually broke off to form his own party. Izetbegovic once candidly said that, presently, multiethnic parties have no future in Bosnia.

29. Similar to the breadline explosion of August 1992, Bosniak TV crews were at the scene and posited Serb responsibility. However, UNPROFOR's expert report was never made public. A New York surgeon, Dr. Sevekat Karduman (Turkish-Moslem), was on duty at Sarajevo Hospital when the dead and wounded came in. He told the Davar newspaper in Tel Aviv that eighty percent of the casualties had deep, open wounds, and fractures and burns below the waist. He noted the near absence of shrapnel in the wounds. UNPROFOR didn't find an impact crater suggesting that, if it was a 120mm mortar, it detonated when it hit a stall. But that would have caused many upper body wounds. An Israeli expert said it may well have been a command-detonated device similar to those used by the Hezbollah.

30. Most of the Croat-Moslem federation structures remained only on paper, particularly the plan for a unified military. In fact, Croat-Moslem tensions have remained high, especially at Mostar.

31. Silber and Little, *Death of Yugoslavia*, pp. 374–375 states that initially the Contact Group's "plan" seemingly lacked authority and vision—that the people involved were unfamiliar with the situation. They cite one staffer trying to locate Banya Luka in Romania.

32. OCSE personnel were permitted to check the border crossings and concluded after some weeks that FY had cut off war supplies.

33. It is interesting that Izetbegovic made the same strategic assessment as did contacts in Pale only weeks later.

34. RSK leader Milan Martic was blamed for rocketing Zagreb and has since been indicted as a war criminal.

35. Honig and Both, *Srebrenica*, The UNPROFOR Dutch battalion was down to 429 soldiers. They suffered from poor morale, felt forgotten and had little regard for Moslem leadership at Srebrenica. They thought that Nasir Oric and his minions were exploiting the enclave for personal gain. After being overrun by the Serbs, they failed to ensure the safety of the civilians who were being bussed away to their destruction. Others were rounded up after trying to escape through the woods (the enclave area was quite large). Executions took place at several locations. It was pre-planned and well organized.

36. At Zepa there were only seventy-nine Ukrainian UNPROFOR troops. The problem with so-called UN "safe areas" is that they were never adequately protected and made safe. The other problem is that they were never disarmed. They all had armed formations inside that time and time again attacked the Serbs.

37. There is no conclusive proof to indicate that the Croatian negotiator was aware that Zagreb's assault would begin on 4 August.

38. It was reported that the US ambassador to Croatia, Peter Galbraith, visited the front in a Croat military vehicle. He later defended his behavior by saying he wanted to ensure that Serb civilians were not harmed. In any case, atrocities did occur. To his credit, however, he did protest about this.

39. The dissension and confusion that erupted on the Serb side during Operation Storm again demonstrated their failure to craft a broad political-military strategy to win the war. If a Greater Serbia was their goal, they did little to advance the project by failing to unify their actions. Milosevic had political problems in Krajina from late 1991 onwards. He later had similar problems with Karadzic in Bosnia. Until the end, he played faction against faction. The BSA fought skillfully in small, set-piece battles. However, with their early dominant control of territory, they felt that they had essentially won the war and only needed to keep the pressure on until Bosnia-Herzegovina capitulated on their terms. Like RSK, they remained in static positions and permitted the initiative to pass to the other sides.

40. The Marcale market tragedy was seized on by UN-NATO to begin a bombing campaign against the BSA. Its object was both to punish and pressure Serb forces at Sarajevo, and to reduce BSA military capabilities in general.

41. It was widely perceived in the West that the Bosnian Serbs were bombed to the negotiating table. This is not true, as they gave Milosevic the green light to negotiate on their behalf as the air campaign was about to get underway. There had been much diplomatic progress through the summer by US envoys Robert Frazure and Richard Holbrooke, who convinced Pale that not only was the Contact Group plan the only game in town, but also that the proposed division of territory was almost the same as what they themselves had proposed earlier.

42. For a few days, NATO and the BSA were at war in Sarajevo. Unfortunately, RFF artillery struck a Serb hospital at Blazuj killing ten and wounding twenty-two. Fifteen Serb civilians, including four children, were killed by a NATO air strike at Doboj.

43. NATO's Implementation Force (IFOR) was extended to mid-1997, and extended again as Stabilization Force (SFOR) to mid-1998. It became clear that it had to remain beyond the latter date.

Chapter 6 – Serbia's "Addams Family"

1. Woodward's first five chapters explain the economic factors contributing towards political breakdown in Yugoslavia, and of Slovenia's and Croatia's orientation towards Austria and Germany. See Silber and Little, *Death of Yugoslavia*, pp. 113–128 on JNA's efforts to disarm the Slovene and Croat TDs as these two republics began to obtain weapons from abroad illegally. When they refused to disarm, Serbia's representative on the federal presidency, Borisav Jovic, bluntly told the Croat Stipe Mesic, "You've chosen war." In early 1991, Milosevic was inclined to let them secede, but to use the JNA to protect the Serbs in Croatia. The JNA, however, believed it had the obligation and right to ensure the integrity of all of the SFRY, bolstering Milosevic's first preference. The result, when fighting broke out, was a muddled policy: a poorly implemented JNA operation in Slovenia, arms to Serbs in Croatia (including militias), and JNA repositioning and intervention.

2. Ljubljana and Zagreb were adamantly opposed to a strengthened federal order, or a stronger Serbia. None, however, expected the SFRY to implode-explode as rapidly as it did. All had pushed the pace!

3. The most egregious example was Zeljko ("Arkan") Raznatovic, who had a string of Belgrade cafes and claimed to be in import-export. With his black leather jacket, diamond-studded Rolex and Levis, Arkan cut quite a figure. He was wealthy, a one-time parliamentarian and a warlord-businessman. According to the *Guardian Weekly* of 8 March 1998 fellow Montenegrin partner, Dragan Joksovic, was killed in Stockholm that February. Joksovic smuggled cigarettes to Sweden with Arkan, probably via Montenegro. Arkan reportedly sent hit men to take revenge for the gang murder. As stated earlier, Arkan was assassinated in January 2000 in Belgrade.

4. The above and following information is from UNHCR's *Refugee Host Family Survey* (Belgrade: Institute of Social Policy, 1993).

5. In April 1997, General Radovan "Badza" (big guy) Stojicic, the deputy interior minister, acting police chief and chief of public security, was gunned down at a Belgrade restaurant. He had been close to Milosevic for years, rising through the ranks as a key player in Kosovo and eastern Croatia. In late October 1997, Mira Markovic's secretary-general of the JUL, Zoran "Kundak" (gun butt) Todorovic, was killed as he exited his car in front of Beopetrol, which he managed. A friend of Milosevic's son was killed in a shopping center underpass earlier in the year. His daughter's boyfriend was shot in a parking lot. There were shifting relations between members of the black market, organized crime, volunteer militias, the police and security organizations, and the SPS—a network of privilege, power, corruption and crime.

6. The *vojna linija* (military line) reportedly operated within the Ministry of the Interior as an unofficial activity charged with supporting the militias in Croatia and Bosnia. Radovan Stojicic, Franko Simatovic, former head of JSO (Special Operations Unit)—"red berets"—and Milosevic aide, and Mihalj Kertes are alleged to have worked for secret police boss Jovica Stanisic for the purpose of arming and training volunteer fighters. Reports cite training camps at Bubanj Potok near Belgrade and Bajina Basta on the Bosnia–Herzegovina border. Seselj's Chetniks, Arkan's Tigers and "red berets" controlled by the ministry were instrumental in ethnic cleansing operations. The *vojna linija* was informally linked to political leaders and businessmen. In early 1997, Stanisic was head of state security and Frenki was his deputy. Kertes ran the federal customs.

7. Magas, Branka, *The Destruction of Yugoslavia* (London: Verso 1993). Even Milosevic critic Magas admits that huge sums of money had been spent in Kosovo since 1974. See pp. 10–11, 19. See p. 47, footnote 56. Kosovo was getting as much as thirty-seven percent of SFRY's total development funds. Chapters 1–3 detail Kosovo's crisis from a left perspective, chapters 3–4 of part 2 deal with economic problems.

8. A year later, the Bosniak threat assessment made its way into the press. Chris Hedges, *New York Times* Service (5 October 1997) cited a clandestine Moslem arms build-up that NATO believed would soon be capable of crushing the Bosnian Serbs. William Droziak of the *International Herald Tribune* (3 December 1997) cites NATO's top commander US General Wesley Clark as saying IFOR must stay to prevent war.

Karadzic is a Montenegrin whose family moved to Sarajevo when he was fifteen. He studied medicine and specialized in psychiatry, as did his wife. He was team physician to the Sarajevo football club and writes poetry. He was one of the founders of the SDS and later became president of RS. As a staunch nationalist, some say that he threatened to rival Milosevic as the leader of the Serbs.

9. The Bosnia-Herzegovina side states it lost 10,615 people in Sarajevo, which included 1,601 children. Fifty thousand were wounded and many invalided.

10. Bosnia-Herzegovina has retained warm ties with Iran, despite US opposition. Hasan Cengic was removed as defense minister, but Bosnia-Herzegovina had senior pro-Iranian army officers who protected the presence of hundreds of mujahideen cadres or special forces personnel. Turkey was training its officers and NCOs. The first batch returned in August 1996 with forty 155mm howitzers concealed in containers for Turkish-Malaysian UN troops. Egypt was supplying artillery. Saudi Arabia, the Emirates, Malaysia and others provided financial support. The US was granting US$100 million in equipment, including forty M-60 tanks, fifteen HU-1 helicopters, eighty armored vehicles, quantities of rifles, machine guns, anti-tank weapons, radios, and generators. The US program was under contract to the US Military Professional Resources, Inc.

11. There has been much speculation over the Spring 1991 meetings between Milosevic and Tudjman at Tito's favorite hunting lodge at Karajordjevo in Vojvodina at which time, supposedly, they agreed to divide Bosnia-Herzegovina. Tudjman has admitted as much on several occasions. The implications were ominous, but have been overtaken by events.

12. At first, Mladic and a number of his senior officers refused to accept Plavsic's decision. Finally, he gave up his command, but continued to hover in the background of RS politics. Finally, after SFOR arrested several suspect war criminals, Mladic went to Belgrade where he presumably enjoyed Milosevic's protection. His role in the Bosnian war was central. UNPROFOR officers respected his reliability and feared his wrath when he was bent on making war.

Mladic is a Bosnian Serb whose father and mother were killed in World War Two. He was a career JNA officer who commanded Knin in early 1992. He hit it off with the Knin rebels and soon after led the BSA. A tough, blunt, bulky officer with a mischievous smile and a steel grip, Ratko is the closest thing that the Serbs have to Israel's Ariel Sharon. He did his utmost to slaughter his enemy, both in battle and in helpless captivity. His daughter committed suicide. He is reported to have had bouts of severe depression.

13. Unbelievably, Arkan's Serbian Unity party in Bosnia received in excess of US$100,000 from OHR. Arkan bragged that the tribunal at The Hague has not indicted him. After Arkan's death, it was disclosed that he had been under a secret indictment by The Hague Tribunal.

14. SPO's appeal has declined because of Draskovic's divisiveness and Danica's meddlesome temper. She once broke a bottle over the head of a guest at a dinner attended by Patriarch Pavle. Vuk did shake up SRS by claiming Seselj's father was a Catholic Croat.

15. Montenegro has never been self-sufficient, always receiving subsidies (first from Russia, then Serbia, Yugoslavia and the SFRY). But it angers many that the VJ continues to acquire properties, some on the Adriatic, which would be suited for tourism. Military construction reportedly provides opportunities for kickbacks.

16. For someone who quipped, "We Serbs may not know how to work, but we do know how to fight," Milosevic has had a fair amount of business experience. He bossed Tehnogas, an industrial group, and then Belgrade's largest bank. He frequently attended meetings of the IMF and World Bank. He probably gained experience useful for UN sanctions-busting (cover companies, cut-outs on Cyprus, etc.). He has dealt with the NatWest bank in London. He seems familiar with how international finance works today, likening the lightning movement of money to "rabbits" that run, hide and remain beyond the control of all except those who are directing the operation.

17. In June 1998, Djukanovic requested the recall of conscripts from Montenegro who were then serving with the VJ in Kosovo.

18. A source who visited northern Albania described young, ill-trained, inexperienced men wearing bits and pieces of uniforms, but with plentiful light arms moving back and forth across the border with Kosovo. They seemed to have little grasp of strategy beyond wanting independence. As they did not identify any leader, my source thinks that the KLA consisted of groups led by their own local

commanders. Some volunteers came down from Western Europe. It was also noted that former Albanian president Sali Berisha's Democratic Party cadres were providing support to the insurgents.

19. Variations on this theme emerged in oral traditions of song before they were finally written down. In fact, there were at least three battles at Kosovo between 1389 and when the Serbians were conquered seventy years later. In the first, even Hungarians and Germans fought with Lazar, and some Serbs sided with the Sultan. Milos Obilic's sacrifice made him a Serb folk hero. A brother-in-law of Lazar, Vuk Brankovic, supposedly left the field of battle at a critical point and is branded a traitor. The true facts are intertwined with myth. More recently, the last big battle took place in November 1915, when 250,000 Serbs fought a retreat with 300,000 Germans and Austro-Hungarians advancing from the north and more than that number of Bulgarians coming in from the east, forcing the Serbs to destroy their guns and go over the Albanian mountains to the sea to meet an Allied force for evacuation to Corfu.

20. Islami, Hivzi, Kosova 1/93, Tirana, pp. 29–34; Abdyli, Ramiz, Kosova 2/93, Tirana, pp. 23–29. *The Institutes of History of Prishtina and Tirana, Historical-Political Review.*

21. Avramov, *Genocide in Yugoslavia*, pp. 175–205. An Italian, and a German, occupation zone, the creation of fascist Albanian militias, Italy's collapse and a German take-over, the establishment of the Skanderbeg SS of 11,000 men; all worked to create conditions whereby a campaign of murder and looting was directed at the Serb population in which thousands were killed. The Balli Kombetar (Ballists) were right-wing nationalists and big landowners in Kosovo, whose militia of 5,000 was wiped out by the Partisans in late 1945. Its leaders, who wanted unification with Albania, either died, were imprisoned, or went into exile. Even Albanians who rallied to the Partisans late in the war proved too nationalistic and were purged. This led to the decision to give Kosovo limited autonomy under Serbia. In 1974, Kosovo was given the fullest autonomy possible, short of actual republic status. Under the 1974 constitution, republics have the right to secede by a majority vote. Belgrade was convinced that a republic in Kosovo would lead to independence in a matter of a few years, with the Serbs becoming the losers.

22. Islami, Hivzi, *Demographic Reality in Kosova* (Kosova Information Center, Prishtina). A birth-rate of twenty-eight per thousand (average 6.6 children) with half of Kosovo's Albanian population under twenty years old has caused a situation of high unemployment and low per capita income.

23. Magas, *The Destruction of Yugoslavia*, pp. 49–60.

24. Silber and Little, *Death of Yugoslavia*, pp. 29–35. They suggest that Kosta Milhajlovic, a Serb economist who became close to Milosevic, was the memorandum's main author. Dobrica Cosic, a popular Serb writer who broke with the YLC in 1968 because of the plight of Serbians in Kosovo, has also been associated with the memorandum. Cosic was jailed for a time and later took other nationalists under his wing. He was FRY president under Milosevic until early 1993. I have relied heavily on Silber and Little, chapters 2 and 4, to describe Milosevic's rise to power.

25. Magas, *The Destruction of Yugoslavia*, pp. 179–190. Vlasi was jailed for fourteen months. Also Silber and Little, *Death of Yugoslavia*, pp. 74–77 for the 28 June 1989 rally at Kosovo.

26. Vickers and Pettifer, *Albania*, pp. 142–165. The first LDK delegation arrived in Tirana in February 1991 and established its liaison office. Ibrahim Rugova later came to Tirana to talk with Ballist émigré representatives who wanted Albanian president Berisha to play the nationalist card to push for Kosovo's "liberation." This issue received strong support in the US where there are some 400,000 ethnic-Albanians and an active Ballist organization. US Republican Senator Robert Dole began to urge independence for Kosovo from 1986. US Congressman Joseph DioGuardia helped to form a Albanian-American Civic League to push Kosovo in Congress. Rights activist Adem Demaci was handed an invitation to visit the US by DioGuardia whereupon he met Tom Lantos, the chairman of the US Congress' House of Representatives Foreign Affairs Committee. A LDK office was set up in Washington.

27. Amnesty International, Yugoslavia, *Ethnic Albanians—Trial by Truncheon* (London: February 1994).

28. In other reports, a Jakup Krasniqi has been cited as a KLA spokesman. KLA members talked vaguely of receiving faxed guidance from abroad. The largest concentration of Albanians in Europe is in Germany where 120,000 are living. Next is Switzerland with about 100,000, where wealthy Kosovar Albanians are said to control narcotics trafficking. Albania is also now a center. This, combined with

perhaps as many as a million weapons loose, would be sufficient to sustain any insurgency. Agence France Press reported on 1 June 1998 how army conscripts at Shkoze simply allowed an arms depot to be looted of hundreds of small arms. Vickers and Pettifer, *Albania*, p. 156, claim Albania has trained guerrillas for Kosovo at Labinot near Elbasan since 1992. Press reports stated some of the KLA had fought in Bosnia. It should be noted that Krasniqi ran the LDK office at Glogovac. It is likely that there are LDK–KLA links.

29. The LDK's advisor for foreign affairs, Dr. Shaqir Shaqiri, had told me in November 1992 that the question of Kosovo for Serbia has more to do with the US$5 billion in mineral wealth that is connected with the Trepca mining complex than it does with the Field of Blackbirds and religious shrines. Indeed, Trepca is a treasure house of lead, zinc, cadmium, gold, silver and coal. It earns millions of US dollars from ore exports. It was reopened by the British after World War One. Interestingly, a Scottish engineer related to Rebecca West that, in the 1920s, Kosovo was dangerous and insecure because of Albanian blood feuds and brigandage and that people were frequently robbed and murdered. He said that this was finally eliminated only after the Serbian gendarmes wiped out whole villages—men, women, and children. See West, Rebecca, *Black Lamb and Grey Falcon* (New York: Viking), p. 940.

Chapter 7 – The Fascist Phoenix

1. Raos, Predrag, "A Capital in Spite of Itself," *Transitions*, March 1998, vol. 5, no. 3, pp. 93–96.
2. Silber and Little, *Death of Yugoslavia*, p. 91.
3. London, Kurt, *Backgrounds of Conflict: Ideas and Forms in World Politics* (New York: The Macmillan Company, 1947). See chapters 1–3. London views nationalist historian Heinrich von Treitschke as an "intellectual standard bearer in the march of Prussianism to National Socialism" (p. 56). Von Treitschke believed in statism and the politics of force. He believed in the form, not the substance of democracy and that small nations are condemned by history to be subject to those who are superior. Hence, he believed the Germans had a historic mission to rule because of their superiority. He viewed war as a moral good. Nietzsche placed "will" at the basis of the struggle for life—the survival of the fittest who are beyond good and evil.
   Bulajic, Milan, *Tudjman's Jasenovac Myth: Genocide Against Serbs, Jews, and Gypsies* (Belgrade: Strucna Knjiga, 1994). I have relied on Bulajic for an evaluation of Tudjman's *Wastelands* and for factual information concerning Jasenovac concentration camp, which follows below in this chapter. Also see *Death Bookkeeping* by Vuksan Cerovic for detailed accounts of genocide kept by the Italian military. Documents and names, Belgrade, IP ZAVET, 1996.
4. Op. cit., Bulajic, Milan, p. 15. Tudjman often treats his listeners and many foreign officials to long historical explanations about the sharp divisions between the Croats and Serbs without making any effort whatsoever to rise above his narrow, nationalistic ethnicity.
5. The famous menu was in the possession of Paddy Ashdown, a UK Liberal Party parliamentarian. Six months later, a stern-faced Tudjman was photographed decorating a bemused Bosnian President Izetbegovic with an elaborate medal and sash, ostensibly as a demonstration of his esteem, and their mutual cooperation.
   Tudjman's *Wastelands* was republished in the US as *Horrors of War: Historical Reality and Philosophy* (New York: M. Evans and Company, 1996). Melady, who became president of Sacred Heart College, also wrote a glowing tribute to Cardinal Stepinac in the foreword. By happenstance, the *Croatia Weekly* cited above has a quote from Melady: "It is no longer a secret that I was sent to the Vatican with the instructions to persuade the Holy See not to support the disintegration of Yugoslavia. I knew that the Vatican believed that Slovenia and Croatia had different cultural histories, that they are different nations, and that they had the right to independence, and I passed this information on to Washington. In that regard, I had a certain influence on the alteration of US policy, although a bit late for Croatia." Hardly a surprising revelation.
6. Information on Dinko and Nada Sakic was obtained from Serbia Info News (www.serbia-info.com/news), which cited a variety of sources.
   Bulajic, *Tudjman's Jasenovac Myth*, pp. 23–24, 28.

7. Avramov, Genocide in Yugoslavia, pp. 243–249.

    The HOP under General Drinjanin forbade its exiled members to enlist in the armed forces of foreign states without permission, and stated that the Ustashe would march again under its own flag. This order was printed in *Danica* newspaper, No. 13, 9 August 1950 in Chicago, Illinois. The paper was edited by Rev. Castimir Majic who described it as, "An American newspaper in the Croatian language dedicated to the cultural enlightenment and spiritual uplifting of Americans of Croatian origin through the American way of life. In harmony with the American tradition of freedom and independence, the *Danica* champions the right of the Croatian people to the reestablishment of their own national state." The newspaper was located at 4851 Drexel Blvd., Chicago.

8. Vilic and Todorovic, *Breaking of Yugoslavia*, pp. 20–24.

9. The document is identified ATTO.WP5, Croatia. Page 3 states, regarding extrajudicial killings, that "…The murders continue a pattern begun in the fall of 1995 of ethnically motivated killing carried out both to intimidate Serbs who stayed behind after Croatia reclaimed these areas and increasingly to discourage those Serbs who fled from returning. The authorities made only a few arrests in these cases…denying that any of the attacks were ethnically motivated. The authorities' attempts to seek out, investigate, and punish those responsible… were inadequate."

10. Kaplan, Robert D., *Balkan Ghosts* (New York: Vintage, 1994). See pp. 9–11 for the contrast in personalities between Strossmayer and Stepinac. Strossmayer was a linguist, an educator and a philanthropist who founded Zagreb University. He bred Lippizaner horses, was a gardener and a connoisseur of good wine. He loved to provide a fine table and charm his guests with his stories. Moreover, he is revered today among Serbs for his ethnic and religious tolerance.

11. Kaplan and others apparently depict Stepinac in ambivalent, naive, essentially weak and tragic terms. That he deserted in World War One from the Austrians to join the Serb army; that he broke off his engagement with his betrothed to become a priest; that he stood up to Tito and withstood five years of solitary confinement, to me, suggest something of much stronger mind. I believe that he viewed the NDH as being in Croatia's and his church's interest.

12. Bulajic, Milan, *Role of the Vatican*, p. 69. I have used this useful compilation for the role of Stepinac, the Roman Catholic church, and the Vatican before, during, and after World War Two, up until the early 1990s.

    I have used Avramov, *Genocide in Yugoslavia*, chapter 6, for information on the rise of the Ustashe, the NDH, the World War Two genocide, and the involvement of the Roman Catholic church and the Vatican. Read for postwar acts of violence by the Ustashe directed against the Yugoslav state.

13. Bulajic, *Role of the Vatican*, p. 158. Bulajic documents that Stepinac was reasonably well informed about what went on at Jasenovac and once became angry when he learned that some Slovenian priests had died there. He wrote a letter to Pavelic that protested this.

14. Zagreb Archbishop Josip Bozanic is quoted by the *Croatia Weekly*: "The beatification of Cardinal Alojzije Stepinac shows that Pope John Paul II supports the cardinal's views and… supports the church gathered around Stepinac. He was an innocent man who was inspired by God." It added that the Croatian Bishop's Conference declared him to be the first beatified martyr to European communism, claiming that in over eighteen years, 126 archives both in the country and abroad were examined, seventy-four witnesses testified, dozens of experts were consulted, all of which determined fourteen reasons for his elevation. The reasons included hatred for the Catholic church, his innocence, testimonies about his "poisoning" by his personal physicians, and the regime's refusal to provide better treatment. Yugoslav doctors stated that Stepinac suffered from a rare blood disease.

15. Djilas, Aleksa, *The Contested Country* (Harvard University, 1991). I have used Djilas to describe the differences between Serb and Croat political forces from Yugoslavia's establishment up to the advent of communist rule in that country. I have used Djilas' account of the elections during the inter-war period and also the circumstances surrounding the announcement of the Sporazum. His work is invaluable, but I am prevented by constraints of space from providing a greater amount of detail.

16. Avramov, *Genocide in Yugoslavia*, pp. 260–269, for the beginnings of the Ustashe movement. Djilas describes the absolute opposition of the communist party to the pre-World War Two government and their periods of flirtation with the Ustashe. No cooperation was possible, however, because of the latter's extreme nationalism.

17. Op. cit., p. 265, refers to the CPP's militant armed wing and how Kosutic met with Mussolini in 1936 and told him that at the right time the CPP would fight with the Ustashe for Croatia. Djilas, *The Contested Country*, p. 132, notes that the CPP's two paramilitary arms went with Pavelic while some of the CPP left wing (if you could call it left) joined the Partisans. Initially, Macek told the Croatian people to cooperate with the NDH, but he refused to participate. Reportedly, he would have been Germany's first choice to head up a quisling regime. He was interned briefly and was then sent to his home village to wait out the war, uninvolved with politics.

18. See Djilas, *The Contested Country*, pp. 128–135 for talks concerning the Sporazum and what resulted. The Yugoslav government, it seems, viewed it as a necessary compromise solution, whereas the Croats looked at it as a step towards full independence.

19. Op. cit., pp. 135–142 tells how Macek sought to confirm the continuation of the Sporazum on the eve of the Axis invasion, and how the Croats carried their differences into Yugoslavia's wartime government-in-exile in London.

20. Over the objections of some, Croatia was formally admitted to the Council of Europe in 1996 after almost four years of waiting.

21. The Bosnian Serbs believed that they could use the talks with Carter to expand upon the Contact Group's offer. They were led on in their thinking, in part, by press reports that the Contact Group was willing to give better terms. To the contrary, the latter was not enthusiastic about Carter's role. A senior US diplomat denied to this writer that Bosnian Serb linkage to Belgrade was offered despite newspaper quotes from anonymous officials that it was.

22. The *New York Times* commented about the return of fascism in Croatia in an article by Chris Hedges, and an editorial and a feature by senior commentator A. M. Rosenthal. It has also been cited from time to time by the Jewish holocaust expert Simon Wiesenthal. The oath in question is *Za dom spremni—* "Ready for the fatherland!"

23. Polls conducted by the Ivo Pilar Social Sciences Institute in April and June 1998 showed the HDZ declining from 32.8 percent to 26.9 percent. The HSP Croatian Party of Rights went from 5.7 percent to 9.6 percent. It further believed that if the HDZ became too cooperative with the West, or too lenient on the Serb issue, many voters would shift to the ultra-nationalist parties of the extreme right. (Source: Vjesnik as republished in *Croatia Weekly*.)

24. Daskalovic, Zoran, "The Confessions Begin," War report, October 1997, pp. 9–10; Traynor, Ian, "Torturers confessions rock Croatia," *Guardian Weekly*, 14 September 1997, p. 5.

25. Anto Furundzija was represented before The Hague Tribunal by an American lawyer from Chicago, Luka Misetic. In a case of rape by Croat soldiers, Misetic argued that the Moslem woman from the Lasva Valley had been treated for post-traumatic stress disorder and that this had not been disclosed by the prosecution. This was ruled a procedural error by a three-judge panel. The trial had to start anew, meaning that the witnesses and the victim, Witness A, had to testify again. Source: A *New York Times* Service article by Marlise Simons appearing in the *International Herald Tribune*, 30 July 1998. Apparently the Chicago Croat-Americans remain active.

    UNTAES head, retired US General Jacques Klein, sincerely tried to make the Erdut Agreement work and was respected for his even-handed approach to reintegration and reconstruction. After he was safely gone, US ambassador to Croatia Peter Galbraith gave a self-serving interview to *War Report* (Dec. 1997–Jan. 1998) wherein he asserted that reintegration was peacefully taking place. For a more accurate assessment, see Chris Hedges, *New York Times* Service, in "For the Serbs, a Croatian Enclave Stands as a Model of Failed Ethnic Integration," the *International Herald Tribune*, 20 March 1998.

26. The organizers of the Jasenovac '89 seminar (October 25–27) distributed a commemorative medal that contained a distinctive U as part of a flower or flame motif. Serbs found it objectionable, intended or not, as an attempt to introduce an Ustashe "U" symbol. This was the same year that Tudjman published his *Wastelands*. On 13 May 1990, some 700 pro-Ustashe exiles and Croat activists held a commemoration at Loiback-Bleiburg, which was broadcast by Radio Zagreb. Pavelic's former bodyguard, Hasan Selimovic, said that Jasenovac had been "too small" to answer the "crimes coming from the east." Dinko Sakic said he was proud of being an Ustashe and that what they had done during the war was for Christianity and Croatia. Srecko Psenicnik, Pavelic's son-in-law and president of HOP, vowed that the spirit of the dead Ustashe, Croat soldiers and Domobrans would inspire another

"resurrection" and that "without Bosnia and Herzegovina, Srijem and Boka Kotorska there is no freedom... no Croatia... and that they are on the threshold of the final Croatian victory.' Bulajic, *Tudjman's Jasenovac Myth*, p. 111. In 1993 Tudjman proposed that the remains of the victims of communism be gathered and buried at Jasenovac, including NDH and Ustashe. A commemoration for Pavelic was held on 28 December, at which time the official statement read, "But for him, this present Croat state would not exist." Op. cit., pp. 122–123.

In March 1998, the Vatican released a long-awaited fourteen-page statement on the wartime role of the Roman Catholic church, which admitted some errors, but which protected Pope Pius XII and also denied that the church contributed to the promotion of racism. It was termed "disappointing" by the Israeli government and too late and too little by a number of Jewish organizations worldwide. One of the more controversial charges is that the Vatican stored 200 million in Swiss francs, mostly in gold coins, for the Ustashe in the immediate aftermath of World War Two. This allegation is based on a US declassified Treasury Department report dating from 1946, which was used in a US television documentary in 1997. The memo stated that the Ustashe moved 350 million in Swiss francs out of Yugoslavia, but 150 million had been confiscated by the British at the Austrian-Swiss border. A Vatican spokesman has since denied the accusation. Unfortunately, the Vatican's records remain off limits to outside scholars and its denials that it supported the Ustashe remain quite suspect in the eyes of many. Croatian music conductor, Ivan Cerovac, wrote in *Vjesnik* that the Split seminar provoked a number of polemics. He singled out Zarko Puhovski, Ivo Banac, and Ivan Paden for criticism because they, "the liberals," had argued that the Catholic church has contributed to errors committed by the Croatian state, judiciary and society, and are unwilling to accept the church's role in the creation of the Croatian state, nor its prominent position. Cerovac censures their opposition to the use of the term *Crkva u Hrvata* (Catholic church of the Croatian people), or "Stepinac's church," which are commonly used. He claimed that Banac went out of his way to cite the existence of Ustashe elements in Catholic missions around the world. (Source: reprinted in *Croatia Weekly*.) Ivo Banac is a US professor of history at Yale University. It was expected that final details concerning the Restitution Act (the fourth such between the Vatican and Croatia) would be signed during Pope John Paul II's October 1998 visit. The act provided for the return of buildings, land, and forest, financial payment for properties not handed over, and subsidies for church social work (educational and humanitarian activities) from public taxes. The state would pay salaries to the clergy and nuns employed in state institutions such as hospitals, the primary and secondary schools, and in universities, theological institutes, and other faculties. (Source: *Croatia Weekly*.)

27. Then seventy-four years old, Tudjman was treated for cancer at the US naval hospital in Bethesda, Maryland, in November 1996. Likewise, ultra-nationalist Gojko Susak was treated for cancer at Walter Reed Army Medical Center in 1995 and at Massachusetts General in Boston in 1997. Reuters reported on 25 July 1998 that Tudjman was rethinking how to justify such a pay raise for himself and also for the Sabor MPs. Reuters reported 22 October 1998 that Ankica Lepej, a clerk at Zagrebacka Banka, had pieced together Tudjman's wife's accounts. The article stated that Mrs. Tudjman ran a children's charity and that she had recently said that she owned only an automobile.

28. Marvin L Stone, former editor-in-chief of *US News and World Report* and a fellow at Zagreb University, was quoted by *New York Times* Service correspondent Chris Hedges as saying, "There is very little diversity now in the Croatian press... The government has either tamed, taken over, or closed all of the independent media." In July 1998, Radio 101 was undergoing managerial turmoil. *Feral Tribune*, as of November 1997, was fending off thirty-four lawsuits, which, if it lost, would cost it US$2.7 million. Tudjman's daughter was suing for US$675,000; Minister of Justice Andrija Hebrang for US$135,000; *Feral's* editor, Viktor Ivanic, was singled out by the US Committee for the Protection of Journalists. Source: Traynor, Ian, *Guardian Weekly*, 23 November 1997.

29. Tudjman used the Croat constitution to retain control of the Zagreb city council mayor's office when elections went against him. The opposition has not won any majorities, only pluralities, and Tudjman could call on national security clauses to prevent the opposition from administering the nation's capital.

30. *New York Times* Service article by Chris Hedges appearing in the *International Herald Tribune* of 28 May 1997.

31. Given President Tudjman's mindset, he must have been very reluctant to permit returns irrespective of pressure from the West. He could serve up a plan for the return of Serb refugees and, at the same time, put the word out through his minions to not only drag their feet, but to take active measures to drive Serbs out and prevent them from returning. As long as most Croats denied their past, and fixated on nationalism, there were few grounds for optimism. This was the state of things as of late 1998. Tudjman, a near-dictator, posed as a friend of the West. And Washington, which first heard appeals on behalf of Croatia from New York's Cardinal Spellman just after the end of World War Two, was stuck with him. Christopher Hitchens is of the opinion that Tudjman was a "wholly-owned subsidiary of the NATO alliance" (*War Report* final issue, no. 58, p. 20).

Chapter 8 – The Good, the Bad, and the Ugly

1. Sulzberger, C. L., *A Long Row of Candles* (Toronto: Macmillan, 1969), p. 64. Sulzberger lived in Sofia in the mid-1930s and relates how MRO's leader was Ivanko Mihailo, who ran ten opium factories. MRO members took their oath over a skull and crossbones, a bible and a revolver. The price for an assassination was US$20. Markov died on 15 September 1978, four days after being injected with poison while he waited for a bus on Waterloo Bridge. It is likely that Bulgarian security killed Markov with KGB technical help. Bulgarian complicity in the attempt on Pope John Paul II gained wide currency in the US, even though an Italian court acquitted the three Bulgarians named for lack of evidence. Claire Sterling's *The Terror Network* was cited by many and magazines such as *Newsweek* and *Reader's Digest* spread the story. Herman, Edward S. and Chomsky, Noam, *Manufacturing Consent* (New York: Pantheon, 1988), demolishes the "Bulgarian connection" and details how Paul Henze, ex-CIA Station Chief in Ankara (a propaganda expert), and Michael Ledeen (Reagan White House advisor), who was deeply involved with Italian security (SISMI), pushed a Bulgarian-Soviet plot concocted by SISMI and the Italian police—a case with obvious flaws that could not hold up in court. Agca did shoot the Pope and remains in prison.
2. The above sayings and the comments below on Bulgarian traits are gratefully borrowed from Sulzberger, *A Long Row of Candles*, op. cit., pp. 62–63.
3. The Macedonian census cited six languages, but not Bulgarian.
4. I suggest that the election was fairly fought, despite blatant US interference, because the BSP had tremendous advantages due to its ample funds and institutional strength established over many years. It preempted much of the UDF program. UDF's popular Petar Beron was forced out by a plodding Zhelev and called an informer. Zhelev also fell out with Filip Dimitrov who was the target of a vicious BSP smear campaign that labeled him a homosexual.
5. Montgomery's 28 September 1993 Senate comments caused an uproar in Bulgaria as they ran counter to a 1991 constitution which ruled out parties based on ethnicity, or religion. The MRF became angry because it did not want to be considered an ethnic party, or have competition from "Turkish" groups. Montgomery included the "Macedonians" in his concerns, irritating everyone except UMO-Illinden, which had some 300 members around Petric-Sandanski. Montgomery was deputy chief of mission during the UDF government. He was hounded by the BSP and had a difficult tour as ambassador.
6. Bulgaria had undoubtedly lost money on direct trade with Yugoslavia. However, there was active smuggling across the borders, and indirect trade through Macedonia had increased by five percent. Some 500 trucks a day were on the road between the two countries.
7. Since 1989, the Roma have suffered the most from factory shutdowns and unemployment. Consequently, many who had escaped from a life of scavenging, or crime, are again at their old occupations. The worst community is the Stoliponovo slum of Plovdiv, where many thousands of Roma and Turks scratch out a livelihood.
8. Georgi Dimitrov was a communist hero who dramatically defended himself and other communists accused by the Nazis of setting fire to the Reichstag in Berlin in 1933. He later headed the Communist International (Comintern) in Moscow; and, after World War Two, was installed by the Soviets as head of the BCP in November 1945. His role during subsequent political purges and show trials cast him in a different light—that of a ruthless communist bent on taking total power. He died in 1949 and was embalmed under glass like Lenin.

9. A UDF white paper entitled "1995—The Unkept Promises of the Bulgarian Socialist Party" detailed the failures of Videnov's government. Holding a majority, it brought to completion only four of 160 draft laws. Laws put forward in the financial-economic areas were so poorly written they had to be returned to committee. Laws of a partisan bent ended up in the constitutional court. Twice, parliament closed because of a lack of legislation. Privatization fell short, and mass privatization was postponed until mid-1996. Bank stabilization was controlled by the BSP, while pyramids and other schemes collapsed. A ten billion leva debt of Agro Business Bank was assumed by the central bank for one leva. Old communists took over some 500 general manager positions at state enterprises. Foreign investment declined 200 percent and another 150,000 people lost their jobs. When applying for full EU membership at Madrid, Prime Minister Videnov failed to attend. Lastly, Bulgaria was the only formerly communist country not to ask to join NATO.

10. Kaplan, Robert D., *Balkan Ghosts* (New York: Vintage, 1994), p. 222, has Lilov responsible for railroading a journalist to internal exile in 1964—a person he didn't even know.

11. Intracom, a company closely associated with the Hellenic Telephone Organization, set up Bulfon (cellular/card phones) with thirty-two percent Bulgarian ownership, with no international tender.

12. Lukanov became deeply involved in Russian oil-gas dealings in Bulgaria, which were said to be mafia-connected. He knew too much. Financial crime climbed rapidly in 1994—fraud, embezzlement, money laundering, tax evasion and illicit trade. By 1996 property crime—theft and protection racketeering–covered seventy-five percent of registered offences. Antiquity theft and smuggling to the West is flourishing. Thousands of cars stolen elsewhere enter Bulgaria for "rehab" and shipment east. In ten years, crime grew 500 percent.

13. Fourteen private banks went into receivership. With the first two, First Private Bank and Mineralbank, the government paid out leva 17 billion in deposit insurance. After others started to close, parliament amended the deposit insurance law and payouts had to await court decisions. The Videnov government finally lowered the floor for ZUNK bonds issued to absorb bad loans to enterprises. Banks had been allowed to account for ZUNKs at par value rather than their much-reduced market value or their actual cost.

14. Investors thought Brady bonds (Bulgarian debt denominated in US dollars), backed by a currency board, might outpace the global Brady index in 1997. Even BankAmerica jumped into Bulgarian Bradys.

15. Jelavich, *History of the Balkans*, vol. 1, pp. 15–18. Again I have used Jelavich to relate the history of the Bulgarians, here and on subsequent pages. Vol. 2 was used for more recent times.
    The ruins of Samuel's fortress rise dramatically from a site just to the north of Lake Ohrid.

16. Kinross, *The Ottoman Centuries*, pp. 37–40. I have used Kinross to describe the coming of the Ottomans to the Balkans and its occupation until after World War One with particular reference to Bulgaria.

17. Op. cit. pp. 57–61, gives Lazar's army superior numbers. It opened with an advance by 2,000 Ottoman archers. Lazar countered, breaking Murad's left flank commanded by his son, Yakub. Bayezid, over on the right, mounted a massive attack. With the battle very much undecided, Lazar's brother-in-law Vuk Brankovic deserted with 12,000 men, possibly having plotted with Murad. This broke the Serbian ranks. Milosh Obravitch stabbed Murad and was executed. Lazar was later beheaded. Bayezid's first act as Sultan was to strangle with a bowstring his young brother Yakub. Kinross says there are several conflicting versions of this battle.

18. Op. cit., pp. 67–69. Thousands of crusaders, knights, and men afoot were slaughtered in captivity on the day after the battle.

19. Op. cit., pp. 85–91.

20. Jelavich leaves off and doesn't pick up again until the eighteenth century. Wheatcroft, Andrew, *The Ottomans* (London: Viking, 1993). A generally sympathetic treatment, which cannot hide the barbarism of Ottoman rule.

21. Kinross, *The Ottoman Centuries*, pp. 509–511.

22. Op. cit., pp. 521–522.

23. Op. cit., pp. 522–524.

24. Op. cit., pp. 525–528. The Russians obtained territory in the Caucasus. The Austrians, in turn, were permitted to occupy and administer Bosnia-Herzegovina. The British, seizing on Turkish weakness,

took over Cyprus. The war came at the time Britain was opening the Suez Canal, its strategic lifeline to its eastern empire in India. Hence, London did not want a complete Turkish collapse and turmoil in the Middle East, which would affect its own interests adversely. Much has been made of Russian losses in Bulgaria, with some citing a plaque at Nevski Cathedral that claims 200,000. Closer are estimates of 27,000 to 36,455 made a few years after the conflict. Russian records, from existing medical entries, cite only 15,567 deaths.

25. Op. cit., pp. 539–543; Jelavich, *History of the Balkans*, pp. 335–348, 366–373. Sulzberger, *A Long Row of Candles*, has Stambolov murdered in Sofia in 1895. Because he wore a chain mail vest, his killers hacked off his arms. He died three days later. His fingers were pickled and put on display.

26. Jelavich, *History of the Balkans*, vol. 2, pp. 37–40, 89–100, 106–125. P. 166 records that, in addition to huge financial reparations, Sofia had to hand over 13,500 cows, 125 bulls, 12,500 horses and 2,500 mules. Its grain production had fallen forty-seven percent. Of 900,000 men conscripted, 90,000 were dead. In fact, from 1912–18 160,000 died and 300,000 had been wounded out of a population of five million. It also had to cope with 200,000 refugees from Greece and Serbia.

27. Op. cit., pp. 166–171. Sulzberger, *A Long Row of Candles*, p. 64, says Stamboliski was stabbed; while bleeding, he was forced to dig his grave; then his hands and ears were cut off, he was shot, and then decapitated. Less dramatic, Jelavich has him in Pazardzhik where MRO-External men captured him. His right hand (which signed the Treaty of Nis) was cut off. He was stabbed sixty times and his and his brother's heads were cut off before they were buried.

28. Jelavich, *History of the Balkans*, pp. 207–209, 221–243, 255–261. For a detailed account of the Soviet takeover in Bulgaria, see Boll, Michael M., *Cold War in the Balkans: American Foreign Policy and the Emergence of Communist Bulgaria 1943–47* (University of Kentucky, 1984).

29. Todorova, Maria, "Improbable Maverick or Typical Conformist: Seven Thoughts on the New Bulgaria," *Eastern Europe in Revolution*, edited by Ivo Banac (Ithaca, New York: Cornell University, 1992), pp. 148–167. In the winter of 1984–85, Zhivkov brought the military and police down on the ethnic-Turks in an effort to Slavify their names and erase much of their culture. Armed militia men went into the villages as if it were a military operation. There were deaths and brutality and a barely suppressed Bulgarian racism was roused again. This had occurred earlier in 1912–13, 1941–44, and in 1971. In just two months, 300,000 ethnic Turks fled to Turkey. By mid-1989, only 160,000 had returned. The West was in an uproar and making good propaganda against Bulgaria. Even the Soviet Union was embarrassed. Zhivkov was an unintelligent imitator of Moscow, whose system of "feudal" patronage had become outdated and backward.

30. Washington has attempted to obstruct Bulgarian arms exports since the early 1990s. It has pressured Sofia to stop selling to certain Middle East countries and from offering its weapons to any group that has the money to pay for them. Bulgaria looks on it as money and jobs, as do many countries.

31. Kozloduy's number one reactor was switched off in August 1997 when two of its turbines stopped. No increase in radiation was noted. In fact, the reactors are of such a type that a Chernobyl meltdown isn't possible. It has four dating from 1974–82 and two from 1987–89. IAEA considers the older reactors outdated and expressed concerns about safety. Western nuclear companies have raised the issue of Soviet reactors worldwide, hoping to gain business.

32. Zhivkov participated in the bloody purges after World War Two when ninety-three leaders from the interwar period were shot. Others were jailed. A few escaped abroad. In a second wave, 2,138 were killed out of 10,897 tried. Later, came purges from power struggles and events in the Soviet Union. Jelavich, History of the Balkans, pp. 292–94, 364–370.

Chapter 9 – Exorcizing the Great Engineers

1. I have relied heavily on Treptow, Kurt W., ed., *A History of Romania* (Iasi: The Center for Romanian Studies [Foundation for Romanian Culture and Studies], 1997). Treptow is an American who is the director of the Romanian center in Iasi. He has a PhD from the University of Illinois and is now resident in Iasi where the center publishes books and the periodical *Romanian Civilization*. The center operates in cooperation with academics internationally and conducts study seminars. It is a good source of information on a country in need of closer examination. I have also continued to use Jelavich,

History of the Balkans, vols. 1 and 2. Lastly, I have shamelessly used Burford, Tim and Richardson, Dan, *The Rough Guide to Romania* (London, 1998), for touristic detail that would have otherwise gone unnoticed. These intrepid travelers and their staff are owed my debt of gratitude.

2. Michelson, Paul E., "Recent Historiography on Romania and the Second World War," *Romania and World War Two* (Iasi: Romanian Center, 1996), pp. 308–309. During the first eighteen months of the war (22 June 1941 to late 1942), Antonescu's regime conducted outrages against Romania's Jews that even impressed the Nazis. Later, it rejected a "final solution" and through a system of subterfuge and double bookkeeping it managed to keep many thousands alive. Jews were transferred from Transylvania where Hungarian practices under Horthy were horrific. Jews survived in Wallachia-Moldavia. Nevertheless, a pogrom at Iasi in June 1941 killed 8,000. Ten thousand died in Chisinau in 1941. An estimated 120–170,000 Romanian Jews were sent to Transnistria. Some 50,000 survived. Romanians killed 40–60,000 Jews at Odessa in late 1941.

3. Kate Connolly in the *Guardian Weekly* of 25 April 1999 agrees that the state of agriculture is deplorable. However, she cites interest by US agro-firms who are aware that Romania's farmland is very fertile with its famed *pamant negru* (black soil). They plan to consolidate holdings whereby the owners will rent their land to a consortium involving Monsanto, Cynamid, Du Pont and FMC. The consortium will provide seeds, fertilizers, chemicals, and modern farming equipment. The farmers will receive about a third of the yield. Some say they will get less, but they can opt out after five years and keep the equipment. The project is expected to involve a small percentage of the five million hectares now under cultivation, out of a nine million hectare total.

4. Funar was once president of the nationalist PUNR. As mayor, he banned the singing of the Hungarian national anthem in church and other displays of Hungarian nationalism. He once called Hungary a suicidal nation, which will try to take Transylvania by force, noting that Romania's army was in Budapest twice in this century. The *European*, May 27–30, 1993. Article by Michael Bond. The same paper claimed Romania's 1.8 million Hungarians were dismayed when that country was admitted to the Council of Europe shortly after Helsinki Watch said that Romania's Hungarians have been "increasingly subjected to a series of abusive policies" at the hands of local officials.

5. Jelavich, *History of the Balkans*, vol. 2, p. 26. In the first half of the nineteenth century, the population of the Danubian Principalities was basically Romanian and Orthodox. In the second half, however, a large influx of Jews entered from Russia. In 1859, 118,000 Jews lived in Moldavia and 9,200 in Wallachia. By 1899, this had increased to 210,000 and 68,000 respectively. The constitution of 1866 stated that only Christians could become citizens. Jews were prevented from buying rural property. Because of restrictions, they tended to congregate in Bucharest and Iasi, working as merchants and traders. In the countryside, they found employment as stewards of large estates, owners of taverns, moneylenders and other jobs that could result in conflict with the local peasant population.

6. *Nine O'Clock*, Bucharest, Monday, 15 February 1999. Article by Anca Popescu, who covered Tirgu Mures' UDMR Magyar Forum.

7. I used the very excellent Rady, Martyn, *Romania in Turmoil* (London and New York: IB Tauris and Company Ltd., 1992), to describe the events of December 1989 and afterwards through the first few years of the NSF. It is also recommended by *Rough Guide* because of its clarity of expression.

8. See *Photo* magazine, February 1990, for epic photographs of the December 1989 revolution as it took place in Bucharest. Also old photos of the Ceausescus enjoying a life of luxury.

9. Jelavich, *History of the Balkans*, vol. 2, p. 205, cites Eminescu as stating that, "A political crime... committed by a private person, ceases to be a crime when it is based on higher views and dictated by the clean notion, even if it be mistaken, of saving the state." Cosma would probably say the same.

10. Additional detail on the political involvement of Cosma and the Jiu valley miners was provided by Banac, Ivo, *Romania After Ceausescu: Post-Communist Communism* (Katherine Verdery and Gail Kligman), pp. 117–147.

11. Rady, *Romania in Turmoil*, p. 194, states that Cosma and Munteanu became friends at a Group for Social Dialogue meeting at Brasov in September 1990. At that time, Cosma claimed that in June they had fallen in a trap laid by the government, that they were used by the NSF. Cosma undoubtedly realized that the students were a force that he could not afford to alienate. As it turned out, in September 1991, they made common cause against the Roman government.

12. Examples of the faulty functioning of the Romanian judiciary in the post-communist era abound. In December 1993, the former head of the Securitate, Iulian Vlad, was released after serving four years of a twelve-year sentence for reasons of good behavior. An estimated 1,000 people died during the December 1989 revolt. In March 1999, two men imprisoned for sixteen years for stealing two rifles and ammunition from the militia in 1983 were released by presidential pardon. Viorel Roventiu and Nicolae Stanciu confessed under torture that they had planned to assassinate Ceauşescu when he visited their town. They were originally to be executed. The sentence was changed to twenty years. It took nine years after Ceauşescu was dead to free them. Cosma, tried in absentia and given eighteen years for undermining state authority, was in March 1999, sentenced to an additional three years for assault and vandalism. This went on appeal. It was well in the Romanian tradition for people to be catapulted from prison to a position of power.

13. Again, in this section I have used Treptow, *A History of Romania*, and Jelavich, *History of the Balkans*. And Robinson, cited previously, makes mention of the Dacians. See pp. 596–606. The latter states that the Dacians fled or adopted the speech and habits of the Roman colonists so thoroughly that they became Latinized. Trajan was born in the Roman colony Italica in Spain. Many of his soldiers were from the 10th Roman Legion, which came out of Catalonia, near Barcelona. Some assert that Romanian is linguistically close to Catalan.

14. Kovach, Tom R., "The 1456 Siege of Belgrade," *Military History*, August 1996, pp. 34–40.

15. The Empress Maria Theresa quote is from Lehrer, Milton G., *Transylvania: History and Reality*, edited by David Martin (Silver Springs, MD: Bartleby Press, 1986). Lehrer was a Jewish American of Romanian immigrant parents who lived in Paris as a journalist and after World War Two was denied an exit permit to leave Bucharest. He died there in 1969. Martin was a foreign policy advisor to US Senator Dodd and the Senate Sub-Committee on Internal Security. The book argues persuasively that the Hungarian record in Transylvania was one of brutal repression of its Romanian population.
Prodan, David, *Transylvania and Again Transylvania: A Historical Expose* (Centrul De Studii Transilvane: Fundata Culturala Romana, 1996). Prodan usefully counters Hungarian claims regarding Transylvania with a wealth of facts.

16. Romania later made significant strides in science: Gheorghe Titeica, Traian Lalescu and Dimitrie Pompei in mathematics; Ioan Cantacuzino, Vactor Babes, Gheorghe Marinescu, Constantin Parhon and Nicolae Paulescu in medicine (Paulescu's pancrine preceded the insulin of the Canadians Banting and Best by eight months); Henri Coanda (jet propulsion) and Traian Vuia in aviation; the Saxon Hermann Oberth in rockets and Stefan Odobleja, cybernetics.

17. Treptow, *A History of Romania* and Torry, Glenn E., *Romania and World War One* (Iasi: Center of Romanian Studies, 1998). Torry is Emeritus Professor of History at Emporia State University, Kansas.

18. Jelavich, *History of the Balkans*, vol. 2, cites Rothschild's East Central Europe. By the middle of the interwar period, Jews controlled the bulk of private capital in export, transportation, insurance, textiles, leather, electro-technical, chemicals, housing, printing and publishing and were strong throughout the legal, medical, journalistic, and banking professions. Though only four percent of the population, Jews constituted about twenty-five percent of the town population in Bukovina, Bessarabia and Moldavia and fourteen percent in rural areas. In Chisinau (Kishinev) and Cernauti, Jews constituted about half of the population. Many store signs were in Hebrew, p. 160. Into this situation, arose the Legionari movement with an ideology that expressed such thoughts as: *Legionari do not fear that you will die too young. For you die to be reborn and are born to die.* And another: *With a smile on our lips, we look death in the eye. For we are the death team that must win or die!* Unfortunately, it was the Jews who did most of the dying. Legionari leader Horia Sima found refuge in Franco's Spain and escaped retribution.

19. Treptow, *A History of Romania*, pp. 423–428, 430–440, 462–478. Informative as well as entertaining is R. G. Waldeck's *Athene Palace* (Iasi: republished by the Romanian Center, 1998).

20. Although there is some historical revisionism afoot regarding Antonescu, there is little doubt that he was a willing partner of Hitler and Nazi Germany. Romania enthusiastically participated in Operation Barbarossa, the invasion of Russia. Its atrocities are well documented. Granted, Antonescu later put some military men on trial and cooperated with the Jewish leader, Wilhelm Filderman, to reduce the death toll. Beevor, Anthony, *Stalingrad* (Penguin, 1999) describes how Soviet forces fell on the Romanian Third Army, which protected the German flanks, leading to a wide encirclement.

21. An interesting sideshow of this period is how the American Office of Strategic Services (OSS) rescued some 1,200 downed airmen who had been held prisoner. It began with Captain Constantin "Bazu" Cantacuzino of the Romanian Air Force flying Lt. Col. Jim Gunn in an ME-109G into a USAAF base at Cerignola, Italy, just a few days after Antonescu fell in August 1944. "Bazu," a pre-war racing driver and pilot, made the return trip in an American P-51. A few weeks later, OSS operative Frank Wisner arrived in Bucharest at the head of a group that attempted to work with Romanian royalist and anti-communist elements. Latham (Jr.), Ernest H., *Romanian Civilization*, vol. 8, no. 3, Winter 1998–99, pp. 3–36.

22. The Ceauşescus, both from peasant families, pushed economic autarky like the Albanians. They also built a power base similar to the Albanian pyramid. See Rady, *Romania in Turmoil*, p. 52, for a schematic of family relationships. As their personality cult grew, they were heaped with honors. Elena studied chemistry, but others wrote scientific papers for her. Because of Romania's stance on various issues, it gained Most Favored Nation trading status with the US in 1975 and enjoyed access to financial credit, computer technology and some military hardware. Nicholae was knighted during a visit to London in 1978. The repressive aspects of the regime were ignored by the West. By the late 1980s, they lived like demigods surrounded by their admirers.

23. A year later, the World Bank and the IMF were again pressing for structural reform while the government wondered how it would meet foreign debt payments of US$2 billion. Its reversal on tax breaks for investors was discouraging news for foreign businessmen who had only brought in US$3.5 billion since 1990. Its leu currency tumbled badly. Central Bank hard currency reserves were only US$1.6 billion. The year's foreign trade deficit could hit US$3 billion.

Chapter 10 – Robin Hood and His Merry Men

1. Never a slave to the job, Greeks nevertheless work hard. Many start at 7 a.m. with a cup of coffee in their belly. Farmers start even earlier. Cigarettes and song keep them going. Not humming, song. Love, or bad luck, fills the morning air. A short break for bread, cheese, sardines, and olives might include retsina, or beer. They are finished by 3 p.m. and go home to the big meal of the day. Then, it's sleep until 6 p.m., whereupon the Greek begins anew. They say they cram two days into one! It might be fishing, the beach, garden, or some project. But for sure, by 9 or 10 p.m. he'll be with family and friends eating and having a little wine. It's the companionship that Greeks love. They will stay up until 12 p.m. or so; the young even later. They are very social. They like jokes and gossip, and to exchange opinions. They laugh easily and often. A wedding, baptism, a name day (many are named after saints), even a funeral, are occasions to exchange the news. Few are idle for long as Greeks must be on the go. Women are much the same and are rarely tied day and night to house, job, or children. The grandparents and relatives play a vital role in making sure the children are taken care of. Lastly, Greeks work to live, not live to work!

2. The promise of *allaghi*, "change," was the Pasok movement's most powerful slogan. It encompassed society itself.

3. Papandreou's Pasok captured a culture of popular protest and struggle, including that of the left during World War Two. A powerful mythology grew out of anti-fascism. Talented composers, artists and writers have dwelt on Greek martyrdom—freedom, or death. Mikis Theodorakis's powerfully moving songs with Maria Farandouri are a must. Listen to Costas Hadzis, that beautiful gypsy, wise-cracking about the Colonels. You don't need to understand Greek. The music alone will work on you. Andreas put on a black leather jacket and appropriated it as his own, like a mantle of anti-capitalism and anti-imperialism. He was Promethean to some, but disappointing to others.

4. In the beginning, when Pasok was more of a movement, it had an organizational structure very similar to the militant parties of the left. A president is elected by a party congress. The executive office of sixteen, plus the president, used to be called the executive bureau, which some thought sounded too much like the communists. A central committee has 140 full members and thirty-five non-voting members. A national council lumps all elected bodies and the party MPs. It has sections for youth, women, labor and international relations. Papandreou developed Pasok's ideology in writings that describe the movement as Marxist, non-dogmatic, and incapable of being reconciled with Leninism.

Pasok claimed to stand for popular sovereignty and social liberation. Andreas was a charismatic leader. If Greeks work hard on the job, they can sometimes be hard to work with. Strong trade unions push to maximize benefits. If it's impossible to reach an agreement, Greeks readily resort to strike action. This goes for both the private and public sectors. Greeks are far from docile employees. They strive to create conditions that satisfy themselves and to carve out a vested interest at their workplace. They are not spare parts to be used and thrown away.

5. On 29 August 1989, some 16.5 million files were said to have been burned in a steel mill furnace outside Athens. Some EYP employees complained about this. Others have wondered how many were microfilmed before their destruction. The figure cited is from Peter Murtagh's *The Rape of Greece* (London: Simon and Schuster, 1994).

6. In 1992, the ND government permitted only private companies to enter the mobile phone business. Stet Hellas (Telestet) bought in for US$102 million (Stet Italy seventy percent, Bell Atlantic twenty-five percent, and Greece's Interamerican five percent). Panaphone bought in for US$218 million (UK Vodaphone 45 percent, France Telecom thirty-five percent, Intracom ten percent, Database Greece ten percent). After Pasok returned to power in 1993, it passed a law permitting OTE to enter the market. Subsequently, OTE's Cosmote was established with twenty-five percent Norwegian participation. Intracom pulled out of Panaphone and is said to be involved with OTE's plans to expand Cosmote's operations in Greece and other Balkan countries. Thus, Kokkalis-Siemens came out on top vis-à-vis Vardinoyiannis-Alcatel and France Telecom, which subsequently sold its Panaphone shares.

7. Intracom came to the attention of the US government in the late 1980s because senior East German officials were visiting its offices and manufacturing plants.

8. The casino deals subsequently became mired in bribery charges, broken contracts and lawsuits. Finally, Simitis opted to reduce Greece's casino operations. Lottery gambling has boomed.

9. *Kathamerini* claimed that account 0709-60-011-025 at Handelsbank in Berlin belonged to Kokkalis and that bribe money was sent from there to a number of other named banks. The report claimed the account was examined by German authorities inquiring into the operations of the East German Stasi security agency. German SPD (Social Democrat) deputy, Freihelm Beucher, once invited Kokkalis to testify before the Bundestag on the past relationship of his company with the East Germans, citing suspicions that embargoed West German technology was passed to East Germany via Intracom. He said there were indications East Germany had a financial stake in Intracom. Needless to say, Kokkalis didn't testify. From 1994, Intracom began participating in a NATO-AWACS project with Boeing, DASA, Ericsson, Siemens, Hughes, and Rockwell.

10. Talk has it that a policeman might collect about 30,000 drachmas a month from an Albanian illegal construction worker. This is US$100, or one week's salary in every month. Obviously, the policeman must know where his man is sleeping (many sleep on the site) and exert some control over him—like keeping his documents.

11. Simitis did law and economics at the University of Marburg in the FRG, the London School of Economics, and earned a PhD in law from Marburg. Under the junta, he helped form Democratic Defense. He had to flee Athens (his wife was arrested). In Germany, he was active with the Panhellenic Liberation Movement (PAK) of Andreas Papandreou. In the mid-1980s, he became minister of agriculture, then minister of economics, in the Pasok government.

The Greek government has retained the help of the US Internal Revenue Service to improve collection of personal income tax. It now requires some proof of where the money came from relative to property purchases. Certain objective criteria were also set up—value of home, office, car and boat—to establish a person's tax obligation. These rules have been imperfectly applied as Greeks deal with their local tax office face to face and argue it out. Tax officers have been jailed for attempted bribery after having approached a taxpayer to arrange a *fakellos*.

12. Clerides was shot down twice. The first time, he escaped from a POW camp and rejoined his unit. The second time, he was sent to the escape-proof Colditz prison in Germany until the war ended.

13. The S-300 has a range of 150 km (ninety miles). If installed near Paphos, the S-300 would have barely reached the southern tip of Turkey in the region of Anamur.

14. Ankara had often accused Athens of providing training for PKK fighters, claiming that camps exist in Greece. However, they have never provided any proof to substantiate their accusations.

15. Greece has provided asylum for any number of political refugees: Palestinians, Iranians who left after 1979, Ethiopians, and others. It had permitted a National Liberation Front of Kurdistan press and information office to operate in Athens as ERNK does in many European cities. The Kurds hold rallies, stage events and collect money for their cause. Greeks view them as being involved in a liberation struggle, not as a terrorist organization. For Ocalan to fall into the hands of the Turks because his situation was handled poorly was a blow to their self-image. Some suspect Simitis ordered Ocalan to be turned over to the Kenyan authorities.

16. In November 1996, Turkey was rocked when notorious murderer and drug dealer, Abdullah Catli, died in a car accident along with a senior police official. An MP from the True Path Party survived. One dead beauty queen, seven pistols, and two silencers were also found. It was revealed that Catli was on the payroll of the police and National Intelligence Organization (MIT) and was used as a hit man against Kurds and left oppositionists. A parliamentary panel corroborated links between politicians, criminals, and security officials. Catli was close to "Grey Wolf" Mehmet Ali Agca, the Pope's assailant. In August 1998, one Alattin Cakici was arrested in France in possession of a diplomatic passport given him by MIT. Cakici had run a right-wing death squad. Ex-prime minister and True Path head, Tansu Ciller, was accused of being a CIA agent; of illegally transferring US$925,000 from Turkey to the US; and evading US$1.6 million in taxes. The charges were later dropped. The US-educated Ciller verbally supported the use of criminals by the state. He has been questioned about a "missing" US$6.5 million from a security slush fund, which some say went to support Grey Wolves activity on Cyprus. In January 1997, Frankfurt judge Rolf Schwalbe accused Ciller of protecting drug families Baibasin and Senoglu in Istanbul, who allegedly belong to an international heroin gang that has its headquarters in Belgium. Scores of political activists and journalists have been murdered in Turkey. Typical was Human Rights Association head Akin Birdal, who was gunned down in his office, but survived multiple wounds. In early 1997, the pro-Kurd People's Democratic Party (HADEP) gave parliament information on 140 mystery killings. Human rights organizations estimate 3,500 persons have been murdered by rightist death squads since the PKK insurgency began in 1984. Hundreds of the disappeared have never been found. Others died in detention where beatings, torture, and rape (even of children) is routine. A March 1994 UK–Ireland report to the Parliamentary Human Rights Group stated that over 1,000 Kurdish villages had been destroyed by security forces and that millions of people have been forced to seek refuge in urban slums. Turkey is a major producer-conduit for narcotics in Europe. Little of the above affects its standing with NATO, or its close alliance with the US.

17. In July 1999, OTE and Dutch telecom bought fifty-one percent of the state Bulgarian Telecommunications Company for US$510 million. This very opaque deal finally fell through.

18. I have relied on Richard Clogg's *A Short History of Modern Greece* (Cambridge University, 1979) and his *A Concise History of Greece* (Cambridge University, 1992), for my very condensed comments on Greece since its independence. Working from one text to the other it was difficult to do footnotes. Suffice it to say, I am very indebted.
   Jelavich, *History of the Balkans*, vols. 1 and 2, were there as well for back-up.

19. The stadium for the 1896 Olympics was donated by the Averoff family of Metsovo in northern Greece. They also bought a battle cruiser which saw service in the Balkan Wars and World War One. The Zappeion Palace was donated by two brothers living abroad. There were many others as well.

20. France's influence was seen from the Greek army's artillery to its officer's tunic and kepi. Greece's army cadets still wear the same in dark blue, white gloves and silver dress dagger.

21. For a great detailed account of the "Catastrophe" read Housepian, Marjorie, *The Smyrna Affair* (New York: Harcourt, Brace, Jovanovich, 1966). The Turks called Smyrna *gavur Izmir* (infidel Izmir). The infidels (Greeks and Christians) were also regarded as *giaours*—infidel dogs!

22. Metaxas hoped that by keeping the British presence to a minimum, he might somehow avoid German intervention.

23. The figure for death by starvation during the first year of the German occupation is extrapolated from Mazower, Mark, *Inside Hitler's Greece* (New Haven: Yale University, 1993), pp. 23–41.

24. Besides Clogg, I used Close, David H., *The Greek Civil War* (London: Longman, 1995).

25. Woodhouse, C. M., *Apple of Discord* (London: Hutchinson, 1948). The author, who was with SOE in Greece during World War Two, takes a less charitable view of EAM-ELAS than Close. Both are very good in their own way.

26. A great help in getting into this tragic period are the very graphic photos of *Life* magazine's Dmitri Kessel, brought out again in *Ellada toy '44*, Athens, Ammos, 1994. Kessel saw it all with outstanding professional skill and sensitivity. A real must!

27. Vafiadis later became a respected Pasok MP who visited the US at the invitation of the George Polk Award Committee.

28. Marton, Kati, *The Polk Conspiracy* (New York: Farrar, Straus, Giroux, 1990). George Polk was a World War Two US navy combat pilot in the Pacific who became a CBS radio correspondent in Greece. He was a critic of US intervention and more so of the Greek government. He was murdered in Thessaloniki in May 1948, most likely by rightists and possibly with the knowledge of the British, who were at that time deeply involved with Greece's politicians, military, and its police and security services. It's a fascinating read and deals with the dismal investigation led by ex-OSS head Bill Donovan. An innocent man was railroaded to jail to "solve" the murder and to pin the crime on the communists, who probably were not involved.

29. Gage, Nicholas, *Eleni* (New York: Random House, 1983), is a moving account of how a mother saved her children from the *pedomazoma*, the communist gathering up of children. Gage, a *New York Times* crime reporter, maintains that it is a true story of his family. The *pedomazoma* included children from three to fourteen years. Most were sent voluntarily, but far too many by the use of coercion. Also read Nikos Kanzantzakis's *The Fratricides* (London: Faber, 1974).

30. Murtagh, Peter, *The Rape of Greece: The King, The Colonels and the Resistance* (London: Simon and Schuster, 1994), p. 52, cites an unnamed retired American diplomat who stated that Karamanlis was appointed prime minister at the insistence of the US government.

31. A good fictionalized mood piece about Lambrakis's murder is *Z* by the Greek author Vassilis Vasilikos. It was made into a film by Costa-Gavras. It provides insight into the psychology of Greek right-wing extremists who lumped all leftists together and viewed them as people who had no right to political expression and as people who should be eliminated.
   The information on Paul and Frederika's income and property is from Murtagh, *The Rape of Greece*, p. 51.
   Murtagh, ibid, states that the Royal National Foundation was estimated to bring in US$20 million a year for the royal family. He says its revenues also included a tax on new, imported cars. This would have affected the wealthy few. Most of the money would have come from cigarettes and the cinema. Murtagh states that the foundation was strictly under Frederika's control and that no one ever knew where the money went, or what it was used for. Both were petty, greedy individuals. They probably used foundation money to support like-minded politicians and conservative causes.

32. Murtagh, op. cit. p. 42–43 states that Papadopoulos had been paid by the CIA since 1952 and that later he worked in liaison with the agency. Former CIA director William Colby in Congressional testimony has stated that Papadopoulos had been on the CIA payroll.

33. Murtagh, op. cit., pp. 106–125 for the events of the coup.

34. Fleming, Amalia, *A Piece of Truth* (Boston: Houghton Mifflin, 1973). Lady Amalia Fleming, the Greek wife of the discoverer of penicillin, and herself a doctor, resisted the junta and was subsequently arrested, tried, jailed and deported. Her account of life under the junta is well worth reading, especially the annex, which provides named details of police-ESA torture.

35. Fallaci, Oriana, *A Man* (New York: Simon and Schuster, 1980). A blend of fact and fiction concerning her life with Alekos Panagoulis. She does well conveying Alekos's devil-may-care exploits and his prison ordeal.
   Murtagh, *The Rape of Greece*, p. 204 for information of junta funding of Nixon's political campaign; Hersh, Seymour M., *The Price of Power: Kissinger in the Nixon White House*, n.p., pp. 137–141 also mentions this. In the early 1960s, Pappas had built a US$125 million oil, steel, and chemical complex in Greece with Standard Oil of New Jersey (Esso). He was close to the junta and allegedly had CIA ties. Hersh states that the agency was a strong supporter of the junta as well. Pappas was the conduit for the 1968 contribution and, in 1972, was a big fundraiser, and was on the "Committee to Re-elect the President."

Some of this information came from Elias Demetracopoulos, an anti-junta journalist-lobbyist in Washington whom the Nixon administration tried to intimidate. Demetracopoulos retold his story to the *Washington Post* in 1997, which added that Henry J. Tasca, who was ambassador to Greece under Nixon, gave secret sworn testimony to the House Intelligence Committee that Pappas had transferred the junta money to Nixon's campaign fund.

36. Again, Murtagh and Clogg for events on Cyprus and the junta's collapse. Greece made good strides towards establishing a multiparty system. While the rules are sometimes bent, or imperfectly applied, Greece today is a functioning democracy. There is a KKE and Left Coalition, neither of which are extremist. Rightists, and a few who support the return of the monarchy, took refuge in ND. It sometimes comes to light that this or that person is still a supporter of the junta, but they are in a tiny minority. I have tried to present Greece as it is. The corruption is much like that in Italy and Spain. The insider corruption elsewhere in Europe is well known. Deals done in America are on an even larger scale, using squads of lawyers to ensure things go smoothly. If you want a more idyllic version read Henry Miller's *The Colossus of Maroussi* or Lawrence Durrell. Greece has many dark corners, but that doesn't make me love it less. It has given me a second home among warm, wonderful people who live on a very human scale surrounded by proud traditions in a beautiful, often abused land. I hope that my Greek friends will understand and forgive me.

Chapter 11 – Kosovo: The Bartered Bride

1. *Kosovo Dossier*, Bina-Belgrade News Agency, 1996, pp. 20–21 cite a JNA officer from Pristina who recalls constant problems with Albanians as a child: school thefts; school-yard beatings; how his bike was often stolen; how he was beaten over the head with his own tire pump. After 1981, it became worse: stone throwing; gang assaults; harassment of children playing, or doing chores outside. The Albanian bus drivers mistreated Serb passengers, refusing to open doors, or sell them tickets, often letting them off far from their stop. Also, of not being served in shops because one was Serbian; of having to wait at the clinic until all of the Albanians were taken care of; how Albanians were given job preference. Serbian job applications might be accepted, but not registered, and then were "lost." The most frequent complaint was preference given to Albanians over Serbs—that is, habitual discrimination.

2. Hedges, Chris, "Kosovo's Next Masters?", *Foreign Affairs*, May–June 1999, pp. 24–42. Hedges says the KLA is ideologically split between the sons and grandsons of the fascist-led clans that fought in World War Two (militias, Skanderbeg SS) and old *kacak* rebels on the one hand, and those that fell under the influence of Hoxha's teachers at Pristina University after 1974, i.e., leftists. He cites a close relationship between the KLA and LDK. He says that some 5,000 Kosovars fought in Bosnia; and goes on to say that Adem Jashari and his brother, Hamza, and others founded the KLA as early as 1991. He cites the "Homeland Calling" fundraising; as well as the likelihood that money came in from the Middle East and other Islamists. At the time of writing, he said that the Serbs claimed some 1,000 mercenaries had joined the war from Albania, Bosnia, Croatia, and abroad from Saudi Arabia, Afghanistan and Yemen, along with a few German, and British instructors. Hedges believes that most volunteers and mercenaries from abroad were Albanians.

   Op. cit., p. 36, states that the Jashari clan ran a black-market smuggling operation. *Jutarnji List*, Zagreb, 23 June 1998, cites ties between Kosovar Albanian narcotics dealers in Italy and KLA. Italian police arrested 125 persons, including Kosovar Albanians, who were using the proceeds of drug sales to purchase arms. Gang member Agim Gazi had bought 200 machine guns for the KLA. It said that the Milan Kosovar gangs are particularly aggressive and tough. In fact, a UN expert on crime claims that the Italian mafia has come to fear the Albanians!

3. The retaliatory attack by Yugoslav police on Donje Prekaz was widely reported in the West, including a somewhat inaccurate and incomplete account in *Vanity Fair* (Eur. July 1998) by Sebastian Junger. According to Serb sources, this was a clash between two well-armed groups. They claim they invited non-combatants to get out and thirty did leave. They also claim that Adem Jashari killed a teen-aged nephew who panicked during the fighting.

4. Information on the Barrett sniper rifle was provided by phone by the Potomac Arms Corporation in Alexandria, Virginia. See 1986 *Shooter's Bible* (Stoeger Publishing Company, South Hackensack, New Jersey), p. 322, paramilitary arms.

5. To my knowledge only Milosevic accepted the accord worked out with Holbrooke. If he had followed it to the letter, the KLA would have been free to reoccupy the territory it had lost.

6. One of the earlier proposals heard from some Albanian leaders was to create a third federal republic. Belgrade refused, as this is what the Kosovars have wanted since 1981, including the right to secede. Provisions for autonomy are written in the existing constitutions and could have been expanded upon. Making constitutional changes, which are unpopular to begin with, would destroy any government.

7. Although there were tensions between Washington and Moscow in 1994–95 over Bosnia, both saw their interests in a settlement that offered a chance for regional stability. Russia was supportive of Dayton. Kosovo is different, however, as all agree it is a part of Yugoslavia. Moscow views Kosovo separatists the same way it does Chechen separatists and was suspicious of the US use of "human rights" to break Belgrade's grip on that province. Rumor has it that Moscow provided information that improved FRY air defense capabilities against NATO. The military, technical and scientific protocol signed with Sergeyev might have included such matters. Russia also has large stockpiles of conventional arms. Ultimately, however, once the bombing began, it gave little assistance. In fact, lack of Russian backing is cited as one of the reasons Milosevic decided to cut a deal with Washington.

8. Walker became Deputy Assistant Secretary of State for Central America in 1985 and worked under Assistant Secretary Eliot Abrams and USMC Colonel Oliver North in support of the Contras in Nicaragua. According to independent prosecutor Laurence Walsh, Walker was involved with organizing bogus humanitarian flights out of El Salvador, which were actually resupply missions for the Contras. From 1988–92, he was US ambassador to El Salvador. During this period "death squads" were very active and were responsible for the murder of Roman Catholic priests, in addition to many hundreds of "leftists"—both activists and suspect sympathizers. All of this was an ongoing human rights outrage. Apparently US concern for human rights cuts differently depending on where Washington sees its national interests.

9. Belgrade's negativism at Rambouillet was because it was a rewrite of Hill's old proposals, which were not negotiable and which had already been rejected. *Nation*, 14 June 1999, p. 50, cites comments by former US foreign service officer George Kenny which he attributes to an unnamed official accompanying Albright: swearing reporters to deep background confidentiality, he bragged that the US "had deliberately set the bar higher than the Serbs could accept," adding that Belgrade needed a "little bombing" to see reason. Kenny, a harsh critic of Milosevic, called Rambouillet a "sham plan… which, in its military appendix B, demanded what would have been an unconditional surrender of Yugoslavia…"

   Kosovo and the Albanian Dimension in Southeastern Europe (Athens: The Hellenic Foundation for European Foreign Policy, 1999). The interim agreement is dated 23 February, the same day that Rambouillet I broke up. Apparently an add on, item 3 amendment to Article I states, "Three years after the entry into force of this Agreement an international meeting shall be convened to determine a mechanism for a final settlement for Kosovo on the basis of the will of the people, opinions of relevant authorities, each Party's effort regarding the implementation of this Agreement, and the Helsinki Final Act, and to undertake a comprehensive assessment of the implementation of the Agreement, and to consider proposals by any Party for additional measures." "Will of the people" seems to be shorthand for a referendum. Several columnists said that Thaci was promised a referendum, that it was an open secret when the meeting ended. Given the fact that the Kosovars will all vote for independence, and the language of this amendment, the future of Kosovo would have been out of the hands of Belgrade.

10. Gelman, Burton, "The Path to Crisis: How the US and its Allies Went to War," *International Herald Tribune,* 19 April 1999, p. 2. He states that Albright pushed for the war after Racak and, by the end of January, Clinton had Blair on board. In addition, "The die was cast for NATO's first war and the most consequential war in Europe since World War Two." He said many miscalculations were made, especially the expectation that Milosevic would give up early in the campaign.

11. "Reflections on the War," *Nation*, 28 June 1999, p. 11. Princeton University professor Richard Falk argues that effective diplomacy wasn't used with Milosevic, that it was mostly threats. The crisis had a

hidden agenda: the need to justify NATO and the Pentagon's desire to wage a technological war with low US casualties. He also cites the need to keep military budgets high. He thinks that the war made a bad situation much worse in purely humanitarian terms. Henry Kissinger said it was ill conceived. Johns Hopkins professor Michael Mandelbaum calls it "a perfect failure."

12. Under activist ambassadors and US defense department teams, both Albania and Macedonia fell under US influence several years ago. The US joined with Israel and Turkey to break the PKK and end a separatist insurgency that threatened Turkey's internal integrity and stability in southeastern Turkey where a major pipeline is planned. Greece was placed under great pressure to end its political support to the PKK. It was required to provide vital sea-air facilities, even when NATO's war was opposed by a large majority of its people. A front-line state in the US-UK effort to contain Iraq (and given its new role in the Balkans), Turkey is additionally a crucial US ally. Finally, it is mainly because of US-NATO intervention that Milosevic failed in his efforts to consolidate territories in Croatia and Bosnia under his control. If he had, Belgrade would have exerted a strong influence in the area, an eventuality opposed by Washington. Given US economic and strategic interests, which now extend to Central Asia, Washington decided to "Balkanize" all of ex-Yugoslavia. It is a policy, it seems, originating from an obsessive "anti-communist" mindset, but was also forged extemporaneously amidst a crisis caused by a state being broken up.

13. If NATO became the KLA's air force, the latter became NATO's ground force. Rumors were rife that the American CIA was giving it support. The respected UK *Guardian* correspondent Martin Walker, after noting that Germany's recognition of Croatia and Slovenia served to break up Yugoslavia, alleged that FRG intelligence chief, Hansjorg Geiger, supplied the KLA. A senior German diplomat confirmed the CIA connection, but denied the latter. He said KLA units had also been provided with satellite phones for the coordination of ground operations and to support NATO air strikes as spotters. He added that the KLA had been provided an office for liaison purposes near NATO's military headquarters in Brussels. True, or not, I had heard that German "commandos" were advising the KLA in the field.

14. *NATO Crimes in Yugoslavia: Documentary Evidence*, vols. 1–2, Belgrade, May and July 1999. An official FRY "White Paper," these 950 pages of documents and photographs show in graphic and gruesome detail that Yugoslavia was hit very hard and that its civil infrastructure and civilian population suffered severe losses. There is nothing quite like photos of a charred corpse to explain what bombs do to humans.

15. Launched out of a pre-air strike build-up, reportedly with the name "Operation Horseshoe," VJ and other units drove the KLA back to the Albanian-Macedonian border, forcing their civilian supporters to flee, or risk being killed. Hedges' article, "Kosovo's Next Masters?," p. 25, said that Serbian ethnic cleansing was mainly for tactical purposes, to deny the rebels civilian support, and was essentially directed at KLA strongholds. But, once the bombing started, rage erupted, which placed the entire civilian population at risk. Some were left alone. Others were rounded-up and driven out. Atrocities occurred when paramilitary and MUP units were involved, often with the VJ in a blocking position. An OSCE report compiled after the war from interviews with Kosovars (*International Herald Tribune*, 6 December 1999, *Wall Street Journal*, 4 January 2000) indicates NATO's attack caused a massive Yugoslav reaction. It also suggests there often were military reasons for what the Serbs did—clearing out invasion and infiltration routes, and areas controlled by the KLA. Interestingly, the German ARD TV Panorama program closely questioned FRG defense officials about "Horseshoe," demanding proof of the plan's existence, proof that FRG allegations that the Yugoslavs planned mass expulsions in advance were not fabricated. OSCE advisor, General (ret.) Heinz Lockwei said that he was denied any official "proof" of the plan that defense Minister Rudolph Scharping had used to publicly justify NATO's bombing campaign.

16. "Kosovo: The Untold Story," *Observer*, 18 July 1999, cites information from the UK Ministry of defense of plans for a ground invasion of Kosovo the first week in September named "Operation B-Minus." It claims that Milosevic agreed to terms three days after Clinton and Blair had agreed to go forward with it. It said a force of 170,000 would have been used (50,000 British) in an invasion expected to last six weeks. NATO approval would have been required in July. Having earlier advised that an air campaign alone wouldn't work, General Clark argued strenuously within the US

administration for approval. Clark set up his planning team, the "Jedi knights," using UK MofD plans for an invasion dating from mid-1998. Still, KFOR commander, General Michael Jackson, reportedly despaired over the lack of direct-ion from NATO headquarters. And, how the plan would win approval from other NATO members, especially FRG's Schroeder, who adamantly opposed a ground invasion, is left unsaid. Also, for Clinton to agree to commit a large US ground force with his eyes always on the US political polls, is questionable.

17. In a speech to the Yugoslav people just after the war ended, President Milosevic stated that 462 VJ and 114 police were killed in the Kosovo conflict. A month later, VJ chief of staff, General Ojdanic, stated losses totaled 524, explaining that sixty-two others were killed in clashes with the KLA after the bombing had stopped, and that thirty-seven were still missing. The numbers appear credible. It would be very hard to hide the "thousands" of military casualties claimed by NATO in a small area like Serbia and Montenegro. Similarly, NATO greatly inflated VJ equipment losses. The USAF Munitions Effectiveness Assessment Team (MEAT) determined that fourteen tanks, eighteen APCs, and twenty artillery pieces had been destroyed, figures close to the numbers cited by Belgrade. US Chairman of the Joint Chiefs of Staff, General Henry Shelton, not only substituted his own greatly inflated report, but suppressed information which had been compiled not only from aerial photographs, but also from the investigations of US ground teams.

18. As pointed out, Rambouillet had made no provision for a Russian contingent in NATO's intervention force, even though it was a member of the Contact Group. And, when the war ended, US Secretary of State Albright insisted that NATO would be at the "core" of any peacekeeping effort. Russia was not explicitly mentioned, although speculation arose as to its possible participation. When Russian troopers unexpectedly arrived in Pristina, KFOR commander General Michael Jackson took the position they should serve as they had in Bosnia, whereas General Clark wanted him to insert NATO blocking troops by helicopter. *Kathimerini*, 4 February 2000, implies that he and Clark argued over this matter. Interestingly, Jackson insists that a ground invasion was not planned. Another question lacking an answer is whether, as some have speculated, if Russia had established a strong air bridge, it and Belgrade would have attempted to hive off northern Kosovo and the Trepca mines for the Serbs, leaving the Albanians the south, and NATO with a fait accompli. This is a tempting idea, but a ploy that would have exposed Serbs to even more risk. Also to split up Kosovo would put paid to FRY's claim to sovereignty. However, partition may result in the end. In *Collision Course: NATO, Russia, and Kosovo*, Praeger, 2005 (forward by Strobe Talbott), John Norris argues that the US and Russia were closer to combat in Kosovo than at any other time since the fall of the Iron Curtain.

19. The *Guardian Weekly*, 1–7 July 1999, carried an article by Chris Hedges which reported widespread allegations that KLA leader Hisham Thaci (war name "snake") was responsible for having his rivals murdered. Also involved were Azem Syla and Xhavit Haliti, along with Albanian security. Thaci reportedly smuggled in arms from Switzerland before the outbreak of fighting and had several million dollars at his disposal. Large sums were paid for weapons of Albanian origin. In April 1999, a KLA commander was murdered who had accused Haliti of profiteering and misuse of funds. At the same time, when the KLA was on the run, Bujar Bukoshi named Ahmet Krasniqi commander of the Armed Forces of the Kosovo Republic (FARK), a rival band. After weeks of tension, Thaci and Albanian security decided to get rid of Krasniqi. He and his companions were stopped by police and disarmed in Tirana, and, after a few blocks, they were stopped again and a hooded hit man shot him. After more killings, arrests, and purges, FARK (comprising 600 ex-JNA officers) was forcibly integrated into the KLA. Bukoshi is of the opinion Thaci is after power as much as he wants independence. The allegations had no effect on Thaci's status as an instrument of US policy in Kosovo, as subsequently he was invited to Washington. In July, he established the Party of Democratic Union in Kosovo, which later became the Democratic Party of Kosovo. Thaci made Bardhly Mahmuti (KLA fund raiser who had lived in Switzerland) its head. Xhavit Haliti (KLA finance boss, and the new owner of the Grand Hotel, in Pristina) is also involved.

20. The *International Herald Tribune*, 20 April 1999, Eric Schmitt and Steven Lee Meyers, reported that many of NATO's bombing targets were civilian facilities run by Milosevic's friends and were bombed to weaken his control, citing petrol and gas facilities run by Dragon Tomic, speaker of the federal parliament and head of Yugo Petrol; Zastava car factory at Kragujevac (employing 15,000) run by

Milan Beko who had been minister of privatization; cigarette factories at Nis and elsewhere said to be linked to Milosevic's son, Marko; Mastrogradnje construction company run by Dejan Kovacevic, minister of construction; a Nis mining company, Duvanksa Industrija, run by Zivota Kosic, minister of energy and mining. The targets were approved by General Clark, General Shelton, and Secretary of Defense Cohen. Other targets included power grids, water pump stations, oil refineries at Pancevo, Novi Sad, and Belgrade; drug, chemical and shoe factories; light aircraft airports, railway stations, bus depots, TV stations and transmitters, bridges, heating plants, a maker of heavy equipment—bulldozers, excavators, and cranes and even clinics and educational facilities. An *IHT* article of 14 May by Michael Gordon cited NATO air chief US General Michael Short as advocating intensified attacks on Belgrade itself. An 18 April piece by Steven Meyer details how General Clark wanted 4,000 targets in FRY, but finally settled for 2,000—a number many felt was arbitrarily too high. Clark expanded the list to include purely civilian targets. He declined an interview.

21. The magnificent frescos of Kosovo and Metohia suggest that the God of the Serbs is an Old Testament God, stern and ever ready to mete out his righteous wrath. Figures are depicted in armor with swords and crossbows, even a muscular Christ.

22. Thaci has been invited to Washington twice, the last such occasion in September 1999 when he and other KLA members were feted at Lansdowne, VA, at a five-day affair hosted by the US Institute of Peace. A "Lansdowne Declaration" was issued calling for independence for Kosovo. Secretary Albright's speech pledged US support. Senator Robert Dole was involved. The institute is located in Washington, D.C. and is federally funded. The US president appoints its head, and the US Senate confirms its leading officers. Such actions by the Clinton administration were designed to openly undermine UNSC resolution 1244.

23. *Kathimereni* of 12 January 2000, Stavros Tzimas, cites the close involvement of the Albanian mafia with Kosovar politicians, naming Albanian Prime Minister Pandelj Maiko as the go-between to Thaci. After KFOR seized US$500,000 from the home of Thaci's brother, Gani, UNMIK head Kouchner and KFOR commander Reinhardt were forced to apologize when Thaci threatened to pull out of the joint administrative council. In other words, Thaci can intimidate UNMIK whenever he wants to. Part two of the OSCE report cited in f.n.17 above states that much of the violence directed at the Serb and non-Albanian population is at the direction of the KLA in a systematic way under the eyes of KFOR both for revenge and to drive people out. The report concluded that stories of mass atrocities by the Serbs are exaggerated and published with little, or no effort, to confirm the actual facts.

24. After much UNMIK confusion, the interim administration seems to be reverting to pre-1989 laws. Kouchner is asking for judges from the international community to serve in Kosovo.

25. Agim Ceku (KLA military chief, IGK defense minister, now head of the Kosovo Protection Corps) was a captain in the JNA in Croatia in 1991. He defected to the Croat ZNG, and, under Tomislav Mercep, participated in the attack on the garrison at Gospic and the subsequent execution of 156 Serbs. He was involved in attacks on Serbian villages and later in the Krajina offensive of 1995. Now a brigadier, Ceku transferred to the Pula corps at Pazin under Damir Krsticevic, who reportedly had attended the US West Point military academy and other staff schools. It's said that Ceku was then introduced to US officers employed by the US-sponsored Military Professional Resources Incorporated (MPRI). Ceku kept his Croatian badge rank when taking over military command of the KLA. No tribunal war crime charges have been brought against Ceku, or Mercep, for that matter.

   In early 2000, KFOR, mostly for public relations purposes, was placed under EU Eurocorps. It was made clear, however, that NATO's General Clark retained actual command. It would seem this permits NATO to take credit when things go right and for the Eurocorps staff to be blamed when things go wrong. By late March, a year after the NATO bombing campaign began, KFOR found itself negotiating with the KLA in an effort to stop it from organizing a new insurgency in Serbia just outside the US zone of control where its fighters had been training in full view of US troops. The KLA soon began operations into the Presevo valley outside of Kosovo where the Albanians are in a majority. Jiri Dienstbier, UN human rights envoy to the former Yugoslavia, stated that, thus far, the UN and NATO mission in Kosovo had been a total failure.

26. A recent UNHCR report cites ethnic exclusion, unemployment, and harassment of non-Albanians in Kosovo, describing them to be at considerable risk. It faults UNMIK for not bringing non-Albanians

into its legal and political structures. It cites a need for KFOR to deploy its forces to protect and escort minorities, allowing that this is essential, but ultimately not sustainable. Concurrently, NATO issued a self-serving report that describes "Operation Allied Force" (OAF) as a huge success, stating it forced the FRY to withdraw from Kosovo and claiming it had "rescued" over a million Albanians. From appearances Camp Bondsteel is a permanent base, not a camp. Extensive roads and structures have been built behind high security fences and barriers, including elaborate recreational facilities. It would seem that it is there for the long haul. NATO's focus is now southeast Europe and eastward.

27. President Clinton appointed a succession of effective, high profile, energy envoys who have pushed US policy in the Caucasus and Central Asia. The agreement to build a 1,730 km oil pipeline from Azerbaijan to Turkey was the result of extensive lobbying and arm-twisting, even among a US petroleum industry unconvinced there is enough oil to justify construction. The line's capacity will be 1 million bpd. Azerbaijan International Operating Consortium (AIOC) is hoping for 7-800,000 bpd at peak production in 2007. Turkey will earn an estimated US$100 million yearly in transit fees. There are also plans to build a US$3 billion gas pipeline westward from Turkmenistan across the floor of the Caspian Sea. Gas and oil quota questions are under discussion. Russia opposes the oil pipeline and claims it is uneconomical. It is obvious that prestige and power relationships are at issue in what was the southern Soviet Union. It involves linkage in many strategic directions, beginning in the Balkans. The US displayed its intentions in 1997 when its airborne troops flew from North Carolina to Kazakhstan and Uzbekistan for NATO Partnership for Peace exercises. NATO has already been invited into Georgia and Azerbaijan and basing sites are under active consideration. Former US national security advisors Zbigniew Brzezinski and Brent Scowcroft; former secretaries of state Alexander Haig, Jr., and James Baker III; and former defense secretaries Casper Weinberger and Dick Cheney have served as consultants, or lobbyists, for various Caspian-Central Asian oil, gas, and pipeline schemes.

28. Cooley, John (ABC news correspondent for the Middle East), *Unholy Wars* (London: Pluto Press, 1999), details how the jihad in Afghanistan against the Soviets has resulted in terrorism against the West and massive heroin trafficking into Europe and America. See pp. 106, 176, 180, 209, 212 on Afghan veterans in Bosnia; pp. 202–203 detail how Algerian Kamareddine Kharban was an advisor to the Bosniaks and how his ties with Iran enabled him to supply weapons to Sarajevo. Petkovic, Milan V., *Albanian Terrorists* (Belgrade: Kalekon, 1998), is a brief on the Kosovo insurgency and support to the KLA from Islamic countries. He cites Iranian operatives who have aided the Bosniaks and Albanians, particularly from Italy: Meghid Sharam, Ali Rezah Bayata, Mahmud Nurani and Kurban Ali Abadhi are named. Bezavah Navabi and Mohsen Nurbakam also worked to provide economic aid. As Cooley points out, the Afghan jihad also fed back into the Algerian civil war. In late 1999, GIA member Ahmed Ressam was arrested as he crossed into the US near Seattle with 90 kg of bomb-making materials. He carried a Bosnian passport. *Middle East International*, 14 January 2000, cites a week-long abortive uprising in Lebanon led by Afghan-Bosnian war veteran, Bassam Kanj, a US citizen. His 200-man *Takfir* group was reportedly connected with Osama bin Laden. A brother of another leader was off fighting in Chechnya.

29. Vickers and Pettifer, *Albania*, pp. 142–185. *Kathamerini*, 6 March 2000. Yoram Schweitzer of Israeli Policy Institute for Combating Terrorism tells how Egyptians from "Islamic Jihad" set themselves up in Tirana, with ties to bin Laden, for the purpose of targeting the US embassy. *Middle East International*, 10 March 2000, reported US defense secretary Cohen cancelled his visit to Tirana because intercepts indicated bin Laden's men there were after a senior US official.

30. As in Bosnia, Turkish troops were welcomed in Kosovo. During NATO's war, the Turks provided support from Bandirma and Balikesir air bases. Ankara's military training and equipment support to Tirana and Sarajevo enhances their position in Kosovo. It is underpinned by large defense contracts in the West. Ankara will spend US$4 billion on 145 attack helicopters and US$6 billion on 1,000 tanks. Germany, France, Italy, and the US are all bidding. On the downside, Turkish security has cooperated with criminals dealing in drugs. The Albanian mafia operates over into Turkey, with its center in Switzerland. In the *Independent*, 10 December 1993, Robert Block and Leonard Loyle report that Albanians control some seventy percent of the heroin drug trade in Switzerland and that 2,000 Kosovars are in jail there for drugs and arms trafficking. The US Drug Enforcement Agency has confirmed to me that the Albanian mafia has a large share of the US heroin market centered in New

York City. The Brussels-based International Crisis Group states that Albania and Kosovo are in the grip of crime and corruption and both are a conduit for drugs and human trafficking to Western Europe. It quotes a UN official who cites the high risk that the international community is endorsing a "narco-mafia" society. He added that huge sums of drug money go to the KLA and groups associated with it. Drugs come from Turkey and are stored in Albanian warehouses.

31. Regarding the new expanded NATO, a Polish diplomat related how the Hungarians had obstructed and delayed their convoys to Kosovo to make Warsaw look bad. Senior US officials, while publicly praising Hungary's contribution to the air war, also told them not to push the Vojvodina issue. We have already seen how Hungary illegally sold arms to Croatia in 1990 and how successive regimes were violently anti-Serb from World War One, throughout the inter-war years, and in World War Two. Avramov's *Genocide in Yugoslavia*, pp. 208–223, details how in 1941 Hungary took Vojvodina and the Banat. In April, 3,500 Serbs were killed, 1,000 at Stirig. Serbs were expelled from Backa-Baranja and Hungarian settlers were brought in. Several thousands of Serbs were interned in camps. In early 1942, Hungarian troops and militiamen sealed off an area between the Tisa and Danube rivers and killed thousands. Their frozen bodies were stuffed in holes in the ice and allowed to stand like statues until the ice began to melt in the spring, whereupon they floated down to Zemun and Belgrade. Novi Sad was emptied of its Serbs and Jews. It's probable that, altogether, some 10,000 Serbs were killed in just one year.

32. Priest, Dana, "How Fear of Losses Kept Super Cobras from Kosovo Action," *IHT*, 30 December 1999. A half billion dollars was spent sending two-dozen AH-64 Apache attack helicopters to Albania. However, the White House, overruling NATO commander General Wesley Clark, kept them under tight control, unused.

33. In August 1999, High Representative Petritsch responded to US press reports *(NYT/IHT)* that Bosniak authorities had stolen over US$1 billion in aid money. In September, a US team headed by James Pardew of MPRI and Robert Frowick, ex-head OSCE Bosnia, arrived in Sarajevo to investigate. In October, former Bosniak army chief, Sefer Halilovic, accused President Izetbegovic of stealing "billions" provided by various Moslem countries. There was a lot of money missing, but the investigation went nowhere. Izetbegovic stepped down from power a year later.

34. After President Clinton told the Bulgarians that the "gain" of reform is worth the "pain," Blagovesta Doncheva had the following to say to the *New York Times* in late 1999: "In the past ten years, the IMF and World Bank have devoured Bulgaria's industries. Insisting on privatization, they had them sold to foreign interests who have sometimes liquidated them. Mass unemployment has been created and the old have been reduced to digging in refuse bins. Children drop out of school, unable to afford books, supplies, and decent clothing. A pension for a lifetime of work might be US$25 a month. Only the young are offered jobs today, and it could be a twelve-hour day for next to nothing. Cheap housing and cheap transportation are a thing of the past, as are free medical care and subsidies for students. The flood of foreign goods is closing our factories. We fell for the talk of democracy and openness. I wish we hadn't." In September 2000, a World Bank report issued at Prague confirmed that the transition from communism to capitalism has been "catastrophic" for the vast majority of the people of Central and Eastern Europe.

35. The US provided US$588,000 for a pipeline feasibility study. The US$1 billion project would be 900 km in length with a capacity of 750,000 bpd of Caspian oil via the Black Sea. New oil finds in the Caspian are projected.

36. Seemingly symbolic of where the UN-NATO mission in Kosovo is headed, German KFOR commander General Reinhardt plunged into a crowd of Albanians in Pristina to press the flesh, only to have his pistol stolen. By March, KLA fighters were training in sight of US army watchtowers in eastern Kosovo and had begun armed attacks against Serbs in the Presevo valley. The so-called Liberation Army of Presevo, Medvedja, and Buganovac (UCPMB) sought to takeover villages in southern Serbia where Albanians are in a majority.

Amnesty International and Human Rights Watch issued reports in early 2000 accusing NATO of violating international law and having committing war crimes. Predictably, the war crimes tribunal brushed these charges aside. Not surprisingly, a US Congressional report gave a bleak outlook for Bosnia-Herzegovina and Kosovo, with possible renewed fighting. KFOR stumbled on secret caches of

KLA weapons amounting to seventy tonnes. And, on leaving Kosovo at mid-year, 2000, Kouchner's deputy UNHCR regional director Dennis McNamara (a New Zealander) roundly castigated UNMIK-KFOR for their tolerance of an organized campaign of violence against the Serbs, Roma, and other minorities that now totaled 500 deaths. *IHT*, 4 July 2000, article by Steven Erlanger.

Epilogue: 2000–2005

1. Aside from the argument that he was simply devising a way to remain in power, Milosevic had for some time looked upon the direct popular election of a president as a constitutional improvement, the same as is done in France and in the US.

2. I am indebted to the *International Herald Tribune* (*IHT*) for its coverage leading up to the election and its aftermath. The items are too numerous to cite, but Steven Erlanger and Roger Cohen's article of 16 October 2000 was particularly helpful.

3. John Lancaster in the *IHT* of 20 September 2000 cited US support to the DOS. He describes it as a US$77 million effort "to do with ballots what NATO bombs could not do: get rid of Slobodan Milosevic..." Michael Dobbs, *IHT*, 13 December 2000, has a detailed account of US political intervention, including the activities of Schoen.

4. As FRY president, Kostunica had foreign policy, control of the army, and little else. Djindjic, as prime minister of Serbia controlled all the other ministries and the police and security organizations. Kostunica was pushed aside and, when FRY was abolished, he had no official position. There was strong resentment between the two.

    In a country where myths and stories of martyrdom abound, the fact Milosevic was taken to The Hague tribunal on June 28 will remain symbolically very powerful. During his marathon trial, Slobodan Milosevic defended himself and the FRY vigorously. He died of a heart attack on 11 March 2006, unconvicted. Large crowds of supporters viewed his body in Belgrade, as well as at his burial at his hometown of Pozarevac—under the linden tree where he first kissed his future wife.

5. *Kathimerini* (English), Stavros Tzimas, of 18 December 2000 provides an excellent background piece and analysis of the UCBPM. They are almost all KLA veterans.

    Times (UK), Anthony Loyd, of 14 May 2002 ("A very dirty little war"), gives a chilling account of the KLA bus bombing, the arrest of suspects, the withholding of information by KFOR, and their eventual release to return to the Kosovo Protection Corps. Transferred to Camp Bondsteel, the prime suspect (linked by DNA to the detonation) later just "disappeared." UNMIK international police say the Americans blocked the investigation. Finally, UNMIK's foreign judges gained access to some NATO intelligence and concluded that the case should go forward. KFOR refused to cooperate and the case ran out of time. The US is particularly reluctant to take any action against the KLA. Some say there is a conspiracy of silence because of past secret US support to the KLA. The Albanian code of *"omerta"* is hard to crack.

6. *Newsweek*, Rod Norland, 26 March 2001 ("Fire in the Mountains"), is an account of the intimate connections between the NLA and the KLA. The war lasted for seven months. It flared up again in August 2003 when a "new" band now calling itself the Albanian National Army (ANA) seized two villages in north Macedonia.

    IHT of 2 April 2001, R. Jeffrey Smith ("The Making of an Insurgent Army in Macedonia"). NLA political chief Ali Ahmeti served for many years in the KLA with Hisham Thaci. The latter was a student activist at Pristina University who went to Albania where he received military training as a member of the KLA.

    Time, 9 July 2001, Andrew Purvis. An account of how US troops rescued NLA fighters at Aracinovo. Another account said the NLA had 120mm artillery and had threatened to shell the capital and an oil refinery. *Kathimerini* (English), 20 July 2001, Stavros Tzimas describes MPRI's relationship with Skopje and alleges that FYROM military chief of staff Jovan Andrevski resigned after it was revealed he passed operational information to MPRI's General Griffith—who allegedly gave it to the NLA. Tzimas says that Griffith had worked closely with KLA military chief Agim Ceku when the latter fought for the Croats, as well as Gazim Orseni who also was a KLA officer and then later became a NLA commander. In late June 2001, Griffith and ex-senior MPRI executive General James Pardew (on US diplomatic assignment) were at a KLA camp in Kosovo. Tzimas asserts that MPRI advised the NLA and that it was rumored that 17 American MPRI trainers were at Aracinovo. An *AP* article in *Kathimerini* (English) dated 3 August 2001 by Misha Savic cites US pressure on Ukraine to put a brake on arms sales to FYROM. US National Security Council chairman Condolezza Rice accomplished this during her visit there in July.

7. Report attributed to Yossef Bodansky, chairman of the US Congressional Task Force on Terrorism and Unconventional Warfare. President Izetbegovic, who died in October 2003, brought thousands of Islamists to fight in Bosnia. A *Guardian Weekly* obituary, 23–29 October 2003, says that "… In opting for ethnic politics, Izetbegovic was as guilty as the Serbian and Croatian fanatics."

8. *AP* article in *Kathimerini* (English) by William J. Kole dated 13 August 2002.

9. As some point out, Milosevic was deposed in the belief that that would take care of the problems— but, in fact, upheaval has continued. In October 2003, Richard Holbrook and Bernard Kouchner returned to the area and emphasized the need for US troops to remain in Bosnia and Kosovo. Since the end of the 1999 war in Kosovo some 1,000 Serbian civilians and other ethnic minorities have been murdered there.

10. *New York Review of Books*, 17 July 2003, Misha Glenny ("The Death of Djindjic").
    New York Review of Books, 15 January 2004, Tim Judah ("The Fog of Justice").

11. *Kathimerini* (English), 13–14 January 2001; the Italian government's accusation has been repeated frequently by prosecutors and cited in the press. Prudentino's Mafia links extend to Naples and Puglia in southeast Italy opposite Montenegro.
    Kathimerini (English), 9 December 2003 AFP article by Bozo Milicic. Former interior minister Andrija Jovicevic accused Djukanovic of "direct involvement" in the sex scandal, saying he protected those charged and witnessed perverted acts by trafficked women. The scandal claimed the careers of several senior officials. It gradually blew over, however, as Djukanovic continued to press for a referendum. It finally was held on 21 May 2006 and narrowly passed the fifty-five percent mark set by the EU. The "yes" vote meant breaking with Belgrade and full independence for Montenegro.

12. *Guardian Weekly*, 10–16 July 2003, article by Ian Traynor. European Stability Initiative for Balkan affairs criticized Ashdown for dictating to the Bosnians, while Ashdown himself has urged Sarajevo to do more to help itself.

13. *Kathimerini*, 4 January 2004 Reuters article by Nedim Dervidbegovic, says that Bosnia is impoverished, ethnically divided, and dependent on massive foreign aid, plus the presence of 12,000 NATO peacekeepers. This is in fact "dysfunctional."

14. *New York Review of Books*, 15 January 2004, cited above. With Serbs Mladic and Karadzic still at large, the Croat Gotovina was arrested in the Canary Islands on December 7, 2005, and sent to The Hague Tribunal. Croat newspaper *Globus*, quoting his defense team, claimed that Gotovina had cooperated closely in the past with U.S. CIA director George Tenent.

15. Newspaper articles too numerous to cite. *IHT*, 16 February 2004, report by Nicholas Wood ("Discontent Fuels Serb's Nationalism") was particularly good. *Nin* magazine journalist Liljana Smajlovic is quoted concerning the outgoing DS party: "These guys have discredited democracy—it's covered with mud."

16. *New York Review of Books*, 15 January 2004, cited above.

17. The author declines to cite the official's name in order to protect the source. His remarks beg for a detailed account of US support to the KLA. It's plausible that support began during the heady days of Berisha and US ambassador Ryerson. It may also have served intelligence needs. From mid-1998, US-KLA contact was open. Judah, Tim. *Kosovo, War and Revenge* (New Haven: Yale University Press, 2000), p. 103. KLA founder member Jashar Salihu said it was begun in 1993, having evolved from earlier groups. It conducted small actions in Kosovo and had its first casualties in January 1997. It became loosely organized in bands in the *kacak* tradition. Soon villagers were rallying to it based on clan loyalty, patriotism, and KLA persuasion.

18. *IHT*, 29–30 November 2003, article by Seth Mydans, cites clashing US-Russian interests in Georgia. *Guardian Weekly*, 4–11 December 2003, report by Nick Paton Walsh, an unnamed Georgian minister claims that the Russian "GRU" has plans to sabotage the Baku-Ceyhan pipeline. It is expected to be in operation by 2006.

19. The US informed NATO of its plans in late 2003 to be better able to deploy to the Balkans, the Middle East, and Central Asia. To support Iraq operations, the US had 1,000 troops at Constanta, Romania, and a smaller group at Burgas, Bulgaria. In late 2005 and early 2006, the US signed long-term agreements with Bulgaria and Romania for the use of a half dozen or more military bases.

20. *Kathimerini* (English), 15 September 1999 interview by Thanassis Tsiganas. With decentralization into federal republics; the arrival of a multiparty political system; overlapping constitutional provisions for social, economic, ethnic-civil rights; with regular workplace and community elections to representative assemblies, in a mixed economy; Yugoslavia was, in 1990, arguably as "democratic" as any number of US-supported regimes. The problem of Kosovo detracted from this, having its complex origins that I have attempted to explain. The FRY's other problem was ingrained US opposition to institutions and practices smacking of "socialism," e.g., social ownership of various enterprises and workers self-management. Tellingly, in early 1989, FYR Prime Minister Markovic (advised by Jeffrey Sachs of Harvard) began to implement World Bank/IMF neo-liberal "shock therapy" that, among other things, sought to eliminate worker's participation in factory management.

Woodward, *Balkan Tragedy*, pp. 160–161. In the spring of 1991, at the urging of Ambassador Zimmerman in Belgrade and Senator Dole, the US Congress passed its Nickles amendment to end economic aid to FRY by May 5 if Serbia hadn't reversed course in Kosovo. However, in June the US Congress expediently amended its Direct Aid to Democracies Act (the Dole bill) to permit US aid to Slovenia and Croatia by bypassing the Yugoslav federal government. This was only days before secession. It would not appear that Washington lacked information, experience, and insight with regard to the FRY. Zimmerman served there before in the 1960s. Brent Scowcroft, chairman of the National Security Council, had once been a military attaché there. Lawrence Eagleburger, Deputy Secretary of State, had been US ambassador. Given how the US ignored outrages against the Kurds in Turkey and genocide in Rwanda, the argument that the US intervened in FRY to protect Croat, Bosniak Moslem and Albanian so-called "rights" holds little water. Ultimately, other considerations and policies drove US policy.

Pressured largely by the US, the UN is expected to begin final status negotiations on Kosovo in late 2005, or in early 2006—amid continuing acts of violence, including against UNMIK itself. Hans Binnendijk of the US National Defense University has admitted that UNMIK has been threatened with an Albanian campaign of terror if independence is not granted soon. This comes after five years of failed effort during which the ratio of per capita reconstruction aid to Kosovo compared to Afghanistan has been 23:1 and the ratio of peacekeepers 24:1. Former interventionists who were quick to blame Belgrade, like David Rieff and Michael Ignatieff, are now more even handed in their assessment of culpability. The latter admits that he and many others were blinded by a "...narcissistic image of ourselves we believed was incarnated in the myth of a multiethnic, multiconfessional Bosnia." This can be said for Kosovo as well. Finally, as this misguided effort to install another failed Muslim state in the heart of Europe goes forward, perhaps some will recall that two of the Saudi 9/11 hijackers—Khalid al-Midhar and Nawaf al-Hamzi—among others, were schooled as Islamic radicals in Afghanistan and Bosnia. Unearned independence for Kosovo's Albanians would be, in Irish observer Brendan O'Shea's words, "...the triumph of ignorance." *International Herald Tribune* articles and editorials, Aug.–10 Oct. 2005. *Harper's Magazine*, Sept. 2005, p. 11. *Nation*, Sept. 26, 2005, p. 14. *Ghost Wars*, Steve Coll (Penguin Books, 2004), pp. 486–488. International Crisis Group, *Kosovo, Toward Final Status,* Jan. 2005. *Studies in Conflict and Terrorism* (Taylor & Francis Inc., 28: 61–65, 2005).

Index